GLOBAL POLITICS

Origins, Currents, Directions

second edition

Allen Sens
University of British Columbia

Peter Stoett
Concordia University

NELSON

™

THOMSON LEARNING

Australia • Canada • Mexico • Singapore • Spain • United Kingdom • United States

NELSON

™

THOMSON LEARNING

Global Politics: Origins, Currents, Directions
Second Edition

by Allen Sens and Peter Stoett

Editorial Director and Publisher:
Evelyn Veitch

Acquisitions Editor:
Kelly Torrance

Marketing Manager:
Murray Moman

Developmental Editor:
Rebecca Rea

Production Editor:
Bob Kohlmeier

Production Coordinators:
Julie Preston and
Helen Jager Locsin

Creative Director:
Angela Cluer

**Cover Design and Interior-
Design Modifications:**
Peter Papayanakis

Cover Images:
PhotoDisc

Copy Editor:
Dawn Hunter

Proofreader:
Betty Robinson

Compositor:
Carol Magee

Printer:
Webcom

**Canadian Cataloguing in
Publication Data**

Sens, Allen G. (Allen Gregory),
1964–
    Global politics : origins,
currents, directions

2nd ed.

Previous ed. written by Peter J.
Stoett and Allen G. Sens.
Includes bibliographical
references and index.
ISBN 0-17-616910-5

1. World politics, 1989–   .
I. Stoett, Peter John, 1965–   .
Global politics.   II. Title.

D860.S86 2001   909.82'9
C2001-930661-X

Brief Contents

Detailed Contents

PART TWO: CURRENTS

PART THREE: DIRECTIONS

Preface

Teaching global politics in Canada is a challenging occupation. Many continuities and enduring concepts require elaboration, and the context in which they are situated is always changing. To make matters worse, the last decade of the twentieth century was a particularly tumultuous one. The collapse of the Communist regimes in Eastern Europe and the disintegration of the Soviet Union brought a remarkably swift and dramatic end to an ideological, geopolitical, and military struggle that defined the post–World War II era. The technological changes that characterized the late 1900s and early 2000s have altered established patterns of economic activity, global communication, and military strategy. Relatively new issues, such as environmental problems and the stability of financial markets, challenge teacher and student alike as they attempt to grasp the complexities of modern international relations.

A common complaint heard from Canadian teachers and students of global politics is the lack of textbooks that are Canadian in orientation. Most texts are American and their examples focus on American foreign policy issues. One crucial function of the first edition of this text was to relate the academic study of global politics more directly to the lives of students who live outside the United States. Since the first edition was received with great enthusiasm, we decided to follow through with a second edition that continues the tradition established in the first but that is enriched by the comments and suggestions supplied by students and teachers. The second rationale for a second edition is more practical: things change. In this field, trying to keep on top of things is a futile gesture. However, it was necessary to update significant portions of the book, and though we may have succeeded in only some aspects, our intent was to make the book as contemporary as possible.

The Cold War between East and West dominated international politics and the attention of policymakers for more than 45 years. Scholars and their students focused on issues such as strategic nuclear and military balance, nuclear arms control, the shifting tides of superpower diplomacy, the politics of alliances such as NATO and the Warsaw Pact, and the extension of the Cold War rivalry into regional conflicts. The politics of the bipolar world have also engaged many members of the public, as the superpower arms race sparked the development of a large peace and disarmament movement. However, it would be a mistake to argue that such Cold War issues excluded other global phenomena, since they occurred in a changing international context that included a growing and ever more integrated global economy; an increasing interdependence between societies and states; a growing divide between rich and poor societies; the increasing activity of nonstate actors such as multinational corporations and nongovernmental organizations; rapid technological advances; and a growing concern over environmental degradation. Nevertheless, the politics of the superpower rivalry, attended by the threat of global nuclear war, was the primary subject of attention in the realm of international affairs.

Today, the issues that attended the superpower rivalry have largely vanished, serving to highlight issues that were submerged under the Cold War agenda or those that emerged at least in part as a consequence of the rapid political changes of the early 1990s. These revelations present nothing less than a psychological challenge. The collapse of the East–West rivalry as the principal focus of global politics has compelled state policymakers to re-evaluate established foreign policy principles and assumptions. For scholars and students of international relations, the end of the Cold War challenged existing theories and models, removed the hierarchy of study, and altered the research and educational agenda. For the interested public, the relative simplicity of Cold War politics was replaced by a bewildering array of crises, problems, and issues that soon muted the optimism that attended the end of the Cold War.

To most Canadians, it appears as though the focus of global politics has been altered toward a more complex set of issues, including the attempts to manage the global economy; the spread of democracy; regional ethnic, religious, and factional conflicts; gender issues; the proliferation of conventional weapons and weapons of mass destruction; threats to the global commons; refugee and population movements; and the information and communications revolution. And yet, a cautionary voice must be raised here. Though it is tempting to speak of the end of the Cold War as the beginning of a new age of global politics, much remains the same. The world is still politically divided into a system of territorial states; conflict and cooperation between states and within states continues; and despite developments in economic interdependence and global communications, the world remains divided between rich and poor, between different civilizations, religions, and ethnicities, and between different modes of domestic governance. In this text we have tried to situate the immense change occurring around us within an understanding of these elements of continuity.

The central aim of *Global Politics* is to introduce readers to the rich and diverse enterprise that is the study of contemporary international relations, encouraging an appreciation of the theoretical roots of divergent perspectives on how the international system operates. The text also establishes the vital historical context required for any understanding of international relations. Furthermore, the book intends to stimulate thoughtful analysis and critical thinking and to promote a healthy skepticism for established wisdom and prevailing assumptions. Finally, *Global Politics* reveals the human element of international relations by providing insights and biographies of individuals who have made an impact on the world in which we live.

Most recently published textbooks are revised editions of works originally published during the Cold War, structured in a manner that reflects Cold War issues and priorities. This text was conceived in a post–Cold War context and designed from the beginning to reflect the contemporary global environment and the issues faced by today's scholars, policymakers, students, and citizens. The Cold War is history (albeit important history), and this book is structured around this fact. To this end, *Global Politics* gives equal attention to the theoretical developments and historical events of the past, the key issues facing us today, and the emerging agenda that confronts us all. (The explicit attention paid to emerging issues marks another significant departure from many standard international relations texts.) As the title suggests, this book looks to the future as much as it looks to the past and the present. The book does not claim to be a crystal ball; it does identify trends and themes and challenges the reader to think about the issues looming on the horizon.

Finally, we stress the fact that this textbook is one of the few that is not American; it is written by Canadian authors, both of whom teach in different regions of Canada, and is intended primarily for a Canadian audience. Naturally, the question of American foreign policy looms large in any treatment of global security and economic or environmental issues, and we have had to devote considerable space to American policy during our discussion of the Cold War period. But American foreign policy need not be the defining question of an entire discipline. At the same time, however, this is not a text on Canadian foreign policy, either. Several excellent examples of those exist already, and we have strived for as global a view as possible.

THE STRUCTURE OF THE BOOK

As our subtitle suggests, *Global Politics* is organized into three parts: origins, currents, and directions. Part One, "Origins," examines the evolution of the international system and the development of related scholarly perspectives up to the end of the Cold War. However, historical material is not merely presented in a chronological fashion. Instead, history is integrated with theory. First, the development of the key contending perspectives in international relations theory is discussed in its historical context. Second, Part One reveals how these contending perspectives tend to focus on different types of historical events or have different interpretations of history. For example, realists emphasize the history of empires, great powers, and wars, while liberals emphasize economic history and the development of interdependence. Critical theorists emphasize historical patterns of hierarchy and dominance and the processes that perpetuate poverty and disempowerment. In short, Part One looks at the history of war, the state, the Cold War, international political economy, international institutions, and law, and it gives us some theoretical background to it all.

In Part Two, "Currents," readers are introduced to some of the key issues on the contemporary international security and economic agenda. We look at today's varied conflict management efforts, the divisive impact of globalization on the world economy, and some principal human rights questions. Part Two is designed to give the reader a snapshot of the contemporary international situation and an improved understanding of the issues that confront today's world. In Part Three, "Directions," items of growing importance on the international agenda are explored. We begin with a discussion of contemporary global environmental problems. Next, we look at population growth and movements, the impact of the information revolution, and sources of potential future conflict. These admittedly selective issues are discussed because, in the view of the authors, they will dominate the future global politics agenda over the long term. Not all these issues will affect Canadians directly, but the connections between Canada's future and the complex trends outside the country are genuine.

An overarching theme emerges, one that links past, present, and future, the continued existence of two trends in global politics: trends of political *convergence* and *divergence*. Trends of *convergence*, or what some prefer to label *integration*, can be identified in economic globalization and interdependence; regional zones of peace, international organizations, and the expansion of international law; the growing volume of international transactions, communication, and travel; the so-called development of a global culture; democratization; and reduced friction between the great powers. Trends of divergence, often termed *fragmentation*, can be identified in the uneven globalization between rich and poor and the information haves and have-nots; the fragmentation of states and intrastate conflict; ethnic, religious, and factional warfare; the development of regional trading blocs; the persistence of interstate conflicts; and the friction between world cultures. The convergence/divergence theme is revisited throughout the book and serves to remind the reader of the risks inherent in making broad generalizations about the nature of global politics.

In Chapter 1, we raise several searching questions about the state of the discipline of international relations and the contemporary evolution of global politics. In our short concluding chapter, we revisit these themes, but we do not aim to provide any concrete answers; rather, we hope to provoke further inquiry, discussion, and debate among readers.

TO THE STUDENT

It is an exciting time to be studying global politics. You are one among the growing post–Cold War generation, a generation that is exposed to a new global political environment with an agenda that is quite different from that which concerned students of international relations during the Cold War. However, as you look to the future of the world in which you live, it would be detrimental to ignore the past. Despite changes in the global political scene and advancements in technology and communications, in some respects little has changed; many of the issues and problems that have plagued the world for decades and even centuries persist today. Discovering that a hot topic today was also a hot topic generations ago can be a humbling experience, but much can be understood from past events and from how current issues are both similar to and different from those events.

Studying international relations is also a large undertaking, for the subject matter is broad, deep, and multidimensional, and many points of dispute and controversy exist. It is tempting for students to focus on certain issues (the environment, war, or the Internet, for example) to the exclusion of others. However, this narrow focus is a mistake, for virtually all subjects in global politics are closely interrelated, and it is impossible to understand one issue in isolation from others. Furthermore, an appreciation of different perspectives is an absolute must. Part of the challenge of any scholarly pursuit is to understand perspectives that differ from your own. When you do this, you gain in two ways: First, you improve your understanding of the basis for disagreements between individuals, groups, and states; and second, you are forced to examine your own personal perspectives and why you believe what you do. In some cases, this process will cause you to change your mind, while in other cases it will not. In any event, you will have gained a critical understanding of different views and ideas about the world.

This book is best viewed as a guide that can direct you through the interrelated subject matter, past, present, and future, of the subfields of global politics. The text introduces the specialized terms, lingo, and jargon that international relations scholars use to describe different phenomena and contending perspectives. (We have put terms that are defined in the glossary in **bold** type.) Of course, a large and rich literature exists on every subject discussed in this text, and you may want to learn more about a particular topic or find materials for research papers. At the end of each chapter, we supply a list of suggested readings and Internet resources to assist you in this task. Further, take care to read the endnotes that accompany each chapter, for they include some of the better-known and valuable sources, and we do not repeat them again under "Suggested Readings."

As a guide, this textbook is only an introduction to the vast topic of global politics. Your instructor may cover other issues, and you may find that you or your instructor do not agree with many of the points made in this book. However, we have tried to be as inclusive and balanced as possible in presenting the subject matter. As individuals, we differ on many aspects of our discipline and agree on many more. While it may be impossible to be completely balanced in such an undertaking (as we learned from preliminary reviews of this book), we have tried to incorporate as many diverse perspectives as possible while retaining content that is traditionally expected of an international relations textbook. Ultimately, it is up to you to develop your own informed opinions and ideas. We are both very interested in receiving any comments you may have regarding the present edition of *Global Politics*, and we invite you to write or e-mail us with them.

We completed our bachelor's and master's degrees in the late 1980s and completed our doctorates in the early 1990s at Canadian universities. Our careers as students and professionals straddle the Cold War and post–Cold War eras. Our experience is one of change and flux, and we, like you, look with excitement and deep concern at the emergent twenty-first century. We hope that this experience gives us a unique qualification as the authors of a text on global politics and that you enjoy reading and using this book.

ACKNOWLEDGMENTS

Many friends, colleagues, and scholars have contributed to the development, writing, and editing of this book. It would be impossible to list all those who have touched our lives and work in meaningful ways over the years, so any attempt that follows is necessarily partial.

We would like to thank the following colleagues whose expertise and assistance have been invaluable: Abbie Bakan, Andre Beauregard, Robert Boardman, Kim Cowan, David Cox, Gerald Dirks, Melissa Gabler, Bill Graf, David Haglund, Kal Holsti, Horst Hutter, Bob Jackson, Brian Job, Eric Laferrière, Jayent Lele, Don Munton, Jorge Nef, Kim Richard Nossal, Kwasi Obu-Fari, Charles Pentland, Evan Potter, Patricia Romano, Doug Ross, Terisa Turner, Henry Wiseman, and Mark Zacher. Our apologies to the many we have left off our list.

We owe a special debt of gratitude to two invaluable research assistants. For the first edition, Dan Wolfish took time from a busy doctoral studies schedule to assist in the preparation of the penultimate draft; and the second edition would not have been possible without the resourcefulness and dedication of Roberta Abbott.

We owe special thanks to the many reviewers commissioned by Nelson Thomson Learning, including John Carson, University of Toronto at Mississauga; Alistair David Edgar, Wilfrid Laurier University; Tom Keating, University of Alberta; Jean F. Mayer, University of Guelph; Alexander Moens, Simon Fraser University; Elizabeth Smythe, Concordia University College of Alberta; Elliot L. Tepper, Carleton University; David Winchester, Capilano College; and Yuchao Zhu, University of Regina. Their comments not only enriched the text and filled gaping holes but also gave us a sense of the current state of the discipline across Canada today. Peter Stoett thanks the Social Sciences and Humanities Research Council of Canada for funding. We would also like to thank the invaluable administrative assistance provided by staff in the Political Science departments at the University of British Columbia and Concordia University.

For the exhaustive editorial, production, and marketing effort at Nelson Thomson Learning we thank all those who worked on the second edition, including, but not limited to, Dawn Hunter, Bob Kohlmeier, Rebecca Rea, Kelly Torrance, Betty Robinson,

Carol Magee, Peter Papayanakis, Natalia Denesiuk, Helen Jager Locsin, Susan Calverley, and Julie Preston.

Most important, we would also like to express our appreciation for the comments offered by our students over the years. Students are the lifeblood of any scholarly enterprise, and ours have provided a wealth of critical insights and suggestions.

Any errors, of course, are our responsibility alone.

DEDICATION

For Pam and Ali

Allen G. Sens
University of British Columbia, Vancouver

Peter J. Stoett
Concordia University, Montreal

A NOTE ON MAPS AND NAMES

In global politics, conflicts (especially territorial conflicts) are often symbolized by disputes over the name of a country or territory. For example, Macedonia is called "the Former Yugoslavian Republic of Macedonia" (FYROM) because the Greek government objects to the use of a name that distinguishes an area within Greece. In addition, the names of many countries change over time, often because of a change in government. For example, the Khmer Rouge changed the name of Cambodia to Kampuchea (today, Cambodia is the common usage once again); Burma has been renamed Myanmar by the military regime in power there (although it is commonly referred to as Burma); and following a revolution in 1997 the African country of Zaire was renamed the Democratic Republic of Congo. Furthermore, separatist or nationalist movements that want to create or re-create their own states often refer to an area of land as their territory. For example, the representatives of the Kurdish people claim parts of Turkey, Syria, and Iran as the territory of Kurdistan, while the leadership of the Palestinian people wants to re-establish an independent state of Palestine in an area now occupied by the state of Israel. The politically sensitive nature of names is compounded by the fact that the use of one name over another is often taken as an indication of political support. This book seeks to make the student aware of such disputes and changes, although space considerations often make this impractical. We have strived to be as balanced and respectful as possible.

PART ONE

Origins

This section lays the foundation for subsequent discussions of contemporary and future issues. It begins with an introduction to the study of global politics, describing the academic field of inquiry widely known as international relations. We then offer a brief history of the evolution of the international political system, including the rise and fall of various empires, the prominent role of the state in the post-Westphalian system, and the wars that have shaped the theoretical perspectives and policy positions of analysts and politicians alike. The next chapter discusses the Cold War and the decision-making theories that were designed to explain behaviour in that context. Chapter 4 discusses the history of the world economy as well as the quite distinct theories that developed to explain that history. Finally, Chapter 5 examines the evolution of international law and international institutions.

This part of the book has three objectives. First, it establishes the historical roots of our own time. Second, it demonstrates how the theoretical perspectives of the field developed out of the experiences of the past. Third, it describes the origin of many of the debates and issues that remain part of the study of international relations today. This foundation will allow us to pursue more contemporary topics in Part Two.

CHAPTER 1

An Introduction to the Study of Global Politics

Let us not imitate the historians who believe that the past has always been inevitable, and thus suppress the human dimension of events.

— Raymond Aron[1]

INTRODUCTION: INTO A NEW CENTURY

The relationship between you and global politics is an interactive one. At the most basic level, you are alive and reading this text because you have not been killed in a thermonuclear war. This point is not trivial since at the height of the Cold War, such an Armageddon-like calamity seemed possible, indeed plausible, to many. Through a combination of accident and dramatic political change, it could become a predominant threat once again in the near future. Today, depending on where we live, we are more immediately threatened by global environmental change, the spread of infectious diseases, the opportunities and dislocation associated with the globalization of the economy, and many other threats to human security.

Every day, billions of people make decisions about what to wear, what to purchase, where to drive, walk, or ride, and how to change society. In making such decisions, every one of us contributes to the vast political space that is global politics. This statement is as true for someone living in Canada as it is for someone living in Pakistan, Uganda, or Micronesia, though the range of choice available is remarkably different. In turn, we are constantly bombarded with media images from the realm of global politics, such as anti-globalization protests in Quebec City and footage of the NATO air war over Serbia. Canadians have witnessed the trials and tribulations of their peacekeepers, taken hostage in Bosnia and accused of human rights violations themselves during the mission in Somalia. However, global politics is much more than image. We are often directly affected by global events, regardless of where we live. Recent increases in world oil prices have had an impact on people in Alberta as well as people in Nigeria; the shift to Chinese rule in Hong Kong has affected the demographic character of Vancouver. The sustained violence in the Middle East in the fall of 2000 prompted demonstrations in the streets of Montreal and Toronto by Canadians who supported either the Israelis or the Palestinians or decried the breakdown of the peace process in general.

Arguably, this interactive relationship between citizens and the world has become more complex as a new century begins. It is quite untrue that, in the good old bad days of the **Cold War** (the so-called **bipolar** era), things were simple. Put bluntly, global politics just cannot be simple! Far too many actors are involved in far too many activities to allow us to characterize the world in simplistic terms. However, the period between the end of World War II (1945) and the fall of the Soviet Union (1991) did permit us to take certain factors for granted. The United States and the Soviet Union were the two principal **state** powers, and although other states had nuclear weapons, these superpowers possessed a clear advantage in terms of firepower and delivery capability. Similarly, before the economic rise of Japan and the development of the European Union, the Soviet Union and the United States had the two largest economies in the world. The United Nations was split along a relatively clear ideological dividing line between the capitalist West, led by the United States, and the centrally planned economies of the East, led by the Soviet Union. Many other countries, such as India, tried to pursue a third or **nonaligned** path in an effort to remain free of dependence on either superpower.

This basic division of humanity has largely evaporated. The important questions the world community faces now are so varied and yet interlinked in character that they seem designed specifically to make teaching and learning about global politics a tremendous challenge. Not only has the geopolitical landscape changed but other issues, such as the environment, human rights, and poverty, are even more visible. We face a new era in which two simultaneous trends have emerged as one of the central paradoxes of our time: *convergence* and *divergence*. While economic, technological, and communicative integration is taking place, so is political fragmentation related to separatist movements, conflict over scarce resources, cultural clashes (what Samuel Huntington has termed the "clash of civilizations"), and other sources of modern conflict.[2] Many of the debates in the study of global politics revolve around whether one of these trends predominates. It would be simpler for all of us if this were clearly the case, but we must deal with the confusing fact that both are happening simultaneously.

This concept is not a novel one, and many other authors have touched on these apparently contradictory trends.[3] Nonetheless, this book is needed to introduce students to the discipline in a new century and beyond, especially those students who do not reside in the United States. Most textbooks tend to be American centred. The key examples and foreign policy dilemmas offered are American ones, reflecting that state's obviously unique position in world affairs. Students in **middle powers** such as Canada, however, appreciate an approach that takes the circumstances of their country (as well as their own personal interests) into account (see Profile 1.1). This textbook strives to present students and teachers with a non-American perspective, one that looks at the difficulties presented by the current global environment from a variety of competing perspectives that do not centre on American foreign policy issues. The task before citizens of smaller states such as Canada, Norway, Australia, Brazil, South Africa, Thailand, and many others is to better understand the global political environment and all that it entails, rather than to maintain national preeminence within it. Some may want to think of themselves not as citizens of states at all, but as global citizens with planetary concerns.

Global politics is a complex congruence of physical and intellectual power, political structures and institutions, and personalities. Studying this congruence has meant adopting a very wide conceptual lens. Commonly, the study of international relations has been considered a part of the larger field of political science. Most political science departments have international relations specialists. However, many universities are moving toward a much more explicitly interdisciplinary approach by, for example, granting degrees in international studies or international relations. We applaud this shift, since political science in the conventional sense is but a small part of the much broader subject matter of international relations. Today, university graduates need to have a strong background that gives them some knowledge about the international environment, and it is not necessary to label them political scientists to achieve this.

PROFILE 1.1 — Canada and Global Politics

Canada's position in the post–Cold War world is an enviable one. Canada faces no traditional military threats to its territory or political independence, possesses a virtually unequalled standard of living and is free from the instability and the conflicts that exist in so many parts of the world. However, this position is no excuse for complacency. Canada depends on a generally peaceful and stable international order for its physical security and its economic health. The Canadian economy is heavily dependent on trade, in particular, trade with the United States, the destination for approximately 83 percent of all Canadian **exports**. Issues such as the future of international institutions, the regulation of international finance, international terrorism and crime, arms control, peacekeeping, human rights, the environment, and many others are of direct relevance to Canadians and the Canadian government. Canada is a significant diplomatic actor, and it belongs to many major international forums and institutions, including the **Group of Eight (G-8)**, the **North Atlantic Treaty Organization (NATO)**, the **Commonwealth**, **La Francophonie**, and the United Nations, to name only a few. Successive Canadian governments have been strong supporters of **multilateralism**, for while Canada does not have the international influence of a great power such as the United States, within international organizations and coalitions Canada can at least have its voice heard.

In 1995, the government of Canada released a statement entitled *Canada in the World*, which described Canada's position in the world in the following terms. It argued that Canada is an economic leader in the age of globalization and that its unique geographic location situates it in the centre of the world economy. It also suggested that "Canada's history as a noncolonizing power, champion of constructive multilateralism and effective international mediator, underpins an important and distinctive role among nations as they seek to build a better order." As we will see, critics who argue that Canada, like any other state, puts self-interest and trade above all other considerations often challenge this proclamation of Canadian virtue.

SOURCE: *CANADA IN THE WORLD*, GOVERNMENT STATEMENT (OTTAWA: DEPARTMENT OF FOREIGN AFFAIRS AND INTERNATIONAL TRADE, 1995).

The discipline's focus is changing as well, away from questions of so-called **high politics**, which concern state security, grand strategies, and the use of military force, and toward so-called **low politics** issues, such as trade and investment, culture, and environmental problems. We are presently concerned with subjects as varied as the investment activities of multinational corporations, the links between trade and human rights in the fast-growing Asia-Pacific region, the work of development agencies in Africa and Latin America, and forestry practices in British Columbia, Brazil, and Indonesia. The Canadian Government has pursued issues such as children affected by war and the ban on landmines as part of a larger effort to promote human security. Indeed, threats to human security are widespread. Despite the action (or, some would argue, because of the inaction) of the United Nations, civil wars continue to rage throughout the world. Ethnic cleansing and genocide continue to be practised (the war in the former Yugoslavia and the genocide in Rwanda stand out as two clear examples in the 1990s, and NATO justified its massive display of military force in Kosovo in 1999 as a response to ethnic cleansing). Many nuclear weapons have been dismantled, but many remain, and others are still in the design stage. Furthermore, the **absolute poverty** in which billions of people live may be seen as a form of structural violence in itself. Violence against women is a major concern, organized crime is flourishing, and environmentalists often portray the assault on global ecosystems as ecocidal.

If global politics is about the pursuit of security (or the freedom from harm), security must be understood in terms of individual, community, ethnic, national, and even global survival. Responding to this broad agenda is the greatest challenge we face in global politics. The horrors of genocide during World War II provided the impetus for the establishment of a universal human rights regime to protect individuals from persecution conducted by the state. However, to varying degrees, ethnic minorities within states (from the Québécois in Canada to the Kurds in Turkey, Iraq, and Syria) continue to feel insecure in a political system dominated by another ethnic group. Their efforts to protect their culture and gain political influence can spark confrontation and conflict. More generally, states often perceive neighbouring states as threats to their continued existence. Such fears continue to ignite arms races, particularly in the South Asia, Asia-Pacific, and Middle East regions. The introduction of nuclear weapons, which have the ability to destroy all life on earth (**omnicide**), made us think in terms of global security. As the recent nuclear tests by India and Pakistan demonstrate, these weapons are still with us, along with the fear of accidents, wars of miscalculation, and proliferation.

Global economic instability has been a concern at least since the Great Depression, which was widely attributed to a lack of international cooperation and to the failure of the United States to exert leadership. Today, this lesson drives the effort of states to maintain and increase the economic and financial multilateralism developed during the Cold War. However, these efforts are often criticized for harming the economic security of less advantaged peoples and regions of the world. Furthermore, the realization that environmental problems such as **acid rain** and global warming are serious threats to all states has increased the propensity to turn to multilateral management efforts. Similarly, an increasing number of issues demand multilateral management, if not by international organizations, then by less formal means. **Unilateral** action becomes much more complicated, and often superfluous, in this context. These issues include migration and refugees, health crises, infectious diseases, women's rights, drug trafficking, cultural protection, and the regulation of the Internet. As such, they all have strong implications for the study and development of security and contemporary international relations; low politics have become high politics.

Some have even suggested that we have moved into a world of "postinternational" politics, an age characterized by the "decline of long-standing patterns" leaving us uncertain about "where the changes may be leading."[4] However, an unmistakable continuity exists: the international system remains fundamentally competitive, as different states, economic players, and ideas battle for dominance. To gain even a cursory understanding of all this, we need to impose clarity. Global politics is a strange and heady conceptual brew, to be sipped with caution.

WHY STUDY GLOBAL POLITICS?

There are many reasons for today's student to study global politics, not least of which—and here we reflect our personal bias without apology—is the sheer excitement of studying politics at the international level and learning more about the world in which we live. Every day, newspapers, television, and the Internet carry news items, features, and discussions on a bewildering array of events happening around the world. Indeed, knowledge may be power, but it must make sense to be of any use.

To some extent, all academic disciplines suffer from what we term the *irrelevancy disease*. In many cases, academics prefer to rely on abstract thinking, which many students find difficult to relate to their daily lives. While some of the theories floating around the discipline seem rather abstract at first glance, the people who study international relations today are often engaged in work that is highly relevant to politicians and the public alike. As greater numbers of people live and work in countries other than their birthplace, the application of international relations theory has become more varied than ever.

A basic education in international relations can also open and supplement career opportunities. Most large-scale businesses are engaged in some form of international activity. Many foreign firms hire domestic nationals to work in their branch companies. Increasingly, many young people are travelling to work or studying abroad and are finding opportunities to learn (and teach) languages and establish careers in other countries. Still others are working with nongovernmental organizations such as aid agencies or as journalists or international lawyers. Regardless of one's eventual career path, it is likely that it will involve contact with people in other countries.

Furthermore, it's a tough world out there, and many people want to make it better, to make a difference (see Profile 1.2). For the majority of global citizens, international events and developments have a very powerful and often devastating influence on their

PROFILE 1.2 Individual Actors on the Stage of World Politics: A Canadian Example

One of the fallen. Red Cross workers held candles during a brief ceremony at Vancouver International Airport as the body of Red Cross nurse Nancy Malloy arrived in Vancouver. (CP Picture Archive/Chuck Stoody)

Nancy Malloy was a Canadian Red Cross nurse and a specialist in hospital administration. A resident of Vancouver, she was born in Brockville, Ontario, in 1945, and held a bachelor's degree in nursing and a master's in business administration. She joined the Red Cross in 1987 and worked in outpost (one-nurse or two-nurse) hospitals in six remote British Columbia communities between 1987 and 1995. She took her first international assignment in 1990, motivated by a personal desire to help alleviate suffering in areas torn by war. She worked in five war zones over the next six years, in Ethiopia (1990), Kuwait (1991), the former Yugoslavia (1993), Zaire (1995), and in Chechnya (1996).

Nancy Malloy arrived in Chechnya in September 1996 as the medical administrator of a Red Cross hospital at Novye Atagi, 20 kilometres south of the capital, Grozny. On 17 December 1996, gunmen broke into the hospital complex during the night and killed six Red Cross workers, including Nancy Malloy. Her tragic and senseless death demonstrates the danger inherent in some types of international humanitarian work; she was the first Canadian Red Cross worker killed in the field. Also killed were Spanish head nurse Fernanda Calado, New Zealand nurse Sheryl Thayer, Norwegian nurses Gunnhild Mykleburst and Ingeborg Foss, and Dutch construction technician Johan Elkerbout. A person need not be a ruling politician to be a hero in world politics, and we are all susceptible to its dark side.

lives. Civil wars, famines, structural adjustment policies, chronic malnutrition, epidemics, pollution and environmental degradation, illiteracy, and many other hardships make life harder than ever. All these problems have important international dimensions, and addressing these problems requires international solutions. And most important, knowledge enables us to challenge, question, and doubt the position and rationales of governments, political leaders, and prevailing orthodoxy on international issues. So the question is not so much how the discipline can be relevant but, rather, whether today's citizens can afford not to know a good deal about the international system.

THE INTERDISCIPLINARY, YET DIVIDED, DISCIPLINE

Formally, and according to academic convention, the field of international relations is divided into several subfields, or what some prefer to term subdisciplines. In this way, international relations scholars can break the enormous amount of material and topics that make up global politics into more digestible sections for investigation and analysis. Though it is a matter of some dispute, depending on whom one asks, we will assume that the study of international relations has four major subfields, and this text will introduce you to each of them.

International relations theory is a body of literature that seeks to explain the nature of the international system and the behaviour of the actors within it.[5] *International security* has traditionally involved the study of conflict and war and the attempts to prevent or control it. Recently, international security specialists have been examining ethnic and religious conflicts, the proliferation of weapons, and the link between the environment and security.[6] The study of *international political economy* grew in the 1960s and 1970s as issues such as trade, finance, foreign debt, and underdevelopment became increasingly prominent in international affairs.[7] Finally, the subfield that examines institutions such as the United Nations is generally referred to as *international organization*, which focuses on means of cooperation such as the establishment of regimes or agreements among states, groups, or individuals.[8] We will deal with international organizations throughout this text, though students should pay particular attention to Chapter 5.

This division of the field into subfields is admittedly arbitrary. Some would argue that other subfields exist, such as foreign policy analysis, international ethics, or development studies, or that many issue-areas, in particular gender studies and environmental problems, have attained the rank of subfields themselves. Yet others would argue that these divisions are superfluous, because such a large overlap exists between the subfields that to separate them is misleading. Provided that we are aware of these objections, however, the divisions allow us to conceptualize the overall project of the study of global politics. Moreover—and this will become increasingly obvious to you as you read this text— those engaged in this project benefit from the collaboration of a large number of specialists from other well-established fields, including experts in comparative and domestic politics, world and local history, economics, geography, psychology, sociology, and anthropology.

When we move beyond the descriptive and analytical and into more prescriptive areas, we engage in *normative* work, in which writers are as interested in putting forth their vision of how the world *should* be as they are in telling us how it is. Normative projects reflect the moral and ethical judgments of the scholar or demonstrate how ethics are acted on by world leaders and diplomats.[9] Some scholars argue further that it is misleading to separate the analytic from the normative, since all investigators have their own biases. At any rate, normative work borrows heavily from the vast literature on ethics and philosophy and ventures into questions concerning the just causes of war, the true meaning of human rights, religious differences, and environmental values. Finally, in this technological age, we also borrow from the *applied sciences*, such as robotics and bioengineering, to describe international developments. In short, the student of global politics must become adept not only at taking a broad approach, but at practising considerable **synthesis** as well.

The discipline is divided further into differences over what the primary *level of analysis* should be. Three main levels of analysis exist—the *individual* level, the *state* or *group* level, and the *systemic* level—although this rough division is open to dispute.[10] The *individual* level of analysis focuses on the decisions of individuals, and the perceptions, values, and experiences that motivate those decisions. Generally, the individual level of analysis emphasizes the role of political leaders, for it is often assumed (perhaps erroneously) that those individuals most influence the course of history.[11] The *state* or *group* level of analysis focuses on the behaviour of individual states, which is often attributed to the form of government one finds at a particular time. It is necessary to look within states as well to determine which groups are influencing foreign policy. For example, the Canadian Liberal government's decision to contribute troops to a United Nations mission in Haiti has been linked to the presence of a strong expatriate Haitian community in a parliamentary by-election riding in Montreal. **Free trade** agreements are supported by the industrial sectors within states that will benefit most from lowering restrictions on trade in their products.

At the *systemic* level of analysis, the actions of states are seen as the result of external influences and pressures on them in relation to their attributes or position in world politics. In other words, the nature of the environment, or system, in which actors find themselves explains their behaviour. The capabilities and resources the actors have at their disposal establish the range of options they might have in any given situation. This emphasis on global structures leads us to an age-old debate within the social sciences concerning the relative causal weight assigned to systems and actors, otherwise known as structures and agents. Does the structure of the system predetermine the actions of actors? Or do humans shape events of their own accord? Many people today view this dichotomy as a false one, forcing us to reduce complex interactions to two essential forces. Rather, one can argue that continual interaction occurs between the individual units of action and the structures within which they operate. Each influences the other, though limitations exist as to how much influence can be projected. A state such as Canada cannot expect to be a dominant player in the current international system, since it is effectively overshadowed by the influence of its southern neighbour, the United States. However, in certain areas, such as peacekeeping and humanitarian assistance, certain Canadians have made extraordinary contributions to multilateral efforts. The modern state's extensive ties to the international system (or, to put it in more controversial terms, the outside world) not only limit its abilities to take autonomous actions but they also provide opportunities (see Profile 1.3).

When we examine the behaviour of actors within a system, as political scientists we are often most interested in discerning their relative influence; that is, we seek to identify who the dominant actors are, be they states, socioeconomic classes, organizations, corporations, or individuals. However, this identification is but half the story, for every form of dominance or control generates opposition. Thus, we seek also to identify and explain the motivations of *counterdominant* actors, which could refer to the Ogoni resisting oppression by the Nigerian government, or it could mean Iraqi military leaders determined to shift the balance of power in the Middle East by invading Kuwait.

Political Leadership:
Pierre Elliott Trudeau, 1919–2000

Searching for peace. Canadian Prime Minister Pierre Trudeau meets with China's Chairman Deng Xaoping in the Great Hall of the People in Beijing in 1983. Trudeau met with Deng to discuss his peace proposals. (CP Picture Archive/ Andy Clark)

In the summer of 2000, Canadians mourned the passing of one their most beloved—and controversial—political leaders, Pierre Elliott Trudeau. Trudeau was prime minister from 1968 to 1979, and again from 1980 to 1984. While he was always occupied with matters of national importance such as the separatist movement in Quebec and the evolution of the Canadian constitution, he was also exceptionally visible on the international stage. Early in his term as prime minister, Trudeau halved Canada's commitment of troops to NATO. He became a friend of Fidel Castro's, despite the American embargo on Cuba. His government recognized the People's Republic of China in 1970. At one point, and against widespread public opposition, Trudeau allowed the Americans to test cruise missiles over Canadian soil. Soon after, he undertook an international peace mission that saw him meet with world leaders to discuss disarmament and other issues. Widely respected for his intellect, Trudeau was known as a charming and, initially, novel statesman when he travelled abroad. As did any Canadian prime minister, he had to deal constantly with the prospects of internal division at home and of external absorption by the United States. Thousands of Canadians paid tribute after his death in 2000, in Ottawa, during a last train-ride home and at a large public funeral in Montreal.

It could refer to ambitious entrepreneurs introducing innovative products to the global market, or it could refer to environmentalists chaining themselves to trees to prevent clear-cut logging. It is too simple to say that dominant actors are conservative and counterdominant actors are radical. Each sphere of human activity differs, and since the political playing field is neither level nor stable, the question of just who is dominant and who is counterdominant is not amenable to an eternal formula. To further confuse the issue, it may be argued that the influence of some actors will be greater than others in times of flux.[12]

We also have to be careful regarding the nature of influence itself. It is impossible to define power here, but power has *hard* and *soft* dimensions.[13] Hard power capability refers to the more obvious: military hardware, technological capabilities, and economic size. In many cases hard power is still put to the test today, as we saw vividly in the U.S.-led Gulf War of 1991 or NATO's intervention in Kosovo in 1999. Soft power refers to the power of ideas, persuasion, culture, and innovation, which possess less tangible qualities. Within the international system, some states have more hard and soft power than others. There are limitations, however, and stubbornness usually reveals them—even the United States could not pressure the government of India to sign a new treaty banning nuclear weapons testing in 1996. But the agent–structure debate noted above continues: should we focus on the power of states per se or on the power of a larger structure, or system, such as the capitalist world economic system, where the soft power of prevailing ideas becomes even more important? Ultimately, this is one of the many analytic questions students need to answer for themselves.

Below, we discuss some of the more prevalent basic perspectives that have been generated by international relations theorists. However, keep firmly in mind the interdisciplinary contributions, and methodological divisions, discussed above.

BASIC PERSPECTIVES ON GLOBAL POLITICS

Charles Lindblom, in the introduction to his book on the purpose and effects of contemporary social science, readily admits, in a discussion of mindsets, "classical nineteenth-century liberalism is my prison. It is not the most inhumane of prisons; its cells are by far larger than those of any other prison I know. Indeed, its construction is such that inmates often succeed in persuading themselves that they are wholly free."[14] This admission acknowledges an important point: we are all, to some degree, trapped within our own particular way of seeing and making sense of the world. As Kenneth Boulding warns, "It is what we think the world is like, not what it is really like, that determines our behaviour."[15] Textbook writers are hardly free of this circumstance; the perspectives of the authors, their origins, and the assumptions they make become part of the book, though we have made every effort to be as inclusive as possible. We might add also that our own perspectives differ sufficiently to add what we hope is a good measure of balance.

Because they reappear in future chapters, it is important to provide a very brief outline of some of the more dominant perspectives in international relations theory in this introductory chapter. Again, we have had to be arbitrary to reflect our own perception of what those perspectives actually are. However, we must keep in mind that all these perspectives have less than concrete manifestations in the work of international relations scholars. In other words, they are best viewed as fluid conceptions, subject to change and manipulation. In fact, as we shall see, these perspectives all took shape in a historical context that informed their development. As the historian Arthur Schlesinger, Jr., has observed, traumatic events (such as war) lead to "skeptical reassessments of supposedly sacred assumptions."[16]

IDEALISM

An idealist perspective assumes the best of human nature: we are essentially cooperative political animals who are occasionally led astray by evil influences into war and conflict, and we have a natural affinity toward the communal, as opposed to the individual, good. When people behave violently, it is because of the institutional or structural setting in which they live. International relations is teleological in that we move either toward some form of world government or toward a self-controlled **anarchy** in which peace will reign. We discuss idealism in more depth in the next chapter.

REALISM

Classical realism, as it has come to be called, is less generous regarding human nature. People are generally nasty self-serving creatures, and political power merely corrupts them further. Political relations are fundamentally about conflict, as unitary rational actors seek their own self-interest. In the case of global politics, the relevant actors are states, which seek their national interest at all times. Military power is the most important expression and guarantor of survival, and the most important issue-area in the field is the threat or actual use of force (everything else is low politics). When it comes to foreign policy and security, states must choose what to do in certain situations purely based on their own self-interest, and we should not be surprised when they choose to go to war. The only way to change this situation would be to make the world system nonanarchic; this system would require a world government, but that prospect is rejected as a virtual impossibility.

Structural Realism

This version of realism focuses on the systemic level of analysis. State actors are still the major players, of course, and they all seek survival in a self-help world. Structures determine behaviour; the structure of the international system is anarchic, lacking a central political authority that can constrain individual states. States have no choice but to maximize their power to reduce vulnerability and promote national interests. International institutions are viewed as mere epiphenomena: they are not important actors in and of themselves but merely reflect the attempts of states to pursue their own ends.

LIBERALISM

Liberalism suggests people can rationally cooperate in the name of self-interest (since what is good for one may be good for another as well). Liberals emphasize the importance of private property, law, free markets, democracy, and justice. Great importance is placed on economic growth, both domestically and internationally. It is believed that more trade leads to fewer wars, since trade instils a sense of cooperation even though it occurs in a competitive environment. In addition, so-called *transnationalist* avenues for international cooperation, such as the creation of international organizations and cultural exchanges, can reduce the chances of war and increase global wealth. Two popular variants of liberalism are in circulation today: complex interdependence and neoliberal institutionalism.

Complex Interdependence

If you blend realism's concern with power and state conflict with liberalism's optimism and emphasis on transnationalist phenomena, you get what Robert Keohane and Joseph Nye, in a seminal work of the 1970s, termed "complex interdependence theory."[17] They argue that economic factors are fast becoming as important as military matters, and that nonstate actors such as **multinational corporations (MNCs)** and **nongovernmental organizations (NGOs)** play important roles alongside states. Further, states are not always rational, coherent actors, since they respond to internal discord. Keohane and Nye intended their theory to be a modification, not a refutation, of realism, but much of what they argued has been subsumed under the liberal banner. We return to this perspective in Chapter 4.

Neoliberal Institutionalism

Idealists and liberals have much in common, including the desire for stronger institutions to facilitate global cooperation. These institutions are often called **regimes,** sets of principles, norms, rules, and decision-making procedures around which actors' expectations converge. They reduce uncertainty and allow people to get on with important transnational business, such as trade, investment, or pursuing human rights improvements. The essential argument here is that the anarchism so instrumental in a structural realist understanding of global politics need not prevent states and individuals from achieving a more harmonious world; in some cases international institutions could actually replace the state as a provider of goods to citizens. We return to these themes in Chapter 5.

CRITICAL PERSPECTIVES

Critical perspectives reject the contemporary order of things as inadequate in terms of social justice. They challenge the other perspectives that serve to reinforce the status quo. Global politics is not only about relations among states; nonstate actors and social forces, such as entrenched classes and popular movements, are also agents of change. History can be seen in terms of the domination, exploitation, and marginalization of one group over another: of the southern hemisphere by the northern European imperialist powers; of women by men; of some races by others. Of course, remarkably different viewpoints exist within this general critical perspective. A very cursory treatment of four of them follows.

Neomarxism and Dependency Theory

The central assumption behind the many strands of this literature is that economic classes are the primary units of analysis in world affairs and that the economic growth experienced by the rich Northern world has come at the cost of others, namely those in the poor Southern world. Economic relations are determined by geography and colonial history. Thus, states rich in natural resources, such as Canada, have gained from exporting them abroad and in particular to large markets such as the United States. At the same time, however, this traps states such as Kenya, Argentina, Zambia, and Peru into dependencies based on staple exports such as tea, bauxite, coffee, tobacco, and wood. Reliance on staple products is exacerbated by relative political weakness. Within underdeveloped states, the upper classes participate in the North–South exploitive relationship, not only reinforcing global inequality but also benefiting from it. This theory is discussed in more depth in Chapter 8.

Feminism

The primary focus of feminism is gender inequality and the critique of the patriarchal systems that perpetuate it. Feminists who study global politics argue that a patriarchal system exists at the international level. Further, dominant academic perspectives, in particular realism, have served only to reinforce the system with gender-specific language and the cult of masculinity surrounding political and military discourse. However, quite distinct versions of feminism exist. Liberal feminists argue that women's participation in world affairs has been too silent or marginalized and that this situation must be corrected; feminists who are more radical argue this correction would be insufficient and that deeper changes are necessary.

Postmodernism

Postmodernists are primarily concerned with how people interpret the world around them and how they act on this understanding. Postmodernists are critical of the positivist aspirations of the traditional theories. They reject the idea that realists, liberals, or Marxists can ever really know anything concrete about global politics (or build objective knowledge about the world), since their personal biases will invariably influence their conclusions. As such, the traditional approaches contribute to the present social injustice brought about by the development of *modernity*, the scientific revolution of the West. Postmodernist thought has many strands as well: deconstructionists emphasize the importance of breaking down popular texts or discourses to understand the power relations they perpetuate, while feminist postmodernists look for gender bias in traditional discourse.

Environmentalism

Although environmental approaches are not unified in any coherent body of theory, environmentalists do agree that liberal theories do not adequately account for the ecological costs of global economic growth, while realism ignores the role played by the state in perpetuating environmental exploitation. Again, many varieties of environmentalism exist, some of which stress dealing with overpopulation, overconsumption, pollution, or the threat to endangered species. More radical approaches advocate reconceptualizing capitalism or redefining human relations. Ecofeminists link patriarchy with ecocide. Nonstate actors are often seen as the most important agents of change, although some radical environmentalists believe in direct action through protest or even acts of violence. Others argue that a need for stronger states is necessary to preserve what's left of the natural world, even if it means limiting human personal freedoms in the process. Chapter 8 reintroduces this perspective.

Another approach, broadly labelled *constructivism*, stresses the impact of intersubjective understandings among political actors on constituting their own identities. This social construction of the self, be it by national leaders, members of international organizations, environmental scientists, or others, determines the normative acceptability of practices and discourses within issue-areas. In short, "it is collective meanings that constitute the structures which organize our actions."[18] We hesitate to include this perspective as an individual one since it is in essence a way of understanding change that borrows from postmodernism and can be applied by a wide range of analysts with roots in the perspectives outlined above, most pointedly, perhaps, those interested in studying international institutions, many of whom come from the neoliberal institutional school.

At this point it would be inaccurate to say that any one perspective dominates the study of global politics. Realism certainly held sway in the United States for much of the Cold War era, but liberal perspectives are at least as prominent today and have often been so in England, Australia, and Canada. Critical perspectives are as popular as ever, especially among students and in the southern hemisphere. As we will see in the following pages, certain issue-areas encourage the appreciation of certain perspectives on global politics. We discuss the nature of those issue-areas in the final section below.

ONWARD!

This chapter has introduced the field of global politics and has argued that an approach that escapes the American focus typical of most texts is needed. But the most central rationale for a new look at this topic is that, as the new century begins, history is moving on. Though the older concepts that have shaped the field, such as state, war, and diplomacy, have retained their significance, we face an era when nonstate actors are often as important, when market forces are changing millions of lives on a daily basis, and when people are attempting to forge new definitions of human rights and dignity. This idea generates a lengthy set of questions—an agenda for study—that requires looking into both traditional and nonconventional areas. A partial list of such questions includes the following:

1. Which theoretical perspective best describes and explains the world? This question is a fundamental one, because different theoretical perspectives provide very different explanations of events and have different sets of priorities.

2. What are the lessons of the past? This is an enduring question in the field, but in the contemporary and future context, it involves the examination of periods in history that more closely approximate our own. The hope is that lessons might be learned about the structure of the current international system.

3. Is the international system fragmenting or integrating? Two phenomena seem to exist side by side in the international system: the break-up and collapse of empires and states, and increasing interdependence and political and economic amalgamation. Is there a trend in one direction or another?

4. Are states becoming obsolete? One trend in international affairs has been the increased permeability and penetrability of state borders. Has the **sovereignty** of the state eroded to the point where we may speak of the imminent demise of the state in world politics?

5. Is geoeconomics replacing geopolitics? With the end of the political, ideological, and military confrontation of the Cold War, many argue that economics is the new arena of competition in the world and that states increasingly measure their relative power next to others in economic, rather than military, terms.

6. What are the causes of war, and how can conflicts be managed or prevented? This is also a question of enduring importance in international relations, but, today, efforts are concentrated on addressing the problem of ethnic or religious wars within states, as well as the protection of civilians during conflict, part of the broader *human security* agenda adopted by Canada during the late 1990s under the guidance of the recently retired Minister for Foreign Affairs, Lloyd Axworthy.

7. How can the proliferation of conventional weapons and weapons of mass destruction be stopped? The flow of weapons of mass destruction, sophisticated conventional weapons, and small arms to areas of tension and conflict is a pressing international concern. How this flow of arms might be stopped is a prominent feature of the contemporary arms control debate.

8. What is the future of the international economy? Are we heading toward an increasingly liberalized world economy characterized by global free trade, or is the world economy heading toward the development of regional trading blocs? Will the global economy be characterized by continued growth or by crisis and economic downturn?

9. Are international organizations getting stronger or weaker? International organizations are a key manifestation of cooperation in international affairs. Some would argue that they serve to enhance and reinforce cooperation. Yet, many international organizations are showing signs of decay, while others are struggling to adapt to a new international environment.

10. How will environmental issues affect global politics? Environmental degradation has emerged as a serious issue between states and within them. The question is whether environmental pressures such as climatic change and resource scarcity contribute to increased cooperation or increased conflict among states and peoples.

11. What will be the impact of the information revolution on global politics? Does the information revolution promise a world of improved communication, understanding, and sharing of knowledge leading to a global community, or a world of the information rich and the information poor?

12. How will increasing migration of people affect global politics? People are on the move around the world, in the form of emigrants, refugees, and migrant workers. Increasing hardship and population pressures in the developing world suggest that even larger population movements will occur in the future, posing hard questions for immigration and refugee policy. Human smuggling is a growing international organized crime activity.

13. What will be the future impact of the power differential between the developing and developed world? An ever-widening gap in economic and political power exists between the richer countries of North America and Europe and the poor countries of Latin America, Asia, and Africa. This question has given rise to the North–South debate.

14. What are the best strategies for development and aid? This issue has been a pressing one since the 1960s, and as the divide between the world's rich and the world's poor continues to widen, the debate over development strategies has taken on a new urgency. Placing more priority on the role of women in development has led to opportunities and new challenges.

These are just some of the many questions students of global politics will face in the coming years. We have, in the most profound sense of the term, entered a new era. As for the argument that with the end of the Cold War and the great ideological battle between liberalism and Communism we are at an epoch similar to the end of history, we would argue that we are instead at a new beginning, one that poses unprecedented challenges to the collective whole and to individuals alike. Even the author widely held to be the most popular proponent of the "end of history" thesis freely admits this possibility. Francis Fukuyama, in the conclusion to his engrossing bestseller *The End of History and the Last Man*, refers to the French–Russian philosopher Alexandre Kojeve, who believed, in the tradition of the German philosopher **Georg Wilhelm Friedrich Hegel**, that "history itself would vindicate its own rationality." Or, as Fukuyama puts it,

> Enough wagons would pull into town such that any reasonable person looking at the situation would be forced to agree that there had been only one journey and one destination. It is doubtful that we are at that point now, for … the evidence available to us now concerning the direction of the wagons' wanderings must remain provisionally inconclusive. Nor can we in the final analysis know, provided a majority of the wagons eventually reach the same town, whether their occupants … will not find them inadequate and set their eyes on a new and more distant journey.[19]

It is that new, and necessarily distant, journey on which the world has embarked at the turn of the century. Above all, this text is designed to provide interested readers with a rough guide for that journey, one that encompasses origins, currents, and directions. Some aspects of the study of global politics are timeless. As one author contends, "diplomacy, in the sense of the ordered conduct of relations between one group of human beings and another group alien to themselves, is far older than history."[20] Some theorists argue that human nature has always been with us and will not change; others insist it can change for the better, or worse, according to circumstances. As our historical discussions in Part One of this book suggest, war and trade—two primary modes of human interaction—have both been around a very long time. We begin with a look at the formation of the nation-state and the problem of war. Although this subject no longer dominates the field as it once did, it remains the most vivid example of the potential consequences of the nation-state system. Chapter 3 explores the Cold War era and the nature of state decision making. Next, we examine political perspectives pertaining to the global economy and its evolution. Our final chapter in "Origins" deals with international organization and international law and in particular with the much-maligned United Nations.

"Currents" deals with more contemporary issues, such as the present security agenda, efforts to mediate peace among belligerents, globalization and marginalization, and human rights questions. Finally, "Directions" forces us to look ahead, however tentatively, at trends that are unfolding before us: environmental problems, potential wars of the future, the increasing and increasingly migratory human race, and the information and technological revolution. We have chosen these themes because they help convey an understanding of the complex convergence/divergence paradox outlined above and because students will no doubt relate to most of them in their everyday lives. Onward!

Endnotes

1. Raymond Aron, *Peace and War: A Theory of International Relations, An Abridged Version* (Garden City, New York: Anchor, 1973 [1966]), 9.
2. Samuel Huntington, "The Clash of Civilizations?" *Foreign Affairs* 72 (Summer 1993), 22–49.
3. The most cited example is Kal Holsti's article, "Change in the International System: Interdependence, Integration, and Fragmentation," in O. Holsti, R. Siverson, and A. George, eds., *Change in the International System* (Boulder, CO: Westview Press, 1980), 23–53.
4. J. Rosenau, *Turbulence in World Politics: A Theory of Change and Continuity* (Princeton: Princeton University Press, 1990), 6.
5. See, for example, J. Dougherty and R. Pfaltzgraff, *Contending Theories of International Relations: A Comprehensive Survey*, 3rd ed. (New York: Harper & Row, 1990); P. Viotti and M. Kauppi, *International Relations Theory: Realism, Pluralism, Globalism*, 2nd ed. (Toronto: Maxwell, 1993); T. Taylor, ed., *Approaches and Theory in International Relations* (Essex: Longman, 1978); C. Kegley, ed., *Controversies in International Relations Theory: Realism and the Neoliberal Challenge* (New York: St. Martin's Press, 1995); R. Keohane, ed., *Neorealism and Its Critics* (New York: Columbia University Press, 1986); and O. Holsti, "Models of International Relations and Foreign Policy," *Diplomatic History* 13 (1989), 15–43.
6. See D. Dewitt and D. Leyton-Brown, eds., *Canada's International Security Policy* (Scarborough, ON: Prentice Hall, 1995). A classic text on conflict management is R. Matthews, A. Rubinoff, and J. Gross Stein, eds., *International Conflict and Conflict Management: Readings in World Politics* (Scarborough, ON: Prentice Hall, 1984). Another subfield, known formally as peace studies, has focused on theories related to cooperation. In fact, the study of peace has a technical name: *irenology*. See J. Starke, *An Introduction to the Study of Peace (Irenology)* (Leyden: A.W. Sijthoff, 1968).
7. A popular text is K. Stiles and T. Akaha, eds., *International Political Economy: A Reader* (New York: HarperCollins, 1991); for a recent Canadian perspective, see D. Drache and M. Gertler, eds., *The New Era of Global Competition: State Policy and Market Power* (Montreal/Kingston: McGill–Queen's University Press, 1991).
8. See R. Riggs and J. Plano, *The United Nations: International Organization and World Politics* (Chicago: Dorsey Press, 1994); J. Ruggie and H. Milner, eds., *Multilateralism Matters: New Directions in World Politics* (New York: Columbia University Press, 1993); and S. Krasner, ed., *International Regimes* (Ithaca, NY: Cornell University Press, 1983).
9. For example, see Michael Walzer, *Just and Unjust Wars* (New York: Basic Books, 1992); F. Kratchvil, *Rules, Norms, and Decisions: On the Conditions of Practical and Legal Reasoning in International*

Relations and Domestic Affairs (Cambridge: Cambridge University Press, 1989); and Robert Jackson, *Quasi-States: Sovereignty, International Relations, and the Third World* (Cambridge: Cambridge University Press, 1990).

10. See J. David Singer, "The Level of Analysis Problem in International Relations," *World Politics* 14 (1961), 77–92; Kenneth Waltz, *Man, the State, and War* (New York: Columbia University Press, 1959); and Robert C. North, *War, Peace, Survival: Global Politics and Conceptual Synthesis* (Boulder, CO: Westview Press, 1990).

11. In fact, much of this work is termed *diplomatic history.*

12. For example, John Naisbitt argues that the larger the system, the more powerful and important are its smaller parts. See *Global Paradox: The Bigger the World Economy the More Powerful Its Smallest Players* (New York: William Morrow, 1994).

13. These two dimensions are outlined in more detail in J. Nye, *Bound to Lead: The Changing Nature of American Power* (New York: Basic Books, 1990).

14. C. Lindblom, *Inquiry and Change: The Troubled Attempt to Understand and Shape Society* (New Haven: Yale University Press, 1990), x.

15. Kenneth E. Boulding, "National Images and International Systems," *Journal of Conflict Resolution* 3 (June 1959), 120–31.

16. See Arthur Schlesinger, Jr., *The Cycles of American History* (Boston: Houghton Mifflin, 1986).

17. For the most recent edition of this work, see *Power and Interdependence*, 3rd ed. (New York: Longman, 2001).

18. Alexander Wendt, "Anarchy is What States Make of It: The Social Construction of Power Politics," *International Organization* 46:2 (1992), 391–425.

19. Francis Fukuyama, *The End of History and the Last Man* (New York: The Free Press, 1992), 339.

20. Sir Harold Nicolson, *Diplomacy*, 3rd ed. (London: Oxford University Press, 1963), 5.

Suggested Readings

Note: Students are reminded to read the endnotes in each chapter for additional relevant readings.

Amstutz, M. *International Conflict and Cooperation: An Introduction to World Politics.* Madison: Brown and Benchmark, 1995.

Art, R., and R. Jervis, eds. *International Politics: Enduring Concepts and Contemporary Issues.* 3rd ed. New York: HarperCollins, 1992.

Calvocoressi, P. *World Politics Since 1945.* 6th ed. London: Longman, 1991.

Gill, S., and J. Mittelman, eds. *Innovation and Transformation in International Studies.* Cambridge: Cambridge University Press, 1997.

Holsti, K.J. *The Dividing Discipline: Hegemony and Diversity in International Theory.* Boston: Allen and Unwin, 1985.

Kegley, C., and E. Wittkopf, eds. *The Global Agenda: Issues and Perspectives.* 4th ed. New York: McGraw-Hill, 1995.

Kennedy, P. *The Rise and Fall of the Great Powers: Economic Change and Military Conflict from 1500 to 2000.* New York: Random House, 1987.

Kuhn, T. *The Structure of Scientific Revolutions.* Chicago: University of Chicago Press, 1962.

Mansbach, R. *The Global Puzzle: Issues and Actors in World Politics.* 3rd. ed. Boston: Houghton Mifflin Company, 2000.

Ponton, G., and P. Gill. *Introduction to Politics.* Oxford: Martin Robertson, 1982.

Rourke, J., ed. *Taking Sides: Clashing Views on Controversial Issues in World Politics.* 7th ed. Guilford: Dushkin, 1996.

Said, A., C. Lerche, and C. Lerche III. *Concepts of International Politics in Global Perspective.* 4th ed. Englewood Cliffs: Prentice Hall, 1995.

Suggested Websites

The Websites listed here are general resource sites. More specific sites are provided at the end of each chapter.

Libraries

Berkeley Sunsite Library Links Libweb
    <sunsite.berkeley.edu/Libweb/>

Carrie: A Full Text Electronic Library
    <kuhttp.cc.ukans.edu/carrie/carrie_main.html>

Gabriel: Gateway to European Libraries
    <portico.bl.uk/gabriel/en/welcome.html>

General Political Science and International Relations Resources

ACUNS External Links
    <www.brown.edu/Departments/ACUNS/NEW_links/>

Berkeley Institute of International Studies

Coombsweb Social Science WWW Virtual Library
    <coombs.anu.edu.au/WWWVL-SocSci.html>

International Affairs Network International Affairs Resources
    <info.pitt.edu/~ian/ianres.html>

Policy.ca: A Non-Partisan Resource for the Public Analysis of Canadian Policy Issues
    <www.policy.ca>

SACIS International Affairs Resources
    <www.library.ubc.ca/poli/international.html>

Stanford University Links Page
    <cisac.stanford.edu/global/links.html>

UN Homepage
    <www.un.org>

Weatherhead Center for International Affairs
    <data.fas.harvard.edu/cfia/>

Yale University Selected Internet Resources: International Relations
    <www.library.yale.edu/ia-resources/resource.htm>

CHAPTER 2

History, Theory, and the Problem of War

One Age cannot be completely understood if all the others are not understood.

— Jose Ortega y Gasset (philosopher and historian)

AN INTRODUCTION TO THE PROBLEM OF WAR

With the dramatic events of the end of the Cold War fresh in our memories, it is tempting to proclaim that a new historical epoch is upon us. But has such a fundamental change occurred that it makes history irrelevant to our understanding of the present and future? The answer is an emphatic no. The end of the Cold War brought enormous changes to the edifice of global politics but few changes to its foundations. We need to look to the past to obtain an understanding of that foundation.

History can provide insights into current issues and problems. For example, any attempt to understand or address the conflicts surrounding the disintegration of Yugoslavia would be incomplete without an examination of the long history of animosity (and cooperation) between the Slovenian, Croatian, Serbian, and Bosnian Muslim (Bosniak) peoples. The division of the Korean peninsula must be understood with reference to World War II and the **Korean War**. It is impossible to understand the persistent national unity question or First Nations's issues in Canada without some knowledge of the colonial legacy in North America. In short, history is all around us, and we ignore it at our peril.

However, we must raise a few caveats about the use of historical material. Rarely is the importance of perspective more evident than when examining history, since many different interpretations of past events exist. States tend to have official versions of historical events, often glorifying the importance and righteousness of their country's actions, or perhaps minimizing the harm caused in their names. For example, Japanese textbooks still omit many of the facts about Japanese foreign policy during World War II (see Profile 2.1).

Scholars of international relations also have divergent views of historical events, depending on their educational and social background, as well as their theoretical orientation. Furthermore, as feminists and postmodernists often argue, historical perspectives can be exclusionary. Many groups—including women and ethnic and religious minorities—argue, quite correctly, that they have been underrepresented in mainstream histories. Finally, history is vulnerable to radical revisions for political ends. For example, those who deny that the Holocaust ever took place are not interpreting history; they are denying it and trying to rewrite it for their own ends. Vigilance against this sort of manipulation is as important as respect for different perspectives (see Profile 2.1).

Abusing History

CONTENT OMISSION IN JAPANESE SCHOOL TEXTBOOKS

In 1997, a Japanese historian named Saburo Ienega won a landmark case before the Japanese Supreme Court. The Court ruled that the Japanese Education Ministry broke the law when it removed certain material from a high-school textbook written by Ienega. Since the 1950s, the Education Ministry has screened Japanese textbooks, removing references to the atrocities committed by the Japanese military in World War II. As a result, generations of Japanese school children have gone through school with only a general or highly sanitized account of Japan's war record, with key events and facts omitted or treated in an incomplete manner. One of the references removed from Ienega's textbook concerned biological warfare experiments conducted by the Japanese military on Chinese subjects during the war. Opposition to such references comes from nationalists (who regard such references as an attack on Japanese pride) and widespread ignorance of Japan's war record (largely a result of the education policy). Others hoped that the Ienega case might finally signal an end to this practice. Successive generations of Japanese textbooks have included more information and facts concerning Japan's role in the war. For example, most textbooks now mention the infamous "comfort women" who were forced into prostitution to serve the soldiers of the Japanese military. However, references to atrocities remain brief and serious omissions are often made. Most textbooks acknowledge only partial responsibility, a key element of the Japanese government's position on Japan's wartime misdeeds. Japan provides an important example of how states and governments can abuse history through censorship and the suppression of unpopular ideas or facts. Because of the Court's decision, the material on biological warfare experiments was restored to Ienega's textbook. However, other references in his book were not restored.

JIM KEEGSTRA AND HOLOCAUST DENIAL

In 1985, an Alberta schoolteacher named Jim Keegstra went on trial in Red Deer, Alberta. Keegstra was charged with willfully promoting hatred against an identifiable group—Jewish people—from 1978 to 1982 while he taught social studies at Eckville High School in Alberta. Keegstra taught his students that Judaism was an evil religion that perverted the laws of God and condoned the harsh treatment of non-Jewish peoples. He implicitly taught his students that the Holocaust was a hoax and that an international Jewish conspiracy—called the "hidden hand"—was working behind the scenes with the support of Jewish financiers to establish a new world order in which there would be one government. According to Keegstra, Jews had infiltrated every institution of society, and this demanded that non-Jews be aware and watchful. Keegstra taught his students that conventional history books had lies in them, and in his classes, he used books and pamphlets from his own library. Class exams and essays were based on these readings and class notes. In most respects, Keegstra's teachings were typical of anti-Semitic views, full of conspiracy theories based on historical distortions and outright inaccuracies, suppression and denial of evidence and fact, and barely concealed hatred. He passed these views on to students in a high-school social studies class as fact, one example among many of the abuse of history by individuals or groups. Jim Keegstra was found guilty, fined $5000, and was prohibited from teaching high school.

We now turn to a brief examination of world history as it is most often described: as the history of war and peace, and the rise and fall of civilizations, states, and empires. It is also a history of the development of the intellectual foundation of contemporary international relations theory and how the experiences of prominent intellectuals have shaped their visions of the nature of international politics. We have two aims here. First, human history can be (and has been) interpreted as a history of conflict. In this sense, what follows is a historical review from a realist perspective, one that most students will recognize. Although the review is not inaccurate, as we will see, it is incomplete. Second, the development of theory has been influenced by developments in history. The two are inseparable, and the changing nature of global politics has stimulated the development of new theories and the adaptation of old ones.

THE ANCIENT LEGACY: THE RISE AND FALL OF CIVILIZATIONS AND EMPIRES

In the Middle East, civilization first developed around 3500 B.C.E., in the basins of three great river systems. The river basin of the Tigris and Euphrates was the cradle for the early Mesopotamian city-states and the Assyrian (1244–605 B.C.E.) and Persian (550–331 B.C.E.) empires. The Nile River basin sustained the great Egyptian empires of the Pharaohs, which rose to the heights of the age of the pyramids (c. 2590 B.C.E.) and the XII (1991–1786 B.C.E.) and XVIII (1570–1320 B.C.E.) dynasties. The Indus River basin and the plain of Ganges was the cradle of India's early Harappa and Mohenjo-Daro civilizations (c. 2550–1550 B.C.E.).

Civilization in the Mediterranean was dominated by successive waves of Greek peoples, who established control over much of the Mediterranean (c. 1150–550 B.C.E.). In Asia Minor (present-day Turkey) the Greek advance clashed with the Persian Empire of Darius and Xerxes. Although Greece resisted conquest, the unity of the Greek city-states collapsed and the resulting Peloponnesian War (431–404 B.C.E.) between Athens and Sparta enabled Macedon, under Philip, to dominate the Greek peninsula (see Profile 2.2).

PROFILE 2.2

Thucydides (460–400 B.C.E.)

Thucydides is regarded as the greatest of the classical Greek historians because of his unfinished account of the Peloponnesian War between Athens and Sparta (Lacedaemon). Thucydides himself was an Athenian general who was exiled from Athens. In exile, he wrote a history of the war that was taking place all around him. His exhaustive and dramatic account can be read as a Greek tragedy, a story of human virtue and human deceit, and an exploration of the origins of war. Many contemporary students of global politics maintain that the themes in the book are applicable across time, culture, and place. Thucydides sought to draw themes and generalizations about the origin of all wars and to offer historical lessons for those who might read his work in the future. For Thucydides, "the growth in the power of Athens, and the alarm this inspired in Lacedaemon, made war inevitable." Thucydides thus identified the cause of war in the fear provoked by shifts in the distribution of power across the Greek city-states. His focus on the importance of power is most graphically illustrated in the famous Melian Dialogue, in which the powerful Athenians say to the less powerful Melians, "for you know as well as we do that right ... is in question only between equals in power, while the strong do what they can and the weak suffer what they must." Thucydides also reflected on the role of prominent individuals in the course of events, and he is considered one of the intellectual founders of political realism.

SOURCE: THUCYDIDES, *THE PELOPONNESIAN WAR*, THE CRAWLEY TRANSLATION (NEW YORK: THE MODERN LIBRARY, 1982), 14, 351.

Philip's son, **Alexander the Great**, conquered a dominion that stretched from Macedon to the Indus River. After Alexander's death in 323 B.C.E., a new power centre developed around Rome in central Italy, and soon expanded over the entire Italian peninsula (510–264 B.C.E.). Bolstered by an extremely effective military and administrative system, Roman rule (first as a republic and then as an empire) eventually stretched from present-day Spain to Mesopotamia. However, the Roman Empire declined due to internal strife and barbarian invasion, and the empire was split in two in C.E. 330 by the establishment of an Eastern empire with its capital at Constantinople (Byzantium). The Western half of the empire fell to invasion in the fifth century, but the Eastern half, the Byzantine Empire, survived another thousand years. The Byzantine Empire eventually fell to Ottoman conquest with the fall of Constantinople in C.E. 1453.

In northern Europe, distinct cultural groups had developed by 800 B.C.E. Much of northern Europe came under Celtic domination by 450 B.C.E. The Slavic peoples established a centre of civilization in what is today central Russia. The decline and fall of the Western Roman Empire in the fourth and fifth centuries exposed Europe to numerous invasions from nomadic peoples living in northern and southern Europe (Goths, Vikings, Vandals, and Magyars), and from larger incursions that originated in central Asia (Huns, Avars, and later the Mongols). These nomadic peoples also invaded Mediterranean Europe, China, India, and Persia, throwing all of these centres of civilization into ruin or near collapse. In northern Europe, the slow recovery from the fall of Rome began with the Carolingian empire (C.E. 751–888). However, this empire fragmented and power devolved to local nobles, ushering in the era of European feudalism and the Middle Ages. From C.E. 1206 to 1696 the Mongol Empire launched repeated invasions into Europe, the Middle East, and Asia, under Genghis Khan and his sons and grandsons. However, the unity of the empire broke down, and Mongol power receded in the face of an expanding Russia and China.[1]

Medieval Europe saw the spread of Christianity and the emergence of settled kingdoms, whose monarchs competed for territory and power. Through expansion, larger kingdoms ruled by dynastic monarchies began to consolidate themselves in Europe between the tenth and thirteenth centuries in what are today the British Isles, Germany, France, and Eastern Europe. This process, as well as the process of agricultural, industrial, and intellectual development, was slowed by climatic change, famine, plague, and war (in particular, the Hundred Years' War between England and France). European recovery from these events began in 1450, as the empires of France, the **Hapsburgs**, Muscovy/Russia, Sweden, and Lithuania all grew through the fifteenth and sixteenth centuries. However, resistance to amalgamation was widespread. The Scots and Irish resisted the expansion of English rule, Italy remained divided (see Profile 2.3), and the efforts of Burgundy and Hungary to establish empires failed. Finally, the religious wars of the Reformation, culminating in the devastating **Thirty Years' War** (1618–48), dominated political, intellectual, and religious affairs (see Profile 2.4).

Despite this instability, this era was one of European exploration and expansion. Originally motivated by a desire to circumvent the controlling influence of the commercial cities (primarily Venice and Genoa) that dominated the medieval trade routes to central Asia and the Middle East, European exploration by Portugal and Spain, and then by France, England, and Holland, brought a European presence to virtually all the inhabited continents. These events produced several lasting outcomes. The focus of political and commercial activity shifted from the Mediterranean to the trading empires of Western Europe. Trade and commerce became truly global in scope. The political and

Niccolo Machiavelli (1469–1527)

Machiavelli was a civil servant and diplomat in the republic of Florence during the Italian city-states period of the fifteenth and sixteenth centuries. These city-states vied for power and influence, and advising the rulers of Florence during this struggle was Machiavelli's profession. When Florence fell in 1512, Machiavelli was without a job, and he spent the final years of his life writing books, including his most famous works, *The Prince* and *The Discourses*. Drawing heavily on his examination of Greek and Roman writings as well as his own experience as a diplomat, he wrote of power, alliances, and the causes of conflict in the Italian city-state system. Much of what he wrote was aimed at the leaders—or princes—of states, advising them on the principles of statecraft, the conduct of their affairs with other princes, the importance of military force, and the lessons of historical experience. For Machiavelli, the security and survival of the state was the paramount concern of the prince; all other concerns were subordinated to this objective. The ends—the security of the state—justified the means necessary to achieve that objective. This Machiavellian approach to politics has often been criticized as amoral. However, Machiavelli argued that rulers must do what is in the best interests of the state; to do otherwise would in fact be immoral. Machiavelli also stressed that his advice to princes was based not on ethical principles or visions of the world as it should be or ought to be, but rather on the way the world was, according to historical and contemporary evidence. To act based on how one felt the world ought to be, as opposed to how the world really was, would be a recipe for disaster. In international relations, Machiavelli's emphasis on interests, power, and the conduct of statecraft is inseparable from the realpolitik tradition of political realism.

SOURCE: NICCOLO MACHIAVELLI, *THE PRINCE* AND *THE DISCOURSES* (NEW YORK: THE MODERN LIBRARY, 1950).

Thomas Hobbes (1588–1679)

Hobbes was an English political philosopher who wrote in the turbulent years of the early seventeenth century, which were dominated by the Thirty Years' War in Europe. In England, Parliament was asserting its power against the monarchy, which would eventually lead to the English Civil War, and Hobbes, a royalist, was compelled to flee to France for eight years. In his writings, Hobbes's primary focus was politics within the state. In his most famous work, *Leviathan*, he depicted the condition of humanity in a hypothetical "state of nature" that would exist in the absence of governmental authority. This condition, he argued, would be characterized by anarchy, "a war of every one against every one," in which there would be "a continual fear and danger of violent death; and the life of man, solitary, poor, nasty, brutish, and short." This condition could only be avoided by the creation of the "Leviathan," a state that or ruler who would establish and maintain order. Without order, there could be no civilization. Realists often describe international relations as a Hobbesian state of nature that lacks a Leviathan in the form of a world government or a dominant power to impose order. Like individuals in a state of nature, states exist in an anarchic environment, in a war of everyone against everyone, in which suspicion, distrust, conflict, and war are inevitable. In such a world, states must pursue their individual self-interests.

SOURCE: THOMAS HOBBES, *LEVIATHAN*, MICHAEL OAKESHOTT, ED. (NEW YORK: COLLIER MACMILLAN, 1974).

economic life of Europe was extended throughout the world, particularly in the form of growing rivalries between the trading empires.

In the Middle East, the spectacular rise and expansion of Islam dominated the period after the fall of Rome. Established by the prophet Mohammed (c. C.E. 570–632), Islam expanded within a century from the Arabian Peninsula to include North Africa and southern Spain, and the western reaches of China and India. After a period of great prosperity and cultural and intellectual development, internal dissension weakened the Arab Empire, which lost some of its territories in southern Europe and the Mediterranean to crusading Christians from Europe in the tenth century. However, Islam experienced a resurgence between 1300 and 1639, led by the Ottoman Empire. By 1354 the Ottoman Empire expanded through the Balkans east of the Adriatic and South of the Danube, and all around the Black Sea. By the time of Suleiman the Magnificent (1520–66), the Ottoman Empire was one of the great empires of the world. In the East, Islam spread through Persia and much of India, expanding to central Asia and the out-lying provinces of China, as well as present-day Indonesia (see Map 2.1). However, the Islamic world began to fracture politically (as the Mughal Empire in India and Safavid Persia clashed with each other and the Ottoman Empire) and religiously (as the **Sunni** and **Shiite** branches of Islam came into conflict). Nevertheless, the Ottoman Empire remained a world power until World War I.[2]

In Asia, civilization began with the development of the first agricultural, hunting, and fishing communities around 4000 B.C.E., in what are today northern China, Southeast Asia, and India. The Shang dynasty (1700–1100 B.C.E.) was the first historical dynasty in China, but like the enormous Harappa and Mohenjo-Daro civilizations of India (2550–1550 B.C.E.), it succumbed to foreign invasion. A period of consolidation and fragmentation of political units in both China and India followed. In India, Chandra-Gupta Maurya seized the Magadhan throne and his dynasty (297 B.C.E.–C.E. 236) succeeded in unifying most of the Indian peninsula under one ruler (see Profile 2.5). Invasion from the north fragmented the empire, which was re-established under the Gupta empires (C.E. 320–410). In China, the Chou Dynasty (1122–221 B.C.E.) replaced the Shang Dynasty. Between 1122 and 771 B.C.E., the empire maintained stability and order based on a feudal system. However, after 771 B.C.E. the empire increasingly frag-mented into independent kingdoms engaged in almost continual conflict, culminating in the Warring States period of 403–221 B.C.E. (see Profile 2.6). The victorious Ch'in Empire in turn collapsed and was replaced by the Han Dynasty (206 B.C.E.–C.E. 220), which established a prosperous and well-administered empire (see Map 2.2, page 29).

Invasions of nomadic peoples prompted the Ch'in Empire and the Han dynasty to build the Great Wall of China. However, the Great Wall could not protect the Han Empire from internal disintegration, and nomadic invaders breached the wall in 304. Recovery was slow, but under the Sui (581–617), T'ang (618–907), and Sung (960–1279) dynasties, China expanded and became prosperous, stable, and intellectually and scien-tifically advanced beyond any other world civilization. Mongol invasion brought a period of decline, but under the Ming dynasty (1386–1644) Chinese power and pros-perity were restored. In Japan, feudal warlords dominated politics until the Tokugawa shogunate unified Japan for 250 years before the forced opening of Japan by the European powers.

In Africa, civilization developed in the Nile tributaries and in east Africa, where the Kingdom of Kush dominated from c. 900 B.C.E. to C.E. 400. Settlers moved through

Map 2.1 The Extent of the Islamic World in 1500

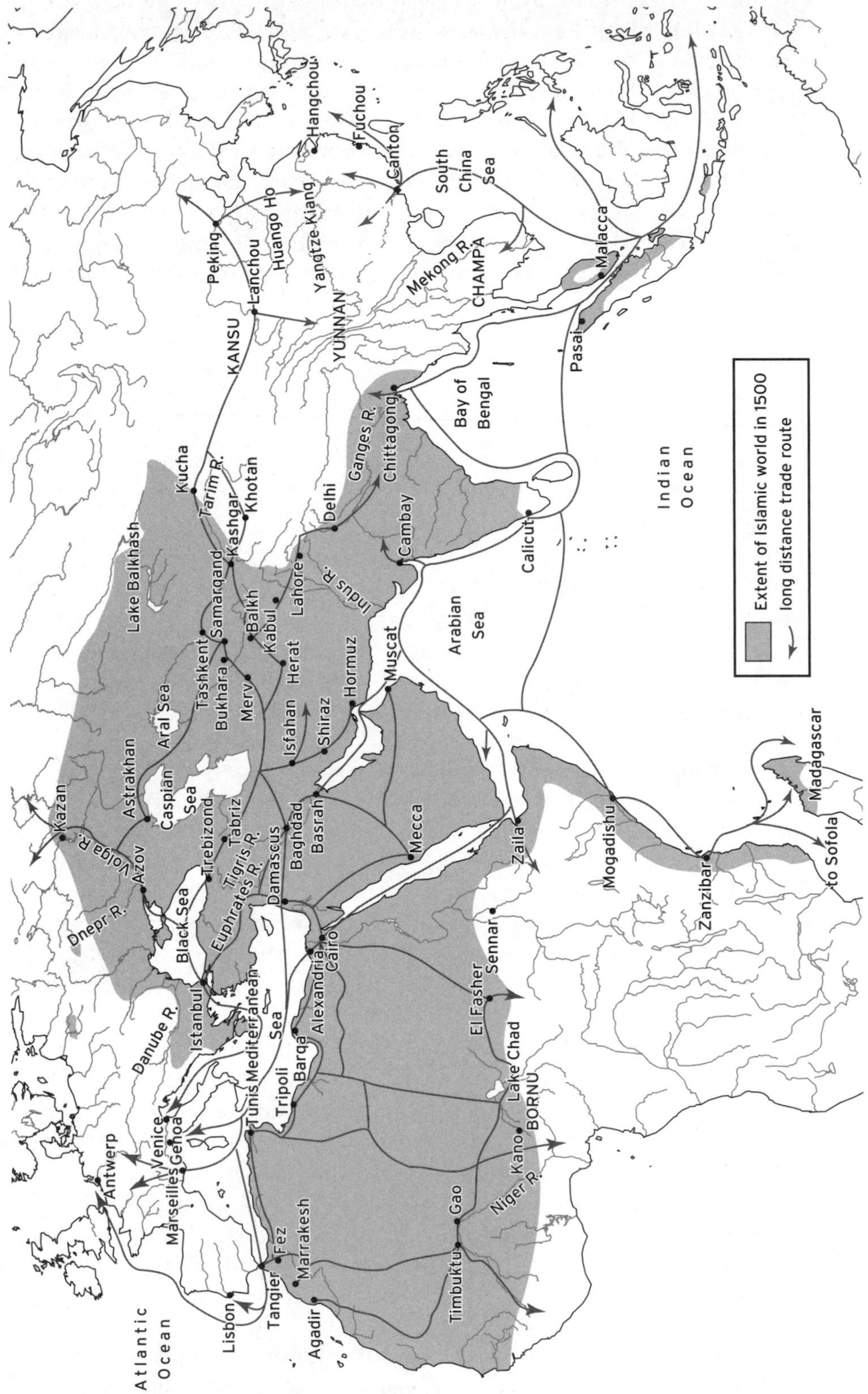

SOURCE: *ATLAS OF THE ISLAMIC WORLD SINCE 1500* (OXFORD: PHAIDON PRESS LTD., 1982), P. 88.

Extent of Islamic world in 1500

long distance trade route

Kautilya (350–275 B.C.E.)

Also known as Chanakya or Vishnugupta, Kautilya was councillor and chief minister to Chandra-Gupta, the founder of the Mauryan Empire. His views survive in the form of the *Arthasastra* (*The Book of the State*), a treatise on the science of politics, which is summarized in six thousand verses. Written primarily for rulers, the *Arthasastra* is essentially a compendium of reflections on human nature and the conduct of political activity. The *Arthasastra* contains advice to rulers on the conduct of war, foreign policy, and empire building. Kautilya argued that war must serve political objectives. The purpose of war is to strengthen an empire, not merely to destroy an enemy. Weakening an enemy before fighting was the key to success in battle and was more important than the force of arms. He advised that rulers should fight weaker states and ally with stronger ones. Kautilya warned that the natural enemies of a ruler were the rulers of bordering empires. However, the rulers of the empires that bordered one's neighbours were natural friends, a piece of advice more commonly captured by the phrase "the enemy of my enemy is my friend." Kautilya also commented on the qualities of the ideal ruler, who, he argued, had to possess good character and a willingness to listen to advisers (like Kautilya). The character of the ruler affected the character of the ruled. He warned about the corrosive effects of injustice and advised the ruler that it was his responsibility to keep the people content if rebellion, chaos, and violence were to be avoided. Kautilya is sometimes called the Indian Machiavelli, but it would be more accurate to call Machiavelli the Italian Kautilya. Many of the themes familiar to the power politics approach can be found in the *Arthasastra*, far removed from the time and context of Machiavelli's Italy.

present-day Ethiopia into southern Africa, and **Iron Age** civilizations developed in central and southern Africa by C.E. 100. Great trading empires developed in Africa over the next thousand years in what are today Zimbabwe, the Democratic Republic of Congo (formerly Zaire), and Ghana. The influence of Islamic expansion into North Africa contributed to the wealth of the Mali, Songhay, and the Kanem Borno Empires, as Arab merchant colonies spread along Africa's north and east coasts. By the arrival of the first Europeans (the Portuguese in 1448), Africa had a thriving trading system based on gold, ivory, copper, and slavery (see Map 2.3).

Portuguese, and later British and Dutch, trading stations spread rapidly in Africa. Trade with Europeans, at first based on gold, shifted to slaves, who were in demand for the colonial sugar plantations in South America and the West Indies. Between 1450 and 1870, some 15 million Africans were shipped across the Atlantic, 90 percent of them to South America and the Caribbean. Some regions of Africa suffered heavily from this trade; others profited. In 1800, most of Africa (except the northern areas held by the Ottoman Empire) remained independent.

In the Americas, the first large civilizations emerged in Mesoamerica (present-day southern Mexico) in the form of the Olmecs and Zapotecs and in the central Andes around 1000 B.C.E. In the fifth century C.E., the Olmecs and Zapotecs were conquered by the invading Maya (C.E. 300–900), who left an enduring cultural legacy in Mesoamerica. In North America large trading and agricultural centres emerged in Hopewell territory (300 B.C.E.–C.E. 550) around the southern Great Lakes. In Central America, Mayan civilization was followed by the Toltecs in the eleventh century and the Aztecs in the

PROFILE 2.6

Sun Tzu

Sun Tzu was a warrior philosopher in fourth-century (B.C.E.) China. His *Art of War*, one of the greatest classical Chinese texts, is one of the most influential books on strategy ever written. The *Art of War* was evidently composed during the Warring States period in ancient China. The period was characterized by competition, shifting alliances, and warfare between the kings who struggled for power in Chou China. Sun Tzu drew heavily on Chinese philosophy—in particular, the Taoist works *I Ching* (the *Book of Changes*) and the *Tao-te Ching* (*The Way and Its Power*)—and Chinese military practices in writing what is in essence a study of the conduct of competition and conflict on any level, from the interpersonal to the international. Most popularly known for its general advice that to win without fighting is best, the *Art of War* emphasizes shunning battle except when victory is assured, avoiding risk, dominating an opponent through psychological means, and using time rather than force to wear an enemy down. The book also includes advice on preparations for war, battle tactics, sieges, manoeuvre, and the use of terrain. Much of the advice emphasizes the importance of achieving advantage over one's enemy before any military engagement. Today, the *Art of War* is studied not only by military leaders but also by politicians and executives who employ it as a window on the political and business approaches of Asian countries and businesses. For international relations scholars, and realists in particular, the themes in Sun Tzu's work reflect the nature of politics and power in anarchic environments. Along with Kautilya, Sun Tzu offers evidence of the existence of power politics themes across time, place, and culture.

SOURCE: SUN TZU, *THE ART OF WAR*, TRANSLATED BY THOMAS CLEARY (BOSTON: SHAMBALA, 1988).

thirteenth century. Aztec expansion, conducted through a combination of alliance and conquest, reached its zenith under Montezuma II (1502–20). In South America several diverse civilizations developed in the Andes and were unified under the Huari and Tiahuanaco empires (C.E. 600–800). These empires collapsed, and unity in the Andes was not achieved until the Inca civilization of the fifteenth century. The Inca Empire expanded between 1438 and 1525 to an area 4000 kilometres long and more than 300 kilometres wide, with a hereditary dynasty and an advanced bureaucracy and infrastructure (see Map 2.4). However, the Spanish on their arrival in the beginning of the sixteenth century overthrew the Aztec and Inca civilizations. Elsewhere, the Portuguese slowly expanded into Brazil, establishing an extensive sugar industry worked by slaves. In North America, colonization was slower, and economic and political activity were based on a wide range of cultural traditions (see Map 2.5).

At this point in history, the rise and fall of civilizations and empires came to be dominated by the slow but steady rise of Europe to a position of global dominance. The legacy of this historical development (also referred to as the rise of the West) remains with us in many forms today, from the nature of the state to the impact of colonialism.

THE MODERN STATE AND THE PEACE OF WESTPHALIA

The modern international system is often called the Westphalian state system. The Peace of Westphalia established a new order in Europe following the Thirty Years' War. From its origins in Europe, this system was extended throughout the world through the expansion of the European empires. With the virtual collapse of the European empires in the second half of the twentieth century, what was left behind was a world of sover-

Map 2.2 China and the Warring States Period (300 B.C.E.)

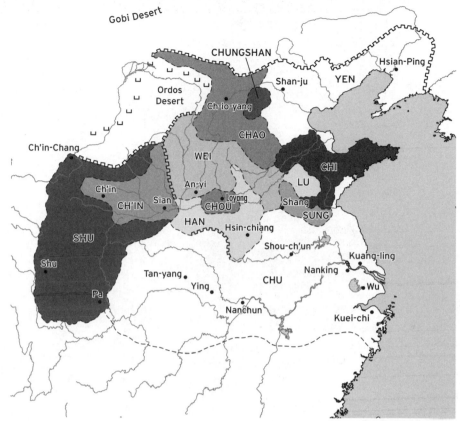

SOURCE: MARTIN VAN CREVELD, *THE ART OF WAR: WAR AND MILITARY THOUGHT* (LONDON: CASSELL AND CO., 2000).

eign states that inherited the territorial, legal, and administrative structures and practices of the European tradition. However, it is important to recognize that the global expansion of the European state system does not provide a complete picture of the modern international system. After all, civilization existed in other regions of the world long before it existed in Europe, and these historical and cultural traditions continue to exert a profound influence on contemporary international relations, just as they did in the past.[3]

The Peace of Westphalia ended the Thirty Years' War in Europe in 1648 (see Map 2.6). Although the principles behind the sovereign state had begun to emerge before 1648, this date is a useful point of differentiation between medieval Europe and modern Europe. In medieval Europe, territorial units were for the most part quite small, and political life within them was extremely localized. Medieval territorial units were themselves not fully autonomous or sovereign; they were under the authority (in spirit if not always in practice) of the Pope or the Holy Roman Emperor. The Peace of Westphalia marked the beginning of the supremacy of the state as a sovereign actor and the beginning of the end of the church's leading political role in European affairs.

Why did this happen? There are a number of reasons. First, the power of the church had been weakened by the splits in Christendom, in particular during the Reformation. The horrors of the Thirty Years' War (in what is today Germany, two-thirds of the population was killed or displaced) revealed the fragility of Christian Europe. The answer was

Map 2.3 African Empires in History

SOURCE: MARTIN GLASSNER AND HARM J. DE BLIJ, *SYSTEMATIC POLITICAL GEOGRAPHY*, 4TH ED. REPRINTED WITH PERMISSION OF JOHN WILEY AND SONS, INC.

the sovereign state, which in principle was to be free from foreign interference in its domestic affairs. The hope was that devastating religious wars such as the Thirty Years' War might be prevented if the domestic affairs of territorial units were recognized as the exclusive reserve of the rulers of states. Second, some of the monarchs of medieval Europe had been slowly acquiring increased economic and military power, which enabled them to expand their territories through the amalgamation and conquest of less powerful political units. Furthermore, the establishment of hereditary monarchies promised increased stability with respect to leadership transition. The expansion of administrative and legal systems, with their power derived from the monarch, improved the capacity of rulers to exert control over their territories and subjects. For these reasons, the state emerged as the dominant political actor in international affairs and took on the distinctive characteristics that we recognize today (see Profile 2.7). As these developments occurred, European monarchies were embarking on the first period of European exploration and empire building. The world was entering the age of the European empires.

THE RISE OF THE EUROPEAN EMPIRES

In Europe, the seventeenth and eighteenth centuries were characterized by the territorial expansion of certain states in Europe and the overseas imperial conquests of the Spanish,

Map 2.4 The Peoples and Civilizations of Central and South America

TARASCAN
1400–1522

Gulf of Mexico

TEOTIHUACAN
100 B.C.E.–C.E. 750

OLMEC
1200–100 BC

Teotihuacán
Tenochtitlán

Chichén Itzá

Uxmet

Mitla

MAYA
100–1542

Piedras Negras

TOLTEC
900–1200

Oopan

AZTEC
1325–1521

ZAPOTEC
and MIXTEC
300–1524

Atlantic

Ocean

CHIBCHA
1200–1538

Zipaquirá

Quito

CHIMU
1000–1471

MOCHICA
2000 B.C.E.–C.E. 700

CHAVIN
1000–500 B.C.E.

Chan Chan

Machu Picchu

Pachacamac

Cuzco

TIAHUANACO
600–1000

Pacific

Ocean

INCA
1200–1535

SOURCE: MARTIN GLASSNER AND HARM J. DE BLIJ, *SYSTEMATIC POLITICAL GEOGRAPHY*, 4TH ED. REPRINTED WITH PERMISSION OF JOHN WILEY AND SONS, INC.

Map 2.5 The Peoples of North America (c. 1500)

SOURCE: "NATIVE AMERICAN PEOPLES," FROM PATRICK K. O'BRIEN, ED., *ATLAS OF WORLD HISTORY* (NEW YORK: OXFORD UNIVERSITY PRESS, 1999). REPRINTED WITH PERMISSION OF OXFORD UNIVERSITY PRESS.

Portuguese, Dutch, English, and French empires. Under Louis XIV France was the most powerful state in Europe in the mid- to late 1600s, but Louis's territorial ambitions provoked repeated alliances against France, which soon became weakened by almost continual warfare. Although formally in existence until 1806, the **Holy Roman Empire** had fragmented into some 300 small principalities and city-states, which were vulnerable to conquest. Prussia (largely through the conquests of Frederick the Great) and Austria under the Hapsburgs (largely through the conquests of Prince Eugene of Savoy) emerged as the dominant states in central Europe. Great Britain, protected from continental wars by the English Channel, carved out a global empire that was the envy of the rest of Europe. The Russian Empire (especially under **Peter the Great** and **Catherine the Great**) expanded to the borders of the Prussian and Austrian Empires in the west, the Ottoman Empire to the south, and China and the Pacific Ocean to the east.

However, revolts rocked the European empires in the second half of the eighteenth century. While the character of the revolts varied—from peasant unrest to a desire for independence in some regions—their origins lay in the spread of the Enlightenment, with its emphasis on the rights of individuals and its rejection of traditional authority. Enlightened monarchs, seeking reform, provoked a backlash of resistance from their aristocracies and provinces. Provinces such as the Austrian Netherlands and Hungary rebelled against the centralization and reform policies imposed by Enlightened monarchs. Overseas colonies, such as the American colonies, Spanish America, and Haiti,

Map 2.6 Westphalian Europe, 1648

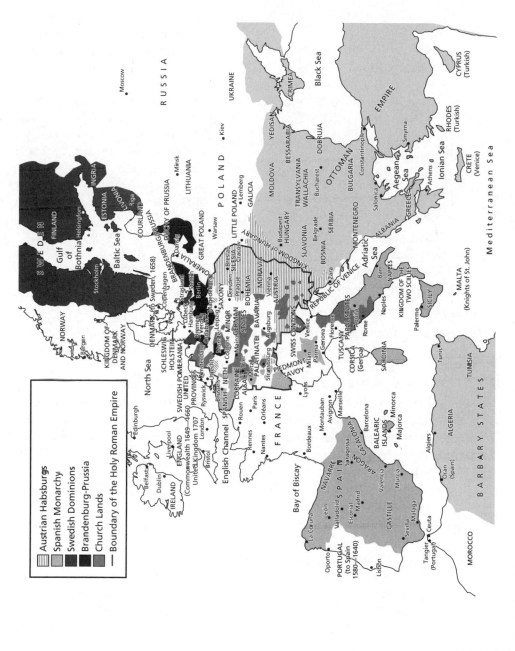

Legend:
- Austrian Habsburgs
- Spanish Monarchy
- Swedish Dominions
- Brandenburg-Prussia
- Church Lands
- Boundary of the Holy Roman Empire

SOURCE: R. PALMER AND J. COLTON, *A HISTORY OF THE MODERN WORLD*, 8TH ED. (NEW YORK: MCGRAW-HILL, 1995). REPRINTED WITH PERMISSION OF THE MCGRAW-HILL COMPANIES.

The Nature of the Modern State

Different theories abound in social science regarding the formation and present role of the state, but in typical international relations discourse, the term *state* refers to political entities with the following qualities:

- They occupy a defined territory.

- They possess a permanent population.

- They are sovereign with respect to other states (that is, they are, in principle, free from interference in their internal affairs).

- They are diplomatically recognized by other states.

- They possess a monopoly on the legitimate use of force, both within and outside their territories.

The terms *nation* and *state* are often used interchangeably in discussions of global politics. However, nation is not the same as state. The state refers to an autonomous institutional and legal structure that controls a defined territory. The state is a political and legal concept. Nation refers to a people who possess a shared sense of common descent and unifying ethnic, religious, or linguistic characteristics. Nation is an ethnic and cultural concept. A nation may exist without a state: two contemporary examples are the Kurdish and the Palestinian nations. A state that has essentially one nation living within its borders is called a nation-state. In practice, very few nation-states exist, because most states in the world today have many nations living within their borders. Canada and the United States are examples of multination-states. The distinction between state and nation is becoming increasingly important in international politics, as in many cases disputes between the nations living within multination-states have led to domestic instability, turmoil, and, in extreme cases, violence.

rebelled against imperial rule and demanded more autonomy or outright independence. Many European regions also sought independence, such as Corsica, Sardinia, Ireland, Serbia, and Tyrol.

Then came the French Revolution (1789–94), which changed the face of Europe. The French Revolution began as a middle-class phenomenon but spread to worker and peasant uprisings. When Austria and Prussia threatened invasion, combining external threat with internal chaos, the monarchy collapsed. A republic was established that ruthlessly suppressed its enemies at home and defeated its enemies abroad. The ideals of the French Revolution spread across Europe: equality before the law, the abolition of feudalism, and the "rights of man." The French Revolution sparked the beginning of the development of modern nationalism, and although initially nationalism was rejected by monarchs and unknown to the poor, it was to become one of the driving forces behind events in Europe.

However, like the Roman Republic, the French Republic did not survive. In 1799 a 31-year-old general named **Napoleon Bonaparte** seized power. During the subsequent **Napoleonic Wars**, Napoleon was practically unbeatable, defeating the armies of Austria and Prussia. By 1810 most of Western Europe was controlled by France. However, Napoleon could not subdue England, nor could he completely conquer the Iberian Peninsula. His invasion of Russia (1812) was a disaster. His final defeat at Waterloo in 1815 ended French dominance in Europe. The **Congress of Vienna** and the formation of the **Concert of Europe** followed, an attempt by the great powers to manage their relations and prevent a recurrence of the Napoleonic Wars. For almost one hundred years, no continent-wide war occurred between the European great powers. However, it is

Karl von Clausewitz (1780–1831)

Karl von Clausewitz was a Prussian military officer, instructor, and strategist who rose to the rank of general in the Prussian army and served on the Prussian general staff during the Napoleonic Wars. His famous work, *On War*, was written after the Napoleonic Wars and his recall to duty in East Prussia in 1830 (he died of cholera in 1831, leaving *On War* unfinished). Virtually unknown when he was alive, Clausewitz had a major influence on all subsequent intellectual thought on war; he viewed it as a timeless phenomenon with its own elements and dynamics. Written in the dialectical and comparative style associated with German idealist philosophy, *On War* is often misunderstood or misinterpreted. For Clausewitz, war is distinguished from other social activity by its large-scale violence, which tends toward absolute war—the highest degree of violence. However, wars usually fall short of this level, because they are mitigated by political goals and the characteristics of societies and their economies and governments. Clausewitz believed that even military force had to be subordinate to the political aims and objectives of the state. War, Clausewitz argued, should not be regarded as separate and distinct from peacetime politics among states. Rather, war should be seen as "a continuation of political activity by other means." In international relations theory, realists regard *On War* as an illuminating treatise of the prominence of the military instrument in the conduct of statecraft.

SOURCE: KARL VON CLAUSEWITZ, *ON WAR*, EDITED AND TRANSLATED BY MICHAEL HOWARD AND PETER PARET (PRINCETON: PRINCETON UNIVERSITY PRESS, 1976), 87.

inaccurate to say that peace prevailed, for several wars took place in this period, such as the Wars of Italian Unification, the **Crimean War**, and the Franco–Prussian War. Nationalism experienced a revival in the 1830s, and Greece, Belgium, and Norway obtained independence. Italy was unified in 1861 and Germany (as the German Empire) in 1871. In both cases, this union was accomplished through a combination of war and the use of nationalism as a political instrument.

The European empires also continued to expand abroad. However, by the nineteenth century the nature of European imperialism was beginning to change. As the Industrial Revolution took hold in Europe, imperial expansion was driven less by the search for trade goods and more by the search for raw materials, markets for products, and territorial competition between the imperial powers. Between 1880 and 1914 the European empires added more than 13.6 million square kilometres (approximately one-fifth of the world's surface) to their colonial possessions (see Profile 2.9). Much of this was acquired in the so-called scramble for Africa, which began in earnest in 1882; by 1914, only Ethiopia and Liberia were independent.

For peoples across the world, colonial rule meant the imposition of arbitrary political boundaries, a profound dislocation in local patterns of commerce, and the dominance of colonial administrations. These administrations ruled through a combination of political and economic coercion and reward, often co-opting local elites into the colonial system of governance. This period was the beginning of the expansion of global capitalism.

Because of the worldwide expansion of the European empires, wars in Europe quickly became global in scope. In North America, wars in Europe between France, England, and Spain broke out in 1744 and 1754, and the supremacy of British naval power resulted in the loss of the French colonial empire in North America and the weakening of the Spanish empire. However, the rebellion of the 13 colonies in 1776 (aided by France) and

The Colonial Legacy

Many of the states that we consider independent today were at one point colonized by imperial powers or listed as *protectorates*. Here we list just some of them. Note that some were colonized by more than one empire over time. For example, the Philippines, a Spanish colony from 1565, became a U.S. possession after 1898 (they were occupied by the Japanese during World War II, then achieved independence in 1946). Note also that many names have changed over time. For example, what is now known as Zimbabwe was once called Rhodesia; and while under British control, Sri Lanka was known as Ceylon. What follows is a partial list of the imperial powers and some of their possessions over the course of the past few hundred years.

BRITAIN

Anguilla, Antigua and Barbuda, Australia, Bahamas, Bahrain, Botswana, Brunei, **Canada**, Ceylon, Dominica, Fiji, Gambia, Ghana, Grenada, Hong Kong, India, Ireland, Kenya, Malawi, Malaysia, Maldives, Malta, Nigeria, Papua New Guinea, Sierra Leone, South Africa, Uganda, Zambia, Zimbabwe

FRANCE

Algeria, Benin, Burkina Faso, Cambodia, Chad, Comoros, Dakar, Djibouti, French Cameroon, French Congo, Gabon, Haiti, Ivory Coast, Laos, Madagascar, Mali, Mauritania, Morocco, Niger, Senegal, Vietnam

THE OTTOMAN EMPIRE

Albania, Algeria, Anatolia (Turkey), Armenia, Bosnia-Herzegovina, Bulgaria, Cyprus, Egypt, Iraq, Jordan, Lebanon, Libya, Qatar, Yemen

SPAIN

Argentina, Bolivia, Chile, Colombia, Cuba, Ecuador, El Salvador, Equatorial Guinea, Guam, Guatemala, Honduras, Mexico, Nicaragua, Paraguay, Peru, Philippines, Puerto Rico, Venezuela

PORTUGAL

Angola, Azores, Brazil, East Timor, Equatorial Guinea, Guinea-Bissau, parts of India, Macao, Mozambique

GERMANY

Burundi, Cameroon, Namibia, Rwanda, Tanganyika (Tanzania), Togo, Western Samoa, other occupations during World War II

ITALY

Ethiopia, Libya, Somalia

THE NETHERLANDS

Dutch Borneo, Dutch East Indies, Dutch West Indies, Suriname

BELGIUM

Burundi, Rwanda, Zaire

DENMARK

Faroe Islands, Greenland, Iceland, north Germany, parts of Norway, Sweden

JAPAN

Bonin Island, Korea, other occupations during World War II

THE UNITED STATES

Guam, Hawaii, Midway, Panama, Philippines, Puerto Rico, Samoa

---

the American War of Independence compelled Great Britain to recognize American independence in 1783. American expansion proceeded rapidly after independence (largely through the Louisiana Purchase, war with Mexico, and war against indigenous peoples). The expansion of the United States continued after the bitter and destructive **American Civil War** with the purchase of Alaska from Russia, and territorial gains through annexation or conquest in the Pacific (Hawaii, Samoa, Midway, and the Philippines) and in Latin America (Cuba and Puerto Rico). The hope of some in the United States for expansion into British North America was thwarted in the War of 1812, and with the formation of Canada in 1867 and its expansion to include western territories. Nevertheless, by 1914 the United States was one of the world's leading powers.

In South America, Napoleon's invasion of the Iberian Peninsula enabled the Spanish and Portuguese colonies to attain independence. These revolutions were carried out by a colonial aristocracy that sought independence, but with minimal social change. For the most part, colonial administrations were replaced by military dictatorships, which were to become an enduring feature of political life in Central and Southern America. In 1823, revolution created the Republic of Mexico. In South America, Spanish power was broken by revolt and military defeat at the hands of Simón Bolívar. Portugal agreed to Brazilian independence in 1822. In postrevolution Central and South America, territorial disputes between the newly independent countries were frequent and violent, and efforts to unite South America into a union failed at the Congress of Panama (1826). Export-driven economic growth and control of land increased the wealth of elites, but the bulk of the population lived in poverty and still does.

In China, dominated by the Ch'ing (or Manchu) dynasty since 1644, trade with Europe—primarily in textiles, tea, porcelain, and opium—had flourished, although the empire was beset with rebellions and internal unrest. By the 1830s, China was the world's largest and most populous empire, but economic and administrative difficulties brought on by its growing population left China vulnerable to the Western powers, which sought to open the Chinese market to their products. The British won the Opium War (1839–42), seized Hong Kong as an imperial possession, and opened five (later many more) treaty ports. Inside these treaty ports, foreigners enjoyed exemption from Chinese law and rule. Other powers—especially Britain, Russia, France, and Japan—then expanded their authority in China, seizing territory and opening more treaty ports. The failure of the Manchu leadership to institute reform and resentment of foreign influence in China led to the so-called Boxer Rebellion in 1900. This strife was suppressed by the foreign powers in China, who in retribution seized more territory and privileges. These actions did not quell the rebellion and disaffection, and on the eve of World War I, China remained unstable and dominated by foreign colonial powers.

PATTERNS IN THE HISTORY OF WAR AND PEACE

Many themes and generalizations have been drawn from this conventional account of global history up to the world wars of the twentieth century. As we will see, these themes formed the foundation of the realist approach to international relations.

- *The recurrence of war and conflict between civilizations, peoples, and empires.* The history of the world is a history of armed struggle. When cooperation does occur, it is based on short-term need or convenience. War is a historical inevitability, and the prudent are prepared for it, even in times of peace. The price for those who are not is political domination or outright conquest.

- *The rise and fall of civilizations and empires.* The explanations for the rise and fall of the great world civilizations and empires are many and varied. First, the fate of these empires is often linked to the emergence and the decline of a single great ruler or the dynasty established. Second, empires have repeatedly been subject to conquest, either at the hands of other empires or from invasion by barbarian peoples. Third, many empires suffer from internal decline due to a combination of economic failure, social decay, and the costs associated with protecting a growing territory. The fortunes of civilizations, empires, and great powers are, therefore, historically fleeting; all eventually decline, to be superseded by others.[4]

- *The political history of the world is primarily the history of the activities of great civilizations, empires, and states.* History is made by the powerful. For some, history can be described in terms of the machinations of **hegemonic powers**, civilizations, great powers, or empires that dominated all others. As a result, smaller or weaker civilizations, empires, and states have not been considered significant in history except as allies or pawns of the powerful.

- *The development of an intellectual tradition on statecraft, drawn from historical experience.* Advice to leaders—kings, princes, or emperors—was the privilege of only a very few individuals, but these individuals represent the beginning of thought on international relations, offering insights into the perspectives of those who lived hundreds and even thousands of years ago. What is revealing about these writings is the extent to which they share common themes about the nature of the conduct of international politics. Writers such as Sun Tzu, Kautilya, Thucydides, and Machiavelli established the intellectual foundation of the realist perspective in international relations. Meanwhile, as we will see, writers such as Mo Ti, Thomas Aquinas, Immanuel Kant, and John Locke established the foundation of the liberal perspective.

- *Diplomatic history and political geography. Before World War II, diplomatic historians conducted most of the research on international affairs.* These historians studied historical patterns and the leaders and officials of empires and states. Political geographers developed theories that promoted the decisive influence of geography on state power in general and the calculations of decision makers in particular. The use of geographic explanations or arguments to characterize political decisions or advocate certain policies became known as political geography or geopolitics. The most famous of these political geographers were Sir Halford Mackinder and Alfred Thayer Mahan (see Profile 2.10). Geopolitical thought has had a profound influence on the conduct of many states and has served as the cornerstone for many national security strategies, including those of the European imperial powers, Nazi Germany, and the United States during the Cold War.

The beginning of the twentieth century was a time of general peace—with a few exceptions, most notably the Russo–Japanese War (1904–05)—and growing prosperity. International developments suggested that long-term peace was in the offing. No major war had occurred in Europe since 1870, and international law on armaments and war had been strengthened at the Hague Peace Conferences of 1899 and 1907. The prevailing sentiment was that increasing trade and industrialization was making war more costly and less likely, an argument that is often made today. However, this sense of optimism began to erode as disputes between the European great powers and their alliances intensified. Nationalist rhetoric grew, an arms race broke out, and war flared in the Balkans (1912–13). Nevertheless, few sensed the impending disaster that would soon befall Europe.

WORLD WAR I

The beginning of World War I is generally marked by the assassination of the heir to the throne of the Austro-Hungarian Empire, Austrian Archduke Franz Ferdinand, at Sarajevo, on 28 June 1914. The assassination of the Archduke set in motion a series of actions and reactions that led the European powers to war. However, while this event

Sir Halford Mackinder and Alfred Thayer Mahan

Map 2.7 The World According to Mackinder

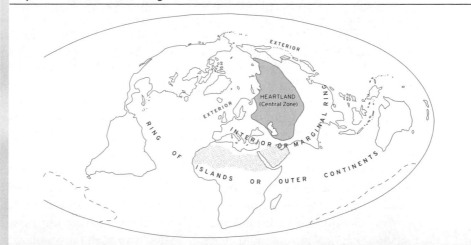

SOURCE: GERARD CHALIAND AND JEAN-PIERRE RAGEAU, *STRATEGIC ATLAS: COMPARATIVE GEOPOLITICS OF THE WORLD'S POWERS*, 3RD ED. COPYRIGHT © 1993 BY GERARD CHALIAND AND JEAN-PIERRE RAGEAU. REPRINTED BY PERMISSION OF HARPERCOLLINS PUBLISHERS, INC.

SIR HALFORD MACKINDER (1861–1957)

Sir Halford Mackinder was a British geographer who wrote a famous paper on "the geographical pivot of history," which he presented to the Royal Geographical Society in 1904. Mackinder argued that the world could be divided into three regions: the Heartland (at the centre of Eurasia); the Interior or Marginal Ring (Europe, the Middle East, and south and north Asia); and the Ring of Islands or Outer Continents (North and South America, Africa, and Australia). For Mackinder, the geographic pivot in world politics was the Heartland. From this view he derived the following geopolitical calculation: whoever controls the Heartland controls the World Island (Europe, Asia, and Africa); whoever controls the World Island controls the world. He concluded that Russia must not be permitted to expand into the lands of the Interior Ring as this would lead to Russian world domination. His theory was influential in Europe, particularly in Germany, where it contributed to the geopolitical views of Karl Hausofer, who advocated *Lebensraum*, German territorial expansion eastward. His theory also influenced U.S. strategy to contain the Soviet Union, which already dominated the Heartland, during the Cold War. Mackinder's

many critics have pointed out that his theory could not explain why Tsarist Russia and the Soviet Union had not dominated the world despite controlling the Heartland. Nor could his theory explain the dominance of the United States for most of the twentieth century. Others criticize his view as a thinly veiled rationale for the maintenance of the British Empire, which controlled territories in the Middle East and south Asia and so served as the guardian of the Interior Ring against aggression from the Heartland.

ALFRED THAYER MAHAN (1840–1914)

Alfred Thayer Mahan was an American naval strategist. His most famous work, *The Influence of Sea Power on History 1660–1783,* influenced the naval doctrines of the United States and the European imperial powers. His central conclusion was that naval powers, rather than land powers, were dominant in history. For Mahan, the principles of naval strategy and naval warfare remained constant, and these principles pointed to one historical theme. Contrary to land power explanations of world politics, the key to state power lay in powerful naval forces supported by a network of overseas possessions and naval bases. From these possessions and bases, naval forces could dominate the seas, and with that dominance came control of the merchant traffic of the world. The influence of Mahan's views was felt in Europe in the struggle for naval mastery between Great Britain and Germany, and in the United States, where it provided a rationale for American imperial expansion during and after the Spanish American War.

may indeed have been the spark that set Europe ablaze, the fuel for the conflict had been accumulating for years. Europe had divided into two hostile alliances: the Triple Alliance of Germany, Austro-Hungary, and Italy; and the Triple Entente of Great Britain, France, and Russia. The latter was wary of the increasing power of Germany and its desire for a place in the sun with the other established imperial powers. The Triple Alliance feared encirclement and the expansion of Russian power in the Balkans. Commercial rivalry, disputes over colonial possessions, and a naval arms race between Great Britain and Germany had intensified the antagonism between these two countries. In all countries enormous national armies could be created rapidly through the mobilization of the citizenry, trained for war through **conscription.** Most European military establishments believed that success in a future war would go to the country that mobilized most rapidly and launched its offensive first. This "cult of the offensive" existed in most countries.[5] In particular, German planning sought to avoid a two-front war against Russia and France simultaneously by attacking and quickly defeating France before turning against Russia. The mood in most societies was one of extreme nationalism (which was often explicitly racist) and faith in the superiority of one's own country and people.

After the assassination of the Archduke, Europe began its slide toward war. The assassination, planned in Belgrade by Serbian nationalists, intensified Austro-Hungarian concerns about the threat Serbia posed to Austro-Hungarian power in the Balkans. Germany, hoping to deter Russian intervention in the Balkans in support of its Serbian ally, issued its famous "blank cheque" of support to Austria. Austria then delivered an ultimatum to Belgrade and declared war on 28 July 1914. Russia, fearing Austrian hegemony in the Balkans, mobilized to support Serbia, a fellow Slavic country. Germany then mobilized and, as called for in prewar planning, attacked France through neutral Belgium. Germany's violation of Belgian neutrality brought Great Britain into the war. The war took on a global aspect with Japan's declaration of war on Germany, the outbreak of fighting between British and German colonial forces in Africa, and the entry into the war of the Ottoman Empire.

For many, war was welcome; nationalist fervour brought cheering crowds into the streets and long lines at recruiting stations. Before its horrors were common knowledge, war held an air of adventure. The mood among decision makers was more sombre. On August 3, following a speech to Parliament in which he confirmed British intentions to enter the war, British Foreign Minister Sir Edward Grey remarked: "The lamps are going out all over Europe; we shall not see them lit again in our lifetime."[6] And yet, throughout Europe, the expectation was that the war would be a short one, with the recently mobilized soldiers home by Christmas.

The German offensive into France, conducted under the **Schlieffen Plan**, failed to defeat France quickly. The firepower of modern weapons soon brought manoeuvres to a standstill, and by October 1914 a front line of trenches, barbed wire, and machine guns

Canada and World War I

We will always remember. Canadian World War I veteran Cyril Edward Martin, of Edmonton, attends the ceremonies commemorating the anniversary of Vimy Ridge battle in Vimy, northern France. The memorial is seen in the background. (AP Photo/Michel Spingler)

Canada entered World War I when Great Britain declared war on 4 August 1914. Canadian Prime Minister Robert Borden had promised Canadian support for the Empire's war effort. Little dissent existed in Parliament as the Liberals under Wilfrid Laurier supported Canada's entry into the war. However, dissent was expressed in French Canada, where many French Canadians opposed Canada's involvement in the war and the increasing sacrifices the war effort entailed.

The First Canadian Division entered the battle lines in France in February 1915, although most of the senior commanders were British. Canadian troops performed admirably in the field during the Battle of Ypres in April 1915. The Canadian contingent in Europe grew rapidly, and a Canadian Corps (composed of three divisions) was established in mid-1915. However, the war had settled into a costly stalemate, and losses at the front made conscription an issue in 1917. The conscription crisis was very divisive, encountering strong opposition in French Canada and among workers and farmers.

In April 1917, Canadian troops seized Vimy Ridge after repeated Allied efforts had failed and suffered 3598 deaths in the process. This success was followed by the Passchendaele offensive, a sobering experience in which the Canadian Corps occupied a few square kilometres of mud and water-filled craters at a cost of 8134 lives. By this time Canadian officers under General Arthur Currie commanded the Canadians. By the end of the war, 56 634 Canadians had been killed and more than 150 000 wounded.

Some maintain that Canadian nationalism was born at Vimy Ridge in 1917—that Canada's service and sacrifice developed a sense of Canadian independence. Sir Robert L. Borden himself was to argue that the war had made Canada an international personality and entitled Canada to a certain independent status. Canada was a signatory to the **Versailles Treaty**, and it received a seat in the League of Nations. Others would point to the political and workplace advances of Canadian women during the war years. Others, however, caution that the conscription crisis and labour disputes divided the country and that, for many, the war meant lost loved ones and shattered lives.

extended from the Swiss border to the English Channel. Offensives designed to break the stalemate by punching through these defensive lines with massive infantry attacks failed repeatedly, with great loss of life. (See Profile 2.11 for Canada's experience.) Germany embarked on a submarine warfare campaign against merchant ships at sea. With the exception of the Battle of Jutland, the massive battleship fleets that had been built during the Anglo–German naval arms race saw little action (the British battle fleet did impose a naval blockade against Germany, blocking German access to products and materials from abroad). The German decision to expand the submarine campaign also brought the United States into the war against Germany on 6 April 1917.

In the east, military defeat and economic chaos had led to the collapse of the Russian war effort and the Bolshevik Revolution of October 1917. The Romanov dynasty was overthrown, and the new **Bolshevik** government sued for peace. With the eastern front secured, Germany transferred its forces west for a final great offensive aimed at defeating Britain and France before the United States could mobilize. The offensive, launched on 21 March 1918, failed with heavy losses, and in July the French, British, and Americans began their counteroffensive, which was to be the decisive turning point of the war. By September, Germany was near defeat. Its armies were exhausted, and its economy was in shambles from the war effort and the British naval blockade. Austria was near collapse. Fearful of domestic unrest and the possibility of a Bolshevik revolution in Germany, the German government sued for an **armistice**, which went into effect on 11 November 1918. Seven months later, on 28 June 1919, Germany signed the Treaty of Versailles.

The consequences of World War I were enormous. More than 13 million people had died, and millions more were wounded. Three empires had collapsed—the Austro-Hungarian, Russian, and Ottoman—and new independent nations emerged in Czechoslovakia, Poland, Yugoslavia, Finland, Estonia, Latvia, and Lithuania (see Map 2.8). As a result, the **balance of power** in Europe had been completely altered. The Russian Revolution had brought a change in government and ideology to Russia that would shape international politics in the years to come. Fear of the Russian Revolution was widespread, as was concern over the emergence of **fascism** as a major political movement. Nationalism, far from eroding in the face of the war, intensified, and the peace settlement left dissatisfied minorities across Europe. The United States emerged as a global power but slowly turned to **isolationism** with respect to European affairs. Finally, dissatisfied revisionist powers emerged on the continent; the Soviet Union sought to regain lost territories, and Italy and Hungary sought revisions of borders.

Under the terms of the Treaty of Versailles, Germany was prevented from possessing a large army or modern military equipment; the province of Alsace-Lorraine was returned to France; Germany's colonies were distributed to the victors; East Prussia was separated from the rest of Germany by the new Poland; the German government was forced to pay reparations; and war guilt was assigned to Germany. The legacy of Versailles would cause much bitterness in Germany, bitterness that would be exploited by Adolf Hitler and the Nazi Party. The ambitions of the revisionist countries and their authoritarian ideologies would clash with democratic, anti-revisionist countries that favoured the status quo. Ultimately, the war to end all wars had merely set the stage for World War II.

THE ORIGINS AND PRINCIPLES OF POLITICAL IDEALISM

The death and destruction caused by World War I resulted in a condemnation of the way international politics had been conducted in the past. The war also created a reaction against power politics, secret diplomacy, arms races, and what was seen as the abuse of unchecked power by the monarchs who led the Central Powers into war. For many, the horrors of World War I served as the final exhibit of the folly of war in human history. A change was required, a change that would alter the international environment in a way that would prevent future wars and eliminate the practices and policies that had made the history of humanity a history of conflict and war. This sentiment prompted the search for a theory of international politics that provided an explanation for all wars and offered directions and policies for preventing them in the future. What emerged from this search was the theoretical framework known as *political idealism*.

Map 2.8 Territorial Changes in Europe after World War I

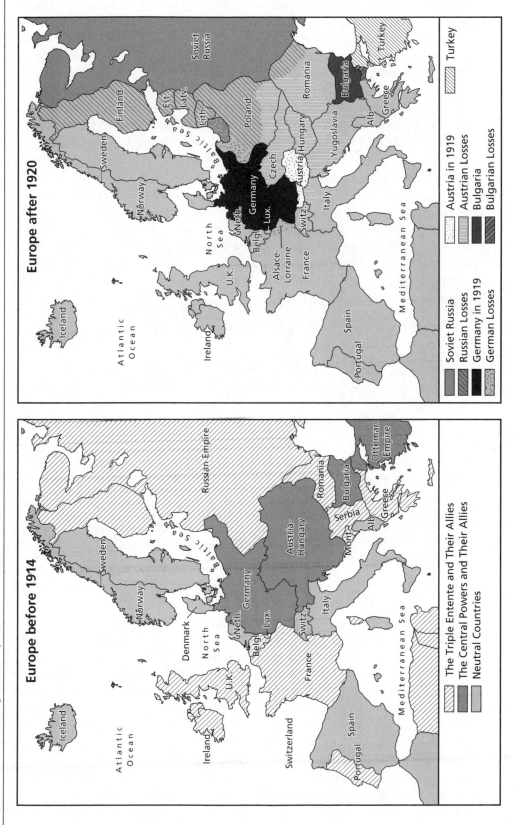

Europe before 1914

Europe after 1920

Legend (Europe before 1914):
- The Triple Entente and Their Allies
- The Central Powers and Their Allies
- Neutral Countries

Legend (Europe after 1920):
- Soviet Russia
- Russian Losses
- Germany in 1919
- German Losses
- Austria in 1919
- Austrian Losses
- Bulgaria
- Bulgarian Losses
- Turkey

SOURCE: GERARD CHALIAND AND JEAN-PIERRE RAGEAU, *STRATEGIC ATLAS: COMPARATIVE GEOPOLITICS OF THE WORLD'S POWERS*, 3RD ED. COPYRIGHT © 1993 BY GERARD CHALIAND AND JEAN-PIERRE RAGEAU. REPRINTED BY PERMISSION OF HARPERCOLLINS PUBLISHERS, INC.

Political idealism has its origins in the philosophical tradition of liberalism, which emerged in Europe in the sixteenth century, although many of the moral principles of liberalism and idealism can be found in earlier works. This philosophical tradition emphasizes the liberty of the individual and the need to protect this liberty from the state. Liberalism, with its focus on individuals as the centre of moral virtue, regards the pursuit of power, authoritarian governance, and intolerance as obstacles to human progress. Some liberal philosophers place their emphasis on building a tolerant, liberal society as the only humane response to pluralism and diversity. Others place more emphasis on the development of capitalism, free trade, and republican democracy as the answer to global problems and the absence of global order. Liberal philosophers include John Locke, Immanuel Kant, Benjamin Constant, John Stuart Mill, Montesquieu, David Hume, Adam Smith, T.H. Green, L.T. Hobhouse, and Thomas Jefferson.

Postwar idealists such as G. Lowes Dickinson, Alfred Zimmern, **Norman Angell**, James T. Shotwell, and U.S. President **Woodrow Wilson** drew on the liberal philosophical tradition. Although these individuals differed on many issues, all idealists shared a number of assumptions about the nature of humanity, the nature of world politics, the experience of World War I, and the road to the future. To varying degrees, idealists assumed the following:

- *Human nature is good.* As a result, assistance and cooperation are possible and natural, motivated by the human qualities of altruism, philanthropy, and humanitarianism.

- *Evil is not innate to humanity.* Evil activity or bad behaviour is the result of bad institutions, states, and structures that motivate individuals to act in a self-interested, distrustful, or aggressive fashion.

- *Social progress is possible.* Human society has developed and improved and will continue to do so.

- *The main problem in international relations is war.* International society must reform itself with the aim of preventing future wars.

- *War can be prevented.* Eliminating bad institutions, states, and structures will eliminate the root causes of war.

- *International cooperation will promote peace.* International organizations and international law will help prevent war.

The policy program of the idealists—their proposed solutions to the problem of war and the issues facing the international system—was expansive and ambitious. Idealists regarded the structure of international relations as a war-making structure that promoted distrust, hostility, conflict, and confrontation. The history of international relations, idealists believed, proved their argument that war was endemic because of the nature of the international system. Idealists believed that by changing the nature of the international system it would be possible to reduce or eliminate war. Their answer was the **collective security** system. Within such a system, all states would agree that in the case of aggression by any state in the system against any other state in the system, all other states would respond to defend the attacked state. In effect, a collective security system sought to make any aggression against any member of the system an act of aggression against all members. As a result, any potential aggressor, faced with the prospect of having to fight every other state in the system, would not engage in aggression in the first place. In this way, peace would be preserved. Idealists also believed that international peace could be encouraged through the development of international organizations, international law, and arms control.

The principles and hopes of political idealism did serve as a guide for postwar efforts to remake the international system, most famously in the creation of the League of Nations and in U.S. President Woodrow Wilson's famous **Fourteen Points**, which influenced the post–World War I settlement. The Covenant of the League of Nations was drafted at the Paris Peace Conference in 1919. The League comprised an assembly and a council of permanent members, which included Great Britain, France, Italy, and Japan, and later Germany (1926) and the Soviet Union (1934). We discuss the operations of the League in more detail in Chapter 5. Between 1920 and 1939, the League considered 66 disputes between states and contributed to peaceful outcomes in 35 of them. The League reflected the idealist perspective's assumption that international organizations would serve to maintain peace and promote cooperation among states on a wide variety of international issues and problems. Peace would be strengthened by the development of international law, including efforts to make war illegal, such as the 1928 **Kellogg–Briand Pact.** Peace would also be strengthened through **arms control**, such as the 1922 Washington Naval Treaty, which restricted the number and armament of battleships in the fleets of the great powers. However, the treaty is also an example of how states pursue their own interests in arms control negotiations; under the treaty some states could have more battleships than others, and naval competition continued in the aircraft carrier and cruiser classes of ships.

The principles of political idealism were neither universally shared nor admired, and the immediate postwar period was characterized by realpolitik behaviour as much as by idealist behaviour. The events of the interwar period and the erosion or failure of many of the key elements of the idealists' reform program removed much of the enthusiasm for idealist assumptions and solutions. Political idealism as a view of the world receded. However, it did not vanish. As we will see in later chapters, many of the key elements of the idealist program remained in place and were employed in the international system long after idealism's golden years had faded. Today, the legacy of political idealism lives on in the principles that form the foundation for arms control, international organizations, and international law.

THE INTERWAR PERIOD

Behind the outward unity displayed by the victorious powers after World War I were serious disagreements, particularly among Great Britain, France, and the United States, over the treatment of Germany. France was the most uncompromising. It had been devastated during the war: 1 355 800 French citizens had been killed and 4 260 000 wounded; almost 300 000 homes had been destroyed; and the country was heavily in debt due to the financial costs of the war effort.[7] The French were not willing to place their faith in Wilson's collective security concept, deciding instead that a system of alliances built against Germany would be the best guarantee of peace. Another matter of dispute was the issue of reparations. France and Great Britain wanted Germany to pay for the entire cost of the war, and Germany began to default on reparations payments as early as 1920. In response, the French government acted unilaterally and occupied the Ruhr Valley in 1923. Within Germany, popular resentment against the Versailles Treaty increased.

In the interwar period, Russia went through the throes of revolution to resurface as a major actor in Europe. Increased economic hardship, growing hunger, and the clear incompetence of the Russian political and military leadership in the war led to the overthrow of the Tsar in February 1917. The Duma, or Parliament, assumed power, but its decision to continue the war alienated the people, leaving it vulnerable to revolutionary organizations of workers, called Soviets, and the return from exile of **Vladimir Lenin**, who promised peace, land, bread, and all power to the Soviets. The provisional government collapsed, and Lenin's Bolsheviks seized power in the October revolution. Lenin's first task was to obtain peace, and despite opposition he accepted unfavourable terms from Germany in return for peace in the Treaty of Brest–Litovsk (1918).

Peace, however, was short lived. Civil war broke out as the White Russian movement, hoping to restore the monarchy, attacked Bolshevik forces with support from intervening armies from Britain, France, and the United States. War weariness broke the spirit of the intervening powers, and by 1921 the Bolsheviks prevailed. The Union of Soviet Socialist Republics (USSR), often called the Soviet Union, was established in December 1922. By 1925 the Soviet Union had recovered economically and was reaching out internationally, even obtaining diplomatic recognition from France, Great Britain, and other European countries. Lenin's death in 1924 eventually brought Josef Stalin to power, who, with his doctrine of "socialism in one country," embarked on a massive program of industrialization and agricultural collectivization, as well as purges of the Communist Party and the Red Army that left millions dead. However, the Soviet Union was firmly established as a great power.

In the Middle East and Asia, the interwar period saw the fall of an empire, chaos in another, and the rise of a new great power. As one of the defeated powers, the Ottoman Empire was partitioned by the victorious states. These humiliations sparked a nationalist uprising led by Mustapha Kemal (Ataturk) that marked the beginning of a secular Turkish state, the heir to the Ottoman legacy. China experienced a period of chaos, instability, and invasion in the interwar period. Successive central leaderships proved incapable of addressing economic problems or the issue of foreign interference in China. Central rule broke down, and provincial warlords assumed local power. Under the leadership of Sun Yat-sen and then Chiang Kai-shek, the Nationalist (Koumintang) Party, allied with the Chinese Communists, attempted to suppress the warlords, end foreign power in China, and reunify the country. After initial success in the north of the country, the alliance between the Koumintang and the Communists broke down. However, Japan intervened in Manchuria in 1931, and Chiang now had to meet two threats simultaneously: the Japanese and the Communist movement in the countryside, led by Mao Tse-tung. Chiang's efforts to crush Mao's Communists forced Mao and his supporters into the famous Long March of 1934–35. The Nationalist and Communist forces were to battle the Japanese until the end of World War II.

The interwar period saw the rise of a new power in Asia: Japan. The Meiji Restoration of 1868 reopened Japan to the world after two hundred years of isolation. Japan embarked on a period of rapid industrialization and established an empire on the mainland. Japan was recognized as a victorious power at the Paris Peace Conference and was given great power status and a permanent seat on the Council of the League of Nations. However, the Great Depression hit Japan hard as the rise of trade barriers around the world hurt the trade-dependent Japanese economy. The government fell, replaced by a military government. These changes, coupled with China's efforts to recover Manchuria (an important source of raw materials and industrial production) from Japan, led to the Japanese fabrication of an attack on a Japanese railway line, which provided the pretext for a Japanese military intervention in Manchuria in 1931. Despite the principle of collective security described earlier, the League failed to respond forcefully, issuing a report in 1933 calling for Chinese control of Manchuria with protection of Japanese interests. In response, Japan walked out of the League of Nations. In 1937, Japan invaded China, and tensions between Japan and the United States escalated over the invasion and trade issues.

The interwar period also saw the rise of two revisionist powers in Europe. In Italy, the fascist leader Benito Mussolini came to power in 1922, and in 1935, Italy attacked Ethiopia. The League responded quickly and forcefully, identifying Italy as the aggressor and voting to implement an embargo on armaments against Italy. However, all other products (including oil, coal, and steel) could still be traded to Italy, and the enforcement of the embargo was never effective. The Italian venture was successful, and in 1936 Mussolini proclaimed Ethiopia a province of Italy. In 1937, Italy withdrew from the League of Nations and annexed Albania in 1939.

In Germany, economic disaster struck. A combination of a weakened economy and the onset of the **Great Depression** in Europe devastated the value of the German mark as inflation spiralled out of control. It was in this economic and political context that the Nazi Party rose to prominence in Germany, on a platform of resentment toward the Versailles Treaty, renewed German nationalism, and **anti-Semitism**. Under Hitler, Germany began to rearm, with no forceful response from Great Britain or France. In 1938 Germany annexed Austria into the Third Reich, and demanded a solution for the Sudetenland Germans, who lived in Czechoslovakia. At Munich, the British and French governments sought to appease Hitler and accepted the incorporation of the Sudetenland into the Third Reich. This region was also Czechoslovakia's main line of defence; when it was annexed, the country was in a hopeless position to resist any further German expansion. In April 1939, Hitler occupied the rest of Czechoslovakia. Subsequent German demands for territory around Danzig from Poland prompted the British and the French to become allies to protect Poland.

In the face of increasing international diplomatic and economic tensions, the League was increasingly unable to act effectively. For most of its history, the League counted only four of the seven great powers among its membership, and as a result it could not serve as the universal organization it was intended to be. The League was further damaged when it could not take effective action against Italian aggression in Ethiopia, Japanese aggression in Manchuria, and later German and Soviet aggression in Europe. The aims of the revisionist powers of the 1930s were fundamentally at odds with the principles of the Covenant. Although some League committees continued to operate during the war, the League was irrelevant as an instrument of peace and security. In April 1946, the League was formally disbanded.

The revisionist powers of the interwar period—Germany, Italy, and Japan—encountered limited resistance to their territorial gains and aggressive acts. Why was this the case? The experience of World War I was clearly a factor; no one wanted to risk another world war. The neutralist position of the United States also weakened the strength of nonrevisionist states. Without U.S. support and active involvement in world affairs, countries such as Great Britain and France lacked the support to decisively respond to aggression, or so they believed. In addition, all countries in the world were grappling with enormous domestic economic problems—international aggression in Manchuria and Ethiopia seemed very far away. Countries had turned inward: the United States had retreated into isolationism; the British behind the English Channel; and the French behind the supposedly impregnable fortifications of the Maginot Line. As a result, the policy toward revisionist countries, in particular toward Germany, became known as **appeasement:** giving in to the demands of revisionist states in the hope that they would soon be satisfied with their gains. Appeasement was not a policy of blind subjection to threats, however. The publics in Great Britain, France, and the United States were opposed to war, and all countries were unprepared for it. Appeasement might satisfy Hitler and Mussolini; if not, it would at least buy time to rearm.

WORLD WAR II: TOTAL WAR

In August 1939, Nazi Germany and the Soviet Union signed the Nazi–Soviet non-aggression pact. The pact was a surprise, since German National Socialism and Soviet Communism were self-declared ideological enemies. A month later, the motivation for the pact would become clear. Hitler invaded Poland on 1 September 1939, and split the gains with the Soviet Union, which had invaded Poland and the Baltic States only days later. Britain and France honoured their pledge to Poland by declaring war on Germany two days later. World War II had begun.

The war rapidly expanded. Utilizing the new tactics of the *blitzkrieg* (lightning war), and seizing command of the air, German forces invaded and conquered Denmark, Norway, the Netherlands, and Belgium. France succumbed as German forces swept around the Maginot Line. Paris fell in June 1940. The Battle of Britain then began, an air campaign in which the German Luftwaffe unsuccessfully attempted to bomb Britain into submission. In the Mediterranean, Mussolini's Italy had invaded Greece, but the failure of the campaign brought Germany into the conflict, and Germany conquered Yugoslavia and Greece in early 1941. German and Italian troops in Africa moved toward Egypt, with the aim of wresting the Suez Canal from British control. In what we might with retrospect label the greatest strategic blunder of all time, in June 1941, Hitler invaded the Soviet Union. Having achieved total surprise, German forces swept through Russia, destroying much of the Red Army in the process. By December, German troops had advanced to within a few kilometres of Moscow. However, the German advance was halted by the Russian winter, lack of supplies, and stiffening Russian resistance around Moscow and Leningrad as Russia began to mobilize its superior resources and population.

In another notable strategic blunder, on 7 December 1941, Japan launched a surprise attack on the United States at Pearl Harbor, home of the American Pacific Fleet. Japan also mounted a swift campaign of conquest in the western Pacific, seizing the Philippines, French Indochina, the Dutch East Indies, Singapore, much of New Guinea, and the Bismarck and Solomon Islands in the South Pacific in the course of a few months. American isolationist sentiment collapsed in the face of the Pearl Harbor attack, and the democratic United States forged an alliance with democratic Great Britain and the Communist Soviet Union—the Allied powers—to oppose Nazi Germany, fascist Italy, and Imperial Japan—the Axis powers.

In 1942 and 1943, the fortunes of war began to turn against the Axis powers. German and Italian forces were repulsed from Egypt. The 1942 German offensive in southern Russia ended in German defeat at Stalingrad. In the Atlantic, after heavy losses to German submarines, more and more merchant ships carrying supplies from Canada and the United States began to get through to Britain. In the Pacific, the Japanese Imperial Navy was defeated in the Battle of Midway and at the Battle of the Coral Sea. The United States then began to embark on a series of campaigns to retake the South Pacific from the Japanese. In May 1943, German and Italian forces in North Africa were defeated. At the decisive battle of Kursk in July 1943, the German summer offensive was defeated, and the Red Army forced the Germans on to the defensive on the entire eastern front. American and British strategic bombing raids against Germany began, damaging German industry and transportation, killing many civilians, and complicating the German war effort.

The decisive blows of the war were struck against the Axis powers in 1944. In June, British, Canadian, and U.S. troops landed in northern France, broke through German defences, and liberated France, Belgium, and the Netherlands. The Soviet Union launched an offensive on the eastern front a few weeks later and by late 1944 had pushed German forces back into Eastern Europe. In 1945, after an unsuccessful German counteroffensive in the west, British and American forces advanced into Germany (see Map 2.9). In January 1945, the Red Army launched a final offensive aimed at Berlin. Adolf Hitler committed suicide on April 30, and on May 7 Germany surrendered unconditionally. Thus would end the career of one of the most influential and darkly troubling

Map 2.9 The War in Europe

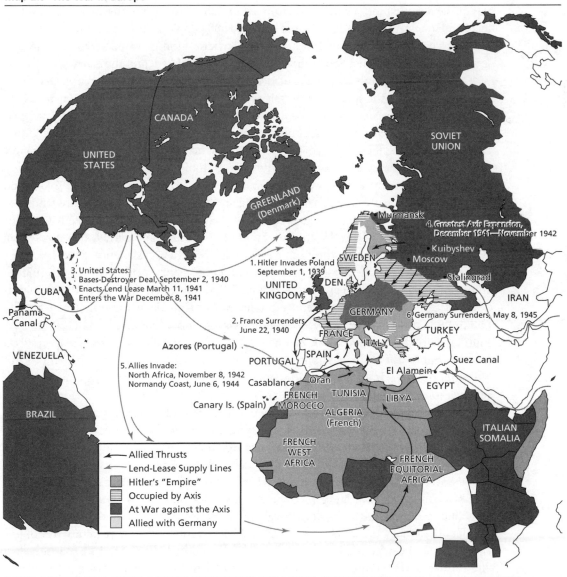

SOURCE: R. PALMER AND J. COLTON, *A HISTORY OF THE MODERN WORLD*, 8TH ED. (NEW YORK: MCGRAW-HILL, 1995). REPRINTED WITH PERMISSION OF THE MCGRAW-HILL COMPANIES.

politicians in modern history. Indeed, one might argue that World War II would not have occurred without the existence of this single man, lending credence to the value of the individual level of analysis discussed in Chapter 1.

In the Pacific, American forces began the reconquest of the Philippines, and the Japanese Navy was eliminated as an effective fighting force at the Battle of Leyte. British and Indian troops retook Burma, and Japan came under air attack from American bases in China and the Marianas Islands. In 1945, the American capture of Iwo Jima and Okinawa secured air bases closer to Japan, enabling the air offensive to be accelerated. Despite the devastation of most Japanese cities and Japan's industrial capacity, the Japanese still resisted, and preparations were made to invade the home islands of Japan (see Map 2.10). The war soon ended but not in a conventional manner. Throughout the war the United States had been engaged in top-secret research to develop an atomic weapon. Such a device had been successfully tested near Alamogordo, New Mexico, in the spring of 1945. In a controversial decision, President Truman authorized the first military use of the **atomic bomb,** which was dropped on Hiroshima on 6 August 1945; its short-term and long-term effects killed more than 140 000 people. A second bomb was dropped on Nagasaki on August 9, one day after the Soviet Union declared war on Japan and invaded Manchuria. On 2 September 1945, Japan capitulated, and the war was over.

The use of the bomb remains controversial even today. Was it necessary? Defenders of the decision cite the enormous casualties that American service personnel would have suffered in any invasion of Japan. Others suggest the atomic bomb was dropped primarily to demonstrate American military might to the Soviet Union. Many argue that the decision to use the bombs against densely populated civilian targets was inhumane, as well as unnecessary. However, the saturation bombing of cities had long been practised by both sides during the war. London, Rotterdam, Dresden, Hamburg, Tokyo, and many other cities suffered extensive bombing and greater casualties than those suffered at Hiroshima and Nagasaki. In this context, the atomic bomb did not seem very different. Nevertheless, to this day the bombings of Hiroshima and Nagasaki retain special symbolic importance, since the atomic era began with their destruction.

World War II was the most destructive conflict in history. Approximately 15 million combatants and 35 million civilians were killed. The Soviet Union alone suffered 20 million casualties—more than the entire population of Canada at the time (for Canada's role in the war, see Profile 2.12). Six million Jews and more than five million others were murdered in the concentration camps of Nazi-occupied Europe (see Chapter 9 on human rights for a discussion of genocide, the Holocaust, and the important **Nuremberg war crimes trials**). Cities and industries across Europe and Asia had been reduced to rubble. A massive rebuilding task faced the survivors. Never before had war so fundamentally affected the lives of civilians. They had become targets of bombing campaigns and had participated in war production.[8] This was the era of what Joseph Goebbels, Hitler's **propaganda** minister, termed "total war."

World War II also had enormous political consequences. The victory of the Allied powers over the Axis powers altered the distribution of power in the world. Borders in Europe changed in accordance with agreements made between **Winston Churchill** and Josef Stalin in 1944 and at the "big three" conference of Roosevelt, Stalin, and Churchill at Yalta in February 1945. The Soviet Union absorbed some 600 square kilometres of territory, which included the Baltic States and land from Poland, Finland, Czechoslovakia, and Romania, recovering what had been lost under the Treaty of Brest–Litovsk. Poland

Map 2.10 The War in the Pacific

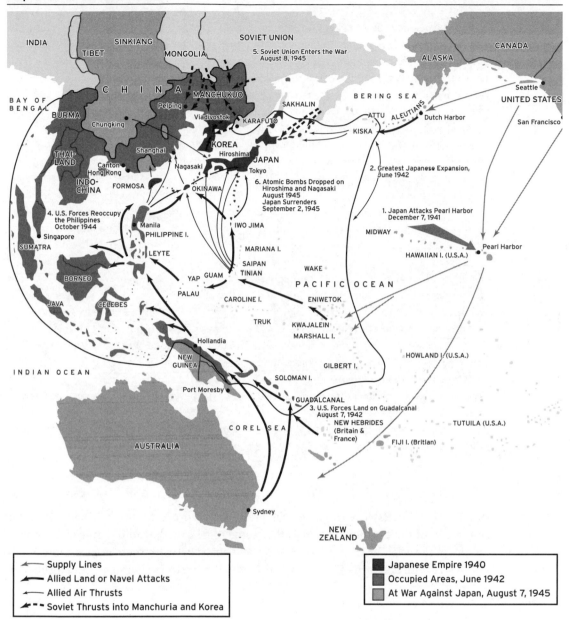

Legend:
- ← Supply Lines
- ◄ Allied Land or Naval Attacks
- ← Allied Air Thrusts
- ◄-- Soviet Thrusts into Manchuria and Korea

- ■ Japanese Empire 1940
- ■ Occupied Areas, June 1942
- ■ At War Against Japan, August 7, 1945

SOURCE: R. PALMER AND J. COLTON, *A HISTORY OF THE MODERN WORLD*, 8TH ED. (NEW YORK: MCGRAW-HILL, 1995). REPRINTED WITH PERMISSION OF THE MCGRAW-HILL COMPANIES.

was compensated with land from Germany, which was divided into four occupation zones. Austria was separated from Germany. In the Far East, Japan lost control over Manchuria, Taiwan, and Korea (which was divided into Soviet and U.S. zones) and suffered the loss of the Kurile Islands, which were seized by the Soviet Union. The war had also ushered in the nuclear era; to say the least, the atomic bomb was to have an enduring impact on international relations. The war also weakened the European colonial powers, and a great wave of decolonization swept the world in the decades after the war, leading to an explosion of the number of independent states. Finally, the end of World War II saw the emergence of two powers—the United States and the Soviet

Canada and World War II

Canada declared war on Nazi Germany on 10 September 1939, seven days after Great Britain. The government of Mackenzie King had envisioned a limited overseas commitment when it entered the war. Opinion in Canada was not as deeply divided as it had been in World War I, and although conscription was once again an issue in 1944 due to battlefield losses, the divisive debates of 1917 were not repeated.

By June 1940 only Great Britain, Canada, and the other Commonwealth countries stood against the Axis. Canada was now committed to a total war and produced vast amounts of ammunition and military equipment in cities such as Hamilton, Toronto, and Montreal. The Royal Canadian Navy bore most of the convoy escort duty early in the war, providing security for the vital merchant shipping lanes to Great Britain. More than 1 100 000 Canadians served during the war, and at its peak, the Canadian Army fielded nearly 500 000 soldiers; most students are surprised to learn that, at this time, the Canadian Air Force and the Navy were among the largest in the world after those of the great powers.

Canadians first fought together in large numbers in the disastrous Dieppe raid in August 1942. The circumstances of the raid are a subject of controversy to this day, since some suggest Allied commanders sent the Canadians to their slaughter. Canadians first saw mass service in the Italian campaign in 1943 and were assigned their own landing beach (along with the United States and Great Britain) in the Normandy invasion of 1944. The Canadian army fought in the Normandy campaign and then liberated much of the Netherlands (to this day, the people of the Netherlands have a deep respect for the sacrifice made by Canadians in liberating their country in the war). More than 42 000 Canadians died in World War II. It may seem surprising now, but Canada ended the war as one of the most powerful countries in the world. This position was the foundation of Canada's postwar *middle power* status and the basis for Canada's postwar internationalism.

Union—that possessed capabilities far greater than those of any other country. The emergence of these **superpowers**, as they came to be called, would define international politics in the postwar era, and suspicion and distrust between them grew rapidly. World War II had ended, but the Cold War, which we will turn to in Chapter 3, had just begun.

POLITICAL REALISM

Not surprisingly, the realist perspective described in Chapter 1 developed following World War II, which many felt provided clear evidence that idealist claims about the progressive inclination of human nature were hopelessly naïve (see Profile 2.13). However, the intellectual roots of realism lay in early writings about war and statecraft in the work of the ancient Greek historian Thucydides, in the writings of Kautilya, in the advice of Sun Tzu, in the philosophies and advice on statecraft of Niccolo Machiavelli, and in the reflections of the English theoretician Thomas Hobbes. These and other writings emphasized the importance of power and self-interest above all other considerations. The realist perspective was thus built on the intellectual heritage of realpolitik.

Early exponents of political realism include E.H. Carr, Hans J. Morgenthau (see Profile 2.14), Kenneth W. Thompson, and Reinhold Niebuhr. As a group, realists made several assumptions about the character of international politics. States were the principal actors

PROFILE 2.13 — The Idealist Perspective and the Realist Perspective

ISSUE	IDEALISM	REALISM
Human nature	Good/altruistic	Evil/selfish
Central problem	War and the establishment of peace	War and security
Key actors	States and individuals	States
Motives of actors	Mutual assistance/ collaboration	Power/national interest/ security
Nature of international politics	Cooperation and community	Anarchy
Outlook on future	Optimistic	Pessimistic/stability
Policy prescriptions/ solutions	Reform the system/ institutions	Enhance power/protect national interests

PROFILE 2.14 — Hans J. Morgenthau

Hans J. Morgenthau was born in Germany in 1904. He received his university education in Germany and practised law in Frankfurt before moving to the United States in 1937, where he was appointed to the University of Chicago in 1943. His most famous work was entitled *Politics among Nations*, first published in 1948. Morgenthau presented a theory of international politics in the book, and his "six principles of political realism" became one of the foundations of the realist perspective:

1. Politics is governed by objective laws that have their roots in human nature, which has not changed since the time of classical China, India, and Greece.

2. States, and their leaders, think and act in terms of interest defined as power, and to understand their actions observers of international politics must think the same way.

3. The idea of interest is the essence of politics and is unaffected by time and place; efforts to transform politics without considering this basic law will fail.

4. Tension exists between moral command and the requirements of successful political action. Morality cannot be applied universally in the abstract but must be filtered through the circumstances of time and place.

5. The moral aspirations of a particular nation are not to be confused with the moral laws that govern the universe.

6. Intellectually, realism maintains the autonomy of the political sphere, as economists, lawyers, or doctors maintain theirs.

Morgenthau, then, argued that international relations is characterized by states pursuing their national interests defined in terms of power. The world is the result of forces inherent in human nature, and is characterized by opposing interests and conflicts among them. For Morgenthau, international politics was governed by universal principles or laws based on the pursuit of the national interest.

SOURCE: HANS J. MORGENTHAU, *POLITICS AMONG NATIONS* (NEW YORK: KNOPF, 1948).

in international politics since no authority in international politics superseded the authority of the state. For the purposes of analysis, states were also taken to be rational, unitary actors, interested above all else in their security and in maximizing their power. The pursuit of power—the ability to make other actors do what they would not otherwise do—was the core aim of international politics.[9] Although most realists would find the following to be an oversimplification of their world view, to varying degrees, realists assumed that

- Human nature is essentially evil (people are selfish and acquisitive).
- The desire for power is instinctive to all individuals and cannot be eliminated.
- As a result, international politics is a struggle for power.
- The international system is anarchic in nature as no central authority or world government exists that is capable of enforcing rules.
- In such an environment, the primary objective of all states is to follow their national interests, defined in terms of power.
- In such an environment, states must ultimately rely on their own efforts to ensure their own security.
- Military power and preparedness is the most important factor in determining state power and security.
- Alliances can increase the security of a state, but the loyalty and reliability of allies should always be questioned.
- International organizations and international law cannot be relied on to guarantee security, as state actions are not bound by enforceable rules.
- Order can be achieved only by the balance of power system in which stability is maintained by flexible alliance systems.

If power is so important, we need to know how to measure it. This task is not easy, conceptually or empirically, since much emphasis has been placed on the tangible, measurable capabilities of states.[10] Such factors include the base assets of a state such as its territory, population, geography, natural resources, and **gross domestic product (GDP).** These elements of power are long-term attributes that generally change slowly over time. They represent the foundation of state power, or what Canadian foreign policy analyst Kim Richard Nossal has termed "relative invariates."[11] Some states are more endowed with these elements than others are by virtue of location or conquest. Frequently, though not exclusively, these states become great powers. Other states stand little or no chance of attaining such status.

For realists, military power is the principal means through which states exercise power in the short term. Military capabilities are the most important measure of state power in war when other power elements are not directly engaged. However, if a war is long, the states with the greater power resources to mobilize and commit to military ends will have the advantage. Estimating the power—especially the military power—of others is a crucial element of international politics, realists argue. As Sun Tzu wrote: "Know the enemy and know yourself; in a hundred battles you will never be in peril." However, tangible, measurable factors (which we termed **hard power** in Chapter 1) are not the entire story. Power encompasses intangibles, power elements that are not easily measured or compared. A state must be able to deploy hard power capabilities in an effective fashion. This ability depends on the unity of purpose within the state, which can be influenced by public opinion, religion, ideology, or nationalism (the conscription crisis in Canada during World War I is an example of such a difficulty, as was the American war effort in Vietnam). The effective deployment of power can also depend on the support a state has obtained in the international system, which may depend, in turn, on the moral legitimacy of its cause, the loyalty of its allies, and the diplomatic and political skills available to the state. Power can also lie in the ability of an actor to set agendas, establish norms of behaviour, and gain wider agreements on rules and regulations that others agree to obey.

The less tangible elements of power (which we call **soft power**) reflect the appeal or attraction of ideas and values. If a state's ideas and values are seen as attractive, they will provide that state with opportunities to exert influence and leadership. For example, some have argued that the United States leads the world in terms of soft power because of its position as the world's leading capitalist marketplace and liberal democracy. Some Canadians (such as former Foreign Minister Lloyd Axworthy) have suggested that Canada has influence in the world beyond its capabilities (especially its military capabilities) because of its emphasis on international cooperation and institutions over the use of military force and coercion. In this view, soft power has enabled Canada to provide leadership on issues such as peacekeeping, the movement to ban landmines, and sanctions against South Africa during the **apartheid** era. This view of soft power rejects the hard power perspective advanced by realists. For their part, realists argue that soft power flows from the ability to exert hard power, and, therefore, hard power remains the central currency of all power in global politics.

ANARCHY AND THE SECURITY DILEMMA

As indicated in Chapter 1, realism is not a monolithic theory, and realism has evolved considerably from its early origins. Classical realists such as Morgenthau and Niebuhr emphasize the role of human nature. Structural realists such as Kenneth Waltz emphasize the anarchic nature of the system as a determinant of state behaviour. The term anarchy implies not complete chaos or absence of rules but rather the lack of a central authority or government capable of enforcing rules.[12] Within states, governments can deter participants from breaking rules, can enforce contracts, and can use their monopoly on the use of coercion to compel citizens to obey the law. No central authority exists to enforce and ensure state compliance with international rules or norms. Consequently, states must become self-reliant if they are to survive. All states must, therefore, be prepared to use force in their own defence, for in an anarchic environment, a state may use coercion or force at any time if the benefits to be gained outweigh potential costs (see the discussion of the stag hunt in Profile 2.15). So states arm themselves for protection against such an eventuality, following the advice of the Latin phrase *Si vis pacem, parabellum*—If you want peace, prepare for war.

In doing so, however, states can find themselves in a situation that scholars have called the **security dilemma**. In this situation, when states take unilateral measures to ensure their own security (such as increasing the capabilities of their military forces), they decrease the security of neighbouring states. Neighbouring states will perceive these measures as threatening and will take countermeasures (increasing the capabilities of their own armed forces) to enhance their own security. These military enhancements will provoke insecurity in other states, which will increase their military capabilities as well. This action–reaction cycle occurs when states increasingly spend resources on military capabilities but make no real gains in the way of security. This dynamic is the basis

The Trouble with Cooperation: The Stag Hunt

The stag hunt is an allegory that originated in the writings of the Geneva-born eighteenth-century philosopher **Jean Jacques Rousseau**. In this allegory, five individual hunters exist in a state of nature, with no government or social structure to determine their behaviour. The hunters have a choice of cooperating to attain a mutually desired goal or defecting from such cooperation if their own individual short-term interests can be satisfied. They can collaborate to capture a stag, which will satisfy the food needs of all five hunters if they share it. To be successful, all five hunters must cooperate to encircle the stag. However, in doing so, it is possible that one of the hunters will encounter a hare, which will satisfy that individual hunter's food needs. That hunter then faces a choice: let the hare go and serve the common interest by continuing the effort to capture the stag, or take the hare and

defect from the group, thus ruining the hunt for the other four hunters, who will not have their food needs satisfied.

The allegory raises several questions about incentives and disincentives for cooperation. If a hunter prefers to cooperate to capture the stag, can the other hunters be trusted to do the same? Is it not in the rational self-interest of a hunter to take the hare? If this is the case, how can the hunters trust each other to cooperate on a hunt for the stag? And if they cannot trust each other, is it not in their interests to take the hare before any of the other hunters do? Indeed, what is the incentive to cooperate at all? The stag hunt allegory illustrates the difficulty of establishing cooperation in an anarchic environment and the corrosive effect short-term self-interest can have on collaborative efforts.

of the many arms races that have occurred between states. Arms races are characterized by periods of high tension and the rapid escalation of the military capabilities of the states engaged. Arms races promote hostility and mistrust and create the conditions in which a crisis could easily lead to misunderstanding, miscalculation, and war. Both world wars described earlier in this chapter can be viewed from this perspective. In the next chapter, we will examine in detail what was, arguably, the greatest security dilemma of all time, the development and evolution of the Cold War.

For realists, the existence of an anarchic self-help system does not mean that the international system lacks order or cooperation. In fact, realists argue that the international system is far from chaotic.[13] In an anarchic system, states can cooperate and do so all the time. States reach trade agreements and form alliances. However, realists argue that this cooperation occurs not for altruistic reasons but because it is in the interests of states to cooperate. Cooperation is simply another reflection of self-help. Furthermore, when states interact they follow international norms and conventions most of the time. Norms are shared expectations about what constitutes appropriate behaviour in the international system.[14] An example of such a norm is the concept of sovereignty, the principle that a state has control over affairs within its own territory, free from external interference by other states. In principle, states are therefore autonomous in that they answer to no higher authority in the international system. Another prominent norm is respect for internationally recognized borders. Despite the fact that most borders in the world today are the result of past wars and international agreements or the legacy of colonial occupation, the territorial integrity of states is regarded as one of the foundations of international stability. Attempts to revise these borders—through conquest or succession—are generally regarded as dangerous or destabilizing events, because a challenge to an existing border is in principle a challenge to borders everywhere. Other norms regulate the conduct of diplomatic relations between states. For example, embassies are considered to be the territory of their home states, rather than that of the host country, and are therefore not subject to interference or the laws of the host country. Finally, as we will see, governments obey a wide variety of international norms, procedures, regulations, and laws every day.

Since cooperation and norms do provide the basis for some order in the international system, anarchy does not mean the absence of order. However, realists emphasize that when it comes to security issues, or so-called high politics concerns, states rely on power to manage relations between them. This reliance has led to the development of the concept of the balance of power.

THE BALANCE AND DISTRIBUTION OF POWER: ALLIANCES AND POLARITY

The term *balance of power* can be used in several ways. The balance of power can be used as a descriptive term to denote the state of the power balance between certain states or groups of states in a certain region of the world. (It was not until the twentieth century and the superpower confrontation that the concern with a global balance of power arose.) It can be used to describe a particular policy of states that may be seeking a balance of power. Most commonly, it refers to a historical phenomenon in which empires and states have repeatedly formed alliances against other states or groups of states. The balance of power is a system of order in an anarchic international system in which states act to ensure that no one state or group of states can come to dominate the system or conquer all other states in the system. This balancing behaviour preserves the system of sovereign states because no one state or group of states can acquire the power to control the entire region (or the world). However, the balance of power does not necessarily mean the preservation of peace. In fact, the balance of power does not exist to ensure peace, but rather to ensure the survival of the state system. The preservation of the balance of power system often requires war to defeat the efforts of certain states to dominate the system.

The concept of the balance of power suggests that if the power of a state or a group of states grows, other states in the system will balance against this growing power. States can balance in one of two ways. They can increase their own power (generally through military spending) or they can engage in **alliances** with other states. Alliances are formal agreements between states that commit them to a common purpose, such as military security. (Those arrangements that are not formalized in treaties and that tend to be of shorter duration are often called *coalitions*.) Alliances are a quick and relatively cheap method of supplementing one's own power with the power of another. Alliances, then, are a form of self-interested cooperation (another term we might use is *marriage of convenience*). Realists argue that the historical frequency of alliances reveals the salience of the balance of power concept.

Generally, alliances form when two or more states share a perceived threat and agree to coordinate their efforts to meet that threat.[15] This agreement may take the form of treaty obligations to assist the other state if it is attacked. In other cases, agreements may extend to high levels of cooperation on political and military issues, including the formation of joint institutions and joint military forces. Alliances are notoriously fluid and changing, and alliance commitments are often broken. When the threat common to alliance members disappears, alliances tend to break up as well, although as our discussion of the **North Atlantic Treaty Organization (NATO)** in subsequent chapters suggests, some alliances have persisted over time, and in many cases states have been reluctant to dissolve them. Why is this the case? A state might be reluctant to defect from an alliance relationship because of concerns that it would acquire a reputation as an unreliable ally. In the future, other countries might be less willing to form an alliance with a state that has a poor reputation for maintaining its commitments and obligations. Alternatively, alliances might survive because self-interested states want to maintain the advantages of the cooperative relationship they have built.

Alliances vary with respect to the commitment of their members and their internal unity, often called **alliance cohesion**. Cohesive alliances have a high degree of shared interests and coordination among their members, and tend to be formally institutionalized. NATO is an example of a highly cohesive alliance that has developed a complex system of political and military cooperation since its inception in 1949. Alliances that are less cohesive have lower levels of coordination and have divergent interests among their membership. Cohesion is important because the ability to form a strong united effort against a threat is the key to a credible alliance; potential enemies are far less likely to attack a cohesive alliance because it seems certain that the members will all honour their commitments. Similarly, efforts by a potential enemy to create rifts in an alliance may not succeed if an alliance is cohesive.

For realists, because states will act to balance the power of other states, the distribution of power in the international system or in regional systems is extremely important. The distribution of power is defined by concentrations of power in a region or in the entire international system and by how many of these concentrations exist.

These concentrations of power are called poles, and the distribution of power is often described in terms of **polarity** (a term borrowed from physics). Polarity describes the number of independent centres or concentrations of power in the system. These poles of power, and the relations between them, determine the polarity of the system; other actors may exist, but they are not decisive in determining system polarity. Changes in the distribution of power may take place slowly, the result of different economic growth rates and technological innovation among states. Some changes in the distribution of power may be very dramatic, the result of a sudden shift in alliances across the states in the system or the sudden weakening of one or more of the powers in a system through internal collapse or defeat in war. When this happens, the polarity of the system may change, and a different kind of system may emerge. For the purposes of study, realist scholars have identified three different kinds of polarity in the history of international relations: multipolar systems, bipolar systems, and unipolar systems. Each system type has a certain distribution of power (polarity), and each is the subject of debate as to its relative advantages and disadvantages.

Multipolar systems consist of three to seven independent centres, or poles, that are relatively equal in power. These systems can be global in scope (the global balance of power), regional in scope (such as the historical European balance of power systems), or localized (such as the Warring States period in Chou China). The stability of multipolar systems is a major issue of debate among realists. Morgenthau argued that such a system is stable (and therefore more peaceful) because enough centres of power always exist to prevent a single power or group of powers from dominating. However, some realists, such as Kenneth Waltz, warn that multipolar systems are inherently unstable, precisely because they are so flexible.[16] In such a system, the actions of one centre of power (such as an attack on another centre of power or a decision to expand its military) can reverberate throughout the system and have unintended consequences (such as system-wide war or an arms race). A special kind of multipolar system is the tripolar system in which three centres of power exist. Tripolar systems are very unstable as there is a tendency for two of the power centres to ally against the third, with no prospect of achieving a power balance to deter war. Historical examples of such power distributions are rare, although some of the characteristics of such systems can be found in the "strategic triangle" between the United States, the Soviet Union, and China during the Cold War.[17]

In **bipolar** systems, two centres of power, either in the form of two predominant states or two great rival alliance blocs, dominate the international system, such as in Greece during the height of the Athenian and Spartan empires, and during the early Cold War between the superpowers and their respective allies. As the Cold War wore on, however, other countries attained more flexibility, largely because of their recovery from the devastation of World War II. As a result, while the superpowers remained militarily and economically predominant, other states increasingly embarked on their own foreign policy agendas and relationships, although these rarely challenged the policy of the superpowers. (In practice, the major allies of the United States maintained more freedom of manoeuvre than did the allies of the Soviet Union.) This system is sometimes referred to as **bipolycentrism.** Realists also disagree on the stability of bipolar systems. Some, such as Kenneth Waltz, argue that bipolar systems are stable because the two centres of power deter each other from rash actions, and they can develop a familiarity that will reduce the chances of miscalculation. Others argue that such a system is inflexible because of the lack of balancing potential; each state sees its position with respect to the other as a **zero-sum game.**[18] As a result, even small changes in the distribution of power between the two centres of power can have destabilizing effects that could lead to war. This became particularly dangerous, of course, in the nuclear age, when all-out war between the two poles can result in the destruction of most life on the planet.

The third configuration is a **unipolar** system, characterized by a single centre of power: a state or a powerful state and its allies dominate the forums, rules, and arrangements governing political and economic relations in the system. Such actors are often called hegemons. Most often, **hegemony** is a reflection of one state's preponderant power in traditional economic and military terms. However, hegemony can also refer to the dominance of certain ideas or certain cultures.[19] The theory of **hegemonic stability** holds that a hegemon can have a stabilizing or ordering influence on a regional system or the international system by performing some of the functions a central government would perform. It can deter aggression or use political and economic pressure to prevent or stop wars between smaller countries. It can provide hard currency for use as a world standard. Two prominent examples of hegemonies in history are Great Britain in the nineteenth century and the United States in the twentieth century. Great Britain's period of dominance occurred after the defeat of France in the Napoleonic Wars. The United States' period of hegemony began with the defeat of Nazi Germany and Imperial Japan at the end of World War II.

It is important to note that scholars of international relations do not always agree on which states have achieved hegemonic status in the past and how long this position lasted. Some scholars would include seventeenth-century Netherlands and sixteenth-century Spain as examples of hegemony. It is also important to note that in practice a hegemon may exist in a multipolar setting (as did Great Britain in the nineteenth century) and in a bipolycentric setting (as did the United States during the Cold War). In such cases, the term hegemony merely describes the existence of a state that is more powerful than all others in the system but is not so powerful that one can speak with empirical confidence of a unipolar system. For example, the Cold War is described as a period of bipolarity, as there were two clearly preeminent centres of power in the system. However, it was also clear that the United States was the more powerful in terms of the influence it exerted over international institutions, rules, and the world economy. As a result, the American role is often described as hegemonic, despite the broader bipolar context.

States that achieve hegemonic status do not retain this status indefinitely. Hegemonic decline will eventually occur over decades or centuries. A combination of domestic internal decay and costly military overextension weakens the hegemonic state. The hegemon will then face the efforts of a challenger to overthrow the hegemon's preeminent position. The transition from one hegemon to another may take the form of a hegemonic war or a peaceful transition in which the first hegemon will be compelled to pass on its status to a rising power.[20] Alternatively, the challenger may fail and the hegemon survive. The status of the United States today is a point of debate among scholars, who disagree as to whether the United States is a hegemon in decline.[21]

WHAT ABOUT THE OTHERS?

What is notable about this discussion of the realist perspective is the lack of reference to most of the other states of the international system. Realists tend to focus on the most powerful actors, or great powers, because these actors define the character of the system (the distribution of power and the polarity of the system), and their actions are, therefore, the most important. There is no question that great powers are tremendously important. Few of them exist at any given point in history, and yet they possess most of the world's power resources at that time. Great powers possess the strongest military forces and the largest economies. Often these capabilities are based on natural endowments of large populations and plentiful resources, as in the case of the United States, Russia, and China. In other cases, these resources might be acquired through expansion, as was the case with the British Empire, or through economic growth and trade, as is the case with Japan. As a result, great powers tend to endure. They can only be defeated militarily by other great powers. They also tend to have global interests and commitments. And on occasion, great powers are formally recognized as such by international structures such as the Concert of Europe or the UN Security Council.

However, the bulk of state actors in the history of international politics have not been great powers. For the most part, historical systems have been composed of a small number of large (powerful) states and a large number of smaller (less powerful) states.

A wider variation of characteristics, resources, and capabilities exists across these states, and as a result, classifying them has been very difficult. The term **middle power** has been used to refer to a group of states that rank below the great powers in terms of power resources and influence in international politics. These states may exert influence within their respective regions, or they may have an international profile on certain specific issues, but for the most part their ability to influence the larger global setting is limited. Some middle powers may be geographically large, such as Canada or Australia, while others may be quite small, such as South Korea or Sweden.

Small powers, or small states as they are more generally known, are countries that have less power capabilities than middle powers and little or no influence on international politics. Small states have smaller economies (although many small states are very wealthy on a per capita basis), tend to have small populations and territories, and tend to have limited power capabilities (such as small militaries) as a result. Small states are generally considered significant only to the extent that they become important in the schemes of the great powers. For example, Belgium has been a small state in Europe since its creation, but it has been important because of its status as a buffer state between Germany and France. Vietnam might be far less well known today but for the engagement of the United States in the Vietnam War and its historical conflicts with China. In addition, regional context is an important factor in judging the importance of states. Some small states in Europe or Asia would be among the most powerful states if they were relocated in different regions of the world. And Brazil, South Africa, and India all have a claim to great power status in their respective regions.

Canada provides a good example of the difficulty inherent in classifying states. Canada has been described variously as a small state, a satellite of the United States, a middle power, and even a "principal power."[22] Canada has one of the leading economies of the world but has a very small military. How is Canada to be ranked in the hierarchy of states?

CONCLUSIONS

In this chapter we have provided a necessarily brief history of global politics, focusing on the expansion and collapse of empires, the formation of the modern state system, and the role of war. We have paid particular attention to the two world wars of this century. We also explored some of the core questions surrounding the issue of war and peace in global politics up to 1945 and how these questions influenced the development of international relations theory. Idealists sought change; they saw the world, particularly the structure of the international system, as fundamentally flawed and attempted to change it. Realists argued that power politics was an eternal reality in history and that efforts to fundamentally alter the nature of international politics were doomed to failure. The failure of collective security during the interwar period led to the rise of the realist perspective in the period following World War II. The next chapter examines in detail the most protracted power struggle in recent history, one that affected all states, small and large: the epic confrontation between the West and the East during the Cold War.

Endnotes

1. For a history of Mongol power, see Robert Marshall, *Storm from the East: From Genghis Khan to Kublai Khan* (Berkeley: University of California Press, 1993).
2. See Albert Hourani, *A History of the Arab Peoples* (Cambridge, MA: Belknap Press, 1991).
3. See Adda B. Bozeman, *Politics and Culture in International History* (Princeton: Princeton University Press, 1960).
4. On the theme of the overextension and decline of empires, see the popular text by Paul Kennedy, *The Rise and Fall of the Great Powers: Economic Change and Military Conflict from 1500 to 2000* (London: Unwin Hyman, 1988).
5. See Stephen Van Evera, "The Cult of the Offensive and the Origins of the First World War," *International Security* 9 (1984), 58–107; and Jack Lewis Snyder, *The Ideology of the Offensive: Military Decision Making and the Disasters of 1914* (Ithaca, NY: Cornell University Press, 1984).
6. Quoted in Barbara W. Tuchman, *The Guns of August* (New York: Bantam Books, 1962), 146.
7. See William L. Shirer, *The Collapse of the Third Republic* (New York: Simon and Schuster, 1969).
8. It is important to note that as Canadian and American men fought abroad, women were recruited into wartime production at home, continuing a fundamental shift in the economic role played by women in advanced capitalist economies that began under similar circumstances during World War I.
9. This classic definition of power is articulated in a famous political science textbook, Robert A. Dahl's *Modern Political Analysis*, 2nd ed. (Englewood Cliffs, NJ: Prentice-Hall, 1970).

10. See Michael P. Sullivan, *Power in International Politics* (Columbia, SC: University of South Carolina Press, 1990).

11. See his *The Politics of Canadian Foreign Policy*, 2nd ed. (Scarborough, ON: Prentice-Hall, 1989).

12. See Hedley Bull, *The Anarchical Society: A Study of Order in World Politics* (London: The Macmillan Press, 1977).

13. Ibid.

14. Dorothy Jones, *Code of Peace: Ethics and Security in the World of the Warlord States* (Chicago: University of Chicago Press, 1991).

15. See Stephen Walt, *The Origins of Alliances* (Ithaca: Cornell University Press, 1987).

16. See Kenneth Waltz, "The Stability of a Bipolar World," in D. Edwards, ed., *International Political Analysis* (New York: Rinehart and Winston, 1970), p. 340. See also John Mearsheimer, "Why We Will Soon Miss the Cold War," *Atlantic Monthly* (August 1990), 37.

17. See Alan Ned Sabrosky, ed., *Polarity and War: The Changing Nature of International Conflict* (Boulder, CO: Westview Press, 1985).

18. See K.W. Deutsch and J.D. Singer, "Multipolar Power Systems and International Stability," in J. Rosenau, ed., *International Politics and Foreign Policy*, rev. ed. (New York: Free Press, 1969), 315–24. In a zero-sum game, one state's gain is automatically perceived as another's loss. Therefore, the outcome of the game is still zero (+1 for the winner, −1 for the loser = 0).

19. The Marxist (Gramscian) tradition in international political economy refers to hegemony as ideational domination by transnational class interests; see Chapter 4. See also S. Gill, *American Hegemony and the Trilateral Commission* (Cambridge: Cambridge University Press, 1990).

20. The most famous treatment of this theory of hegemonic stability and transformation is probably Robert Gilpin's *War and Change in World Politics* (Cambridge: Cambridge University Press, 1981). See also R. Keohane, *After Hegemony: Cooperation and Discord in the World Political Economy* (Princeton: Princeton University Press, 1984).

21. This debate is crystallized in two popular works: Paul Kennedy, *The Rise and Fall of the Great Powers: Economic Change and Military Conflict from 1500 to 2000* (London: Unwin Hyman, 1988); and Joseph S. Nye, Jr., *Bound to Lead: The Changing Nature of American Power* (New York: Basic Books, 1990).

22. See D. Dewitt and J. Kirton, *Canada as a Principal Power: A Study in Foreign Policy and International Relations* (Toronto: John Wiley and Sons, 1983). For further discussion, see Kim Richard Nossal, *The Politics of Canadian Foreign Policy*, 3rd ed. (Scarborough, ON: Prentice-Hall, 1997), 52–68, and Andrew Cooper, *Canadian Foreign Policy: Old Habits and New Directions* (Scarborough, ON: Prentice-Hall, 1997), 9–21.

Suggested Readings

Asimov, Isaac. *Asimov's Chronology of the World: The History of the World from the Big Bang to Modern Times.* New York: HarperCollins, 1991.

Barraclough, Geoffrey, ed. *The Times Atlas of World History.* Maplewood, NJ: Hammond, 1978.

Brown, Michael, Sean Lynn-Jones, and Steven Miller, eds. *The Perils of Anarchy: Contemporary Realism and International Security.* Cambridge: MIT Press, 1995.

Bull, Hedley. *The Anarchical Society: A Study of Order in World Politics.* London: Macmillan, 1977.

Dockrill, Michael. *Atlas of Twentieth Century World History.* New York: HarperCollins, 1991.

Dougherty, James E., and Robert L. Pfaltzgraff Jr. *Contending Theories in International Relations.* 3rd ed. New York: Harper and Row, 1990.

Doyle, Michael. *Ways of War and Peace.* New York: Norton, 1997.

Gabriel, Jurg Martin. *Worldviews and Theories of International Relations.* New York: St. Martin's Press, 1994.

Gianfranco, Poggi. *The State: Its Nature, Development, and Prospects.* Stanford: Stanford University Press, 1991.

Holsti, K.J. *The Dividing Discipline: Hegemony and Diversity in International Theory.* Boston: Allen and Unwin, 1985.

———. *Peace and War: Armed Conflicts and International Order 1648–1989.* Cambridge: Cambridge University Press, 1990.

Knutsen, Torbjorn L. *The History of International Relations Theory: An Introduction.* Manchester: Manchester University Press, 1992.

Rothstein, Robert L., ed. *The Evolution of Theory in International Politics.* Columbia, SC: University of South Carolina Press, 1991.

Spegele, Roger. *Political Realism and International Theory.* Cambridge: Cambridge University Press, 1996.

Tilly, Charles, ed. *The Formation of National States in Western Europe.* Princeton: Princeton University Press, 1975.

Suggested Websites

Horus' History Links
<www.ucr.edu/h-gig/horuslinks.html>

EuroDocs: Western European Primary Historical Documents
<www.lib.byu.edu/~rdh/eurodocs/>

Index of Resources for Historians
<www.ukans.edu/history/VL/>

CHAPTER 3

The Cold War

DECISION MAKING IN THE NUCLEAR AGE

To the extent that the nuclear threat has deterrent value, it is because it in fact increases the risk of nuclear war.

— Robert S. McNamara[1]

Restraint? Why are you so concerned with saving their damn lives? The whole idea is to kill the bastards. At the end of the war if there are two Americans and one Russian left alive, we win.

— General Thomas Power, Commander of U.S. Strategic Air Command in the 1960s[2]

THE COLD WAR: POWER POLITICS ASCENDANT

The Cold War seems distant now, but just a decade ago it dominated our understanding of global politics.[3] Citizens of every state on earth were put at risk by the nuclear arms race. Canadians would have been caught in a horrific crossfire if nuclear war had occurred. A high level of animosity existed between East and West, between the ideologies of the Communist command economies (the so-called second world) and democratic liberal capitalism (the so-called first world), between the red scare and the American imperialists, between the commies and the Yankees, between the pinkos and the fascists—the list of quaint phrases depicting each side seemed endless. The Cold War was a comprehensive ideological, geopolitical, military, and international rivalry between the two superpowers (and their respective allies and **client states**) that became increasingly global in scope as the postwar era matured. Thankfully, as its name implies, the Cold War never became a global hot war; the vast military capabilities of the superpowers never directly fought each other. Instead, the Cold War was fought in the international arena through diplomacy, ideological rhetoric, arms races, regional **proxy wars** and interventions, and the competition for allies and military bases around the world.

We can destroy you. The testing of nuclear weapons by the United States and the Soviet Union was the most visible expression of Cold War animosity.

The Cold War was not the only issue in post–World War II international relations; decolonization had greatly increased the number of states in the world, human rights had gained in popularity, the global economy had grown dramatically, and many non-state actors had risen in prominence. Nevertheless, the dominant characteristic of this era was the superpower rivalry; international issues cannot be addressed or examined in isolation from this fact. An examination of the history of the Cold War reveals several themes that persisted until the collapse of the Soviet Union:

- *A cyclical pattern of confrontation and cooperation.* The Cold War was characterized by periods of high tension and crisis between the superpowers alternating with periods of a relative relaxation of tensions and increased levels of cooperation.

- *The nuclear stalemate.* For most of the Cold War, especially after the late 1960s, each superpower was vulnerable to complete destruction by the nuclear arsenal of the other. Nuclear deterrence became the dominant military strategy of the Cold War.

- *The development of informal rules and mutual understandings.* Over time, the superpowers established formal and informal understandings and agreements that often guided relations between them. When these agreements or understandings were violated in the view of one of the superpowers, tensions between the countries increased.

- *Political pragmatism versus ideological rhetoric.* During the Cold War, both superpowers professed the superiority of their respective ideologies. However, both superpowers sacrificed the principles of their respective ideologies if geopolitical considerations demanded it. For example, both superpowers supported allies with political systems antithetical to their own.

- *Superpower involvement in regional wars.* Although the two superpowers avoided direct warfare, both used or supported allies and client states in wars directed against their opponent's allies and clients. These wars are referred to as proxy wars. For example, Cuba's involvement in the Angolan Civil War was a proxy for direct Soviet involvement. For the many people caught up in these regional conflicts, the Cold War was hardly a period of stability.

For other countries in the international system, the Cold War was the context for much of their foreign policy decision making. Many countries voluntarily sought security arrangements and alliances with the superpowers. Most of the countries of Western Europe joined the United States and Canada in the North Atlantic Treaty Organization (NATO), which bound its members to come to the assistance of any member should it be attacked. This alliance, of course, was built against the threat posed by the Soviet Union. The Warsaw Treaty Organization (WTO), more commonly called the **Warsaw Pact,** joined the countries of Eastern Europe with the Soviet Union in an alliance against NATO. The Warsaw Pact, however, was much more tightly controlled from Moscow; Poland, Hungary, the former Czechoslovakia, and other Eastern European states were expected to be compliant partners and suffered ill consequences if they objected. Twice the Soviet Union used force to keep its Eastern European allies in line: in Hungary in 1956 and Czechoslovakia in 1968.

Around the world, states established relationships with the superpowers based on a combination of ideological affinity and pure self-interest. Both superpowers established a network of client states around the world to which they gave varying degrees of diplomatic, economic, and military assistance. The United States gave large amounts of assistance to countries such as Israel, Iran (before the Iranian Revolution), Pakistan, and South Korea. The Soviet Union supported North Korea, Cuba, Vietnam, and Syria. Very few countries succeeded in following a neutral path, such as Switzerland, Austria, and Sweden. Some countries such as India, Indonesia, and Egypt sought to distance themselves from the Cold War by forming the **Nonaligned Movement (NAM)** but never succeeded in becoming a major political force, since few if any countries could escape the fact that international issues were invariably affected by the behaviour of one or both superpowers. To varying degrees, all countries had to accommodate this fact when making foreign policy decisions.

The aim of this chapter is to explore the origins, character, and collapse of the Cold War. This task is a crucial one because our own time is often defined as a post–Cold War era. This identification begs the question of what has changed since the end of the Cold War and what has not. This chapter also examines an important area of study within global politics: the study of decision making. This area developed dramatically during the Cold War, because the consequences of intentional or accidental nuclear war were so great. Today, these decision-making theories are valuable tools in our search for how the decisions that shape global politics are made.

THE ORIGINS OF THE BIPOLAR ERA

The Cold War began with the swift erosion in cooperation between the Western Allies and the Soviet Union during 1946 and 1947. However, the seeds of the Cold War were planted in the latter half of World War II, when distrust and friction began to develop between the Western Allies (primarily the United States and Great Britain) and the Soviet Union. Each side was suspicious of the other's ultimate intentions, although distrust was held in check by the larger interest in continued cooperation to defeat Nazi Germany and Imperial Japan. However, when the war ended, their differences became more evident and tensions quickly escalated. In a short time, the former allies had become adversaries.

Was the superpower rivalry inevitable? After all, the Western Allies and the Soviet Union had cooperated during World War II despite their differences, and both had expressed a desire to maintain that cooperation in the postwar period. Suggestions were made that coexistence might have been possible through the establishment of spheres of influence in which the other side would agree not to interfere. The membership of the United States and the USSR in the newly created United Nations (UN), which was mandated to preserve world peace, offered hope that cooperation would continue. Nevertheless, relations between the West and the East deteriorated to open hostility and rivalry and paralyzed the principal organ for conflict resolution in the UN, the **Security Council**. This hostility and rivalry had several origins and took on many forms. The Cold War had an ideological dimension, a geopolitical dimension, a strategic dimension, and an international dimension. Together, these established the character of the Cold War.

THE IDEOLOGICAL DIMENSION

The Cold War had an important ideological content, for the superpower rivalry was characterized not only by military or geopolitical competition but also by a confrontation between two antagonistic political, economic, and social systems. In a sense, the Cold War was a confrontation between two different ways of life, a competition to determine which system performed best and which could build a better and more just society. On the one hand, the majority of Western countries and their peoples perceived Marxism-Leninism as a fundamentally authoritarian political ideology that stifled the political and economic freedom of the individual. Communism threatened the overthrow of Western liberal democracy and the free market economic system. On the other hand, the ideological pronouncements of the Soviet Union characterized the West as a bastion of capitalist interests that controlled the world economy and was bent on surrounding and then destroying the Marxist-Leninist revolution in Russia. Capitalism and Communism could not coexist, and the Soviet Union had to do what it could to accelerate the historical inevitability of Communist revolutions around the world. U.S. Secretary of State James Byrnes once argued, "there is too much difference in the ideologies of the U.S. and Russia to work out a long term program of cooperation."[4]

During the Cold War, a persistent and intense debate raged in government and academic circles (as well as in the general public) about whether the USSR was an expansionist power. For many, particularly early in the Cold War, the answer to this question was yes: the Soviet Union was a messianic, expansionist power bent on expanding its power and influence in the world through direct aggression and the support of Communist national liberation movements abroad. For these **hawks,** Marxist-Leninist ideology was a blueprint, a guide, for Soviet actions. Just as Hitler's book *Mein Kampf* had outlined the plans and world view of that dictator, the ideological writings of Lenin and Stalin and the pronouncements of Soviet leaders outlined the plans and world view of the Soviet leadership. However, many argued otherwise. These **doves** argued that the foreign policy of the Soviet Union was essentially defensive, concerned primarily with preserving and protecting the Soviet state. While the Soviet Union would take advantage of opportunities to increase its power or expand its influence, it would not take undue risks in the pursuit of such opportunities. Ideology was not a guide to Soviet policy; at best, it was a perceptual lens through which the Soviet leaders saw the world. Soviet behaviour actually had more in common with the policies of Russia's tsars. It was power politics that drove Soviet policy, not ideology.

As the Cold War dragged on, the ideological intensity of the superpower competition receded, as did the hostility of the rhetoric between the two countries. However, ideology remained the cornerstone of the confrontation between the United States and the Soviet Union. The competition between the two systems manifested in extreme nationalism (or patriotism) in both countries, and even in periods of **détente,** it surfaced in sports, the arts, scientific achievement, and space travel. In the 1980s, the ideological rhetoric of the Cold War intensified when Ronald Reagan became president of the United States. Reagan took a hawkish view of the USSR, believing that the Soviet Union was the root of all evil in the world. The ideological animosity of the Cold War also existed between allies of the United States and other Communist countries in the world. The ideological rivalry of the Cold War was not uniform across all countries, however. Canada, for example, had better relations with Romania and Cuba than did the United States. In fact, Canada's relatively friendly relations with Cuba remain a central point of contention in Canada–U.S. relations today.

THE GEOPOLITICAL DIMENSION

As indicated above, ideological rivalry does not provide a complete characterization or explanation for the events of the Cold War. Just as important was the geopolitical rivalry between the superpowers. The preeminence of the United States and the Soviet Union at the end of the Cold War led them naturally to regard each other with suspicion. As Robert Tucker has observed: "The principal cause of the Cold War was the essential duopoly of power left by World War II."[5] In other words, the structure of the international system at the end of World War II led each superpower to regard the other as a rival. The ideological differences between the two countries only exacerbated this situation.

At the heart of the geopolitical rivalry was the position both superpowers found themselves in at the end of World War II. In the West, the Soviet Union was perceived as an imminent security threat. The governments of Western Europe and Japan felt particularly threatened because of the proximity of Soviet forces to their own borders. In Canada, concern arose about the threat the Soviet Union represented to the postwar order.[6] In the United States, the Soviet threat was cast in the geopolitical context of Halford Mackinder and his view of the world (see Chapter 2). The Soviet Union, after all, seemed to occupy the "heartland," and was poised to expand along the "interior ring" along the way to dominating the "world island"—and thereafter the world. From this position, the Soviet Union had the tremendous geopolitical advantage of the interior lines of transport and was thus poised to expand anywhere along a wide perimeter (see Map 3.1). To contain the USSR, the United States and its allies were forced to defend a wide perimeter all around the heartland of Eurasia.

However, in the Soviet Union, the geopolitical position of the country was regarded in a rather different fashion. We can simulate a Soviet geopolitical view of the world by using a polar projection of the world (see Map 3.2). The difference is striking. No longer does the Soviet Union seem poised to strike out in any direction with the advantage of the interior lines. Instead, the Soviet Union is encircled, and the long border of the Soviet Union is threatened by enemies and security concerns. Any potential effort to break out of this encirclement or to conduct military operations from the USSR would encounter some of these enemies or threats. In Europe are the NATO countries, backed by the power of the United States. In southern Europe are the NATO countries of Greece and Turkey, which dominate the straits between the Black Sea and the Mediterranean. In the Middle East lies the Muslim world, a security concern because of the fear that this region could have an influence in the Islamic republics of the Soviet Union. To the east is China, a great ideological competitor by the second half of the Cold War, and Japan, a close ally of the United States. From the perspective of Soviet planners, then, the geopolitical position of the USSR was not an enviable one.

THE STRATEGIC DIMENSION

Both superpowers and their respective allies maintained large conventional military forces throughout the Cold War. An immense amount of time, money, and effort was devoted to the maintenance of these forces and their training, equipment modernization, and deployment around the world. By the late 1980s the size of these conventional military forces was immense. In particular, Europe was host to the large armies of NATO and the even larger armies of the Warsaw Pact. However, the strategic character of the Cold War was defined by nuclear weapons and the nuclear arms race between the United States and the Soviet Union. The nuclear weapon was a revolutionary development in the history of warfare, a fact dramatically punctuated by the two bombs dropped on Japan at the end of World War II.[7] Ironically, the weapons were so destructive, and the consequences of their use so enormous, that the military usefulness of such weapons came under question. But if nuclear weapons could not be usefully employed

Map 3.1 The Western Geopolitical View of the World

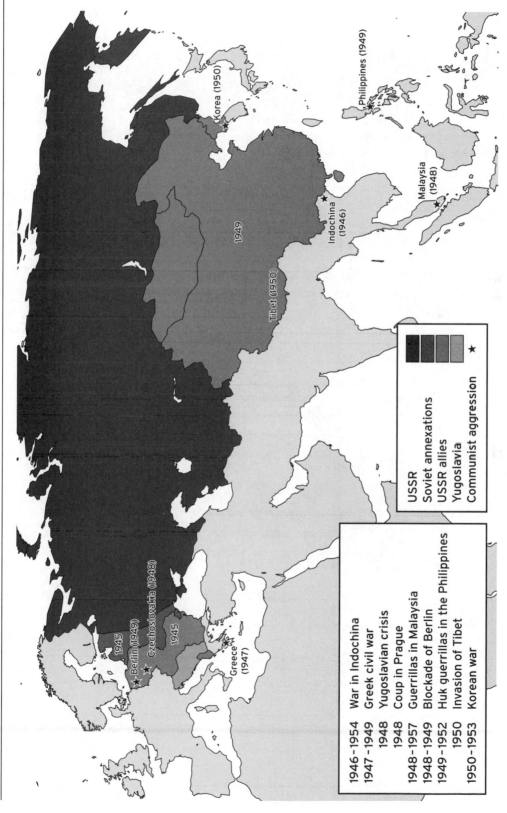

				★

USSR
Soviet annexations
USSR allies
Yugoslavia
Communist aggression

Korea (1950)

Philippines (1949)

Malaysia (1948)

Indochina (1946)

1949

Tibet (1950)

Berlin (1949)

Czechoslovakia (1948)

1945

1945

Greece (1947)

1946-1954 War in Indochina
1947-1949 Greek civil war
1948 Yugoslavian crisis
1948 Coup in Prague
1948-1957 Guerrillas in Malaysia
1948-1949 Blockade of Berlin
1949-1952 Huk guerrillas in the Philippines
1950 Invasion of Tibet
1950-1953 Korean war

SOURCE: GERARD CHALIAND AND JEAN-PIERRE RAGEAU, *STRATEGIC ATLAS: COMPARATIVE GEOPOLITICS OF THE WORLD'S POWERS*, 3RD ED. COPYRIGHT © 1993 BY GERARD CHALIAND AND JEAN-PIERRE RAGEAU. REPRINTED BY PERMISSION OF HARPERCOLLINS PUBLISHERS, INC.

Map 3.2 The Soviet Geopolitical View of the World

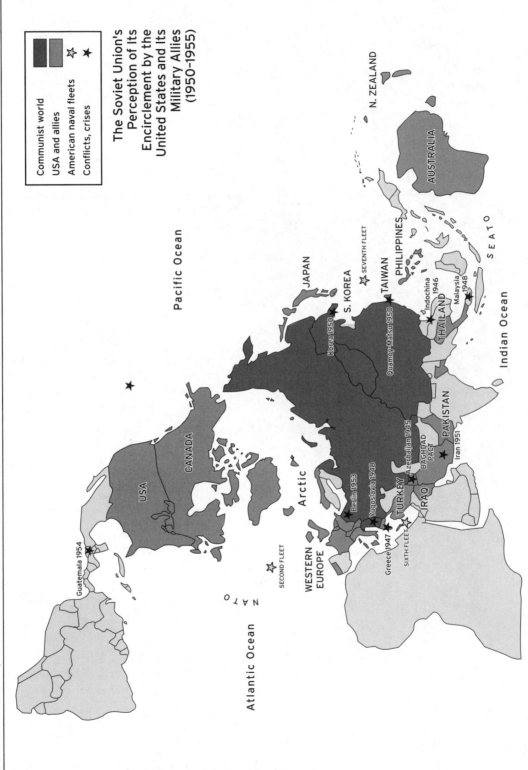

The Soviet Union's Perception of Its Encirclement by the United States and Its Military Allies (1950–1955)

Communist world
USA and allies
American naval fleets
Conflicts, crises

Pacific Ocean

Atlantic Ocean

Arctic

Indian Ocean

NATO

SECOND FLEET

SIXTH FLEET

SEVENTH FLEET

SEATO

USA

CANADA

WESTERN EUROPE

TURKEY

IRAQ

PAKISTAN

JAPAN

S. KOREA

TAIWAN

PHILIPPINES

THAILAND

AUSTRALIA

N. ZEALAND

Guatemala 1954

Greece 1947

Berlin 1953

Yugoslavia 1948

Azerbaijan 1945

BAGHDAD PACT

Iran 1951

Korea 1950

Quemoy-Matsu 1950

Indochina 1946

Malaysia 1948

SOURCE: GERARD CHALIAND AND JEAN-PIERRE RAGEAU, STRATEGIC ATLAS: COMPARATIVE GEOPOLITICS OF THE WORLD'S POWERS, 3RD ED. COPYRIGHT © 1993 BY GERARD CHALIAND AND JEAN-PIERRE RAGEAU. REPRINTED BY PERMISSION OF HARPERCOLLINS PUBLISHERS, INC.

on the battlefield, what could they be used for? In short, they were useful only for preventing their use by others. In other words, nuclear weapons were instruments of mutual **deterrence** not fighting.

Deterrence is a policy of preventing or discouraging an action by confronting an opponent or opponents with risks they are unwilling to take. The actor doing the deterring is a *deterrer*, and the actor being deterred is a *deterree*. A potential aggressor will likely be deterred when the probability of victory is low or the costs of a war (whatever the outcome) are high. Two broad types of deterrence strategies are

- *Deterrence by denial.* A deterree will not start a war because it is convinced it cannot achieve its objectives. Deterrence by denial was a prenuclear phenomenon, based on the view that powerful military forces and high levels of military preparedness could discourage an attack by one country against another.

- *Deterrence by punishment.* A deterree will not start a war because of the threat that it will receive unacceptable damage in return. The enormous destructive power of nuclear weapons, coupled with advanced delivery systems, made deterrence by punishment feasible.

Nuclear deterrence defined the military relationship between the superpowers during the Cold War. Even though the nuclear arsenal of the United States was superior to that of the USSR at least until the mid-1960s, the explosion of the Soviet atomic bomb in 1949 had ended America's nuclear monopoly, and forced both leaderships to confront the consequences of a nuclear war between them. By the mid-1960s, a rough parity, or equivalence, existed between the arsenals of the two superpowers; the nuclear arsenals of the United States and the Soviet Union were capable of inflicting unacceptable damage on the military forces and civilian population of the other in the event of a nuclear war. If both superpowers could annihilate the other in a war, neither would start such a war. This equivalence was referred to as **mutual assured destruction (MAD)**. During the Cold War both superpowers devoted massive resources to the development and maintenance of enormous nuclear forces so that there could be no doubt that their arsenals possessed an assured retaliatory capability, which made each country capable of devastating the other under any possible set of circumstances (see Figure 3.1). To this end, both countries built and deployed their arsenals so that even if a large portion of their nuclear forces were destroyed, enough weapons would survive to devastate the other country.

As the Cold War progressed, the size and destructive potential of the nuclear arsenals of both superpowers led to a growing realization that all-out nuclear war between the two countries would be devastating to more than just the superpowers. Not only would the United States and the Soviet Union be destroyed but the effects of nuclear radiation and the possibility of nuclear winter (the cooling of the global climate from the ejection of dust and debris into the atmosphere) raised the question of whether humanity itself would survive a nuclear war. This fear of omnicide, coupled with the enormous expenses of the nuclear arms race, fostered the development of large peace movements and antinuclear movements in most Western countries during the Cold War, dedicated to stopping the nuclear arms race and promoting arms control and disarmament.

THE INTERNATIONAL DIMENSION

The Cold War rapidly became a fixture of international politics. Not only was the Cold War an immediate concern in North America and the Soviet Union, it had a visible

Figure 3.1 The Nuclear Stockpile

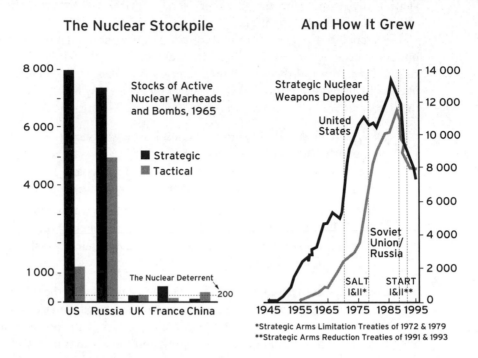

The Nuclear Stockpile

And How It Grew

Stocks of Active Nuclear Warheads and Bombs, 1965

■ Strategic
■ Tactical

The Nuclear Deterrent

US   Russia   UK   France   China

Strategic Nuclear Weapons Deployed

United States

Soviet Union/ Russia

SALT I&II*

START I&II**

1945 1955 1965 1975 1985 1995

*Strategic Arms Limitation Treaties of 1972 & 1979
**Strategic Arms Reduction Treaties of 1991 & 1993

impact in Latin America, Europe, Africa, the Middle East, and in south and east Asia (for the impact of the Cold War on Canada, see Profile 3.1). Indeed, no region was uninfluenced by the superpower confrontation, and crises and confrontations occurred with startling frequency. In the early years of the Cold War, tensions were high and confrontations were numerous, including the Soviet refusal to pull out of Iran in 1946 and reports of Soviet involvement in the Greek Civil War. These events prompted U.S. President Harry S. Truman to adopt the policy suggestions put forward by **George Kennan**. Postwar U.S. attitudes toward the Soviet Union were decisively influenced by Kennan, a junior official in the United States' embassy in Moscow. Instructed to analyze the postwar intentions of the Soviet Union, Kennan responded with a famous "long telegram," in which he argued that the USSR regarded the United States as its foremost international opponent, and that as long as the United States remained strong, Soviet power could not be secure. In an anonymous published statement of his beliefs in the influential journal *Foreign Affairs* in 1947—the famous "X" article—Kennan argued that the Soviet Union represented a dangerous blend of an autocratic ruler (Stalin), a revisionist and messianic ideology (Marxism-Leninism), and a violent and expansionist history. Kennan recommended the political containment of the Soviet Union until the internal nature of the Soviet Union changed and along with it, its foreign policy.[8]

Truman soon declared "that it must be the policy of the United States to support free peoples who are resisting attempted subjugation by armed minorities or outside pressures."[9] This commitment came to be called the **Truman Doctrine**, and was the first articulation of what was to become America's grand strategy during the Cold War: the **containment** of the perceived expansionist and revisionist power of the Soviet Union. The aim of containment was to prevent the spread of Communist ideology around the world, to prevent any direct aggression by the USSR, and to prevent the Soviet Union

Never again. Japanese students offer *Orizuru*, or folded paper cranes, hoping for world peace and in the memory of atomic bombing victims at the Peace Memorial Park in Hiroshima, western Japan. (AP Photo/Chiaki Tsukumo)

from expanding its influence in the world. Virtually all U.S. foreign policy action, from foreign assistance to military intervention to diplomacy, was directly related to or influenced by the objectives of containment. Kennan, however, did not support the emphasis placed on military containment. He felt that the Soviet threat was primarily political and that it could not be met entirely by military means.[10] As tensions between the United States and the Soviet Union escalated, further crises followed, including the American decision to establish the Federal Republic of Germany, a Communist coup in Czechoslovakia in 1948, the Soviet blockade of West Berlin of June 1948, the Communist victory in China in 1949, Chinese behaviour in Tibet, numerous Taiwan Strait crises, and the Korean War in 1950. The Cold War era was also characterized by mass decolonization as the former European empires finally crumbled, and both superpowers competed for allies among newly independent countries.

Europe, which would be the focal point of the superpower competition for much of the Cold War, was divided. The concern of the United States and other Western governments was that the Soviet Union might gain control of Western Europe, either through direct conquest or by having Communist parties taking control in the war-devastated region. To prevent this, the United States launched the **Marshall Plan**, a program of U.S. financial assistance to rebuild the economies of Western Europe, and in 1949, the United States, Canada, and several European allies established NATO, a formal alliance arrangement that solidified the American and Canadian commitment to Western Europe. Throughout the Cold War, half the world's total defence spending would be devoted to the superpower standoff in Europe. Germany itself was divided into zones of occupation, with three-quarters of the country (and three-quarters of the former capital, Berlin) held by the Western Allies—the United States, France, and Great Britain—and the rest held by the Soviet Union. The most prominent confrontations of the early Cold War were centred on the status of Berlin. The Berlin crises of 1948 and 1961, in which the Soviet Union attempted to gain full control of the city, led to armed confrontations, but not to war. Across Germany, a fenced and guarded line—which Winston Churchill was to call the "iron curtain" in 1946—dramatically symbolized the division of Europe. In 1961, East Germany built the **Berlin Wall**, separating East and West Berlin, and forcibly preventing Berliners from communicating or travelling across this divide.

In China, the nationalists under Chiang Kai-Shek and the Communists under Mao Tse-Tung had battled invading Japanese forces during World War II. However, the evacuation of the forces of the defeated Japanese left the nationalists and the Communists to battle over control of China. Despite assistance from the United States, Chiang-Kai Shek was defeated by the Communists and forced to flee to the island of Formosa, which is today known as Taiwan. On 1 October 1949, the People's Republic of China (PRC) was proclaimed. To the capitalist West, the "loss" of China to Communism was the first of what have been called the two shocks of 1949 (the second shock was the explosion of the

Canada and the Cold War

During the Cold War, Canada was a close ally of the United States and a member of the Western club of countries. Some have argued that Canada was duped or forced into adopting this postwar foreign policy and that the country was little more than a puppet of the United States. However, although the flexibility of Canadian governments was limited, Canada adopted the foreign policy it did during the Cold War largely by design. Canadian foreign policy was based on an appraisal of Canadian interests in the Cold War world. The reality was that Canada was strategic territory, as any attack on the continental United States would devastate Canada as well. As a result, Canada joined in combined efforts to deter or prevent war by participating in NATO and the North American Air Defence (later Aerospace) Agreement. Canada's economy was heavily dependent on a stable international trading system (built by the United States) and on trade with the United States itself. Since Canada is a democratic country, Canadian governments and the majority of the Canadian people were suspicious and even hostile to Communism as a political and economic system. In other words, Canada was a status quo state, comfortable with its position in the world under the *Pax Americana* and interested in the prevention of instability or war.

However, this comfort did not mean that Canada did not exert an independent foreign policy. Canada was a strong supporter of the UN throughout the Cold War and was a key contributor to United Nations peacekeeping (which contributed to efforts to prevent regional wars from becoming larger conflagrations that might draw in the superpowers). Canada consistently advocated multilateralism during the Cold War, largely because multilateralism gave it an opportunity to participate in cooperative efforts and institutions, giving Canada a voice in international affairs. Canada also took an independent stand on South Africa, was critical of U.S. policy toward Cuba, and established good diplomatic relationships and a good reputation in much of the developing world. However, successive Canadian governments took care not to alienate the United States; Canadian criticisms of U.S. policy in Central and South America and Vietnam were muted as a result.

first Soviet atomic bomb). Continued fighting between the nationalists and the Communists on mainland China led to a U.S.–Taiwan defence pact in 1954, which was put to the test when nationalist possession of the two small islands of Quemoy and Matsu were threatened by mainland China in 1954–55 and 1958.

Ideological differences, distrust, and Chinese resentment of what they perceived as domineering Soviet attitudes led to the Sino–Soviet split of the early 1960s. Thereafter, the Soviet Union and China were geopolitical and ideological competitors in the world. The two countries engaged in direct although relatively minor military clashes along their disputed common border. During the rest of the Cold War, the Soviet Union devoted approximately one-third of its military resources to guarding the Sino–Soviet frontier. The two countries also engaged in rhetorical sparring matches, each claiming to represent the true path to Communism. The threat posed by Soviet power prompted China to establish a rapprochement with the United States, which culminated in a visit by U.S. President Nixon in 1972. The Sino–Soviet split led to debate over whether the split was fundamentally ideological or geopolitical, similar to the debate over the origins of the Cold War.

In June 1950 the Korean War broke out when Communist North Korea attacked South Korea. In response, the United States and 15 allied countries sent military forces to South

Korea. This deployment was done under the collective security provisions of the United Nations, although in practice the United States dominated both the political and military direction of the war. The USSR had walked out of the Security Council over the issue of Chinese representation and so was absent (and could not cast a **veto**) when the vote was taken to give UN authorization to the U.S.-led collective security operation. (The Soviet Union would never walk out of the Security Council again.) Allied forces pushed the North Koreans back toward the Chinese border, with the intent of unifying the country. China then intervened, sending more than 300 000 "volunteers" into North Korea, who pushed U.S., Korean, and allied forces back in retreat. A stalemate followed near the original border along the 38th parallel, and the war ended in a truce in 1953 (see Profile 3.2). The Korean War heightened Western fears of Communism and revealed that conventional wars could still occur in an era of nuclear weapons and that clashes between the West and the Communist world could occur in the form of proxy wars.

After this period of crisis and the death of Stalin in 1953, the Cold War thawed to some extent. Nikita Khrushchev emerged as the new General Secretary of the Communist Party of the Soviet Union. The first U.S.–Soviet Summit meeting was held at Geneva in 1955. However, the spirit of Geneva did not last long. In 1956, the Soviet Union crushed a rebellion in Hungary. In the Suez Crisis of the same year, Israel, France, and Great Britain invaded Egypt. The European states were clinging to imperial prestige and resented Egypt's **nationalization** of the Suez Canal. The Soviet Union threatened to intervene on behalf of Egypt, one of its allies in the region. The United States, which opposed the actions of its allies in Egypt, compelled them to accept a proposal forwarded by Canadian Foreign Minister Lester B. Pearson for a ceasefire and a UN interpositionary force in the region. Great Britain and France withdrew, and Israel pulled its forces back. Though peace in the region would be short-lived, the Suez Canal crisis signalled the end of European dominance in world affairs, the beginning of superpower management of crises, and the introduction of modern peacekeeping.

PROFILE 3.2 Canada and the Korean War

On 25 June 1950, North Korea invaded South Korea. The next day, under U.S. request, the UN Security Council passed a **resolution** calling on member states to respond to halt North Korean aggression. The Canadian government agreed in principle with the U.S. position, but was noncommittal about sending troops. Initial Canadian contributions involved naval vessels and transport planes. Not until August 7 did the St. Laurent government, under criticism at home for its inaction, commit ground troops to Korea. Canada was anxious that the operation in Korea be controlled and managed by the UN. It was thought that multilateral management of the conflict would restrain American impulsiveness. However, the Korean War was fought largely by American and South Korean forces, and the political decision making was dominated by Washington. This situation led to some criticism in Canada that the Canadian government was too closely tied to that of the United States, a critical theme that persisted throughout the Cold War. Canadian troops joined the 27th Commonwealth Infantry Brigade in February 1951 and later formed the 25th Canadian Infantry Brigade Group operating as part of a Commonwealth Division. Canadian troops took part in a number of battles, and by the war's end on 27 July 1953, Canadian troops had suffered 312 killed and 1577 wounded in what came to be known as Canada's "forgotten war."

MISSILE EQUIPMENT
MARIEL PORT FACILITY

The visual evidence. The U.S. Defense Department released these pictures in Washington, on 8 November 1962, saying that they were taken from over the Mariel naval port in Cuba on 4 November 1962. The department identified ships at dockside as Soviet freighters. The photo at the upper left is a close-up of missile equipment in the outlined area below. (AP Photo/file)

Cold War intrigue also spread to the Caribbean. In 1959, the United States attempted to overthrow Fidel Castro's revolution by supporting the **Bay of Pigs** invasion by Cuban exiles. The invasion failed and served to drive Castro further into the Soviet camp. In 1960, an American U-2 spy plane was shot down over the Soviet Union. These incidents culminated in the 1962 Cuban Missile Crisis in which the United States and the Soviet Union came closer to all-out conflict than they would at any time during the Cold War. The crisis was precipitated by the construction of medium-range ballistic missile launch sites on the island of Cuba. These sites, built to offset Cuba's strategic inferiority and to help deter another invasion of the island, were detected by U.S. aerial reconnaissance. Soviet merchant vessels carrying missiles were also detected as they sailed to Cuba. U.S. President John F. Kennedy imposed a naval blockade of Cuba to prevent the landing of the missiles and to force the removal of the bases. The world seemed headed toward war when the USSR agreed not to station missiles in Cuba in return for an American promise not to invade the island. The fear prompted by the Cuban Missile Crisis led both superpowers to establish closer ties, agreeing in 1963 to a Limited Test Ban Treaty that banned atmospheric nuclear tests, as well as to a Moscow–Washington telephone hotline, and a variety of scientific, cultural, and space and aviation agreements.

However, Cold War competition continued around the world (see Profile 3.3). Both superpowers supported allies and client states in the developing world with political, financial, and military assistance. In addition, both the United States and the Soviet Union supported insurgency movements in the allied and client states of the other superpower. The pattern of support did not necessarily reflect ideological positions. In many cases, the United States supported governments and movements that were authoritarian and undemocratic (though not opposed to the investment of American capitalists), while the Soviet Union often supported governments and movements that could scarcely be called Communist. Proxy wars continued, the largest of which occurred in Vietnam, where warfare had persisted since World War II during the painful retreat of French colonialism.

In the Vietnam War, the United States backed a succession of authoritarian governments in Saigon against an internal insurgency mounted by the Viet Cong and supported by Communist North Vietnam (which in turn was supported by the Soviet Union and China). The United States, concerned with expanding Communist influence in Asia, committed itself to preventing a Communist takeover in Vietnam. In the face of continued Communist successes in South Vietnam, what was initially a small U.S. involvement (in the form of military advisers) soon escalated to the deployment of more than 540 000 U.S. troops by 1968. The Americans engaged in massive saturation

PROFILE 3.3 — The Domino Theory and Other Zero-Sum Views

During the Cold War, successive American administrations committed the United States to combating the spread of Communism whenever and wherever it took place, a perspective that was shared to varying degrees in many other Western capitals. This commitment grew from the fear that if one country in a region fell under Communist rule, then the other countries in that region would also be at risk. Therefore, Communism had to be prevented from taking root in even the smallest and remotest of countries. This concept came to be called the *domino theory*, after the practice of lining up domino pieces on end one after the other, close together. Tipping over one domino causes the rest of the dominoes to fall. The domino theory suggested that Communism could spread in the same way: once one country fell, its neighbours would inevitably fall as well. This fear contributed to American efforts to prevent the spread of Communism around the world, most prominently in Korea and Vietnam. Another analogy was *salami tactics* in which the world was represented as a salami. Communism was taking over the world slice by slice, country by country. Yet another instrument was the use of world maps that showed Communist countries in red. As more countries fell to Communism, more red appeared on the map. This method contributed to the fear that the Soviet Union was "painting the map red." All these conceptualizations were based on a zero-sum view of the Cold War; the perception was that a gain for one side was an equivalent loss for the other side, so both superpowers found themselves engaged in struggles for countries that, in many cases, their residents had never even heard of.

bombing campaigns, intervened in Cambodia, and also introduced a modern variation of an ancient practice, **ecocide**: the deliberate destruction of the environment to root out enemy forces. However, the United States failed to defeat the insurgency in South Vietnam or to prevent supplies and reinforcements from the North from reaching the South. The Vietnam War divided the American public and compelled the Nixon administration to seek an end to the war. The Paris Peace accords of 1973 led to a pullout of all American troops from South Vietnam, which fell to the North in 1975. Approximately 58 000 Americans were killed in Vietnam, and more than one million Vietnamese perished. The Vietnam War, often billed as the first war the United States had lost, had a profound impact on the American psyche, as many questioned the rightness of the war and were hesitant to support the deployment of U.S. forces to future crises. The failure in Vietnam was compounded by the energy crisis of the 1970s, created by the 1973 Arab oil embargo against the United States and the fall of the U.S.-backed Shah of Iran at the hands of a rebellion led by Islamic clerics in 1979.

Nonetheless, the development of strategic nuclear parity between the United States and the Soviet Union, as well as the cooperative arrangements that were established in the mid- to late 1960s, laid the foundation for détente. Both superpowers also had domestic rationales for cooperating with the other: U.S. President Richard Nixon was seeking Soviet assistance to end the Vietnam War, while Leonid Brezhnev (who came to power in 1964) hoped that trade and technology transfers from the West could help invigorate a stagnating Soviet economy. By 1969, tensions between the two superpowers began to relax. The trade relationship between the two countries expanded. Visits and cultural exchanges increased. And the superpowers reached new agreements on arms control, including the **Strategic Arms Limitation Treaty (SALT)** I in 1972 and SALT II in 1979. These agreements placed limits on the size of the superpowers' nuclear arsenals. However, tensions between the superpowers remained. The United States voiced its opposition to continued Soviet involvement in the developing world, which the Soviet leadership resented. The Soviet Union was disappointed with the economic benefits détente was supposed to bring.

The final blow to détente was the Soviet invasion of Afghanistan in 1979. U.S. President Jimmy Carter responded by enunciating the Carter Doctrine, which committed the United States to protecting its interests in the Persian Gulf by any means necessary, including military force. He also organized a boycott of the 1980 Moscow Olympics, suspended U.S. grain exports to the Soviet Union, and dramatically increased defence spending. The invasion of Afghanistan was to prove as much of a quagmire for the Soviet Union as Vietnam had been for the United States. The Soviet Union was unable to fully suppress Afghan resistance to the invasion, and the Soviet army was to suffer 13 000 dead and 35 000 wounded by the resistance fighters, who were given financial and weapons support from the United States through Pakistan.

If the invasion of Afghanistan soured U.S.–Soviet relations, the election of President Ronald Reagan in 1980 ushered in a period sometimes referred to as Cold War II. President Reagan and his supporters came to power with a very hostile view of the Soviet Union, which was reflected not only in his public speeches and proclamations but also in the policies of his administration. The Reagan administration accelerated the military buildup initiated by President Carter, proposed the development of a space-based ballistic missile defence system called the Strategic Defense Initiative (popularly known as "Star Wars"), and enhanced U.S. support to insurgency movements in Soviet client states (in particular in Nicaragua and Angola). Escalating tensions between Washington and Moscow fuelled increasing concerns about the possibility of war and growing opposition to the nuclear arms race in the form of a growing antinuclear movement.

However, in 1985 Mikhail Gorbachev became the leader of the Soviet Union and embarked on a course of economic and political reform. To facilitate this reform effort, Gorbachev sought improved relations with the West. His overtures to Western governments—particularly in the area of arms control—changed the tone of the East–West relationship. Although distrust and misunderstandings continued, tensions eased and confrontations were few. As we will see later in this chapter, Gorbachev's reform program was to prove ultimately unsuccessful. Nevertheless, his arrival on the international scene marked the beginning of the end of the Cold War.

THE STUDY OF FOREIGN POLICY DECISION MAKING

During the Cold War, international relations scholars began to take an interest in how states (and, to a lesser extent, other actors) made foreign policy decisions. This growing interest created a distinct area of study in international relations that continues to fascinate. Scholars had a natural interest in how governments reached decisions that could have devastating consequences and in how the breakdown of decision-making systems, and the possibility of miscalculations and errors, might lead to crises or even wars. Scholars working in this area of study borrowed ideas and concepts from psychology (with its interest in motives and perception), economics (which examines the decisions of consumers in terms of tradeoffs and preferences), and business administration (with its interest in efficiency and organizational culture). The field was grounded in rational choice theory, which makes certain controversial assumptions about the decision maker.

In general terms, foreign policy is "the concrete steps that officials of a state take with respect to events and situations abroad." Foreign policy is "what individuals representing the state do or do not do in their interactions involving individuals, groups, or officials elsewhere in the world."[11] Foreign policy, then, is the public policy of a state, implemented in the environment external to the state. However, this definition excludes non-state actors and the influence of domestic politics. Of course, we must remember that nonstate actors, such as the Holy See, multinational corporations, and humanitarian relief organizations, can make decisions relevant to events and situations abroad. We must also be aware that domestic decisions can have foreign policy consequences; in fact, the boundary between domestic and international issues has been eroding steadily. For example, Canada's protection of its domestic magazine industry was recently a subject of examination by the **World Trade Organization (WTO),** which found that Canada's protection of this industry violated the rules of the WTO. In short, foreign policy decision making involves more than just the consideration of state actors.

As defined by James Dougherty and Robert Pfaltzgraff, Jr., "decision making is simply the act of choosing among available alternatives about which uncertainty exists."[12] The primary concern of decision-making theory is process, rather than outputs or actual decisions. When actors make decisions, these decisions are made in a larger context, which influences the nature of the decision. This context includes

- *The external environment.* The broader setting in which the decision must be made includes the kind of issue confronting the actor, the position and power of the actor with respect to others, and the influences and pressures that are being exerted on the actor by others.

- *The internal environment.* The domestic setting in which the decision must be made concerns the nature and structure of the political system, the role of key decision makers, the influence of public opinion or interest groups, the influence of domestic political factors (such as elections), and the role of certain bureaucracies in foreign policy decision making.

- *The perceptions of the decision makers.* The perceptual lenses of individual decision makers can have a major influence on decision making. How individuals in the process see the world and the actors in it is a key determinate of actor behaviour.

- *The time constraints.* The temporal setting (the amount of time the decision makers have in which to reach a decision) is crucial. If a decision is required quickly, it will be made in a different way than if the decision being made concerns long-term planning.

We are used to thinking of foreign policy decisions as they are portrayed by Hollywood: high-charged scenarios where life and death decisions have to be made by heroic characters. Of course, some real world crises, such as the Cuban Missile Crisis, are quite literally a matter of life and death. Indeed, during crises rational decision-making processes tend to break down.[13] Very little time is available to gather information and test it for accuracy, and communications between individuals and groups may be disrupted. Insufficient time may be available to formulate a comprehensive set of options and to consider their advantages and disadvantages. Decision makers tend to fall back on prevailing views or assumptions and ignore or dismiss contrary opinions or information. Stress and sleep deprivation may affect the ability of decision makers to make reasoned choices. Emotions become more intense and are a greater factor in decisions. Mistakes and errors are made with greater frequency, with fewer opportunities to catch and correct them. As a result, at a time when the issues at stake are very important and when the need for an effective decision is most urgent, the decision-making procedures and systems designed to make effective, reasoned outputs may break down.

However, the vast majority of policy decisions are not made in this tense context; in fact, most foreign policy is the result of lengthy deliberation. Two main models of decision making are used, and they offer alternative explanations of how decisions are made by actors in the international system (although they are primarily focused on states). The **rational actor model** argues that decisions are made in a rational fashion by decision makers. The **bureaucratic politics model** suggests that decision outputs are the result of competition and bargaining among different interests within government.[14]

THE RATIONAL ACTOR MODEL

You will recall that the realist perspective, which dominated academic discourse on international relations during the Cold War, assumes that states are rational actors. In the rational actor model of decision making (also called the *classical model*) decisions are regarded as the product of a largely unified and purposeful process based on considerations of available alternatives aimed at selecting the best option. In other words, decisions are the result of a rational process of choice designed to maximize outcomes. The rational choice process has four steps:

1. *Recognize and identify the problem.* Recognizing that a decision must be made, and identifying the nature of the problem, is the first step in any rational process of decision making.

2. *Establish objectives and aims.* The next step involves considerations of one's goals with respect to the issue at stake. These goals must be established based on judgments about interests and preferences, in addition to expectations about prospects for success.

3. *Establish options.* Next, possible alternative decisions must be formulated and considered in the context of available resources, capabilities, and potential reactions by other actors.

4. *Select an option.* Finally, the best option available—in terms of satisfying the goals of the actor and having the best chance of success—will be selected.

As a result, decisions are the product of a careful cost–benefit analysis process.

However, decision making in the real world can seldom exist in such a pure or comprehensive theoretical form. In practice, decision making is impeded, constrained, or bounded by a number of factors.[15] The ability of individuals to process information and operate effectively under pressure varies. The information that decision makers receive may be incomplete or inaccurate. Time constraints may also force decision makers to make choices under pressure without the advantages of careful deliberation. Decisions may also be made based on **satisficing**,[16] which occurs when decision makers examine their available alternatives until they encounter one that meets their minimum standards of acceptability. They then select that alternative without proceeding to examine any further options, even though better ones may be available. Finally, decision makers will seldom select an option that carries a high level of risk. Instead, decision makers will bypass such options and decide on those that entail fewer prospects for gains but also fewer risks.[17] Decision makers are risk averse rather than risk acceptant; even Saddam Hussein's decision to invade Kuwait in 1990 may be explained with reference to the idea that he did not realize he risked an American counteroffensive.

Obviously, the pure rational decision-making model is an ideal type. Government officials do not make decisions in vacuums; the external environment is often of crucial importance. In liberal democracies such as Canada, two variables often have immense influence: interest groups and public opinion. Interest groups comprise individuals who share common perspectives and goals on particular issues and seek to influence the decisions made on such issues. For the leaders of states, these societal interests must often be accommodated, although in practice the influence of various groups and the openness of the political system to such groups varies considerably. Interest groups can take a wide variety of shapes and forms, including political parties, professional associations, business coalitions, labour unions, churches, senior citizens, veterans groups, and activist organizations such as human rights or environmental groups. These groups engage in two levels of activity: lobbying and public awareness campaigns.

Lobbying occurs when representatives of interest groups meet with decision makers in an attempt to change or influence their views on an issue. In some cases rewards may be offered to the decision maker in return for taking a particular stand on an issue. In countries where corruption is a serious problem, rewards may take the form of bribes or favours of various illicit kinds. In other cases, interest groups may take their case directly to the public in an effort to influence public attitudes and wishes about certain issues. In this way, interest groups can achieve their aim by compelling decision makers to respond to larger public pressure. Public awareness campaigns can take the form of written or electronically disseminated material, protest rallies and marches, and seminars. For example, nongovernmental organizations raised international awareness of the global landmines problem by using the Internet. The profile of this campaign compelled governments of states such as Canada to respond to the issue with the creation of a global landmines treaty. In practice, interest groups may have goals or views that clash with the interests of broader society (however those might be defined), and wealthy clients can hire lobbyists who are more effective. As a result, the influence of interest groups has often been derided as counterproductive and a threat to reasoned decision making in a democratic society.

Public opinion is a general reference to the range of attitudes held by the people in society. Public opinion is especially important in democratic political systems, although it is not irrelevant in authoritarian systems. To win public support for their foreign policies, governments will launch information or propaganda campaigns. These campaigns can vary considerably, from efforts by governments to explain and justify their actions to blatant distortions and falsifications of evidence. In democratic political systems, public opinion can be gauged through polls, which can influence government action. In some cases, governments may embark on a foreign policy venture to increase their popularity or to distract the public from domestic problems. This ploy is sometimes called "wagging the dog," from which the title of a popular motion picture is drawn. An example of this phenomenon is the 1982 Falklands War, in which the military government of Argentina seized *Las Malvinas* (the Falklands) in an effort to revive its sagging popularity at home. It worked, but only for a short time as Great Britain retook the islands by force. The Argentine government fell shortly thereafter. The same argument could be applied to the British government of Margaret Thatcher, which was low in the polls before the crisis and may have used the British military response to bolster its domestic popularity.

As any pollster knows, public opinion is rarely monolithic. In fact, different components of the population may hold different views on the same issue. Frequently, public opinion can be uninformed and tend toward simplistic views and beliefs, which can complicate the efforts of decision makers to explain their policies or the constraints facing the country on a certain issue. As a result, public opinion can send mixed or contradictory signals to government decision makers. Public opinion can also change and, therefore, compel governments to act in haphazard and unpredictable ways. For example, in 1992 media coverage of the war and famine in Somalia created public opinion pressure on the U.S. government to lead a multinational force (which included Canada) to support the relief effort and end the war. Less than a year later, 18 U.S. soldiers were killed in an ambush and one soldier's body was dragged through the streets of Mogadishu. U.S. public opinion shifted dramatically against U.S. involvement in Somalia, and the U.S. withdrew shortly thereafter. However, it would be a mistake to assume that governments are always at the mercy of swings in domestic public opinion; governments can (and often do) pursue foreign policy actions that are deeply unpopular.

Nevertheless, public opinion does not have the same level of influence over foreign policy issues that it does over domestic issues. Foreign policy decision makers generally have more autonomy from both public scrutiny and public input, because states need to act in a relatively coherent fashion in international affairs and because diplomacy tends to be both less visible and more secretive. Therefore, international affairs is often regarded as the exclusive reserve of a foreign policy elite, composed of elected and unelected government officials, some business elites, journalists, lobbyists, and experts.

THE BUREAUCRATIC POLITICS MODEL

The bureaucratic politics model makes very different assumptions about the nature of the decision-making process. This model suggests that decision-making outputs do not reflect a process of the rational consideration of alternatives by individuals but rather are the result of the process of competition or bargaining among bureaucratic units with divergent perspectives on the issues.[18] Decisions are the result of pulling and hauling between government agencies. What bureaucratic interests are involved in this process? Governments have become increasingly dependent on foreign policy bureaucracies, which provide a source of expertise on the issues and have the staff and instruments at their disposal to execute the decisions of governments. Many of these bureaucratic units are engaged in the decision-making process. In Canada, for example, the Prime Minister's Office, the Department of Foreign Affairs and International Trade, the Department of National Defence, the Department of Finance, and parliamentary committees have input into foreign policy decision making.

The assumption of the bureaucratic politics model is that those who represent different bureaucratic interests within the decision-making structure will hold different views on the issue confronting the decision makers. This assumption is premised on the idea that where an individual stands on an issue depends on where that individual sits; individuals representing the Department of Foreign Affairs may have a very different view of how the Canadian government should act than individuals from the Department of Finance or from the Canadian International Development Agency. Also at stake in this bureaucratic process—whether it involves struggling or bargaining—are the prestige, influence, and perhaps the budget, of the bureaucratic agency.

Another influence that organizations can exert on decision making is through the organizational process by which they implement or execute decisions. The organizational process model suggests that decisions are neither the result of a rational process of choice nor the result of competition or bargaining among bureaucracies. Instead, decision-making outcomes are the result of the constraints imposed on decision makers by the bureaucratic organizations that execute the decisions of policymakers. These constraints come in the form of standard practices or routines called standard operating procedures

(SOPs). Because these SOPs reflect what an organization is prepared or equipped to do, they can limit the range of choices available to the decision maker. In other words, the organization responsible for executing a decision may not be capable of performing the desired tasks. In effect, the capabilities, preparedness, and contingency plans of an organization often determine the range of choice available to decision makers.

THE INDIVIDUAL, THE GROUP, AND THE ROLE OF PERCEPTION

Perception plays a crucial role in the decision-making process. Perception can have an impact on decision making on two levels: the level of the individual and the level of the group or organization. At the level of the individual, all decision makers have different and often unique life experiences, preconceptions, personal beliefs, value systems, prejudices, and fears that influence their perspective of the world. As a result, considerable attention has been devoted to the perceptions of individual decision makers and the link between these perceptions and their decisions. This study can be done through content analysis (the exploration of themes in speeches and writings), examinations of personal histories, or the discovery of operational codes in which routine and method act as an influence on personal beliefs.[19]

In short, we all possess perceptual lenses through which we view the world. Individuals examine and process information through these perceptual lenses, which leads to some of the following tendencies in decision making:

- *Worst-case analysis.* Decision makers tend to regard their own decisions as objective responses, while attributing hostile motives to the decisions of others.
- *Mirror imaging.* Decision makers can form similar images of each other ("we are peaceful, they are warlike," etc.) that reinforce mutual hostility. Decision makers can also make the mistake of believing that other decision makers are mirror images of themselves and that they will act in the same manner.
- *Wishful thinking.* Decision makers may have a personal attachment to a certain outcome, and may overestimate the chances of achieving that outcome.
- *Historical analogy.* Frequently, decision makers will employ history as a guide to policy, a process that can be beneficial or counterproductive, depending on the appropriateness of the analogy and the similarities with the current issue.
- *Affective bias.* All decision makers have learned or intuitive preconceptions of issues or actors. Decision makers tend to be more accepting of information that confirms their predispositions and less accepting of information that challenges those preconceptions.
- *Grooved thinking.* Decision makers may categorize information or events into a few basic types, and in some cases information and events may be unsuitably categorized, which can lead to inappropriate foreign policy responses.
- *Uncommitted thinking.* Decision makers may have no opinions on certain issues and questions and may vacillate or flip flop among different views of the issue and the different options available to respond to it.
- *Committed thinking.* Alternatively, decision makers may have a strong commitment to certain beliefs and views that remain consistent over time and are difficult to change.

At the group level, the dynamics that take place between individuals within a decision-making body (whether it be the foreign policy team of a state, or the decision-making body of a nonstate actor) can also influence the decision-making process. In some circumstances, the influence of group dynamics can promote a rigorous and systematic approach to the problem by accounting for a number of individual differences expressed by those in the group. In effect, the group can promote rationality by encouraging deliberation and debate. However, group dynamics may also interfere with the rationality of a decision-making process. Groups can develop shared mindsets or belief systems—in essence, dominant views—that individuals within the group are afraid to challenge. Psychology experiments have shown that when a group of six people are shown two lines on a screen and five of the six people (who are accomplices to the experiment) say that the lines are of equal length when in fact they are not, the sixth individual is likely to agree with the group rather than make the correct assessment. This phenomenon is called **groupthink**.[20] In addition, groups and organizations have their own cultures, perceptual lenses, and value systems; and information and ideas that are in accordance with these belief systems are passed up the organizational ladder. Those ideas that are not in accordance with the group's prevailing views are discarded or are subjected to intense scrutiny. In extreme cases, those who advocate policies at odds with the prevailing view may be ostracized or isolated from the group.

These conceptual models of decision making can be valuable instruments for students of international relations, as the models can be used to derive alternative explanations for why decisions were made. For example, in May of 1998 India tested a series of nuclear warheads, tests that established India as a declared nuclear power. Why did India conduct these tests? One explanation is derived from the rational actor model. India tested nuclear warheads because the government felt that it was the best option in the face of India's security concerns about Pakistan and China and that the tests would bolster India's power and prestige in the world. The bureaucratic politics model suggests that the tests were the outcome of competing interests within the Indian state, with the pro-test factions led by the military and nuclear science establishments emerging victorious. Alternatively, the tests could have been an effort (and a successful one at that) to rally public support behind the new government led by the Bharatya Janata party. In other words, the tests were driven by domestic political considerations. By using these decision-making models to analyze historical and contemporary events, we can gain a richer understanding of the nature of the decisions made in the arena of global politics.

PLAYING THE GAMES

Another instrument used to study the decisions of policymakers is **game theory**, which is further derived from a rational choice model. Game theory is a branch of mathematics concerned with modelling behaviour and outcomes under certain proscribed conditions. Two or more actors are provided with a set of alternative policy choices, and each is provided with a set of payoffs that are dependent on both their policy choice and the policy choices of others. In other words, the expected utility (the payoff or gain) is influenced by the decisions of others. Therefore, the policy choices of the players are influenced not only by their policy preferences but also by their expectations about the policy preferences of others. Game theory attempts to predict the outcomes of games by anticipating the preferences of the players. The outcomes of games can also be affected by altering the payoffs or gains that the actors receive. Some games are zero-sum games in which a loss by one actor is considered a gain for the other. Other games are non-zero-sum games in which it is possible for both players to gain (or to lose).

Game theory is employed by some scholars in international relations to model the behaviour of states under certain conditions. It should not surprise us that models that assume rationality and utility maximization are often employed by realists. In particular, a game called Prisoner's Dilemma has been used by realists to demonstrate how the character of an environment can lead actors to make rational, self-interested choices that will leave them worse off than if they cooperate with one another. The actors in the game do not cooperate because no basis for trust exists among them; this situation is roughly equivalent to the security dilemma discussed in the previous chapter. We will briefly examine two of the more popular games models employed.

Prisoner's Dilemma is the most common; it centres on a story of two prisoners who have committed a crime, such as armed robbery. The two prisoners are placed in their own cells and are unable to communicate with each other. The prosecutor knows that the two prisoners have committed the crime but requires a confession to get a conviction on the charge of armed robbery. Otherwise, the prosecutor only has enough evidence to get a conviction on the lesser charge of possession of a gun. The prosecutor offers the following deal to each prisoner:

> If you confess, and your partner does not, you will go free and your partner will go to jail for armed robbery for 10 years. If your partner confesses, and you do not, your partner will go free and you will go to jail for armed robbery for 10 years. If you both confess, you will split the penalty for armed robbery, and you will each go to jail for five years. If you both do not confess, you will both be convicted for gun possession and will serve a penalty of one year.

The game assumes there is no possibility for retaliation, that this is an isolated case, and that the prisoners only care about their own individual interests. Given these payoffs, the outcome of the game is clear: both prisoners will confess to the crime of armed robbery. The logic for such a decision is based on the following calculation of individual interest by each prisoner:

> I should confess, because if I confess and my partner does not, I will go free and my partner will go to jail. If I confess and my partner also confesses, I will still go to jail, but for a shorter term than I would if I didn't confess and my partner did. Under no circumstances should I not confess, for I cannot trust my partner to do the same.

Both prisoners will serve fairly long sentences when they could have served a short one by trusting each other to keep quiet. The Prisoner's Dilemma game can be represented by the following chart:

| | PRISONER A | |
PRISONER B	CONFESS	DO NOT CONFESS
Confess	5, 5	0, 10
Do not confess	10, 0	1, 1

This chart is called a *payoff matrix* and illustrates the choices and payoffs facing each prisoner. Therefore, if both prisoners confess, they each get 5 years in prison. If prisoner B confesses and prisoner A does not, prisoner B goes free while prisoner A receives 10 years in prison for armed robbery. If both prisoners do not confess, they receive one year in prison for gun possession charges. In international relations theory, this game has been used to illustrate how countries may find themselves in arms races. It is in the interest of both countries not to engage in an arms race, for they will expend vast sums of money and yet end up no more secure than they were before. However, neither country can afford to trust the other by not arming itself, for if one country armed and the other did not, then the country that did not arm would be at a disadvantage. So both countries arm, even though both states would do better to avoid an arms race altogether.

Another game often employed by international relations scholars is called Chicken. Chicken is drawn from a practice allegedly popular among North American teenagers in the 1950s and immortalized by James Dean in the movie *Rebel Without a Cause*. Two cars are driven toward one another, on a collision course, at high speed on a narrow stretch of road. The first to swerve to avoid the imminent collision is "chicken" and suffers a corresponding drop in prestige. The driver who does not swerve wins an increase in prestige at the cost of the other driver's reputation. If both drivers swerve, they both lose prestige but not as much as they would have if they had swerved alone. If they both do not swerve, they will collide and be killed or seriously injured. As they approach each other, the two drivers may take actions that are designed to signal their commitment to stay on course, such as accelerating, raising their hands off the steering wheel, or removing the steering wheel and throwing it out the window (thus entirely removing the ability to swerve).[21] The following payoff matrix applies:

	DRIVER A	
DRIVER B	**SWERVE**	**DO NOT SWERVE**
Swerve	–2, –2	–5, 5
Do not swerve	5, –5	–10, –10

This game is used to model international crises in which countries are on a collision course toward war; the country that blinks or backs down first "loses." If neither country backs down, the outcome may be a costly or devastating war.

As mentioned earlier, the study of decision making grew rapidly in popularity among scholars during the Cold War. This interest grew largely because the decisions made in Washington and in Moscow were so significant for the international system. Because decisions made in these capitals could have led to conflict or even nuclear war, a natural interest in the character and dynamics of decision making emerged. The study of foreign policy decision making remains important today, although it has lost its apocalyptic significance with the end of the Cold War.

THE END OF THE COLD WAR: POWER POLITICS DESCENDANT?

The combination of the superpower confrontation during the Cold War, the regional wars that broke out around the world, and the nuclear arms race all served to provide ample ammunition to realists. The Cold War seemed to confirm much of the premise and dynamics of the power politics approach to explaining the international system and international relations. However, as we will explore over the next few chapters, some significant new trends began to take shape in the Cold War world, including the development of an increasingly interdependent world economy, the growth of international institutions and organizations, heightened concern over the environment, increased international travel and communication, and the widening gap between the rich and the poor. These trends began to challenge the accuracy of the realist framework. Nevertheless, it was the end of the Cold War that removed the shadow of the superpower rivalry and brought these trends from the back burner of international relations to the front of the international agenda. Few international events have been as dramatic as the end of the Cold War. The revolutions against Communist rule in Eastern Europe, the reunification of Germany, and the collapse of the Soviet Union itself took place within a startlingly short time—from mid-1989 to the end of 1991—and changed the face of global politics. The Cold War ended not with a hegemonic war (as many had feared and anticipated) but with the disintegration of one of the two poles of power in the world. It is crucial to explore the question of how this could have happened.

The Soviet Union experienced increased economic stagnation during the rule of Leonid Brezhnev. By the time Mikhail Gorbachev came to power in 1985, the problems facing the Soviet Union were enormous. The economy was performing poorly and in some sectors was actually shrinking. By the 1980s Japan had overtaken the USSR as the world's second-largest economy. Soviet central planning had created an economic structure that was inefficient, obsolete, and incapable of meeting the demand for food and even basic consumer items. The Soviet Union's two vital energy resources, coal and oil, were becoming more difficult to extract. The USSR had become the world's largest importer of grain, with a quarter of its own crops rotting in the fields because of a poor distribution system. The military budget was absorbing approximately 20 to 25 percent of the country's gross national product (GNP), as well as 33 percent of the country's industrial force, 80 percent of its research and development personnel, and 20 percent of its energy output. In addition, the Soviet Union subsidized its allies, spending more than U.S.$20 billion a year. The workforce suffered from poor morale, with strikes and demonstrations taking place in many cities. Food rationing had to be reintroduced. Life expectancy and infant mortality compared unfavourably with the West. The closed nature of the Soviet system, which restricted access to information and controlled television, newspapers, and books, was unable to take advantage of the computer and information revolution.[22]

Gorbachev's solution to these problems was to implement a reform program based on three elements: **glasnost** (openness) to broaden the boundaries of acceptable political discussion; **perestroika** (restructuring) to reorganize the old economic system by introducing limited market incentives; and democratization to increase the involvement of the people in the political process. It was Gorbachev's hope that this program would revitalize the Soviet economy while the Communist Party remained in power. Gorbachev never envisioned that his reforms would fundamentally alter the nature of political power in the USSR; he was a reformer, not a revolutionary (see Profile 3.4). To embark on this program of domestic reform, Gorbachev required a favourable international environment. He required good relations with the West to obtain Western aid so that resources could be diverted from military spending to the civilian economy. Gorbachev embarked on a foreign policy that saw him reach out to the West with arms control proposals and summits with Western leaders. He also withdrew Soviet forces from Afghanistan.

However, Gorbachev's domestic program did not yield the desired results. In fact, the opposite occurred, as the living standard of the average Soviet citizen actually began to fall. By the end of the 1980s, the contradictions in the Gorbachev reform program were evident. In the attempt to reorganize the economy, the old system was dismantled, while no new legal or reformed banking system was put in place to allow market forces to

Mikhail Gorbachev

Hailed in Canada. Former Soviet Union President Mikhail Gorbachev presents the James S. Palmer Lecture at the University of Calgary, 12 October 2000. (CP Picture Archive/ Andrian Wyld)

The last leader of the Soviet Union (from 11 March 1985 to 25 December 1991), Mikhail Gorbachev was the architect of the reform program that initiated a chain of events that was to culminate in the collapse of the USSR. After studying law in Moscow (graduating in 1955), Gorbachev worked his way through the ranks of the Communist Party organization, eventually becoming responsible for agriculture. He became a full **Politburo** member in 1980, and after the deaths of Brezhnev's successors (Yuri Andropov and Konstantin Chernenko), Gorbachev became General Secretary of the Central Committee of the Communist Party of the Soviet Union. He embarked on an ambitious program of political and economic reform, what he called "the new political thinking" on domestic and foreign policy issues. This reform was dramatically displayed in Gorbachev's approach to arms control, a cooperative relationship with Europe, and a hands-off approach to the Eastern European countries (even when they were throwing off Communist rule).

While Gorbachev's international diplomacy earned him international acclaim and won him a Nobel Peace Prize in 1990, at home he was increasingly unpopular, and his reform program had unleashed forces that were soon spiralling out of control. Central control over the economy was lost, nationalism spread and intensified, the constituent republics of the USSR began to agitate for more autonomy, and the political spectrum in the USSR diverged into radical reformers and conservatives. Ultimately, the reform program was rendered obsolete by the political events surrounding the break-up of the Soviet Union.

In retrospect, Gorbachev was one of the great reformers in world history, but his efforts were inadequate in the face of a system that required transformation rather than mere reform. Outside contemporary Russia, Gorbachev is remembered as the Soviet leader who did more than any one individual to make the end of the Cold War peaceful by acquiescing to the freedom of Eastern Europe. However, within Russia, Gorbachev is vilified as the man who caused the collapse of the Soviet Union and increased the misery of the average citizen. The last leader of the Soviet Union remains far more popular abroad than in his own country.

operate. The result was economic decline, unemployment, and a drop in production. Glasnost served to expose the inefficiencies and corruption of the economic system and increasingly of the government and the Communist Party itself. Within the USSR, some wanted to slow reform and maintain many of the characteristics of the old economic system, while others wanted to accelerate reform and remove the old system entirely. Gorbachev was increasingly isolated politically between these two factions, and his credibility and influence began to wane.

By the late 1980s the end was near. The last gasps of the Soviet Union began in 1989. In a series of revolutions in Eastern Europe—some peaceful, others violent—the ruling Communist parties in those states were swept away with no response by Gorbachev. The

Tearing down the Wall. An unidentified West Berliner swings a sledge-hammer, trying to destroy the Berlin Wall near Potsdamer Platz, on 12 November 1989, where a passage was opened nearby. (CP Picture Archive/John Gabb)

Berlin Wall, the symbol of the Cold War division of Germany and the division of Europe, was officially opened on 7 November 1989, although citizens of both countries had been singing and dancing on the wall and taking picks and hammers to the Cold War symbol for days. Germany, divided during the Cold War, was reunified on 3 October 1990. The Warsaw Pact, the Soviet Union's alliance system in Eastern Europe, was dissolved. Although Germany and Eastern European countries would now have to struggle with political and economic reform and the legacy of more than 40 years of Communist rule, the Europe of the Cold War had vanished.

Within the USSR, increasing disaffection with the central leadership in Moscow led to demands for an increased devolution of powers to the constituent republics. A new Union Treaty was to be signed on 20 August 1991 that would have weakened the power of the centre. However, on August 19, a coup attempt was mounted while Gorbachev was away on vacation, and power was taken by an eight-person council.[23] The coup was based in three overlapping groups in the central leadership: the state bureaucracy, military and industrial interests, and the security forces, which all felt threatened and marginalized by the reforms and devolution of powers to the republics. However, the coup failed, largely because key elements of the internal security apparatus and the military refused to support it. Instead, many backed Boris Yeltsin, a former Communist Party official who had been elected Chairman of the Supreme Soviet of the Russian Republic in May 1990 and President of the Russian Republic (the largest of the 15 republics) in June 1991. Faced with public opposition and without control of the army, the junta caved in, and Gorbachev was brought back to Moscow. However, the central government began to simply wither away as governments in the republics gathered increasing power in their own jurisdictions. Gorbachev was quite literally president of a federal bureaucracy detached from the republics and possessing little real authority. The final blow fell with the Ukrainian vote for independence on 1 December 1991, which effectively scuttled the attempts to revive a Union Treaty. Declarations of independence from other republics followed. On December 8 the **Commonwealth of Independent States (CIS)** was formed as a coordinating framework for most of the former republics of the USSR (only the Baltic States are nonmembers). In the last week of December 1991, the Soviet flag was taken down from the Kremlin in Moscow. The Soviet Union had disintegrated, and the Cold War was over.

PONDERING THE END OF THE COLD WAR

For almost half a century, the Cold War defined global politics. Virtually everything deemed internationally newsworthy was directly or indirectly related to the Cold War, whether it was the announcement of new defence spending projects, the negotiation of a new arms control agreement, or the outbreak of a war somewhere in the world. Everyone feared the ever-present threat of nuclear war and the unspeakable yet certain devastation such a war would bring. Indeed, it is possible to speak of a Cold War generation for whom nuclear annihilation was a constant possibility (it still is, but the threat is much less intense). For this generation the Cold War affected domestic politics as well. In the democratic industrialized world, the fear of Communism led to suspicion and often suppression of domestic Communist movements. In some countries, witch hunts were conducted to purge government, the arts, and society of Communist influences. The most famous of these efforts took place in the United States in 1952–53 under Senator Joseph McCarthy, whose use of accusation and innuendo with no substantial evidence gave rise to the term *McCarthyism*, an extreme example of the general tendency during the Cold War to regard with suspicion those who were sympathetic to or supportive of Communism and the Soviet Union (or China). In other countries, anti-Communism was used as an excuse to suppress dissident movements, Communist or non-Communist, often with the larger purpose of maintaining a political and military elite in power. For example, hundreds of thousands of people died in Indonesia as a result of a bloody anti-Communist purge by the Suharto government in 1965. In Communist countries, political freedoms were almost nonexistent, and state-controlled media emphasized the evils of the capitalist West. Reports of international events, when they occurred, were invariably cast in terms of Western plots against the Communist world.

For governments, the Cold War was the foundation of the foreign policies of most states. Patterns of tension and conflict around the world either originated in the Cold War or were influenced by it. Events such as the Berlin Airlift and the Cuban Missile Crisis were a direct result of Cold War tensions between the superpowers. Conflicts in Africa, the Arab–Israeli wars, the conflicts between India and Pakistan, and wars such as in Vietnam and Afghanistan had local or regional origins but took on a Cold War dimension through the direct or indirect involvement of the superpowers. At the same time, Cold War considerations also formed the basis for much cooperation among states. This cooperation took a variety of forms, including the creation of alliances aimed at a common enemy (such as NATO and the Warsaw Pact), the sale of arms to client countries, and arms control agreements between the principal antagonists, the United States and the Soviet Union.

Intellectually, the Cold War contributed to a sense of predictability and order in world affairs. The most predominant concern was maintaining a stable superpower relationship and keeping the Cold War cold. A general consensus (although by no means universal) emerged in most countries with respect to foreign affairs and defence policy. Broadly supported by their publics, governments maintained their alliance commitments and a certain level of defence spending. In scholarly circles, the Cold War seemed to vindicate much of the realist perspective, and academic work concentrated on issues such as strategic stability, deterrence, and arms control. The Cold War fed an interest in the history and politics of the Soviet Union, and *kremlinology* became an important area of study. This does not imply that scholarship during the Cold War was stale or uniform. On the contrary, major theoretical debates took place. Most prominent perhaps was the clash between behaviouralists, who wanted to quantify global politics, and traditionalists, who maintained that history, not data analysis, was still the best teacher. This debate ended in an agreement to disagree. An increased interest in economic interdependence fostered the rise of liberal perspectives, and a growing academic voice for and from the southern hemisphere pushed theories about imperialism and dependency to the fore.

However, when it came to the study of international security issues, the discourse was dominated by the superpower standoff.

Because the end of the Cold War meant the end of conditions that had been so pervasive and all encompassing, it left a conceptual and intellectual aftershock. Political leaders, scholars, and the public began to ask fundamental questions about the nature of global politics, questions that were seldom asked during the Cold War. Little thought had been devoted to what a post–Cold War world would be like. No plans were made for such an eventuality, and some, like John Mearsheimer, suggested that we would come to miss the Cold War, with its familiarities and certainties.[24] However, a post–Cold War agenda, driven by international events, slowly took shape and new points of debate emerged. We will explore these issues in Part Two of this book.

In the former Communist world, the end of the Cold War has been much more traumatic. Economic hardship, social decay, and environmental problems abound in many of the countries that are trying—with various degrees of enthusiasm—to restructure their economies and open their political systems. In particular, the collapse of the Soviet Union left many people in Russia wondering what had happened. Post–Soviet Russia embarked on a rapid program of economic reform designed to bring capitalism to the country. The reforms, coupled with the resistance of powerful bureaucratic and industrial interests, have caused massive disruptions in the economy. While a few new rich prosper, life for most Russians has gotten worse, not better. The sense of pride associated with being citizens of one of only two superpowers has vanished, replaced by the realization of the country's fragmentation and the humiliation of declining standards of living and an erosion of personal safety in the face of growing crime rates. The formerly well-funded sectors of Russian society and industry are also deeply troubled. A poorly led, poorly prepared, and cash-starved military performed poorly in the suppression of Chechnya, a small region in the Caucasus that sought independence. Scientists who worked in the huge Soviet military-industrial complex have struggled to support their families; some have resorted to suicide. The military and the arms industry are willing to sell arms to generate revenue, and a recent trend toward the sale of advanced weapons systems—including a controversial nuclear technology sale to Iran—raises concerns about the proliferation of sophisticated weapons, including weapons of mass destruction.

Some fear that the state of affairs in Russia could lend itself to extremist leadership. Conditions in Russia today are disturbingly similar to those that existed in **Weimar Germany**, and those conditions were instrumental in enabling Adolf Hitler to rise to power. Russian President Vladimir Putin was popular largely for his no nonsense approach to Chechen separatists. Putin won power in presidential elections in March 2000 (elections marred by fraud), but many worry that his government shows too much enthusiasm for centralized power and too little enthusiasm for the rule of law. In addition, old patterns of suspicion and hostility remain intact in Russia. When a Russian nuclear submarine sunk in the Barents Sea in August 2000, some Russian military officials were quick to blame Western military operations for the accident.

WHY DID THE SOVIET UNION COLLAPSE?

Realism has been attacked for its failure to predict the end of the Cold War. In truth, however, none of the theoretical frameworks employed by international relations scholars can claim a better record in this regard. Nevertheless, with the benefit of hindsight, we can isolate several factors that offer potential explanations for the fall of the

The Potemkin Village Analogy

The Potemkin Village analogy originates with the story of a Russian prince named Grigori Potemkin, a favourite of the famous Tsarina of Russia, Catherine the Great. Potemkin had helped organize her imperial tour of the southern provinces of the Russian Empire in 1787, taking great efforts to make the tour as spectacular as possible. This effort included the construction of attractive false fronts, or façades, for many of the buildings and towns along the Tsarina's route to impress Catherine with the prosperity of the empire, a pros-perity that was at least in part an illusion manufactured by Potemkin. This story is used as an analogy for the state of the Soviet Union by the 1980s, a Potemkin Village, a superpower that was in truth a superpower in military terms only. This façade of strength, while significant, obscured the fact that the Soviet Union was sliding deeper into economic decline, with most of its citizens cynical about the political and economic system and struggling to maintain their meagre standard of living.

Soviet Union. In general, these factors point to a superpower that was in increasingly dire straits, a superpower that had become a "Potemkin Village" and was facing an unpromising future (see Profile 3.5).

In retrospect, many observers in the West were well aware of the problems facing the USSR. However, they underestimated the extent to which these forces were undermining the Communist Party of the Soviet Union, which after all could call on massive military forces, a large internal security apparatus, and state control of political and economic life to maintain its power and keep order in the country. The autopsy following the collapse of the USSR has yielded the following perspectives and explanations for this dramatic event:

- *Containment and the arms race.* One explanation is that the grand strategy of containment by the United States worked. The cost of the nuclear arms race, the cost of maintaining a massive military establishment, and the cost of supporting allies in Eastern Europe and overseas bankrupted the Soviet Union. Unable to devote resources to the revitalization of its civilian economy and boost sagging consumer and agricultural production, the USSR simply spent itself into its grave. This position is taken by many realists in the West, in particular in the United States, who argue that the policy of firm containment and high defence spending contributed to the end of the Cold War and a Western victory. Western liberals argue that, in fact, the containment policies of the West may have pro-longed the Cold War. Soviet leaders could use the threat posed by the West as a rallying point for political support and as an excuse to maintain high levels of defence spending and centralized control over the economy. Without an external threat to distract attention from domestic hardships, the USSR may have embarked on reform (or even collapsed) far earlier. George Kennan, the original author of containment, argued in 1992 that "the general effect of cold war extremism was to delay rather than hasten the great change that overtook the Soviet Union at the end of the 1980s."[25]

- *Imperial overstretch.* Another explanation can be found in the theories of power transition and imperial decline. Using the theories publicized by Yale historian Paul Kennedy, this explanation suggests that empires tend to expand until they overstretch themselves. The costs of these commitments burden the economy at home, which undercuts the long-term capacity of the economy to sustain itself. By this explanation, the USSR took on too many commitments in the world, which forced it to devote scarce resources to client states such as Cuba, Syria, and Vietnam. The Soviet Union supplied such countries with financial assistance, preferential trade terms, and weapons. The war in Afghanistan burdened the economy even more in the early 1980s. The costs of these commitments drew already scarce resources out of the country, resources that could have been used to reinvigorate the Soviet economy.

- *Domestic decline.* The most widely accepted explanation of the collapse of the Soviet Union is that the Communist system simply did not work very well. The command economy that had been so successful in guiding the rapid industrialization of the Soviet economy later served to hinder reform and innovation. Consumers suffered from shortages of even basic goods and endured long lineups for food items. Industries in the civilian sector turned out poorly manufactured goods developed and built not for the consumer but to fulfill production **quotas** set by the state. Agricultural techniques stagnated and led to poor distribution and massive waste. Worker morale declined, as exhibited in the famous Soviet workers' proverb: "They pretend to pay us, and we pretend to work." New technologies and techniques could not be absorbed into the Soviet economic system, which became increasingly entrenched in a heavily bureaucratized political system that favoured the elite few—the *nomenklatura*—but was resistant to change. More important, the ruling elites had lost their legitimacy, a legitimacy based at least in part on the idea of building toward a better future. In many of the Soviet Union's regions, nationalism and ethnic identity were growing out of disaffection with the political centre. The collapse of the Soviet Union was therefore the result of a failed economic system, one that could not sustain itself, let alone compete with the West, which was entering the electronic and information age.

- *Gorbachev's reforms.* Another explanation argues that the reform program of Mikhail Gorbachev was the most important reason behind the collapse of the USSR. Gorbachev sought a middle way to reform between the command economy and market forces. However, no middle way was to be had, and the poorly conceived reform program was doomed from the beginning. This misdirected reform effort made an already bad situation worse, creating such desperation and discontent that the centre lost its grip on power. A different reform program might have succeeded. Alternatively, the old system might have been kept in place, despite its inefficiencies, and the Soviet Union would still exist. The Soviet system was badly run down, but in trying to fix the system, Gorbachev broke it.

- *The triumph of democracy and the market.* Finally, liberals argue that the collapse of the Soviet Union represented a victory for democracy and the market as systems of governance. The virtues and advantages of an open political system, the efficiencies of a market economy, and the capacity to innovate and adapt to changing conditions and technology served as a standard against which all other systems were measured. Clearly, the Communist system did not measure up. The average Soviet citizen was becoming increasingly aware of the living standards enjoyed in the West, and this was a source of increasing concern and embarrassment to the Soviet leadership. This explanation argues that soft power played an important role in the end of the Cold War.

WHY DID THE COLD WAR NOT BECOME A HOT WAR?

The Cold War was characterized by periods of high tension, crises, proxy wars, and a conventional and nuclear arms race between the superpowers and their allies. Why did these differences and confrontations not lead to a global war between the United States and the Soviet Union? First among the reasons was the nuclear stalemate between the two countries. The leaders of both countries knew that if a conflict between them developed into a war, there was a very good chance that the war would escalate to the use of nuclear weapons, resulting in a strategic nuclear war that would at the very least devastate both societies.

The Cuban Missile Crisis proved to be the catalyst for a growing realization that to avoid a nuclear war, the superpowers would have to manage their relationship rather than engage in eternal conflict. As a result, both countries exercised caution in their relationship because the consequences of miscalculation were so significant. The superpowers established a hotline between Washington and Moscow to facilitate communication in a crisis. Over time, informal rules were established between the two countries, such as the acknowledgment of spheres of influence in which the other would not overtly interfere and consultation and communication during times of war or crises in regions such as the Middle East and Asia. The leaders of both countries met in summits, arrived at cooperative arrangements such as cultural exchanges and trade agreements, and signed several arms control treaties. All these efforts served to enhance the communication and cooperation between the United States and the Soviet Union and were a reflection of the awareness of both countries that the Cold War had to be kept cold.

CONCLUSIONS

This chapter began with an examination of the various themes and dynamics of the Cold War, an omnipresent reality in global politics after World War II, which influenced virtually every aspect of international life. The tense relationship between the superpowers and the nature of the nuclear arms race fuelled the growth of decision-making analysis as a subfield of the study of international relations. However, as we will see in later chapters, the international system began to experience some significant changes in the latter half of the Cold War period, changes that served to challenge the accuracy and applicability of the power politics approach. We now turn to an examination of one of these changes: the growth of economic interdependence in the global economy.

Endnotes

1. "The Military Role of Nuclear Weapons: Perceptions and Misperceptions," *Foreign Affairs* 62 (1983), 59–80.
2. Jeremy Isaacs and Taylor Downing, *Cold War: An Illustrated History* (Toronto: Little, Brown, and Company, 1998), 232.
3. The term *Cold War* originates in the fourteenth century and refers to the long conflict between Muslims and Christians for the control of Spain.
4. Quoted in Charles W. Kegley, Jr., and Eugene R. Wittkopf, *World Politics: Trend and Transformation*, 5th ed. (New York: St. Martin's Press, 1995).
5. Robert W. Tucker, "1989 and All That," *Foreign Policy* 69 (Fall 1990), 94.
6. See Denis Smith, *Diplomacy of Fear: Canada and the Cold War 1941–1948* (Toronto: University of Toronto Press, 1988).
7. Lawrence Freedman, *The Evolution of Nuclear Strategy* (London: The Macmillan Press, 1983).
8. X [George F. Kennan], "The Sources of Soviet Conduct," *Foreign Affairs* 25 (July 1947), 566–82.

9. Quoted in John Lewis Gaddis, *Strategies of Containment: A Critical Appraisal of Postwar American National Security Policy* (New York: Oxford University Press, 1982), 64–5.

10. Ibid., p. 40.

11. James N. Rosenau, "The Study of Foreign Policy," in James N. Rosenau, Kenneth W. Thompson, and Gavin Boyd, eds., *World Politics: An Introduction* (New York: Free Press, 1976), 16.

12. James E. Dougherty and Robert L. Pfaltzgraff, Jr., *Contending Theories of International Relations: A Comprehensive Survey*, 4th ed. (New York: Longman, 1996), 457.

13. Michael Brecher, *Crises in World Politics: Theory and Reality* (New York: Pergamon Press, 1993).

14. The seminal work on decision-making models was written by Graham T. Allison, in *Essence of Decision: Explaining the Cuban Missile Crisis* (New York: Harper and Row, 1971). See also Jonathan Bendor and Thomas H. Hammond, "Rethinking Allison's Models," *American Political Science Review* 86 (1992), 301–22.

15. Herbert A. Simon, *Models of Bounded Rationality* (Cambridge, MA: MIT Press, 1982).

16. See Herbert A. Simon, *Models of Man* (New York: Wiley, 1957).

17. Jack S. Levy, "An Introduction to Prospect Theory," *Political Psychology* 13 (June 1992), 171–86.

18. David A. Welch, "The Organizational Process and Bureaucratic Politics Paradigms: Retrospect and Prospect," *International Security* 17 (1992), 112–46.

19. See Robert G.L. Waite, "Leadership Pathologies: The Kaiser and the Fuhrer and the Decisions for War in 1914 and 1939," in Betty Glad, ed., *Psychological Dimensions of War* (Newbury Park: Sage, 1990), 143–68; and Alexander George, "The 'Operational Code': A Neglected Approach to the Study of Political Leaders and Decision-Making," *International Studies Quarterly* 13 (1969), 199–222.

20. Irving L. Janis, *Victims of Groupthink: A Psychological Study of Foreign-Policy Decisions and Fiascoes* (Boston: Houghton Mifflin, 1972).

21. In the movie, James Dean and his protagonist race toward a cliff in separate cars; the one who jumps out of the car first loses. The other driver is killed when his door jams and he goes over the cliff; this may be a more appropriate analogy, after all.

22. David Mackenzie and Michael W. Curran, *A History of the Soviet Union,* 2nd ed. (Belmont, CA: Wadsworth, 1991), 474–75.

23. In a rather embarrassing episode, Canadian government officials decided to reach out to the coup leaders, stating they would communicate with them in the near future.

24. John Mearsheimer, "Why We Will Soon Miss the Cold War," *Atlantic Monthly* (August 1990), 35–50.

25. George Kennan, "The G.O.P. Won the Cold War? Ridiculous," *New York Times* (21 October 1992), A21.

Suggested Readings

Bottome, Edgar M. *The Balance of Terror: A Guide to the Arms Race.* Boston: Beacon Press, 1971.

Catudal, Honore M. *Nuclear Deterrence: Does it Deter?* Atlantic Highlands, NJ: Humanities Press, 1985.

Craig, Paul P., and John A. Jungerman. *Nuclear Arms Race: Technology and Society.* New York: McGraw-Hill, 1986.

Gaddis, John Lewis. *The United States and the Origins of the Cold War, 1941–1947.* New York: Columbia University Press, 1972.

———. *The Long Peace.* New York: Oxford University Press, 1987.

George, Alexander L. *Bridging the Gap: Theory and Practice in Foreign Policy.* Washington, DC: United States Institute of Peace, 1993.

Geva, Nehemia and Alex Mintz, eds. *Decision Making in War and Peace: The Cognitive Rational Debate.* Boulder, CO: Lynne Rienner, 1997.

Harvard Nuclear Study Group. *Living With Nuclear Weapons.* Toronto: Bantam Books, 1983.

Lafeber, Walter. *America, Russia and the Cold War, 1945–1990.* 6th ed. New York: McGraw-Hill, 1991.

McKeown, Timothy, and David Caldwell, eds. *Diplomacy, Force, and Leadership: Essays in Honor of Alexander George.* Boulder, CO: Westview Press, 1993.

Neack, Laura, Jeanne Hey, and Patrick Haney, eds. *Foreign Policy Analysis: Continuity and Change in Its Second Generation.* Englewood Cliffs, NJ: Prentice-Hall, 1995.

Nogee, Joseph L., and Robert H. Donaldson. *Soviet Foreign Policy since World War II.* 4th ed. New York: Macmillan, 1992.

Roberts, Jonathan M. *Decision-Making during International Crises.* New York: St. Martin's Press, 1988.

Robertson, Charles L. *International Politics since World War II: A Short History.* 2nd ed. New York: John Wiley and Sons, 1975.

Sakwa, Richard. *Gorbachev and His Reforms, 1985–1990.* New York: Prentice Hall, 1990.

Smith, Denis. *Diplomacy of Fear: Canada and the Cold War, 1941–1948.* Toronto: University of Toronto Press, 1988.

Smith, Hedrick. *The New Russians.* New York: Random House, 1990.

Vertzberger, Yaacov Y.I. *The World in Their Minds: Information Processing, Cognition, and Perception in Foreign Policy Decisionmaking.* Stanford, CA: Stanford University Press, 1990.

Suggested Websites

U.S. Diplomatic History Resources Index
  <faculty.tamu-commerce.edu/sarantakes/stuff.html>

Cold War Hot Links
  <www.stmartin.edu/~dprice/cold.war.html>

CHAPTER 4

Political Perspectives on the World Economy

The British taste for tea ... could not have been cultivated in that damp little island had it not been able to export its cheap textiles to Southern Asia, albeit to sell them in captive colonial markets, along with common law, cricket and railways.

— Malcolm Waters[1]

AN INTRODUCTION TO INTERNATIONAL POLITICAL ECONOMY

The global economy we so readily refer to today has been a long time in the making. Historians and anthropologists alike might argue that long before the advent of the modern state era, the spread of culture was facilitated first and foremost by the growth of **trade** between groups, **nations**, states, and empires. The development of capitalism in Europe and its expansion around the world had established European dominance in the global economy by the seventeenth century. Today capitalism remains the primary socioeconomic system in the world. It is clear that we are living in an era in which trade, financial flows, technology, international cooperation, and economic interdependence make the world economy appear to be a place of great convergence. World economic output continues to expand: in the year 2000, world economic growth was estimated at 4.9 percent, the fastest growth rate in 16 years.

However, many analysts dispute this image. Rather than view the global marketplace as a progressive one in which wealth is eventually attained by most participants and war becomes less likely as trade and investment ties promote interdependence and coopera-tion, they argue that the growth of wealth in some areas has come at the expense of poverty, dislocation, and violence in other areas. The world is increasingly polarized between the generally rich states of the northern hemisphere and the generally poor states of the southern hemisphere. This polarization is at the root of the north–south debate, which is reflected in different opinions about international financial institutions and in diplomatic disputes at international conferences on environmental and develop-ment issues. Trade has certainly increased international contact and cooperation throughout human history, but it has also produced empire and warfare as strong states dominate weaker ones. The attempt by poor southern states to catch up to rich northern ones and achieve the same level of affluence has not been particularly successful, although there are notable exceptions. According to this relatively negative view of the global economy, the future looks bleak as well, since the technological advances of the industri-alized world mostly will benefit only the richest portion of the world's population.

Those who study the vast field of *international political economy (IPE)* are interested in the relationship between economics and politics. They examine the evolution of the global economy, its current structure, and the strain between the state and an increasingly interdependent world economy. In this chapter we will examine the origins and the character of the contemporary international economic system. The chapter will then expand on the chief distinctions between various contending perspectives on international political economy.[2] The *liberal perspective* has the most currency today; it is the position largely favoured by international business and the pro-trade governments that govern many trade-dependent states, such as Canada. Another perspective, that of *economic nationalism*, prefers to accept the basic outlook of political realism outlined in the previous chapters and insists that the state is still the primary actor in global politics and economics. *Marxism, neomarxism,* and *dependency theory* stress the role of dominant socioeconomic classes and marginalization of the worker and characterize the world economy as exploitative. Critical theories such as *postmodernism* and *feminism* focus on the issue of marginalization of political perspectives and groups on a global scale. We will return to these critical perspectives in Chapter 8, where we discuss globalization and its counterpart, marginalization.

ECONOMIC POLITICS ASCENDANT?

This chapter makes no attempt to educate the reader on purely economic matters; a wealth of literature written by economists is readily available.[3] Our focus here is on the interaction between political and economic forces, forces that are so interwoven that it is often difficult to discern between the two. The United Nations, for example, is well known as a political institution. Yet, through the work of its development agencies and the associated **International Monetary Fund** (IMF), it is certainly an economic actor as well. When the prime minister of Canada personally promotes increased trade in the Pacific region, he or she is acting in the capacity of a political actor, although an economic agenda is being followed. At the same time, economic matters can transcend political ones and vice versa. A particularly dramatic example of the separation of commerce from politics occurred in the Crimean War of 1854–56. While England was at war with Russia, London banks floated loans for the Russian government! In July 1996, the Taiwanese and Chinese state-run oil companies signed a joint exploration agreement, a two-year deal covering an area in southeast China, and cross-border investment between the two economies continues to climb—despite very strained diplomatic relations between the two. Human rights campaigners are often critical of the ability and willingness of large corporations to invest in countries where human rights abuses occur, such as Burma or Indonesia or Nigeria. Consumer **boycotts** and state **sanctions** may limit such investment, but whether companies invest is by and large a decision made by multinational corporations, not by governments.

As we discussed in Chapters 2 and 3, much of the attention devoted to the study of international affairs has focused on warfare and military security concerns. This focus does not mean that economics was ignored in the conduct of international affairs or in the study of global politics. In fact, it has long been recognized that economic power is a necessary foundation for military power. Nevertheless, economics was often categorized as one of the concerns of low politics rather than high politics for several reasons. First, World War II focused attention on military security issues and the Cold War focused attention on the geopolitical and ideological competition of the superpowers. Second, nuclear weapons were thought to have transformed international politics, and it was believed that both conventional weapons and economic dimensions of power would be less important as a result. Third, international economic issues were relatively uncontroversial after the war because the United States dominated the global economy and could easily set the majority of rules and norms of the postwar order. Other countries focused on rebuilding their devastated economies and were incapable of or unwilling to challenge the United States on economic issues.

However, by the latter half of the Cold War, the profile of international issues began to increase, and by the 1990s economic issues were the leading priority for most states. The ascendance of economic issues can be attributed to the following factors:

- *The decline of the dominant position of the U.S. economy.* For much of the early Cold War, the United States was the world's only economic superpower (the closest competitor was the Soviet Union, with an economy half the size of the U.S. economy). However, in the latter half of the Cold War, the U.S. economy entered a period of what some describe as decline, and many observers concluded that the era of U.S. economic dominance was over.

- *The rise of other state economies.* During the Cold War, other states recovered from the devastation of World War II and became increasingly important actors. The economies of Western Europe and Japan emerged as economic centres of power, and several countries in East Asia—led by the Four Tigers of Hong Kong, Taiwan, Singapore, and South Korea—experienced high levels of economic growth.

- *The rise of multinational corporations (MNCs).* The emergence of MNCs—corporations with operations in several countries—as major economic actors in the world challenged prevailing views about the dominance of states as economic actors. As the size and resources of MNCs grew, so did debates about their impact on global trade and their role in the economic development of poor countries.

- *Increasing global interdependence.* During the Cold War it became increasingly evident that economic activity in the form of trade, financial flows, and monetary policies, facilitated by advances in communications technology, was linking the economies of states together to an unprecedented extent. This interdependence was reflected in the growth of economic institutions and organizations designed to promote economic transactions across states. These organizations became just as prominent as international institutions built around military security objectives (and in some instances more so).

- *The oil shocks.* In 1973 and 1980 the oil-rich states of the Middle East (and Venezuela) had a profound influence on international politics through their manipulation of the supply of oil. The heightened international significance of the oil-producing states increased the attention paid to the economic dimension of international relations and increased the external debt of many southern states in the process.

- *The collapse of the Soviet Union.* The fall of the Soviet Union dramatically illustrated the importance of economics as a foundation for state power. As discussed in Chapter 3, the USSR's decline and eventual collapse were due largely to the failure of its economic system. As well, the fall of the USSR removed the military and ideological threat to the West; as a result economic issues became more prominent.

You may recall that Chapters 2 and 3 focused on a historical and political perspective that emphasized the politics of war and peace. International political economy scholars (of all different perspectives) see global history differently. They focus on economic developments and on the relationship between economics, politics, society, and power. As we will see, some examine global history in the context of trade and the development of the rich, great powers, others through a framework of imperialism and economic dominance, and still others through a prism of postmodernity or gender. However, we cannot hope to understand the contemporary global economy without a brief examination of the leading concepts in IPE, the various perspectives that have evolved, and the history of the global economy.

TERMS AND CONCEPTS IN INTERNATIONAL POLITICAL ECONOMY (IPE)

Questions about regimes are central to IPE, especially the question of leadership in those regimes. **Regimes** are sets of norms, principles, rules, and decision-making procedures around which actors' expectations converge.[4] Regime analysts often stress the need for sound leadership, even perhaps for what is termed **hegemonic stability**, a situation in which the leader is sufficiently strong to provide the **public good** with a safe and secure environment in which to pursue common economic growth. One could even point to the ancient Roman Empire as a hegemonic system. The British assumed such a role following the defeat of Napoleon. After World War II the United States emerged in this key leadership role in the West. Today, debate continues over whether the United States is in a position to exert hegemonic leadership in the future, given its own financial problems and the rise of other economic powers such as Japan and Germany. Non-American students may find such a question yet another example of American introspection, but the importance of the American economy is simply undeniable.

Trade and investment are important components of the modern IPE. For our purposes, trade refers to the buying, selling, or barter of goods and services across the borders of states. When a Vancouverite buys a product from Toronto, this exchange is not considered international trade (although it is often called interprovincial trade). If one were to purchase it from Seattle, however, it would qualify as an instance of international trade. A state has a trade surplus when it exports more than it **imports**; it has a trade **deficit** if imports exceed exports. This balance has become more difficult to measure today, when so many goods and services are passed on through electronic means. Investment refers to the inflow of capital (in the form of money or capital goods such as machinery). Analysts often differentiate between venture capital (high-risk investments made in search of high profits abroad) and patient capital (long-term investments made with the expectation of gradual profits). Two immediate distinctions should be made here: **foreign direct investment (FDI)** occurs when a company constructs facilities in another country; **portfolio investment** occurs when foreign investors buy shares in domestic firms. One can also engage in portfolio foreign investment with the purchase of government bonds, in effect lending foreign governments money for a price (see Profile 4.1).

Both trade and investment take place in a world where governments routinely intervene, to differing degrees, to protect the interests of their own economies. The most common form of restriction on trade is the **tariff**, which is in essence a sales tax that discriminates against certain products. This tax makes that commodity more expensive to import from foreign producers than to purchase from domestic producers, thus discouraging its purchase. At one point, tariffs were a primary source of government income for states such as Canada that relied heavily on trade. Recently, tariffs have become less important as they have been lowered in many sectors through global and

The Balance of Payments

The **balance of payments** is an accounting system for recording a state's financial transactions with the outside world. The balance of payments comprises two accounts: the *current account* and the *capital account*. The first includes exports and imports of merchandise (cars, radios, CD-ROM drives), exports and imports of services (management consulting, information), investment income and payments (dividends and interest income earned from foreign investments along with payments to foreigners who have invested in the home country), and foreign aid and other transfers (human-itarian relief, loans and grants, the sale of military weapons). The capital account includes short-term and long-term investment inflows (foreign investment in the home state) and outflows (investment abroad). States with a highly troubled balance of payments may borrow money from the International Monetary Fund or sell bonds to make up the difference. One other account is important: a state's *official reserves*, which represent the foreign currencies, gold, and other financial assets accumulated by its central bank to pay for imports and meet other financial obligations.

regional negotiations. **Nontariff barriers**, however, are increasingly important today. They consist of quotas on the number of imports allowed, subsidies to industries at home, and standards and regulations. Foreign investment is often directly controlled by governments, which are concerned about the economic and cultural implications of too much foreign investment. For some time, India had a policy that disallowed foreign purchase of more than 49 percent of an Indian firm. Canada restrained foreign investment while Pierre Trudeau was prime minister with the establishment of the Foreign Investment Review Agency (subsequently scrapped by the pro–free trade Progressive Conservative government of Brian Mulroney). At the same time, states actively promote their own ability to export both goods and capital through agencies such as the Export–Import Bank in Washington and the Export Development Corporation in Ottawa.

THINKING ABOUT THE INTERNATIONAL POLITICAL ECONOMY

Because of the complexity of the global economy and the varied status of the countries and peoples within it, theoretical approaches that seek to describe, explain, and provide policy solutions to problems differ tremendously. We will introduce two perspectives of international political economy: neomercantilism and liberalism. Each perspective encourages a different understanding of the events and processes discussed in this chapter. We then proceed to examine more critical perspectives. You will notice that these theories have resonance in the broader IR (International Relations) theories outlined in Chapter 1, and the idealism/realism split outlined in Chapter 2.

ECONOMIC NATIONALISM AND THE NEOMERCANTILIST APPROACH

Economic nationalism and neomercantilism are most easily associated with the realist perspective; that is, they stress the importance of the self-serving state in the global economy. The economic policies of states are designed to pursue power and enhance wealth, which are then utilized to pursue more power. In this process the state is obligated to intervene in economic affairs. Neomercantilist economic policies are designed to promote domestic growth by generating trade surpluses with other economies. Because this surplus can only come at the expense of one's trading partners (who must then have a trade deficit), neomercantilism is often referred to as a **beggar-thy-neighbour economic policy.** States will pursue relative gains; what counts is their economic position relative to other states.[5] The tools of neomercantilist economic policies are currency devaluations, tariffs, quotas, and **export subsidies**.

The term *neomercantilism* is derived from the mercantilist economic policies of the imperial era, when empires sought to accumulate precious metals by exporting as much as possible and importing as little as possible to achieve a favourable **balance of trade**. In the modern era, in which the state rapidly evolved into the trading state,[6] economic nationalists have argued that the state should interfere with regularity in the global marketplace to protect its economic interests. Some states, such as Japan, have been known as especially mercantilist in the modern setting because they strongly protect their domestic markets, allowing limited goods and services within, while they actively promote Japanese products and Japanese foreign investment abroad. Canadian Prime Minister Jean Chrétien took a group of government and business representatives to many foreign lands to pursue contracts, and this group was popularly dubbed "Team Canada"; reactions on the appropriateness of a state's leader playing such a direct role in trade promotion are mixed.

Despite the limited success of the **General Agreement on Tariffs and Trade (GATT)** negotiations in reducing tariffs, the 1970s ushered in a new era of **protectionism**, which resulted from several events. The boom in oil prices brought on by the OPEC cartel, the shift from fixed to flexible **exchange rates** that occurred as the United States finally gave up its role as the guarantor of international monetary stability, rising competition from export-led industrializing states such as Japan and the newly industrialized countries (NICs), and increased trade subsidies and barriers imposed by the European Community all perpetuated a climate of uncertainty. A major recession in the early 1980s, brought on partly by another steep rise in the price of oil, further contributed to this environment. Those threatened by job displacement in the industrialized northern states put considerable pressure on governments to slow down the pace of trade liberalization and impose protectionist measures to preserve sectors of the economy. A notable example was the agricultural sector in Western European states. In the United States, large trade deficits inspired virtual panic among economic nationalists.[7]

Economic nationalism remains an influential perspective in most states, despite growing international trade and regional and global free trade agreements. Anti–free trade movements have maintained or increased their popularity in most countries, supported by individuals and groups concerned about jobs, social programs, and culture. As a result, neomercantilists insist that the state is still the primary actor in the global political economy. MNCs are simply instruments of the states in which they house their headquarters. The opening of the world economy to increased trade has not led to a borderless world, as the proponents of *globalization* proclaim, but to one in which the state continues to act as a protectionist force. Free trade agreements simply reflect the fact that certain states feel free trade will benefit them and increase, rather than decrease, the power they wield in the world.

LIBERALISM AND NEOLIBERALISM

Dissatisfaction with the realist perspective grew in the 1960s and 1970s, the result of increasing economic interdependence and cooperation, the development of international institutions, and evidence of the decline in military power (as old imperial states lost their empires and the United States lost the Vietnam War). As a result, many scholars argued that an alternative to realism was necessary. This belief was intensified after the end of the Cold War, when realism was assailed for failing to predict the fall of the Soviet Union. In addition, many felt that realism could not address crucial post–Cold War issues such as the environment, economic inequality, and the information and communications revolution. This view stimulated a re-examination of classical liberalism and political idealism (see Profile 4.2).

Liberalism originates in the early work of prominent European writers such as Immanuel Kant (see Profile 4.3) and Adam Smith.[8] Smith was particularly important; by 1800 his book *Wealth of Nations* had been translated into every Western European language except Portuguese. In it Smith attacked **mercantilism**, arguing that the functions of government should be limited to defence, internal security, and the arbitration of disputes between citizens. The market would best allocate goods according to supply and demand. Since some countries or climates could produce a commodity more cheaply than others, it made sense to Smith that countries should specialize in those areas and exchange commodities abroad (this idea is the dogma of comparative advantage). In this way, all countries would generate more wealth, even though they were all doing so in their own self-interest.

This last factor is important, since liberalism assumes that people are rational in the sense that they pursue their own self-interests and seek to maximize their gains. As

PROFILE 4.2 Realism, Liberalism, and Critical Theories Compared

ISSUE	REALISM	LIBERALISM	CRITICAL THEORIES
Human nature	Evil, selfish	Good, cooperate for mutual gain	Variable
Central problem	War and security	Encouraging cooperation on global issues	Marginalization
Key actors	States	Individuals, MNCs, "penetrated" states, and international institutions	Classes, groups
Motives of actors	Power, national interest, security	Justice, peace, prosperity	Power, greed
Nature of international politics	Anarchy; economic growth will not overcome state conflicts	Interdependent; economic growth will promote peace	Hierarchy, dominance, exploitation
Outlook on future	Pessimistic; stability; states will pursue neomercantilist policies	Optimistic; progress is possible; economic growth is good for all	Pessimistic unless policy solutions are achieved
Policy prescriptions and solutions	Enhance power; protect national interests	Develop institutions and regimes to encourage cooperation	Revolution, transformation, social change

Immanuel Kant was a German philosopher who wrote as the Enlightenment was sweeping through Germany in the eighteenth century. He wrote his most famous work, *Perpetual Peace*, in 1795. Based on the experience of the wars of the French Revolution, Kant argued that there were two possible futures for humanity: the end of all hostilities through international agreements or the perpetual peace of the cemetery of humankind after an annihilating war. *Perpetual Peace* is written as a contract similar to the diplomatic documents of the day; in this sense, it is a model for the establishment of international peace through international agreements between states. In it Kant proposes the following: the establishment of a system of conduct among states, including the principles of sovereignty, noninterference, and eventual disarmament; the conversion of authoritative states into republican states (which are less likely to go to war than the former); the development of an international federation of free states with a republican constitution that respects the sovereignty of its members; and the creation of conditions for universal hospitality and growing commerce across state borders. Kant believed that these measures would lead to peace among all peoples, a peace that would be reinforced by the natural tendency of states to engage in commerce rather than war with one another. Kant believed that humans had the ability to learn and progress through experience and that humanity and international society could be transformed. *Perpetual Peace* is one of the foundations of intellectual thought on international organization, international law, and the efforts to solve the problem of war.

Smith once wrote, "it is not from the benevolence of the builder, the brewer, or the baker that we expect our dinner but from their regard to their own interest."[9] On the international scene, classic liberals assume (along with the realists and economic nationalists) that states will similarly act in their own self-interest. However, liberal thought has expanded a great deal since the days of Adam Smith, and contemporary liberal thought is often referred to as *neoliberal*.

Neoliberal thought has wide variations. Some neoliberals employ a structural approach to their examination of global politics. Others concentrate on systems of governance (democratic states versus authoritarian states). Still others focus on international economic interdependence and the international flow of people and communications. Finally, neoliberal institutionalists focus on the impact of international institutions and nongovernmental organizations. Together, the neoliberal tradition holds the following views on the nature of world politics:

- States are not unitary actors, nor are they necessarily rational.
- No hierarchy of issues exists; economic and nonmilitary concerns can dominate a state's agenda.
- International politics is characterized by patterns of interdependence and transnational forces.
- The state has eroded in significance and can no longer claim exclusive sovereignty or control over its economy or society.
- Nonstate actors such as MNCs, international institutions, and NGOs are important actors in global politics.

- As interdependence and international cooperation grow, war decreases in value as an instrument of state policy.

Mark Zacher and Richard Matthew found that liberals believe that human society—at even the global level—is gradually evolving toward greater human freedom, conceived in terms of "increases in physical security, material welfare, and opportunities for free expression and political influence."[10] Thus, history is viewed as progressive. Realists essentially reject this perspective, arguing that the history of world politics is largely cyclical (war follows peace and on it goes). In addition, liberals stress the need for international cooperation. This cooperation can mean simple trade arrangements that facilitate good relations between states, or it can mean adherence to the norms and rules proscribed by international institutions that in effect help people overcome the parochialism of the nation-state and participate in a global economic and political community. Liberals also tend to believe that, in line with their progressive notion of history, a process of modernization is taking place, which follows from the scientific and intellectual revolutions that have shaped modern European and American culture and politics. Zacher and Matthew believe that the key components of this concept of modernization are "liberal democracy, interdependencies (commercial and military), cognitive process, international sociological integration, and international institutions."[11] Liberals see the individual (as opposed to the state or classes within states) as the primary political actor in world politics and believe that mutual human interests must be pursued to reach optimal outcomes, be it in terms of trade, investment, or diplomacy. As people become more interdependent through increased interaction, so too will their interests become intertwined, within and across borders. This interdependence leads to a mutual vulnerability that encourages cooperation and understanding and to the welcome expansion of one of the perspectives introduced in Chapter 1, *complex international interdependence.*[12]

This perspective stresses the importance of nonstate actors, such as nongovernmental organizations (NGOs) and, especially, international business. The state is conceived as a disaggregated unit; in other words, it is not seen as a unitary actor but rather as being composed of many, often conflicting, actors that operate on the world stage. Thus, "when nations negotiate, often the toughest bargaining is not between nations but within them."[13] Part of the liberal perspective suggests that, much like within domestic or internal society, a civic order exists that operates beyond the bounds of strict state regulation. Internationally, one can even argue that a global civil society exists that consists of structures that shape world affairs, such as common public concerns and voluntary associations engaged in issues of trade, cultural expression, religion, science, and production.[14]

For liberals, protectionism is seen as a counterproductive force that should be eliminated through institutional processes such as the GATT/WTO negotiations. More directly, trade leads to peaceful relations, since it creates a context of mutual respect if not need. Immanuel Kant wrote in his famous "Essay on Eternal Peace" (1795): "It is the spirit of commerce which cannot coexist with war, and which sooner or later takes hold of every nation." One might be critical of this assumption, for commerce has helped start wars as well as avoid them (as the Opium War of 1839–42 illustrates). Nevertheless, the link between trade and peace is central to liberal thought, and many liberals argue that it was the beggar-thy-neighbour trade policies of the Great Depression that led to World War II.

The modern manifestation of liberal thinking in international political economy is the concept of *globalization*, the idea that the world is shrinking because of increased interdependence related to trade ties and technological advances that provide investors with opportunities on a 24-hour basis. Capital is as mobile as ever, and though the neomercantilists often persevere in maintaining border controls over the import and export of goods, international organizations such as the WTO are facilitating the gradual emergence of a truly global market economy. We do not expand on this theme here because it is the main subject of Chapter 8. However, we should note that most governments, economists, and corporate executives tend to accept this liberalist transition as gospel. The perspectives outlined below challenge this view.

MARGINALIZATION AND CRITICAL PERSPECTIVES

The realist and neoliberal perspectives have, by and large, dominated the field of international relations in Europe and North America. However, other perspectives have developed over the last few decades that have attained great analytic and policy relevance, including *Marxism* and *dependency*, *postmodernism*, and *feminism* (we discuss the *sustainable development* perspective in Chapter 8). At the core of these critical perspectives on global politics is the view that disparities in global wealth go hand in hand with disparities in global political power. The rich countries of the world tend to dominate political deliberations on global economic issues. Poor countries have little input. Within countries, the poor often have little in the way of a political voice and little representation in government. The same can be said for women and for many minorities around the world. As a result, an important theme in the study of the divide between rich and poor peoples is the extent to which certain groups are economically and politically marginalized or otherwise excluded from participation in mainstream political and economic life. This study has led to the development of numerous intellectual perspectives and ideological movements that focus on the root causes of this marginalization. These perspectives and movements are dedicated to the emancipation of the politically and economically disadvantaged, whether they are the proletariat, poor states, minority groups, or women.

MARXISM, NEOIMPERIALISM, AND DEPENDENCY THEORY

Many observers argue that the principal conflict the world faces today is that between the rich and the poor, both in terms of underdeveloped southern states and the more affluent northern ones, and in terms of marked discrepancies in the standard of living of citizens within those states. The rise of international trade in goods and services as well as foreign investment has come at the expense of the southern states. The historical legacy of colonialism has resulted in a world order that is biased against the former colonies. Despite the use of development aid—or, some would even insist, because of it—poverty has persisted in many states in Africa, Latin America, and Asia. This poverty results in a central strain in the international system; as one journalist put it, "The rich get richer and the poor get resentful."[15] Borrowing from the intellectual tradition of Marxism, neomarxists and dependency theorists argue that poor states and poor peoples have been marginalized in the global economy as a direct result of the legacy of colonialism and the structure of the contemporary international economic order. Today, exploitation is achieved through the activities of multinational corporations. As the southern states became mired in external debt in the 1970s and 1980s, international agencies such as the IMF also began to play a significant role in this exploitation by ensuring that debt payments were made and made on the rich countries' terms.

The origins of Marxism lie in the writings of **Karl Marx** (1818–83), who studied law and philosophy and wrote about history. In league with Friedrich Engels (1820–95), Marx campaigned for a socialist Germany. Marxism itself is a branch of thought emerging from the French Revolution, the British Industrial Revolution, and German philosophy. Marx insisted on a materialist world view, implying that the world is constructed in our minds by the economic structure of society and that the means of production (technology, invention, natural resources, property systems) determine our religious, philosophical, governmental, legal, and moral values and institutions. What the bourgeoisie had done in France, Marx believed, the proletariat, or working class, could do elsewhere. According to Marxism, then, classes are the social engines of history. The state is conceived as a vehicle of the ruling economic class; it exists primarily to serve their interests and not those of the public. Marxist thinkers such as **John Hobson**, **Rosa Luxemburg**, and Vladimir Lenin wrote about the international impact of capitalism, which they considered to be the primary cause of imperialism (see Profile 4.4).[16] As the domestic economies of the European powers ran out of markets, it became necessary to expand into the colonial areas to find new markets, natural resources, and a place to export capital.

International thinking along Marxist lines has taken many paths. One of the more influential modern variants has been **dependency theory**, which argues that southern states have become trapped in a system of exploitation, one that forces them to be dependent on the north for capital and locks them into an unfair trading relationship. Inspired largely by the Latin American states' relationship to the United States, dependency theory suggests that the world system evolved from European imperialism to the disadvantage of those in the periphery. The wealth of the north was derived in part from the poverty of the south. States in the south were complicit, because the ruling classes in the periphery also benefited from the system. An important link existed between local capitalists, the underdeveloped state apparatus, and multinational corporations (or, put

PROFILE 4.4   Lenin and Monopoly Capitalism

Though Lenin's place in history is well known, his role in the formation of an intellectual perspective on international political economy is less celebrated. In a pamphlet published at the end of World War I ("Imperialism: The Highest Stage of Capitalism"), Lenin argued that the war had resulted from competition among the major capitalist powers, which had reached the stage of monopoly capitalism, "in which the division of all territories of the globe among the great capitalist powers has been completed." Imperialism resulted from the concentration of production in combines, cartels, syndicates, and trusts; the competitive quest for sources of raw materials; and the development of banking oligarchies. Under these conditions, imperialism was inevitable and not a matter of choice. The principal exporters of capital would be the dominant powers in the international system. Critics argue that this essentially economic explanation does not take into account other causes of imperialism, such as the search for glory and recognition. Lenin's ultimate creation, the Soviet Union, is dead, but to many concerned with the plight of the southern hemisphere, his ideas still form the core of their thinking.

another way, transnational capital). In addition, even the working classes in the north gained from this exploitative relationship. Thus, some theorists, such as Andre Gunder Frank, proclaimed that the real choice was between underdevelopment and revolution.[17] The world was not interdependent; it was hierarchical and exploitative.

Neomarxists and dependency theorists share several assumptions and views regarding global politics:

- The most important actors in global politics are dominant economic interests or socioeconomic classes.

- The state, and war, is an instrument of the ruling classes, though states play an important role, exercising some autonomy from the former in their pursuit of legitimation and capital accumulation.

- States and their ruling elites are bound into a hierarchical structural relationship characterized by patterns of dominance and dependence.

- A wide differential in power exists between the rich and the poor.

- For the marginalized and dependent states and peoples everywhere, revolution and the overthrow of the world capitalist system are the only hope for change. However, since this prescription of "delinking" from the world economy has proven elusive, many advocate major reform in both domestic and international systems instead.

Though not a Marxist, Norwegian Johan Galtung has written of a system that he feels perpetuates structural violence. It is a world system in which the division of labour forces the workers in southern states to do menial labour while the northern investors and traders benefit; in which the southern states themselves are fragmented and unable to develop positive trade relations; and in which the elites of the south have gradually evolved to the point where they have much more in common with northern elites than with their own citizens.[18] However, the past two decades have seen tremendous economic growth in what Immanuel Wallerstein, one of the main writers from a *world-systems perspective*, calls the *semi-periphery*, most notably the Asian NICs and Tigers, and this growth challenges the notion that the global economy can be so clearly separated into north and south. Though it has fallen out of fashion in many circles, the dependency perspective remains an important one in the north–south question. However, it would seem that the overwhelming majority of states have decided to play the global capitalist game, and to play it with often surprising enthusiasm, rather than to pursue a more revolutionary or autonomous path to development. But then, one might well ask who has made this decision, the people of the south or a transnational capitalist elite?

THE POSTMODERN CHALLENGE

The theories and approaches to world politics discussed in this book are all products of the positivist tradition in the sciences and the humanities. Positivism is based on the scientific method of inquiry, concerned with facts and phenomena rather than speculation or faith. On this basis, positivists believe that progress can be made in building knowledge about the social and political world. Postmodernists, in contrast, are post-positivists because they call for an examination of the underlying assumptions of positivist thought. Postmodernism is a broad intellectual movement that has come to the study of global politics over the past 10 years.

In brief, postmodernists believe that positivists (whether they are realists, liberals, or Marxists) are not capable, as they claim, of building objective knowledge about the world. For postmodernists, we cannot truly understand reality because how we see the world is socially constructed by subjective images that have their origins in our formative experiences, our cultures, our educations, our languages, and our political perspectives. "Reality" is, therefore, inherently intangible and subjective and is dependent on the nature of the viewer, not on the existence of an objective world. Postmodernists argue that individuals who have inherited the Western tradition have performed the bulk of research work in the sciences and humanities. This hegemonic intellectual tradition serves to marginalize other perspectives and non-Western thought. At the heart of the postmodern research agenda is an investigation into how power distribution in a relationship affects policy and scholarship. Every analysis, or policy, is constructed in such a way as to perpetuate or enhance a power relationship.[19]

The aim of postmodern scholars is to deconstruct existing international relations theory and texts and to expose their assumptions and distortions. In this way, postmodernists seek to show how positivist efforts to understand an objective reality are based on fallacy and pretension. Postmodernists, then, challenge the very epistemological base of the discipline, suggesting that the study of global politics has been based on the acceptance of positivism in the social sciences and that this is no longer warranted. A common complaint, however, is that postmodernists make little effort to construct their own theories describing and explaining global politics. Social constructivism, introduced in Chapter 1, does seek to offer plausible explanations of how interactions among various agents help to shape their identities and, thus, their behaviour, but it is difficult to label this approach as a purely postmodern one. Similarly, many theorists have incorporated the work of Antonio Gramsci into their analyses, suggesting that the world capitalist system is dependent on the perpetuation of hegemony not in the balance-of-power sense but in the ideational context. The managers of the world economy rely on a broad acceptance of many neoliberal precepts, such as faith in the positive impact of economic growth, to justify the gaps in wealth that exist.

FEMINIST PERSPECTIVES

Feminist literature de-emphasizes the state and instead focuses on gender relations, specifically on the political and economic marginalization of women within states and in the world as a whole. All the perspectives on the global economy introduced so far focus on relations between states or classes but not between males and females as they interact within the context of economic and political structures. We should note that feminist literature is not monolithic. Many feminists who study or participate in world affairs consider themselves liberal feminists; they advocate the increased involvement of women in international relations not because it would fundamentally alter the structure of global politics and economics but rather because women should have an equal right to the power and wealth that can result from that involvement. Indeed a growing body of literature focuses on the role of important individual women in the foreign policy-making process.[20] However, it is obvious that women have always played an important role in questions of peace and war even as they have been excluded from the top echelons of power. Women have often been vocal in the peace movement as well; for example, the Women's International League for Peace and Freedom was "the first organization to condemn the terms of the treaty of Versailles after World War I, correctly predicting how its harsh terms would not contribute to real peace."[21]

Other authors have focused on the role of gender in the exploitative processes that characterize the global economy. As the international division of labour changes, its impact will be felt by some more than others; for example, the move toward export-led production in the microelectronics sector in Asia has been facilitated by the employment of low-wage yet efficient female workers, generally believed by MNC employers to have smaller fingers and more patience. Class and gender exploitation work together. An awareness of the dividing line of gender must be reflected in development policies; the field of international development ignored the important role played by women in national and local economies. By the 1970s a movement began to counter this ignorance, and slowly an entire body of literature encouraged development assistance policies to adopt what has become known as the *Women in Development* (WID) approach.[22]

One of the major complaints of feminist scholars interested in global politics is that women are often made invisible by traditional international relations analysis, with its focus on the high politics of military security, a "man's world, a world of power and conflict in which warfare is a privileged activity."[23] As a result, much of feminist criticism has been directed at realism for promoting a masculine view of the world that diminishes human rights and development and rationalizes aggression. In addition, feminists challenge the traditional definition of security and seek to broaden the security agenda to include health, nutrition, education, family planning, food, and security. Feminist studies of IPE have stressed the effect of the world economy on women and their economic marginalization. Postmodern feminists are concerned with rejecting the claim that the history of international relations has been written objectively: "Since all historical inquiries grow out of the inquirer's linguistic frame, the results follow all too predictably from the hegemonic power of the Western White males initially responsible for the linguistic structure. The writing of history ... is not about truth-seeking; it's about the politics of historians. One man's truth is another woman's falsity."[24]

The feminist perspective operates at two levels: First, the argument is made that the role women play in the global economy is essential and must be recognized in any salient analysis, whether the researcher is looking at structural adjustment programs, the international sex trade, the microelectronics production industry, the generation of intellectual capital, or any other field. Similarly, the role women have played in historical developments, including the great ages of imperialism, should not be overlooked simply because history has not, by and large, been written by them. Second, there is a rejection of the dominant realist values and an emphasis on the values of self-worth, community development, cooperation, peace, and sustainable development. While it remains to be seen whether some of these values can infiltrate the halls of academia and become dominant in the field, there can be little doubt that the feminist critique of traditional international relations theory has had a profound impact on the thinking of both younger and older scholars. The larger question may well be whether, in an economic world still dominated by males, feminist perspectives can have a serious impact on actual policy decisions.

THE EVOLUTION OF THE GLOBAL ECONOMY

Given the postmodernist and feminist warnings about the selective nature of historical narrative, we proceed with caution to present a very brief overview of what we deem to be some of the more significant developments in the history of the world economy. Keep in mind that the perspectives above, from neomercantilism to neomarxism, will offer differing points of emphasis and arrive at differing conclusions and predictions. We merely present a basic overview.

Throughout history, groups of people have traded with one another. Trade over wide geographic areas developed around 200 B.C.E. with the rise of the Roman Empire in the west and the Han Empire in the east. Trade flourished within these empires, and luxury goods traded between the empires via the famous Silk Route and by sea routes connecting Indian and Persian ports with those in the Mediterranean. Trade nearly collapsed after the fall of the Roman Empire and the invasion of India and China by barbarian peoples. Long-distance trade routes were reopened between C.E. 570 and 1000, centred around ancient trade routes and cities such as Bruges, Venice, Baghdad, Samarkand, and Hangchow. A variety of products, ranging from Asian spices to Flemish woollens, were in heavy demand, and merchants began travelling to sell them. As economic activity and wealth grew, demand for exotic luxury items increased. By C.E. 1100, trading centres had been established all over Europe, from Italy to the Baltic, from England as far east as Bohemia. In 1317 the Venetians produced the Flanders galleys, commercial flotillas that made regular passage between the Adriatic and the North seas. In the 1400s, trade flourished in Europe, and financial empires based on international banking rose in importance (for example, the Fuggers of Augsburg and Medicis of Florence).

Extensive long-distance trade did not begin until about 1500. With the adoption of the mariner's compass and improvements in ship design and building, it became possible to sail the open seas, out of sight of land, and still get—roughly—where one wanted to go. The Portuguese were the first to build a sea-based commercial and political empire, but all the major European nations, including the Spanish, Dutch, French, and others, would soon follow. As a result, just as the Westphalian state system was extended around the world through the expansion of the European empires (see Chapter 2), the economic system of Europe was extended around the world in a similar fashion. The economic and trading systems of non-European empires and civilizations initially survived (and even thrived), but increasingly they were reduced to colonial status by the political and economic dominance of the European empires. In this way, the seeds of the current north–south debate were sown.

Asia had long been a source of many highly valued commodities, such as silk and cotton fabrics, rugs, jewellery, porcelains, sugar, and spices (the remarkable rise of Asia–Pacific trade in the late 1900s is not as surprising when we take this historical context into consideration). But the new sea route to the east and the discovery of America in the late 1400s brought a vast increase in trade not only in luxury items but also in bulk commodities like rice, sugar, and tea. Older commercial activities were transformed by the widening of markets. Spain increasingly drew cereals from Sicily, the Netherlands drew food from Poland, and the French wine districts ate food from northern France. Russia and the Baltic States entered the commercial scene with the growth of shipping and related industries. Trade had become a way of life for many people by the middle of the past millennium.

Arguably, the opening of the Atlantic in the sixteenth century was the real beginning of a global economy. In this period, the economic dominance of the Mediterranean and the Middle East receded, as western and northern Europe became the new centres of economic activity with trade links to the Americas, Africa, and Asia. The Portuguese and Spanish were the first to profit, and they retained a near monopoly through most of the sixteenth century, but their eventual commercial and military decline made room for the British, French, and Dutch empires. However, this economic activity had a dark side. First, the slave trade was one of the largest activities in the world economy. The arrival of European traders in Africa greatly increased the traditional sub-Saharan and Arab slave trades; between 1500 and 1850 White traders forced almost 10 million Africans to the Americas, most of them to the newly opened plantations of the Caribbean, Brazil, and the United States. Second, the colonial powers were adamant about protecting their trade routes and markets. For example, the famous Opium War (1839–42) was caused primarily by British traders, who insisted on trading opium to addicts of the drug in China despite official Chinese protestations. In 1839 opium in British warehouses was destroyed, and in retaliation the British sent warships and troops to attack China's coastal cities (such as Hangchow, Hong Kong, and Canton). Eventually, the victorious British received a $20 million indemnity and temporary colonial possession of Hong Kong, and they opened ports to the opium trade. The Opium War also weakened Imperial China, leaving it vulnerable to demands for treaty ports and trading concessions by Russia, Japan, France, and Germany. Hong Kong was finally returned to Chinese rule at the end of June 1997.

Another great expansion of international trade took place when systems of delivery—ships and trains—acquired new capabilities in the nineteenth century. World trade grew threefold between 1870 and 1913, before being curtailed by World War I. Most trade at that time took place between imperial powers such as Great Britain and France (and, toward the end of this period, the United States and Germany) and their colonies; the latter would export primary products such as natural resources, and the parent country would export finished products (this pattern of trade persists today in many sectors). Opening up borders to trade was not an easy development, since governments were highly protective of domestic markets and could use the colonies to attain raw materials instead of trade with each other. The defeat of the Corn Laws, which had imposed high tariffs on imports of grain into England, was one of the first major victories for free trade. The Anti–Corn Law League, established in 1838, was composed mostly of industrialists and wage earners, all of whom sought to establish lower corn prices with freer trade. The British land-owning aristocracy, however, wanted to protect English agriculture from the onslaught of cheaper, continental products. Pressure from the League and a famine in Ireland ultimately led to the Corn Law's repeal in 1846. Great Britain, by that time the most powerful economic actor, would become dependent on imports for food and was thus committed to an interdependent global economic system.

However, it was not just the movement of goods that was shaping the emerging global economy. Between 1845 and 1914 some 41 million people migrated to the Americas, especially the United States, from Europe. Others went to Australia and South Africa (see Chapter 11). This migration and the stagnation of industrialized European economies led to the development of the export of capital. British, Dutch, French, Belgian, Swiss, and eventually German investors tried to increase their incomes by buying the stocks of foreign business enterprises and the bonds of foreign businesses and governments. They organized companies of their own to operate in foreign states; and banks began granting loans to each other across the Atlantic. As early as the 1840s, half the annual increase of wealth in Great Britain was going into foreign investments. By 1914 the British had U.S.$20 billion in foreign investments, the French about U.S.$8.7 billion, and the Germans about U.S.$6 billion (these were huge sums of money at the time). The sums went into the Americas, the less affluent regions of Europe, and then after 1890 to Asia and Africa. However, in World War I the British lost about a quarter of their foreign investments, the French about a third, and the Germans lost everything.

Investment, trade, and monetary policy in the eighteenth, nineteenth, and twentieth centuries were largely influenced by capitalist principles. Capitalism involves the ownership of means of production and the employment of labourers to produce goods that are then sold on domestic and international markets. As an economic system, capitalism is prone to cycles of boom and depression, the most notable example of the latter being the long depression that set in about 1873 and lasted to about 1893. The growth of capitalism depended partly on the technological changes that ushered in the Industrial Revolution, but in the strict economic sense it was contingent also on a willingness to grant credit and gamble with it. Sometimes this gamble works, in the sense that profits are realized and loans are paid back; other times it does not, and the willingness to loan and gamble recedes. During times of recession, governments began to take a more active role in the economy. Previously, governments had adopted a hands-off or *laissez-faire* approach to their economies, except in the case of tariffs. Governments began taking measures to combat the essential insecurity of private capitalism, adopting additional protective tariffs and social insurance and welfare legislation, and allowing trade unionism to grow in some areas. After 1880, the old orthodoxy of nineteenth-century unregulated, laissez-faire capitalism diminished in an era of interventionist governments.

Investment and trade were both facilitated by the near-universal adoption of the gold standard. England had adopted the gold standard in 1816, when the pound sterling was legally defined as the equivalent of 113 grains of fine gold. This standard led many investors to keep money in London in the form of sterling on deposit, and this money, along with the military defeat of Napoleon, gave rise to London's reputation as the centre of the world economy. Western Europe and the United States (the latter was growing into a major economic power, though the American Civil War would forestall this) adopted an exclusively gold standard in the 1830s; a person holding any *civilized* money (pounds, francs, dollars, marks, etc.) could turn it into gold at will, and a person holding gold could turn it into money. Thus citizens from states with different currencies could trade with confidence that the money changing hands could be transformed. Until 1914 exchange rates between the currencies remained very stable, though the gold standard was hard on countries with little gold, and it produced a gradual fall in prices, especially between 1870 and 1900, because (until the gold discoveries in South Africa, Australia, and Alaska in the 1890s) the world's production of gold lagged behind the expanding production of industrial and agricultural goods.

In the 15 years before World War I, world trade experienced a huge increase. German exports grew more rapidly than British exports at this time, and some historians feel this severe economic competition was one of the primary factors leading to the "war to end all wars" itself. The war would help usher in another economic system, put in place by Lenin's Bolsheviks after the Russia Revolution in 1917 (see Chapter 2). This rejection of capitalism by Russia produced a wave of fear that other states in Europe or North America might experience a similar revolution. The new Soviet state would pronounce itself owner of all the means of production and, after World War II, would participate in an alternative trade system involving itself and other states based on the socialist economic model.

After World War I, production was at an all-time high, due especially to the mass production of the automobile. However, much of the postwar boom was based on credit and stock market speculation. The Great Depression began as a stock market crisis in New York in October 1929. The crisis was related to speculation; stockbrokers (and many ordinary citizens as well) had purchased large amounts of stock on credit, pushing up stock prices. When prices began to fall, owners of stock had to sell off enough stock to pay back the money they had borrowed, and this snowballed into a huge sell-off: between 1929 and 1932 the average value of 50 industrial stocks traded on the New York Stock Exchange dropped from $252 to $61, and 5000 American banks shut down.[25]

Americans stopped exporting the capital other states were becoming dependent on, and as Americans stopped buying foreign goods, world trade decreased. The failure of a leading European bank in Vienna in 1931 sent shock waves across Europe. Massive unemployment was experienced across the globe and states adopted policies designed to protect themselves. The gold reserve in Britain that had supported the pound sterling declined, and investors converted their pounds into other currencies they felt would be safer. By 1931 Britain had devalued the pound and gone off the gold standard, and other countries soon followed suit. Governments manipulated their currencies to keep up exports (i.e., they devalued it, making it cheaper to buy their goods).[26] States turned to strict **bilateral** trade instead of the embryonic multilateral system that had been flourishing and in some cases resorted to actual barter (exchange of goods without money involved). Tariffs were raised, first by the United States in the famous Smoot–Hawley tariff of 1930 (see below) and then by others countries, which had the effect of shutting down trade in some products (such as agricultural products) almost entirely, while quotas were introduced for others. An International Monetary and Economic Conference met in London in 1933, but participants were unable to free trade from these restrictions.

In Germany, Adolf Hitler rode to power on a wave of post-Versailles discontent and tremendous inflation rates. The German economy, in shambles after World War I, did begin to recover as a result of the Dawes Plan. In 1924 an American banker, Charles G. Dawes, proposed a plan under which war reparations would be lowered and bank loans would be extended to Germany to enable it to pay the reduced reparations. Money flowed into Germany from the United States, financing economic recovery and the payment of reparations to Great Britain and France. These reparations payments were in turn used to pay off the debt these countries owed to the United States. The importance of the U.S. economy in this arrangement was highlighted in 1929, when the stock market crash stopped the flow of U.S. dollars to Europe. When the Germans could no longer pay their reparations, the British and French could no longer pay their war debts to the United States. To pay these debts, the British and French governments sought to increase their exports to the United States to obtain currency to pay their debts. However, protectionist sentiment (to protect domestic industry) in the United States was high, and the Smoot–Hawley tariff of 1930 raised tariffs against foreign imports to the United States to their highest levels ever. The result was that British and French exports were shut out of the United States. The Smoot–Hawley tariff hampered international trade, blocked collection of war debts, and initiated a chain reaction of protectionism around the world, including the 1932 Ottawa Agreements, which established favourable tariff agreements for the Commonwealth. The tariff also exported the depression to Europe, which, without U.S. dollars, could not finance its debt burdens. The result was economic disaster; businesses closed and unemployment soared. Just as it did in Germany, economic nationalism contributed to political nationalism and the rise of extremist movements, which capitalized on the frustration and resentment over high unemployment and falling living standards. Democratic governments fell in Japan, Austria, and Eastern Europe (with the exception of Czechoslovakia).

The rise of fascism in Spain, Germany, and Italy, and Japanese expansionism in Asia would eventually lead to World War II, but many analysts argue that the effect of the

Great Depression and the fall of the multilateral trading system as it had evolved to that point were partly responsible as well. During the war economic production became war oriented. According to Alvin and Heidi Toffler, the United States manufactured nearly six million rifles and machine guns, more than 300 000 planes, 100 000 tanks and armoured vehicles, 71 000 naval vessels, and 41 billion rounds of ammunition.[27] The United States had built up considerable gold reserves during the 1930s and benefited further from trade with the Allies. As a result, the most powerful military power emerged as the most powerful economic power after the war. Theorists of imperialism and neomercantilists alike would argue that this legacy of economic dependence on military production is still a major factor in contemporary international political economy.

BRETTON WOODS AND THE DEVELOPMENT OF THE LIBERAL INTERNATIONAL ECONOMIC ORDER

Recall that the instability that characterized the interwar period is often attributed to U.S. reluctance to join the League of Nations and provide a leadership role in the world economy. The United States refused to accept the mantle of leadership and fill the void left by the diminishment of the British Empire, which had previously wielded great power within the world economy through the common use of the pound sterling.[28] After the tumult of World War II, the beliefs of British economist John Maynard Keynes (see Profile 4.5) came to dominate the economic discourse and policies of the industrialized

---

PROFILE 4.5   # John Maynard Keynes (1883–1946)

Keynes was one of the most influential economists of the twentieth century. In his first important book, *The Economic Consequences of the Peace* (London: Macmillan, 1919), Keynes questioned the wisdom of the postwar settlement that imposed heavy reparations on Germany. In his classic text *The General Theory of Employment, Interest and Money* (1938), he challenged the conventional economics of the time. The prevailing wisdom—one that has resurfaced in many states in the past few decades—was that the state, or more precisely governments, should not intervene in the economy. Keynes argued that this philosophy was harmful during downswings in the economy and that the state *should* intervene in the economy, encourage low interest rates, and adopt a fiscal policy that injects money into the economy through increased public expenditure or lower taxes. Although his call for government spending placed him on the left of the political spectrum, Keynes could hardly be considered a socialist, for he believed that the market could best determine the production of goods.

Keynes was an economic adviser to the British government and drafted proposals for the establishment of an International Clearing Union after World War II. In this system, nations with trade deficits would be able to maintain participation in the global economy by drawing on the Union, which other states would help fund. The International Monetary Fund and the International Bank for Reconstruction and Development perform a function similar to that of Keynes's proposed Union. Although the Keynesian outlook fell into serious disrepute among industrial countries when it was discovered that deficit spending led to insurmountable levels of public debt, the idea that it is the government's responsibility to create jobs to keep an economy alive survives. A famous Keynesian economist, who was educated at the University of Guelph, is John Kenneth Galbraith.

nation-states. In July 1944, even before the end of World War II, representatives of 44 countries met at Bretton Woods, New Hampshire, to construct a stable postwar international economic system. This system came to be called the **Bretton Woods system**, and until 1971 the plans developed at Bretton Woods were to form the foundation of what would be called the liberal international economic order (LIEO), the international economic system of the noncommunist world.

The first priority of the Bretton Woods conference was to establish an international financial structure based on fixed currency rates. Floating exchange rates were blamed for the instability and ultimate collapse of the international economy in the interwar period. At Bretton Woods, all countries agreed to fix (or *peg*) their currencies to the U.S. dollar at a specified rate of exchange and to maintain that rate. The U.S. dollar, in turn, was fixed (or pegged) to gold, at an exchange rate of U.S.$35 an ounce. The United States pledged that it would exchange dollars for gold at any time. As a result, all countries knew the value of their currency in U.S. dollars (and ultimately in gold). They knew this value would not fluctuate unpredictably, because states could borrow from the International Monetary Fund (see below) to prevent a weakening of their currency and because any change in exchange rates required international negotiations. As a result, the international monetary system would be predictable and stable. The U.S. dollar became the central unit of account in the international system, used by states to maintain the value of their currency (by using dollars to sell or buy their own currency internationally), to purchase products needed for postwar reconstruction, and to store financial reserves.

The Bretton Woods negotiations also established two institutions to help manage the system and perform central banking functions. The International Monetary Fund (IMF) was created to facilitate trade. The IMF had to approve changes in the fixed exchange rate system and possessed a credit fund of U.S.$8.8 billion to lend to countries that were experiencing downward pressure on the value of their currencies. The **International Bank for Reconstruction and Development (IBRD)**, also known as the World Bank, was created to assist war-torn countries in rebuilding their economies by providing short-term financing (see Profile 4.6). Later, both the IMF and the World Bank became prominent lenders to developing countries, a role they still perform today, although not without criticism. Together, the IMF and the IBRD are known as the "twin institutions" of the Bretton Woods system.

After World War II it became clear that the Americans wanted to provide the leadership that was lacking in the interwar period. Within the field of IPE, some scholars mix realist with liberal assumptions to suggest that an effective global economy needs a strong leader for it to function; this is the concept of hegemonic stability introduced in Chapter 2. The leader provides financial stability and military security. Although it was clear soon after the war that the Soviet Union, with its commitment to a noncapitalist path, would have none of this, it was also clear that all the other states with large economies, most of which had emerged from the war with a great deal of reconstruction necessary, were willing to accept American leadership. The United States provided much of the funding for the creation of the United Nations, the IMF, and IBRD and came to the aid of the Bretton Woods system when it was threatened in 1947.

In 1947, the problem was a dollar shortage. Quite literally, too few U.S. dollars were circulating in the international system. As discussed above, dollars were in demand for a number of crucial functions, but if enough dollars were not available, what then? More dollars had to be disbursed into the international system if Bretton Woods was to sur-

The IBRD (the World Bank)

The IBRD was established at the Bretton Woods Conference in 1944 and is located in Washington, D.C. After the postwar reconstruction of Europe, the Bank began to focus on southern development. It has supported more than 6000 projects in 140 countries, offering over U.S.$300 billion in financing. The Bank operates on a weighted voting system, meaning that the more a state contributes, the more say it has in what the Bank does and does not do. Obviously, then, Bank decisions are dominated by the United States, Japan, Germany, and other wealthy states. In 1957 the Bank established the International Finance Corporation (IFC) to assist poorer states in obtaining finance from private lenders, and in 1960 the International Development Association (IDA) was established. The IDA made 50-year interest-free loans to poorer states. In the 1970s the activities of the Bank accelerated under a campaign to eliminate poverty, and aid was linked to economic and social reforms. Critics charge that the Bank has contributed to the perpetuation of poverty by favouring large-scale infrastructure projects that benefit the wealthy and cause environmental damage. The Bank has attempted to reform its previous approaches, but a public campaign (entitled "Fifty Years Is Enough!") waged in the mid-1990s called for its dissolution. Today, the Bank is active in assisting the former Communist states and lending to the Middle East to support the peace process.

vive. The answer was a massive program of aid to foreign countries so that they would be able to buy the U.S. goods they required for reconstruction. The most famous of these programs was the Marshall Plan under which 16 Western European countries received more than U.S.$17 billion between 1948 and 1952. The United States also tolerated trade protectionism in Europe and Japan to revive the European and Japanese economies (and thus create more consumers for U.S. products in the future). As a result of the Marshall Plan and trade protectionism abroad, the United States experienced massive balance of payments deficits; that is, more money was flowing out of the country than was coming in. Although this deficit was not a concern in the late 1940s and early 1950s, by the late 1950s the balance of payments deficit was becoming a problem, and by 1960 the Bretton Woods system was again in trouble.

THE DECLINE AND FALL OF THE BRETTON WOODS SYSTEM

By 1960, the problems facing the Bretton Woods system were in many ways different from the ones it faced in 1947. The persistent balance of payments deficits experienced by the United States meant that more and more dollars were in circulation in the international system. The deficits, caused by U.S. military activities around the world, military and economic aid, and private investment in foreign countries, were increasingly out of control. The dollar shortage had turned into the dollar glut. In 1960, for the first time, more dollars were in circulation than there was gold in U.S. reserves. This imbalance meant that the United States would not be able to exchange gold for dollars at $35 an ounce. Not surprisingly, many began to question the strength of the U.S. dollar as a reserve currency and feared that it would be devalued. As a result, many holders of U.S. dollars began to convert their dollars into gold, creating the first *dollar crisis*.

Other developments also threatened the position of the dollar. The economies of Western Europe and Japan had recovered from the war, and the need for U.S. dollars and

U.S. products lessened. The IMF was moving away from reliance on the U.S. dollar toward special drawing rights (SDRs), a basket of major currencies that could be drawn on by countries in search of financing. (Because SDRs were a blend of currencies, they were seen as more stable than gold or U.S. dollars.) The expenditures of the Vietnam War and President Lyndon Johnson's War on Poverty had also eroded the competitiveness of the U.S. economy. And finally, in 1971, the United States experienced a balance of trade deficit (with more goods imported into the country than were exported) for the first time. This deficit threatened jobs at home and increased international tensions as the U.S. government blamed Western Europe and Japan for maintaining undervalued currencies (currency values that did not reflect the true cost of goods and services in those countries). This undervaluing in turn made foreign products more attractive for consumers in the United States, which contributed to the U.S. balance of trade deficit.

On Sunday, 15 August 1971, the Nixon Administration responded to the eroding position of the U.S. economy by announcing that it would no longer exchange dollars for gold. A tariff was placed on goods entering the United States, and the U.S. dollar was devalued to increase exports.[29] For all intents and purposes, the Bretton Woods system had collapsed. This collapse had two general consequences. First, the international monetary system was transformed. With the collapse of the fixed exchange rate system, the value of currencies now floated freely in international financial markets. The value of a currency was now based on perceptions of the strength and health of a state's economy. Market forces, rather than government intervention, determined a currency's value. The financial predictability of Bretton Woods vanished, replaced with the volatile financial markets we are familiar with today (see Profile 4.7). Second, it was apparent by 1971 that the United States could no longer unilaterally regulate the international monetary system (or the global economic system for that matter). Economic power had become more dispersed in the international system, and although the United States was still by far the world's largest economy, it was no longer capable of exerting leadership unilaterally, and other countries were no longer willing to unconditionally accept that leadership. The management of the international economy began to shift from a hegemonic management system to an increasingly multilateral management system.

The global economy faced another challenge in the wake of the collapse of Bretton Woods: the formation of the **Organization of Petroleum Exporting Countries (OPEC)**. In 1960, four Middle Eastern states and Venezuela had formed OPEC, initially to fight proposed oil price cuts by oil companies and later to pressure transnational oil corporations to give host-country governments a greater share of the immense profits being made. By the early 1970s OPEC was winning significant concessions and had raised the price of oil. It is important to keep in mind that oil has been the predominant fuel of industrialization since the latter half of the twentieth century, especially in the United States, Western Europe, and Japan.[30] OPEC is a **cartel**, a producer's organization that seeks to raise the price of a good by reducing its supply through controls on production. In 1973, in reaction to U.S. support for Israel in the 1973 Arab–Israeli War, OPEC countries initiated a cutback in oil production and imposed an oil embargo against the United States. World oil prices rose dramatically, from $2.50 a barrel in 1973 to $11.65 in 1974 (a barrel is a standard measure for petroleum, equivalent to 42 gallons or 158.86 litres). The *oil shock* created havoc in the West and particularly in the United States, the world's leading importer of oil. World recession followed, as countries had to spend more for energy. Dollars also flowed to OPEC countries in such huge amounts ($70 billion in 1974 alone) that the supply of dollars in the international system depressed the value of the dollar still further. Some equilibrium was achieved when oil prices began to decline in the late 1970s due to a

Money and Floating Exchange Rates

Money performs several different functions in the international economy. Currencies must be accepted and recognized so that actors possessing currency can use it to purchase goods and services from other actors. Money serves as a store of value, and money must be a standard of deferred payment so that actors will be willing to lend money knowing that the money will still have purchasing power when the loan is repaid. This belief is important because the value of money can erode through inflation. Inflation occurs when the supply of money exceeds the value of goods and services produced in an economy. As a currency becomes inflated, it loses purchasing power and becomes a poor store of value and less acceptable as an exchange for the payment of debts. As a result, governments around the world try to keep inflation as low as possible.

Changes in currency exchange rates occur when international evaluations of a country's economy and its ability to maintain the value of its money change due to political or economic events or trends. If a country has a healthy and growing economy, its currency will rise relative to other currencies (one unit of the currency will buy more of another currency) because it becomes more desirable as a store of value or a medium of exchange. If, however, a country's economy is performing poorly, its currency will fall relative to other currencies (one unit of the currency will buy less of another currency) because it is less desirable as a store of value or a medium of exchange. Of course, since all currencies are floating relative to each other (see Profile 4.8), the exchange rates between them are dependent on the relative performance of their economies. Who makes these international evaluations of the performance of state economies? International organizations, governments, banks and financial institutions

(such as investment houses), corporations, and individuals all contribute to the general appraisal of a state's economy (although in practice certain institutions play a greater role than others). A lot of activity in international financial markets is based on currency speculation. Currency speculation is an effort to make money by buying it and selling it at a profit. In essence, speculators gamble (based on economic and political indicators) that the value of a currency in the future will be more than it is today. So they will buy the currency today, store it, and sell it when the value of the currency is higher (thus making a profit).

As a result, the capacity of a state government to influence the value of its own currency is limited, because the value of the currency is based on what others think of the state's economy. However, governments will try to act in support of their currencies, because the value of a currency (and especially its stability relative to other currencies) is extremely important for exporters and importers of goods and services, since they must purchase or sell their goods and services across state borders in accordance with current exchange rates. Governments will therefore try to follow responsible fiscal policies so as not to damage the value of their currency. Governments intervene by buying or selling their own currency in the international system, thereby increasing or decreasing the value of the currency by affecting the international demand for it. One of the great challenges of the post–Bretton Woods system was adjusting to the fact that the value of currencies could fluctuate quite dramatically and that this fluctuation was due to forces largely out of state control. Today, changes (even small changes) in the value of currencies are important knowledge, whether you are planning a holiday or managing a government's financial reserves.

fall in demand through conservation efforts, reduced consumption, the discovery of new deposits elsewhere, and a shift to alternative sources of energy. However, another oil shock followed after the Iranian revolution in 1979, as world prices of oil shot up to $50 a barrel. Global recession once again followed, although, again, conservation measures and the

Canada and Floating Exchange Rates

Like most other currencies, financial markets largely determine the value of the Canadian dollar. Currency traders, buyers, speculators, banks, and foreign governments evaluate the attractiveness of the Canadian dollar on the basis of the health of the Canadian economy, the economic policies of Canadian governments, and political developments in Canada. If the Canadian economy shows disappointing trends (such as lower growth), the Canadian dollar is less attractive to foreign currency holders and the value of the Canadian currency will decline. Similarly, if the Canadian government follows economic policies that are viewed as fiscally irresponsible (such as increased budget deficits), the value of the Canadian dollar will decline. Political developments may also cause the value of the Canadian dollar to fluctuate. For example, in the 1997 federal elections in Canada, early returns indicated a possible minority government for the Liberal Party. A minority government may have meant instability in Canada's political scene, and the value of the Canadian dollar dropped as speculators, banks, and governments found the Canadian dollar less attractive. As the election results showed a slim Liberal majority government, the dollar rebounded somewhat on international markets. Canada, like most countries, is faced with two dilemmas in this market-oriented monetary environment. Canadian governments must make economic policy with an eye on the possible reaction of international financial markets, and this constrains the government's ability to make decisions based on domestic needs. The Canadian government must also decide when to intervene to prop up the dollar by buying Canadian dollars on international markets (thus creating a demand for Canadian dollars, which increases the value of the currency). Doing this, of course, costs money. Because Canada is a major exporter and importer, currency fluctuations are of tremendous importance to the Canadian economy.

exploitation of new sources of oil eventually reduced pressure on world oil prices. However, to this day many of the world's leading industrial economies (especially those in Europe and Asia) are heavily reliant on Middle Eastern oil. In fact, many would argue that the war in the Persian Gulf in 1991 was related directly to the strategic importance of oil. Oil is also a key factor in the politics of export-dependent states such as Nigeria. (It can also be argued that the sudden influx of *petrodollars* to Western banks encouraged the latter to make hazardous loans to southern state governments, bringing on the Third World debt crisis.)

Despite the economic dislocation and hardships (as well as the political friction) created by the immense changes to the international economic system, states in the developed world began to rely more and more on multilateral instruments to manage the global economy. The world was effectively divided into two trading blocs (using that term loosely), the capitalist Western camp and the socialist Eastern camp. Moscow formed **COMECON**, the **Council for Mutual Economic Assistance** (which included the Eastern European states) in 1949. A nonaligned movement also existed, consisting of states that would trade with either side, led by India, Indonesia, Egypt, and other postcolonial states. Despite this political division, not only did trade increase in the absolute sense, reflecting increases in production in several key states such as the United States, Germany, and Japan, but the industrialized capitalist states institutionalized negotiations aimed at enhancing economic production and decreasing the interference of governments that set tariffs and nontariff barriers. The two most prominent global arrangements were the General Agreement on Tariffs and Trade (GATT) and the **Group of Seven (G-7)** (recently expanded to the G-8 to include Russia as a political member).

The GATT was a treaty binding its members to certain rules concerning international commerce. These rules included the principles of nondiscrimination (all GATT members were to be treated equally by all other GATT members), reciprocity (all countries had to make concessions to make the opening of markets universal), and national treatment (foreign products had to be treated the same way as domestic products). Only 23 countries attended the first GATT conferences in 1947. Originally, the authors of the Bretton Woods system had desired the establishment of a powerful International Trade Organization (ITO). However, the U.S. Congress objected to an exception for imperial trading systems. The GATT system proceeded without the ITO, focusing on a series of trade negotiations (see Profile 4.9). The aim of GATT was to reduce barriers to trade and financial flows. Canada has been an avid supporter of the GATT regime.[31]

PROFILE 4.9 **Multilateral Negotiations under the GATT and Number of Participants**

1. Geneva, 1947: 23 states
2. Annency (France), 1949: 13 states
3. Torquay (Britain), 1950–51: 38 states
4. Geneva, 1955–56: 26 states
5. Dillon Round, 1960–61: 26 states
6. Kennedy Round, 1964–67: 62 states
7. Tokyo Round, 1973–79: 99 states
8. Uruguay Round, 1986–93: 107 states

Note: Rounds 4 to 8 all took place in Geneva.

Though the GATT succeeded in reducing tariffs and facilitating increased levels of world trade, the 1970s saw a rise in protectionism. The most recent round of negotiations (the eighth) may have been the most difficult. The Uruguay Round began in 1986 and involved 107 countries (including the individual members of the European Union). Only the Soviet Union and China sat out the negotiations. On 15 April 1994, at Marrakesh in Morocco, the final result of these lengthy negotiations (some refer to the GATT as the "General Agreement to Talk and Talk") was released to the public. Under this new world trade agreement, 123 countries agreed on a set of rules that would reduce tariffs by approximately one-third. Since 1994, more states have signed the agreement, and the countries that are party to the Uruguay Round agreement account for 90 percent of world trade. The agreement also put into place a complicated series of regulations on intellectual property rights, promoting fair trade in agriculture and services, and promoting growth in developing countries. Finally, the agreement also established the World Trade Organization (WTO) and appointed Renato Ruggiero, from Italy, as the first director of the WTO. (We will explore the WTO further in Chapter 8.)

Since 1975, another (far more exclusive) forum has met to discuss and reach agreements on economic issues. The Group of Seven (G-7) countries are Canada, France, Germany, Great Britain, Italy, Japan, and the United States. Initially known as the Group of Five (G-5) before the admission of Canada and Italy in 1976, the G-7 is not an international organization. Rather, it is a forum for discussion and coordination on a wide range of political and economic issues. In short, the G-7 has a deliberative function (to create understanding and awareness), a directive function (summits establish agendas and priorities), and a decisional function (members reach joint agreements on

The big boys wave to the world. Prime Minister Jean Chrétien waves as he stands with G-8 leaders (left to right) Russian Prime Minister Sergei Stepashin, Japanese Prime Minister Keizo Obuchi, Chrétien, U.S. President Bill Clinton, German Chancellor Gerhard Schroeder, French President Jacques Chirac, British Prime Minister Tony Blair, Italian Prime Minister Massimo D'Alema, and EU President Jacques Santer during the official photo in Cologne, Germany, 19 June 1999. (CP Picture Archive/Tom Hanson)

programs, targets, and time-tables). Summits of the leaders of the G-7 countries are held on a yearly basis. In the early years of the G-5/G-7, the primary role of the forum was to coordinate the management of exchange rates and domestic interest rates. This role is significant because it signalled the inability of the United States to manage the global economic system on its own, and it committed the largest economies of the free world to cooperation on economic policy to attempt to manage the international economy. In addition, the early meetings marked the return of Japan to global prominence.

The G-7 summit in 1994 was held in Naples, where leaders agreed to revitalize international economic institutions and integrate the former Communist countries into the global economic system more rapidly. This summit was also notable for the fact that Russian President Boris Yeltsin was invited. Although Russia was not invited to become a full economic member of the forum, it has attended the G-7 summits every year since Naples (leading some to refer to the G-7 as the G-8 or simply the Eight). In 1995 the G-7 summit was held in Halifax, where leaders discussed the collapse of the Mexican peso and the progress achieved in creating new financial institutions. In recent years the G-7 summits have addressed a wide range of political issues, including the war in the former Yugoslavia and the environment, raising questions about whether the G-7 is becoming something akin to an elitist concert of powers. Membership in the G-7 has also become an issue. As a forum for the world's largest democratic market economies, the G-7 membership is rather anachronistic. If economic size were the sole measure of membership, for example, Canada would no longer be a member of the group. Canada's continued membership in the G-7 is a reflection of Canada's international diplomatic profile, its tradition of involvement in international economic and political issues, and the unwillingness of other G-7 countries to discuss the politically sensitive issue of membership criteria. In another relatively exclusive forum, the **Trilateral Commission**, economic experts from North America, Europe, and Japan meet to discuss future relations. The 29 states in the **Organisation for Economic Co-operation and Development (OECD)** carry out research and consultations on promoting free trade and economic efficiency and OECD countries produce two-thirds of the world's goods and services. The organization is often criticized as a rich countries' club, though Mexico and South Korea have both won admission.

As we have seen, the global economy has evolved considerably since the end of World War II, through a combination of long-term trends (such as economic growth, trade, and the decline of U.S. dominance, or hegemony, in the system) and short-term shocks (such as the collapse of Bretton Woods, the oil shocks, and the fall of the Soviet Union). In general, the politics of the global economy have evolved from a largely unilateral or hegemonic management of the system to a multilateral management effort. The global economy we live in today is the product of a conscious effort to create an open trading system at the end of World War II and of the subsequent political and economic events that shaped the twentieth century.

CONCLUSIONS

As the Cold War ended, the global economy was as complex as ever. A clear dividing line remained between rich and poor, largely in north–south terms. However, it was becoming quite apparent that the Soviet Union and the Eastern European states were in economic disarray. They had to be integrated into the world economy somehow, and they embarked on a program of privatization that, initially at least, caused a great deal of hardship. China was charting a new course toward greater privatization and was experiencing rapid economic growth based on cheap labour and increased exports. Other Asian countries were also continuing down the export-led development path with record growth, although the Asian financial crisis of 1997 (see Chapter 8) would slow this down. The United States had entered into **NAFTA** with Canada and Mexico, and the European Union was forging ahead with its problematic economic and political integration. Sub-Saharan Africa and Latin America were still mired in development dilemmas related to debt and democracy. The environmental problems that had resulted from years of global industrialization and population growth became topics of great concern as the world prepared for the United Nations Conference on Environment and Development, held in Rio de Janeiro, Brazil, in 1992.

Poverty and wealth, the two central themes of economic history, continue to coexist. So, too, do the central perspectives on international political economy we have outlined. In this chapter, we have examined the field of international political economy and emphasized the inherent links between economic and political systems on both a national and international scale. We have provided a necessarily sketchy outline of the recent evolution of trade and finance in the international economy and outlined two competing perspectives that attempt to explain these changes—economic nationalism and liberalism—as well as two of the more robust critical perspectives, one based on theories of imperialism and inequality between north and south, the other based on a feminist critique of the traditional approach to the study of international relations as a whole and the global economy in particular. In Chapter 8, we will look at the modern world economy and discuss some of the prevalent concerns facing those who study international political economics today. We turn now to an examination of what many analysts feel is the principal facilitator of both peace and economic progress on a global scale, the international institution.

Endnotes

1. Malcolm Waters, *Globalization* (London: Routledge, 1995), 66–67.
2. Liberalism, economic nationalism, and Marxism are widely accepted as representative of the basic schools in the subdiscipline of international political economy; perhaps the best known account of this is produced in Robert Gilpin's *The Political Economy of International Relations* (Princeton: Princeton University Press, 1987).
3. See, for example, P. Krugman and M. Obstfeld, *International Economics: Theory and Policy* (New York: HarperCollins, 1991); and J.D. Richardson, *Understanding International Economics: Theory and Practice* (Boston: Little, Brown and Company, 1980).
4. For standard texts, see S. Krasner, "Structural Causes and Regime Consequences: Regimes as Intervening Variables," in S. Krasner, ed., *International Regimes* (Ithaca, NY: Cornell University Press, 1983), 1–22; M. Zacher, "Toward a Theory of International Regimes," *Journal of International Affairs*

44(1) (1990), 139–58; and O. Young, "The Politics of International Regime Formation: Managing Natural Resources and the Environment," *International Organization* 43(3) (1989), 349–75.

5. Robert Gilpin, *The Political Economy of International Relations* (Princeton: Princeton University Press, 1987).

6. For what has fast become a classic text, see R. Rosecrance, *The Rise of the Trading State: Commerce and Conquest in the Modern World* (New York: Basic, 1986).

7. The U.S. trade deficit rose from $25 billion in 1980 to $160 billion in 1987; it fell to $91 billion in 1992 (*Economic Report of the President* (Washington, 1993)) but was at $114 billion in 1997 (*New York Times*, 20 February 1998, p. C1).

8. I. Kant, *Perpetual Peace* (1795; Indianapolis: Bobbs-Merrill, 1957); A. Smith, *An Inquiry into the Nature and Causes of the Wealth of Nations* (1776; New York: Modern Library, 1976). We should note that Robert Keohane and others insist that liberalism "does not purport to provide a complete account of international relations. On the contrary, most contemporary liberals seem to accept large portions of both marxist and realist explanations." From "International Liberalism Reconsidered," in J. Dunn, ed., *The Economic Limits of Politics* (Cambridge: Cambridge University Press, 1989), 165–94, 175.

9. B. Mazlish, ed., *The Wealth of Nations* (Indianapolis: Bobbs Merrill, 1961), book I, ch. 2, 15.

10. Mark Zacher and Richard Matthew, "Liberal International Theory: Common Threads, Divergent Strands," in C. Kegley, ed., *Controversies in International Relations Theory: Realism and the Neoliberal Challenge* (New York: St. Martin's, 1995), 107–50, 117.

11. Ibid., 117.

12. R. Keohane and J. Nye, eds., *Power and Interdependence: World Politics in Transition* (Boston: Little, Brown, 1977). A previous volume edited by the same authors was of equal importance: *Transnational Relations and World Politics* (Cambridge: Harvard University Press, 1972).

13. F.W. Mayer, "Managing Domestic Differences in International Negotiations: The Strategic Use of Internal Side Payments," *International Organization* 46 (1992), 793–818.

14. P. Wapner, "Politics beyond the State: Environmental Activism and World Civic Politics," *World Politics* 47 (1995), 311–40, 313.

15. Carlye Murphy, *Washington Post National Weekly Edition* (19 November to 25 November 1990, 18).

16. J. Hobson, *Imperialism: A Study* (1902; Ann Arbor: University of Michigan Press, 1965); R. Luxemburg, *The Accumulation of Capital* (1913; London: Routledge and Kegan Paul, 1971); V.I. Lenin, *Imperialism: The Highest Stage of Capitalism* (1917; New York: International Publishers, 1939). See also A. Brewer, *Marxist Theories of Imperialism: A Critical Survey* (London: Routledge and Kegan Paul, 1980).

17. Most famously, Frank's *Latin America: Underdevelopment or Revolution* (New York: Monthly Review, 1970). For an excellent review of dependency theory, see M. Blomstrom and B. Hettne, *Development Theory in Transition, The Dependency Debate and Beyond: Third World Responses* (London: Zed Books, 1984); and Peter Evans's classic, *Dependent Development: The Alliance of Multinational, State, and Local Capital in Brazil* (Princeton: Princeton University Press, 1979). See also Samir Amin, *Accumulation on a World Scale: A Critique of the Theory of Development*, Vols. 1 and 2. (New York: Monthly Review Press, 1974).

18. See Johan Galtung, *The European Community: A Superpower in the Making* (London: Allen and Unwin, 1973).

19. For a spirited discussion and defence of this broad yet emergent thinking, see especially James Der Derian, "Post-Theory: The Eternal Return of Ethics in International Relations," in M. Doyle and J. Ikenberry, eds., *New Thinking in International Relations Theory* (Boulder, CO: Westview, 1997), 54–76.

20. See, for example, N. McGlen and M. Sarkees, *Women in Foreign Policy: The Insiders* (New York: Routledge, 1993).

21. L. McDonald, "Women Theorists on Peace, War and Militarism," paper presented at the Meetings of the International Sociological Association, Amsterdam (May 1996), 11. See also G. Bussey and M. Tims, *Women's International League for Peace and Freedom 1915–1965* (London: Allen and Unwin, 1965).

22. See G. Sen and C. Grown, *Development, Crises and Alternative Visions: Third World Women's Perspectives* (New York: Monthly Review Press, 1986). On class and gender on an international scale, see M. Mies, *Patriarchy and Accumulation on a World Scale* (London: Zed Books, 1986).

23. J. Ann Tickner, "Hans Morgenthau's Principles of Political Realism: A Feminist Reformulation," *Millennium* 17(3) (1988), 429; see also C. Enloe, *Bananas, Beaches and Bases: Making Feminist Sense of International Relations* (London: Pandora, 1989); and S. Whitworth, *Feminism and International Relations* (London: Macmillan, 1994).

24. J. Appleby, L. Hunt, and M. Jacob, *Telling the Truth about History* (New York: Norton, 1994), 244.

25. On the causes and consequences of Black October 1929, see J.K. Galbraith, *The Great Crash: 1929* (1954; Boston: Houghton Mifflin, 1988).

26. As J. David Richardson writes, under these conditions a "vicious vortex of depreciation upon depreciation can develop. Its result is that very few countries succeed in overdepreciating because everyone is trying to. Therefore very few countries insulate themselves fully from the world recession. International exchange becomes chaotic, and nationalistic recrimination abounds." *Understanding International Economics*, 197.

27. A. Toffler and H. Toffler, *War and Anti-War: Survival at the Dawn of the 21st Century* (Boston: Little, Brown and Company, 1993), 40. See also N. Polmar and T. Allen, *World War II: America at War, 1941–1945* (New York: Random House, 1991).

28. C. Kindleberger, *The World in Depression 1929–39* (Berkeley: University of California Press, 1973).

29. See F. Block, *The Origins of International Economic Disorder* (Berkeley: University of California Press, 1977). This tariff increase especially angered Ottawa, since Canada and the United States had such a close trading relationship by that time.

30. As two authors have noted, "one of the great anomalies of nature is the immense concentration of huge, easily accessible, and cheap oil supplies in the Middle East and particularly in the Gulf region. Saudi Arabia alone is conservatively estimated to be endowed with over 25 per cent of the world's proven reserves. On the other hand, consumption is concentrated in the industrialized West and Japan." A.A. Kubursi and S. Mansur, "The Political Economy of Middle Eastern Oil," in R. Stubbs and G. Underhill, eds., *Political Economy and the Changing Global Order* (Toronto: McClelland and Stewart, 1994), 313–27, 324. See also D. Yergin, *The Prize: The Epic Quest for Oil, Money and Power* (New York: Simon and Schuster, 1991).

31. See Frank Stone, *Canada, the GATT and the International System* (Montreal: Institute for Research on Public Policy, 1984).

Suggested Readings

Amin, S. *Accumulation on a World Scale: A Critique of the Theory of Underdevelopment.* New York: Monthly Review Press, 1974.

Baran, P. *The Political Economy of Growth.* New York: Monthly Review Press, 1967.

Black, J.K. *Development in Theory and Practice: Bridging the Gap.* Boulder, CO: Westview, 1991.

Braudel, F. *Civilization and Capitalism: 15th–18th Century.* 3 vols. New York: Harper and Row, 1981, 1982, 1984.

Brawley, M. *Turning Points: Decisions Shaping the Evolution of the International Political Economy.* Peterborough, ON: Broadview, 1998.

Cox, R. *Production, Power, and World Order.* New York: Columbia University Press, 1987.

Doyle, M., and J. Ikenberry, eds. *New Thinking in International Relations Theory.* Boulder, CO: Westview, 1977.

Elsenhans, H. *Development and Underdevelopment: The History, Economics, and Politics of North-South Relations.* New Delhi: Sage, 1991.

Gill, S., and D. Law. *The Global Political Economy: Perspectives, Problems, and Policies.* Baltimore: Johns Hopkins University Press, 1988.

Grant, R., and K. Newland, eds. *Gender and International Relations.* Bloomington: Indiana University Press, 1991.

Johnson, H., eds. *The New Mercantilism.* Oxford: Oxford University Press, 1974.

Jones, R.J.B., and P. Willetts, eds. *Interdependence on Trial: Studies in the Theory and Reality of Contemporary Interdependence.* New York: St. Martin's, 1985.

Keenes, E. "The Myth of Multilateralism: Exception, Exemption, and Bilateralism in Canadian International Economic Relations." *International Journal* 50 (4) (1995), 755–78.

Kindleberger, C.P. *The World in Depression, 1929–1939.* Berkeley: University of California Press, 1973.

Knorr, K. *Power and Wealth: The Political Economy of International Power.* New York: Basic, 1973.

Polanyi, K. *The Great Transformation: The Political and Economic Origins of Our Time.* New York: Beacon Press, 1944.

Spero, J.E. *The Politics of International Economic Relations.* New York: St. Martin's, 1977.

Strange, S. "Protectionism and World Politics." *International Organization* 39 (Spring 1982), 233–59.

Strange, S., ed. *Paths to International Political Economy.* London: George Allen and Unwin, 1984.

Wilber, C., and K. Jameson, eds. *The Political Economy of Development and Underdevelopment.* 5th ed. New York: McGraw-Hill, 1992.

Suggested Websites

Resources for Economists on the Net
    <econwpa.wustl.edu/EconFAQ/EconFAQ.html>

Economics Internet Resources
    <www.wcsu.ctstateu.edu/socialsci/ecores.html>

International Monetary Fund
    <www.imf.org/external/index.htm>

WWW Virtual Library in Economics
    <www.hkkk.fi/EconVLib.html/>

Alta Plana: International Economics Gateway
    <www.altaplana.com/gate.html>

World Wide Web Virtual Library of International Development Cooperation
    <www.alcazar.com/wwwvl_idc/index.html>

International Institute for Sustainable Development

Devline

United Nations Development Programme

WWWomen

WomensNet
    <www.igc.org/igc/gateway/wnindex.html>

Organisation for Economic Co-operation and Development

CHAPTER 5

International Institutions and Law

*We the Peoples of the United Nations, determined to save suc-
ceeding generations from the scourge of war, which twice in our
lifetime has brought untold sorrow to mankind, and to reaffirm
faith in fundamental human rights, in the dignity and worth of the
human person, in the equal rights of men and women and of
nations large and small, and to establish conditions under which
justice and respect for the obligations arising from treaties and
other sources of international law can be maintained, and to promote social progress and better standards of life in larger
freedom.... Have Resolved to Combine Our Efforts to Accomplish
These Aims.*

— Preamble, *The Charter of the United Nations,* 1945

INTRODUCTION

The UN building in New York is the diplomatic centre of world politics. Here, one can witness a remarkable range of activity: the gathering of representatives from every recognized state on earth in the **General Assembly**; the fervent activity of specialized agencies and programs aimed at implementing the UN's goal of increasing the standard of living of all peoples; the power politics intrigues among the often divergent permanent five (P-5) members of the Security Council; and the expression of world opinion through the resolutions adopted by the General Assembly. Today, many high-school and university students participate in Model United Nations Conferences, held in places as diverse as Toronto and Cairo, which provide a highly educative experience. UN-related Websites are popular destinations on the Internet. It is still a defining moment of statehood to become a member of the General Assembly: since 1989, more than 30 new states have joined the UN, from Andorra to Uzbekistan. Every September, various heads of state or their foreign ministers make sure to find time to deliver a speech to the General Assembly in New York. The UN's significance is undeniable, though one can debate its overall effectiveness when it comes to realizing the promises of the UN Charter.

However, even a tentative understanding of the contemporary UN system necessitates a broader examination of the role of international organization in global politics today. For the UN, though one of the most developed and multifunctional international organizations, is but one example of a wide variety of institutions that have been created around the convergence of interests and ideas. Despite futuristic and probably impulsive predictions, the UN has not evolved into a world government, complete with standing armies, powers of jurisprudential enforcement, democratic legitimacy, or the ability to

A challenging occupation. United Nations Secretary-General Kofi Annan addresses members of the General Assembly during the start of the UN Millennium Summit at the UN headquarters in New York, 6 September 2000. (CP Picture Archive/Richard Drew)

redistribute the world's wealth. Nor has it disintegrated (as pessimists assumed was inevitable) like its predecessor, the League of Nations.

An *international organization* (IO) is what Plano and Olton term a "formal arrangement transcending national boundaries that provides for the establishment of institutional machinery to facilitate cooperation among members in security, economic, social or related fields."[1] Generally, two types of international organizations exist: intergovernmental organizations (IGOs) and nongovernmental organizations (NGOs). All IGOs share a number of characteristics. First, they comprise states and only states (although in some cases nonstate actors may be represented). Second, IGOs are created by treaties between states and, therefore, have a legal standing under international law. Third, they hold regular meetings attended by delegates from member states. Those delegates represent the policies and interests of their respective countries. Fourth, IGOs have permanent headquarters and an executive secretariat that runs the day-to-day activities of the organization. Finally, IGOs have permanent administrative employees who work for the organization and do not represent their governments; rather, they are international bureaucrats. Although these employees do not give up their citizenships, they serve the organization, not their respective states.

Different perspectives on global politics place the role and future of international organizations at different points along a spectrum ranging from powerlessness to autonomy. What is clear, however, is that these organizations have proliferated in number, especially in the twentieth century. In 1909, there were 37 IGOs. In 1960, there were 154, in 1987 there were 381, and there are presently more than 400 IGOs. As we will see, these organizations perform a wide variety of functions in the international system, and states have increasingly interacted and cooperated with each other through the mechanisms provided by IGOs. In addition, such institutions are vital to smaller states, such as Canada, that have many connections to the international diplomatic scene but a limited capacity to influence international events on their own.

It is important to recognize the wide scope of activities in which international organizations engage. The UN, for example, is involved in issue-areas as diverse as international and civil war, technology, gender relations, humanitarian assistance and disaster relief, literacy, pollution abatement, decolonization, human rights and international law, disarmament, important treaties such as the Non-Proliferation Treaty, and significant conferences such as the Population Summit in Cairo in the fall of 1994. The various specialized agencies and programs of the UN are rough indicators of the range of activity that converges in the political space of the UN system alone. This includes the International Research and Training Institute for the Advancement of Women, the United Nations Population Fund, the Office of the UN Disaster Relief Coordinator, the **International Civil Aviation Organization**, the World Intellectual Property Organization, all of the UN-mandated peacekeeping operations in effect around the globe, UNAIDS, and many others.

It would be improper to examine international organizations without reference to the context in which they operate. World politics has changed in many ways over the course of the UN's 55 years. Not only has the Cold War come and gone but new actors have become involved in world politics to the point that some argue that they actually have as much influence as states or government decision makers themselves. These new actors include perhaps most obviously the board members of huge multinational corporations but they also include members of nongovernmental organizations such as relief agencies and environmentalist groups. As well, we have seen the rise of a particular single actor, the **secretary-general**, from the preconceived role of an international bureaucrat to that of a globetrotting mediator, and an often controversial one at that (see Profile 5.1). With the post-bipolar international structure, we have a Security Council that has been rather receptive to American influence. While states such as Canada remain committed to the UN by contributing finances and personnel for peacekeeping operations, impatience is growing in many capital cities about the UN's inability to live up to some of its promises.

PROFILE 5.1 A Canadian at the Top of the UN Bureaucracy

A large responsibility. Louise Frechette, left, stands with UN Secretary-General Kofi Annan at a news conference at the UN, 12 January 1998. Frechette, Canada's Deputy Defence Minister, was named UN Deputy Secretary-General, fulfilling Annan's pledge to appoint a woman to the second-highest post in the world organization. (CP Picture Archive/Todd Plitt)

In early 1998 another Canadian, Louise Frechette, made headlines when she was appointed to the post of Deputy Secretary-General, a key Secretariat administrative post. Ms. Frechette, born in Montreal and a graduate of the Université de Montreal, has enjoyed a long career in diplomacy, joining the Canadian Department of Foreign Affairs and International Trade (at the time known as the Department of External Affairs) in 1971 and serving in a variety of diplomatic postings. These posts include Canada's Ambassador to Argentina and Uruguay, Assistant Deputy Minister for Latin America and the Caribbean, and Canada's Ambassador to the UN in New York (a post subsequently held by Robert Fowler). She has also served as Canada's Deputy Minister of National Defence before joining the UN Secretariat for her challenging position there. She is partially responsible for the conduct of the thousands of Secretariat employees.

Many Canadians, such as Yves Fortier, Stephen Lewis, Elizabeth Dowdeswell, Lester Pearson, Douglas Roche, and Maurice Strong, have played high-profile roles at the United Nations.

At the same time, the issue-areas that international organizations (IOs) deal with have multiplied as IOs have become increasingly concerned with developmental, industrial, environmental, and human rights issues. For example, the World Bank lends money for development (or, according to some critics, underdevelopment) in the southern hemisphere. The UN Environmental Programme (UNEP) helps coordinate various policies and the work of agencies aimed at environmental protection.

Several different kinds of IGOs exist. The UN is a *multipurpose, universal membership* organization. It serves many functions and can be joined by all states in the international system, providing the Security Council's permanent members and two-thirds of the General Assembly agree.[2] As of 2000 the United Nations had 188 member-states (up from only 51 when the UN was established in 1945) and the organization includes more than 30 major agencies and programs such as the International Labour Organization (ILO), the Food and Agriculture Organization (FAO), the UN Educational, Scientific and Cultural Organization (UNESCO), the International Maritime Organization (IMO), the **UN Conference on Trade and Development (UNCTAD),** and the UN Development Programme (UNDP), in addition to those mentioned earlier. Multipurpose, universal membership organizations may be contrasted with *regional* and *functional* organizations, which manage issues at a regional level or are designed for a specific purpose. In fact, most IGOs fall into the latter category. The most famous regional IGO is the European Union, which was known as the European Community (EC) before 1994; indeed, the EU has coordinated policies to such a degree that it is often called a *supranational* institution. Other multipurpose regional organizations include the Organization of American States (OAS), the Association of Southeast Asian Nations (ASEAN), and the **Arab League**. Single-purpose, or functional, regional organizations include the **Asian Development Bank**, the North Atlantic Treaty Organization (NATO), the Northwest Atlantic Fisheries Organization (NAFO), and the Organization of Petroleum Exporting Countries (OPEC). Lest we think only the UN has potential global membership, we should keep in mind the existence of open-membership organizations that have single functions, such as the various UN agencies[3] mentioned above, the International Organization for Migration (IOM), and the International Whaling Commission (IWC). Not all states have joined these organizations, but they could if they desired.

INTERNATIONAL ORGANIZATIONS AND REGIMES IN HISTORY

International organizations have been around for a long time in the form of religious or political institutions such as the powerful Roman Catholic Church. Indeed, the political administration of territories occupied by the Roman Empire and, much later, of the European Great Powers, could technically be labelled embryonic forms of IOs, since they involved political interaction and structure across frontiers. The Olympic Games, which organized peaceful competition among Greek city-states, were another early ancestor of the modern IO.[4] We could include in our examples of IOs arrangements among states to maintain power and order, such as the Concert of Europe (see Chapter 2). But when we speak of modern, formal IOs, such as the League of Nations (1919–46) and the current UN system (1945–present), we are discussing relatively recent phenomena.

IOs have been established for at least two main reasons. The first is practicality. Once the nation-state system was established and contacts between states expanded, it became clear that governments would have to maintain linkages that facilitated communication and coordination. As economic interdependence between states grew, it became necessary to establish new lines of communication and to reduce the probability of unexpected events. Trade relations are very dependent on order, the ability to expect payment for goods, fair treatment in foreign markets, freedom from piracy, and other factors. Second, IOs can be set up to serve a much broader purpose, such as the establishment or maintenance of world order and peace—this is the official mandate of the UN itself, which was established following the most destructive war in global history. However, we should stress how these rationales complement each other. Simply put, most functional organizations are based on some set of guiding principles (or ideals), but their creation is also necessitated by the practical circumstances surrounding them. For example, two early IOs still in operation today are the **International Telecommunications Union** (1865) and the **Universal Postal Union** (1874), both created for rather specific purposes (telegraphs and postage between nations).[5] Another early IO with a clear functional purpose was the **International Office of Weights and Measures**, established in 1875. Yet behind this functional cooperation was a belief, held by participating government and industry representatives, that telegrams, mail, and common measurement standards were good for business, if not for world peace itself. Liberal values on international political economy, as discussed in the previous chapter, surface again here: increased trade and communication is assumed by many to be the best path toward a peaceful international system.

IOs perform a wide variety of functions and roles in global politics:

- IOs serve as instruments of action. Increasingly, states act through IOs when pursuing joint objectives, in part because multilateral action through an IO has an increased moral weight or legitimacy. It also reflects the diffusion of power in the international system. Many military alliances are IOs; NATO is but one example.

- IOs function as forums for communication and conflict management. They offer a physical location that enables state delegations to meet and converse. In this way, IOs can facilitate cooperation, reduce misunderstandings, and promote dialogue. It is for this reason that the UN is sometimes referred to as the "world's safety valve." IOs can also offer conflict management services in the form of mediators, observers, and peacekeeping personnel.

- IOs serve regulatory functions in the international system. IOs can establish international standards and protocols to regulate everything from medicine and postal services to meteorology and civilian nuclear power. The extent of such regulation, however, remains limited; critical theorists suggest this regulation is another manner of controlling for deviance in the world capitalist system.

- IOs can also perform distributive functions. IOs can assist in the transfer and distribution of finances, goods, and services (from loans to oral rehydration pills) around the world. Critical theorists suggest that IOs protect wealth rather than distribute it.

We can see, then, that it is tempting to conclude that IOs are similar in their wide range of functions to domestic governments. Although early IOs performed many of these roles, the first major effort at international organization in the twentieth century was the League of Nations.

THE LEAGUE OF NATIONS

As discussed in Chapter 2, the League of Nations was created at the end of World War I. Two basic principles underlay the League's system of peace maintenance. First, members agreed to respect and preserve the territorial integrity and political independence of other states. Second, any war or threat of war was considered a matter of concern to the entire League. While the major emphasis of the League's *Covenant* was on maintaining international peace and stability, some recognition was also given to promoting economic and social cooperation. The Covenant did not provide any special machinery for overseeing these efforts, though a commitment was included for the establishment of one or more organizations to secure "fair and humane conditions of labor for men, women and children" (Article 23), and an autonomous International Labor Office (ILO) was established as part of the Treaty of Versailles (the ILO is still in existence as the International Labour Organization).

League organization centred around three major organs: the *Assembly*, to which all member-states belonged; the *Council*, to which a select few belonged; and the **Secretariat**. The League also established a *Permanent Court of International Justice* in 1921 to resolve disputes between members of the international community. From the outset the Permanent Court of International Justice's role was not considered of primary importance, mirroring the present International Court of Justice in the UN system, which retains some symbolic significance but is not a decisive factor in world affairs. The League Assembly and the Council were the two main deliberative organs of the League. In both organs, each state possessed one vote. The Assembly was primarily responsible for discussing important issues confronting either individual members of the League or the international community as a whole. The Council was primarily responsible for discussing the maintenance of peace.

Originally, the Council was to be composed of five permanent and four elected members. However, since the United States never joined (the U.S. Senate did not ratify the Treaty of Versailles, preferring its old isolationist foreign policy), Great Britain, Italy, Japan, and France were the original permanent members. Germany was given Permanent Council status on its admission to the League in 1926, and the Soviet Union was given the same status in 1934. Germany and Japan would eventually withdraw from the League, and the Soviet Union was expelled in 1939 for its invasion of Finland.

Despite the failure of the League to prevent war, it did enjoy some success. The operations of the Secretariat, which was charged with administrative duties, were widely regarded as a success. As Egon Ranshofen-Wertheimer has observed, "The League has shown that it is possible to establish an integrated body of international officials, loyal to the international agency and ready to discharge faithfully the international obligations incumbent upon them. It was not for lack of executive efficiency that the League system failed."[6] Beyond this administrative precedent, the League of Nations established or incorporated bureaus and committees dealing with disease, communications, traffic in arms, slavery, drugs, labour, women, and children. In 1925, it played an important role in bringing about the peaceful resolution of the Greek–Bulgarian border dispute. By 1921, 48 members had joined the League and by mid-1929 46 states had ratified the 1928 Kellogg–Briand Pact, in theory committing signatories to the peaceful settlement of disputes. The League considered 66 disputes and conflicts between 1920 and 1939, and in 35 of them, it was able to contribute to a peaceful resolution. The League was linked to several semi-autonomous organizations, such as the Economic and Financial Organization, the Health Organization, the Organizations for Communications and Transit, the High Commissioner for Refugees, and the Intergovernmental Committees on the Drug Traffic, Traffic in Women, the Protection of Children, and Intellectual Co-operation. Nevertheless, despite the Wilsonian idealism that surrounded the formation of the League, its "primary purpose, like that of the Concert of Europe, was to assist in the management of a multipolar balance of power, not to replace it with a universal system."[7]

Unfortunately, the League's ability to alleviate serious disputes was limited. As discussed in Chapter 2, when the Japanese launched a series of attacks against Manchuria in 1931, some Council members, including Great Britain and France, were unwilling to apply economic and military sanctions, which seriously undermined the League's ability and willingness to discourage members of the international community from resorting to arms to achieve their objectives. Another serious blow to the League's credibility came in 1935, when the League was unable to deter Italy's invasion of Ethiopia, although the economic sanctions imposed on Italy were the first on behalf of the international community, setting an important precedent for the use of economic sanctions by the UN.

Several reasons have been advanced for the League's demise. Some attribute it to the absence of the United States and, during shorter periods, to the absence of the Soviet Union and Germany. Others attribute its collapse to the inherent deficiencies of its Covenant, including Article 5, requiring unanimity on all major Assembly and Council decisions. Yet, in the critical tests, such as Japan and Ethiopia, it appeared to be the lack of political will among the members of the League, rather than the available machinery, that was primarily responsible for the League's failings. Finally, the aggressive foreign policies of the Axis powers made a successful League impossible. The League of Nations, reduced to insignificance by the cataclysm of World War II, was officially disbanded in April 1946.

THE UNITED NATIONS ORGANIZATION

It is common knowledge that plans for the UN had begun far before the end of World War II. The term "United Nations" originated in the *Washington Declaration* of 1942 in which 26 Allied countries pledged to fight Germany, Japan, and Italy; before that, the *Declaration of Principles* (the **Atlantic Charter**) expressed similar concerns. By October 1943, the governments of the United States, Great Britain, the Soviet Union, and China were prepared to issue a clear statement of their intention to establish a general international organization. That year further steps were taken to create several agencies that would eventually fall under the auspices of the UN or that would come to be closely associated with it. The **Food and Agriculture Organization (FAO)** was established during 1943, and, as a result of the Bretton Woods Conference in 1944, the IMF and the IBRD were created.

However, it was not until the Dumbarton Oaks conversations of 21 August 1944 that representatives from the United States, Great Britain, and the USSR (China participated in the second phase of negotiations) began to map out a blueprint for a new world body. At the famous **Yalta Conference** of February 1945, progress was made on filling several of the technical gaps that remained open at the Dumbarton Oaks Conference. Two important conferences took place before the eventual historic meeting in San Francisco where the Organization was officially born. In February and March 1945, representatives from the United States met in Mexico City to discuss their plans for a general international organization with their Latin American allies. In the same month, a committee of jurists representing virtually all the states that would attend the San Francisco conference met in Washington to discuss the creation of an **International Court of Justice (ICJ)**, which would replace the Permanent Court of Justice established under the League of Nations.

Canadian Delegation for the United Nations Conference in London, 18 January 1946. Vincent Massey, Canadian High Commissioner to the United Kingdom (left) stands next to Minister of Justice Louis St. Laurent, Secretary of State Paul Martin, and Associate Under-Secretary of State for External Affairs Hume Wrong. (CP Picture Archive)

Robert Fowler. From 1995 to 2000, Robert Fowler served as Canada's Ambassador to the United Nations. Fowler also served as head of the United Nations Angolan Sanctions Committee. Canada's current Ambassador to the United Nations is Paul Heinbecker. (CP Picture Archive)

Why was it important to begin discussing plans for the creation of the United Nations before the war was over? According to Inis Claude, two main reasons existed. First, as former U.S. Secretary of State Cordell Hull pointed out, if negotiations for an international organization had been left to the end of the war, it would have been much more difficult to reach a consensus on how to create the organization, since politicians would be too preoccupied with political, economic, and social issues at home. Second, it was extremely important to avoid creating an unnecessarily close relationship between the UN and the peace settlement. In other words, the founders of the UN did not want it to appear as if the rights and obligations contained in the UN Charter were being imposed on states as part of the peace settlement, which appeared to be the case with the League. Rather, the UN was to be created expressly for "all peace loving nations," which opened the possibility of accepting postwar Germany and Japan, to assemble in the hope of bringing about lasting peace.[8]

In addition, it is important not to dismiss the psychological and political factors motivating diplomats from countries such as Canada to support the creation of the UN. Simply put, Canadians believed that the United States had to be engaged in postwar affairs and saw the UN as a means to ensure this. A great deal of support existed among several governmental and nongovernmental bodies in the United States for the UN, although to gain support for the organization, several American leaders had to emphasize that the UN was an entirely new organization. Yet a close reading of the UN Charter indicates that although this document is approximately four times longer than the League's Covenant, it nonetheless contains many of the same features. Not unlike the Covenant, the Charter refers to the principal organs of the UN and the functions each should perform. Moreover, it clearly sets out the primary purpose of the UN, the maintenance of international peace and security, and how this commitment can be fulfilled. Furthermore, like the Covenant, the Charter emphasizes the inherent responsibility of all member states to deter aggression.

The climactic event in the long and arduous process of building a new international organization took place in San Francisco in the spring of 1945. Representatives from 50 nations deliberated for two months before they could agree on the final version of the UN Charter. On 26 June 1945, the Charter was signed, but it was not until 10 January 1946 that the first session of the General Assembly was held in London. Eventually, UN headquarters would be moved to its permanent home in New York City, a building now easily recognized around the world (see Profile 5.2). Although initial hopes for the organization were high (especially in Canada), the superpower confrontation effectively paralyzed the UN's capacity to mount collective security efforts. This incapacity did not mean that the UN was inactive. On the contrary, the UN performed many other crucial functions, most prominently in the process of decolonization, peacekeeping, and aid and development.

The UN has six principal organs (see Figure 5.1). At the heart of the UN is the *General Assembly* (GA), a forum in which all states can send representatives to sit in session, present opinions, and vote on resolutions, which need a two-thirds majority to pass (see Profile 5.3). It is true that GA resolutions cannot force other UN members to act; however, since those resolutions are considered by many to carry the weight of world opinion, they remain significant. The GA also makes key decisions regarding who gets to join the organization, what the Economic and Social Council (ECOSOC) does, and the spending powers of the organization. The GA has exclusive authority over the budget of the UN and elections to the Security Council and ECOSOC but needs a recommendation from the Security Council to take action on the appointment of the secretary-general, UN membership, and amendments to the Charter. The Assembly and Security Council are jointly responsible for electing the judges of the International Court of Justice (ICJ).[9]

PROFILE 5.2   Locating the United Nations

What if you had built a world organization on which a new global order was to be based but didn't know where to put it? Locating the UN was, in fact, one of the first problems that the organization faced. This question was obviously important since it was initially believed that a truly global organization could hardly be located anywhere closely affiliated with a major power, such as in Washington or Moscow, and it would be unsafe to locate it in an unstable state where political authority itself was contested, such as in China or soon-to-be independent India. In all probability, the idea of locating the UN in a southern state was never taken seriously; the first southern hemisphere location of a UN agency was in Nairobi, Kenya, and this was the headquarters of the UN Environmental Programme established in the early 1970s. Germany, Japan, and Italy were (of course) out of the question as hosts of the new UN, as was any truly neutral place, such as the inaccessible Antarctic. The Swiss, hosts to the League of Nations and the first temporary location of the General Assembly of the UN, were reluctant to assume the responsibility of long-term UN involvement; they refused to host a UN capable of making decisions related to the use of force, which is of course precisely what Chapter 7 of the UN Charter authorizes the Security Council to do. (Though Switzerland has not joined the UN because of its foreign policy of neutrality, it does claim to abide by UN Resolutions and hosts many UN-related agencies.) Europe was in a state of financial chaos and most of its capital cities were literally in physical ruin. The only country in a position of relative economic strength was the United States, and it was the American industrialist and philanthropist John Davison Rockefeller Jr. (1908–79) who supplied the initial capital to build the UN in New York City.

Figure 5.1 The United Nations System

THE UNITED NATIONS SYSTEM

International Court of Justice	General Assembly (GA)	Economic and Social Council (ECOSOC)	Security Council	Secretariat	Trusteeship Council

- Main and other sessional committees
- Standing committees and ad hoc bodies
- Other subsidiary organs and related bodies

▲ **UNRWA**
United Nations Relief and Works Agency for Palestine Refugees in the Near East

■ **IAEA**
International Atomic Energy Agency

▲ **INSTRAW**
International Research and Training Institute for the Advancement of Women

▲ **UNCHS**
United Nations Centre for Human Settlements (Habitat)

▲ **UNCTAD**
United Nations Conference on Trade and Development

▲ **UNDCP**
United Nations International Drug Control Program

▲ **UNDP**
United Nations Development Programme

▲ **UNEP**
United Nations Environment Program

▲ **UNFPA**
United Nations Population Fund

▲ **UNHCR**
Office of the United Nations High Commissioner for Refugees

▲ **UNICEF**
United Nations Children's Fund

▲ **UNIFEM**
United Nations Development Fund for Women

▲ **UNITAR**
United Nations Institute for Training and Research

▲ **UNU**
United Nations University

▲ **WFC**
World Food Council

▲ **WFP**
World Food Program

▲ **ITC**
International Trade Centre UNCTAD/GATT

- **FUNCTIONAL COMMISSIONS**
  - Commission for Social Development
  - Commission on Crime Prevention and Criminal Justice
  - Commission on Human Rights
  - Commission on Narcotic Drugs
  - Commission on Science and Technology for Development
  - Commission on Sustainable Development
  - Commission on the Status of Women
  - Population Commission
  - Statistical Commission

- **REGIONAL COMMISSIONS**
  - Economic Commission for Africa (ECA)
  - Economic Commission for Europe (ECE)
  - Economic Commission for Latin America and the Caribbean (ECIAC)
  - Economic and Social Commission for Asia and the Pacific (ESCAP)
  - Economic and Social Commission for Western Asia (ESCWA)

- **SESSIONAL AND STANDING COMMITTEES**

- **EXPERT, AD HOC AND RELATED BODIES**

■ **ILO**
International Labour Organization

■ **FAO**
Food and Agriculture Organization of the United Nations

■ **UNESCO**
United Nations Educational, Scientific and Cultural Organization

■ **WHO**
World Health Organization

World Bank Group

■ **IBRD**
International Bank for Reconstruction and Development (World Bank)

■ **IDA**
International Development Association

■ **IFC**
International Finance Corporation

■ **MIGA**
Multilateral Investment Guarantee Agency

■ **IMF**
International Monetary Fund

■ **ICAO**
International Civil Aviation Organization

■ **UPU**
Universal Postal Union

■ **ITU**
International Telecommunication Union

■ **WMO**
World Meteorological Organization

■ **IMO**
International Maritime Organization

■ **WIPO**
World Intellectual Property Organization

■ **IFAD**
International Fund for Agricultural Development

■ **UNIDO**
United Nations Industrial Development Organization

■ **GATT**
General Agreements on Tariffs and Trade

- Military Staff Committee
- Standing committees and ad hoc bodies
- Peacekeeping operations

▲ **UNTSO**
United Nations Truce Supervision Organization
June 1948 to date

▲ **UNMOGIP**
United Nations Military Observer Group in India and Pakistan
January 1949 to date

▲ **UNFICYP**
United Nations Peacekeeping Force in Cyprus
March 1964 to date

▲ **UNDOF**
United Nations Disengagement Observer Force
June 1974 to date

▲ **UNIFIL**
United Nations Interim Force in Lebanon
March 1978 to date

▲ **UNIKOM**
United Nations Iraq-Kuwait Observation Mission
April 1991 to date

▲ **UNIVEM II**
United Nations Angola Verification Mission II
June 1991 to date

▲ **ONUSAL**
United Nations Observer Mission in El Salvador
July 1991 to date

▲ **MINURSO**
United Nations Mission for Referendum in Western Sahara
September 1991 to date

▲ **UNPROFOR**
United Nations Protection Force
March 1992 to date

▲ **UNOSOM**
United Nations Operation in Somalia
April 1992 to date

▲ **ONUMOZ**
United Nations Operation in Mozambique
December 1992 to date

▲ **UNOMIG**
United Nations Observer Mission in Georgia
August 1993 to date

▲ **UNMIH**
United Nations Mission to Haiti
September 1993 to date

▲ **UNOMIL**
United Nations Observer Mission in Liberia
September 1993 to date

▲ **UNAMIR**
United Nations Assistance Mission in Rwanda
June 1993 to date

▲ United Nations programs and organs (representative list only)
■ Specialized agencies and other autonomous organizations within the system
• Other commissions, committees and ad hoc and related bodies

SOURCE: *CANADIAN REFERENCE GUIDE TO THE UNITED NATIONS* (OTTAWA: DEPT. OF FOREIGN AFFAIRS AND INTERNATIONAL TRADE). REPRINTED BY PERMISSION.

Member-States of the United Nations as of July 2000

MEMBER (DATE OF ADMISSION)

Afghanistan (19 Nov. 1946)

Albania (14 Dec. 1955)

Algeria (8 Oct. 1962)

Andorra (28 July 1993)

Angola (1 Dec. 1976)

Antigua and Barbuda (11 Nov. 1981)

Argentina (24 Oct. 1945)

Armenia (2 Mar. 1992)

Australia (1 Nov. 1945)

Austria (14 Dec. 1955)

Azerbaijan (9 Mar. 1992)

Bahamas (18 Sep. 1973)

Bahrain (21 Sep. 1971)

Bangladesh (17 Sep. 1974)

Barbados (9 Dec. 1966)

Belarus (24 Oct. 1945)

Belgium (27 Dec. 1945)

Belize (25 Sep. 1981)

Benln (20 Sep. 1960)

Bhutan (21 Sep. 1971)

Bolivia (14 Nov. 1945)

Bosnia and Herzegovina (22 May 1992)

Botswana (17 Oct. 1966)

Brazil (24 Oct. 1945)

Brunei Darussalam (21 Sep. 1984)

Bulgaria (14 Dec. 1955)

Burkina Faso (20 Sep. 1960)

Burundi (18 Sep. 1962)

Cambodia (14 Dec. 1955)

Cameroon (20 Sep. 1960)

Canada (9 Nov. 1945)

Cape Verde (16 Sep. 1975)

Central African Republic (20 Sep. 1960)

Chad (20 Sep. 1960)

Chile (24 Oct. 1945)

China (24 Oct. 1945)

Colombia (5 Nov. 1945)

Comoros (12 Nov. 1975)

Congo (20 Sep. 1960)

Costa Rica (2 Nov. 1945)

Côte d'Ivoire (20 Sep. 1960)

Croatia (22 May 1992)

Cuba (24 Oct. 1945)

Cyprus (20 Sep. 1960)

Czech Republic (19 Jan. 1993)

Democratic People's Republic of Korea (17 Sep. 1991)

Democratic Republic of the Congo (20 Sep. 1960)

Denmark (24 Oct. 1945)

Djibouti (20 Sep. 1977)

Dominica (18 Dec. 1978)

Dominican Republic (24 Oct. 1945)

Ecuador (21 Dec. 1945)

Egypt (24 Oct. 1945)

El Salvador (24 Oct. 1945)

Equatorial Guinea (12 Nov. 1968)

Eritrea (28 May 1993)

Estonia (17 Sep. 1991)

Ethiopia (13 Nov. 1945)

Fiji (13 Oct. 1970)

Finland (14 Dec. 1955)

France (24 Oct. 1945)

Gabon (20 Sep. 1960)

Gambia (21 Sep. 1965)

Georgia (31 July 1992)

Germany (18 Sep. 1973)

Ghana (8 Mar. 1957)

Greece (25 Oct. 1945)

Grenada (17 Sep. 1974)

Guatemala (21 Nov. 1945)

Guinea (12 Dec. 1958)

Guinea-Bissau (17 Sep. 1974)

Guyana (20 Sep. 1966)

Haiti (24 Oct. 1945)

Honduras (17 Dec. 1945)

Hungary (14 Dec. 1955)

Iceland (19 Nov. 1946)

India (30 Oct. 1945)

Indonesia (28 Sep. 1950)

Iraq (21 Dec. 1945)

Ireland (14 Dec. 1955)

Israel (11 May 1949)

Italy (14 Dec. 1955)

Jamaica (18 Sep. 1962)

Japan (18 Dec. 1956)

Jordan (14 Dec. 1955)

Kazakhstan (2 Mar. 1992)

Kenya (16 Dec. 1963)

Kiribati (14 Sept. 1999)

Kuwait (14 May 1963)

Kyrgyzstan (2 Mar. 1992)

Lao People's Democratic Republic (14 Dec. 1955)

Latvia (17 Sep. 1991)

Lebanon (24 Oct. 1945)

Lesotho (17 Oct. 1966)

Liberia (2 Nov. 1945)

Libyan Arab Jamahiriya (14 Dec. 1955)

Liechtenstein (18 Sep. 1990)

Lithuania (17 Sep. 1991)

Luxembourg (24 Oct. 1945)

Madagascar (20 Sep. 1960)

Malawi (1 Dec. 1964)

Malaysia (17 Sep. 1957)

Maldives (21 Sep. 1965)

Mali (28 Sep. 1960)

Malta (1 Dec. 1964)

Marshall Islands (17 Sep. 1991)

Mauritania (7 Oct. 1961)

Mauritius (24 Apr. 1968)

Mexico (7 Nov. 1945)

Micronesia (Federated States of) (17 Sep. 1991)

Monaco (28 May 1993)

Member-States of the United Nations as of July 2000 (cont'd)

Mongolia (27 Oct. 1961)

Morocco (12 Nov. 1956)

Mozambique (16 Sep. 1975)

Myanmar (19 Apr. 1948)

Namibia (23 Apr. 1990)

Nauru (14 Sept. 1999)

Nepal (14 Dec. 1955)

Netherlands (10 Dec. 1945)

New Zealand (24 Oct. 1945)

Nicaragua (24 Oct. 1945)

Niger (20 Sep. 1960)

Nigeria (7 Oct. 1960)

Norway (27 Nov. 1945)

Oman (7 Oct. 1971)

Pakistan (30 Sep. 1947)

Palau (15 Dec. 1994)

Panama (13 Nov. 1945)

Papua New Guinea (10 Oct. 1975)

Paraguay (24 Oct. 1945)

Peru (31 Oct. 1945)

Philippines (24 Oct. 1945)

Poland (24 Oct. 1945)

Portugal (14 Dec. 1955)

Qatar (21 Sep. 1971)

Republic of Korea (17 Sep. 1991)

Republic of Moldova (2 Mar. 1992)

Romania (14 Dec. 1955)

Russian Federation (24 Oct. 1945)

Rwanda (18 Sep. 1962)

Saint Kitts and Nevis (23 Sep. 1983)

Saint Lucia (18 Sep. 1979)

Saint Vincent and the Grenadines (16 Sep. 1980)

Samoa (15 Dec. 1976)

San Marino (2 Mar. 1992)

Sao Tome and Principe (16 Sep. 1975)

Saudi Arabia (24 Oct. 1945)

Senegal (28 Sep. 1960)

Seychelles (21 Sep. 1976)

Sierra Leone (27 Sep. 1961)

Singapore (21 Sep. 1965)

Slovakia (19 Jan. 1993)

Slovenia (22 May 1992)

Solomon Islands (19 Sep. 1978)

Somalia (20 Sep. 1960)

South Africa (7 Nov. 1945)

Spain (14 Dec. 1955)

Sri Lanka (14 Dec. 1955)

Sudan (12 Nov. 1956)

Suriname (4 Dec. 1975)

Swaziland (24 Sep. 1968)

Sweden (19 Nov. 1946)

Syrian Arab Republic (24 Oct. 1947)

Tajikistan (2 Mar. 1992)

Thailand (16 Dec. 1946)

The former Yugoslav Republic of Macedonia (8 Apr. 1993)

Togo (20 Sep. 1960)

Tonga (14 Sept. 1999)

Trinidad and Tobago (18 Sep. 1962)

Tunisia (12 Nov. 1956)

Turkey (24 Oct. 1945)

Turkmenistan (2 Mar. 1992)

Uganda (25 Oct. 1962)

Ukraine (24 Oct. 1945)

United Arab Emirates (9 Dec. 1971)

United Kingdom of Great Britain and Northern Ireland (24 Oct. 1945)

United Republic of Tanzania (14 Dec. 1961)

United States of America (24 Oct. 1945)

Uruguay (18 Dec. 1945)

Uzbekistan (2 Mar. 1992)

Vanuatu (15 Sep. 1981)

Venezuela (15 Nov. 1945)

Viet Nam (20 Sep. 1977)

Yemen (30 Sep. 1947)

Yugoslavia (24 Oct. 1945)

Zambia (1 Dec. 1964)

Zimbabwe (25 Aug. 1980)

The *Security Council* comprises five permanent members, including the People's Republic of China, France, the Russian Federation, the United Kingdom, and the United States. Each of these states has a veto over any substantive matter that comes before the Council. There are also 10 nonpermanent members (originally there were six), elected by the General Assembly in accordance with an agreed geographical formula for two-year terms. A substantive matter (as opposed to a procedural one) requires nine positive votes and the absence of a veto to pass in the Council. The Council meets whenever the Secretary-General decides a matter has come up that demands its attention. Simultaneous translation allows it to operate in six official languages: Arabic, Chinese,

English, French, Spanish, and Russian. Sydney Bailey and Sam Davis write that one diplomat, Victor Andres Belaunde of Peru, "used to choose a language to suit his mood: French when he wanted to be precise, English when he wanted to understate, Spanish when he wanted to exaggerate."[10] The Security Council is still the primary organ dealing with questions of international peace and security, and in particular **collective security**, a concept embraced originally by the UN's founders despite its apparent failure during the interwar period (see Profile 5.4). Canada has been elected six times to a nonpermanent seat on the Council: 1948–49, 1958–59, 1967–68, 1977–78, 1989–90, and 1999–2000.

The *Economic and Social Council* (ECOSOC) comprises 54 members elected by the General Assembly for a term of three years. ECOSOC has established several regional and functional commissions and other bodies, considers general policy questions regarding economic and social development, and makes recommendations. A third UN Council, the Trusteeship Council, was set up to help manage trust territories after World War II but is no longer a relevant body. The *Secretariat* is the administrative arm of the organization comprising the Secretary-General and staff appointed by that person. Staff members are supposed to act as truly international civil servants, discarding any national obligations they may have toward their home state. The Secretariat has been trusted with increasingly important matters since the formation of the UN, and the Secretary-General has participated in, or has had representatives participate in, many diplomatic missions through the "good offices" function. The other important organ of the UN, the *International Court of Justice* (ICJ), is discussed in our examination of international law.

Despite the UN's profile in the world, and despite the wide variety of political, economic, and social functions it performs, the organization is deeply troubled, perhaps more so than at any other time in its history. Many people hoped that the end of the Cold War would free the UN to act as an instrument of global conflict management and collective security as its founders had intended. However, the UN was beset by problems in the 1990s and early 2000s. The most serious of these problems is the funding crisis.

PROFILE 5.4 | **Collective Security and the UN**

Collective security is a system of international order in which all states respect recognized territorial boundaries and in which aggression by any state is met by a collective response. In other words, an attack on one will be considered an attack on all and dealt with accordingly. This ideal differs from collective defence systems, which are traditional alliances aimed at potential aggressors outside the membership of the system. Collective security is an ideal system that has yet to be fully realized by the international community. The League of Nations was a collective security organization, as is the United Nations. The United Nations

rarely exercised its collective security provisions during the Cold War, due to the use (or threatened use) of the veto. It came close to doing so in the Korean War, but the Soviet Union was absent from the Security Council vote on Korea. Some argue that the response to Iraq's invasion of Kuwait in 1990–91 was an instance of collective security in action; others insist it was merely an example of American-orchestrated power. NATO chose to avoid the Security Council altogether when it launched its air war over Serbia in 1999, aware that the Russians and Chinese would most likely veto military action.

The regular budget of the UN is approximately U.S.$1.2 billion, and the money is paid to the UN in the form of dues from member states (peacekeeping costs are assessed separately). However, many members have not paid their dues, and as a result the UN was owed approximately U.S.$511 million for the regular budget and U.S.$1.6 billion for peacekeeping costs in 1997.[11] The United States is the single largest debtor state. Although the Americans made a payment of $264 million in 1999, it still owed 65 percent of the total $2.51 billion owed the UN that year ($1.831 billion for peacekeeping, $644 million for the regular budget, and $35 million for the criminal tribunals for the former Yugoslavia and Rwanda).[12] Without this money, the UN is virtually bankrupt, and lack of funds has severely constrained UN activities. The UN has also been criticized for being unrepresentative, with the composition of the Security Council reflecting the old distribution of power and excluding emergent countries (especially Japan and Germany, as well as developing countries). The UN has also been criticized as overly bureaucratic and resistant to reform. Finally, the UN can only be as effective as its members want it to be. National interests, concerns over protecting sovereignty, and economic and political disputes between states continue to plague the UN. Indeed, many countries (especially in the developing world) want to avoid a stronger UN; they are concerned that the UN could become an instrument used by rich states to dominate or intimidate others. Contrary to the blatantly erroneous allegations of some individuals, the UN is nowhere close to becoming a world government with any kind of supranational powers.

References to the UN system will appear throughout the rest of this text. Opinions diverge on the utility of the UN. For example, on the one hand, in December 2000 the UN agreed to reduce American dues for the first time in 25 years but only after a bitter debate. Reduction of American dues was a key U.S. condition for repayment of its outstanding debt. U.S. dues have been cut to 22 percent of the UN budget (down from 25 percent), and the U.S. share of UN peacekeeping costs was reduced to 27 percent (down from 30 percent). However, many in the U.S. Congress feel that this amount is still too high, and as of early 2001, opposition remained to the payment of America's outstanding debt to the UN. Smaller states such as Canada tend to be supportive of the institution.[13] Canada and other countries have shown consistent dedication to paying UN dues and contributing to peacekeeping missions. Despite the fact that the UN has not succeeded in achieving all the goals that advocates would like, the UN performs so many valuable functions that if it did not exist, it would likely have to be created. However, in the end the UN does what its members allow it to do, and, much like the League of Nations, the political will of its members sets the limitations.

NON–UN IGOs

The UN, of course, is not the only IGO in the international system. While space does not permit an exhaustive survey, here is an overview of some other prominent IGOs that have special relevance for Canada.

- *The North Atlantic Treaty Organization.* NATO (also informally called the Atlantic Alliance) was established in 1949 to deter a Soviet invasion of Western Europe. (Canada was a founding member.) After the Cold War, NATO adopted a New Strategic Concept, which reduced its standing military forces and created a force structure oriented toward crisis response. NATO has established close relationships with other European institutions and has become actively involved in peacekeeping operations in the former Yugoslavia. In a controversial action, NATO embarked on a bombing campaign against Serbia in 1999 in response to human rights abuses in the Serbian province of Kosovo. NATO has also strengthened its cooperation with countries in Eastern Europe and has been involved in arms control on the continent, especially the Conventional Forces in Europe (CFE) Treaty. NATO had had 16 members since 1982, but in July 1997 it announced a controversial decision to invite Poland, Hungary, and the Czech Republic to join by 1999. NATO headquarters is in Brussels, Belgium.

- *The Commonwealth*. The origins of the Commonwealth lie in the British Empire. World War I, the adoption of the famous **Balfour Declaration** at the 1926 Imperial Conference, and its formal creation in 1931 under the Statute of Westminster were the defining events in the formation of the Commonwealth and the independence of its early members (which included Canada and Newfoundland). The Commonwealth expanded during the decolonization era, and in 1965 a Secretariat was established. A major issue facing the Commonwealth during the Cold War was the apartheid regime in South Africa. The collapse of apartheid led to the readmission of South Africa in 1994. Today, human rights, democracy, and development are the major concerns of the Commonwealth (see Profile 5.5). Another important cultural and political organization with ties to Canada's colonial past is La Francophonie.

PROFILE 5.5 **Membership in the Commonwealth**

The 54 Commonwealth states have an estimated 1.7 billion citizens. Members are listed below:

Antigua & Barbuda	Kiribati	Solomon Islands
Australia	Lesotho	South Africa
Bangladesh	Malawi	Sri Lanka
Barbados	Malaysia	St Kitts & Nevis
Belize	Maldives	St Lucia
Botswana	Malta	St Vincent & the Grenadines
Brunel Darussalam	Mauritius	Swaziland
Cameroon	Mozambique	Tanzania
Canada	Namibia	The Bahamas
Cyprus	Nauru	The Gambia
Dominica	New Zealand	Tonga
Fiji Islands	Nigeria	Trinidad & Tobago
Ghana	*Pakistan	Tuvalu
Grenada	Papua New Guinea	Uganda
Guyana	Samoa	United Kingdom
India	Seychelles	Vanuata
Jamaica	Sierra Leone	Zambia
Kenya	Singapore	Zimbabwe

*Pakistan was suspended after a military coup in the country in October 1999.

- *The Organization of American States.* According to its own literature, the OAS is the oldest regional organization in the world, with its origins in the 1826 Congress of Panama. The Charter of the present OAS was signed in 1948 and entered into force in 1951. The OAS has a troubled history, both because of the political instability of Central and South America and because of the disturbing tendency of the United States to engage in unilateral action (including invasions and interventions) in the region. As a result, the OAS has been frequently maligned as ineffective and dominated by Washington. Today, the principal activities of the OAS are focused on democratic values, trade, and economic development. The OAS has also played a minor role in political oversight and mediation, frequently deploying election observers and negotiating teams. The OAS had 35 members n 2000 (Canada joined in 1990) and is headquartered in Washington, D.C.

NONGOVERNMENTAL ORGANIZATIONS

In Chapter 4, we mentioned the growing importance of nongovernmental organizations (NGOs) in world affairs—those run for profit, which are more typically termed multinational corporations (MNCs), as well as those dedicated to a particular cause or representing social movements. NGOs are not only significant actors in their own right but they often interact, sometimes on a permanent basis, with multilateral intergovernmental venues.

Scholar James Rosenau has written of the "bifurcation of global structures into the old state-centric world and the relatively ascendant multicentric world, composed of sovereignty-free actors including MNCs, ethnic minorities, subnational governments and bureaucracies, professional societies, and transnational organizations."[14] Most visibly, the rising influence of groups like Amnesty International, CARE, Médecins sans frontières, and the International Red Cross/Red Crescent is viewed as a positive contribution to human rights and humanitarian issues. While NGOs may not have the military power or diplomatic resources of states, they do possess an inherent ability to change shape, to submerge and resurface, and to make decisions rapidly, all important tools of survival. Meanwhile, the international organizations that form the core of state-centric diplomacy, in particular the immense UN system, can act as channels or conduits between the state and the NGO community.

While NGOs may not have access to the same resources as states, they are increasingly important and visible actors in the global system. In 1972 about 2100 NGOs existed; in 1982 more than 4200 had been established, and by 1993 more than 4800 had been registered with the Union of International Associations in Geneva. Current estimates run as high as 40 000 international nonprofit NGOs. Most are private organizations, founded by individuals or groups and funded from donations, grants, IGO budgets, or governments. These individuals or groups do not formally represent their states or governments, although they continue to be citizens of states, and many do collaborate extensively with governments. It is impossible to list the wide variety of NGO activities here, but a partial list would include the following:

- *Humanitarian NGOs.* These NGOs undertake aid efforts to assist in the alleviation of human suffering. The International Committee of the Red Cross (ICRC) provides medical assistance to victims of war and armed conflict. CARE International provides developmental and emergency care to poor peoples and victims of natural disasters and conflicts. Save the Children focuses on alleviating child poverty.

- *Human rights NGOs.* Human rights NGOs monitor and investigate human rights abuses worldwide and put pressure on governments to improve their human rights records or take action against other governments with poor human rights records. The most prominent example is Amnesty International.

- *Scientific and technical.* Scientific and technical NGOs work to increase scientific cooperation, achieve standardization, and promote research and development. Examples include the Council of Scientific Unions, the International Peace Research Institute, and the European Space Agency.

- *Sports.* Sporting organizations manage international sporting events and frequently find themselves involved in world politics, as sport is often employed for political purposes (such as the ban on South African athletes or boycotts of the Olympics). The International Olympic Committee (IOC) is the most prominent sport-related NGO.

- *Professional associations.* Professional associations exist to promote the interests of their members and interaction among them. Examples include the International Chamber of Commerce (which promotes climates favourable to business interests) and the International Federation of Airline Pilots.

- *Environmental.* Environmental NGOs promote awareness on environmental issues and often mount protests and publicity campaigns to this end. Two well-known environmental NGOs are Greenpeace and Friends of the Earth.

- *Women's issues.* Women's NGOs exist to promote the political and economic advancement of women. Examples include the Commission on the Status of Women (a commission of ECOSOC) and the parallel Women's Forum, and the Associated Country Women of the World.

- *Philanthropic organizations.* A large number of trusts and foundations provide grants and sponsor projects on a variety of international issues. Although not strictly NGOs because they are chartered under the domestic law of one state, organizations such as the Ford Foundation and Rockefeller Foundation have supported the NGO community and continue to do so.

- *Religious.* A large number of religious NGOs exist, including the Roman Catholic Church, the World Jewish Congress, and the World Union of Catholic Women's Organizations.

NGOs perform many functions in global politics: they facilitate communication between interested individuals; they can act as pressure groups to change government policies; they can offer information-gathering resources, often when no other reliable source exists; they can distribute aid and knowledge; and they can play an important role in the formulation of state or IGO policy in cooperation with governments. Indeed, there is a growing tendency toward institutionalized interaction between official multi-lateral organizations and NGOs with more specific agendas. Such hybrids include the Arctic Council, which is composed of eight Arctic states—Canada, Denmark (for Greenland), Finland, Iceland, Norway, the Russian Federation, Sweden, and the United States—as well as three initial permanent participant groups—the Inuit Circumpolar Conference; the Saami Council (Scandinavia, Finland, and Russia); and the Association of Indigenous Minorities of the North, Siberia, and the Far East of the Russian

Federation (see Profile 5.6). It is not insignificant that these groups have been guaranteed a permanent status on the Council, even if they will have less influence than the formal governments involved. The Council is supposed to be a "high-level permanent intergovernmental forum to provide for co-operation, co-ordination and interaction among the Arctic states, the Arctic indigenous communities and other Arctic inhabitants on common Arctic issues [including] economic and social development, improved health conditions and cultural well-being."[15] In another somewhat ironic example, even legislators have an NGO, the Parliamentarians for Global Action. Here we see the ultimate meshing of the public sector and the nonprofit NGO.

At the UN, NGOs have consultative status in many agencies. As LeRoy Bennett writes:

> The most sought-after consultative status is granted by the Economic and Social Council. The breadth of ECOSOC's mandate explains the large number of NGOs that have been granted consultative status, including more than 800 organizations divided into three categories according to the extent of their involvement in ECOSOC's program.... The relationships between United Nations agencies and hundreds of NGOs demonstrates the impossibility of effectively separating public from private organizations.[16]

Bailey and Daws argue that NGOs play an important role within ECOSOC, "so long as they do not try to usurp the functions of governments."[17] Others, such as David Keen, who is concerned with refugees' rights, argue that while NGOs can contribute

immensely to such UN-related activities as humanitarian relief, "this trend nevertheless carries risks. It represents a shift in welfare responsibilities away from government-funded bodies in the UN towards organizations largely funded from private contributions.... Linking the welfare of millions with private charity—which is unpredictable and makes planning difficult—seems a poor alternative to establishing an international system in which refugees' rights to welfare are guaranteed by regularized public contributions and clear legal obligations."[18]

Some analysts even suggest that transnational environmental activist groups, such as the World Wildlife Fund, Friends of the Earth, Greenpeace, Conservational International, and Earth Island Institute are formative agents in the development of a new world civic politics.[19] A wide variety of actors cluster around certain issue-areas; for example, the 1994 annual meeting of the International Whaling Commission attracted representatives from more than 90 NGOs. Similarly, in the political arena, groups such as Amnesty International and Human Rights Watch play a key role in monitoring and exposing violations of human rights by governments. Others, such as CARE International, play a constructive role in both long-term and emergency development and relief efforts. And NGOs, domestic and international, have always been the active force behind what has been broadly labelled the *peace movement* in both the international and domestic contexts.[20] However, the tendency to equate NGO activity with the broader political concept of civil society may be criticized as an oversimplification, as we would then have to include organizations such as the National Rifle Association and even pro-racist groups with internationally organized memberships. One can also include transnational criminal activity, since drug smuggling, money laundering, and other illicit activities are clearly international and, just as clearly, highly organized.

Throughout the remainder of this text we will refer often to various NGOs that have been involved in global politics. Whether we are on the verge of a new global civic politics is highly debatable, but we are undeniably living in an era in which nonstate actors have increased their ability to influence the work of governments and international organizations alike.

INTERNATIONAL LAW

Many would argue that international law has its origins in the Roman Empire, when Roman judges had to settle disputes between persons of different regions with conflicting local customs. Roman law held that no custom was necessarily right, that a higher universal law existed that was inherently fair and would apply to all. This *natural law*, or *law of nature*, would arise from human reason and nature itself, and it would derive its force from being enacted by a proper authority. This authority, attributed (not surprisingly) to the emperor, was called *majestas*, or sovereign power. Thus the central question of international law remains the achievement of global standards that can be applied within the context of respect for the individualism of different localities and geographic areas of the world (see Profile 5.7). In addition, the international legal system, like the Westphalian state system and the international economic system, resulted from the expansion of the European empires. As a result, Western values and legal concepts dominate international law and are often the source of considerable friction between Western countries and the Islamic and Asian world.

International law is often dismissed as a strong force in world politics because it is based on voluntarism, on states' willingness to commit themselves to its realization, rather than on any body capable of enforcing it. Though no legal authority exists that

PROFILE 5.7 — Hugo Grotius (1583–1645)

Grotius was a Dutch jurist and diplomat (in Swedish service). His most famous work, *De Jura Belli et Pacis (On the Law of War and Peace)*, is regarded as one of the intellectual foundations of international law. Grotian thought offers an alternative perspective on international relations from that of Machiavelli or his English contemporary Thomas Hobbes. This perspective, referred to as the *Grotian tradition*, seeks to establish order and escape anarchy in the international system through the creation of international law. For Grotius, the origins of international law rested in natural law principles and in treaties and covenants established between states. In addition, Grotian thought recognizes the existence of values and norms that influence the behaviour of states and help to maintain order among them. Grotius believed that international law should be binding on states even in the absence of a central authority to enforce them. In this sense, Grotius was advocating the building of a world as it ought to be, rather than describing the world as it existed.

Four key Grotian ideas have had an enduring legacy in international relations:

1. States should refrain from interference in the internal affairs of others, by not seeking to impose their ideologies (in Grotius's time, Catholicism and Protestantism) on others.

2. A law of nature exists that is higher than human affairs but can be known through reason.

3. Acceptance of the principles of this natural law is the only escape from anarchy.

4. An assembly of nations ought to be created to enforce such laws.

In international relations theory, Grotius is recognized as one of the key founders of the concepts behind international law and international organizations.

---

can enforce international law in the same way domestic courts can enforce national laws, as LeRoy Bennett writes, an assessment "of the deficiencies of international law may lead erroneously to the conclusion that no legal principles operate across national boundaries, but an inadequate system does not signify the absence of any system."[21] In the study of international law, formal *public* international law encompasses the affairs of states, while *private* international law largely concerns the affairs of companies doing business in the international arena. The latter is the more lucrative for aspiring lawyers, while the former is, arguably, the more important for its implications for global politics. We should distinguish between what some authors label *progressive development* and *codification*. The first aims at developing new law (*lex ferenda*), while codification aims essentially at clarifying existing law (*lex lata*). In practice, a bit of both occurs.

International law is derived from many sources, including treaties, customs, and legal scholarship. Of these, *treaties* are the most important, since they are largely seen to bind states to agreements. Tens of thousands of bilateral and multilateral agreements exist today, a sign of the spread of diplomatic activity as well as faith in international law. Treaties are assumed to be binding on successor governments, no matter how those governments come into power. Many treaties, however, have escape clauses that permit states to withdraw their obligations without penalty, and other clauses that allow disputants to use the World Court to settle arguments over their interpretation.

Arguably, the most important treaty is the *Charter of the United Nations*, which enshrines the primacy of the principle of state sovereignty, the most important principle in contemporary international law. The UN Charter attempts to strike a balance between the principle of state sovereignty and the need for collective responses to international issues. For example, although states that sign the UN Charter do commit themselves to collective security and in theory surrender some of their sovereign authority to make foreign policy decisions to the greater body called the United Nations, it is the Security Council, comprising a mere 15 members (5 of which, we will recall, have disproportionate power as permanent members), that ultimately decides when collective security has been breached and when the UN can take action. In addition, in practice many states have not contributed to collective security or peacekeeping efforts by the UN. Participation is largely voluntary, and no system exists to force or compel states to contribute to UN operations. Another example of the protection of sovereignty in the Charter is the contrast between supranational jurisdiction and two conflicting perspectives on the legitimate prosecution of crimes. The *territorial principle* suggests that courts in the country where the crime is committed should have first crack at prosecution. The *nationality principle* implies that states can assert their jurisdiction over the conduct of nationals anywhere, including outside their home state.

International law is also derived from *customary law*, which stresses the validity of repeated modes of interaction over time; in what is known as the positivist sense, actual customs that occur over time can be said to constitute some form of lawlike behaviour, while natural or divine law (said to have come from the heavens) is rejected. Customary law has an important psychological element in the sense that it requires "a conviction felt by states that a certain form of conduct is *permitted* by international law."[22] For example, in the so-called *Fisheries Case* in the International Court of Justice (*United Kingdom vs. Norway, 1949–51*), the United Kingdom complained that Norway had reserved an exclusive fishing zone for its nationals within a four-mile zone (about 6.5 kilometres) that had been drawn according to several fixed points along the coastline instead of using the configuration of the actual coastline itself. The Court found that Norway had been using this method for decades without any objections by other states and that, therefore, it was permissible under customary international law. The ICJ can also refer to *legal scholarship*, the judgments of international arbitrational bodies such as itself, as well as the writings of highly respected experts in the field, when arriving at decisions.

If no global police force exists to enforce international law, are there mechanisms at least to encourage compliance? The short answer is yes. States that reject or deliberately disobey international law can be subject to **reprisals** (actions that would have been illegal under international law may be legal if taken in response to the illegal actions of another state). The most extreme example of this action is the outright declaration of war on a state, as was seen when Iraq violated the sovereignty of Kuwait, and the Security Council voted in November 1990 to authorize the use of force against Iraq. (Cuba and Yemen voted against the relevant resolution, and China abstained.) Bilateral or multilateral sanctions can also be applied.[23] In the bilateral case a state will suspend or reduce its customary trade relationship with another state, and in the multilateral case a number of states will join to impose sanctions on a target state. As we will see in Chapter 7, it is debatable how effective sanctions really are. For example, some say sanctions helped change apartheid South Africa, while others (such as former British Prime Minister Margaret Thatcher) argue that South Africa changed despite them. Less doubt remains, however, that multilateral sanctions will have a greater impact on the offending state than will bilateral sanctions. A sanctioned state can, over time, assume the status of a *pariah* in the world community. Nigeria, Burma, Iraq, Iran, Serbia, and Libya are examples of states that have achieved this dubious distinction. When more powerful states violate international law, however, much less is done by the world community.

Certain conventions related to international diplomacy must be mentioned at this stage. Embassies in foreign states are considered part of the embassy state's territory. As such, the laws of the embassy state apply there, not the local laws of the land. When Iranian students seized and occupied the American embassy in Iran in 1979 following the Islamic revolution there, it was widely considered a breach of international law. Since host governments are expected to use force to protect the sanctity of embassies, the Iranian government was condemned as an accomplice. Another important convention is the extension of diplomatic immunity to foreign diplomatic staff (though there are some constraints on their right to travel). Because this means the law of the local state does not apply to foreign diplomats, the worst a state can do to a diplomat suspected of engaging in criminal acts is expel that person from the country. This treatment opens up room for espionage activities and can elicit a rather indignant response among the local population.

International criminal law has been defined as a "complex set of norms and conflict-resolving mechanisms adhered to by sovereigns within a particular jurisdictional unit, through agreement or the use of sanctions."[24] As such, it encompasses slavery, terrorism, hijacking, drug trafficking, genocide, piracy, acts against the peace, acts of aggression, and war crimes. Obviously, a great deal of overlap exists between many of these crimes, and jurisdictional overlap between them and domestic legal systems also exists. We deal with many of these potential breaches of international law in the other chapters in this book since it is a continual—and controversial—aspect of any issue-area in world affairs.

Sometimes, the concerns of private and public international law converge in a single case. For several years, three judges from the United States, three from Iran, and three from other countries have been quietly negotiating the issue of financial compensation following the Iranian revolution in 1979. The Iran–United States Claims Tribunal meets in an unmarked building on the outskirts of The Hague. As Abner Katzman writes, "despite the backdrop of political bitterness, the daily hearings in the marble and wood-paneled chambers have resolved almost 4000 cases arising from expropriations, the freezing of assets, and broken contracts. That has meant about $2.1 billion (U.S.) for American claimants and about $9 billion to Iranians, with a billion more in interest." The tribunal also facilitated the settlement of a $61.8 million payment the Americans made to Iran after the cruiser *USS Vincennes* shot down an Iran Air A-300 Airbus over the Persian Gulf on 3 July 1988. The Airbus case had been before the ICJ for years before both sides decided it would be easier to deal with through the tribunal.[25]

However, this case is by no means typical, since political divisions will often undermine attempts to achieve consensus and healthy compliance levels with international law. The prevalent cynicism about the efficacy of international law is understandable. However, that a body of legal thought and historic precedents pertaining to international relations exists at all is impressive. In a speech to the General Assembly of the UN in New York, the former president of the ICJ, Judge Nagendra Singh, argues we should not be

> mesmerized by the simplistic notion of politics and law as antipoles. On the contrary, the law made by treaties is a law made by political decisions the law codified in conventions is a law confirming the opinio juris of political entities while the law of custom registers the regularity of State conduct. But in all three the keynotes are balance and reconciliation, tolerance and mutual regard in a nutshell, the evidence that politics can, and must, transcend the partisan, the provisional, and the parochial.[26]

Others, such as Theodore Couloumbis and James Wolfe, are less sanguine:

> Without worldwide consensus on vital international issues, without central global authorities, without a legislature, without effective courts, given the existence of large autonomous subjects with powerful military establishments, given further the permanent companion of human history called war … in these circumstances, all that international law can hope to accomplish is to limit violence [and] to substitute for it at times.[27]

The UN has developed a complex network of international legal specialists and governmental representation over the years. Two important bodies are the International Law Commission, which is an independent body of 34 legal experts who meet once a year in Geneva to work on the codification of existing laws, and the Sixth Committee of the General Assembly, the Legal Committee. It is filled with governmental representatives that report to the Assembly on current developments in international law and draft conventions. Although many other parts to the giant puzzle of contemporary international law exist, the most prominent institution is the International Court of Justice, also known as the World Court.

THE INTERNATIONAL COURT OF JUSTICE

Established in 1946, the ICJ is the principal judicial organ of the UN and meets at The Hague in the Netherlands. Its 15 judges are elected by separate votes (simple majorities required) in the Security Council and the General Assembly, and they are intended to reflect the world's leading civilizations and judicial systems. The judges serve nine-year terms. Decisions are taken in private by a majority vote, the quorum being nine. Cases are brought before the ICJ voluntarily when both states seek a ruling, but the Court also provides **advisory opinions** at the request of the General Assembly, individual states, or any of the specialized agencies. All members of the UN belong to the Court, although many have opted out of accepting its compulsory jurisdiction (the ability to call states before it at will and enforce decisions). Article 36 of the ICJ Statute says that states may agree in advance to adhere to compulsory jurisdiction. In 1946 the United States made a reservation (known as the *Connally Amendment*) that asserts the right to exclude disputes believed to fall under domestic jurisdiction, and most states have adopted similar reservations. Thus the ICJ is nothing like a domestic court of law.

Most states have signed the treaty establishing the Court, but only about a third have signed the Optional Clause, which would give the Court unconditional jurisdiction in certain cases.[28] The United States withdrew from the Optional Clause when it refused to allow the Court's 1986 decision regarding the mining of Nicaraguan harbours to affect its foreign policy. Israel has withdrawn its acceptance of the Optional Clause as well. Canada put forth a reservation over the issue of extending Canadian sovereign jurisdiction in Arctic waters in the early 1970s.[29] However, literally hundreds of bilateral and multilateral treaties contain clauses agreeing that the parties will submit any disputes over the terms of the treaty to the ICJ. And the Court has jurisdiction over a number of specialized human rights conventions, including the Convention on Genocide, the Supplementary Convention on the Abolition of Slavery, the Slave Trade and Institutions and Practices Similar to Slavery, the Convention on the Political Rights of Women, the Convention Relating to the Status of Refugees, and the Convention on the Reduction of Statelessness. The ICJ also works in conjunction with other legal bodies. For example, the European Convention for the Protection of Human Rights and Freedoms (1950) allows individuals to petition the European Commission on Human Rights, which may ask the European Court of Human Rights to enforce the relevant UN Convention.

In some cases, states employ the ICJ as a mediator. For example, in 1992, El Salvador and Honduras used the Court to settle territorial disputes along six stretches of border, three islands, and territorial waters. The disputes had been one of the causes of a war in 1969. The commonly accepted five-judge panel was headed by a Brazilian, and included judges from El Salvador, Honduras, Britain, and Japan. The Court drew borders in the ruling that gave about two-thirds of the total land to Honduras and split the territorial waters among both countries and Nicaragua, and all the relevant governments pledged to abide by the decision. Thus, a potentially violent conflict was avoided by the use of the ICJ. Canada and the United States have similarly used the Court to determine fishing rights off the East Coast.

The Court has also gone beyond its role as mediator and passed commentary. It recently found that the use or threat to use nuclear weapons is "generally illegal under international law." The Court added that it was impossible to say whether the weapons would be illegal to use in self-defence, however. This hardly challenges the theory of deterrence, which, as we saw in Chapter 3, is based on the idea that nuclear weapons would only be used in self-defence anyway. This opinion was also a nonbinding one sought by the General Assembly, and the presiding judge, Mohammed Bedjaoui of Algeria, had to break a 7–7 tie on crucial paragraphs of the ruling. Yet, despite all this ambiguity, many have interpreted the Court's ruling as a strong push toward the negotiation of a Comprehensive Test Ban Treaty, which has so far escaped the nuclear weapons states despite the indefinite extension of the Non-Proliferation Treaty in 1995. Canada's former disarmament ambassador, Douglas Roche, believes the Court was telling the nuclear five "to get on with it."[30] However, it is rather con- testable whether an ICJ ruling on such a matter will have any significant influence when it comes to a topic state leaders tend to hold so dear to national security.

THEORY AND INTERNATIONAL ORGANIZATIONS

Three interpretations of the role and influence of international organizations stand out in the literature on international organizations (IOs). The central question pursued here is how much influence and autonomy IOs have in the contemporary world system. We have seen already that both intergovernmental organizations (IGOs) and nongovern- mental organizations (NGOs) have increased in size and scope. But has this change resulted in a commensurate increase in their abilities to affect human behaviour? Are they actually capable of making independent decisions, free from the constraints of members' objections? Are they places where the interests and expectations of various actors merely converge, or have they assumed a causal role in global politics themselves?

First, in the case of multinational corporations (MNCs) and NGOs, these organiza- tions have some automatic freedom from governments since they are not official repre- sentatives of states and exist to pursue their own objective, be it profit, charity, or value promotion. However, powerful though they may be, they are still subject to the national laws that exist where they operate, as well as the constraints imposed by the interna- tional system. But what about intergovernmental organizations themselves? The three main perspectives on the question of the role of IGOs are simplified immediately below. Keep in mind that one can view the question of the effect of international law in much the same manner.

1. IGOs are seen as mere instruments of foreign policy: they are little more than political arenas in which members (states) pursue their self-interests.

2. IGOs are seen as "intervening variables"; that is, IGOs and international regimes intervene between causes and outcomes in world politics. As a result, they have some limited influence in global politics.

3. IGOs can be seen as autonomous and influential actors, able to command their own resources and significantly alter the international system.[31]

Before elaborating on each of these, we should recall the broader theoretical perspectives we have introduced so far. For realists, IOs are seen largely as a possible means to foreign policy ends. In other words, they are viewed primarily as instruments of foreign policy for powerful states. The P-5 members of the UN Security Council, for example, are best seen as an elite group of nuclear states because of the veto system. No resolution can pass through the Council without the approval or abstention of all P-5 countries. This position is quite realistic with regard to IOs, since governments maintain great control over them and often use them to pursue foreign policy. However, many argue that the realist position underestimates the potential for cooperation in an age when nongovernmental actors have increasing influence in world affairs.

Critical theorists, despite pragmatic exceptions, tend to take a cynical view of most IOs. They represent, indeed contribute to, a system based on north–south (or, to use the language of dependency theory, *core–periphery*) exploitation. The base of international society remains the social production process, which has evolved into a world capitalist system. This system is characterized by an international division of labour in which core (mostly northern) states specialize in the **capital-intensive production** of sophisticated manufactured goods, and peripheral states (mostly southern) concentrate on the labour-intensive production of raw materials and agricultural commodities. Governments and international organizations are in effect the administrative superstructure of this world system. Since most IGOs are funded by rich states and staffed by government bureaucrats, they tend to represent the interests of the ruling elite and as such serve to obstruct meaningful global change or revolution. This being said, some NGOs are often praised by both socialists and feminists for challenging conventional power structures, and another strain of thought emphasizes the potential of the UN to one day serve as a mechanism for redistributing the world's wealth or resources. Some feminists view the UN as a conduit to disseminate their perspective as well, and events such as the 1993 Women's Rights Conference in Beijing lend credence to this position.

Liberals tend to see the most potential for IOs, so much so that the literature refers to *liberal institutionalism* as a genuine perspective. The core here is a belief that regimes and institutions can facilitate agreements among rational utility maximizers. They operate as modifiers of state behaviour or, as Stephen Krasner and others put it, as "intervening variables." Although diplomacy is still the prerogative of states, the IOs to which they belong (and, in the broader sense, the regimes) at least partially shape their behaviour. Some would suggest that IOs are perhaps even supplanting the state in importance. In other words, IOs are gaining autonomy from the governments that send representatives to them and have an independent voice in world affairs. Within the liberal perspective we may identify at least two prevalent strains of theory: *functionalism* and *regimes analysis*.

FUNCTIONALISM

Integration theorists have written of the gradual establishment of supranational governments, be they along federal or confederal lines. **Functionalism**, with roots in the writings of David Mitrany, emerged as a branch of such thinking following World War II.[32] Functionalists envisioned such integration as a process arising out of technical cooperation among nation-states, and in the behaviouralist era (1960–70), neofunctionalists stressed the role of mutual self-interest in the construction of institutions whose success would "spill over into other areas of interaction."[33] In the development of larger political communities, form should follow function. IOs should be constructed according to the specific needs they can satisfy for the citizens of states, and eventually those citizens will come to realize that their loyalty to the nation-state is itself misplaced. The European Union has been the traditional source of empirical inspiration for functionalism and neofunctionalism. Regional economic arrangements are heralded as embryonic political communities, since a "regional market's institutional machinery, its harmonization of economic policies, and the spillover effect of its successes may help create an awareness within the region of the advantages of the integrative process."[34]

For functionalism to make sense, it must be manifested at the institution-building level: the granting of authority to supranational entities in which a scientific or technocratic consensus determines policy. Although examples of this authority occur in limited areas, it is not possible to talk seriously of apolitical international relations. First, policies will reflect the operative ideologies of the decision makers, regardless of how objective their research and suggestions might be. Second, the sacrifice of state sovereignty such institutions demand can be viewed as a short-term commitment, rather than the kind of permanent obligation required to transform global politics. Third, aware of the possibility that political interests will usually interfere with scientific or technocratic calculations, political scientists have been rather skeptical about the idea of functionalist bodies capable of freeing themselves from the political demands of individual members. Neofunctionalists argue that, in some cases, self-interest will be best pursued by such cooperation, which will then spill over into other areas. However, the evidence in terms of a neofunctionalist trend in the continuing evolution of the European Union (often considered the most fertile proving ground for neofunctionalism) seems rather bleak.[35]

One observation that flows from the functionalist literature has a special resonance for global politics today: the notion that the modern state is not equipped to deal with the daily needs of contemporary citizens. In a certain sense, little doubt exists that a growing number of states, due to ecological and other problems, are incapable of effective governance. Lynton Caldwell writes of the potential spread of what he terms socioecological insolvency, wherein "a state has exhausted its material means of self-support and no longer provides to its people the elementary services of government."[36] Furthermore, functionalism stressed the possible emergence of some form of global technocratic social democracy and predicted the formation of groups of international scientists acting in concert to influence policy. These groups are commonly referred to as "epistemic communities."[37] However, none of these developments necessarily means the end of the sovereign state system or the end to conflicts between states.

REGIME ANALYSIS

It is more common today for students of international organizations to discuss institutionalism rather than integration, accepting the inconvenient fact that the nation-state just will not go away. Oran Young's differentiation between institutions ("social practices consisting of easily recognised roles coupled with clusters of rules or conventions governing relations among the occupants of those roles") and organizations ("material, extant entities that possess legal sovereignty and physical artifacts, such as office buildings") is helpful.[38] Clearly, the first category offers more analytic depth. This category is currently manifested in academic inquiry by what has been popularly labelled *regime analysis*, stemming from the neoliberal preoccupation with the concept of interdependence in world politics. To cope with this interdependence, states form regimes, defined succinctly by Stephen Krasner as sets of norms, principles, rules, and decision-making procedures around which actors' expectations converge. Regimes do not change the fundamental structures of political power, but they may influence the ultimate outcome of behaviour emanating from the international system.[39] Of course, one may be more or less enthusiastic about just how "intervening" these variables are. This intervention does not always seem to matter in its current usage; the term regime has acquired fantastic flexibility. A loose definition of what exactly constitutes a regime or institution—a tight definition would be unnecessarily constraining—leads to the conclusion that most areas of international collaboration are regimes whether or not some hegemonic leader provides the "public good" of leadership. What were once functionalist projects, for example, have become regimes.[40]

Regime analysis may seem a shallow, even cosmetic, perspective by those obsessed with grand theories that attempt to explain everything. Others argue that any study of regimes must reflect the social constructions or *normative contexts* that influence these interactive activities. The identification of the latter can only be an imprecise enterprise, perhaps largely determined by the intellectual perspective of the observer. This contribution belongs to the social constructivists mentioned in preceding chapters, who suggest that agents and structures co-evolve as participants acquire intersubjective understandings of each other and themselves. Prolonged exposure to certain institutions will affect the perceptions of policymakers and thus their policies, for better or for worse.

International institutions do help us define acceptable behaviour, though this is not an inherently progressive function. This process of definition may involve delegitimization: redefining certain types of behaviour as illegitimate and attempting to proscribe it. In these cases we see the development of *global prohibition regimes*: they are guided by norms that "strictly circumscribe the conditions under which states can participate in and authorize these activities and proscribe all involvement by nonstate actors."[41] Slavery is often used as an example of an international activity that came to be viewed as inhumane by key actors in the global system, which led to a global prohibition regime outlawing the world slave trade.

At the same time, regulatory regimes have a corresponding positive function, to legitimize behaviour that is taking place. This legitimation could include, for example, behaviour that is arguably hazardous to environmental health, such as the spread of nuclear power, which is one of the stated goals of the International Atomic Energy Agency. The tendency to equate regime formation with a progressive evolution in world affairs overlooks the dual nature of institutions and organizations that have both promotional and regulatory roles. Finally, mainstream regime analysis is often criticized for overlooking the contemporary role of nongovernmental actors, despite the fact that the rise of such actors helped promote thinking about interdependence.

CONCLUSIONS

This chapter has argued that international organizations are still highly relevant in global politics. We offered a brief historical look at international institutions in history, including the development of the League of Nations and the United Nations. Next, we discussed international law and some of its key terminology before turning to a look at the International Court of Justice. Though international law has limited direct utility and relies on consent rather than any strong coercive powers, it contributes to the popularization of important issues, such as the validity of nuclear weapons, and can promote human rights and compliance with regime agreements designed to preserve the environment. However, certain states will consider themselves above the law, and this belief leads to a crisis of legitimacy for institutions such as the ICJ. As the noted scholar Martin Wight once commented, international law has a tendency to "crawl in the mud of legal positivism."[42] Yet international law remains a core component of efforts to build a more tightly knit global society—for better or for worse.

We finished the chapter by discussing theoretical perspectives pertaining to the role of IOs and international law. Critical theorists feel that IOs and international law serve the interests of the more powerful states or classes. Neoliberal institutionalists hold a more positive view of institutions and organizations, regarding them as important actors that can be used to lower levels of conflict and promote greater understanding and well-being. Students might reflect on this question of the influence and autonomy of IOs when reading the remainder of this book, since IOs factor into all of the issue-areas we examine. One of the more fundamental questions concerns what IOs—and their context, the global political system—look like in the post–Cold War era, which is remarkably different from the bipolar system that preceded it. The next section of this book provides an overview of the issues that dominate contemporary global politics.

Endnotes

1. J. Plano and R. Olton, *The International Relations Dictionary,* 4th ed. (Santa Barbara: ABC-CLIO, 1988), 416. This dictionary has become standard in the international relations field.
2. The permanent members include China, France, Russia, the United Kingdom, and the United States. It is still a matter of some contention regarding which states belong to the UN, since China has resolutely disallowed the Republic of Taiwan from joining. China claims Taiwan is still part of mainland China. Switzerland has refused to join the UN at this time, protecting its policy of neutrality (collective security would commit it to taking sides in a UN-approved war).
3. This difference may lead to understandable confusion for the nonspecialist. The agencies of the UN (WHO, UNESCO, etc.) are in and of themselves international organizations, with working constitutions and general and executive assemblies. However, they are generally considered part of a larger organizational entity, the UN Organization.
4. The games were held from 776 B.C.E. to C.E. 393, every four years at Olympia in honour of Zeus; they resumed in their present format in 1896. At present, the International Olympic Committee is a universal-membership, single-purpose IO, with headquarters in Lausanne, France.
5. The ITU was originally created as the International Telegraph Union; the title was changed in 1934. The ITU became a UN Specialized Agency in 1947. Headquarters are in Geneva. See G. Codding and A. Rutkowski, *The International Telecommunications Union in a Changing World* (Dedham, MA: Artech House, 1982). The UPU was established when the first International Postal Convention was

signed, creating the General Union of Posts, changed to the UPU four years later. Stamp collectors will recognize the importance of the Convention, which gave every member-state full use of postal services throughout the world. Headquarters are in Berne, Switzerland, where the International Copyright Union is also stationed. See G. Codding, *The Universal Postal Union* (New York: New York University Press, 1964).

6. *The International Secretariat* (Washington, 1945), 428.

7. Barry Hughes, *Continuity and Change in World Politics: The Clash of Perspectives*, 2nd ed. (Englewood Cliffs: Prentice-Hall, 1994), 73.

8. Claude's classic text is *Swords into Ploughshares*, 4th ed. (New York: Random House, 1971).

9. See K. Jacobsen, *The General Assembly of the United Nations* (New York: Columbia University Press, 1978).

10. *The United Nations: A Concise Political Guide,* 3rd ed. (London: Macmillan, 1995).

11. See *Crisis and Reform in United Nations Financing.* Report of the United Nations Association–USA Global Policy Project. United Nations Association of the United States of America, 1997, p. 1.

12. *New York Times* (11 June 1997); and UN Press Release GA/AB/3310, 5 October 1999: "Secretary-General and Under-Secretary General for management address 5th committee as it takes up improving UN financial situation."

13. See F.H. Suward and E. McInnis, "Forming the UN, 1945," in D. Munton and J. Kirton, eds., *Canadian Foreign Policy: Selected Cases* (Scarborough, ON: Prentice-Hall, 1992), 4–18, for more on the initial Canadian position.

14. For a concise summary, see Rosenau's article "Normative Challenges in a Turbulent World," *Ethics and International Affairs* 6 (1992), 1–20. A (much) lengthier exposition is found in his *Turbulence in World Politics: A Theory of Change and Continuity* (Princeton University Press, 1990).

15. Press Release, Department of Foreign Affairs and International Trade, Government of Canada, 19 September 1996.

16. L. Bennett, *International Organizations: Principles and Issues,* 6th ed. (Englewood Cliffs: Prentice Hall, 1995), 272.

17. S. Bailey and S. Daws, *The United Nations: A Concise Political Guide*, 3rd ed. (Lanham, MD: Barnes and Noble, 1995).

18. *Refugees: Rationing the Right to Life* (London: Zed, 1992), 40.

19. P. Wapner, "Politics beyond the State: Environmental Activism and World Civic Politics," *World Politics* 47 (1995), 311–40; J. Fisher, *The Road from Rio: Sustainable Development and the Nongovernmental Movement in the Third World* (Westport: Praeger, 1993); J. McCormick, *Reclaiming Paradise: The Global Environmental Movement* (Bloomington: Indiana University Press, 1989); and P. Willetts, ed., *"The Conscience of the World": The Influence of Non-Governmental Organizations in the UN System* (Washington: Brookings, 1996).

20. R. Angell, *Peace on the March: Transnational Participation* (New York: Van Nostrand Reinhold, 1969); for a Canadian history, see T. Socknat, *Witness against War: Pacifism in Canada 1900–1945* (Toronto: University of Toronto Press, 1987).

21. L. Bennett, *International Organizations*, 180.

22. M. Akehurst, *A Modern Introduction to International Law,* 3rd ed. (London: George Allen and Unwin, 1977), 35.

23. On sanctions, see especially M. Doxey, *Economic Sanctions and International Enforcement,* 2nd ed. (New York: Oxford University Press, 1980).

24. C. Bassiouni and V.P. Nanda, eds., *A Treatise on International Criminal Law: Crime and Punishment,* Vol. 1 (Springfield: Charles Thomas, 1973), 5.

25. A. Katzman, "U.S., Iran Claims Settled Quietly," *The Globe and Mail* (March 20, 1996).

26. Reprinted in *The International Court of Justice,* 3rd ed. (The Hague: ICJ, 1986), 144.

27. *Power and Justice: Introduction to International Relations,* 3rd ed. (Englewood Cliffs: Prentice-Hall, 1986), 259.

28. This is Article 36 of the Statute of the ICJ, which provides in Section 2 that any party can recognize as compulsory the jurisdiction of the Court in legal disputes concerning the interpretation of a

treaty, any question of international law, the existence of any fact which, if established, would constitute a breach of an international obligation, and the nature or extent of the reparation to be made for the breach of an international obligation. By July 1993, only 56 states had filed declarations of acceptance of the optional clause.

29. See K. Kirton and D. Munton, "Protecting the Canadian Arctic: The Manhattan Voyages, 1969–1970," in K. Kirton and D. Munton, eds., *Canadian Foreign Policy: Selected Cases* (Scarborough: Prentice-Hall, 1992), 205–26, 220.

30. *The Globe and Mail* (9 July 1996), A8. For a broad discussion of this important theme, see N. Singh and E. McWhinney, *Nuclear Weapons and Contemporary International Law,* 2nd ed. (Dordrecht: Martinus Nijhoff, 1989).

31. For another summary, see Charles Pentland, "International Organizations," in J. Rosenau et al., eds., *World Politics* (New York: The Free Press, 1976), 624–39.

32. Mitrany's classic text is *A Working Peace System: An Argument for the Functional Development of International Organisation* (London: RIIA, 1943).

33. Most famously, see E. Haas, *Beyond the Nation-State* (Stanford: Stanford University Press, 1964); and A. Groom and P. Taylor, eds., *Functionalism: Theory and Practice in International Relations* (London: University of London, 1975).

34. R. Riggs and J. Plano, *The United Nations: International Organizations and World Politics* (Chicago: Dorsey, 1988), 290.

35. See, in particular, M. Huelshoff and T. Pfeiffer, "Environmental Policy in the EC: Neo-Functionalist Sovereignty Transfer or Neo-Realist Gate-Keeping?" *International Journal* 47 (1) (1992), 136–58.

36. L. Caldwell, *International Environmental Policy: Emergence and Dimensions,* 2nd ed. (Durham: Duke University Press, 1990), 328. We expand on this theme in Chapter 11.

37. See Peter Haas, "Introduction: Epistemic Communities and International Policy Coordination," *International Organization* 46 (1) (1992), 1–35.

38. O. Young, *International Cooperation: Building Regimes for Natural Resources and the Environment* (Ithaca: Cornell University Press, 1989), 32. For example, the University of British Columbia is an organization, and the Canadian postsecondary school system is an institution; the International Atomic Energy Agency is an organization, the nonproliferation regime is an institution; the Las Vegas Wedding Parlour is an organization, and marriage is an institution.

39. For standard texts, see S. Krasner, "Structural Causes and Regime Consequences: Regimes as Intervening Variables," in S. Krasner, ed., *International Regimes* (Ithaca, NY: Cornell University Press, 1983), 1–22; R. Keohane, *After Hegemony: Cooperation and Discord in the World Political Economy* (Princeton, NJ: Princeton University Press, 1984); M. Zacher, "Toward a Theory of International Regimes," *Journal of International Affairs* 44 (1) (1990), 139–58; and O. Young, "The Politics of International Regime Formation: Managing Natural Resources and the Environment," *International Organization* 43 (3) (1989), 349–75.

40. For example, see P. Sands, "EC Environmental Law: The Evolution of a Regional Regime of International Environmental Protection," *Yale Law Journal* 100 (8) (1991), 2511–23.

41. E. Nadelmann, "Global Prohibition Regimes: The Evolution of Norms in International Society," *International Organization* 44 (4) (1990), 481–526.

42. M. Wight, "Why Is There No International Theory?" in H. Butterfield and M. Wight, eds., *Diplomatic Investigations* (Cambridge, MA: Harvard University Press, 1968), 29.

Suggested Readings

Archer, C. *International Organizations.* 2nd ed. London: Routledge, 1992.

Baehr, P., and L. Gordenker. *The United Nations Reality and Ideal.* New York: Praeger, 1984.

Boyd, A. *Fifteen Men on a Powder Keg: A History of the United Nations Security Council.* New York: Stein and Day, 1971.

Brownly, A. *Principles of Public International Law.* 4th ed. New York: Oxford University Press, 1990.

Cox, R., H. Jacobsen, et al. *The Anatomy of Influence: Decision Making in International Organization.* New Haven: Yale University Press, 1973.

Falk, R. *The State of Law in International Society.* Princeton: Princeton University Press, 1970.

Falk, R., with S. Kim and S. Mendlovitz, eds. *The United Nations and a Just World Order.* Boulder, CO: Westview, 1991.

Franck, T. *Judging the World Court.* New York: Priority, 1986.

Goodrich, L. "From League of Nations to United Nations." *International Organization* (February 1947), 3–21.

Grieco, J. "Anarchy and the Limits of Cooperation: A Realist Critique of the Newest Liberal Institutionalism." *International Organization* 42 (Summer 1988), 485–507.

Haas, E. *Why We Still Need the United Nations: The Collective Management of International Conflict, 1945–1984.* Berkeley Institute of International Studies, University of California, 1986.

Haggard, S., and B. Simmons. "Theories of International Regimes." *International Organization* 41 (Summer 1987), 491–517.

Henkin, L. *How Nations Behave: Law and Foreign Policy.* New York: Praeger, 1970.

Hoffmann, S., and K. Deutsch, eds. *The Relevance of International Law.* Garden City: Doubleday-Anchor, 1971.

Huntington, S. "Transnational Organizations in World Politics." *World Politics* 25 (April 1973), 333–68.

Jacobsen, H. *Networks of Interdependence.* 2nd ed. New York: Alfred Knopf, 1984.

Kratochwil, F. *Rules, Norms, and Decisions on the Conditions of Practical and Legal Reasoning in International Relations and Domestic Affairs.* Cambridge: Cambridge University Press, 1989.

Kratochwil, F., and J.G. Ruggie. "International Organization: A State of the Art on the Art of the State." *International Organization* 40 (Autumn 1986), 753–75.

Rosenau, J., and E.-O. Czempiel, eds. *Governance Without Government Order and Change in World Politics.* Cambridge: Cambridge University Press, 1992.

Ruggie, J.G. "International Regimes, Transactions, and Change Embedded Liberalism in the Postwar Economic Order." *International Organization* 36 (1982), 379–415.

Strange, S. "Cave Hic Dragones: A Critique of Regime Analysis." *International Organization* 36 (Spring 1982), 479–96.

von Glahn, G. *Law Among Nations: An Introduction to Public International Law.* New York: Macmillan, 1965.

Walters, F. *A History of the League of Nations.* London: Oxford University Press, 1952.

Weber, S. "Institutions and Change." In M. Doyle and G.J. Ikenberry, eds. *New Thinking in International Relations Theory.* Boulder, CO: Westview, 1997.

Suggested Websites

Note: The best place to begin any search for international organizations is at
<www.un.org>.

WashLaw Web
<www.washlaw.edu>

The Fletcher School of Law and Diplomacy

Cyberspace Law Journal
<www.cybersquirrel.com/clc/cybersites.html>

The Global Policy Forum

International Court of Justice
<www.un.org/law/index.html>

The United Nations Home Page

Union of International Associations

PART TWO

Currents

This section is designed to explore the issues and debates that characterize contemporary global politics. In the preceding section we presented an overview of the historical and intellectual roots that have contributed to the evolution of the international system and our understanding of it. Although we will still make use of historical reflection, we move now into more contemporary matters, such as current security concerns and conflict management techniques; the globalized world economy and its many environmental, cultural, and poverty-related concerns; and the debate over human rights in international affairs. As we will see, the dual process of convergence/divergence continues to define the political landscape. We have tried to provide as complete an overview of current world affairs as possible but make no claim to have captured them all in the brief space of four chapters. Readers are, as usual, encouraged to look further using the suggested readings, endnotes, and Websites provided at the end of each chapter.

CHAPTER 6

International Security after the Cold War

The supreme importance of the military instrument lies in the fact that the ultimate ratio of power in international relations is war.

—Edward Hallett Carr[1]

INTRODUCTION: THE CHANGING NATURE OF SECURITY STUDIES

In many respects, the study of international security (often called *strategic studies*) is a post–World War II phenomenon. The subject matter of international security studies is very broad, but several consistent lines of inquiry occupy the attention of those working in the field:

- Theoretical work on the origins and causes of conflict in the international system
- National security and research on potential military threats (often called *threat analysis*)
- Nuclear deterrence and nuclear strategy
- Arms control (especially nuclear arms control)
- Studies of military organizations, civil–military relations, and military history
- The study of alliances
- Regional security studies with a focus on regional security dynamics

As we saw in Chapter 2, some of these issues have been explored by philosophers, historians, and advisers throughout history. What distinguished strategic studies in the bipolar Cold War period was the prominence of nuclear weapons in the discourse. In the early Cold War period, much of the attention of scholars working in the area was devoted to the implications of the atomic bomb and what it meant for military strategy and for international relations. When parity developed between the superpowers, the focus turned to the study of nuclear deterrence and the theory and practice of implementing nuclear weapons into national security strategies. As the Cold War progressed, arms control became a more prominent issue, as did peace studies, which emphasized conflict resolution and conflict prevention strategies. As a result, three main questions of inquiry in international security studies during the Cold War arose:

1. What is the best way to deter war, and how can deterrence be made most effective?

2. How can war be limited so restricted levels of military power can be used to achieve restricted political goals?

3. How can the arms control process serve the goal of a stable and peaceful world?

While bipolarity and nuclear weapons were the central subjects of concern, attention was also directed toward conventional (non-nuclear) warfare, regional wars (especially in the Middle East and South Asia), the proliferation of nuclear and conventional weapons, and the study of so-called *low-intensity conflicts* (*LICs*), largely in the southern hemisphere. For the most part, American scholars and practitioners dominated the study of international security during the Cold War.

The end of the Cold War had a profound effect on the study of international security. Concern with the nuclear balance between the superpowers and arms control has now faded into the background. Today, a wide range of other security issues has moved to centre stage. Profile 6.1 illustrates how the security agenda has shifted since the end of the Cold War and highlights the major issues that occupy the attention of scholars today. Generally, the new international security agenda is far more diverse and varied than in the past. It is important to note that most contemporary security issues are not really new; most of them (such as regional conflicts and terrorism, to name only two) were issues during the Cold War period as well. However, the end of the Cold War served to bring these issues to the immediate concern of governments, publics, and scholars. In fact, the change has been so fundamental that international security studies has been transformed by an increasingly broad and diverse range of topics and conceptions of security. These include

- *State security*. This is the traditional focus of security studies, and it remains relevant today. Here, the focus is on state interests such as the protection of territory, the independence of political institutions, and the defence of a way of life. Other interests may include strategic territory and allies abroad, and access to vital resources such as oil.

- *Group security*. The focus of this growing area of study is ethnic, religious, clan, or factional groups. The issues of group security revolve around minority rights, economic and political grievances, **self-determination**, and in some cases separatism. In most violent conflicts today, some or all of the actors involved are groups.

- *Human security*. Here, the focus is on the individual as the object of security and the freedom of individuals from violent or nonviolent threats to their rights, their safety, and their lives. The human security agenda has developed considerably in recent years, led by countries like Canada that are pursuing issues such as landmines, the International Criminal Court, war-affected children, and child labour.

- *Environmental security*. Here, the object of security is the ecology of the earth. Environmental security concerns include global and local ecological degradation and its impact on human communities. Environmental security can only be achieved through sustainable economic and social development. This concept of security is an important element of the ecopolitics approach we discuss later in the book.

These nonstate-centric conceptions of security have enriched security studies. A term that used to be synonymous with the protection of the interests of a state is now used in reference to a wide variety of concerns and issues. State security remains important, but other actors and issues are recognized as important as well.

PROFILE 6.1 — The International Security Agenda: Cold War and Post–Cold War

COLD WAR		CONTEMPORARY	
East–West	Preoccupation with super-power confrontation as the source of the next world war	North–South	Growing awareness of global disparities and poverty as a source of conflict
Interstate	Study of wars between states	Intrastate	Study of wars within states: ethnic, religious, and factional conflicts between sub-state actors
Nuclear strategy	Focus on deterrence and nuclear weapons programs	Nuclear, biological, and chemical (NBC) proliferation	Concern with the spread of nuclear weapons to more states or substate groups
Alliances	Study of alliance formation, East and West blocs	Zones of peace and instability	Study of actors and structures (especially institutions) in peaceful regions as compared with warring regions
Military	Focus on military security and military as foreign policy instrument	Economic, social, and environmental	Examination of economic conflict, resource wars, and environmental degradation as a root cause of wars
High-intensity conflict (HIC)	Focus on large-scale wars between powerful states and development of sophisticated weapons	Low-intensity conflict (LIC/ conventional weapons proliferation)	Focus on insurgency wars and spread and production of conventional armaments around the world
War in Europe	Concern with NATO/Warsaw Pact HIC in Europe	Regional conflicts	Concern with outbreak and spread of war and instability in the world's regions
Superpower arms control	Effort to control superpower arms race especially with agreements on nuclear weapons	Global arms control	Effort to control spread of weapons around the world
Escalation	Concern that conventional war would escalate to nuclear war	Spillover	Concern that regional conflicts could spread to neighbouring areas

Our aim in this chapter is to explore the problem of interstate and intrastate war, a traditional concern of security studies that remains relevant today. This chapter will then address security challenges that have grown in prominence with an increasingly interdependent world: the proliferation of weapons; terrorism; and the growth of international organized crime. Emerging security issues are addressed in Chapter 13.

THE NATURE OF WAR IN INTERNATIONAL POLITICS

War is a period of armed hostilities within or between states or other collectivities (such as ethnic groups or political factions). In war, killing and physical destruction are both expected and condoned, although the participants are expected to follow the boundaries and constraints established by existing laws or norms. War is distinguished from other

Figure 6.1 Twentieth-Century Wars and War-Related Deaths, 1900–1995

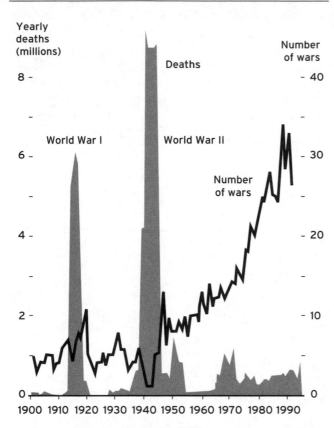

SOURCE: REPRODUCED WITH PERMISSION, FROM *WORLD MILITARY AND SOCIAL EXPENDITURES*, 1996 BY RUTH LEGER SIVARD. COPYRIGHT © 1996 BY WORLD PRIORITIES, BOX 25140, WASHINGTON, D.C., 20007 U.S.A.

forms of organized political violence by casualty rates: in this respect, the most commonly accepted definition of war is an armed conflict in which there are 1000 or more combat-related deaths in any given year of the conflict.

In an effort to identify larger patterns in the history of warfare, the Correlates of War Project (COW), directed by J. David Singer, collected data on warfare from 1816 to 1980. The COW project identified 216 interstate wars in that period. The conclusion of Singer and his associates is that no identifiable trend in the frequency of interstate wars exists. However, Jack S. Levy suggests that if the historical period under examination is widened, a clear trend is identifiable. Levy examined warfare over five centuries and found that the number of wars has declined steadily since the sixteenth century, with a slight increase in the twentieth century.[2] Another identifiable trend is the increase in the destructiveness of war, particularly in terms of the toll on human life. Since 1500, there have been 589 wars in the world, which have caused 141 901 000 deaths.[3]

Patterns in war-related deaths and the frequency of war between 1900 and 1995 are shown in Figure 6.1.

In the post–World War II era, several trends can be identified. Between 1945 and 1995, 187 wars took place in the international system. Wars between great powers are absent in this period, although great powers have been involved in wars (such as Korea, Vietnam, the Falklands, and the Gulf War). Instead, the bulk of these wars have taken place between or within smaller countries and more confined geographic regions. Interstate wars have been remarkably absent in North America (none since 1913–15), Western Europe (none since 1945), and South America (none since 1941, excepting the Falklands war, which was fought between Argentina and Great Britain). However, interstate wars have been frequent and destructive in other regions, most notably in the Middle East and in Asia. Another trend is the frequency of intrastate conflicts. As Kalevi Holsti has observed, of the 187 wars between 1945 and 1995, only 58 (31 percent) were interstate conflicts.[4] The rest took place within states, and most of these conflicts occurred outside Europe and North America. The destructiveness of war, in terms of the toll on human life, has increased exponentially since 1945. In the twentieth century, four times more people have died in wars than in all wars in the previous 400 years.[5] Increasingly, the victims of war are civilians. In World War I, 15 percent of the fatalities were civilians. In World II, this percentage rose to 65 (including Holocaust victims). In wars since 1945, more than 90 percent of casualties have been civilians.[6]

One encouraging trend can be found in the decline of financial resources devoted to military ends. Since the end of the Cold War, there has been a downward trend in world military spending. In 1999, world military spending totalled U.S.$780 billion, the lowest level of expenditure since 1966 and a decline from the peak of U.S.$1.3 trillion in 1987. Most of this reduction, however, comes from the dramatic fall in military expenditures in Eastern Europe and the former Soviet Union.[7] The sum of U.S.$780 billion, most would argue, still represents a tragic waste of valuable financial resources better spent elsewhere (for example, the entire UN budget including peacekeeping operations has rarely exceeded $5 billion).

Finally, technological capabilities have increased the destructive potential of armies. An intimate relationship has always existed between technological advances and military effectiveness. From the development of iron and steel, the English longbow and the Asian composite bow, gunpowder, the rifle, the machine gun, the tank, the airplane, the missile, and the power of the atom, new weapons have had a decisive impact on the battlefield and a consequent impact on the fortunes of the societies that possessed them. In other cases, the employment of existing technologies has led to battlefield success. Technique, as much as technological innovation, contributed to the successes of Napoleon's France and Hitler's Germany. However, each new generation of weaponry has increased the ability of armies to kill and destroy, and in the latter half of the twentieth century, this ability was extended over vast distances, a development made possible by the airplane and the missile. As we discussed in Chapter 3, our technology has reached the point where we are now capable of destroying more than societies and civilizations; we are now capable of destroying ourselves as a species.

THEORIZING ABOUT THE ORIGINS OF WAR

Not surprisingly, many efforts have been made to understand the phenomenon of war and to explain its cause. The difficulty with this enterprise is our inability to confidently generalize from one war to the next. After all, every war has unique multifaceted causes; monocausal explanations tend to be oversimplistic. Wars have started over tangible issues such as territory, wealth, colonies, economic interests, freedom of navigation, the destruction of enemies, and independence. Wars have also been fought over intangibles such as ethnic, religious, cultural, and ideological values; national pride; and revenge. The obstacle to establishing the universal origins of war has been captured effectively by Quincy Wright: "A war, in reality, results from a total situation involving ultimately almost everything that has happened to the human race up to the time the war begins."[8] A daunting analytic task!

We can, however, build narrower categories of possible explanations of war by exploring the three levels of analysis introduced in Chapter 1: causes of war at the individual level, the state or group level, and the systemic level. Using the *individual level* of analysis, we would find the cause of war in ourselves, in our nature as a species. But where does this nature come from? Most of the world's religions have an explanation for the origins of evil acts by human beings. Early psychologists suggested that humans are inherently aggressive, and, therefore, war is inevitable. In a letter to Albert Einstein, Sigmund Freud suggested that humans possess a death instinct, a desire to destroy and kill.[9] Konrad Lorenz, an anthropologist, referred to humans as killer apes, one of very few species that kills its own kind.[10] Social Darwinists argue that aggression is a function of the survival of the fittest, with the weak peoples of the world conquered by the strong. Behavioural sociologists, however, suggest that aggressive and violent behaviour is not innate but learned. Human society developed in such a way as to reward aggressive individuals and aggressive social organizations. These traits were in turn passed on to future generations. Some feminists have argued that aggression is related to gender, with most males being more aggressive than females (whether through biology or social conditioning). Still other theories suggest that the origins of war lie in individual personalities and misperception.[11] The problem with these explanations of war is that human behaviour is often cooperative or philanthropic (even more often than aggressive or violent). Most conflicts are resolved peacefully, and most humans are not at war with others all, or even most, of the time.

The *state* or *group* level of analysis suggests that the cause of war is to be found in the social and political characteristics of states or groups. Put simply, some states or groups are more prone to war than others. Cultural determinists such as anthropologist Margaret Mead argue that war is an invention and that some cultures never experienced war, such as some of the Indigenous peoples of the South Pacific.[12] However, most societies and civilizations have experienced war. An enduring debate exists over what kinds of states or groups are inherently more warlike, and, not surprisingly, the prevailing consensus has changed over time. Today, it is generally held that states or groups with authoritarian internal structures are more warlike. Authoritarian states are often referred to as "bad states" or "rogue states"; the leaders of such states are isolated from the will of their peoples and lack any checks or controls on their exercise of power. The authoritarian leaders of substate groups are often called *warlords*. In contrast, democratic states are regarded as inherently peaceful, an assumption we will examine further in the next chapter. However, in the past, monarchies were regarded as stable and responsible forms of government, while republics were seen as impetuous, aggressive, and dangerous. During the Cold War, democratic states regarded themselves as inherently peaceful and Marxist states as inherently aggressive, while Marxist states regarded capitalist states as warlike, seeking markets abroad through imperialism and combating other imperialist states in the process. On other occasions, great powers have been seen as aggressive actors, while small states, lacking such power, were less war-prone. Echoes of this sentiment can be found in some Canadian attitudes toward the United States. In other words, the conception of what is a war-prone form of social organization has changed over time and according to political or ideological perspectives.

Finally, the *system level* or *structural theory explanation* finds the origins of war in the nature of international politics itself. As discussed in Chapter 2, this view is widely held by structural realists. The principal source of war is anarchy (the absence of central authority) and the distribution of power (the number of poles in the system). Individual aggressiveness and the internal character of states and groups are less important as explanatory factors. Wars arise not necessarily from belligerence, but because, as Kenneth Waltz argues, "There is nothing to prevent them."[13] The insecurity of an anarchic environment will lead to the security dilemma, arms races, and competing alliances (see Chapter 2). One of the more popular systemic-level explanations of war has been the concept of hegemonic war. Some realist scholars have suggested that history oscillates between **long cycles** of war and peace between great powers, with a general war breaking out approximately every 100 years.[14] Long cycle theory is based on the rise and decline of hegemonic powers; at their height, they maintain systemic stability by establishing order, usually in the form of rules governing trade and security. However, as these hegemonic powers decline due to overextension, costs of empire, and the rise of challengers to their position, the preeminence of the hegemon is delegitimized and war breaks out between the declining hegemon and its challengers. At the conclusion of the war, a new hegemon emerges and the cycle begins anew. In this view, the outbreak of war is linked to the fortunes of hegemonic powers.

INTERSTATE WARFARE AFTER THE COLD WAR: THE GULF WAR

War between states is still a problem in international politics. On 28 August 1991, Iraq invaded and occupied neighbouring Kuwait. Although the precise motives for doing so remain unclear, Iraq had claimed (with little justification) a right to Kuwait as a province of Iraq. It is more likely that Iraq's dire economic situation at the end of its war with Iran prompted Iraqi leader Saddam Hussein to seize the oil-rich country of Kuwait for both immediate economic gain and long-term control over a significant portion of Middle East oil reserves. The Iraqi invasion of Kuwait was condemned by almost every country in the world, and at the UN a series of resolutions called for Iraqi withdrawal, imposed severe economic sanctions against Iraq, and eventually authorized the use of force against Iraq. A U.S.-led military coalition began to deploy military capabilities to the Gulf, initially to defend Saudi Arabia against Iraqi attack but then to prepare for an offensive military operation should it be required.

Great Britain, France, Saudi Arabia, Syria, Egypt, Canada, and many other countries joined the coalition (which received its mandate from the UN Security Council). By the time war broke out, the coalition had amassed 750 000 personnel in the Gulf, three-quarters of them American. Public opinion in most coalition countries was not solidly behind the war; antiwar demonstrations took place in many countries. However, once the war began, public support increased. This change has been attributed to the *rally around the flag effect* and to carefully managed (and controversial) media coverage of the war.

Iraq responded by taking Western civilians in Iraq hostage and attempting to mobilize Islamic sentiments against the coalition. Saddam Hussein attempted to link his withdrawal from Kuwait to Israeli withdrawal from the occupied territories. He attempted to widen the war by involving Israel, hoping to break up the coalition between Western and Middle Eastern countries. Iraq also deployed more than 400 000 troops to defend its gains in Kuwait. However, in terms of both troop and equipment quality, the Iraqi army, though formidable, was no match for the modern armies fielded by the United States, Great Britain, and France. In the end, diplomacy failed; Saddam Hussein was unwilling to meet coalition demands that he withdraw unconditionally from Kuwait, and economic sanctions were judged (prematurely in the minds of many critics) as too slow by an impatient Bush administration in Washington.

The military campaign began on 17 January 1991, with a 40-day air campaign against Iraq and Iraqi forces in Kuwait. Iraqi air defences were destroyed, and the coalition controlled the air for the rest of the war. Iraq responded by launching Scud missile attacks against Saudi Arabia and Israel, which failed to cause serious damage or bring Israel into the war. The war ended with a 100-hour ground offensive into Iraq and Kuwait, which succeeded in routing Iraqi forces. A ceasefire was called on 27 February 1991. Iraq was forced to abide by all UN Security Council resolutions, including the renunciation of claims to Kuwait, the payment of reparations for the war, and the destruction of its weapons of mass destruction program. The costs of the war were high. In monetary terms, the war cost more than U.S.$150 billion, most of the bill footed by Saudi Arabia, Kuwait, Germany, and Japan. The coalition suffered approximately 240 casualties, while estimates of Iraqi military casualties range between 20 000 and 85 000. Estimates of Iraqi civilian deaths range between 2300 and 20 000. The war also caused the displacement of four to five million people, mostly migrant workers living in Iraq, Kuwait, and Saudi Arabia,[15] and led to Kurdish uprisings in the north of Iraq and Shiite Muslim uprisings in the south. These were brutally suppressed by Saddam Hussein until the UN declared these areas safe havens, protected by coalition air power. The environmental impact of the war was also enormous. Iraq intentionally released vast quantities of crude oil into the Gulf in an effort to foul Saudi Arabian coastal areas, destroying fish and wildlife habitat. During their retreat from Kuwait, Iraqi forces blew up hundreds of Kuwaiti oil wells, which sent oil smoke into the atmosphere over a wide area.

The Gulf War remains controversial. Was the military campaign necessary? To what extent was the war fought over oil? Why did the United States (or any other country) not make forceful diplomatic warnings to Iraq during the early days of the crisis? Why was more support not given to the rebellions in Iraq at the end of the war? Was the Gulf War an example of future conflicts in the post–Cold War era, or was it unique? Finally, Saddam Hussein remains the leader of Iraq, and although Iraq is crippled as a military power, the armed forces are strong enough to maintain the regime in power through force and intimidation. UN sanctions remain in force against Iraq, aimed at pressuring Saddam Hussein to destroy his weapons of mass destruction program. These sanctions are increasingly controversial, as they have harmed Iraqi civilians and hindered the country's rebuilding efforts. (We examine the issue of sanctions in Chapter 7.) Additional air strikes have been launched against Iraq since the end of the war (including those by the new Bush administration in February 2001) in an effort to compel Iraq to cooperate fully with UN weapons inspectors seeking to dismantle Iraq's weapons of mass destruction program and to maintain the no-fly zone. Despite these controversies, two conclusions can be drawn from the Gulf War: interstate war remains possible after the Cold War; and the United States is by far the most powerful political and military actor in the world (although the war was largely financed by Japan, Germany, and Saudi Arabia).

INTERSTATE WARFARE AFTER THE COLD WAR: ETHIOPIA AND ERITREA

Interstate wars do not only involve the most powerful states of the world. On 5 June 1998, Ethiopian aircraft began a bombing campaign against Eritrea, followed by a land force invasion on June 12. Thus began a war between two poor states in the Horn of Africa. For 17 years, Eritrean resistance movements had fought for an Eritrea independent of Ethiopian rule. Their goal was realized in 1993, and in a spirit of reconciliation both countries made extensive commitments to economic partnership. However, economic disputes soon broke out between the two countries. Eritrean independence had left Ethiopia landlocked, and conflict over the terms of the economic partnership and Ethiopian access to the Red Sea became increasingly heated. Old grievances and ethnic conflicts exacerbated the tension. By 1998, the countries were engaged in economic warfare against each other.

Eritrean troops then seized an economically important province of Ethiopia, provoking the June offensive by Ethiopia. The war raged through the remainder of 1998 and through 1999, with neither side gaining a decisive military advantage over the other. Casualties were high, with the number of dead estimated at between 70 000 and 100 000. The war displaced more than 650 000 civilians. The battles of the war were reminiscent of World War I: "The death toll is high because the combatants use the weaponry of the Korean War, the tactics of the first world war, and the medical establishments of the 19th century."[16] By April 2000 the war was reduced to border skirmishes. The civilian population in the war zone suffered horribly from drought, famine, disease, ethnic cleansing, and mass deportations. Aid was diverted to the war effort, and the civilian infrastructure was largely destroyed. With neither side able to achieve victory, both countries signed a peace agreement in December 2000, agreeing to international assistance to demarcate a border and to the deployment of a UN peacekeeping force. It is hoped that this agreement will lead to a lasting peace, ending a two-year interstate war.

The Gulf War and the Eritrean–Ethiopian war remind us that interstate wars may still occur in an era of intrastate conflict and transnational security concerns. Furthermore, examples abound of high levels of tension and rivalry between states in the contemporary international system that could lead to future wars:

- *Greece and Turkey* both claim control over islands in the Aegean Sea and have clashed over the control of Cyprus, an island divided between Greek Cypriots and Turkish Cypriots.

- *India and Pakistan* have fought three wars since the end of World War II and continue to clash over territorial and religious issues. In 1998, both countries tested nuclear weapons, raising the prospect of a nuclear war in South Asia.

- *China, Vietnam, Malaysia, Brunei, and the Philippines* are the principals in a dispute over the Spratly Islands, a chain of small volcanic outcroppings in the South China Sea. Small violent clashes have occurred over the possession of these islands and the right to exploit fishing and mineral resources and conduct oil exploration in the territorial limit around them. China has further tensions with *Taiwan and the United States.*

- *Israel and Syria* have fought each other in the Arab–Israeli wars, and continue to dispute possession of the **Golan Heights**. Their interests and allies also clash in Lebanon.

- *North Korea and South Korea* have not fought each other since 1953, but despite an improvement in relations in 2000 (including a meeting between the leaders of the two states), a very high level of tension remains on the Korean peninsula.

- *Peru and Ecuador.* Since the last major war between these two countries in 1941, they have clashed over their disputed border. The latest border skirmishes took place in 1995.

Warfare between these states remains a very real possibility, and of course other interstate wars could break out almost anywhere with virtually no warning. Many states in the world continue to regard their neighbours with suspicion, continue to have unresolved territorial or political disputes, and have a history of conflict.

Another use of force by states also remains relevant in contemporary international politics: the use of coercive diplomacy and military intervention during crises. Threatening to employ military force to achieve political objectives remains a prominent tool of state diplomacy. Military forces do not actually have to be employed in war to be useful; the threat of their use can compel, or coerce, other states into a certain course of action. In strategic studies parlance, crises occur when states attempt to force other states to alter their behaviour. Crises have been frequent and widespread in the international system, with 390 crises erupting between 1918 and 1988. Almost all states have been involved in international crises.[17] Furthermore, states also employ military force in a limited fashion, through military intervention in ongoing conflicts and wars between other actors. Between 1945 and 1991, 690 cases of direct military intervention occurred in the world.[18] By their very nature, military interventions carry the risk of precipitating war or widening an existing war.

We must, therefore, be cautious in proclaiming the post–Cold War world an era of intrastate war and transnational security issues. Wars between states remain possible, even if relatively few examples have occurred in recent years. Nevertheless, the problem of intrastate war is more immediately relevant in light of the wars being fought in the world today, and the concern over transnational security threats has risen dramatically. We now turn to an examination of these contemporary security issues.

ETHNIC, RELIGIOUS, AND FACTIONAL CONFLICT

As indicated earlier in this chapter, one of the most noticeable trends in international security is the extent to which traditional conflicts between states—interstate conflicts—have been less frequent, while conflicts within states—intrastate conflicts—have been numerous. In fact, the vast majority of recent conflicts have occurred at the substate level. These conflicts are often generically referred to as *ethnic conflicts*, but not all intrastate conflicts are ethnic conflicts. In many cases, they may be conflicts between religious communities, clans, or political factions, and some would argue that class relations are central factors in most of them. As a result, in this chapter we use the term *communal conflicts* to describe wars that take place between communal groups of all types at the substate level.[19]

Intrastate conflicts have been a feature of international politics for a long time. Those causing at least 1000 civilian and military deaths have occurred 162 times from 1816 to 1992.[20] Since World War II, intrastate wars have broken out more often than wars between states. In the 187 military conflicts in the world between 1945 and 1995, 129 were internal conflicts (69 percent).[21] Another study has estimated that between 1945 and 1991, 258 identifiable cases of ethnic conflict occurred in the world.[22] What is new is that communal wars are virtually the only kind of wars currently being fought, and so ethnic, religious, and factional groups are arguably the most important source of conflict in the contemporary international system.[23] In 1999, 27 major armed conflicts erupted in the world, and all but two of these were intrastate conflicts.

THE NATURE OF COMMUNAL GROUPS

Communal groups come in many forms (see Profile 6.2), but they all share one important quality: a sense of common identity. Ted Robert Gurr calls this shared sense of identity a "psychological community" that is enduring and differentiates the group from others.[24] This sense of identity gives the group the internal **solidarity** and the capacity for collective action. Without this quality (if group identification is weak) there is seldom the potential for organized collective action by the group. Communal identities can be based on one or more of the following characteristics:

- Ethnicity (race, custom)
- Historical experience or myth
- Religious beliefs
- Region of residence
- Familial ties (clan systems)

It is important to note that communal group identity is not a menu or checklist of items that identify a group. Communal identity is bestowed on individuals by virtue

Types of Communal Groups

NATIONAL PEOPLES

Ethnonationalists: large regionally concentrated peoples with a history of autonomy and independence objectives (Kurds, Croats, and Québécois)

Indigenous peoples: descendants of conquered original inhabitants with cultures sharply different from dominant groups (Aboriginals in Canada and Australia, Masai in Africa, Dayaks in Borneo)

MINORITY PEOPLES

Ethnoclasses: ethnically or culturally distinct peoples descended from immigrants or slaves, usually of low-status economic position (descendants of African slaves in North America and Latin America, North Africans in France, Koreans in Japan, Romany in Europe)

Militant sects: groups that derive their status and activities from religious belief (Sunni, Shiite, Druze in Lebanon, Jewish peoples, Baha'i in Iran)

"Communal contenders": distinct peoples, tribes, or clans in heterogeneous societies

Disadvantaged: subject to political or economic discrimination (Apartheid South Africa)

Advantaged: preponderance of political or economic power (Sunni in Iraq, Tutsi in Rwanda, Anglo-Saxons in United States)

SOURCE: ADAPTED FROM TED ROBERT GURR, *MINORITIES AT RISK: A GLOBAL VIEW OF ETHNOPOLITICAL CONFLICTS.* COPYRIGHT © 1993 BY THE ENDOWMENT OF THE UNITED STATES INSTITUTE OF PEACE. REPRINTED WITH PERMISSION BY THE UNITED STATES INSTITUTE OF PEACE, WASHINGTON, D.C.

of birth, but it is not a fixed or permanent characteristic of all individuals within a group. Communal identity may be more or less active in some individuals at any given time, depending on the issues at stake. Communal identity also has a voluntary element, in the sense that individuals within a group have a certain element of choice over how much they want to identify themselves by communal group loyalty. Some of these communal characteristics are more subject to individual choice than others are. Obviously, physical characteristics are not a matter of choice. However, observing religious beliefs or social customs is more subject to individual choice.

Communal groups are also not static or unchanging. The self-identity of communal identities may vary over time. Some communal groups may assimilate into other groups and become less distinguishable as a separate group. The unity of some groups may be influenced by their position within a larger society. On the one hand, if a group comes under external pressure (for example, a threat to its religious beliefs or social customs), its sense of identity and capacity for communal action may increase. On the other hand, if the group has its basic desires accommodated within a larger social structure, the identity and capacity for action may decline. Communal identity can also be affected over time by other social constructions. Myth and legend, passed down from generation to generation, can keep beliefs, values, and shared history alive. Communal identity can also be reinforced and even constructed through schooling and social life. Nation-states aspire to communal status; the modern state spends time and money on fostering group coherence at the national level. In some cases, such as in Canada or the former Czechoslovakia, the effort is partially unsuccessful or fails completely because substate communal loyalties persevere.

EXPLAINING COMMUNAL CONFLICT

Why do communal conflicts break out? It is tempting to point to a particular causal factor and declare that it is the cause, and the only cause, of that conflict. In some cases, this declaration may be accurate. In most cases, multiple causal factors are behind the outbreak of a communal conflict, and while some may be more readily apparent than others, no one factor is solely to blame. This fact must be kept in mind when exploring the genesis of these conflicts. Communal conflicts may originate in one or more of the following situations.

1. *Grievances.* One communal group within a society may have a grievance against other groups or against the state itself. These grievances may take several forms, including:

   - *Economic grievances.* Communal conflicts can be conflicts over entitlements and resources and the right or power to control them. In this sense, communal conflicts are struggles against entrenched economic discrimination. Often, one communal group will control these resources and the means of distributing them, and this control will lead to conflict between the advantaged and the disadvantaged groups.

   - *Political grievances.* Communal conflicts may be conflicts over political rights and freedoms. In this sense, these conflicts are struggles against political discrimination, which may take the form of efforts to gain the right to vote, practise a religion, travel, organize, or secure protection from human rights abuses. In addition, the conflict may be a struggle for representation in the institutions of the state, in government, the army, the police, or the bureaucracy.

2. *Autonomy and independence.* In other cases, conflict may develop out of the desire of a communal group for greater political and cultural autonomy or independence. It is perhaps ironic that many intrastate conflicts are motivated at least in part by a desire by one or more communal groups to establish a state. Most communal groups regard a certain defined territory (which they may or may not occupy) as part of their ethnic endowment or as their natural homeland. Conflict may develop over territorial rights and interpretations of possession between rival communal groups that claim the same stretches of territory.

3. *Social change.* In other cases, conflict may erupt when a communal group feels threatened by change. This change may take the form of the threat posed by industrialization or commercialization or by government policies that threaten their political, economic, territorial, or cultural position in society. In such cases, communal groups will mobilize in defence of their way of life. Because this way of life is at the core of self-identity of the individuals within a group, emotions run high; individuals are committed to the issues at stake in a very personal manner.

4. *Primordialism.* Another explanation is that communal conflicts develop out of the hatreds that various particular communal groups feel for one another. These hatreds usually have a long historical record, and the communal groups involved have long memories of past injustices perpetrated generations before. This explanation suggests that communal conflicts start at the *grassroots* level between peoples and that these hatreds drive political events.

5. *Incitement by leaders.* Another explanation suggests that communal conflicts can be sparked by self-aggrandizing nationalist leaders, who incite nationalist, ethnic, or religious bigotry for their own political ends. Such leaders may

attempt to mobilize public support for their goals of territorial expansion or ethnic purification by vilifying other communal groups. Alternatively, nationalist leaders may create scapegoats for economic and social hardships at home. This explanation suggests that communal conflicts begin at the elite level, and drive events at the grassroots level.

6. *State nationalism versus ethnonationalism.* Conflicts can originate in a clash between the state and ethnic groups. The nation-state is built on an internal tension between the sovereignty of the state based on territorial demarcation and the imposition of this sovereignty on the ethnic, cultural, and religious divisions of the world. Only 10 percent of all states in the world are ethnically homogeneous. Only half of all states in the world have one ethnic group that makes up as much as 75 percent of the population. All other states are far more diverse. In the effort to achieve domestic social unity, political leaders have sought to emphasize a sense of common identity based on loyalty to the state; this loyalty is challenged by loyalty to a communal group.

7. *The loss of the political centre.* Finally, a structural explanation for communal conflict suggests that when state, regional, and international forces are too weak to maintain order and protect the security of individual groups within the country, communal groups are plunged into a condition of anarchy. In the contemporary international system, this cause has taken a number of forms. One is the collapse of old imperial systems and colonial orders, which left behind weak and unstable states that continue to be beset with internal problems. Another explanation is the recent collapse of states, such as the Soviet Union and Yugoslavia, both of which left a patchwork of newly independent states and peoples in their wake. Another is the phenomenon of weak states and the collapse of failed states. When states and empires collapse, the human geography of their territory resembles a quilt, a patchwork of peoples with islands and enclaves of one group often surrounded by others. In such situations, a security dilemma can develop among peoples as it has developed among states. Other groups are seen as potential threats, and attempts to protect group security become interpreted as hostile acts by neighbours, starting (or renewing) a cycle of mistrust or hostility.

THE NATURE OF COMMUNAL WAR

Intrastate wars have a very different profile than the wars of the past. As Kalevi Holsti has observed, "There are no declarations of war, there are no seasons for campaigning, and few end with peace treaties. Decisive battles are few. Attrition, terror, psychology, and actions against civilians highlight 'combat.' Rather than highly organized armed forces based on a strict command hierarchy, wars are fought by loosely knit groups of regulars, irregulars, cells, and not infrequently by locally based warlords under little or no central authority."[25]

In particular, the violence and brutality of contemporary communal conflicts has shocked and appalled most observers, and this sentiment is in no small part responsible for the many international efforts to terminate or manage these conflicts. However, wars have always been brutal; even so-called good or just wars have been extremely destructive. In World War II, for example, entire cities were laid waste in an effort to destroy manufacturing facilities and to weaken the morale of the civilian population. What is it about communal conflicts that strikes such a chord of repulsion? Is it the fact that images of these wars have been presented to viewers on television? Is it because the relatively small number of casualties involved enables us to sympathize with the victims on an individual level in a way that we cannot with the abstraction of high casualties? Or is there a qualitative difference between these wars and interstate conflicts?

One significant difference may be the extent to which civilians are intentional targets in communal conflicts. Attacks on civilians are widespread for several reasons. Civilians are the centre of group power, the source of soldiers, food, and support, and so they are attacked to weaken the military potential of the communal group. In addition, because communal groups are often closely intermingled, the early stages of communal conflicts tend to involve violence or open warfare between close neighbours. Finally, and perhaps most insidiously, because territorial gain is reflected in the composition of people living in that territory, forcing populations to leave is, therefore, a cornerstone of military campaigns. A new term, **ethnic cleansing**, has been coined to refer to this practice. Ethnic cleansing is the forced removal of peoples from their area of residence (see Chapter 9). In communal conflicts, that territory can then be conquered by bringing in people of the victor's communal group. Then, and only then, is the territory taken.

The instruments of ethnic cleansing include forced deportation, mass murder, and the destruction of homes and property, spreading terror and compelling people to flee the area in search of safety. Fear and terror are, therefore, weapons in communal conflicts. Rape has also been used as an instrument of terror in such conflicts, most notably in the former Yugoslavia and in Rwanda. Beyond the pain and trauma to individuals, rape spreads fear among the female population, compelling the women of a communal group to flee. Once the women are gone, communities are completely uprooted. In addition, in many societies, women who have been raped are considered undesirable as a mate, reducing the chances that they will have children. If a pregnancy results from the rape, that child will be of mixed heritage. Therefore, rape is also an attack on the very ability of a communal group to reproduce itself. For all these reasons, the violence of communal conflicts is regarded as especially brutal, even by the standards of behaviour found in the history of warfare.

The following case studies provide vivid illustrations of the dynamics of communal conflict. What is evident is that many similarities exist between intrastate conflicts around the world but that understanding the origins and dynamics of each conflict requires careful consideration of the circumstances and societies unique to each war.

THE CASE OF YUGOSLAVIA: COMMUNAL CONFLICT IN A FRAGMENTED STATE

The violence in the former Yugoslavia is one of the great tragedies of the post–Cold War period. The Yugoslavian state was created following the disintegration of the Austro-Hungarian and Ottoman empires, with Serbia and Montenegro forming the core of the new state and Slovenians and Croatians joining out of concerns over Italian expansionism. In World War II, Yugoslavia was conquered by Nazi Germany, but during the occupation numerous acts of violence and brutality were perpetrated by all ethnic groups against each other, as well as those perpetrated by occupation forces. Memories of this violence resurfaced in the 1990s. Yugoslavia was a federal state composed of eight republics and provinces, presided over by the dictator Josef Tito. When Tito died in 1980, the federal structure and the federal Army became dominated by Serbia, alienating Slovenia and Croatia, which sought to leave the federation and declare independence. Violence broke out in 1990, with skirmishes between Serbian minority militia and the

Croatian police. Both Slovenia and Croatia declared independence in June 1991. The Serbian-dominated federal army was instructed by Serbian President Slobodan Milosevic to use force to keep Slovenia and Croatia in the federation, but the army failed and withdrew from Slovenia in 1991 and from Croatia in 1992.

In April 1992, war spread to Bosnia, where the Bosnian Muslim government, having declared independence, wanted to preserve a multiethnic state. However, nationalist movements in the Serbian and Croatian regions of Bosnia sought independence and eventual amalgamation with Serbia and Croatia respectively. Months of savage fighting followed, characterized by ethnic cleansing, artillery bombardment of cities, and battles for control of land bridges linking ethnic enclaves. The initial success of the Bosnian Serbs was reversed by a combination of a Muslim–Croat alliance, the withdrawal of support from Serbia (the result of UN sanctions), and the intervention of NATO in support of the UN. At the end of 1995, after more than three years of war, a peace was brokered in Bosnia, leading to the Dayton Agreement and the deployment of a NATO-led peace-keeping force. The long-term success of this agreement is still uncertain, but at the very least, it has brought relative peace to a region torn apart by the violent disintegration of a state at the hands of warring ethno-religious communal groups.

THE CASE OF SOMALIA: CLAN CONFLICT IN A FAILED STATE

Somalia emerged as an independent state out of colonial Africa in July 1960. However, it was a state deeply divided along clan lines. In 1969, Major-General Mohammed Siad Barre seized power and attempted to establish a socialist state. Opposition to Barre's rule grew in the 1970s and 1980s, and he was forced to rely on his own clan to maintain power. In January 1991 Barre was ousted by a coalition of opposition clans after a long period of strife that devastated much of the country. The opposition clans soon fell to bickering among themselves over the question of who was to rule in post-Barre Somalia. Warfare between rival clans broke out, and 16 months of war followed, destroying what was left of the infrastructure of Somalia.

A humanitarian disaster of enormous proportions, originating in drought and war, gained the attention of the international community, which responded in an effort to bring humanitarian relief and peace to Somalia. Yet while the humanitarian relief effort was largely successful, the peace efforts were not. Clan conflict continued in Somalia, with UN peacekeepers and American-led coalition forces engaging in armed clashes with local warlords. The international presence was withdrawn in March 1995, and sporadic violence between the rival clan factions has continued. The country remains deeply divided, with no central government and poor prospects for long-term peace and development.

THE CASE OF CHECHNYA: THE RUSSIAN STATE AGAINST AN ETHNIC GROUP

A centuries-old history of conquest, repression, and deportation has left a legacy of bitter relations between Moscow and the peoples of the Caucasus region. This bitterness was especially true of Chechnya, the most homogeneous Muslim republic in the Russian Federation. When the Soviet Union collapsed in 1991, Chechen leaders claimed the right of self-determination and independence for Chechnya. The Russian government maintained that Chechnya was part of Russia. Neither leadership demonstrated any willingness to compromise, and Chechens increasingly ran their own affairs in defiance of the political authority of Moscow. In 1994, the Russian government under Boris Yeltsin decided to use military force to crush Chechen independence. The first round of violence lasted two years, resulting in 100 000 casualties and nearly 400 000 refugees. Most of the major cities and towns of Chechnya were devastated by indiscriminate artillery and air bombardment, including the capital, Grozny. The war was very unpopular in Russia. A ceasefire in August 1996 saw the withdrawal of Russian troops from Chechnya and an agreement to defer the status of Chechnya for five years. During the ceasefire, the Chechen leadership continued to defy Moscow and Russia continued its attempts to destabilize the Chechen leaders.

In August 1999 war returned to Chechnya as the Russian government sought an end to the conflict. The so-called Second Chechen War received more popular support in Russia after a series of bombings in Moscow was attributed to Chechens. The Chechen people (and indeed all people of the Caucasus) have been demonized in Russia as criminals or radical Islamists. Through the indiscriminate use of firepower and the deployment of 90 000 troops, Russia now controls most of Chechnya, although it has been unable to eliminate Chechen resistance or to impose complete authority over all of the breakaway republic. Despite the evident horrors of the war, international reaction to the Russian campaign was muted. Most countries verbally condemned the Russian government but, in an effort to maintain good relations with Russia, cited the right of the Russian government to maintain internal order in its own territory. The legacy of both Chechen wars is a destroyed civilian infrastructure, a countryside ridden with landmines, and a population living in destitution with a fierce hatred of Moscow. Chechnya requires a massive reconstruction effort, and it is unlikely to receive such an effort from the very government that waged war on it.[26]

These examples are only a few of the ongoing and potential intrastate communal conflicts in the world. Other important conflicts with a communal dimension include

- *Israel and the Palestinian people.* This decades-old conflict between the Jewish and Palestinian peoples, who both claim the same territory as their own, has defied efforts to build a permanent peace. In 2000, a peace process unravelled and led to renewed violence between Israel and Palestinians. After 300 Palestinians and 38 Israelis were killed, peace talks resumed in late 2000 and continued into 2001. However, significant differences (such as the status of Jerusalem and the return of Palestinian refugees) have yet to be resolved, and the violence continued as this edition was written.

- *The Kurds.* The Kurdish people are an ethnic group living in a large territory currently controlled by Turkey, Iraq, Iran, and Syria. Kurdish efforts to establish their own state (Kurdistan) have led to periodic violence and terrorism by Kurdish separatist groups and brutal suppressions of Kurds by the governments of Turkey and Iraq.

- *The Sudan.* In the intrastate war in Sudan, Christian militias and the Muslim government have clashed over territory, separatist claims, and control of scarce resources.

- *Indonesia.* In Indonesia, conflict between groups and between separatist movements and the Indonesian government have occurred in several regions of the country, including Aceh, the Moluccas, Timor, and Irian Jaya. These conflicts accelerated in 2000, raising fears that the Indonesian state might collapse.

Communal conflicts appear to be the wave of the future, and we will return to this theme in Chapter 13. Another factor that even a casual observer of these conflicts could not help but notice is the presence of weapons. It seems as though conventional weapons from tank and artillery pieces to small arms, hand grenades, and landmines are readily available everywhere on the post–Cold War map. We turn now to a discussion of the weapons proliferation problem.

THE PROLIFERATION OF WEAPONS

The proliferation of weapons comes in two forms. Vertical proliferation refers to increases in the number of weapons possessed by individual states; horizontal proliferation refers to the spread of military capabilities across states. In the contemporary international system, the most prominent proliferation concern is with the horizontal spread of weapons of mass destruction (nuclear weapons, chemical weapons, and biological weapons). Also of concern is the horizontal spread of conventional weapons, which include a wide variety of weapons systems such as fixed-wing and rotary aircraft, naval vessels, missiles, and armoured vehicles, as well as smaller individual weapons such as assault rifles and landmines. The proliferation of weapons is regarded with anxiety because regional arms races can exacerbate existing tensions or raise levels of distrust and hostility. In addition, should war break out, the parties to the conflict will be equipped with modern weapons technology capable of high levels of destruction. Concern also exists that substate groups such as terrorist organizations are acquiring increasingly sophisticated weapons systems. The control of the spread of weapons systems and weapons technology is, therefore, regarded as an important contribution to both preventing war and reducing the level of violence in future wars.

THE PROLIFERATION OF NUCLEAR WEAPONS

One of the greatest concerns today is the prospect of the spread of nuclear weapons capabilities to more states and perhaps to substate actors. In the 1960s it was thought that as many as 20 countries would have the bomb within a decade. Today, 8 countries possess nuclear weapons, with 4 more acquiring them but subsequently giving them up. However, these facts are no cause for complacency. As many as 30 countries in the world now have the requisite level of technological expertise and economic development to become nuclear weapons states. Currently, 7 states are *declared* nuclear powers, with the eighth (Israel) maintaining an *undeclared* status. Several other states have been attempting to develop a nuclear weapons capability as well (see Profile 6.3).

Some scholars—in particular, structural realists—have argued that nuclear weapons can have a steadying effect on regional stability.[27] As Kenneth Waltz argues, "the presence of nuclear weapons makes states exceedingly cautious.... Why fight if you can't win much and might lose everything?"[28] Thus, nuclear proliferation may increase regional stability, by creating a multilateral nuclear peace. However, the prevailing view is that the spread of nuclear weapons is inherently dangerous.[29] Simply put, if more decision makers have the option of using nuclear weapons, then nuclear weapons are more likely to be used. The prospects for accidental or unauthorized nuclear release will increase, especially as many new nuclear weapons states may not invest the same effort or resources into the development of effective command and control systems. In addition, small nuclear arsenals may be more vulnerable to preemptive strikes, thus increasing the incentives to use nuclear weapons first in crisis or war. The social and environmental costs of nuclear arms races are tremendous, as the Russians and Americans are well aware.

PROFILE 6.3 — Nuclear Weapons States: Past, Present, and Future

NUCLEAR WEAPONS STATES	FORMER NUCLEAR WEAPONS STATES	FUTURE NUCLEAR WEAPONS STATES?
United States (1945)	South Africa[b]	Algeria
Russia (1949)	Ukraine[c]	Iran
United Kingdom (1952)	Belarus[c]	Iraq[d]
France (1960)	Kazakhstan[c]	Libya
China (1964)		Syria
Israel (1969)[a]		Japan[e]
India (tested 1974) (tested 1998)		North Korea
Pakistan (1992) (tested 1998)		

[a] Undeclared nuclear weapons state
[b] South Africa developed nuclear weapons in the 1970s but unilaterally dismantled the weapons and the program.
[c] Ukraine, Belarus, and Kazakhstan all inherited the nuclear weapons on their soil after the collapse of the Soviet Union, but all three relinquished possession of those weapons.
[d] Required by Gulf War ceasefire to eliminate all nuclear-related facilities and materials
[e] Regarded as a very distant threat at this stage

Why do states want to acquire nuclear weapons? Several rationales may motivate state leaders to develop a nuclear weapons capability. First, they may want to acquire nuclear weapons for security reasons, perceiving a threat from another country and seeking the bomb to act as a deterrent, as a war-fighting instrument, or as a weapon of last resort. Certainly, these reasons were important considerations in the decision by the Soviet Union and Pakistan to develop a nuclear capability. Second, state leaders may seek the prestige such a capability would bring to a country: nuclear weapons are equated with modernization and development. This idea was a factor in the Chinese and Indian nuclear weapons programs. Others might be seeking security, autonomy, and independence, the ability to be self-reliant when it comes to nuclear weapons. These factors were important in the motivation behind the development of France's *Force de Frappe*. Alternatively, some countries might develop (or attempt to develop) nuclear weapons because of isolation (South Africa) or ambition (Iraq). As we saw in Chapter 3, another possible explanation is the influence of domestic politics; nuclear weapons may be acquired to advance the interests of domestic groups, industries, and bureaucracies.[30]

What is required to become a nuclear weapons state? For any country seeking to develop nuclear weapons, several steps must be taken. First, the political will to develop the weapons must exist. Canada, for example, could build nuclear weapons tomorrow, but successive Canadian governments have decided not to do so. Second, a country must acquire the knowledge base required to build nuclear weapons. A country must develop its own nuclear scientists and technicians or purchase the services of foreign scientists and technicians. Some worry proliferates today that nuclear expertise from the former Soviet Union may be available to would-be nuclear weapons states. Working conditions and opportunities for scientists and technicians in the former Soviet Union are poor, and the concern is that they will be willing to sell their services and knowledge to the highest bidder. Third, a country must build the nuclear, industrial, and manufacturing infrastructure required to build a bomb. This infrastructure may involve the construction of a nuclear reactor, processing plants for nuclear material, and laboratories and manufacturing facilities. All this infrastructure takes time to build, is costly, and can be detected if the program is a clandestine one. Fourth, the country must acquire fissile material—highly enriched uranium or plutonium—for the bomb. This acquisition is often the most difficult challenge for would-be nuclear states, for this material is rare and must be purchased from abroad or mined and processed at home. Finally, a bomb design must be adopted and a decision made to assemble and deploy the weapons. A test may be necessary, although computer modelling has improved to the point where a country can have a high expectation that its bomb will work even if it is not tested. We will explore international efforts to prevent the proliferation of nuclear weapons in the next chapter, but the greatest obstacles to the spread of nuclear weapons remain the technical difficulty, costs, and long time frame associated with a nuclear weapons program.

Of course, states are not the only actors who may be interested in acquiring nuclear weapons. Concern is increasing that nuclear weapons may fall into the hands of substate groups, especially terrorist organizations. This fear has been magnified by recent revelations about the availability of materials from the former Soviet Union on the international black market, particularly in Europe.[31] While the concern is considerable, the likelihood of a terrorist organization acquiring a nuclear device or the capability to produce one is remote. Terrorist organizations may not be able to achieve their goals with a weapon so destructive, and its use (or the threat of its use) might be counterproductive. Developing such weapons is not easy and is beyond the resources of most substate actors. Stealing a weapon is also a difficult proposition, but even if a warhead could be obtained, the terrorists would still have to find someone with the knowledge to detonate the bomb, which is a rare talent. Nevertheless, the threat of nuclear terrorism cannot be ignored, because the use of even trace amounts of plutonium as a terrorist tactic is a possibility and because the implications are so enormous.

A Nuclear South Asia

One of the most significant developments in nuclear weapons proliferation after the Cold War took place in May 1998. From May 11 to 13, India conducted five nuclear tests, and Pakistan followed suit with six tests between May 28 and 30. While India had tested a nuclear device in 1974 and Pakistan was thought to have nuclear weapons by 1992, these tests heightened tensions in South Asia and increased awareness of the dangers of nuclear proliferation. International condemnation was swift, as countries such as the United States, Japan, Australia, and Canada imposed sanctions on India and Pakistan. Although the sanctions hurt both economies (especially Pakistan's), neither country showed any indication of renouncing its nuclear weapons program. Although both countries were accused of violating international norms on nuclear testing and damaging the nonproliferation regime, Indian and Pakistani officials argued that such accusations were hypocritical. After all, they argued, most of their accusers possess nuclear weapons or benefit from the security provided by them. Did not India and Pakistan have the same right as sovereign states to respond to their own security requirements?

As we indicated in Chapter 3, the relevance of nuclear deterrence did not end with the Cold War. Nuclear deterrence is alive and well in South Asia, with concerns that two countries that have fought three wars might fight a fourth war with nuclear weapons. These concerns were exacerbated by the development of ballistic missiles by both countries. However, the nuclear tests might have imposed the same threat of mutual annihilation on India and Pakistan that existed between the superpowers during the Cold War. Indeed, on 20 February 2000 the leaders of India and Pakistan inaugurated the first bus service between the two countries in 50 years, using the occasion to reinforce their desire for peace and to avoid a nuclear war. It seemed that the nuclear weapons might compel the two states toward a closer political relationship, much in the same way the United States and the USSR established a closer (though still antagonistic) relationship as the Cold War progressed. However, in the summer of 2000, a border skirmish in Kashmir between Pakistani-backed separatists and the Indian military increased tensions between the two countries and illustrated that the possession of nuclear weapons would not necessarily prevent conflict between them.

In Chapter 3 we discussed some varying explanations for why India and Pakistan tested nuclear weapons in 1998. Several factors played a role in India, including the enthusiasm of nuclear scientists, the Indian government's desire to increase domestic support, the threat from Pakistan and China, and the desire to be seen as a great power. Pakistan's government was under enormous pressure to respond to the Indian tests and not appear weak. Growing conventional military inferiority meant nuclear weapons promised security from India. The Pakistani military, a strong force in Pakistani politics, was largely in favour of the tests. Public opinion in both countries was solidly behind the tests, with large crowds celebrating in an atmosphere of national fervour. There were dissenters: in 1998, thousands of protestors marched in India and Pakistan to oppose the tests. It is possible that these groups will be the beginning of growing regional anti-nuclear movements similar to those that existed in the West during the Cold War. As one Indian commentator lamented, "A country that has nearly half its population living in absolute poverty, that has an illiterate population more than 2.5 times that of Sub-Saharan Africa, that has more than half its children over the age of four living in malnourishment can never be a superpower."[32] To outsiders, foreign governments, and opponents of nuclear weapons, the tests were sadly inappropriate for two countries mired in poverty and struck a serious blow to efforts to reduce nuclear armaments in the world.

THE PROLIFERATION OF CHEMICAL AND BIOLOGICAL WEAPONS

Although the proliferation of nuclear weapons has attracted most of the attention of scholars, government officials, and the public, the proliferation of chemical and biological weapons may be a more urgent and pressing concern. Chemical and biological warfare involves the dissemination of chemicals or living organisms over military or civilian targets. The primary vector—that is, the medium through which the chemical or biological warfare agent reaches a human being—is the atmosphere, although these weapons can be transmitted to humans through water and surface contact as well. *Chemical agents* include mustard gas, phosgene, cyanide, and the nerve agents sarin, soman, and tabun, among many others. Biological weapons are living organisms that multiply within the host, killing it. *Biological agents* include plague dysentery, typhus, anthrax, small pox, yellow fever, and botulism. Research and development have produced newer and deadlier chemicals, and biotechnology has led to the development of a whole series of engineered bacteria and viruses.

Chemical weapons were used extensively in World War I. Chemical and biological weapons were used by the Japanese Imperial Army in China during World War II. Chemical weapons were used by the United States in Vietnam, in the form of napalm, defoliants, and tear gas. There were persistent allegations of chemical weapons use in

Tea, anyone? Three British soldiers, wearing chemical and biological protective gear, sit in front of portraits of members of the Saudi royal family in a hotel lobby while waiting for the all-clear siren during a Scud missile alert in Dhahran, Saudi Arabia, during the Persian Gulf War in 1991. (AP Photo/J. Scott Applewhite)

Afghanistan and in Cambodia. During the Iran–Iraq war (1980–88), Iraq used chemical weapons at the front against Iranian troops and also used chemical weapons against a Kurdish rebellion in northern Iraq. In 1995, nerve gas was used in a terrorist attack in the Tokyo subway system.

Chemical weapons have limited utility against well-trained and equipped troops. Against such forces, they are largely of nuisance value, forcing soldiers to wear hot, cumbersome, and restrictive protective clothing, which increases the time required to perform even basic tasks. Biological weapons have a limited battlefield utility, as they take time to incapacitate or kill. However, both chemical and biological weapons can be devastating against unprotected military personnel or civilians, which is why they are classified as weapons of mass destruction.

Why would political or military leaders want to acquire chemical or biological weapons? Some countries may acquire such weapons for use on the battlefield, particularly if their prospective opponent is not well equipped with protective clothing. One concern raised by the use of gas by Iraq during the Iran–Iraq war was that it demonstrated the utility and effectiveness of such weapons against unprepared opponents. Other countries may acquire these weapons for deterrent purposes, reasoning that if they possess such weapons, other countries will be reluctant to attack them. Compared with the costs associated with nuclear weapons, chemical and biological weapons are relatively inexpensive to develop and produce. As a result, chemical and biological weapons have been called "the poor state's nuclear weapon." Furthermore, the technology to produce such weapons is readily available and accessible; much of the equipment used does not vary widely from fertilizer or chemical industry technology. The materials required are also not difficult to obtain; the *precursors*, or component chemicals, for most chemical weapons are common industrial compounds that can be purchased openly on the international market. Research facilities need not be large or expensive (and are therefore difficult to detect). In short, countries unwilling to invest the time in or expense of developing nuclear weapons may find chemical or biological weapons an effective and economical alternative (see Profile 6.4).

Another concern is that chemical and biological weapons will fall into the hands of substate groups. The Tokyo subway attack illustrates that such weapons are well within the resources and expertise level of substate organizations, and the vulnerability of civilian populations to attack from chemical or biological weapons is self-evident. Chemical or biological agents could be dispersed over population centres or farmland by light aircraft or remote-controlled vehicle, or introduced into the water supply of a major city. Transportation facilities, individual buildings, or public areas are all vulnerable to smaller-scale attacks.

PROFILE 6.4 States with Chemical and Biological Weapons

CHEMICAL WEAPONS		BIOLOGICAL WEAPONS	
Confirmed	United States, Russia, Iran, Iraq	Confirmed	Russia*
Probable	Afghanistan, Burma, China, Egypt, Ethiopia, Israel, Kazakhstan, North Korea, Syria, Taiwan, Ukraine, Vietnam	Probable	China, India, Iran, North Korea, Pakistan, Syria, Taiwan
Suspected	Chile, Cuba, France, South Korea, Libya, Pakistan, Somalia, South Africa, Thailand	Suspected	Egypt, Libya

* Russia admitted to possessing biological weapons in 1992. The United States stopped production in 1969, although it continued to fund laboratory research into biological weapons.

SOURCES: *STOCKHOLM INTERNATIONAL PEACE RESEARCH INSTITUTE YEARBOOK, 1995: ARMAMENTS, DISARMAMENT, AND INTERNATIONAL SECURITY* (NEW YORK: OXFORD UNIVERSITY PRESS, 1995), 340–41.

THE PROLIFERATION OF CONVENTIONAL WEAPONS

Although weapons of mass destruction receive more publicity, conventional weapons have been responsible for the overwhelming majority of deaths and casualties in the world's wars since 1945. Most casualties have been caused by light weapons, such as military rifles, grenades, rocket launchers, and mines (see Profile 6.5). The problem of conventional weapons proliferation has three dimensions: the legal international arms trade, the covert arms trade, and the indigenous development and production of weapons.

The bulk of conventional weapons that exchange hands in the international system do so through the perfectly legal international arms trade, consisting of arms deliveries between governments and between corporate manufacturers and governments. The world arms trade has contracted considerably from Cold War levels, but that contraction seems to have stopped and the arms trade has stabilized for the last few years. In 1998 the value of world arms transfers totalled U.S.$21.9 billion (at constant 1990 prices), a negligible decline from the 1994 total of U.S.$22 billion, but a 73 percent drop from the peak of U.S.$83 billion in 1984.[33] Traditionally, the bulk of the arms trade has consisted of transfers from the industrialized countries to the developing world. Since the 1970s, three-fourths of all weapons shipments were transfers to the developing world. In the last decade of the Cold War, developing states spent U.S.$430.6 billion on weapons purchases. Most major weapons systems—armoured vehicles, naval craft, aircraft, and missiles—were delivered to the Middle East. This pattern has continued in recent years. In 1998, arms transfers to the developing world accounted for 65 percent of the global arms trade. Since 1995, Asia has imported 40 percent of all arms transfers. In 1998, Europe accounted for 28 percent of imports, the Middle East 24 percent, and Africa and Latin America together accounted for 4 percent. Taiwan was the leading arms importer in the world between 1994 and 1998, importing U.S.$13.11 billion worth of arms (see Figure 6.2). The leading supplier states remain the industrialized countries, with the United States accounting for 56 percent of all transfers in 1998 (see Figures 6.2 and 6.3).

Weapons Proliferation and Human Security: The Global Landmines Problem

Landmines are designed to explode automatically in response to pressure or the proximity of an individual or vehicle. Because they are easy to make and deploy, and are cheap (as little as $3 to $15 for simpler mines), they have become very common in intrastate wars around the world. As a result, an estimated 60 to 110 million landmines are buried around the world in 64 countries. More mines are laid every year, while extraction rates are low: every year UN or private de-miners take out 100 000 mines. Extracting the mines already buried could take 1100 years (at current extraction rates) at a cost of U.S.$33 billion.

The human costs of landmines are horrific; landmines kill approximately 10 000 people a year and maim another 20 000. It is estimated that there are presently 250 000 "mine amputees." Mine injuries are painful and crippling, involving costly treatment and lengthy rehabilitation. They are also an obstacle to post-hostilities recovery and development, rendering land unusable for crops or grazing and preventing safe passage on roads or trails. Mines are indiscriminate: they kill men, women, children, combatants, and noncombatants (as well as livestock), in many cases long after the war in which they were laid is over. Landmines represent a serious threat to human security in countries like Cambodia, Angola, and Bosnia.

Efforts to ban the stockpiling, production, and export of landmines grew in the 1990s. A UN resolution called for a moratorium on landmine exports (with then Secretary-General Boutros Boutros-Ghali giving the matter his personal attention), and NGOs such as the International Red Cross and the International Campaign to Ban Landmines increased their pressure on governments. By 1996 Canada had begun to exert international leadership on this issue, imposing a unilateral moratorium on the production, export, and operational use of anti-personnel landmines. In 1997, Canada led a successful campaign to conclude a global anti-personnel landmine treaty, which was signed in Ottawa on December 2 of that year. The treaty bans the use, production, transfer, and stockpiling of anti-personnel mines and obligates signatories to destroy their stock of mines. Canada also contributes to mine-clearing efforts. The Canadian Armed Forces contributes to mine-clearance operations around the world, and the government of Canada contributes funds for mine clearance, medical treatment, rehabilitation, and artificial limbs. However, key countries did not sign the treaty, including the United States, Greece, Turkey, Russia, China, India, Pakistan, Iraq, and Iran. The treaty also cannot solve the problem of the mines already buried. Nevertheless, the treaty was a major diplomatic and arms control success and a significant breakthrough for the human security concept.

SOURCE: "THE UNITED NATIONS AND MINE CLEARANCE," OVERVIEW—JUNE 1995, UNITED NATIONS DEPARTMENT OF HUMANITARIAN AFFAIRS, INTERNATIONAL MEETING ON MINE CLEARANCE, GENEVA, 5–7 JUNE 1995.

The downward global trend in arms sales is the result of three factors. The end of the Cold War and the collapse of the Soviet Union greatly reduced the availability of armaments from that country (which had been responsible for three-fifths of world arms exports between 1985 and 1989). Strained budgets in the south, even among the relatively wealthier countries of the Middle East, mean that less money is available for the purchase of weapons systems. Indigenous weapons production in an increasing number of countries has reduced the extent to which they are reliant on weapons purchased from abroad. Nevertheless, the global trade in armaments remains very lucrative and a subject of considerable dismay to those concerned with the economic development of these countries and the improvement of the quality of life for their citizens.

Figure 6.2 Leading Suppliers of Major Conventional Weapons, 1991–1998

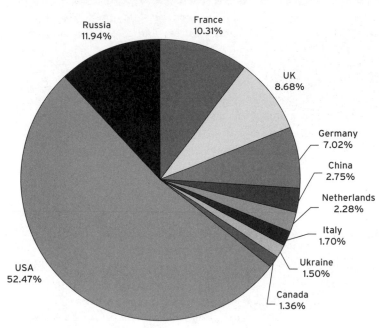

Russia 11.94%

France 10.31%

UK 8.68%

Germany 7.02%

China 2.75%

Netherlands 2.28%

Italy 1.70%

Ukraine 1.50%

Canada 1.36%

USA 52.47%

SOURCE: *SIPRI YEARBOOK, 1999* (STOCKHOLM: STOCKHOLM INTERNATIONAL PEACE RESEARCH INSTITUTE, 1999).

Another point of concern is the quality of many weapons now being purchased. Because of the shrinking nature of the international arms market, the level of competition has escalated. As a result, many of the very best weapons are up for sale, and many countries are purchasing weapons that represent significant improvements over their past inventories. Particular concern exists over the spread of ballistic missile capabilities, which could be used to deliver nuclear, chemical, or biological weapons in various regional settings. In addition, many countries are acquiring sea-skimming anti-ship missiles, modern tanks, new fighter aircraft, and submarines.

Competition has also led most arms companies to offer generous offset packages to prospective buyers, which take a variety of forms. The importing country might be permitted to manufacture certain components of the weapon domestically under licence (and perhaps in time the entire weapon). Some offset packages permit the permanent transfer of technology to the recipient country. Governments may assist their own arms industries by lifting export restrictions on certain armaments. In other cases, governments may offer financing or credit to prospective buyers to secure the contract for their own arms industry. The arms industry itself is also in the process of transformation. Just as global economic interdependence has facilitated the internationalization of civilian business, finance, and manufacture, it has also facilitated the internationalization of the arms industry. Weapons systems can now use components and technology from a variety of different countries and corporations. Why do governments allow, encourage, and help weapons manufacturers sell their product abroad? In some cases, hard currency is the main motivation, especially if that country is in dire need of cash. For some countries (such as Russia), military hardware is one of the few viable exports and hard currency earners in the country's economy. Jobs are another incentive to secure arms deals abroad. Producing states will encourage arms exports to maintain production activity and the employment that activity brings. Producing states may also want to maintain their manufacturing capability (sometimes called the defence industrial base) and keep their production lines open for future sales. As long as the production line is busy, the skilled workforce, design teams, and manufacturing facilities will remain intact. If the production line has to close down, these assets may be lost. Finally, producers may want to encourage sales abroad to lower the unit cost of the weapon. If a weapons system has a long production run and large numbers are produced, the costs of that weapon on a

Figure 6.3 Leading Recipients of Major Conventional Weapons, 1991–1998

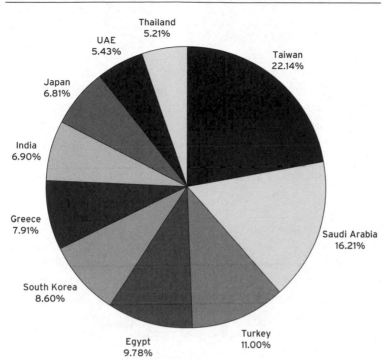

SOURCE: *SIPRI YEARBOOK, 1999* (STOCKHOLM: STOCKHOLM INTERNATIONAL PEACE RESEARCH INSTITUTE, 1999).

per unit basis will be lower than if the weapons system was manufactured in lower quantities. The larger the production run, the lower the costs of each individual weapons system, making the weapons system more affordable, both for foreign buyers and for domestic purchasers.

The covert arms trade is harder to track. The value of the covert trade in armaments (or *gunrunning* as it is sometimes called) is estimated at between U.S.$2 billion and $10 billion per year.[34] The weapons are sold by international arms dealers who specialize in brokering weapons sales or who purchase weapons and stockpile them for sale on the black market. The weapons may have been stolen from military stocks, diverted from their original destinations, or purchased in war-torn regions from individuals who or groups that have a large surplus of weapons available for sale to any bidder. In some cases, weapons may be sold by companies that fail to observe embargoes or export rules, sometimes with the tacit approval of governments. The weapons are then transported through transshipment points to their buyers. Even in the former Yugoslavia, under a multilateral arms **embargo**, more than U.S.$2 billion worth of armaments was covertly shipped into the country in 1993.[35]

Another characteristic of conventional weapons proliferation is the development of indigenous production of weapons systems, which has occurred for several reasons. Many countries have developed the technological infrastructure and expertise to manufacture more modern weapons systems. Other countries have manufactured certain weapons or components under licence and have acquired production rights over time. For other countries, the ability to produce modern weapons is an indicator of their technical and industrial expertise. This phenomenon has two worrying implications. First, efforts to increase controls over the proliferation of weapons will be complicated by the fact that more and more states are producing their own weapons and relying less on purchases from abroad. Second, the growth of indigenous production means that more countries are producing weapons for export, increasing the number of producer states in the world.

As we will see in the next chapter, concern over the proliferation of all types of weapons systems has led to the creation of a number of international efforts to control the global spread of armaments.

INTERNATIONAL TERRORISM

Few international events have the emotional impact that incidents of terrorism generate. In many cases, incidents are often broadcast around the world, even as they transpire, by the global media. Images and stories of horror, death, injury, and kidnapping are paralleled by revelations or speculations concerning the political motive for the attacks. The surprise that attends most acts of terrorism contributes to this international impact; without warning, a plane is hijacked, a bomb explodes, or individuals are kidnapped or taken hostage. And yet, many more cases go unnoticed or unreported. People living in Canada have been fortunate; Canada has been relatively unscathed by terrorist activity. Although there can be no doubt that international terrorists use Canada as a travel conduit or a place where a small minority of sympathetic individuals might be found, incidents of terrorism in Canada have been rare. The FLQ Crisis and the activities of Direct Action are the exceptions rather than the rule (see Profile 6.6).

Terrorism directly or indirectly affects the policies of all actors in global politics, and terrorist activity often stretches across borders and regions. In this sense, it is a transnational security concern. It affects the decisions of governments and the way multinational corporations do business and is on the agenda of both IGOs and NGOs. Military and police forces must be equipped and prepared to respond to terrorist acts. Huge sums are spent every year on counterterrorism and security measures at airports and public places. It influences the travel decisions of tourists and causes a perpetual state of anxiety in many societies.

Terrorism is far from a recent phenomenon. Terrorist incidents, or the causes that motivate them, often have deep historical roots. Traditionally the weapon of the weak, terrorism has been employed as a political instrument by individuals or groups seeking to reject authority, generate social change, promote revolution, or spread fear. Historical examples of the use of terrorism include the Zealots, a Jewish sect that appeared in C.E. 6 and used assassinations in an effort to force the Roman Empire out of Palestine. In the

---

PROFILE 6.6 | **The FLQ Crisis**

Although it is not a case of international terrorism, the FLQ Crisis in Canada is the most prominent example of terrorism on Canadian soil. The Front du Libération du Québec (FLQ), a self-styled revolutionary movement advocating independence for an "oppressed Québec," engaged in a series of bombings in Montreal in 1969. The FLQ kidnapped the British Trade Commissioner for Quebec, James Cross, and Quebec Minister of Labour Pierre Laporte (who was subsequently murdered). In response, Prime Minister Pierre Trudeau invoked the War Measures Act, calling in the Armed Forces, which patrolled Montreal streets, restricting travel and movement. The Royal Canadian Mounted Police, using broad local powers of seizure and arrest to locate the FLQ, arrested more than 400 suspects, of whom 62 were brought to trial and 20 were convicted. The FLQ was eliminated as an organized group. Trudeau's decision remains controversial, with some calling it a scar on Canada's civil liberties record and an abuse of state power over its citizens. Others argue that the government had to respond forcefully to terrorism. The FLQ was crushed and full rights and liberties were swiftly restored. After the crisis, the federal government embarked on measures to address some of the grievances of the French community, including increased investment in French-speaking areas.

Middle East between 1090 and 1275, Muslims known as *hashashin* (from which the word "assassin" originates) carried out many political and religious killings on behalf of their political and spiritual leaders. At the end of the nineteenth century, political assassinations by anarchists claimed U.S. President William McKinley, French President Sadi Carnot, the Empress Elizabeth of Austria, and Spanish Prime Minister Antonio Canovas. World War I began with an act of terrorism—the assassination of Austrian Archduke Franz Ferdinand—by a Serbian terrorist organization called the Black Hand.

Terrorism is not only committed by individuals or groups. Although the image of the small terrorist organization operating in a clandestine fashion in the city or countryside is the most popular conception of terrorism, much of the terrorism in the world is planned and executed by states against their own citizens. Such **state terrorism** differs from state-sponsored terrorism, which is the support of terrorist individuals or groups by a government. State terrorism also has deep historical roots: even that golden moment of liberty, the French Revolution, saw state terrorism employed as a tool of the French Republic to get rid of its enemies. State terrorism is employed by states within their own borders to suppress dissent and silence opposition. Such campaigns frequently involve massive human rights violations, an issue we shall return to in later chapters.

THE ORIGINS AND CAUSES OF TERRORISM

Definitions of terrorism are notoriously difficult to construct, in part because terrorism is a politically charged word, often used inappropriately for political purposes. The familiar adage "one person's terrorist is another's freedom fighter" illustrates the relative nature of the term. Many different types of terrorism occur, and it is difficult to establish a single definition that accounts for all of them. Walter Laqueur defines terrorism as "the substate application of violence or threatened violence intended to sow panic in a society, to weaken or even overthrow the incumbents, and to bring about political change."[36] Cindy Combs defines terrorism as "a synthesis of war and theatre, a dramatization of the most proscribed kind of violence—that which is perpetrated on innocent victims—played before an audience in the hope of creating a mood of fear, for political purposes."[37]

State terrorism is designed to eliminate political opposition; the killers and torturers that engage in it are paid for their work, which can even become routine for them. But what causes the nonstate terrorist to commit acts of violence against innocent people? Researchers have put forth the following explanations.

Individual Psychology

Some researchers suggest that the root cause of terrorism is the psychological makeup of the individuals who participate in terrorist activities. In particular, psychologists and psychiatrists suggest that personality disorders or even mental illness may explain terrorist activity.

Ideological Fanaticism

Terrorism can originate from the commitment of individuals and groups to a particular political idea and their efforts to promote this political idea through violence. Ideologies such as Marxism-Leninism, fascism, and extreme racism offer a framework for interpreting social injustice and inequality and identifying those responsible, and provide a program of action to build a better society. Terrorists are thus committed to the idea of social change through violence.

Religious Fanaticism

Terrorist acts may originate in religious extremism, drawn from literal interpretations of religious beliefs. Often, religious fanaticism employs a belief system that is in fact a perversion of the principles of that religion. Terrorist acts are carried out by individuals or groups seeking to advance their religious views, secure religious rights or freedoms, or wage a holy war against their religious enemies.

Grievance and Cycles of Violence

Terrorist acts may originate with the grievances of a particular group. This group may be the target of discrimination and repression, which may include economic, political, or religious persecution. In some instances, this persecution may be violent. In such cases, terrorist acts may be efforts to strike back against an opponent, whether it is an oppressive regime or another group.

Nationalism and Separatism

Terrorism may also originate from the desire of individuals within a larger community for greater political autonomy or even full independence. While this desire often originates with a history of grievances, the specific aim of the terrorist activity is to advance the political independence of a group.

Activist Fanaticism

Terrorist activity may also originate from a very specific issue or controversy that provokes certain individuals or groups to violence. The aim of such violence is to prevent certain political or social activity or to force their belief systems on others. Such issues include abortion, animal rights, racial superiority, and environmental protection.

Another characteristic of terrorism deserves brief mention. Terrorism is seldom successful. While terrorist activity is designed to promote a cause, it can often have the opposite effect. Terrorist activity can alienate other supporters of the cause who do not believe that violence is the appropriate instrument for advancing their interests or beliefs. Terrorism can also discredit moderates, who become associated with the violence even though they have no connection to it. While a harsh backlash against terrorists by a central authority can drive more people to the terrorists' cause, these measures can also lead to persecution and repression of the people or group the terrorist organization is supposedly fighting for.

THE CHANGING CHARACTER OF INTERNATIONAL TERRORISM

Is international terrorism on the rise? In terms of the number of incidents of international terrorism per year, the trend is downward. International terrorist activities surged in the 1980s to a peak of 665 incidents in 1987. The number of incidents declined during the 1990s, falling to a 25-year low of 296 incidents in 1996 before rising to 392 incidents in 1999.[38] Nevertheless, terrorist incidents tend to be spectacular and highly publicized; as a result, governments are compelled to respond and make discernible gains in the battle against international terrorism because of public outrage. One must question whether international terrorism deserves all the attention it receives. Without diminishing the impact that terrorist activity can have on individual lives, some doubt arises as to whether international terrorism presents a significant threat to national and international security when compared with other security issues.[39] However, concern exists that terrorism, if unchecked, will spread and become more frequent, undermining democratic norms and individual rights, provoking authoritarian actions by governments, and creating the impression of disorder and vulnerability.

Another characteristic of contemporary international terrorism is the growing link between different terrorist individuals and groups. An international terrorist network exists, although estimates of its extent vary. Terrorist groups may share membership or cooperate in the execution of terrorist acts. They may share or exchange training facilities, weapons and explosives, information, and finance. Modern international terrorist movements are part of a wider web of underground suppliers, which make many terrorist movements increasingly self-sufficient and less reliant on client states to sponsor their activities.

Finally, the objectives of many terrorist groups are somewhat different from the political aims of traditional terrorist organizations. The aims of what Walter Laqueur has called "postmodern terrorism" are not political; they are inspired by religious or cult beliefs or by racial hatred. Perhaps most disturbing of all is the trend away from hijackings and the targeting of specific individuals and toward more indiscriminate killing (see Profile 6.7).[40]

COMBATING TERRORISM: APPROACHES AND METHODS

Can international terrorism be stopped? One strategy is to eliminate its root causes. To the extent that terrorism is rooted in grievances, injustices, and desire for autonomy or independence, efforts to address such grievances or desires could reduce or eliminate terrorist activity. However, this approach presumes that governments are willing to accommodate the wishes of terrorist groups; in fact, public opposition to such measures may be very strong. In many regions of the world, poverty, despair, hatred, and other social ills are so pervasive that eliminating the terrorism that develops from such conditions would require revolutionary changes, and governments are committed to preserving the status quo, not inducing revolution.

PROFILE 6.7 **The Tokyo Subway Attack**

In March 1995, 12 people were killed and more than 5000 injured by a poison gas attack on several Tokyo subway lines. The attack was carried out by members of a religious cult known as *Aum Shinrikyo* (Supreme Truth), a well-financed organization with more than 10 000 members in Japan and some 100 000 abroad. Asahara Shoku founded the cult in 1994 and taught of an imminent Armageddon for modern society, which he believes was corrupt. Although many more casualties have been caused by bombings and shootings, the Aum Shinrikyo acts are especially disturbing. For the first time, chemical weapons have been used on a large scale in an urban terrorist act. The cult maintained front companies and laboratories that employed highly skilled technicians and scientists to develop and produce the gas used in the subway attack. Second, the cult was a religious organization, not a political one, and was interested in promoting a theological outcome, not one designed to advance a political agenda or extract concessions from the Japanese government. As such, its actions cannot be responsive to political change designed to eliminate the root causes of terrorism.

A day at the market. Victims are treated at the scene of a car bomb explosion in Market Street, Omagh, 115 kilometres west of Belfast, Northern Ireland. The bomb tore apart the crowded centre of this market town, killing at least 27 people and injuring some 200 others. (AP Photo/ Paul Mcerlane. From an amateur video)

A second strategy is to employ military force against terrorist organizations or the states that sponsor their activities. Such counterterrorist operations might include the use of highly trained teams of police or military personnel in large-scale search operations or the bombing of terrorist training grounds and facilities from the air. The United States justified the bombing of Libya in April 1986 and the use of **cruise missiles** against alleged terrorist facilities in Afghanistan and Sudan in August 1998 as anti-terrorist operations. However, the usefulness of the military against terrorist organizations is limited. Terrorist organizations are hard to track because they are often small, compartmentalized into highly secretive cells, and composed of committed individuals. The prospect for infiltration or informants, therefore, is quite low. Military operations against terrorists also face tactical and political obstacles. Terrorist facilities are often located in sponsoring states, and any attack against them would have to take into account the military capability of the host state as well as the political repercussions of attacking its territory. Often, military force is a very blunt instrument: attacking terrorists or their facilities can lead to the deaths of innocent individuals. Further, it can create martyrs for the terrorist cause, something most governments want to avoid.

A third strategy is to strengthen domestic and international law. However, in democratic societies, strengthening domestic law to combat terrorism is a serious matter, raising the danger of excessive restriction of freedoms and a slide into **authoritarianism** in the name of combating subversion (many people felt that the Canadian federal government did just this with the War Measures Act during the FLQ crisis, described earlier). Internationally, states can establish bilateral agreements on extradition of terrorists for trial. For example, the political exception rule allows defendants accused of terrorist acts to claim that they were engaged in political acts of conscience so that they are not subject to extradition. The bilateral United States–United Kingdom extradition treaty removes this rule from certain acts of terrorism, such as skyjacking. A number of international multilateral treaties on terrorism also exist, though many states have yet to sign them (see Profile 6.8). States also share intelligence and occasionally cooperate in anti-terrorist activities.

Finally, publicity is a major objective behind terrorist activities. Acts of terrorism bring attention not only to the attack itself but also to the individuals and groups who carried out the act, the cause or aim they purport to achieve, and the grievances or injustices they are struggling against. Terrorism attracts the attention of the media, the public, and government officials and elected leaders. The role of the media in covering terrorist incidents is controversial. Some argue that media coverage of terrorist incidents encourages terrorism (by providing terrorists with the publicity they seek) and that such

1963	Tokyo Convention on Offences and Certain Other Acts Committed on Board Aircraft	1973	Convention on the Prevention and Punishment of Crimes against Internationally Protected Persons, Including Diplomatic Agents
1970	The Hague Convention for the Suppression of Unlawful Seizure of Aircraft	1979	International Convention on the Taking of Hostages
1971	Convention to Prevent and Punish Acts of Terrorism Taking the Form of Crimes against Persons and Related Extortion That Are of International Significance	1999	International Convention for the Suppression of the Financing of Terrorism
1971	Montreal Convention for the Suppression of Unlawful Acts against the Safety of Civil Aviation		

coverage lacks sophistication and a high level of informed comment. Others argue that a free media is an essential component of a free society and that media reporting on terrorism, as long as it remains within appropriate ethical and legal boundaries, should not be constrained.

INTERNATIONAL ORGANIZED CRIME

Traditionally, organized crime has been regarded as a domestic political problem for societies and governments. While this is still largely the case, criminal activity has become increasingly internationalized. Today, transnational organized crime has been identified as a serious global security issue by the G-7/G-8, the UN, and the **Organization of American States (OAS)**. Indeed, at the 1995 G-7 summit in Halifax, the states declared that such activity represented a growing threat to the security of the G-7 countries.[41] Transnational crime has been identified as an international security issue for the following reasons:

- International criminal activity has escalated in terms of monetary scale and international scope. The world's organized crime syndicates are estimated to gross U.S.$1.5 trillion a year. The retail value of the global drug trade alone has been estimated at between U.S.$400 billion annually (about 8 percent of world trade).[42] Drugs flow from production centres to virtually every region in the world.

- Organized crime has expanded into international banking, investment, finance, and business activity. The German Federal Intelligence Service has reported that economic crime is the "world's largest criminal growth area."[43] Before it was exposed, the infamous Bank of Credit and Commerce International (BCCI) served as a money laundering and criminal finance system for organized crime. For most of its 1.4 million depositors, the BCCI was a bank like any other. The amount of money laundered by organized crime (hiding the origin of dirty money so it can be used openly) is estimated at U.S.$500 million a year.

- Criminal organizations have become threats to governments. In Italy, the Mafia has used assassinations and bombings to intimidate the Italian government and Italian law enforcement authorities. In Colombia drug cartels have killed judges and politicians.

- Criminal organizations can erode the social fabric of a country, undermining political authority and corrupting the economic and political leadership of states and their governments. In some cases, however, this is because criminal organizations actually improve the standard of living of rural workers or inner-city youths, whereas governments neglect them.

- In some countries, organized crime represents a threat to the conventional economy and the ability of the government to manage it. In Russia, organized crime accounts for a major portion of economic activity that is beyond government regulation and taxation. According to international crime analyst Louise Shelley, "the most lucrative element of post-Soviet transnational criminality lies in the area of large-scale fraud against government."[44]

- Worrisome indications exist that organized crime may be involved in the international sale of materials required for the production of weapons of mass destruction, in particular nuclear materials, which have appeared in small quantities for sale in Europe.

- The distinction between organized crime and terrorist and guerrilla movements is blurring as terrorist and guerrilla organizations obtain funding from the sale of drugs and as governments funnel money from illegal arms sales to guerrillas.

Organized crime exists in virtually all societies in all regions of the world, but the United States, Canada, Mexico, Colombia, Italy, Russia, China, and Japan harbour particularly powerful criminal organizations. Many of these organizations have been increasing their cooperation with one another across state and regional boundaries. In North America, the Mafia or *Cosa Nostra* dominates organized crime. Its activities include drug trafficking, union control and corruption, loan sharking, illegal gambling, and financial fraud. Mexican crime organizations smuggle drugs on behalf of the South American drug cartels and smuggle illegal immigrants (with the assistance of the Chinese Triads) into the United States. In Italy, the Mafia dominates, with operations in more than 40 countries. In Russia, the Russian *mafiya* has expanded rapidly, making inroads into North America and Europe. Their activities include slavery, theft, extortion, murder, money laundering, and poppy production (for the world heroin market). In Asia, the Six Great Triads (based largely in Hong Kong and Taiwan) form the largest and oldest criminal network in the world. They are involved in drug trafficking, arms trafficking, illegal immigration, gambling, prostitution, fraud, and product piracy. The Japanese *Boryokudan,* or *Yakuza* (the name used in the West for Japanese organized crime syndicates), also operate throughout Asia.

The expansion of crime into an international activity and the growing communication and cooperation among organized crime syndicates has been facilitated by the growth of global interdependence. Other contributing factors include the collapse of Communism in the Soviet Union and the growth of capitalism in China, which have removed social barriers to criminal activity in those countries. The establishment of free trade areas and customs unions (especially in North America and Europe) has facilitated the flow of criminal goods and services across borders. The weakening of state authority in many countries has eroded the capacity of police and judicial systems to combat organized crime; and, of course, many governments are quite literally supportive of, and supported by, organized crime.

Criminal organizations often form alliances and agreements, designed for mutual benefit. For example, Colombian cocaine trafficking syndicates have exchanged cocaine for heroin provided by Nigerians. The Sicilian Mafia has cooperated with the Colombian drug syndicates, providing access to their distribution system in Europe in exchange for access to the Colombian distribution system in the United States to recapture the market share they had lost to Asian heroin producers.[45] Of course, these arrangements between criminal organizations are often fleeting and are based purely on self-interest; few other incentives hold such alliances together. In addition, the world of international organized crime is also one of conflict, as criminal organizations often seek to eliminate their competitors by whatever means necessary.

The line between organized crime and terrorism and guerrilla movements used to be very distinct: terrorists were motivated more by ideological objectives. In contrast, criminal organizations were interested in increasing their sales, markets, and revenues. Terrorist goals included the weakening of the state and the social and political order. Criminal organizations had an interest in economic stability so that they could pursue their business activities. However, the lines between the criminal, the terrorist, and the guerrilla are blurring. Many terrorist organizations are increasingly engaged in profit-generating criminal activity, and many criminal organizations have embarked on campaigns of politically inspired violence. Criminal and terrorist or guerrilla organizations are also engaging in cooperation. As former director of the Central Intelligence Agency James Woolsey warned, "In Latin America powerful drug groups have established ad hoc, mutually beneficial arrangements with terrorist groups such as the Sendero Luminoso in Peru and the Revolutionary Armed Forces of Colombia, or FARC ... insurgents are sometimes paid to provide security services for drug traffickers, they often 'tax' drug operations in areas they control, and, in some cases, are directly involved in drug cultivation."[46] Of course, one would need a fine-toothed comb indeed to discover all the connections to organized criminals and terrorists Mr. Woolsey's organization has fostered over the years!

As the operations of criminal organizations have become increasingly international, the effort to combat international crime has involved greater cooperation and coordination of effort between countries. The United States, for example, has developed a very high level of cooperation with many South American countries to assist in the effort against the drug cartels. This cooperation involves agreements on punishments and extradition, law enforcement coordination, intelligence sharing, and military cooperation. As international crime is only likely to increase, measures such as these may become increasingly common as governments seek to join forces to combat criminal organizations that possess resources greater than those of many states. Meanwhile, the demand for drugs in the United States, the real source of the Colombian cartel's wealth, continues. Until this demand is reduced, there is little hope that the drug trade can be defeated. The United States continues to wage a largely futile war on drugs in the Caribbean and South America. In 2000, the United States spent U.S.$1.3 billion on mostly military aid to Colombia alone to combat the drug problem. Critics charge that this military aid is undermining Colombian democracy, ignoring the social plight of Colombia's poor, and supporting paramilitary groups that have been accused of human rights violations.

CONCLUSIONS

In this chapter, we have explored some of the major issues facing international security in current global politics. Is the world a more dangerous place after the Cold War? It is true that the end of the Cold War made the world safer from the threat of global nuclear war. Another positive is that the likelihood of a great power war remains low. However, the sad fact is that the world is significantly safer only for people living in North America, most of Europe, and, perhaps, Japan. In much of the rest of the world, there has been no respite from regional wars or the threat of the outbreak of such wars. Indeed, it is possible to speak of the world in terms of zones of peace and zones of instability. Zones of peace, such as North America and Western Europe, enjoy relative peace and freedom from the threat of war, a high level of prosperity, and high levels of economic and political cooperation. Within zones of instability, wars rage unchecked, the threat of war looms over daily life, prosperity is a distant hope, and economic and political cooperation is limited or fragile. The question is, Which of these zones will widen in the future? Will more regions become increasingly stable and free of conflict, or will instability and violence spread?

We have also looked at weapons proliferation, intrastate conflict, international terrorism, and transnational organized crime. These are just some of the issues that are presently shaping the current international security field, and we will encounter others in subsequent chapters. International efforts to prevent, control, or manage warfare and international security concerns are collectively known as conflict management efforts. We will explore these efforts in the next chapter.

Endnotes

1. *The Twenty Years' Crisis* (London: Macmillan, 1942), 139.
2. J. Levy, *War in the Modern Great Power System, 1496–1975* (Lexington: University Press of Kentucky, 1983), 117.
3. Ruth Leger Sivard, *World Military and Social Expenditures 1991* (Washington, DC: World Priorities, 1991), 20.
4. See Kalevi J. Holsti, *The State, War, and the State of War* (Cambridge: Cambridge University Press, 1996), 22.
5. Ruth Leger Sivard, *World Military and Social Expenditures 1991* (Washington, DC: World Priorities, 1991), 20.
6. See G. Strada, "The Horror of Landmines," *Scientific American* (May 1996), 40.
7. See *SIPRI Yearbook, 1999* (Stockholm: Stockholm International Peace Research Institute, 1999).
8. Quincy Wright, *A Study of War*, vol. 1 (Chicago: University of Chicago Press, 1942), 17.
9. S. Freud, *Civilization, Society, and Religion*, edited by A. Dickson, translated by J. Strachey (New York: Penguin Books, 1985), 357.
10. K. Lorenz, *On Aggression* (New York: Harcourt Brace, 1966).
11. See R. Jervis, *Perception and Misperception in International Politics* (Princeton: Princeton University Press, 1976), 154; and M.G. Hermann, "Explaining Foreign Policy Behaviour Using the Personal Characteristics of Political Leaders," *International Studies Quarterly* 24 (March 1980), 8.
12. See John Keegan, *A History of Warfare* (New York: Alfred A. Knopf, 1993), 86–9.
13. Kenneth Waltz, *Man, the State, and War* (New York: Columbia University Press, 1959), 232.
14. See G. Modelski, *Exploring Long Cycles* (Boulder, CO: Lynne Rienner, 1987), and W. Thompson, *On Global War: Historical-Structural Approaches to World Politics* (Columbia, SC: University of South Carolina Press, 1988).
15. See L. Freedman and E. Karsh, *The Gulf Conflict 1990–1991: Diplomacy and War in the New World Order* (Princeton: Princeton University Press, 1993), 408–9.
16. "Africa's Forgotten War," *The Economist* (8 May 1999), p. 41.
17. M. Brecher, *Crisis in World Politics: Theory and Reality* (Oxford: Pergamon Press, 1993), 68–9, 171.

18. See Herbert K. Tillema, "Foreign Overt Military Intervention in the Nuclear Age," *Journal of Peace Research* 26 (May 1989), 179–95, and *Overt Military Intervention in the Cold War Era* (Columbia, SC: University of South Carolina Press, 1996).

19. This term is employed by T.R. Gurr, *Minorities at Risk: A Global View of Ethnopolitical Conflicts* (Washington, DC: United States Institute of Peace, 1993).

20. See M. Small and J.D. Singer, *Resort to Arms: International and Civil Wars, 1816–1980* (Beverly Hills: Sage, 1982); J.D. Singer, "Peace in the Global System: Displacement, Interregnum, or Transformation?" in C.W. Kegley, Jr., ed., *The Long Postwar Peace* (New York: HarperCollins, 1991), 56–84; and P. Wallenstein and K. Axell, "Armed Conflict at the End of the Cold War, 1989–1992," *Journal of Peace Research* 30 (August 1993), 331–46.

21. Holsti, *The State, War, and the State of War*, 22.

22. D. Carment, "The International Dimensions of Ethnic Conflict," *Journal of Peace Research* 30 (May 1993), 137–50.

23. M. Esman, *Ethnic Politics* (Ithaca, NY: Cornell University Press, 1995); S. Griffiths, *Nationalism and Ethnic Conflict* (New York: Oxford University Press, 1993); J.A. Spence, "Introduction and Overview," *International Affairs*, Special Issue on Ethnicity and International Relations, 72 (July 1996).

24. Gurr, *Minorities at Risk*, 3.

25. Holsti, *The State, War, and the State of War*, 20.

26. See Gail Lapidus, "Contested Sovereignty: The Tragedy of Chechnya," *International Security* 23 (Summer 1998), 5–49.

27. See B. Bueno de Mesquita and W.H. Riker, "An Assessment of the Merits of Selective Proliferation," *Journal of Conflict Resolution* 26 (June 1982), 283–306; J. Mearsheimer, "The Case for a Ukrainian Nuclear Deterrent," *Foreign Affairs* 72 (Summer 1993), 50–66; and K. Waltz, "Nuclear Myths and Political Realities," *American Political Science Review* 84 (September 1990), 731–45.

28. *The Spread of Nuclear Weapons: More May Be Better*, Adelphi Paper No. 171 (London: International Institute for Strategic Studies, Autumn 1981), 5.

29. See L. Dunn, *Containing Nuclear Proliferation*, Adelphi Paper No. 263 (London: International Institute for Strategic Studies, 1991); K. Kaiser, "Non-Proliferation and Nuclear Deterrence," *Survival* 31 (March/April 1989), 123–36; and S. Miller, "The Case against a Ukrainian Nuclear Deterrent," *Foreign Affairs* 72 (Summer 1993), 67–80.

30. For three models of weapons proliferation incentives, see S. Sagan, "Why Do States Build Nuclear Weapons? Three Models in Search of a Bomb," *International Security* 21 (Winter 1996/97), 54–86.

31. See R. Molander and P. Wilson, "On Dealing With the Prospect of Nuclear Chaos," *The Washington Quarterly* 17 (1994), 32.

32. Tavleen Singh, "Get Back to Basics," *India Today*, 8 June 1998.

33. *SIPRI Yearbook, 1999* (Stockholm: Stockholm International Peace Research Institute, 1999), and *World Military Expenditures and Arms Transfers, 1995*, United States Arms Control and Disarmament Agency (Washington: United States Government Printing Office, 1996), 9.

34. "The Covert Arms Trade," *The Economist* (12 February 1994), 21.

35. Ibid., 21.

36. Walter Laqueur, "Postmodern Terrorism," *Foreign Affairs* 75 (September/October 1996), 24–36.

37. Cindy Combs, *Terrorism in the Twenty-First Century* (Upper Saddle River, NJ: Prentice Hall, 1997), 8.

38. See *Patterns of Global Terrorism, 1999* (Washington, DC: United States Department of State, 2000).

39. See J. Simon, "Misunderstanding Terrorism," *Foreign Policy* (Summer 1987), 104–20.

40. Laqueur, "Postmodern Terrorism," 25.

41. Robert Chote and Peter Norman, "Leaders Zero In on Crime and Nuclear Safety," *Financial Times* (19 June 1995), 5.

42. *Human Development Report 1999* (New York: United Nations, 1999).

43. Karl-Ludwig Guensche, "BND Warns against New Mafia Methods," FBIS Report, AU0507132496 Berlin *Die Welt* (5 July 1996), 2.

44. Louise I. Shelley, "Transnational Organized Crime: An Imminent Threat to the Nation-State?" *Journal of International Affairs* 48 (Winter 1995), 485.

45. See Shelley, "Transnational Organized Crime."

46. James Woolsey, "Global Organized Crime: Threats to U.S. and International Security," Address for the Centre for Strategic and International Studies, Washington DC, 26 September 1994, 1.

Suggested Readings

Betts, Richard K., ed. *Conflict after the Cold War: Arguments on Causes of War and Peace*. New York: Macmillan, 1994.

Bueno de Mesquita, Bruce. *The War Trap*. New Haven, CT: Yale University Press, 1981.

Cashman, Greb. *What Causes War: An Introduction to Theories of International Conflict*. New York: Lexington Books, 1993.

Claude, Inis L., Jr. *Power and International Relations*. New York: Random House, 1962.

Coker, Christopher. *War in the Twentieth Century: The Impact of War on Modern Consciousness*. London: Brassey's, 1994.

Creveld, Martin van. *Technology and War: From 2000 B.C. to the Present*. New York: Free Press, 1989.

Freedman, Lawrence, ed. *War*. New York: Oxford University Press, 1994.

Gilpin, Robert. *War and Change in World Politics*. Cambridge: Cambridge University Press, 1981.

Holsti, K.J. *Peace and War: Armed Conflicts and International Order 1648–1989*. New York: Cambridge University Press, 1991.

Kegley, Charles W., Jr. *International Terrorism: Characteristics, Causes, Controls*. New York: St. Martin's Press, 1994.

Sederberg, Peter C. *Fires Within: Political Violence and Revolutionary Change*. New York: HarperCollins, 1994.

Vasquez, John A. *The War Puzzle*. Cambridge: Cambridge University Press, 1993.

Suggested Websites

Stockholm International Peace Research Institute

Center for Defense Information
<www.cdi.org>

War, Peace and Security Guide
<www.cfcsc.dnd.ca>

International Relations and Security Network

CrisisWeb

Physicians for Global Survival
<www.web.net/~pgs/>

Conflict Management in Global Politics

We are here to choose between the quick and the dead.

—Bernard Baruch, 1946[1]

RESPONDING TO THE INTERNATIONAL SECURITY AGENDA

In Chapter 6, we examined some of the key issues and challenges facing the contemporary international system from a security studies perspective. This chapter explores the instruments and tools of conflict management, including direct and indirect diplomatic interaction, arms control and disarmament, the use of international organizations and law, peacekeeping and humanitarian intervention, and economic statecraft. Our aim in this chapter is to evaluate what could be called the international conflict management tool kit. What instruments have been developed to control, prevent, or otherwise manage security challenges in global politics? To what extent have these instruments been useful or found wanting? Like the study of international security, the study of *international conflict management* has evolved with changing agendas and new challenges. As we will see, traditional conflict management instruments have been adapted to the post–Cold War setting with mixed results.

THE NATURE OF DIPLOMACY

Diplomacy is purposeful communication between states. It involves state leaders (and increasingly the leaders of communal groups) as well as career diplomats and bureaucrats. While diplomacy is an everyday feature of international life, it is also the foundation of efforts to prevent, contain, and manage international conflict.

Public and private diplomatic affairs are highly formalized events, characterized by painstaking attention to tradition and protocol. For example, when a **head of state** makes a formal visit to a foreign country, an elaborate reception protocol demands a formal reception at the airport, a red carpet, a greeting line of dignitaries, an honour guard (dutifully inspected by the visitor), a band (playing the national anthem of the visitor), an escorted motorcade to a hotel or the seat of government, and at least one formal state dinner. While the receptions for visitors or diplomats of lesser rank are not as elaborate, they are no less established as conventions. Though

Is all this just formality? Prime Minister Jean Chrétien and U.S. President Bill Clinton stand at attention on the south lawn of the White House in 1997 during a state arrival ceremony for the prime minister. (CP Picture Archive/Tom Hanson)

many of the trappings of past diplomatic practice have been discarded, many of the key traditions, such as diplomatic immunity, linger in contemporary diplomacy. As we discussed in Chapter 5, states that have embassies in foreign countries can legitimately lay claim to that space as part of their own territory. This principle of **extraterritoriality** is a cornerstone of diplomatic tradition. According to Garret Mattingly, it evolved in the early days of the Westphalian state system, when states "found they could only communicate with one another by tolerating within themselves little islands of alien sovereignty."[2]

Diplomatic protocol prevents individuals, groups, and states from clashing on issues of symbolism and prestige and maintains the image that diplomats, officials, and leaders of equivalent rank are treated as equals. Formality and protocol also reduce the chances that personalities will interfere with communication between governments, but they are not always successful. Miscommunication occurs often in global politics, sometimes with tragic results. Personalities are often a crucial influence on affairs of state. Canadians, for example, have often expressed an interest in the personal relationship between the prime minister and the president of the United States, and they have expressed anxiety when the two leaders do not get along (John Diefenbaker and John F. Kennedy) and when they seem to get along too well (Brian Mulroney and Ronald Reagan).

However, diplomacy has undergone some significant changes, particularly in the latter half of the twentieth century. Decolonization and increased global interdependence have forced diplomatic services to adjust to larger numbers of states and a much wider variety of language and cultures. Some Canadian embassies now have more staff than the entire Canadian foreign policy establishment employed before World War II. Developments in global communications have made contact between governments and their representatives abroad virtually instantaneous. Gone are the days when diplomatic pouches would outline broad policy and give a diplomat considerable leeway to make decisions. In addition, governments now maintain active links to a wide variety of international organizations and nonstate actors.

As indicated in Chapter 3, foreign policy remains a relatively closed area of government activity. Nevertheless, open availability of information about international events and the increased relevance of public opinion in many countries have made diplomacy a much more public affair, and this has many implications. The views and opinions of professional career diplomats may be rejected or ignored by political leaderships if no public support exists for such measures. Conversely, public opinion may compel leaders to act in ways that are contrary to the advice of the diplomatic service. In one sense, then, public opinion may cause the diplomacy of a state or group to be more reflective of the body of the people; however, it may lead to rash or dangerous diplomacy designed primarily to capture votes. In addition, businesses, NGOs, academics, and bureaucrats have increased opportunities for interaction that can have an impact on international diplomacy (this is sometimes called *track two diplomacy*).

Finally, increasing importance is attached to summit diplomacy, the formal meeting of heads of state and government. Summit diplomacy has both its advocates and its detractors. Summits can enable leaders to establish a personal rapport and remove the frustrating constraints of the slow and bureaucratic diplomatic process. The **Camp David** accords, which brought Egyptian President Anwar Sadat and Israeli Prime Minister Menachem Begin together at President Jimmy Carter's official Maryland retreat, resulted in a peace agreement between two countries that had fought four wars in the past 30 years. (A similar attempt by Bill Clinton in 2000 was less successful.)

However, summitry can lead to ill-advised decisions made by leaders without adequate consultation with experts or time for reflection. At the Yalta Summit in 1945 (discussed in Chapter 2) between Winston Churchill, Franklin Roosevelt, and Josef Stalin, Roosevelt acquiesced to an agreement that would divide Europe into spheres of influence and pave the way for Soviet domination of Eastern Europe. (It is unclear, however, whether he had any real choice in the matter.) Summits have also been criticized as being little more than photo opportunities and cocktail parties, often leading to no substantive progress or involving only the signing of agreements worked out in advance by diplomats. They can also attract large protest gatherings, as demonstrated during the Summit of the Americas in Quebec City in April 2001.

DIPLOMATIC TECHNIQUES AND CONFLICT MANAGEMENT

Throughout history, states and groups have used similar basic diplomatic techniques, which can essentially be reduced to the use of threats and promises. The effectiveness of diplomacy as a conflict management instrument depends heavily on one variable: whether a set of proposals can be developed that each party prefers over reaching no agreement at all or over using violence to settle their dispute. In the absence of a set of outcomes acceptable to all sides, diplomacy will fail as a means of preventing, controlling, or managing conflict. Conflict management diplomacy is about facilitating and encouraging the development of such sets of proposals.[3] One of the ironies of diplomacy as a conflict management tool is that in periods of war or crisis, at precisely the time when effective diplomatic communication is most valuable, such communication is least frequent. Often, countries in a dispute will break off diplomatic relations, necessitating a reopening of communication or the involvement of a third party.

Several diplomatic techniques have been employed to facilitate conflict management efforts.

Signalling

States and groups use signals to communicate intent and commitment. Signals may be very direct, coming in the form of speeches, written statements or proclamations, or direct diplomatic contact with individual representatives of other states or groups. Statements expressing Canada's displeasure over the Iraqi invasion of Kuwait and the Nigerian regime's execution of several political opponents in 1996 are examples of direct signalling. At other times, signals may be indirect and may come in the form of deliberate symbolic actions such as official or unofficial visits, the recall of ambassadors, or displays of military power. The problem with all signals is that they can be misunderstood or misinterpreted and sometimes missed altogether. Some signals can be very circumspect. In a particularly famous example, China invited the U.S. table tennis team to visit China during an international table tennis tournament in Japan in 1971. After some deliberation, it was decided (correctly) that this was an overture by the Chinese leadership to improve relations between China and the United States. Thus, the term *ping pong diplomacy* was coined.

Bargaining and Negotiation

Another technique is the use of bargaining, an attempt to reach an agreement on issues of symbolic or substantive value to all parties. Bargaining and negotiation (bargaining in a formal setting) is all about establishing how such symbolic and substantive desires and aims will be exchanged and divided among the parties to the mutual agreement of all. Not all agreements will be equally beneficial to all sides; in fact, some agreements will be very unequal. This imbalance occurs because parties to a dispute bring different means of leverage to the bargaining or negotiation process. Leverage originates with power capabilities, and these can be employed by offering rewards, issuing threats, or appealing to sentiments of friendship, allegiance, or shared ideology or religion. When one or some parties have leverage over the others, unequal arrangements are frequently (though not always) the result.[4] Over time, several tactics for successful negotiation have emerged:

- Discourage zero-sum views of the issues.
- Establish a fair compromise to ensure a lasting settlement.
- Avoid ultimatums and posturing; encourage dialogue and debate.
- Avoid humiliating one's opponents.
- Blend rewards and threats.
- Avoid personal *ad hominem* attacks on the other party.
- Look for bridges, solutions that are acceptable to both sides but different from the positions taken at the beginning of negotiations.
- Look for nonspecific compensation, in which one side gets what it wants but gives up something that was not part of the original dispute or discussion.
- Divide the issue into separate and more manageable subjects for agreement.

Third-Party Mediation

Third parties, whether they are individuals, groups, organizations, or states, can be invited by the parties to assist the process of reaching a settlement. Third parties can offer a number of services, which include

- Providing **good offices** (acting as a conduit for communication), a role performed on two separate occasions by U.S. Secretaries of State Henry Kissinger and James Baker in their "shuttle diplomacy" flights between Middle East capitals during negotiations; this role is a primary function of the secretary-general of the UN.
- Providing a neutral site for negotiations (a role often performed by Switzerland and specifically the city of Geneva).
- Clarifying facts and evidence (which may involve providing figures or conducting fact-finding missions).
- Acting as a mediator by becoming active in negotiations, making suggestions that might be agreeable to all sides, and breaking deadlocks when they occur.
- Acting as an arbitrator (making a judgment on the dispute and establishing a fair settlement) with the consent of the parties.
- Acting as an adjudicator (making a judgment with reference to international law).

Naturally, any international actor entrusted with such roles must be respected by all sides, be perceived as neutral with little or no agenda of its own, and be capable of performing such tasks.

DIPLOMACY AS A CONFLICT MANAGEMENT INSTRUMENT

The record of diplomatic efforts to prevent, control, or manage conflicts is mixed. Certainly there have been spectacular failures, most notably in the weeks before the outbreak of World War I. Of course, when wars do break out, any diplomatic efforts to prevent them are by definition failures. However, there have been successful cases of diplomatic conflict management, and most conflicts between actors in the international system are resolved peacefully through diplomatic means. In 1987, Indian military exercises prompted the mobilization of the Pakistani army. Within days, the two countries were poised on the brink of war, with an implicit threat of nuclear hostilities. However, because of diplomatic exchanges between the two countries, both sides backed away from hostilities that neither wanted. Also in 1987, but in a multilateral setting, Costa Rican President Oscar Arias designed a peace accord for Central America involving Costa Rica, El Salvador, Nicaragua, Honduras, and Guatemala. All parties agreed to eliminate restrictions on dissent, offer political amnesty to rebel movements, hold national elections, negotiate ceasefires between governments and rebel groups, deny the use of their territory to rebel groups from other countries, and cut off superpower aid to rebel groups. It was a remarkable achievement, and although never fully implemented, the Arias Plan won Oscar Arias the 1987 Nobel Peace Prize. Other areas where negotiations are vital include the Indo–Pakistani dispute over Kashmir, the ongoing dialogue between North and South Korea, the various Balkan states (following the fall of the Milosevic regime in Serbia in 2000), and the peace agreement signed by Ethiopia and Eritrea in December 2000. Two of the most watched diplomatic conflict management efforts today are the Middle East peace process and the Northern Ireland peace process, and we expand briefly on these below.

Diplomacy and Conflict Management in the Middle East

Since the late 1940s, the key component of the Middle East peace process has been the Israeli–Palestinian conflict. Other actors such as Syria and Egypt and various armed groups in Lebanon are also part of the conflict management equation, but a lasting peace in the Middle East is heavily dependent on an Israeli–Palestinian accommodation. At the root of the conflict is land: both Israelis and Palestinians claim the same territory, and so conflict management efforts have concentrated on issues such as control of land, Palestinian self-rule, control of Jerusalem (which both sides regard as their indivisible capital as well as a holy centre), Palestinian refugees, Israeli settlements on the West Bank, economic opportunity for Palestinians, and access to water resources. For decades, this conflict resisted all efforts at diplomatic management, with the Palestine Liberation Organization (PLO) and the government of Israel using acts of terror, assassinations, military action, civil disturbance (such as the Palestinian youth uprising, or *Intifada*) and economic coercion to promote or protect their interests.

A breakthrough occurred in September of 1993. Israeli and PLO officials had been meeting in secret in Oslo, Norway. With the mediation of the Norwegian government, negotiators reached agreement on a Declaration of Principles signed in Washington by Israeli Prime Minister Yitzak Rabin (who was assassinated in 1995) and Yasser Arafat on 13 September 1993. In this declaration, Israel recognized the PLO as the legitimate representative of the Palestinian people, and the PLO recognized Israel's right to exist and renounced terrorism. The declaration also included the goals of future negotiations, the most important of which was Israeli withdrawal from the Gaza strip and the West Bank, and self-rule for Palestinians in those territories. A follow-up Interim Agreement signed in 1995 provided for the phased transfer of some land to Palestinian control, the phased withdrawal of Israeli forces from those areas, easier movement for Palestinians between Gaza and the West Bank, and greater freedom for the Palestinian economy, which is heavily dependent on Israel. In return the PLO agreed to prevent further terrorist attacks

Violence in the Middle East, 2000. Following the funeral of 14-year-old Majid al-Hawamdeh, killed in clashes with Israeli soldiers in the West Bank town of Ramallah, Palestinians engage Israeli troops on the outskirts of Ramallah. Live fire was shot from both sides. Israeli Prime Minister Ehud Barak told his cabinet that Israel needed a "timeout" to reassess the tattered peace process, a move that would put on hold years of negotiations with the Palestinians. (CP Picture Archive/Jerome Delay)

on Israel. Since the signing of these agreements, progress has been slow. Renewed terrorist attacks by Palestinian splinter groups caused Israel to suspend implementation, while the continued development of Israeli settlements in the West Bank caused consternation among Palestinians. The economic situation for most Palestinians has worsened, and Palestinian refugees are becoming increasingly impatient for their chance to return home. Some progress was made: an agreement to divide the city of Hebron was reached in 1997, and both sides renewed their commitment to peace in the Wye River Memorandum in 1998. However, progress ground to a halt again, and on 10 July 2000 Israeli Prime Minister Ehud Barak and Yasser Arafat held a summit, with the mediation of U.S. President Bill Clinton, in an effort to break the deadlock. The talks broke up on July 25 over disagreement about the future of Jerusalem. A controversial visit to Jerusalem by Ariel Sharon (who was recently elected prime minister) in the fall of 2000 sparked outbreaks of violence, and by the end of 2000, 300 Palestinians and 38 Israelis had been killed. The international community has struggled with how to respond to this latest round of violence in the Middle East.

Diplomacy and Conflict Management in Northern Ireland

The conflict in Northern Ireland has its origins in the Protestant English conquest of Catholic Ireland in the early seventeenth century. It has since become a conflict involving nationality, sovereignty, and self-determination. English dominance in Ireland was secured by William of Orange at the Battle of the Boyne in 1690. Catholic resistance and revolt through to the early twentieth century (including the famous Easter Rising in 1916) increased sentiment in England for Home Rule in Ireland. This idea was opposed by Protestants as a recipe for absorption into the Catholic majority. After the Irish Civil War (1919–21) between the British and the Irish Republican Army (IRA) ended in a truce and the independence of southern Ireland in 1922, sectarian violence in the north continued between Catholic Nationalists or Republicans who wanted the six counties of Northern Ireland united with the south, and Protestant Loyalists or Unionists who wanted Northern Ireland to remain under British rule. The period between 1920 and 1969 was relatively calm, but sectarian violence returned in what has been called the modern "time of troubles" in which more than 3225 people were killed. The IRA was revived and began a campaign of violence against Protestants. The British Army returned to Northern Ireland to restore stability. However, after the shooting of unarmed protestors in Londonderry in 1972 (known as *Bloody Sunday*) and the imposition of direct rule from London, the British Army was regarded as an occupying force by most Catholics. Bombings and shootings by the IRA and extremist Protestant organizations continued through to the early 1990s. As with so many conflicts, most people and parties in Northern Ireland want a peaceful settlement, but extremist violence has polarized the two sides and made compromise and reconciliation difficult. Many diplomatic efforts have been made to resolve the conflict, but they have foundered because of refusals to negotiate or the outbreak of violence.

A new round of peace talks began in 1996, under the mediation of U.S. Senator George Mitchell. Present were the Irish and British governments, and after the IRA announced a ceasefire and came to the table in 1997, all the major parties were present. Working under a deadline imposed by Mitchell, a diplomatic breakthrough occurred on 10 April 1998. The settlement was called the Belfast Agreement, but it is commonly called the Good Friday agreement. The agreement included the following: Northern Ireland would remain a part of Great Britain as long as a majority of people wanted it; an assembly would be established in Northern Ireland for self-governance; institutions would be established to develop more cooperation between Northern Ireland and the Republic of Ireland; and the civil rights of Catholics would be established and protected. The agreement went to a referendum and passed by a large majority. Elections were held for the new assembly in June. However, violence did continue in the all too familiar forms of bombings, assassinations, and attacks on property.

Tensions rose during the infamous *Orange Marches*, which commemorate the Battle of the Boyne. In late 1999, the implementation of the Good Friday agreement stalled. The new assembly was suspended by the British government when the IRA refused to disarm. All sides have pledged to work toward peace and revive the Good Friday agreement, so diplomacy may still be given a chance in a conflict that has resisted resolution for decades. However, violence remains a dreaded possibility as the two sides struggle to deal not only with each other but also with the more militant sects within their own groups.

These cases illustrate how diplomatic conflict management efforts can overcome deep divisions and distrust, but they also illustrate the enormity of the challenges facing diplomatic efforts to resolve conflicts. For diplomacy to be a successful conflict management instrument, the parties to a dispute must prefer a negotiated settlement to other available alternatives (such as war or achieving no settlement at all). This is not always the case, and if one or more parties to a dispute are not interested in negotiations or bargain in bad faith or refuse to compromise on certain issues, diplomacy stands little chance of success. Even when there is a commitment from all parties to achieving a settlement, they may have difficulty controlling their own people in order to implement the results of negotiation.

As a result, the outcomes of diplomatic conflict management efforts may be many and varied. Results can include an improved climate between the parties to a dispute; the establishment of a basis for further negotiation; the creation of a short-term agreement to settle an immediate problem; or the establishment of a firm basis for a lasting peace. However, results can include the creation of an agreement that becomes a point of dissatisfaction or humiliation for one of the actors or a breakdown in negotiations and the collapse of diplomatic efforts. Diplomatic outcomes will not necessarily eliminate the possibility of future disputes between the parties, but diplomatic effort is a crucial instrument for resolving conflicts in global politics. Without it, recourse to armed struggle is often the consequence.

DISARMAMENT AND ARMS CONTROL

The main assumption behind disarmament and arms control efforts is that weapons contribute to the outbreak of war, a position juxtaposed with the view that peace and stability can only be attained through balances of power or through preparation for war.[5] Advocates of disarmament and arms control argue that the frequency of war can be reduced by eliminating threatening or destabilizing weapons; preventing arms races that increase tensions and hostility and absorb financial resources; promoting mutual trust and confidence; and limiting the destructiveness of war if it does occur. In certain periods in history, the idea of disarmament and arms control has been well received. The destructiveness of World War I led to several arms control efforts. After World War II, the development of the atomic bomb and the nuclear arms race between the superpowers vastly increased the sense that something had to be done to control the development and production of these weapons. Peace movement organizations sponsored rallies, marches, and concerts dedicated to ending the arms race. Here we see nonstate actors playing in what was previously a very state-centric game. In the contemporary post–Cold War period, interest has surged in existing arms control arrangements (as well as in the prospects for creating new ones) that are relevant to transnational security issues.

At this point, an important distinction must be made. Disarmament efforts seek to drastically reduce or eliminate all weapons as an important step toward the elimination of war itself. Arms control, however, aims at regulating the growth of weapons and sometimes (but not always) reducing arms levels. The aim of **arms control** is not the eradication of weapons or the elimination of war but the reduction in the risk of war through efforts to stabilize the status quo, build confidence between states and groups, encourage the peaceful resolution of disputes, and discourage the use of force. Therefore, "arms control is fundamentally a conservative enterprise. Disarmament seeks to overturn the status quo; arms control works to perpetuate it."[6]

Not surprisingly, then, few historical examples of disarmament efforts exist. Some of the more notable follow:

- In sixth-century B.C.E. China, several states formed a disarmament league that contributed to a century of peace.

- In 1817, Great Britain and the United States signed the Rush–Bagot Treaty, which demilitarized the Canada–U.S. border and called for the dismantling of a number of military vessels on the Great Lakes, establishing the basis for what would become the world's longest undefended border.

- At the end of World War I, U.S. President Woodrow Wilson called for national disarmament to the lowest point consistent with domestic safety, a provision later watered down to disarmament to the lowest level consistent with national safety, which could mean almost anything.

- The League of Nations sponsored a World Disarmament Conference in 1932, which attempted to ban offensive weapons but foundered on the definition of which weapons were defensive and which were offensive.

- The United Nations has held a number of special sessions on disarmament since its inception in 1946.

Other examples of disarmament are forced measures (such as the restrictions placed on German armaments in the Versailles Treaty and on Japan after World War II) or are unintentional, caused by chaotic conditions within a state (such as the effect of the Iranian Revolution on the Iranian armed forces, or the effect of the decline of the Russian economy on the Russian armed forces today). In short, disarmament has a very limited historical record, although, as we will see, a new trend toward disarmament efforts may be developing.

In contrast, the historical record of arms control agreements is vast and varied. In almost all cases, arms control efforts have attempted to ban the production or deployment of a specific weapon (or a variant of a weapon) or to restrict the number of weapons a signatory is allowed to possess. For example, in the eleventh century an effort was made by the Second Lateran Council to ban crossbows, and in 1868 the St. Petersburg Declaration banned explosive bullets. The 1899 and 1907 International Peace Conventions at The Hague banned a number of weapons (including poisonous gas). At the Washington Naval Conferences (1921–22), the United States, Great Britain, Japan, France, and Italy agreed to fixed ratios for the number of capital ships in their battle fleets, a production moratorium on new ones, and the scrapping of a significant number of those extant.

During the Cold War, two broad types of arms control agreements existed. The most prominent of these were the bilateral agreements established by the two superpowers. In addition, several multilateral arms control agreements involving other countries were established. Some of these multilateral arrangements were directly related to the Cold War, while others were intended to have a wider, universal effect. Some arms control agreements covered a specified territory or region, while others had a global, or system-wide, scope. Many of these agreements survive to this day and form the foundation of contemporary efforts to address the transnational security issues of the post–Cold War world.

BILATERAL ARMS CONTROL DURING AND AFTER THE COLD WAR

Bilateral agreements cover issues that concern two states. Compared with multilateral agreements, they tend to be easier to achieve because negotiators only have to concern themselves with one set of interests and differences. During the Cold War, superpower arms control focused on nuclear weapons and on ways to reduce the prospects for nuclear war. The signing of arms control agreements often accompanied larger efforts to improve the relationship between the United States and the Soviet Union in periods of détente. In addition, some arrangements were made in an informal manner: U.S. President Jimmy Carter and Soviet Foreign Minister Andrei Gromyko promised each other that their countries would never be the first to use nuclear weapons. This pledge was never made formal in an agreement, despite the efforts of "no first use declaration" advocates. NATO maintained the right to retaliate with nuclear weapons throughout the Cold War. In 1993 the new Russia confirmed the right to use nuclear weapons to defend itself.

Profile 7.1 reflects the impressive scope of bilateral arms control agreements between the United States and the Soviet Union/Russia (Russia has assumed the USSR's treaty obligations). Among the most important formal agreements were the **Strategic Arms Limitation Treaty (SALT)** and the **Strategic Arms Reduction Treaty (START)**. Signed in 1972, SALT I placed limits on the number of **intercontinental ballistic missiles (ICBMs)** and **submarine-launched ballistic missiles (SLBMs)** deployable by both sides for five years. SALT I also placed limits on the deployment of **antiballistic missiles (ABMs)** in the so-called ABM Treaty. In 1979, the more comprehensive SALT II agreement placed a ceiling of 2250 on the number of ICBMs, SLBMs, heavy bombers, and air-to-surface ballistic missiles (ASBMs) permitted by each side. After the 1979 Soviet invasion of Afghanistan, SALT II was never ratified by the United States Senate, although

PROFILE 7.1

Major Bilateral Arms Control Agreements between the United States and the Soviet Union/Russia

DATE	AGREEMENT	PRINCIPAL AIMS
1963	Hotline Agreement	Establishes a direct radio and telegraph communications link between Moscow and Washington (updated with a satellite communications link in 1971)
1971	Nuclear Accidents Agreement	Creates a procedure for notification of a nuclear accident or unauthorized detonation and establishes safeguards to prevent accidents
1972	SALT I Interim Agreement	Limits number of ICBMs and SLBMs allowed by each side
1972	Anti-Ballistic Missile Treaty	Limits deployment of anti-ballistic missile systems to two sites (later reduced to one in a protocol in 1974) and prohibits development of space-based ABM systems
1973	Agreement on the Prevention of Nuclear War	Superpowers agree to consult in the event of the threat of nuclear war
1974	Threshold Test Ban	Restricts underground testing of nuclear weapons over the yield of 150 kilotons; broadened in 1976
1977	Convention of the Prohibition of Military or Any Other Hostile Use of Environmental Modification Techniques	Bans weapons that threaten alteration or modification of the environment
1979	SALT II (not ratified)	Restricts number of strategic delivery vehicles permitted by both sides
1987	Nuclear Risk Reduction Centers Agreement	Establishes facilities in both capitals to manage nuclear crisis
1987	Intermediate Range Nuclear Force Treaty (NF Treaty)	Eliminates U.S. and Soviet ground-launched intermediate-range nuclear weapons in Europe
1990	Chemical Weapons Destruction Agreement	Bans further production of chemical weapons and calls for reduction in weapons stockpiles to 5000 tons each by 2002
1991	START (Strategic Arms Reduction Treaty)	Reduces nuclear arsenals by approximately 30 percent
1992	START I Protocol	Commits Russia, Belarus, Ukraine, and Kazakhstan to strategic weapons reductions specified in START I
1993	START II	Reduces strategic nuclear arsenals to 3000 (Russia) and 3500 (United States) by 2003; bans multiple-warhead land-based missiles

both countries continue to abide by the basic provisions of the treaty. The criticism of both SALT I and SALT II was that neither agreement actually reduced the number of weapons held by the superpowers; all they did was introduce restrictions on the numbers of weapons that could be deployed in the future.

In June 1982, the Reagan administration initiated a new round of talks, called the START negotiations. The subject of much criticism for their lack of productivity, the talks finally bore fruit in July 1991 when the superpowers signed the START Treaty, which committed both sides to reducing their nuclear arsenals by one-third. This dramatic agreement was made possible largely by the changing climate brought about by the tail end of the Cold War. However, critics charged that the agreement would only reduce the nuclear arsenals of the superpowers to the levels that existed in 1982, the year the START negotiations began. With the fall of the USSR, the Russian government did not speak for all of the nuclear weapons in the former Soviet Union, which now included Ukraine, Belarus, and Kazakhstan. After a period of intense negotiation (in particular with Ukraine, which had a powerful domestic constituency favouring the retention of nuclear weapons), all three countries signed the Lisbon Protocol to the START agreement in May 1992. This agreement obligated them to eliminate all nuclear weapons on their territories and sign the Non-Proliferation Treaty (NPT). All these countries have now done this, and in the process have joined South Africa as the only countries to have dispossessed themselves of nuclear weapons. Despite these obstacles, at a summit in Washington in June 1992, President Bush and President Yeltsin surprised the world by agreeing to a Joint Understanding under the START agreement that would reduce the nuclear arsenals of the superpowers by 60 percent—to 3000 warheads for Russia and 3500 warheads for the United States—by the year 2003 (later 2007). Formally signed as the START II Agreement in January 1993, the agreement is also significant in that it eliminates multiple warheads on all land-based ICBMs and restricts SLBM warheads to no more than 1750. Thus the START II agreement has been hailed for enhancing strategic stability, by eliminating the weapons that would be most useful in a first strike by either side. See Figure 7.1 for a comparison of the number of nuclear warheads held by the United States and Russia under START.

MULTILATERAL ARMS CONTROL DURING AND AFTER THE COLD WAR

Several multilateral arms control arrangements specifically aimed at Cold War security priorities were also concluded after 1945. Some of the more significant agreements have become important components of the effort to address contemporary security concerns (see Profile 7.2). In the post–Cold War world, the emphasis on transnational security issues (which by definition require the engagement and cooperation of a large number of countries) has increased the focus on multilateral arms control arrangements. In particular, interest has been renewed in agreements controlling the spread of nuclear weapons and agreements covering the spread of chemical, biological, and conventional weapons.

As we discussed in Chapter 6, the proliferation of nuclear weapons is a prominent international security issue. Two agreements figure prominently in the global effort to control the spread of nuclear weapons: the Non-Proliferation Treaty (NPT) and the Comprehensive Test Ban Treaty (CTBT). The NPT is the most important international treaty on the issue of nuclear proliferation. Signed in July 1968 and renewed every five years, the NPT had 187 signatories in 2000. At the April 1995 renewal conference, the

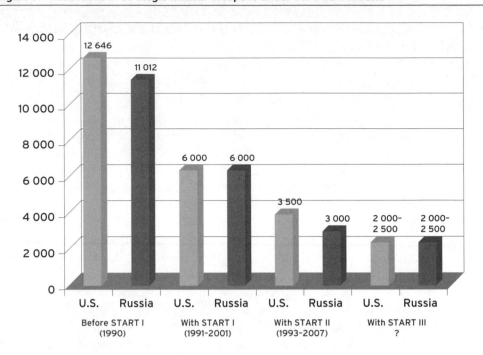

SOURCE: CENTER FOR DEFENSE INFORMATION AND FEDERATION OF AMERICAN SCIENTISTS.

NPT was extended indefinitely. The NPT binds its signatories to several provisions. Nuclear weapons states are obligated not to transfer nuclear weapons or related technology to non-nuclear weapons states. In turn, non-nuclear weapons states are obligated not to try to acquire nuclear weapons or related technology. Materials related to nuclear energy are exempt from these provisions; the NPT was designed to facilitate the spread of peaceful nuclear technology. Peaceful nuclear explosions are permitted, and all signatories pledge to work toward universal nuclear disarmament. The International Atomic Energy Agency (IAEA) is charged with verifying compliance with the NPT through constant monitoring of nuclear facilities in signatory countries and the use of on-site inspections. The NPT has been the subject of considerable criticism as it binds only its members and not all nuclear weapons states are signatories (e.g., Israel, Pakistan, and India). Despite the efforts of the IAEA, some non-nuclear weapons states, such as Iraq and North Korea, have managed to come very close to acquiring nuclear weapons, bringing charges that the IAEA is ineffective as a **verification** and compliance mechanism as it lacks (among other things) sufficient resources and an enforcement capacity. Finally, the NPT is criticized for its role in encouraging the spread of nuclear energy. This role has been considered questionable in its own right, and civilian reactor programs can be the first step in acquiring a bomb. However, the NPT does maintain the norm that the spread of nuclear weapons is dangerous and should be avoided. The NPT, along with a network of agreements among suppliers of nuclear technology, does add another obstacle to keep potential nuclear weapons states from acquiring the weapons. Without the NPT, a bomb would be much easier to build and develop.

The CTBT also has a long history. Since the late 1950s, periodic efforts have been made to ban all nuclear tests. A Partial Test Ban Treaty signed in 1963 by the United

Major Multilateral Arms Control Treaties and Agreements

DATE	AGREEMENT	PRINCIPAL AIMS
1959	Antarctic Treaty	Prohibits military use of the Antarctic, including nuclear weapons testing
1963	Limited/Partial Test Ban Treaty	Prohibits testing nuclear weapons in the atmosphere, underwater, and in outer space
1967	Outer Space Treaty	Prohibits testing or stationing any weapons in space, and bans military manoeuvres in space
1967	Treaty of Tlalelco	Creates Latin American nuclear weapons-free zone
1968 (1995)	Nuclear Non-Proliferation Treaty	Prohibits transfer of nuclear weapons and technology to non-nuclear states
1971	Seabed Treaty	Prohibits deployment of weapons of mass destruction (including nuclear weapons) beyond a 12-mile (20-kilometre) coastal limit
1972	Biological Weapons Convention	Prohibits production and stockpiling of biological weapons
1977	Environmental Modifications Convention	Bans use of technologies that can alter global weather patterns or ecology
1981	Inhumane Weapons Convention	Prohibits or restricts certain fragmentation weapons, incendiary weapons, and treacherous weapons
1985	South Pacific Nuclear Free Zone (Roratonga Treaty)	Prohibits testing, acquisition, or deployment of nuclear weapons in the South Pacific
1986	Confidence Building and Security Building Measures and Disarmament in Europe (CDE) Agreement	Requires prior notification and on-site inspection of military exercises
1987	Missile Technology Control Regime (MTCR)	Restricts export of ballistic missiles and technology
1990	Conventional Armed Forces in Europe (CFE) Treaty	Limits numbers of five categories of weapons in Europe (extended to former Soviet Union states in 1992)
1992	Open Skies Treaty	Permits surveillance and verification flights over signatory countries
1993	Chemical Weapons Convention	Requires all stockpiles and production facilities to be destroyed within 10 years
1993	UN Register of Conventional Arms	Calls on states to submit sale and receipt information on seven categories of conventional arms to a central registry
1996	Comprehensive Test Ban Treaty	Requires all signatories not to test nuclear weapons
1997	Global Land Mines Treaty	Requires all signatories to destroy stocks of landmines and not produce or export them

States, Britain, and the USSR (and joined by France in 1974 and China in 1980) did not include underground tests, a step that would constrain the development of new types of nuclear weapons. In the 1990s, several countries (including the United States) followed unilateral moratoriums on testing. With the signing of the CTB Treaty on 24 September 1996, more than 90 countries committed themselves not to test nuclear weapons.[7] The CTBT now has 160 signatories (with 69 countries having ratified the treaty by early 2001). The CTBT also prohibits peaceful nuclear explosions, closing an important loophole in the NPT. However, India and Pakistan, two nuclear weapons states, have refused to sign the CTBT. India has argued that the treaty provisions violate its sovereignty, and Pakistan will not sign until the security situation in South Asia changes (meaning until India signs).

The two most important mechanisms designed to address the problem of chemical and biological weapons proliferation are the Chemical Weapons Convention (CWC) and the Biological Weapons Convention (BWC). The CWC was signed in January 1993 and entered into force in April 1997. It is an ambitious and forward-looking treaty, aimed at disarmament rather than arms control. The signatories to the CWC are obligated to complete the destruction of all of their chemical weapons and production facilities within 10 years of the treaty entering into force. Signatory countries must declare whether they possess chemical weapons or manufacturing facilities and provide a precise inventory of both, along with plans for their destruction. Signatories are also obligated to declare whether they have received chemical weapons from another country or whether they have transferred them to another country. The CWC also has a complex verification system in which countries may mount challenge inspections in other countries to verify compliance. As of February 2001, 174 countries had signed the CWC. The United States ratified the treaty in 1997. However, once again the CWC only binds its signatories, and the ease with which chemical weapons can be manufactured has led to suspicion that clandestine chemical weapons facilities may evade the attention of the world community.

The Review Conferences of the BWC have convened periodically since the signing of the BWC (1972) and its entry into force (1975). The BWC was the first multilateral arms control effort aimed at eliminating an entire class of weapons of mass destruction. The BWC prohibits the development, production, and stockpiling of biological weapons, although it does not explicitly ban their use since the 1925 Geneva Protocol for the Prohibition of the Use in War of Asphyxiating, Poisonous, or Other Gases and of Bacteriological Weapons of Warfare had already done so. However, the BWC has been heavily criticized for lacking a verification system and allowing signatories to continue research into biological weapons and protective measures for defensive purposes.

For much of the Cold War, discussion of arms control addressing the problem of conventional weapons proliferation was minimal. One mechanism in place (and it is still in place) was the end-user certificate, which accompanied any shipment of weapons. The end-user certificate specified the country of final delivery and prohibited that country from diverting the weapons to any other country. This mechanism was subject to the effects of bribery (paying border officials to ignore the certificate), counterfeit certificates, and smuggling. During the Cold War, much of the effort directed toward conventional arms control was aimed at the conventional balance of forces in Europe. However, as concern over the spread of conventional weapons has increased, greater attention has been placed on establishing controls over such weapons. Some examples of non-nuclear multilateral arms control efforts are the Conventional Forces in Europe (CFE) Treaty, the Missile Technology Control Regime (MTCR), and the UN Register of Conventional Arms. The CFE Treaty grew out of the Mutual and Balanced Force Reduction Talks (MBFR), which were conducted from 1973 to 1988. The aim was to reduce the levels of conventional weapons in Europe maintained by both NATO and the Warsaw Pact. The MBFR talks were generally unproductive, but they laid the foundation for the CFE Treaty, signed by 23 European states in November 1990. The treaty entered into force in 1991 and was extended to include the newly independent states of the former Soviet Union in 1992. The treaty classifies weapons into five broad categories of Treaty Limited Equipment (TLE) in a geographic area from the Atlantic Ocean to the Ural Mountains in Russia (the so-called Atlantic to the Urals, or ATTU, zone). All countries have allowable limits in TLE, which they cannot exceed, although in practice most countries maintain arsenals lower than what they are permitted under the CFE. However, the CFE has been criticized, as countries in Europe have "cascaded" more modern armaments to other countries, which have in turn sold their old weapons on the international market.

The MTCR is an informal arrangement designed to control the spread of **ballistic missile** technology. As such, it is not a treaty, nor is it legally binding on its membership. Formed in 1987 by seven producers of ballistic missile technology, the MTCR initially covered nuclear-capable missiles and was later expanded in 1993 to include chemical-capable and biological-capable missiles as well. The MTCR now comprises more than 30 states. However, because the MTCR is not a treaty, compliance is voluntary. In 1993, China (which had pledged to abide by the provisions of the MTCR) was found to have transferred ballistic missile components to Pakistan and reserves the right to do so with North Korea and Iran.

The UN arms register was created in 1991 by a UN General Assembly resolution. The register is an attempt to establish an information service to track arms shipments around the world in seven categories of weapons: tanks, armoured combat vehicles, heavy artillery, combat aircraft, attack helicopters, warships, and missiles and missile systems. Ideally, states will submit information to the register on any exports and imports of weapons. It is hoped that this information will increase the transparency of arms transfers around the world and so reduce the secretive nature of arms transfers and the tensions and suspicions this secrecy can create. Critics of the registry argue that it places no real limits on the transfer of weapons and is entirely dependent on the willingness of states to provide information about their arms sales and purchases. In addition, the register can only compile information on the open arms trade; it has no effect whatsoever on the covert arms trade and may, in fact, increase it.

The human security agenda has promoted a variety of arms control activities and proposals. As we discussed in Chapter 6, the human security agenda focuses on the individual, so arms control efforts to further the cause of human security are aimed at the weapons that do most of the killing in today's wars. The Global Land Mines Treaty is the most prominent example of this kind of arms control and is quite possibly a model for the future. Efforts are underway to develop arms control agreements on cluster bombs and the proliferation of light weapons. It remains to be seen whether the success of the landmines treaty can be replicated and whether the major states that have so far refused to sign the treaty, namely the United States, Russia, and China, will sign and ratify in the near future.

CRITICS OF ARMS CONTROL

Both disarmament and arms control efforts have been subjected to heavy criticism. This criticism has varied with the nature of agreement under discussion, but several critical themes have emerged consistently over time.

- Arms control is risky and even dangerous because success depends on trusting one's opponents not to cheat.

- Because the word of one's opponents is not to be trusted, arms control compliance must be verified, a complicated and difficult task.

- Arms control agreements will be violated in times of crisis or war.

- Weapons cannot be effectively banned because the knowledge to manufacture them exists.

- Those weapons that are banned or restricted have little military utility and are not considered useful weapons.

- Arms control agreements only succeed in channelling arms competitions into weapons system types that are not banned or restricted (the SALT limits on missile numbers led to the deployment of multiple warheads on missiles).

- Technological developments can render arms control agreements obsolete or ineffective.

- Making agreements with authoritarian governments is ill advised, because they are more apt to cheat and are able to conceal this cheating with greater effectiveness.

- Arms control agreements only bind signatories, not nonsignatories, who may proceed with arms build-ups or the manufacture of certain banned weapons.

- Arms control arrangements are often violated. (There were 12 alleged uses of chemical or biological weapons between 1975 and 1981 that violated the BWC, and more than three-quarters of all nuclear tests were conducted after the Partial Test Ban Treaty went into effect.)

In response to these criticisms, advocates of disarmament and arms control maintain that states and groups have entered into arms control negotiations with deceitful purposes. States have used arms control to gain an advantage over an opponent. In some cases, states have made arms control proposals while they are ahead in the arms race. In other cases, states have sought to use arms control to permit weapons and capabilities where they have advantages and to restrict weapons and capabilities where they are at a disadvantage. At times, arms control has been used to subjugate other states. Many arms control advocates also suspect that states enter arms control arrangements as public relations exercises. Until governments around the world are committed to the idea of disarmament and arms control for the mutual long-term benefit of all, the capacity of disarmament and arms control measures to live up to their promise of a more peaceful world will be limited.

There is no doubt that the end of the Cold War created a climate that facilitated the negotiation of many far-reaching arms control agreements. In addition, agreements such as the CWC represent a significant increase in both the aims and the provisions of arms control. The trend may be toward attempts to control weapons that are seen as especially inhumane or indiscriminate. However, any optimism must be tempered by several sobering facts. First, governments continue to direct more resources toward researching and developing new weapons than to attempts to control weapons. Second, military and political leaders remain wary of disarmament and arms control as a means of strengthening their security. Trusting in the word and restraint of others remains perilous in an anarchic, self-help international system. As a result, military preparedness remains a primary instrument of state security. Third, leaders are reluctant to engage in arms control either because they want to attain a certain military capability (be it nuclear weapons or ballistic missiles) and are unwilling to commit themselves to an agreement not to acquire it, or because they possess a superiority in a certain military capability and see no reason why they should accept constraints on it. Fourth, increasingly, arms control is not a matter of East and West (as it was in the Cold War), but a matter between the north and the south, with southern governments viewing global efforts to prevent the spread of certain weapons as discriminatory acts by the rich nations anxious to perpetuate their military superiority. Fifth, an increasing number of states are becoming capable of developing and manufacturing sophisticated weapons systems, making the process of reaching an arms control agreement among a larger and larger number of states an increasingly difficult proposition. Finally, when it comes to arms control, expectation has always exceeded results. Arms control cannot be regarded as a panacea, for true international security "depends not as much on arms or arms control as on reducing as much as possible the sources of conflict in international situations and on finding effective nonviolent means of resolving the conflicts that remain."[8]

INTERNATIONAL LAW AND CONTROLS ON WAR

Efforts to prevent or control war through international law have concentrated on two issues: the prohibition or outlawing of war as an instrument of policy, and the imposition of rules and regulations to establish a lawful conduct in war. Many efforts have been made to prohibit war, although many of these efforts were qualified in some way. The Hague Conventions of 1899 and 1907, for example, bound signatories to seek a peaceful resolution to their disputes before resorting to force. Presumably, if no peaceful resolution could be found, war was permissible. The Bryan Treaties of 1913–14 banned declarations of war by one state against another before an arbitration committee had met to consider the circumstances of the conflict. The Covenant of the League of Nations bound League members to renounce aggression, and the signatories to the 1928 Kellogg–Briand Pact forfeited the right to go to war (see Profile 7.3).

The Charter of the UN (Article 2/4) prohibits the use or threat of force in the international system, and a 1974 General Assembly resolution banned aggression. However, none of these efforts has succeeded in achieving the real goal of banning the use of military force, war, or aggression.

Partly because of the historical record of attempts to prohibit war, much of the body of international law on war concerns its conduct. As early as 1400 B.C.E. agreements had been established concerning the treatment of prisoners, and poisoned weapons were outlawed in India in 500 B.C.E. Modern legal efforts to control war have focused on establishing rules of conduct that distinguish between combatants and noncombatants (civilians), and between the battlefield (where the fighting takes place) and zones of peace. However, as warfare increased both in geographic scope (especially in the two world wars of the twentieth century) and in number of civilian deaths, these distinctions lost much of their salience.

The Kellogg–Briand Pact

Formally known as the Treaty Providing for the Renunciation of War as an Instrument of State Policy, the Kellogg–Briand Pact was originally a treaty agreed to by the governments of the United States and France in 1927. The American Secretary of State Frank B. Kellogg and the French Foreign Minister Aristide Briand agreed to outlaw war between their two states. The enthusiasm of the U.S. government led to an open offer to other governments to sign the treaty; by 1934, 64 states (most of the states in the world at that time) were signatories. However, the hopes of the treaty were never realized. Most signatories placed caveats on their commitment to the renunciation of war; Japan, for example, insisted on the right to wage war in self-defence, while Great Britain insisted on its right to intervene militarily in areas of the world of interest to it (meaning its colonies). The treaty contained no enforcement mechanism and was unable to respond to acts of aggression. The treaty was also signed by states that had clear expansionist or revisionist ambitions. As a result, the treaty has been derided as an example of the emptiness and futility of efforts to outlaw war.

International law has also focused on defining war crimes such as genocide (see Chapter 8), and on the prohibition or restriction of specific types of weapons. Modern efforts at the latter are largely derived from two special UN conferences on Conventional Weapons held at Lucerne in 1974 and Lugano in 1976. These conferences laid the foundation for the three protocols of the 1981 Inhumane Weapons Convention, which banned different types of weapons systems. Protocol I covers fragmentation weapons, banning the use of toxic fragments and fragments that are undetectable by X-ray. Protocol II covers treacherous weapons, prohibiting booby traps, the use of mines against civilians, the placement of mines, and the recording of minefields. Protocol III covers incendiary weapons, prohibiting the use of incendiary weapons against civilians, and attacks on the natural elements unless they are used as cover for military movements.

Despite the letter of international law, these provisions are frequently violated. To use the example of landmines, today many mines are manufactured out of plastic, which is difficult to detect by X-ray. Mines are also laid indiscriminately, and their locations are seldom recorded by communal group militias or insurgency groups. Few, if any, enforcement mechanisms exist supporting the observation of international law in war. In fact, the efforts to build and apply such a law—the Nuremberg and Tokyo war crimes trials and the war crimes trials in Bosnia and Rwanda—have been criticized as victors' justice, imposed on the losers of a conflict by the winners. Furthermore, in many conflicts around the world, little or no awareness exists of the laws of war, and very little will to follow them, particularly in local communal conflicts. International law also has difficulty keeping up with technological developments; many new weapons systems are not covered by international law. Nevertheless, international law on war establishes norms of conduct and the inhumane nature of certain weapons systems; to violate these norms is to invite international condemnation and the loss of legitimacy.

INTERNATIONAL ORGANIZATIONS AND CONFLICT MANAGEMENT

International organizations perform several tasks and roles that are both directly and indirectly related to conflict management. They can act as a forum for debate and discussion, assisting members to become familiar with one another, reducing the chance of misunderstanding or misinterpretation, and providing an opportunity for actors to float or test proposals or ideas to gauge the initial reaction of others. In this capacity, international organizations can also act as a steam valve for international conflict and crises, permitting political leaders to accuse and condemn their opponents without resorting to violence. This ability can be particularly useful when public opinion back home demands a verbal response, especially in cases where doing nothing best serves the interests of peace. Of course, governments can also be criticized for avoiding substantive action on an issue by raising it in an international forum but doing little else.

International organizations can provide third-party mediation services in times of crisis or war. Because they are established actors with a permanent location and membership, they can provide physical facilities, staff, and diplomatic support for negotiations. The UN provided intermediaries that facilitated the ceasefire in the Iran–Iraq War. Other members of the organization can also encourage the parties to a dispute to come to a settlement and offer rewards and threats to that end. International organizations can establish fact-finding and information missions designed to obtain more objective sources of evidence and information. In other cases, the staff or leadership of the organization itself may become involved in facilitating an agreement. In 1988, UN Secretary-General Javier Perez de Cuellar and UN diplomats helped develop the plan under which Soviet forces withdrew from Afghanistan. Finally, with the agreement of the parties to a dispute, international organizations may act as arbitrators.

How can the international community constrain unilateral actions? To act as a collective, international organizations require the consensus of their membership (depending on the voting procedure of the organization). If states or groups want to act as a collective, with the advantages of added legitimacy that joint action provides, then some states or groups will have to compromise or alter their positions so that a common stance can be reached. In this way, organizations can help alter outcomes in such a way as to enhance peace by inhibiting or restraining certain members from aggressive actions. For example, Canadian (and European) support for NATO is partly attributed to the constraining effect of NATO on the United States.

Finally, international organizations can promote peace and stability by establishing norms and principles of conduct and governance among their members. Members must often commit to the rejection of aggression and military force as means of resolving disputes. Over time, this norm of nonviolence may become so pervasive that governments and substate groups will no longer regard military force as an option in the conduct of their affairs with each other. Karl Deutsch referred to such groups of countries as "security communities," which share common values, predictability of behaviour, and mutual responsiveness (the capability and willingness to respond quickly to one another).[9] In addition, international organizations will seek to promote domestic values and systems of governance that are regarded as stabilizing and nonaggressive. Examples include the **Organization for Security and Co-operation in Europe (OSCE)**, which is built on the promotion of the principles of democracy and the protection of human rights, and the Organization of American States (OAS), which maintains a unit for the promotion of democracy. Of course, a neomarxist perspective would reject this as yet another example of Western cultural imperialism.

In recent years, emphasis has shifted toward regional multilateral organizations as conflict management instruments. The hope is that they may contribute to regional peace and security by encouraging and facilitating cooperation among their members, establishing norms for the peaceful resolution of disputes, and acting as conduits for regional efforts to manage conflict. Among the many examples of the involvement of regional organizations in conflict management efforts are the following.

- *The North Atlantic Treaty Organization (NATO).* NATO has altered its political purpose to the maintenance of stability and has changed its military structure to respond to crises. The organization has created two consultative instruments to strengthen cooperation between its members and the states of the former Warsaw Pact and Soviet Union: the Partnerships for Peace (PFP) and the Euro–Atlantic Partnership Council (EACP) replacing the North Atlantic Cooperation Council (NACC). NATO has achieved a higher level of political and military cooperation among its membership than virtually any other organization in the world and engaged in military strikes against Serbia in 1999.

- *The Organization of American States (OAS).* Founded in 1948, the OAS was preoccupied with the issue of the spread of Communism to Latin America during the Cold War. Initially heavily influenced by the United States, the membership took an increasingly anti-U.S. stand later in the Cold War, unanimously opposing the intervention in Grenada in 1983. Since the Cold War, the central task of the OAS has been the promotion of mutual security, regional economic and social development, nonintervention and sovereign equality, the peaceful settlement of disputes, and democracy and human rights. Although the OAS is linked to the Rio Treaty, a security pact among the countries of the Western hemisphere, it has rarely been involved in security issues. An indication that this stance may be changing came with the involvement of the OAS in the termination of several insurgency conflicts in Central America in the 1990s.

- *The Organization of African Unity (OAU).* Established in 1963, the OAU was built on the concept of Pan-Africanism and the encouragement of decolonization. Created to promote African solidarity in world affairs, the cooperation of African countries, and the defence of the sovereignty and territory of African countries, the OAU has had some success in mediating conflicts. However, it has failed to address more complex interstate and intrastate disputes such as the Nigerian Civil War, the Ethiopia–Somalia War, and the civil wars in Angola and Mozambique. More recently, the OAU was unable to mediate a settlement to the communal conflict in Somalia or to the Ethiopian–Eritrean War, though a ceasefire has been reached in the latter. Despite efforts to improve its crisis response capabilities, the OAS remains deeply divided and short of financial resources. Another African regional organization, the **Economic Community of West African States (ECOWAS)**, dominated by Nigerian participation, has had mixed results in its efforts to manage the conflicts of West Africa.

- *The Arab League.* Formed in 1945, the Arab League was designed to promote cooperation between Arab countries on economic and social affairs, communications, culture, and health. Egypt was expelled for making peace with Israel in 1979 but was readmitted in 1987. As a mechanism for conflict management, the Arab League has not been very successful; most of its proclamations and plans have gone unheeded. It was unable to broker a resolution in the events leading up to Iraq's invasion of Kuwait and ended up authorizing its member states to cooperate with the U.S.-led coalition against Iraq. Tensions over this decision led several states to boycott the League, which has been largely dormant since.

- *The Association of Southeast Asian Nations (ASEAN)*. ASEAN was formed in 1967. Formally a mechanism for regional cooperation, ASEAN has addressed a widening range of issues from trade liberalization to refugees to the drug trade. ASEAN has moved slowly into the realm of security issues. It played a significant role in ending the Vietnamese occupation of Cambodia. Today, ASEAN is the basis for regional political and security arrangements, including joint military exercises. ASEAN members are involved (often as a collective) in larger Pacific-wide cooperation initiatives, such as the Asia/Pacific Economic Cooperation (APEC) arrangement. In 1993, ASEAN expanded its security role with the creation of the ASEAN Regional Forum (ARF), to which Canada contributes expertise.

In part, this trend toward regionalism in conflict management is due to the troubles facing the UN (see Chapter 5). Short of money and resources, the UN has found it increasingly difficult to maintain its current obligations and programs and even harder to undertake new operations and tasks. However, the turn to regional organizations is also a function of the belief that they are more effective as conflict management instruments within their respective regions than are extraregional or universal organizations such as the UN. Indeed, the UN Charter calls explicitly for cooperation between the two levels.

Regional organizations do have advantages when addressing crises or wars within their own region. First, their members will be more familiar with local disputes and tensions and will place the conflict in the hands of locals rather than in the distant headquarters of the UN. Second, regional organizations may not be constrained by disagreements among countries at the UN. To the extent that a regional consensus exists on a response to a crisis or conflict, a local mechanism may prove more capable of a response than a divided UN Security Council (or General Assembly). Third, regional organizations, by virtue of their geographic proximity, are better able to respond quickly than the UN is, particularly if a peacekeeping or interventionary force is required. In some cases, regional organizations may have better capabilities than the UN and a more streamlined political and military decision-making structure (this is certainly the case with NATO).

However, regional organizations also have some drawbacks. First, the fact that local actors are involved may lead some of these actors to pursue their own interests in the crisis or conflict. Similarly, the parties to a dispute may feel that local actors and regional organizations lack the requisite neutrality and impartiality to act as mediators or facilitators. An extraregional actor may be advantageous in such cases. Second, regional organizations are often incapable of offering sufficient rewards (such as economic aid) or acting on threatened punishments (such as economic sanctions). Most lack the economic resources and military capabilities to undertake significant action. In many cases they are unable under their respective charters to undertake such actions, and they are unable to enforce their will on states by any means other than moral appeal. Third, most regional organizations in the world do not have a high level of political or military cohesion. The members of such organizations are often deeply divided, and a meaningful consensus is often very difficult to achieve. Nonetheless, the potential certainly exists for regional organizations to play an increased role in conflict management, especially in cooperation with other organizations or extraregional actors.

FROM UNITED NATIONS PEACEKEEPING TO HUMANITARIAN INTERVENTION

From its inception, the UN was first and foremost a security institution, designed to establish peace and security in the post–World War II world. As stated in the first sentence of the Preamble to the Charter, the UN was intended to "save succeeding generations from the scourge of war."[10] The UN was designed as a collective security system, and the UN Charter committed member states to resolve their differences peacefully and refrain from the use of force.[11] However, the UN Charter also recognized the limitation of collective security as experienced by the League of Nations; under Article 51 of the Charter UN member states retain the right of self-defence, and under Article 52 member states retain the right to engage in regional arrangements (such as alliances) to protect their security. The UN system is also built around the state as the key unit in global politics, a unit that enjoys the principle of sovereignty and freedom from interference in its domestic affairs. In matters of security, the UN Charter strikes a balance between the collective security provisions of the UN and the rights and the sovereignty of states.

The conflict management provisions of the UN are found in Chapters 6 and 7 of the UN Charter. Chapter 6, entitled "Pacific Settlement of Disputes," calls on member states to resolve their disputes through "negotiation, enquiry, mediation, conciliation, arbitration, judicial settlement, resort to regional agencies or arrangements, or other peaceful means of their own choice." The UN Security Council is able to investigate disputes to determine whether they endanger international peace and security, and in that eventuality, make recommendations for methods of resolution. Chapter 7, entitled "Action with Respect to Threats to the Peace, Breaches of the Peace, and Acts of Aggression," is the heart of the collective security function of the UN. In Article 40, the UN Security Council may call on the parties to a dispute to abide by Security Council resolutions concerning the conflict. In Article 41, the UN Security Council can then call on member states to observe measures directed at the parties to a dispute that do not involve the use of force (these are commonly sanctions in some form). Finally, if these measures prove inadequate, the Security Council can invoke Article 42, which reads:

> Should the Security Council consider that measures provided for in Article 41 would be inadequate, it may take such action by air, sea, or land forces as may be necessary to maintain or restore international peace and security. Such actions may include demonstrations, blockade, and other operations by air, sea, or land forces of Members of the United Nations.

Chapter 7 also specifies the obligation of member states to provide forces, facilities, and transit rights for such operations.

The Cold War had a profound influence on the UN, but the most fundamental consequence was the inability of the UN to perform its collective security function because of the divergence between the veto-holding permanent members of the Security Council. Only the Korean anomaly (see Chapter 3) stands as an example of UN collective security in action during the Cold War.

As a result, the most visible and significant conflict management role performed by the UN since its creation has been peacekeeping. Between 1945 and 2000, the UN has created 54 peacekeeping operations (41 of them between 1988 and 2000), a remarkable achievement considering that peacekeeping is an entirely improvisational activity and is not even mentioned in the UN Charter. The origin of UN peacekeeping lies in the use of observer and truce supervision missions, a tradition drawn from the experience of the League of Nations.[12] In 1947, the General Assembly established an observer mission along the Greek border to ascertain whether the Greek Communists in the Greek Civil War were receiving aid from their Communist neighbours (they were). Despite the partisan nature of the mission, much was learned about the deployment, formation, and principles of conduct governing such missions. In June 1948, following the Arab–Israeli War of that year, the UN established the United Nations Truce Supervisory Organization (UNTSO) to supervise and observe the truce in Palestine. UNTSO was given the task of investigating incidents, building confidence at the local level, defusing tensions and incidents of violence, and acting as a conduit for communication. In 1949, after a UN-facilitated ceasefire ended a war between India and Pakistan, the UN established the Military Observer Group in India and Pakistan (UNMOGIP). UNMOGIP was responsible for providing information on troop movements, investigating incidents, and assisting with the maintenance of order. Both UNTSO and UNMOGIP are still in place today. However, the term "peacekeeping" was not coined until 1956, when the Suez Crisis prompted (under the suggestion of Canadian Secretary of State for External Affairs Lester B. Pearson) the creation of the first United Nations Emergency Force (see Profile 7.4).

These early experiences laid the foundation for UN peacekeeping during the Cold War. Over time, a set of conventions about the composition, aims, and tasks of peacekeeping operations emerged, which were for the most part consistently followed in most UN peacekeeping operations. The conventions of what came to be called traditional peacekeeping included

- *Impartiality.* No side should be seen as being favoured by the UN peacekeepers. Unlike Chapter 7 collective security operations, UN peacekeeping did not identify an aggressor (although an individual's acts could be condemned and blame assigned). The maintenance of this impartiality was essential if the missions of the UN were to be successfully carried out.

PROFILE 7.4 The United Nations Emergency Force

The Suez Crisis was precipitated by the nationalization of the Suez Canal by Egypt on 26 July 1956. Three months later, Israel, France, and Great Britain invaded Egypt. Israel was seeking to damage the Egyptian military in a preemptive war, while France and Great Britain were attempting to seize the canal. The invasion was widely condemned by the international community, including the United States. Under pressure from domestic opposition and from Washington, the warring parties agreed to a ceasefire on November 6–7. In previous weeks, Canada had proposed the creation of a UN force and had supplied a draft resolution and presented it to the General Assembly for approval. The creation of UNEF satisfied many interests. France and Great Britain were spared some of the embarrassment of being forced to obey the United States. UNEF enabled the United States to achieve an end to the war without direct intervention. UNEF allowed Canada to prevent a serious rift between the United States and Great Britain. Egypt secured the canal, and Israel obtained a ceasefire after having damaged the Egyptian armed forces. Launched on 4 November 1956, under a UN General Assembly resolution, the mission was mandated to secure and supervise the cessation of hostilities and facilitate the withdrawal of France, Great Britain, and Israel from Egyptian territory, and to serve as a buffer between Egyptian and Israeli forces. UNEF began to deploy after the ceasefire was in place. It reached a strength of 6000 personnel, from Brazil, Canada, Colombia, Denmark, Finland, India, Indonesia, Norway, Sweden, and Yugoslavia. UNEF I was expelled from Egypt in 1967, and another Arab–Israeli war soon followed.

- *Nonhostile and lightly armed personnel.* As UN peacekeepers were not present to engage in offensive military operations and could not appear to be a coercive presence, UN peacekeepers were unarmed or lightly armed (generally with service rifles and sidearms) for self-defence only.

- *Consent.* Respect for state sovereignty required the UN to obtain the consent of the parties to a dispute before a UN force could be dispatched. The UN presence also depended on host consent to remain in place. These first three conventions formed the foundation of the modalities of traditional UN peacekeeping and were closely interrelated.[13]

- *Keep, but don't make, the peace.* UN peacekeepers could not create the conditions for their own success; in other words, a peace had to be in place before the peacekeeping operation was deployed. Put simply, there had to be a peace to keep; UN peacekeepers could only facilitate and reinforce a larger peace process.

- *Military personnel.* UN operations were carried out primarily by individuals with military status. These individuals were trained, equipped, and organized; were deployable overseas; and were disciplined and under firm command and control.

- *Proper authorization.* UN peacekeepers had to be dispatched under UN authorization (or by organizations authorized to do so by the UN). In practice, this has meant the Security Council (although some early missions were authorized by the General Assembly), which also established the mandate for the mission (the legal and operational boundaries of the mission) and the rules of engagement (the legal and operational boundaries of the personnel in the mission).

- *Reliance on member states.* As the UN had no army, UN peacekeeping operations were entirely dependent on contributions of money, personnel, and equipment from member states. In practice, small states and middle powers (such as Canada) provided most of the forces, as the great powers generally lacked impartial credentials.

- *Nonterritoriality.* Peacekeeping operations did not attempt to seize or hold territory. UN peacekeepers did not occupy territory against an opponent; they patrolled a zone or line that had been negotiated by the parties to a dispute. They had no legal claim to that territory, nor did they exercise sovereignty over it.

Based on these principles, the tasks of traditional UN peacekeeping included interposing between belligerents, gathering information and facts, observing ceasefire lines and reporting violations, supervising the withdrawal of belligerent forces, defusing tensions, preventing or controlling the outbreak of violence, assisting in the maintenance of order, acting as mediators and buffers between the parties to a dispute, and engaging in humanitarian tasks. For the most part, UN peacekeeping operations during the Cold War conformed to the above principles and tasks. The exception was the United Nations Operation in the Congo (ONUC), in which the UN became involved in a civil war (see Profile 7.5). While the Congo experience was sobering, UN peacekeeping missions continued to be mounted throughout the Cold War, with some missions lasting for decades. UN peacekeeping operations thus occupied a middle ground between Chapter 6 and Chapter 7 of the UN Charter, leading to their description by former UN Secretary-General Dag Hammarskjöld as "Chapter Six-and-a-half" operations. Up to the end of 1987, 13 UN operations were underway in the world, deploying a total of 10 000 personnel. Peacekeeping is one of the most visible and respected of UN functions, and UN

The Congo Crisis was precipitated by the independence of the Congo from Belgium on 30 June 1960. Violent disorder spread throughout much of the country between the government and rebellious groups and regions, prompting Belgium to intervene in its former colony. The Congo appealed to the UN for help, and on July 14 the UN Security Council authorized a peacekeeping mission for the Congo. The UN force in the Congo was initially mandated to remain neutral in the conflict. However, the secession of Katanga province, the assassination of the Congolese prime minister, and the threat of a wider war prompted the UN Security Council to use more forceful measures to restore law and order, enforce a ceasefire, prevent civil war, and evacuate Belgian forces and foreign mercenaries. The force was expanded from 17 500 in 1960 to almost 20 000 by July 1961. UN forces participated in the suppression of the secessionist movement in Katanga, which eventually brought peace to the country. However, the Congo operation had damaged the peacekeeping instrument. Disputes arose between participating states about how to implement the new mandate and how much force was permissible. The Soviet Union and its allies accused the United States and Western countries of political interference in the UN mission and refused to pay for their share of mission costs. The fact that the UN had become involved in a war and in the politics of a state made many countries, both contributing states and developing states, wary of future UN peacekeeping operations. Future UN operations were usually very circumscribed, cautious, and traditional in nature.

peacekeepers were collectively awarded the Nobel Peace Prize in 1988. Canadian troops played a prominent role in UN peacekeeping missions throughout the Cold War.

However, the character and qualities of peacekeeping operations began to change by 1990–91 for several reasons. First, with the end of the Cold War, communal conflicts have been prominent features of the international security agenda, and such conflicts have often been identified as threats to international peace and security. As such, they have come to the consideration of the UN. Second, the UN Security Council, freed from the dynamic of the Cold War, has been more readily able to reach agreement on the creation of peacekeeping forces, and the use of the veto has declined dramatically. Third, there was much optimism that the UN would be able to perform as the instrument of international peace and security the way the drafters of the UN Charter had intended. This optimism was reflected in *An Agenda for Peace*, a document prepared in 1992 by Secretary-General Boutros Boutros-Ghali, in which he proposed to enhance the role of the UN in international peace and security:

> In these past months a conviction has grown, among nations large and small, that an opportunity has been regained to achieve the great objectives of the Charter—a United Nations capable of maintaining international peace and security, of securing justice and human rights and of promoting, in the words of the Charter, "social progress and better standards of life in larger freedom." This opportunity must not be squandered. The Organization must never again be crippled as it was in the era that has now passed.[14]

As a result, the number of peacekeeping operations mounted by the UN surged. Whereas between 1948 and 1978, 13 missions were created (with no new ones established between 1979 and 1988), between 1988 and 1998, 36 new missions were established. In August 2000, the UN operated 15 missions.

Not only did UN missions experience a surge in frequency, the missions themselves experienced a number of qualitative changes. These changes included

- *Increased size.* The size of many UN operations increased dramatically. The big three UN operations of the post–Cold War period—the United Nations Transitional Authority in Cambodia (UNTAC), the United Nations Protection Force in the Former Yugoslavia (UNPROFOR), and the second United Nations Operation in Somalia (UNOSOM II)—all deployed more than 20 000 personnel at their peak. During the Cold War, only the UN operation in the Congo (ONUC) approached this size. Several other UN operations also deployed more than 6000 personnel, including the United Nations Confidence Restoration Operation (UNCRO), the United Nations Mission in Haiti (UNMIH), and the United Nations Mission for Rwanda (UNAMIR).

- *Deployment within states.* Most post–Cold War UN peacekeeping operations have been conducted within the borders of states. As a result, while peacekeeping personnel may still perform missions associated with traditional peacekeeping, such as supervisory, observer, or interpositionary tasks, they are doing so not between states but between warring parties within states.

- *Lack of consent.* In some post–Cold War UN operations, the principle of consent has changed dramatically. UNPROFOR and UNOSOM II were both authorized under Chapter 7 of the UN Charter, and such operations are not, at least in principle, bound by the consent provision of traditional peacekeeping. In practice, both UN operations took place in areas without a central government to provide consent. In these cases, the UN sought consent from the next highest level of authority: the warring communal groups and factions themselves. However, the universal consent of all such groups was not seen as a prerequisite for deployment, as a peacekeeping force could not have its existence dependent on one local faction leader. At the local level, however, consent remained very important, as peacekeepers often could not operate successfully on a day-to-day basis without the cooperation of local leaders.

- *Operations in hostile environments.* Many post–Cold War UN peacekeeping missions were deployed in areas where there was no peace to keep. Negotiated arrangements among the warring factions were either nonexistent or fragile, and many warring factions had not given consent or were at best ambivalent about the UN's presence. UN peacekeepers have been deployed in war zones and in areas of virtual anarchy and civil disorder. As a result, UN contingents attempting to facilitate the delivery of humanitarian relief or to establish safe areas for refugees have encountered obstruction and threats and have come under armed attack both from organized communal groups and from lawless bands of armed individuals who are not under firm political control.

- *Increased use of force.* The UN has also demonstrated a greater willingness to employ force and the threat of force during peacekeeping missions, in part because of the erosion of the principle of consent. However, the UN was widely criticized (particularly in UNPROFOR and UNOSOM II) for standing by while humanitarian relief supplies were blocked, while human rights abuses were perpetrated, while cities were bombarded, and while UN personnel were obstructed and abused. In response, the UN employed a greater level of force against warring parties and UN contingents became more heavily armed. However, this placed UN peacekeepers at risk of retaliatory attacks, led to civilian casualties, and undermined the impartiality of the UN force.

• *Proliferation of mission tasks.* The scope of UN missions has also changed. UN contingents now perform a much wider range of mission tasks. These include electoral support or management (Cambodia), judiciary and policy reform (El Salvador), refugee resettlement (Mozambique), facilitation of the delivery of humanitarian relief supplies (former Yugoslavia), disarmament of warring factions and weapons cantonment (former Yugoslavia), mine clearing and education (Cambodia), and protection of safe areas (former Yugoslavia). As a result, UN operations now include a wide variety of functional experts, such as civilian police, electoral personnel, human rights experts, and information specialists, and often involve close cooperation with aid and humanitarian relief agencies.

• *Peacebuilding and national reconstruction.* Many of the above tasks have a long-term objective: the reconstruction of a viable, stable country, including the repair of infrastructure, the creation of democratic political processes, and the entrenchment of law and civil society. This ambitious process is based on the belief that establishing ceasefires and a peace arrangement is not enough; the underlying conditions for peace must be created if a UN effort is to be successful over the long term. As Boutros-Ghali put it, "UN operations now may involve nothing less than the reconstruction of an entire society and state. This requires a comprehensive approach, over an extended period. Security is increasingly understood to involve social, economic, environmental, and cultural aspects far beyond its traditional military dimension."[15] This objective has transformed UN peacekeeping operations from almost exclusively military operations to missions coordinating a vast aid and development effort.

As a consequence of the changing nature of peacekeeping operations and the different environments in which they were operating, UN peacekeeping experienced what can only be described as a time of troubles in the post–Cold War period. Highly publicized UN failures in the former Yugoslavia, Somalia, and Rwanda revealed the mismatch between traditional peacekeeping and the intrastate communal conflicts of the post–Cold War world.

Yugoslavia

The UN experience in Yugoslavia was, at best, mixed. Although the UN Protection Force (UNPROFOR) succeeded in facilitating the delivery of humanitarian relief to the civilian population, the UN failed to end hostilities in Bosnia-Herzegovina. UN personnel were the targets of intimidation and harassment, were shot at, and were taken hostage. All sides during the Bosnian war routinely defied the UN. In one incident

Peacekeeping in the midst of war. A young boy points a fake gun at a peacekeeper in Bosnia. (CP Picture Archive/Tom Hanson)

that has become a symbol of UN futility in Bosnia, peacekeepers protecting a UN safe area around Srebrenica found themselves outgunned by the Bosnian Serbs and withdrew, leaving the Muslim inhabitants to their fate. It was the shifting nature of the military balance on the ground, the intervention of NATO, and the use of air strikes that prompted the signing of the Dayton Accord in 1995. The implementation of the settlement was facilitated by the deployment of 60 000 NATO troops.

Somalia

The UN experience in Somalia was almost a complete failure. The UN Operation in Somalia (UNOSOM I) was initially deployed to facilitate the delivery of humanitarian relief supplies. The obstruction of UN and aid agency efforts and the continued fighting in Somalia prompted the creation of the U.S.-led Unified Task Force (UNITAF), authorized under Chapter 7 of the UN Charter. While UNITAF was initially successful in achieving order, it became involved in a shooting war against one of Somalia's factions. Because of casualties to U.S. forces, UNITAF was deactivated and UNOSOM II replaced it. However, the failure to establish a peace settlement and the continued fighting in Somalia led to the withdrawal of UNOSOM II in March 1995. Although many lives were saved, Somalia is no closer to political stability today than it was before UN intervention.

Rwanda

The call for the creation of a UN force for Rwanda came on the heels of the Somalia imbroglio. A conflict between the Hutu government and the Tutsi-led Rwandan Patriotic Front (RPF) had been raging for decades. A peace settlement (the Arusha Accords) was signed in August 1993, and the United Nations Assistance Mission for Rwanda (UNAMIR) began deploying later that year. However, in 1994 an orchestrated genocide began in Rwanda. The UN force commander, Canadian General Romeo Dallaire, has often argued that if he were given more troops and an appropriate mandate, he could have prevented the worst of the genocide. In fact, neither was forthcoming and UN member states (remembering the Somalia experience) actually reduced the size of UNAMIR. By then, half a million people had died, and many more would die as the world watched and did nothing. It was not until months later (after the genocide was over) that the UN increased the size of its peacekeeping force in Rwanda, largely by way of a French intervention, which gave rise to further questions about neutrality.

The story of post–Cold War UN peacekeeping is not entirely one of failure. The UN made some progress in reinforcing peace in Cambodia (UNTAC) and Angola (UNAVEM), although the peace process in Angola has subsequently crumbled. Mozambique (UNOMOZ) is widely regarded as a success, and the UN has made some progress in restructuring the police and the judiciary in El Salvador (ONUSAL). In Haiti, the UN effort has succeeded in bringing an end to civil disorder and the worst human rights abuses. However, these relative successes have been obscured by the high-profile failures in Yugoslavia, Somalia, and Rwanda (a complete list of completed and current UN peacekeeping operations can be found at the UN Website at <www.un.org>).

Because of these failures, the credibility of the UN as an effective conflict management instrument has been called into question. Much of the criticism has been directed at the UN itself. Former UN Assistant Secretary-General for Political Affairs Giandomenico Picco has argued that "neither the post–Cold War climate nor civil wars can rightfully be blamed for the failures that have beset the United Nations since 1991. One must look to the workings of the United Nations itself."[16] Saadia Touval argues that

It is increasingly apparent that the United Nations possesses inherent characteristics that make it incapable of effectively mediating complex international disputes. It does not serve well as an authoritative channel of communication. It has little real political leverage. Its promises and threats lack credibility. And it is incapable of pursuing coherent, flexible, and dynamic negotiations guided by an effective strategy.[17]

The UN has also been criticized for its inability to manage the peacekeeping operations it has mounted. UN peacekeeping missions have been plagued by a variety of operational problems, including poor communication with UN headquarters in New York; a shortage of long-range transportation and tactical airlift; the uneven quality of troop contributions and incompatibility of equipment; little or no capacity to gather information or intelligence; and slow reaction times, with as much as six months passing before a UN operation is ready to be deployed. A situation faced by Canadian General Lewis Mackenzie while serving with UNPROFOR in the former Yugoslavia dramatically illustrates UN shortcomings. The general, requiring a decision from UN headquarters in New York, was unable to contact anyone on the telephone because he placed his call after office hours.

Another important factor affecting the capacity of the UN is peacekeeping fatigue. Simply put, states are less willing to contribute money and resources to UN operations. The surge in peacekeeping operations in the late 1980s and early 1990s created enormous demands on UN budgets and on contributing states. In 1988 the UN ran 5 operations with some 10 000 soldiers, at a cost of U.S.$230 million. In the peak year of 1994, the UN ran 13 operations, deploying some 70 000 personnel, at a cost of almost U.S.$4 billion annually.[18] As peacekeeping missions have become more modest in size and scope, costs have fallen, from U.S.$1.4 billion in 1996 to under U.S.$1 billion in 1999. As of 1999, member states owed the UN U.S.$1.75 billion in peacekeeping dues.[19] The increased costs and risks involved have made countries increasingly cautious about contributing to UN peacekeeping. This caution, in turn, compromises the ability of the UN to mount successful operations. As Boutros Boutros-Ghali warned in 1993, "Our renaissance remains in question; demands made upon the United Nations are not being matched by the resources to do the job."[20]

In the face of such problems, some attempts have been made to improve the capacity of the UN to create and deploy peacekeeping missions. The Department of Peacekeeping Operations (DPKO) has created a 24-hour situation centre that provides UN headquarters with command, control, and communications capabilities. In 1992, the Department of Humanitarian Affairs (DHA) established a Humanitarian Early Warning System. In 1993 a Standby Arrangements program was developed to establish a roster list of forces and capabilities that contributors were willing to make available to the UN on short notice. An equipment stockpile was established at Brindisi, Italy. In 1995, Canada released a set of proposals on establishing a United Nations Rapid Reaction Capability. The UN has established a rapidly deployable peacekeeping headquarters designed to react swiftly. Larger proposals have also been forwarded, including the long-standing suggestion that the UN should possess its own army. However, this idea has foundered because of opposition from most member states who fear the creation of a military instrument under UN control and because of the prohibitive costs of such a venture. In August 2000, the UN released the "Report of the Panel on UN Peacekeeping Operations," otherwise known as the Brahimi Report. The report recommended (among other things) an extensive restructuring of the Department of

Peacekeeping Operations, an improved capacity to react rapidly to crisis, and an enhanced headquarters capable of better planning and coordination. It remains to be seen to what extent the recommendations of the Brahimi Report will be implemented.

Concerns exist about the extent to which peacekeeping operations are becoming dominated by the great powers, especially the United States. While peacekeeping used to be performed almost exclusively by small and middle powers, it is now common for the great powers to be engaged, with all of the implications concerning neutrality and impartiality. However, as UN operations have become larger and more expensive, the involvement of the great powers has been considered essential because UN peacekeeping missions require increasingly more capabilities to perform their mission, particularly in the areas of logistics and transport, communications, and tactical mobility (especially by air). Concerns that peacekeeping is becoming hostage to the interests of the great powers must be balanced with the reality that without the diplomatic and often the material support of the great powers, peacekeeping missions could not be mounted.

UN peacekeeping is still a valuable conflict management instrument in the international system. Ongoing missions continue to contribute to the maintenance of peace around the world, and in future conflicts and crises, the mechanism of UN peacekeeping will continue to be a conflict management option. For example, a peacekeeping mission is expected to deploy to the Ethiopian–Eritrean border in support of the peace agreement between the two countries. However, the effectiveness of peacekeeping in the future will be determined by three factors: (1) the careful consideration of the demands of a proposed mission and the mandates and capabilities required to carry it out; (2) the willingness of contributing states to offer money and resources, including troops; and (3) the willingness of the parties to a dispute to stop fighting and begin the process of building a peace.

With UN peacekeeping increasingly regarded as unsuited to the challenges of major regional conflicts and gross violations of human rights, states have turned to regional organizations or "coalitions of the willing" that are unburdened by the constraints of the UN system. The interventions in Kosovo and East Timor are two examples of so-called *humanitarian intervention*, efforts to respond to humanitarian crises or gross violations of human rights using military force. Humanitarian intervention can, of course, be conducted through the UN (many recent peacekeeping missions could be described as humanitarian interventions), but in recent years the term has increasingly referred to efforts mounted by regional organizations or coalitions of the willing operating with UN authority (this is sometimes called "contracting out") or without UN authority. Either way, the role of the UN is diminished in such cases.

NATO and Humanitarian Intervention against Serbia

Since the creation of Yugoslavia, Kosovo has been a predominantly ethnic Albanian province of Serbia. Tensions escalated between the Albanian majority, which called for increased autonomy or outright independence, and the Milosevic government in Belgrade. Violence broke out between Albanian separatists (later called the Kosovo Liberation Army, or KLA) and the Serbian police in the early 1990s. The violence intensified in 1998 and 1999 as an increasingly indiscriminate government campaign aimed at suppressing the KLA escalated into ethnic cleansing disturbingly similar to the kind witnessed in the Bosnian War. Incidents of mass murder became increasingly frequent and a serious refugee crisis developed inside and outside Kosovo. NATO threatened Serbia with air strikes unless the campaign against ethnic Albanians stopped. The Serbian government agreed to attend talks at Rambouillet, France, but refused to sign a peace agreement that would have given Kosovo considerable autonomy and provided for a future referendum on independence. Today, controversy exists as to whether Rambouillet was a good faith effort at negotiation or a NATO ultimatum. What is clear is that it was Milosevic's last chance to avoid the use of force against Serbia. On 24 March 1999, NATO began a bombing campaign against Serbia that would last 78 days until, on June 10, the Milosevic government accepted NATO demands to withdraw its security forces from Kosovo. On June 12, NATO began deployment of Kosovo-force (K-FOR) to restore law and order, demilitarize the KLA, and assist the UN with the restoration of civilian authority. They remain there as this book goes to print.

NATO's campaign against Serbia remains controversial. Critics charge that NATO acted illegally, as no UN resolution was ever passed authorizing the air campaign (K-FOR did have UN approval). Not enough time or effort was given to diplomacy. The bombing campaign itself was criticized as excessive and more damaging to civilian targets than to the Serbian military. NATO had violated the rights of a sovereign state and had in effect severed Kosovo from Serbia by force. Critics also charged that NATO was being selective. Why did it intervene against Serbia but not against Algeria (embroiled in a brutal civil war) or in Chechnya (under assault by Russia)? Supporters of the NATO campaign argued that Serbia had violated international law, rejected diplomatic overtures, and had engaged in ethnic cleansing, which demanded a swift reaction before more Albanians died and the region became destabilized. To do nothing, supporters argued, would allow ethnic cleansing to continue and risk a wider Balkan war. The air campaign was conducted to avoid civilian casualties as much as possible, and in any case Milosevic could have stopped the bombing by agreeing to terms far earlier. Serbia may have been a sovereign state, but by committing violations of human rights, it had given NATO countries little choice and every right to intervene. NATO could not be expected to intervene everywhere; not intervening in Algeria or Chechnya did not make intervening in Kosovo wrong.

The legacy of NATO's campaign is mixed and the future of Kosovo uncertain. The bombing devastated the Serbian economy, with the lower damage estimates placed at U.S.$4 billion. Estimates of civilian deaths range from 500 deaths to the Serbian government claim of 2000. NATO is a dirty word among the Serbian people, who maintain that their country was unjustly attacked. In Kosovo, which is now a de facto NATO protectorate, the return of something resembling normal life and a general gratitude toward NATO must be balanced against high unemployment in a destroyed economy and Albanian violence against the Serb minority. K-FOR has struggled to provide protection for Kosovar Serbs, and some 130 000 have fled to Serbia. Ethnic tolerance is hard to find in Kosovo. At the end of 2000, the government of Slobodan Milosevic was overthrown by a popular uprising and new elections brought Vojuslav Kostunica to power. It remains to be seen whether this new leadership will mark the beginning of a new and better future for Kosovo, even as UN war crimes inspectors exhume bodies from mass graves.[21]

Humanitarian Intervention in East Timor

East Timor was a Portuguese colony for almost 500 years. In 1975, it was invaded by Indonesia and subjected to a brutal occupation that saw at least 200 000 deaths between 1975 and 1980 alone from executions, starvation, and military operations. East Timor became a symbol of the world's failure to respond to such human rights disasters. In 1998, a leadership change in Indonesia opened the way for a UN-supervised referendum on independence. However, violence perpetrated by pro-Indonesian militias supported by the Indonesian Army required the postponement of the referendum. Finally, on 30 August 1999, an extraordinary 98 percent of registered voters went to the polls despite threats of physical violence. Almost 80 percent voted against remaining tied to Indonesia. The pro-Indonesian militias reacted with a campaign of violence and intimidation, which rapidly escalated into the pillaging of East Timor. Faced with a humanitarian crisis, an Australian-led coalition developed plans for an intervention force to restore order and protect the East Timorese people. The proposed force received UN approval on September 15, and on September 20, an Australian-led force of 8000 personnel began arriving in East Timor with the consent of the Indonesian government. The force moved quickly to establish order and forced the militias out of East Timor. In February 2000 the Australian-led force withdrew and was replaced by a UN peace-keeping force. In cooperation with the Timorese people, the UN is now engaged in a process that will lead to East Timorese independence by 2001 or 2002.

It is difficult to find a critic of the Australian-led humanitarian intervention in East Timor because of the circumstances of the intervention, which included a clear moral purpose, UN authorization, and the consent of the Indonesian government. In this case, the circumstances were quite different from those confronted by NATO in Kosovo. However, some critics wonder why it took so long for the international community to respond to Indonesia's brutality in East Timor (which had lasted for almost 25 years). For most of that time, governments traded with Indonesia, participated in international organizations with Indonesia, and held summits with Indonesian leaders (such as the now-infamous APEC summit in Vancouver in 1997). It took a change in East Asia's security environment (a consequence of the end of the Cold War), a change in the Indonesian government, the collapse of the Indonesian economy in the Asian financial crisis, and another humanitarian crisis to create the conditions for the outside world to respond to one of the longest lasting human rights outrages in the world.[22]

Many welcome the idea of humanitarian intervention as a positive development because it represents a willingness to act in support of human rights and international humanitarian law and against those regimes that perpetrate atrocities against groups of people. The alternative—to stand by and do nothing or wait for sanctions to work—is simply unacceptable. Critics argue that humanitarian intervention is seldom purely humanitarian, is selectively and inconsistently applied, and results in the deaths of innocent civilians and the destruction of civilian infrastructure. The legal, moral, and political terms of this debate are now an important issue in the study of conflict management.

ECONOMIC STATECRAFT, DEMOCRACY, AND CONFLICT MANAGEMENT

Economic instruments have also played a significant role in conflict management. One such instrument is trade; recall how the liberal perspective asserts that wars can be prevented through the promotion of economic interdependence. Another economic instrument is the use of economic sanctions. Finally, a widely held proposition in recent years suggests that democracies do not fight one another and that war can be prevented by promoting democracy around the world.

INTERDEPENDENCE AS A CONSTRAINT ON WAR

Liberals have long argued that growing economic ties between countries (in areas such as trade, finance, and shared production) will reduce incentives to go to war. Richard Cobden wrote that free trade would unite states, making them "equally anxious for the prosperity and happiness of both."[23] Just before the outbreak of World War I, Norman Angell argued that the increasing level of trade between countries was making war "commercially suicidal."[24] States had to choose between old power politics methods and peaceful trade. Since war was no longer profitable, states would choose the latter. Undaunted by the outbreak of World War I, Angell went on to make the same argument in the 1930s. War broke out, he argued, because state leaders failed to understand that war no longer pays; World War I only confirmed this point.

The argument that economic interdependence promotes peace has experienced a rebirth since the surge in global economic activity of the past few decades. States are mutually vulnerable to the damage war would cause. War disrupts trade, eliminates markets, compromises the joint production of goods, and complicates access to resources. Richard Rosecrance argues that states have a choice between becoming "trading states" (emphasizing wealth through commerce) or "territorial states" (emphasizing gains through territorial expansion). In the modern global economy, states will choose the former. For Rosecrance, in an interdependent world the "incentive to wage war is absent … trading states recognize that they can do better through internal economic development sustained by a world wide market for their goods and services than by trying to conquer and assimilate large tracts of land."[25] In addition, war has become increasingly costly (especially when nuclear weapons might be involved), both in terms of the monetary costs of fighting a war and in terms of destruction. For all these reasons, as economic interdependence between countries grows, they will be less inclined to go to war because they would lose the gains and value of trade and incur the high costs of war. Put simply, interdependence promotes peace because states can do better through trade than through conquest: don't invade—trade.

The opposing (realist) view is that economic interdependence does not promote peace; in fact, it encourages war because interdependence means dependence and vulnerability. States are dependent or vulnerable if they are forced to rely on others for imports of crucial goods or resources, which could be cut off or used as political blackmail. As a result, dependent states have an incentive to go to war, to secure access to vital resources. Kenneth Waltz suggests that states in an anarchic international system will want to "control who they depend on or to lessen the extent of their dependency."[26] For their part, critical perspectives assert that economic interdependence facilitates greater exploitation and thus causes more conflict.

The historical record concerning the relationship between interdependence and war is uncertain and the subject of considerable debate. Both perspectives cite the World War I and interwar period as evidence supporting their claims. For liberals, the 1920s was a period of high interdependence, and in that period there were no wars. In the 1930s, when protectionism led to the erosion of interdependence, tensions increased and war broke out. Realists point out that before World War I the European powers had reached unprecedented levels of trade among themselves, but despite this, world war did break out. In the 1930s rising tensions and eventual war were caused by the rise of revisionist states. This debate is unlikely to be resolved in the near future; since the variables that can lead to war are so numerous, it is very difficult to isolate the impact of interdependence.

SANCTIONS AND CONFLICT MANAGEMENT

Economic sanctions are "deliberate government actions to inflict economic deprivation on a target state or society, through the limitation or cessation of customary economic relations."[27] Economic sanctions, therefore, are coercive instruments. Nevertheless, they have been employed as instruments of conflict management in the international system. Economic sanctions may take several forms, including trade boycotts, embargoes, or restrictions on financial interactions (such as access to overseas assets or international financial institutions). Sanctions may be imposed unilaterally by one state, or multilaterally, by a group of states (or by the membership of an international organization). When sanctions are imposed, the sending or initiating countries might have a number of possible goals or aims:

- Compliance: "to force the target to alter its behaviour to conform with the initiator's preferences"
- Subversion: "to remove the target's leaders or overthrow the regime"
- Deterrence: "to dissuade the target from repeating the disputed action in the future"
- International symbolism: "to send messages to other members of the world community"
- Domestic symbolism: "to increase its domestic support or thwart international criticism of its foreign policies by acting decisively"[28]

The use of sanctions has deep historical roots. In his history of the Peloponnesian War, Thucydides describes a trade embargo put in place by Athens against Megara, a Spartan ally. Under Napoleonic domination, most of continental Europe limited grain sales to Great Britain. However, the use of sanctions increased dramatically in the twentieth century. One study found that since World War I, economic sanctions have been used 120 times, with 104 of those examples occurring since World War II.[29] The increased use of economic sanctions as an instrument of policy can be explained by the attractiveness of sanctions as a policy choice. Diplomatic measures, although they may carry the weight of the displeasure of one country against another or the force of global or world opinion, tend not to have the same strength as other instruments for two reasons: (1) the leverage one can exert against a target state is limited, and (2) the sending or initiating countries incur few costs, so diplomatic measures are less credible as expressions of will or commitment. Military measures, however, are both costly and risky, although they may have a greater chance of succeeding than would diplomatic efforts. States may, therefore, find economic sanctions an attractive option because although costs are involved (the severing of some or all economic ties with the target state), they do not carry the costs of military action and have more credibility than mere diplomatic measures.

Despite the frequency of their use, the effectiveness of economic sanctions in achieving their goals has been limited at best. The consensus is that when results are measured against goals and objectives, economic sanctions usually fail and often harm the most vulnerable people in target states. One study found that between 1914 and 1989, "although sanctions were successful in 34 percent of 115 cases ... success has become increasingly elusive in recent years.... The success rate among [the 46] cases begun after 1973 was a little less than 26 percent."[30] Several possible explanations exist as to why the success rate of economic sanctions is so low:

- The target state is usually able to find alternative sources of supply or markets for its exports (for this reason, unilateral sanctions are frequently ineffective, and most sanction efforts are multilateral in nature).

- In target states, sanctions may provoke nationalist sentiments and a willingness to sacrifice in the name of resistance against outside interference.

- Sanctions may do the most harm to the very people they are supposed to benefit. Authoritarian rulers who care little for the economic hardships of their people will not be swayed by sanctions. The people will suffer for the actions of their leadership. As Jim Hoagland has observed: "The logic of the policy seems to be to make unarmed citizens desperate enough to rise up and throw off the brutal regimes that other powers are not willing to use the world's best armies to topple."[31]

- Sanctions are often undercut by the actions of domestic companies, the companies of other countries, or by foreign governments. The longer sanctions last, the greater the likelihood that they will erode and collapse.[32]

- The imposition of sanctions can actually increase the power of undesirable political elites in the target country, as the sanctions can be used to justify their increased control over the country, or create a lucrative environment for black market activity. Sanctions can also create a "rally around the flag" effect that can boost the popularity of an authoritarian leader.

- Sending or initiating countries can have inflated expectations about the utility of sanctions. Economic deprivation has never been a reliable means of forcing political change; the political context is usually a more important factor in the political outcome.[33]

The success of sanctions appears to depend on several variables. First, the relationship between the state (or states) sending the sanctions and the target is very important. If the target state is less economically powerful than the sending states, or is a close trading partner of the sending states, economic sanctions will have a greater effect on the target country. Second, when sending countries impose sanctions quickly and decisively, and when sanctions do not involve significant economic hardships for sending countries, the sanctions will have greater credibility, for they reflect firm resolve and will be sustainable over time. Third, clear conditions must be established for the lifting of sanctions. In other words, it must be clear to the target country why the sanctions were imposed and what actions they must undertake to have them lifted. Furthermore, if objectives are broad and general, sanctions will not have the same chance of success as if the objectives are specific and clearly defined. Sanctions should, therefore, be imposed to give the target country an incentive to change certain specific policies rather than as a general punishment for a broad range of actions. Finally, sanctions will be more effective if an internal faction exists within the target state that supports the imposition of sanctions and can exert domestic pressure against the government using sanctions as a political argument for changing a policy; this was certainly an instrumental factor in the case of apartheid South Africa (see Profile 7.6). It is likely that sanctions will continue to be a frequently used instrument in conflict management. Compliance with stated goals is not the only objective of sanctions. They remain a valuable tool to signal disapproval and are an important alternative to the use of military force. Sanctions are also versatile as they can be used to respond to a wide variety of security concerns.

A DEMOCRATIC PATH TO PEACE?

The idea that democracies are inherently peaceful forms of government is not unique to the post–Cold War era. Immanuel Kant suggested that constitutional governments and

Sanctions

QUALIFIED SUCCESS AND THE CASE OF SOUTH AFRICA

The South African apartheid regime was a prominent human rights issue during the Cold War. Apartheid institutionalized racial separation and discrimination against the Black majority in South Africa, and to end this system sanctions were imposed on South Africa from a variety of sources. The UN imposed a voluntary arms embargo against South Africa in 1963, and this was made mandatory in 1977. Many other countries, including Canada, began to impose stronger unilateral sanctions against South Africa as well. In addition, campaigns in many countries led many corporations and social institutions (such as universities) to divest themselves of their interests and operations in South Africa. However, stiffer multilateral sanctions against South Africa could not be imposed because of the opposition of Great Britain and the United States. Both countries argued that sanctions would only hurt the Black African majority in South Africa. Instead, the Reagan administration opted for a policy of **constructive engagement** in 1981. Critics charged that the United States was being soft on South Africa because of its importance as a source of raw minerals and its opposition to Communism in Africa. However, in 1985 Congress overrode a presidential veto and imposed harsh economic sanctions against South Africa. In 1989, F.W. de Klerk came to power in South Africa, intent on reform. He released the long-time jailed leader of the **African National Congress (ANC)**, Nelson Mandela, and opened negotiations with the ANC, which, in 1993, led to the dismantling of apartheid, to universal democracy, and to a Black majority government. Sanctions were lifted, and South Africa was no longer an isolated country.

Did sanctions succeed in this case? The consensus is that they played a role; the South African economy was certainly damaged by sanctions, as trade fell, debt rose, loans were not renewed, foreign investment declined, and growth rates declined. Two questions remain. How much of this economic damage was due to sanctions, and how much was due to falling world prices for gold (a key South African foreign exchange earner)? What would have happened had a hard-line South African leader determined to resist sanctions come to power, instead of the reform-minded de Klerk? In any event, the South African example does stand as a success story for sanctions.

QUALIFIED FAILURE AND THE CASE OF THE GULF WAR

When Iraq invaded Kuwait in 1990 the international community responded with diplomatic expressions of opposition and economic sanctions. These sanctions were organized through the United Nations and included a total ban on imports and exports to and from Iraq, with the exception of humanitarian imports such as medicine and some foodstuffs. Iraq was a vulnerable target, as its main export was oil (with only two routes of egress, both easily blocked), and it was heavily dependent on food imports. The stated goal of sanctions was to compel Saddam Hussein's government to withdraw from Kuwait. It was also hoped that sanctions would promote the overthrow of Saddam Hussein. However, confidence in sanctions was never very high, and the military option was developed as quickly as possible and eventually used to force Iraq from Kuwait.

Why were sanctions not given time to work? First, many suspected they would not work because of the authoritarian nature of the Iraqi regime. Saddam Hussein could maintain power through brutality and intimidation and use the hardships that sanctions would create among the people of Iraq to increase support for his regime. Second, it was also felt that sanctions would take a long time to work, perhaps 12 to 18 months, if they would work at all. Concerns were raised that some countries would not maintain sanctions for that long and that the fragile coalition of countries built up against Iraq would fracture over time. As a result, Iraq would retain Kuwait and go unpunished and would emerge as a dangerous and powerful country in the Middle East that would control a significant percentage of Middle East oil supplies. Economic sanctions were, therefore, abandoned in the case of Iraq.

Since the end of the Gulf War, Iraq has remained under UN sanctions. The goal of the sanctions is to compel Saddam Hussein to cooperate with UN weapons inspectors seeking to destroy Iraq's weapons of mass destruction program (with the additional hope that Saddam may be toppled). Maintaining the sanctions has become increasingly controversial. Critics charge that the sanctions are causing extensive human suffering inside Iraq, while Saddam himself remains untouched. Supporters argue that sanctions remain the only lever available (other than the use of force) to pressure Iraq to give up its weapons of mass destruction and to prevent more aggressive behaviour by the Iraqi regime.

their respect for international law would be a constraint on war. However, the idea of a democratic peace took on a new significance after the Cold War. A belief prevails in most Western countries that democracies rarely, if ever, fight one another (although they do fight nondemocratic states). It follows that if you expand the number of democracies in the world, you will increase the chances of peace. This was one of the pillars of United States foreign policy during the Clinton administration, which promoted the concept of "enlargement of the world's community of market democracies" as a replacement for the Cold War strategy of containment.[34] According to former U.S. President Bill Clinton, "enlargement" is in the interest of United States because "democracies rarely wage war on one another."[35] Enlargement is to be achieved by encouraging democracy in Eastern Europe, in the former Soviet Union, and in the southern hemisphere.

The argument that democracies do not fight one another is based on two assumptions. First, the domestic institutional structures of democratic states act as a constraint on war. Democracies must answer to their citizens, and the financial and human costs of war might result in a government losing the next election. In addition, there are constraints on leaders in democracies; the checks and balances that exist in parliamentary and republican systems will help prevent warlike or renegade leaders from coming to power. Authoritarian governments, in contrast, have fewer constraints, and are thus more likely to engage in aggressive or warlike behaviour. Second, the norms of democratic governance promote the peaceful resolution of disputes. Democracies are governed by the rule of law and by norms and principles that seek to establish a balance between the rights of the individual and the common good. As a result, democracies use **adjudication** and bargaining to avoid violent conflict, externalizing their internal behaviour, and so advocates of the idea of a democratic peace argue that they will be more likely to negotiate, adjudicate, and bargain when disputes arise between them. As Bruce Russett suggests, "the culture, perceptions, and practices that permit compromise and the peaceful resolution of conflicts without the threat of violence within countries come to apply across national boundaries toward other democratic countries."[36] Michael Doyle agrees, suggesting that democracies that "rest on consent, presume foreign republics to be also consensual, just and therefore deserving of accommodation."[37]

However, the idea of a democratic peace has been challenged. First, critics argue that institutional constraints will not necessarily prevent wars between democracies. If they did, they would prevent democracies from going to war against any kind of opponent. The fact that democracies have often gone to war (although not necessarily with other democracies) raises doubts about the salience of democratic constraints on war. Public opinion has, in fact, favoured war: American public opinion favoured war with Spain in 1898, and the publics of Europe enthusiastically welcomed war in 1914. Second, democracies have nearly gone to war with each other on numerous occasions. In one study, Christopher Layne argues that in four cases of near-war between democracies (the United States and Great Britain in the Trent Affair of 1861; the United States and Great Britain in the Venezuela Crisis of 1895–96; France and Great Britain in the Fashoda Crisis of 1898; and France and Germany in the Ruhr in 1923), war was avoided only because one side backed down because of fears that a war would end in defeat or quagmire.[38] Third, there have been very few democracies in history, and as a result there have been fewer opportunities for conflict and warfare between them. Furthermore, most states are rarely at war, so it should be no surprise that democracies are rarely at war.[39] Fourth, democracies have actually fought one another. Or have they? Here the problem is the definition of democracy. World War I saw democratic states fight one another. However, some debate exists as to whether Germany was a democracy and how democratic any of the combatants were in the realm of foreign policy decision making.[40] In another ambiguous case, the United States Civil War was a war that occurred within a democracy. Although this war has been dismissed as only a civil war, the War between the States did have the character of an interstate conflict. In any case, why did the democratic institutions of the United States not save the country from civil war?

The debate over the idea of a democratic peace has profound policy implications. For example, should Canada support the spread of formal democracy in the hope that it will lead to a more peaceful world? Is it not possible that the effort to encourage or promote democracy will drag Canada (or other countries) into interventions and even wars in the cause of the democratic peace?

CONCLUSIONS

This chapter has explored some of the conflict management instruments available to actors in global politics. As we have seen, conflict management efforts in global politics are plagued by several obstacles, most notably the problem of compliance, trust, and self-interest. Many actors sign international agreements or take on obligations but do not abide by them. Other actors refuse to engage in bilateral or multilateral conflict management efforts because they do not trust other countries to live up to their obligations. Many conflict management instruments founder because global actors do not believe it is in their best interests to pursue such a course.

Conflict management is by its very nature a cooperative enterprise, and as we have seen, cooperation in a world that is at least in part anarchic is a difficult enterprise (see the discussion on game theory in Chapter 3). As a result, conflict management tends to be a very controversial subject. Despite the less than illustrious history of conflict management, some cause for optimism remains. Emerging transnational security issues may compel international actors—especially states—to increase their efforts to establish more rigorous and effective arms control agreements in the future. Peacekeeping, by both regional organizations and the UN, continues to offer hope, and economic statecraft will also be employed by states in the name of conflict management. But can all this diplomatic activity really affect the condition of individuals in the contemporary age? Our next chapter, which examines global inequities, will address this question.

Endnotes

1. From his speech to the First Meeting of the Commission to Deal with the Problems Raised by the Discovery of Atomic Energy and Other Related Matters, Hunter College, The Bronx, New York, 14 June 1946.

2. Garret Mattingly, *Renaissance Diplomacy* (Baltimore: Penguin, 1964), 244.

3. For a highly readable and general text on negotiation, see R. Fisher and W. Ury, *Getting to Yes: Negotiating Agreement without Giving In* (Boston: Houghton Mifflin, 1981).

4. See K. Boulding, *The Three Faces of Power* (Newbury Park, CA: Sage, 1990); and W. Habeeb, *Power and Tactics in International Negotiation: How Weak Nations Bargain with Strong Nations* (Baltimore: Johns Hopkins University Press, 1988).

5. For a recent discussion, see R. Johansen, "Swords into Plowshares: Can Fewer Arms Yield More Security?" in C. Kegley Jr., ed., *Controversies in International Relations Theory: Realism and the Neoliberal Challenge* (New York: St. Martin's Press, 1995), 224–44.

6. J. Kruzel, "Arms Control, Disarmament, and the Stability of the Postwar Era," in C. Kegley Jr., ed., *The Long Postwar Peace* (New York: HarperCollins, 1991), 249.

7. See R. Johnson, "The In-Comprehensive Test Ban," *Bulletin of Atomic Scientists* 52 (November/December 1996), 30–5.

8. Kruzel, "Arms Control, Disarmament, and the Stability of the Post–Cold War Era," 268.

9. See K. Deutsch et al., *Political Community and the North Atlantic Area* (Princeton: Princeton University Press, 1957).

10. See *Charter of the United Nations and Statute of the International Court of Justice* (New York: United Nations), 1.

11. See Article 2/4, *Charter of the United Nations and Statute of the International Court of Justice*, 4.

12. For case studies of peacekeeping before the creation of the UN, see A. James, *Peacekeeping in International Politics* (New York: St. Martin's Press, 1990).

13. For more discussion of these principles and their interrelated nature, see F.T. Liu, *United Nations Peacekeeping and the Non-Use of Force*, International Peace Academy Occasional Paper Series (Boulder, CO: Lynne Rienner, 1992).

14. *An Agenda for Peace: Preventive Diplomacy, Peacemaking, and Peacekeeping* (New York: United Nations, 1992), 1–2.

15. B. Boutros-Ghali, "Beyond Peacekeeping," *New York University Journal of International Law and Politics* 25 (Fall 1992), 115.

16. "The UN and the Use of Force: Leave the Secretary General out of It," *Foreign Affairs* 73 (September/October 1994), 14.

17. Saadia Touval, "Why the UN Fails," *Foreign Affairs* 73 (September/October 1994), 45.

18. See Barbara Crossette, "UN Chief Chides Security Council on Military Missions," *The New York Times* (6 January 1995), A3.

19. "United Nations Peacekeeping Operations," Internet, <http://www.un.org/depts/dpko>, 20 June 2000.

20. Quoted in Paul Lewis, "United Nations Is Finding Its Plate Increasingly Full but Its Cupboard Is Bare," *The New York Times* (27 September 1993), A8.

21. See Barry Posen, "The War for Kosovo: Serbia's Political-Military Strategy," *International Security* 24 (Spring 2000), 3–50; William Arkin, "Smart Bombs, Dumb Targeting?" *Bulletin of the Atomic Scientists* 56 (May/June 2000), 46–54; and Adam Roberts, "NATO's Humanitarian War over Kosovo," *Survival* 4 (Autumn 1999), 102–23.

22. See James Cotton, "The Emergence of an Independent East Timor: National and Regional Challenges," *Contemporary Southeast Asia* 22 (April 2000); and James Traub, "Inventing East Timor," *Foreign Affairs* 79 (July/August 2000), 74–89.

23. Richard Cobden, *The Political Writings of Richard Cobden* (London: T. Fisher Unwin, 1903), 225.

24. Norman Angell, *The Great Illusion*, 2nd ed. (New York: G.P. Putnam's Sons, 1933), 33, 59–60. Or as the great rock artist Frank Zappa once commented, there won't be a nuclear war in our time "because there's too much real estate involved."

25. Richard Rosecrance, *The Rise of the Trading State: Commerce and Conquest in the Modern World* (New York: Basic Books, 1986), 24–5.

26. Kenneth Waltz, *Theory of International Politics* (New York: Random House, 1979).

27. D. Leyton-Brown, "Introduction," in D. Leyton-Brown, ed., *The Utility of International Economic Sanctions* (New York: St. Martin's Press, 1987), 1–4.

28. J. Lindsay, "Trade Sanctions as Policy Instruments: A Re-Examination," *International Studies Quarterly* 30 (June 1996), 153–73.

29. See G. Hufbauer, J. Schott, and K. Elliott, *Economic Sanctions Reconsidered: History and Current Policy*, 2nd ed. (Washington, DC: Institute for International Economics, 1990).

30. K. Elliot, "Sanctions: A Look at the Record," *Bulletin of the Atomic Scientists* 49 (November 19), 32–5.

31. See J. Hoagland, "Economic Sanctions Sometimes Do More Harm Than Good," *The State* 11 (November 1993), A12.

32. See Hufbauer et al., *Economic Sanctions Reconsidered*, 100–1.

33. Ibid., 94.

34. (Former U.S. national security adviser) Anthony Lake, "From Containment to Enlargement," United States Department of State, Bureau of Public Affairs, *Dispatch* 4 (39) (September 1993), 3.

35. William Clinton, "Confronting the Challenges of a Broader World," United States Department of State, Bureau of Public Affairs, *Dispatch* 4 (39) (September 1993), 3.

36. Bruce Russett, *Grasping the Democratic Peace: Principles for a Post–Cold War World* (Princeton: Princeton University Press, 1993), 31.

37. Michael Doyle, "Kant, Liberal Legacies and Foreign Affairs," Part One, *Philosophy and Public Affairs* 12 (Summer 1983), 205–35, 230.

38. C. Layne, "Kant or Can't: The Myth of a Democratic Peace," *International Security* 19 (Fall 1994), 5–49.

39. D. Shapiro, "The Insignificance of the Liberal Peace," *International Security* 19 (Fall 1994), 50–86.

40. Layne, "Kant or Can't," 40–4.

Suggested Readings

Anderson, M.S. *The Rise of Modern Diplomacy*. New York: Longman, 1993.

Berdal, Mats R. "Whither UN Peacekeeping?" *Adelphi Paper* 281 (October 1993).

Bundy, McGeorge, William J. Crowe, Jr., and Sidney D. Drell. *Reducing Nuclear Danger: The Road Away from the Brink*. New York: Council on Foreign Relations Press, 1993.

Diehl, Paul F. *International Peacekeeping*. Baltimore: Johns Hopkins University Press, 1993.

Durch, William J. *The Evolution of UN Peacekeeping* (New York: St. Martin's Press, 1993).

Fisher, Roger, and William Ury. *Getting to Yes*. Boston: Houghton Mifflin, 1981.

Fisher, Roger, et al. *Coping With International Conflict: A Systematic Approach to Influence in International Negotiation*. Upper Saddle River, NJ: Prentice Hall, 1997.

Grieves, Forest L. *Conflict and Order*. Boston: Houghton Mifflin, 1977.

Hufbauer, Gary Clyde, Jeffrey J. Schott, and Kimberly Ann Elliott. *Economic Sanctions Reconsidered: History and Current Policy*. 2nd ed. Washington, DC: Institute for International Economics, 1990.

James, Alan. *Peacekeeping in International Politics*. New York: St. Martin's Press, 1990.

Jensen, Lloyd. *Bargaining for National Security: The Postwar Disarmament Negotiations*. Columbia: University of South Carolina Press, 1988.

———. *Negotiating Nuclear Arms Control*. Columbia: University of South Carolina, 1988.

Lasswell, Harold D. *Politics: Who Gets What, When, How*. New York: Meridian, 1958.

Martin, Lisa L. Coercive Cooperation: *Explaining Multilateral Economic Sanctions*. Princeton, NJ: Princeton University Press, 1992.

Talbott, Strobe. *Deadly Gambits*. New York: Random House, 1985.

Telhami, Shibley. *Power and Leadership in International Bargaining: The Path to the Camp David Accords.* New York: Columbia University Press, 1990.

Viotti, Paul R., ed. *Conflict and Arms Control.* Boulder, CO: Westview Press, 1991.

Weston, Burns, ed. *Toward Nuclear Disarmament and Global Security.* Boulder, CO: Westview Press, 1984.

Suggested Websites

Center for Defense Information

UN Peacekeeping
<www.un.org/peace/>

Federation of American Scientists

CHAPTER 8

Globalization, Regionalization, and Marginalization in the World Economy

If present trends continue, economic disparities between industrial and developing nations will move from inequitable to inhuman.

—James Gustave Speth,
UN Development Programme Administrator[1]

As almost every factor of production—money, technology, factories, and equipment—moves effortlessly across borders, the very idea of an American economy is becoming meaningless, as are the notions of an American corporation, American capital, American products, and American technology. A similar transformation is affecting every other nation.

—Robert Reich, former U.S. Secretary of Labor[2]

OUR CENTRAL PERSPECTIVES ON THE WORLD ECONOMY REVISITED

This chapter begins with a re-examination of the central perspectives of international political economy introduced in Chapter 4, and adds a fifth perspective, that of environmentalism. Next we present a survey of some of the key issues that are playing a role in transforming the world economy as well as our understanding of the subfield of international political economy (IPE).

As this chapter's title suggests, a lot is going on in the world economy, which partially reflects the convergence/divergence theme with which we opened this book. The components of the world economy are increasingly interlinked and, on the surface, look more and more like a single (albeit rather chaotic) entity. We are beginning to formulate ideas about what the implications of this transformation are, for the system as a whole, for individual countries and corporations, and even for individual people. At the same time, much of the economic integration that has occurred has been at the regional, as opposed to truly global, level; some analysts suggest a three-fold or four-fold trade bloc system is gradually establishing itself, one that might preclude the grander globalization many neoliberals would prefer. Other analysts remind us that poverty and relative powerlessness continue to escalate in many regions of the world, despite the creation of wealth elsewhere. This phenomenon is called *marginalization* and is the topic to which we return in the final pages of this chapter.

Beyond these trends, we have seen some major developments over the past few years. Foremost among them was the 1997–98 Asian financial crisis, which had a ripple effect throughout the world economy. Foreign investors and currency speculators have come to play a huge role in the daily economic life of countries, and when they remove their money, the chaos is immediate and long lasting. Government debt has been reduced in some cases (Canada, for example, has managed balanced budgets in recent years), but it has soared in others, especially in Asia. Women of all ages have become even more integrated with the modern production process than ever before, but often under exploitative conditions. Energy production remains a central issue with geostrategic salience. The attempts to manage the global economy, from the proposed **Multilateral Agreement on Investment (MAI)** to the autumn 1999 meeting of the World Trade Organization, have met with vocal opposition from protest groups concerned with the impact of globalization on cultural, employment, military, environmental, and other contemporary factors. A rift between regional and global approaches coexists, with a growing rift between north and south.

Before discussing the present global economy, however, we must refamiliarize ourselves with the central perspectives offered in Chapter 4. The economic nationalist is primarily concerned with the health and security of the nation-state itself; economics is simply a means to ensure or, better yet, increase both. This view is best seen as an economic extension of the realist perspective. Whereas the economic nationalist sees states struggling to survive or prosper, liberals see individuals maximizing their profits in the global marketplace and states playing the role of minimalist managers of the world economy. However, neoliberal institutionalists believe rational actors will converge in common institutions and regimes to facilitate this process. The Marxist perspective rejects both these interpretations as mere deflections from the real structure of economic power, a class-based system that has spread to global proportions and works to keep the majority of people poor while a few, protected by the state system, get richer. Postmodernists argue what is needed is a re-examination of all these theories, and the principles on which they are based, so that we can see the underlying power relations inherent in discourse. In particular, the role of gender—usually ignored by the dominant perspectives—needs to be isolated and studied.

We turn now to a necessarily cursory introduction to yet another perspective, one that has come to be more apparent in the space of recent decades. As we discuss in Chapter 10, the environment has emerged as a major issue in global politics. Increasingly, political economists are recognizing the importance of the environment as both a causal variable and an ongoing concern in their work. One might argue this importance has led to the point where a new perspective is emerging in the study of international political economy. After this, we focus on the hotly debated term "globalization" and ask what it really means. Next, we examine several key factors in the contemporary global economy, such as the role of women, energy production, government debt, the centrality of the marketplace, and the split between regional and global efforts to manage world trade and investment. Finally, we discuss the continued gap between rich and poor.

ADDING THE ENVIRONMENTAL PERSPECTIVE

Little doubt currently exists that the environmental problems caused by the global economy have become serious issues. Our discussion in Chapters 10, 11, and 13 should make this very evident. Some would suggest that these issues warrant the adoption of a new approach and that we can no longer separate the world's economy from the earth's ecology at the conceptual or policy level. The most widely publicized endorsement of this opinion was the important report *Our Common Future*, the result of what has come to be known as the Brundtland Commission, which preceded the United Nations Conference on Environment and Development in Rio de Janeiro in 1992.[3]

An environmental perspective would keep the question of sustainable development front and centre. Rather than focus on the need for perpetual economic growth, it would suggest that human societies must learn to live within some sort of boundaries or limitations. This idea must be reflected at the international level by careful monitoring of the impact of industrialization and the use of various measures to ensure that trade does not increase present strains on the biosphere. Natural resources would be appreciated for more than their market value; they would assume intrinsic worth. Conflicts over resources between states and substate groups would receive much attention as indications of the future path of international relations. Most basically, an environmental perspective would emphasize the idea that "if economic activity is to result in sustainable forms of development, environment can no longer be regarded as a factor separate from and secondary to economic decision-making; it must be fully integrated into the economic decision-making process in government, industry, and the home."[4]

This perspective has a split, however, and it is a rather large one. The mainstream, or more conventional, approach emphasizes regime formation and maintenance processes and is most closely aligned to the liberal perspective. The argument here is that we need to focus on the limitations mentioned above, and this can be done without radical changes in the structure of the world economy. Governments can collude for good as well as bad, and they can work together with the necessary commitment to ensure that environmental management becomes important at several diplomatic levels. The Earth Summit (or UNCED—see Chapter 10) was an example of high-profile diplomacy, but the real work is done on a less glamorous scale when bureaucrats and scientists shape and implement cooperative policies in areas such as conserving wildlife, preventing pollution of the commons, and even working to limit global warming. In short, the mainstream approach is neo-institutional and accepts the premise that enlightened self-interest can bring states to create regimes encouraging further cooperation on environmental and other issues.

The other side of the environmentalist perspective is much closer to our critical perspectives. It sees the environmental crisis as a reflection of more fundamental problems related to humankind's attitude toward the environment and, as important, each other. The environmental problems liberals feel are manageable are instead regarded as signs that there must be severe changes in the global economy, a move away from north–south exploitation, a move toward less competition, and the acceptance of perspectives such as ecofeminism. Ecofeminism "stresses the link between structural violence against women and the overexploitation of the environment."[5]

Canadian international political economist Eric Helleiner has summarized what a "green IPE perspective" might look like and how an international power structure might appear under such a vision: "As in the medieval period, the key organizing principle would be 'subsidiarity'—that is, power would be concentrated at the lowest level possible and delegated upwards only when absolutely necessary."[6] A link exists between this branch of the environmental perspective and the urge for decentralization stressed by noted political environmentalists such as E.F. Schumacher and, more radically, the anarchist Murray Bookchin.[7] Similarly, the environmental destruction caused by warfare and military preparation is seen as a consequence of a flawed international structure that currently rewards aggression and militarism, and thus, a broader peace movement is needed to contribute to the achievement of sustainability. The nation-state has been a prime cause of the problems we face, and the solution to the environmental crisis is in the hands of people, social movements, and nongovernmental organizations.[8] If left to nation-states, the search for capital will continue to drive environmental policy; to quote the Argentinean mining secretary, "in Argentina, we would never think of subordinating the interests of development to the interests of the environment."[9]

The environmental perspective provides one key criticism of the processes of globalization. We turn now to a discussion of that term, used so often that it has become unclear what exactly, if anything, it means.

WHAT IS GLOBALIZATION?

It is such a common term today that *globalization* is often accepted, without much examination, as an inevitable path of world development. But when did we begin thinking about a borderless world in which transnational forces, spurred on by technological developments (especially in the field of communications), are shrinking the globe? One might argue this has been a long-term human project, begun when humans first began communicating, and it will perhaps end soon with the global domination of liberal democracy and capitalism. Seen this way, globalization may be the logical end of history; other stages (the city-state system, feudal Europe, the nation-state system) of global development have merely been the means to this end. Others, however, might reject such a teleological approach or see the current era as the beginning of a new history, one marked by the forces of Western culture and their spread throughout the globe, resistance to them, and continued disparities in wealth and future prospects.[10] Some even suggest that global capitalism, driven by its own "manic logic," is creating an inhumane world.[11]

Perhaps the most succinct definition of globalization is offered by Malcolm Waters in his short but fascinating book on the topic. As a sociologist, Waters is more interested in the relationships inherent in global shifts. He defines globalization as a "social process in which the constraints of geography on social and cultural arrangements recede and in which people become increasingly aware that they are receding."[12] Waters believes globalization has always been taking place, proceeding through the "fits and starts of various ancient imperial expansions, pillaging and trading oceanic explorations, and the spread of religious ideas." This path was interrupted by the European Middle Ages, a period of "inward-looking territorialism" but then picked up again in the fifteenth and sixteenth centuries, when the Copernican revolution convinced humanity that it occupied a globe (instead of a flat endless plain) and when European expansion took the ideas that today still shape the global economy—market-based trade, for example—to distant lands where people had previously lived in "virtually complete ignorance of each other's existence."[13]

Others, such as the renowned Canadian international political economist Robert Cox, argue that the analysis of what Cox terms the "globalization thrust" must ultimately begin with an understanding of the internationalization of production:

> The internationalizing process results when capital considers the productive resources of the world as a whole and locates elements of complex globalized production systems at points of greatest cost advantage. The critical factor is information on how most profitably to combine components in that production process.... Producing units take advantage of abundant, cheap, and malleable labour where it is to be found, and of robotization where it is not.[14]

While Waters's explanation rests more on the spread of ideas, Cox relies more on a *materialist* explanation (stressing the political implications of economic forces).

International relations theorists have very mixed reactions to the assertion that we are in a new stage in the process of globalization. Realists point to the stubbornness of the institution of state sovereignty; anyone travelling across a border and dealing with the officials stationed there to protect it realizes very quickly that borders still exist! Though the functionalist school (see Chapter 5) believed international institutions would eventually supplant the state, they did not have the multinational corporation (MNC) in mind. Further, it is very difficult to soundly argue that the UN is anywhere near becoming a world government. For their part, Marxists would reject globalization as the continuation of older forms of **imperialism.** In fact, they would be apt to wonder what all the fuss is about, since this process has been continual since the beginning of the expansion of the ruling elite in ancient societies.

Perhaps globalization, if it is occurring at all, is the modern equivalent of what development theorists earlier referred to as *modernization.* The latter term was harshly criticized because it implied that only Western states were modern and that those developing states that had failed to reach the point of mass consumption societies were unmodern, perhaps because of geographic, cultural, or even personality traits prevalent in their societies. Thus, one might argue that the pressure to globalize, to become even further involved with the world economy and its regimes, is a destructive one that implies that non-Western societies have no choice, if they want to be with it, other than to adopt the conventional attributes of the West: capitalism, commercial culture, secular governance, and an emphasis on the here and now.

The further argument exists that an emerging global corporate culture is pervading the workplace on an unprecedented scale. Thus the idea that we are moving from a Fordist economy, in which relatively highly paid assembly-line workers receive the benefits of a welfare state, to one in which firms have more impact on workers' lives by encouraging them to actively participate in the design of the production process, even encouraging the establishment of a corporate culture. While it is difficult to establish whether such a trend exists, the emergence and success of giant industrial producers such as Toyota, which demand more concentration and production from employees in Western states such as Canada, suggests a shift in this direction (see Profile 8.1).

Still others would insist that the very concept of globalization, and its continual promotion by the corporate elite, belittles the strong cultural differences that exist today. One author argues that the world is still fundamentally divided into at least eight civilizational systems, the Chinese (Confucian–Taoist–Buddhist), Hindu, Islamic, Japanese (Shinton–Buddhist–Confucian), Latin American syncretist, Islamic, non-Islamic African, and Christian.[15] Does a secular vision of globalization, based on markets and investment and common values, do justice to the inherent diversity of humanity? What about the major split, presented as axiomatic by some analysts, between the Eastern and Western, or Islamic and Christian, communities? What about the differences within every nation-state, between rich and poor, between ethnic groups, between male and female? In short, can the forces of globalization overcome the realities of human diversity and environmental diversity? Perhaps **homogenization** is further off than we would believe.

Examining the idea that globalization will produce some sort of global culture, Canadian author Randall White asks:

> Just what could some authentic global culture possibly be? To take just the most obvious point, how would it deal with the at once simple but highly complex fact that in the world at large today we do not all speak anything like

"Toyotism"

Toyota is a very successful automobile manufacturer with branch plants in Canada. "Toyotism" consists of several principles that are held as guiding lights for large firms; it is based on the Japanese model of industrial production. These principles include

- *Strategic management,* which demands long-term outlooks and results in policies such as low price setting to get a product off the ground.

- *Just-in-time inventory systems.* To minimize inventory levels (stocks) of mate-

rial at all stages of the production process, the material is delivered only when needed. This system can be a weakness in the event of transportation problems.

- *Managerial decentralization,* giving workers a greater role in the design process, which is generally done in a nonunionized working environment.

SOURCE: K. DOHSE, U. JURGENS, AND T. MALSCH, "FROM 'FORDISM' TO 'TOYOTISM'? THE SOCIAL ORGANIZATION OF THE JAPANESE AUTOMOBILE INDUSTRY," *POLITICS & SOCIETY* 14 (2) (1985), 115–46.

the same language? In the face of such monumental questions ... globalization ideology as a practical matter can only fall back on something that bears a close resemblance to the old imperialism that really did exist, but that the world at large now rightly regards as too repugnant for the future.[16]

What is perhaps most pernicious about the globalization idea is that it suggests some superior force is at work driving us all toward convergence along the Western model. It is common for both corporate executives and politicians to talk of globalization as if it were inevitable and as if those who do not succumb to its tide will lose out in the future. If this is true, then there is little use in even thinking about setting alternative courses. It suggests further that we must, perhaps grudgingly, accept the fact that many people will be harmed by the process as others gain. The author of a recent report on the UN Human Development Index, for example, believes a "new vision of global solidarity is needed to match the push for globalization. Without this vision and action, globalization will become a monster of gargantuan excesses and grotesque inequalities."[17] Of course, many would argue that the monster is already upon us.

We turn now to a brief treatment of several of the pertinent factors shaping the world economy today, but remember that these factors are at work within the context of the environmental problems and the process of globalization discussed above.

WOMEN IN THE WORLD ECONOMY

An area that deserves special mention, because it is often overlooked altogether, is the role women are currently playing in the global economy. More women are in the formal workforce than ever, but we should keep in mind the immense importance of the non-formal work that women (and many men) do to reproduce the labour that drives formal production. In other words, the world economy would surely grind to a halt were it not for those who clothe, teach, and care for children. For that matter, the predominantly male workforce in many areas is also fed and clothed by women.

The workforce in the industrialized states has undergone significant demographic change since women began working in factories during the world wars. Many economies have shifted to a service and information orientation (see Chapter 12), and this shift has meant that more women are in positions of decision-making power.

Governments have often supported or encouraged this transition with employment equity programs. From a liberal feminist perspective, then, progress has been made—though just how much progress is still a matter of considerable debate. For example, a large international sex trade, which relies primarily on female labour, is a mainstay of the contemporary global economy, and it is often based on coercion. The Asian Coalition Against Trafficking in Women estimates that 200 000 Bangladeshi women were forced to work in Pakistan in the last decade and that as many as 30 000 Burmese women are trafficked into Thailand each year. Similar cases have been reported regarding Filipino women in Japan, and many other cases exist elsewhere.[18]

Among academics and politicians alike, much more attention has been paid in recent times to the role of women in development. Countries such as Canada have made women central players in their development assistance programs, though with mixed results. This is part of a more general, and welcome, move away from large infrastructural projects designed to bring Western-style growth to impoverished areas and toward focusing instead on smaller-scale development that involves local communities. International agencies, such as **UNICEF**, have been involved with acquiring bank loans for women in small-business sectors in countries such as Egypt and Pakistan. In many southern states, women have organized cooperatives, income-producing businesses that range from garment production to food processing.[19]

This focus on women in development is important because their labour does not always show up in economic statistics, yet without it the world economy would stop moving. Still, most of the **malnourished** and undereducated children in the world are female. Among the southern regions, only in Latin America do women's literacy rates even approach those of men. In addition, there is an increasing tendency for large MNCs to employ women in countries such as Indonesia and Malaysia for assembly work in export-oriented sectors such as electronics. While this employment may appear as progress to some, freeing women from the constraints of rural life, others argue it amounts to a form of gender-discriminatory slavery, since the women work long hours and are paid very little for their efforts. Investors prefer female workers because they have smaller hands, greater endurance, and, because of cultural backgrounds in Islamic states such as Indonesia, they are less likely to organize unions.

Ecofeminists, meanwhile, argue that despite all the media attention paid to the environment, industrialized Western society still doesn't understand the link between violence against women and environmental exploitation. The world economy remains heavily dependent on the extraction of large amounts of resources, for both fuel and products. Violence against women remains a widespread phenomenon, especially in times of war, as witnessed in the former Yugoslavia in the early 1990s. Efforts have been made at numerous levels to deal with both types of exploitation; the type of deep change ecofeminists call for, however, is a long way off. We return to women's rights issues in Chapters 9 and 11.

THE POLITICAL ECONOMY OF ENERGY PRODUCTION AND CONSUMPTION

The world economy is powered by a vast infrastructure of energy production, distribution, and consumption; without it, the wheels of the global economy simply would not turn. The primary sources of industrial energy today remain oil (at 38 to 42 percent) and coal (at slightly over 30 percent), though natural gas use is rising quickly and makes up almost a quarter of world energy production. It is clear that fossil fuels are by far the largest energy sources in the present context. Though hydroelectricity and nuclear power remain in use, large dams are notorious for creating environmental damage, and nuclear power has proven highly expensive and sometimes dangerous (see Profile 8.2). We should note also that citizens in North America consume far more resources per capita than any other continent (Canadians are the second highest energy consumers on a **per capita** basis, after the U.S.).[20] Consumption is also very high in Western Europe, Japan, and the former Soviet Union. Some of this consumption is due to the cold winter climates in these places, but it also reflects highly consumptive lifestyles. By comparison, citizens in South Asia and Africa consume very little energy. Europe and Japan are far more efficient in their use of energy than North America, and the former Soviet Union is probably the least efficient of all. The Western states are net importers of energy, and the Middle East, with its high levels of oil deposits, is the greatest net exporter of energy, though others, such as Laos, are net exporters of hydropower as well.

Oil remains synonymous with power and wealth. It is relatively cheap (if environmentally dangerous) to transport; it provides exporters, including Russia, Mexico, Venezuela, and Nigeria, but especially the Persian Gulf states (Kuwait, Saudi Arabia, Iran, the United Arab Emirates, Qatar, Bahrain, Oman, and—until sanctions shut down its exports—Iraq) with hard currency. To ensure a steady supply of oil from the Middle East, the area was colonized by the Europeans early in this century and inundated with American MNCs after that. As we saw in Chapter 4, OPEC's oil price increases brought on worldwide confusion and **recession** in the early 1970s and 1980s. Though the Bush administration in the United States and the UN Security Council emphasized the importance of protecting Kuwait's **sovereignty**, it is quite clear that dependence on Middle Eastern oil was an important contributory factor in causing the West to go to war against Iraq in 1991 following its invasion of Kuwait.

PROFILE 8.2 Fuel in Nuclear Arms?

Nuclear power remains the most expensive and often-criticized form of power production. The costs are so high that it would be impossible to maintain nuclear power without significant government subsidies. It has a very limited future in most countries, and, though Japan and France maintain active and expanding nuclear programs, problems exist there as well. In Canada, meanwhile, Ontario Hydro and Atomic Energy of Canada have put forth a proposal to process surplus United States weapons-grade plutonium from leftover Cold War stockpiles and turn it into fuel for Canada's nuclear power plants. Canada's reactors currently run on uranium, but a facility to be built in the United States would produce mixed oxide fuel, a mixture of pluto-

nium and uranium that can be used in CANDU reactors. After being used in this manner, the plutonium would be in a form difficult to use in the construction of nuclear weapons. This fact puts opponents of nuclear energy, most of whom were also vocal opponents of the Cold War nuclear weapons build-up, in a somewhat awkward position, since the project would represent a Canadian contribution to disarmament but would also legitimize nuclear power and leave Canada with additional nuclear wastes to deal with. For members of the peace and disarmament movement who oppose nuclear power, it is a tough ethical choice.

SOURCE: M. MITTELSTAEDT, "HYDRO, AECL BID TO PROCESS PLUTONIUM," *THE GLOBE AND MAIL* (19 JULY 1996), A3.

As Hanns Maull writes, the two chief concerns regarding the control of oil are price stability and access:

> Price stability does not necessarily mean stable prices; it implies only that prices move smoothly, without drastic jumps, roughly in line with world inflation and towards the cost of alternative sources of energy. Access is defined as the availability of supplies in sufficient quantities over time without major disturbances.[21]

The chairman of Exxon, one of the world's largest oil multinationals, once complained that predicting oil prices was much like "trying to paint the wings of an airplane in flight."[22] When OPEC was founded in 1960, the price of oil was determined by that of Saudi Arabian light, a medium-density oil used as a standard for crude-oil prices until 1980. The price then was about U.S.$2 per barrel. An Arab oil embargo after the Middle East war of 1973 caused widespread panic buying, and **OPEC** was able to raise the price of crude to $11.50 a barrel by 1974. By January 1980, after the Iranian revolution induced further panic buying, Saudi Arabian light was selling for as much as $36 a barrel. These prices not only contributed greatly to the recession of that time but forced Western states to focus on alternative sources (such as North Sea oil) and conservation. The current benchmark oil is in fact North Sea Brent Blend, which has varied markedly over the past few years with price fluctuations related to the Gulf War, oil gluts, Iraq's partial re-emergence on the world market, high demand from the United States for heating oil, and rising energy demand worldwide. World crude oil demand rose in the 1990s by nearly 12 percent, driving world prices for crude oil to nearly $40 a barrel in late 2000. Approximately 40 percent of that crude oil comes from the OPEC countries.

According to estimates published in *The Economist*, by 2010 the industrialized northern states will consume less than half of the world's energy; the former Soviet bloc will consume a sixth, and what they term developing countries (the south) will consume 40 percent of the world's energy. The World Energy Council suggests that by 2020, more than 90 million barrels of oil will be consumed daily and that coal output will almost double to 7 billion tonnes. So, too, will natural gas demand double, reaching 4 trillion cubic metres. This huge increase in energy demand will result from the increasing industrialization of the Latin American and, especially, Asian regions.[23] China, the world's sixth-biggest oil producer (ahead of Venezuela), became a net oil importer at the end of 1993. It will probably have to rely heavily on the Middle East for its supply, further complicating the geopolitical situation there, and to the prospect of oil deposits in the heavily contested South China Sea. Ultimately, many analysts believe that a global conversion toward alternative fuel sources must take place, and in particular to the renewable resources such as wind, geothermal, and solar power that many environmentalists have advocated for decades. This conversion is especially important for developing countries: in India, for example, two million small power plants are turning cow dung into electric power and cooking fuel.[24] However, we should be very cautious about assuming that this transition can take place on a truly global scale. Though their benefits are real, these technologies are still expensive propositions and are in no position to replace oil or coal. Natural gas may be the steppingstone toward renewable energy sources; compared with other fossil fuels, it is clean and still relatively cheap. It releases less carbon when burned, contains little sulphur (responsible for acid rain), and if the technology is right, it releases fewer nitrogen oxides as well.

Optimistically, the push for increased efficiency by environmentalists and managerial elites alike will force states like China and the United States to mitigate the potential excesses of development and further explore renewable energy sources. Technological improvements and even lifestyle changes in the West have, in some cases, reduced energy consumption, though overall it continues to rise. Most states have an avenue toward energy self-sufficiency; Canada has huge oil and natural gas reserves, for example. But the current pace of industrialization around the world and the uncertainties associated with oil prices make it difficult to suggest that the more advanced industrialized states have achieved any form of everlasting energy security; one might argue that their dependence and resulting vulnerability have increased.

THE PREVALENCE OF GOVERNMENT DEBT

Another factor contributing to government vulnerability in the contemporary world economy is public debt. While Keynesians and others argue that a certain amount of government debt can be beneficial, as borrowing or deficit financing can allow states to intervene in the economy when necessary, an excess of debt is restrictive in a number of ways. The two major types of governmental debt today are internal and external. In both cases, governments are limited as to what they can accomplish because of the need to pay the interest on their debt loads. Governments must attempt to attract foreign investment to make up annual deficits in spending and to service their debts. In doing so, they must impose a harsh fiscal discipline on their society to create an attractive economic climate for would-be investors. Furthermore, attracting foreign investment leaves the country vulnerable to foreign ownership. It is a vicious circle, and cutting back too quickly on deficit levels is very painful for citizens of southern and northern states alike. Critics charge that international institutions such as the International Monetary Fund (IMF) have been primarily concerned with securing the interests of northern investors and banks and not the needs of the south.[25]

It should not come as a complete surprise that oil was involved in the creation of this variable of uncertainty. The extra profits generated by OPEC's price revolutions in the early 1970s and 1980s had to be invested somewhere, and the banks that accepted these so-called **petrodollars** became quite desperate to lend them out to potential customers. Thus southern states were often enticed to borrow large sums to finance development schemes, only to fall into irreparable debt by the early 1980s. Oil exporters such as Venezuela and Mexico assumed high oil revenues in their development plans and borrowed heavily against future earning; falling oil prices have thus increased their debt load as well. Though many Asian states, with strong economies focused on production for export, had managed to pay off large percentages of their debt, several of them were forced to borrow from the IMF following the Asian financial crisis of 1997; countries in Latin America and Africa have generally been even less able to begin seriously tackling their debt. We should note, however, that the world's largest debtor, by far, is the United States, but given the strength of its economy and currency, there is little pressure on the United States to pay this debt off anytime soon.

To pay the interest on their loans without defaulting, many states have had to accept short-term loans from the IMF, which attaches certain conditions to its loans, such as downsizing government and increasing trade. These **structural adjustment program (SAP)** loans make it difficult for a government to maintain legitimacy among the majority of its people, who feel they are bearing the brunt of the costs. Cuts to health and educational services, for example, hurt the poor the most. Protest can often lead to repression by the state, furthering the cycle of violence and economic despair. Yet many of the southern states that are in great debt, such as Brazil, Argentina, and Nigeria, remain strong regional military powers, spending valuable resources on military equipment often supplied through the northern states. Meanwhile a vague promise made by the United States in 1999 to lessen Third World debt has yet to be realized.

THE TRIUMPH OF THE GLOBAL MARKET?

The state-run economies that formed half of the East–West divide during the Cold War have largely collapsed. Although some states, like China and Cuba, retain the rhetorical vestiges of socialism, they too have turned to what we might loosely label **marketization** (characterized ideally by the introduction of private property, free competition between firms, and the use of foreign capital). North Korea remains steadfastly committed to a noncapitalist path, but it is literally in shambles, with a large part of the population suffering from malnutrition and starvation. Former Soviet-bloc states are now labelled "economies in transition" and are striving to emulate the Western model. Further, as states struggle to deal with vast debt loads, the trend is toward decreasing the interventionary role of the state by lowering government spending on education, health care, and general welfare. The IMF has often insisted on such policy changes in developing states with high foreign debt loads, but that it has occurred in industrialized states as well suggests that a broader change in government philosophy emerged in the 1980s and 1990s, one in tune with what is often termed a neoliberal or neoconservative agenda.[26]

The creation and implementation (in 1995) of the World Trade Organization (WTO) is viewed as further evidence that a global marketplace is evolving, one that integrates most countries (even Russia and China are determined to join). The Geneva-based WTO was initially expected to increase world trade by up to U.S.$200 billion a year, with one-third to one-half of the gains going to developing countries, but it is too early to assess this optimistic prediction.[27]

Another shift of great importance is the rise of the ever-active market in **currency speculation**. Daily turnover on foreign-exchange markets has grown to around U.S.$1.5 trillion, about the same as the total currency reserves of the world's central banks. In 1992, the exchange rate mechanism (ERM) of the **European monetary system** fell apart, and in 1994 the Mexican peso took a huge plunge, which led to IMF and U.S. efforts to bail out investors (mostly Americans). Similar problems surfaced in the once-vibrant Asian stock markets in 1997. These events have led to fears that the power of these markets, based largely on speculative purchases and quick sales, has challenged the ability of the nation-state to control its own economic fortune. This fear has led to calls for measures to moderate these activities and generate revenue from them for international charitable projects. In fact, more than 20 years ago, an economist named James Tobin suggested that a tax be levied on international currency exchanges. Different analysts have suggested different figures, but the usual amount is 0.1 percent on all foreign currency trades, which alone would raise well over $100 billion a year. Such a tax, it is often argued, would limit the amount of speculation international investors engage in, and the resultant revenue could be used for international humanitarian purposes, such as paying for peacekeeping operations, or paying off the debt owed by the United Nations. However, it would be difficult to convince market-oriented governments that this type of intervention is justified, and, as an article in *The Economist* points out, unless every state participated, "trading would simply shift to tax-free havens. Also, financial wizards would quickly devise dodges: rather than trade yen for dollars, say, they might agree to swap Japanese government bonds for American Treasuries."[28] Finally, the increasing use of the **Internet** for commercial transactions would make such a taxation scheme even more difficult to implement.

Though the state still plays a major role in the economies of all countries, and especially in the industrialized north, a withdrawal of the state is certainly taking place as governments are forced to deal with debt loads. Yet, if we have seen a triumph of the market on an almost global scale, it is not by accident. One need not accept the entire ideological thrust of Marxism to agree with critical theorists that the economic elite has a tremendous impact on the formation of government policy. This statement is as true in matters of trade as it is in domestic issues. Governments explicitly incorporate the private sector in foreign policy decision making and in domestic market production. Few countries make this incorporation as evident as does Canada; when the international trade minister travels to a foreign state he or she is accompanied by a virtual army of representatives from businesses and Crown corporations seeking to break into new markets with products and expertise. For example, recent "Team Canada" trips to China resulted in sale of Canada's CANDU nuclear reactors. This sale has generated some criticism, since (1) the federal government waived the usual environmental assessment procedure, and China does not have a strong reputation on such matters, and (2) the sale of the reactors was financed in part by the Canadian Export Development Corporation in Ottawa, meaning essentially that Canadian taxpayers have subsidized an ailing nuclear industry at home and supported a Chinese regime many find repugnant.

The visiting delegations are quite extensive, as opposed to the old days of behind-the-scenes diplomacy. For example, the business delegation that accompanied then International Trade Minister Art Eggleton to Russia and Poland in October 1996 included high-level representatives from more than 50 major Canadian companies, such as Alcan Canada-Vostok, Atomic Energy of Canada, Bombardier Regional Aerospace Division, Canadian Imperial Bank of Commerce, Dreco Energy Services, McCain Foods, Molson Breweries, Northern Telecom, Nortel, the Saskatchewan Wheat Pool, and many others.[29] This begs the question of what, precisely, governments should be doing in world affairs. Beyond providing the most rudimentary of national defence against invasion, should governments exist primarily as a mechanism to extend trade opportunities abroad? Or do they exist to promote and protect the quality of life, or to attain the status of a winner in the global economy? Are the concerns of development and human security being sacrificed for economic gain? At the same time, if a government is elected primarily with a mandate to create jobs, and if increased government spending is not a realistic option due to previously attained debt loads, then perhaps a strong pro-trade foreign policy orientation is its only viable option, and one that would be supported by much of the voting public.

If the market has won over the hearts and minds of a transnational economic elite, it may not have done so among the millions of people who continue to forge their own path of development somewhere else. It would be a gross overgeneralization to argue that all that is left is **capitalism** with minimal state interference. From the quiet fields of agrarian communities around the world, to the streets of the bustling megacities, people are engaged in forming their own substate arrangements and interpersonal relationships. For example, female workers have formed many cooperative ventures to produce textiles in Guatemala; women in Kenya have founded the Green Belt movement, planting millions of trees to stop **desertification**; artistic communities in many northern states form mutually supportive networks; unique regimes in environmental management are being forged as we grapple with problems of the commons. There is much more to the global political economy than the amorphous entity we refer to as the market, and though the conventional path of socialism may well be dead, with its stench of economic failure and political repression, a new one may be emerging, one that is being cleared by the survival strategies implemented by people in both hemispheres.

This discussion of the centrality of the marketplace in the global economy and of the inherent weaknesses of even the strongest states dependent on imported energy sources and on foreign capital suggests that the state as a political entity no longer exhibits the same amount of control over its destiny as it may have in earlier, less complicated (or less globally integrated) days. We are often told that this lack of self-control, or subjection to the exigencies of external factors, is part of the new global economy, but this would be a false picture. States are actively engaged in establishing regimes and institutions and rules and regulations, on both a global and a regional level, to manage the global economy.

MANAGING GLOBAL TRADE LIBERALIZATION: THE WTO

The push toward freer trade continued with the conclusion of the GATT Uruguay Round. The WTO effectively replaced the GATT Secretariat in Geneva. As mentioned in Chapter 4, the authors of the Bretton Woods System had originally envisioned the establishment of an International Trade Organization (ITO) that would have the same legal status as the IBRD and IMF and contribute to the development a free trade–based global economy. It was not until 1995, however, that the WTO was established instead. Biannual ministerial meetings are supposed to dictate WTO direction, and this council has subsidiary working bodies that specialize in areas of trade such as goods, services, the environment, and intellectual property. Countries accused of unfair trading practices must answer to the council, and other states are legally permitted to impose countervailing sanctions and to receive whatever compensation the WTO panel judges appropriate (see Profile 8.3). This system is, in fact, a big step, since GATT outcomes were often ignored, but this process does give rise to complaints (in particular by economic nationalists) that the WTO represents the subordination of national sovereignty to an international organization without accountability to the citizens of individual states.

Given the apparent strength of this new institution and given the shift to a market-based world economy that is producing the effect of globalization described above, one might think that a truly global liberal trading order is emerging. Or is it? The opposition to globalized liberalization is widespread, as evidenced at the "battle in Seattle," which disrupted the 1999 WTO General Meeting (see Profile 8.4). Everyone from environmentalists to trade unionists resents the idea that a disconnected body in Geneva can make decisions that have a large impact on national development issues. Similar opposition, spread through the Internet, was discernible during the failed OECD negotiations for the establishment of the Multilateral Agreement on Investment (MAI), which would have taken the basic principles of trade agreements such as NAFTA and internationalized them, protecting international investors from government interference.[30] Beyond this, there are practical limitations to a global trading system. Protectionism still exists, though it may in some cases be disguised. Trade disputes are frequent in the international system, such as the following prominent examples: the serious split between the United States and the European Union on agricultural subsidies; the efforts of southern states seeking greater access to northern markets; the debate over genetically modified organisms and other health and environmental issues; and the debate over enforcing intellectual property rights. In addition to the efforts of the WTO and the controversies that swirl around it, a number of regional organizations in the world have been developed to manage trade.

The WTO and Canada: Good News, Bad News

Decisions made by the WTO will help some governments achieve their goals while they will hamper others. It will become increasingly difficult to promote free trade in some products and yet remain protectionist with others. Compare the two accounts below for an idea of how the WTO will sometimes give but sometimes take away.

CANADA AND THE JAPAN LIQUOR TAX CASE

In October 1996, the WTO Appellate Body requested that Japan change its liquor tax regime to remove barriers to imports of a wide variety of distilled liquor products (ranging from whisky to gin). In Japan, imported distilled liquor is taxed at significantly higher rates than competing Japanese distilled spirits such as *shochu*. Canadian distillers want to sell their products in Japan at what they consider fair prices. This was the first Appellate Body ruling involving Canada and was the second complaint involving Japanese barriers to imported liquor. In 1987 a panel under the GATT upheld a complaint by the European Commission that Japan's liquor tax law gave a competitive advantage to Japanese distilled liquor. Although Japan changed its law, *shochu* continued to receive preferential tax rates. Under WTO rules, the Appellate Body report must be adopted within 30 days of being circulated to WTO members. Japan will then have 30 days to notify the WTO Dispute Settlement Body of its plans for implementing the report's recommendation. "I am very pleased with this ruling, a first for Canada," said Art Eggleton, Canada's international trade minister at the time. "It will end a long-standing dispute, and we expect that it will lead to higher Canadian exports to the Japanese distilled liquor market. I urge Japan to carry out the ruling quickly."

CANADA AND THE MAGAZINE CASE

In January 1997, a WTO panel ruled that the Canadian government's efforts to support the Canadian magazine industry violated world trade rules, finding that Ottawa was at fault for preventing the sale of magazines containing mostly U.S. editorial content. The case was filed by the Office of the U.S. Trade Representative at the Geneva-based WTO and followed a prolonged effort by Time Warner Inc. to establish an edition of *Sports Illustrated* magazine in Canada. The decision was regarded as a serious blow to Canadian government efforts to protect the cultural sector from Americanization. The decision by a WTO panel rejected Ottawa's attempts to prevent *Sports Illustrated* from publishing a Canadian edition with mostly U.S. editorial content. However, this was only part of the ruling, since the three-member panel also struck down key policies that supported the entire Canadian magazine industry and protected it from all-out competition, including preferential postal rates, a tariff restriction, and an up to 80 percent tax on split-run magazines. "We lost," said a Canadian governmental official. Canada now faces a choice of either implementing the WTO ruling or allowing Washington to establish trade barriers against Canadian products equivalent to protectionist measures directed against U.S. magazines. Though the Canadian government has vowed to fight the ruling, it is difficult to see how that would be possible within WTO rules.

SOURCES: (LIQUOR LAWS) DEPARTMENT OF FOREIGN AFFAIRS AND INTERNATIONAL TRADE, *NEWS RELEASE*, 4 OCTOBER 1996; (MAGAZINES) D. FAGAN AND L. EGGERTSON, "CANADA LOSES MAGAZINE CASE," *THE GLOBE AND MAIL* (17 JANUARY 1997), A1.

MANAGING REGIONAL TRADE LIBERALIZATION

Much of the free trade debate and dialogue in the world is, in fact, oriented toward regional trade agreements. These agreements are sometimes called *preferential trade agreements*, because they represent regions, or zones, of preferred terms of trade among participating countries. In Europe, a process of economic integration has been under

The Battle in Seattle

Civil disobedience is a time-honoured method of expressing one's opposition to government policies. An estimated 40 000 people took to the streets in Seattle in 1999 to register their opposition to the WTO as a regulatory body. Their main concern, although they had an impressive variety of concerns overall, was that the WTO was being granted too much power—the ability to make key decisions affecting people's health, environment, employment, and other issues. For many, the WTO represented the dark side of globalization. The sheer number of protestors surprised local authorities, and when a small minority became violent, the police responded with arrests and tear gas. Inside the WTO meetings, the ministers of member states were unable to reach a consensus on the issues that divided them. The meeting broke up with little in the way of substantive agreements. The protestors had made their point, but the governments of the world could not make the WTO meetings a success, possibly because of the increased public awareness brought about by the debate over globalization. Similar, though less violent, protests were mounted during the IMF annual meeting in Washington in April 2000 and the Summit of the Americas in Quebec City in April 2001. Seattle, Washington, and Quebec City are likely just the beginning of a global campaign of protest against the institutions of globalization.

way since the 1950s. In 1957, the European Economic Community (EEC) created a **customs union** covering all products among its members. In 1967, the EEC and two other European institutions became the European Community (EC), with an enlarged membership of 12 states by 1986. The EC marked the successful elimination of most of the remaining impediments to the free flow of goods, labour, and capital across the borders of member states. In 1994, the EC became the **European Union (EU)** after the Maastricht Treaty of late 1991 was ratified. The EU now has 15 member states, and under the terms of the **Maastricht Treaty,** the states are committed to the development of a monetary union, which has already resulted in the establishment, and partial implementation, of a common currency, the **Euro**.

The process of integration in Europe has provoked protest over the loss of state control over national economies, social institutions, and culture. These concerns continue to plague the operation of the EU and the ability of governments to reach common policies on controversial issues. In particular, efforts to coordinate political and military policy through the EU have not been particularly successful. Nevertheless, the EU is the most highly integrated and institutionally developed of the world's trading areas, leading some to argue that the EU will soon become a supranational organization, perhaps even a "United States of Europe." In reality, the EU is far from this since member countries remain politically sovereign, although they have agreed to share decision-making responsibility and place some of the authority to make decisions in the hands of the EU. This strategy is sometimes called *pooled sovereignty*. The economic power of the EU (centred on the economic strength of a united Germany) is felt throughout Europe, and it acts as a centre of gravity for economic activity across the continent.

The present European Union, however, is moving beyond efforts at economic integration and toward monetary union as well. Other EU members are tired of relying principally on the German economy and its central bank, the Bundesbank, which tends to raise interest rates quickly whenever inflation becomes a possibility.[31] Once the Euro becomes a common currency, monetary policy will be set by a federated central bank.

This is a huge step, one unlikely to be repeated elsewhere. For example, it would be difficult to imagine the Federal Reserve of the United States and the Bank of Canada allowing some other agency to determine monetary policy for both states, though it is obvious that American monetary policy has a tremendous impact on the Canadian economy.

However, full acceptance of the Euro will not come easily, though it is in use in 11 member states as of 2001. The Euro has not proven strong against the American dollar. The Germans will have to sacrifice the relatively solid deutschemark and their position as financial leader in Europe. Germany felt it imperative that states earn the right to use the Euro, and the 1991 Maastricht Treaty stipulated key attributes that states must have to be allowed to participate in the new regime. For example, they must limit their government deficit to 3 percent of gross domestic product (GDP). They must ensure that their national debt does not exceed 60 percent of GDP; they must avoid currency devaluations for two years before the onset of the Euro; and, not surprisingly, they must keep their inflation rate within 1.5 percentage points of the average rate of the three EU members with the lowest inflation. These are tough standards for most European states, especially those with less stable economies, such as Spain and Portugal; and they further alienate citizens in countries such as France and Ireland that only narrowly accepted the Maastricht Treaty in the first place. In 1996, the 15 EU members began a yearlong negotiation to prepare for the future of the Union, including the possible entry of 12 states from Eastern and Southern Europe. Germany seeks to reduce the role currently played by the national veto, relying instead on majority votes to enact changes. Britain strongly disagrees, insisting on its right to maintain the veto system. On serious matters of foreign policy, such as defence, common front or not, it is highly unlikely the veto will be abolished.[32]

However, the biggest question international relations scholars ask about the evolution of the European Union concerns its long-term effect on the institution of state sovereignty. As seen in Chapter 2, the right to make decisions regarding the national economy, as well as the right to have an independent currency, has been viewed as fundamental to sovereignty. The new EU threatens this, since states are gradually giving increasing responsibility to a supranational institution and may even achieve a common currency among them.[33] Also of great interest is the European Court of Justice ruling that a member state can be sued for damages for failure to honour EU law. The case involved Spanish fishing companies that had set up shop in the United Kingdom to avoid the quota assigned to Spain. The British denied 84 Spanish fishing companies the right to fish from the United Kingdom. Britain may be obliged to pay the companies roughly U.S.$45.8 million in compensation for lost potential income. The court set three conditions for determining whether an individual or a company is justified in taking a member state to court: when "the government violates rights conferred on individuals; does so in a 'sufficiently serious' manner; and when the victim can show clearly that damages occurred as a result of the state's action."[34]

Whether the Euro comes into effect across the EU, the changes that have characterized European integration have set landmarks in the transition of world politics from a state-based power game to a transnational economic one. Genuine concerns exist about the viability of the project, but no one can deny that, despite centuries of animosity among the great powers of Europe, there is a higher level of policy coordination than ever. However, we should be very careful about using the EU as a prototype for future regionalism. In fact, it is a common criticism of the neofunctionalist school that it used the European Community as an embryonic standard that simply is not exportable elsewhere. Europe has a very high standard of living (though there are differences within the region, which the EU is supposed to attempt to rectify); it has global connections in both trade and diplomacy; and it has had the military protection of the United States. Clearly, the EU should be considered a unique situation, and other free trade agreements, like NAFTA, are not intended to induce the same level of economic and political integration (though NAFTA's more vocal Canadian critics argue it will ultimately have this effect).

At the same time, we can argue that there is a noticeable trend toward regional integration in trade and investment and the creation of political mechanisms to facilitate this (see Profile 8.5). Under the Free Trade of the Americas (FTAA) negotiations, we could well have a free trade area from Alaska to Argentina by the year 2005. The Pacific states could become more closely integrated by that time, with Japan and China vying as regional leaders, and the **Association of South East Asian Nations (ASEAN)** states forming a bloc. And Europe's integration, both economic and political, will probably continue. These integrations present a potential tri-regional model of the future world economy: the Americas, Europe (with Eastern Europe, Russia, and Africa connected, though unlikely to be made prosperous), and Asia, with increased cooperation between these regions.

Such a model contrasts in style and, ultimately, purpose, with the more global approach encouraged by the WTO. Those liberals who argue that peace follows commerce might be concerned that dividing the world into three large trade zones will encourage a tripolar mentality that could even lead to military conflict as the interests of the three areas begin to conflict. Others, especially those from the Marxist tradition, argue that each area will be a political empire of the dominant power and its capitalist

---

PROFILE 8.5

The Canada–Chile Free Trade Agreement

Countries continue to sign bilateral free trade agreements, as well as multilateral agreements. Rather quietly, the governments of Canada and Chile signed a free trade agreement, which is not part of **NAFTA**. The agreement's key features, from the Canadian standpoint, are as follows:

- Immediate duty-free access for 75 percent of Canadian exports and the elimination of Chile's 11 percent import **duty** on almost all remaining industrial and resource-based goods over five years.

- Much better access for a range of agricultural goods. For example, tariffs for durum wheat, which represents 35 percent of exports in this sector, will be eliminated immediately.

- Significant new protection for Canadian investments in Chile, including an agreement to automatically grant Canadian

investors the benefits of any future liberalization, and an undertaking to negotiate a bilateral double taxation agreement.

- The creation of a Free Trade Commission and a secretariat to ensure the timely and effective resolution of disputes.

- Side agreements on environment and labour, the first agreements of this nature ever signed by the government of Chile.

Should Chile grant even better access for certain agricultural products in a future trade agreement with the **MERCOSUR** countries (Argentina, Brazil, Paraguay, and Uruguay), Canada will automatically have similar access for milling wheat, wheat flour, and oilseed products.

SOURCE: GOVERNMENT OF CANADA, *NEWS RELEASE*, NO. 211, 18 NOVEMBER 1996.

classes. Thus, imperialism continues in a highly integrated fashion, and imperial powers inevitably come into conflict as resources grow scarce and expansionism becomes the driving norm (this was, partially, Lenin's explanation of World War I).

Some of globalization's proponents, however, might argue that regional integration is just a step along the road to a harmonized global economy. It occurs simultaneously as the world economy develops as well; the two processes reinforce rather than challenge each other. And, as regional organizations form, the political machinery of multilateralism is created. Though it has become almost habitual among students of international political economy to refer to the European Union as the primary example of regional neofunctionalism, other situations exist in which states are engaging. A famous example, of course, is the North American Free Trade Agreement (NAFTA), which includes Canada, the United States, and Mexico, and may soon include several Latin American countries as well. The Canada–U.S. Free Trade Agreement was signed in January 1989, between the two countries that exchange more goods and services than any other two in the world. This bilateral arrangement was expanded in 1992 with the addition of Mexico. NAFTA provides for the increased flow of goods and services across the borders of these states, especially in agriculture, automobile products, and clothing and textiles. The agreement was not without considerable controversy. There were (and still are) many concerns in Canada that NAFTA is a threat to Canadian sovereignty and culture and that NAFTA might threaten safety regulations and environmental protection in Canada, as well as social programs such as health care. Others were concerned that jobs would leave Canada and head to Mexico, where salaries are lower. Advocates of NAFTA responded that Canadian sovereignty, social programs, and standards are protected under NAFTA and that little or no evidence suggests that NAFTA has led to job losses in Canada. Similar concerns about jobs were voiced in the United States, while in Mexico some expressed fears about becoming an economic colony of the United States.

Two side agreements accompanied NAFTA, one on labour and one on the environment. These were made largely to counter opposition on the grounds that NAFTA would promote the degradation of labour standards, wages, and the environment. The environmental agreement created the Commission for Environmental Cooperation (or CEC, headquartered in Montreal), and it has filtered funding to many NGOs that have developed projects related to sustainable development. Examples include a project by the Air and Waste Management Association (Ottawa) to advance air quality in Hamilton, Ontario, and Monterrey, Mexico; the development of nonwood forest products in Oaxaca, Mexico; and an education/water quality monitoring project for Colonia residents in El Paso County/Valle de Juarez. However, critics charge that NAFTA, by encouraging investment along the U.S.–Mexican border, is designed primarily to keep Mexicans there (and not migrating northward) and will inevitably result in a lessening of environmental protection in the already heavily polluted region. The CEC has been criticized as an ineffective watchdog, having no real power to force any of the states to improve environmental standards.

In Asia, Japan is the regional leader, although the rise of China as an economic power may pose a long-term threat to that distinction. In Asia, however, regionalism is far less defined and far less institutionalized. In part, this difference is due to the tradition of bilateral economic diplomacy in Asia, as well as fear of Japanese political hegemony (with the memory of World War II still fresh in people's memories). Nevertheless, some regional arrangements have taken shape, most notably ASEAN, established in 1967 to promote economic, political, and social cooperation among its members. ASEAN now comprises seven countries with the admission of Vietnam in 1995. A far more ambitious project in Asia was the establishment of the Asia-Pacific Economic Co-operation (APEC) forum in 1989 (see Profile 8.6). At the summits of 1993 and 1994, the 18 Asian and North American members of APEC committed themselves to "free and open trade and investment" by 2020.

However, 1997 was a tumultuous year for many of the Asian economies as the Asian financial crisis engulfed the region. Many explanations are available for the currency crisis, and we can hardly approach doing them justice here. Some blame the over-

extension of Japanese and other local banks; some blame the decision to make several key currencies, previously pegged to the U.S. dollar, convertible, attracting foreign currency speculation; others blame the herd-like mentality of investors, who panic when they see trouble and thus cause much more trouble. The "crony capitalism" that characterized some of the economies is often cited as well: since politicians have had such a strong personal involvement in the economy, corruption was rampant. After China devalued the Yuan (its currency) in 1996, there was a glut of exports in the inter-Asian market. The Japanese economy was in the midst of a prolonged slowdown. There was overdevelopment in the sense of artificial prices and doomed investment in the real estate sector. As the Thai, Indonesian, Filipino, and Malaysian economies began to tumble, the rest of the world hoped Japan would step in to bail them out, much as the U.S. had done with Mexico in 1995; but it did not. The crisis affected economies as far away as Russia and Brazil. Political institutions in Asia were affected as well: Thailand pursued a new constitution and there were changes in government in Indonesia and South Korea. Countries were forced to sell off domestic industries and, as usual, the poor were hit hardest of all, with little support following massive layoffs. Asian economic elites moved their money to safer locations, such as the United States and Western Europe.

Though many of these economies are on the road to recovery, dealing with the crisis has furthered the regional need to depend on international financial institutions and the policies of what critical political economists refer to as the Washington Consensus: privatization, liberalization of markets, devaluation, deregulation, austerity, and a smaller public sector (except in police power). After the crisis, with shaken confidence, Asia continues on the path toward greater economic integration.

Will these economic regions coalesce into antagonistic trade blocs? Many fear that political and economic friction between countries, as well as pressure from disaffected publics, will promote protectionism and provoke trade wars between regions. Economic regionalism will turn into political regionalism, and the world will become Balkanized and divided in a scenario not dissimilar to the interwar experience. Others are more optimistic, arguing that economic regions are beginning to overlap in their membership and that virtually all countries have a stake in the continued health of the global economy.

While it is impossible to forecast the long-term outlook of the world economy, we can say that both the trend toward regional integration and the broader trend toward globalization will continue in the near future. Barring a major military confrontation, which is always a possibility, trade among nations will probably increase as economic growth continues, which will please most liberals, some economic nationalists, few environmentalists, and even fewer neomarxists.

THE CENTRAL ROLE OF MULTINATIONAL CORPORATIONS

Another characteristic of the contemporary global economy is the expansive rise of the MNC. Although large corporations have always been influential in the industrialized states, they have a long history of investing and operating in other countries. American, European, and Japanese MNCs are the largest and most powerful. As early as the 1960s, the power of MNCs led to questions about the primacy of the nation-state.[35] In particular, the dominance of American multinationals has caused Canadians, Europeans, and Central Americans to worry about the influence of American corporate commercialism on their cultures (in the Canadian case, a short-lived spate of Canadian nationalism arose out of these concerns).[36] MNCs are regarded either as necessary suppliers of investment and technical knowledge or predatory entities that perpetuate the underdevelopment of poor countries.

The sheer size of modern MNCs is intimidating. The Ford Motor Company, for example, has operations in 30 countries and employs more than 300 000 people worldwide. Some MNCs have a large number of subsidiary corporations. For example, PepsiCo's include Bata Shoes, Unocal, Texaco, and a large line of PepsiCo products such as Pepsi, 7-UP, Hostess Frito-Lay, Pizza Hut, Taco Bell, and Kentucky Fried Chicken. Corporate mergers have accelerated the growth of some MNCs: In 2000, the French car manufacturer Renault took over Nissan; in the pharmaceutical sector Glaxco Wellcome merged with SmithKline Beecham in an effort to capitalize on the drug potential of the human genome project; and America Online merged with Time Warner, creating a company with a market value of U.S.$340 billion (although the drop in tech stocks in the latter half of 2000 reduced this figure by $140 billion). In some cases, MNCs produce goods from components that are manufactured in different countries and assembled in the market country. Sometimes, they share ownership of a subsidiary with another MNC, or with the host government, because of legal requirements or to reduce risk. These arrangements are called *joint ventures*, and many such ventures operate in the former Soviet Union and in China. In some cases, MNCs decide not to invest directly in other countries, instead choosing to establish licensing arrangements with foreign companies or governments, permitting them to produce products in return for a fee and share of the profits. Today, many firms are engaged in what are commonly referred to as **interfirm alliances**: subcontracting, partial mergers, and interfirm agreements all designed to minimize the amount of government interference. Critics argue the proposed MAI, discussed above, would further compromise governments' ability to control MNC activities.

MNCs are extremely powerful economic entities, and their significance in the global economy has grown as world trade has expanded. In 1978, the 430 largest MNCs accounted for more than U.S.$1.8 trillion of global economic output. In 1994, the 37 largest MNCs in the world produced more than U.S.$3 trillion of goods and services, over 10 percent of world economic output.[37] It is striking that when the annual sales of the largest MNCs in the world are compared with the annual GNP of states, more than one-third of the world's largest economic units are MNCs. Even more stark is the fact that while the UN has an operating budget of approximately U.S.$1.2 billion, the world's largest MNCs have annual revenues over U.S.$100 billion.

MNCs are also significant because of their numbers: there are approximately 37 000 MNCs in the world, with some 170 000 affiliates, or subsidiaries. Few countries in the world do not host an MNC or a subsidiary within their territorial boundaries. Furthermore, MNCs have a great deal of control over the global capacity to manufacture products, sell services, and provide finance, and they are leading developers of technology and services. Most of the largest MNCs are in the manufacturing sector (Mitsubishi, General Motors), oil (Exxon, Royal Dutch/Shell Group), and electronics (IBM, AT&T). In other sectors, financial corporations are among the world's largest MNCs. In this sector, Japanese banks dominate, with 23 of the 50 largest banks in the world headquartered in Japan (where domestic laws permit them to expand into a wide variety of financial services, unlike U.S. banks, which are restricted by law to specific financial services, such as brokerage or insurance). However, recent events in Asia suggest that the era of Japanese banking prowess may be at an end. The service sector also has many large MNCs, including McDonald's and Wal-Mart.

MNCs' influence can be measured by the familiarity with which we recognize the household names IBM, Hitachi, Microsoft, General Electric, Du Pont, PepsiCo, Eastman Kodak, Toyota, Mitsui, Volkswagen, Bayer, Renault, Michelin, Ciba-Geigy, Seagram, Thomson, Fiat, Philips, Unilever, and others. The products, logos, and advertising campaigns of these corporations have become part of popular Western culture. As these products are marketed around the world, they become visible reflections of Western presence, or what critics would term instruments of **cultural imperialism**.

The role played by MNCs in the global economy is a controversial one. Some see MNCs as agents of their home states, used by states to further their own economic and even political interests in the world. Indeed, some MNCs have become deeply involved in the politics of host countries, even to the point of engineering the overthrow of governments. A famous example of this is the involvement of International Telephone and Telegraph (ITT) in the events that led to the overthrow of the Allende government in Chile in 1973. Others see MNCs as essentially benign actors, acting in the interests of their shareholders and motivated by profit, and essential to the efficient development, production, and distribution of goods and services in the global economy. Still others see MNCs as exploitative actors, preying on cheap labour markets and raw materials, and selling the resulting products at huge profit margins. For example, in the early 1990s, many Nike shoes were manufactured in Indonesia, where the typical worker was paid $1 a day in 1991 (minimum wage legislation and labour rights are seldom enforced in Indonesia). A pair of Nike shoes can cost more than $100 in Canada (Nike profits for 1991 were reported at U.S.$287 million). For critics of MNCs, situations like this are repeated in all economic sectors in poor countries around the world (see Profile 8.7).

THE GREAT DIVIDE: THE POLITICAL ECONOMY OF THE RICH AND THE POOR

The gap between the rich and the poor peoples of the world is enormous, whether this is measured in terms of economic statistics or quality of life. This gap is often described in terms of a generally rich northern hemisphere and a generally poor southern hemisphere. In practice, however, there are significant exceptions to this generalization; for example, North Korea is relatively poor, while Australia is relatively rich. Nevertheless, issues surrounding poverty and development are often cast in terms of a north–south debate. Similarly, the term "Third World" is still in use, although it is in decline (see Profile 8.8). Countries are also classified along "rich" and "poor" lines, with the countries of the developed world having attained a high level of wealth through industrialization and technological development, relatively equitable levels of income distribution, and high standards of living in stable civil societies. In contrast, countries of the "developing world" have lower levels of wealth, agricultural or subsistence economies, and inequitable income distribution in societies dominated by small elites. From this distinction has grown the term **less-developed country (LDC)**.

However, it is important to remember that there are rich and poor in both the developed and developing worlds; indeed, poverty is a serious problem in most of the world's leading industrialized economies, and an extravagant upper class is often visible in the south. Furthermore, some groups tend be more marginalized than others from the benefits of the economy, especially minority groups and working-class women. Nevertheless, however one classifies the problem, the reality of economic inequality in the world is staggering, and for many this is the most serious global issue facing the world today. As we will see, considerable dispute exists over the most appropriate and effective means of addressing and alleviating the gap between the rich and the poor. Liberals see this gap as

PROFILE 8.7 — The Debate over MNCs: Do They Exploit Southern Countries?

YES	NO
1. MNCs decapitalize less-developed countries (LDCs). MNCs take more money in profit out of LDCs than they invest.	1. MNCs provide investment. MNCs invest a lot of their own money and attract foreign investors as well.
2. MNCs are obstacles to social progress. The profit motive makes MNCs unresponsive or opposed to progressive political change.	2. MNCs support peaceful domestic environments. MNCs require peace to operate effectively, and therefore have an interest in long-term stability.
3. MNCs contribute to inequality. MNCs create an elite socioeconomic class in LDCs, isolated from the poor majority.	3. MNCs create jobs. They have an interest in a capable workforce and provide training and education.
4. MNCs discourage indigenous development. They oppose efforts by LDCs to industrialize, as this would create domestic competition.	4. MNCs promote development. MNCs help create modern infrastructure, share technology and technique, and therefore create conditions conducive to domestic growth.
5. MNCs create dependence. LDC economies come to depend on MNCs for investment, technology, and markets.	5. MNCs increase fiscal resources of LDCs. MNCs create royalties and tax revenues for LDCs.
6. MNCs use LDCs as sources of raw materials. MNCs extract raw materials for a low price and manufacture products abroad, forcing LDCs to purchase expensive finished products.	6. MNCs give LDCs access to world markets. They provide a channel to markets for products as well as markets for purchase, enabling LDCs to access the global marketplace.

a natural component of uneven growth in the world economy that will even out over time. Marxists and dependency theorists see it as a legacy of imperialism and exploitative colonial rule, which continue in a different form to this day. Postmodernists would explain it as a legacy of intellectual domination of Western approaches to politics, the marginalization of other traditions, and a reflection of racism. Feminists see it as a legacy of economic and political approaches that have marginalized women. Let us look further at the state of inequality in the global economy today.

THE STATE OF INEQUALITY: ECONOMIC AND HUMAN DIMENSIONS

The northern hemisphere contains one-quarter of the world's people but consumes two-thirds of its goods and services. The southern hemisphere contains three-quarters of the world's people but consumes only one-third of its goods and services. Of the U.S.$23 trillion world GDP in 1993, $18 trillion was in the industrialized economies, and only $5 trillion was in the developing countries, which contain 80 percent of the world's population.[38] This very general measure illustrates the extent to which the world is divided in terms of distribution of wealth. This division is exacerbated by the fact that

The "Third World"

Throughout this text, we have avoided using the term "Third World." The term has been criticized as demeaning to less-developed states. However, although obvious ethnocentricity has been involved in labelling the developed capitalist states the "First World," the term Third World was first used to indicate a non-American, non-Soviet path of political and economic alignment. Over time, however, it slipped into general usage as meaning the southern states with low GNPs, and here it quickly began to make less sense, not only because there are large discrepancies in GNP figures among these states, but because, with the end of the Cold War, there is no longer a distinct Second World of communist states. Alternative phrases have proliferated over the years: developing states, less-developed states, underdeveloped states, the periphery, the Third World, the south, and the Majority World. The broader question is not really which is appropriate, since they are all derived from political perspectives, but whether any sort of label is appropriate, given the diversity of states and peoples in the developing world. Enormous differences exist in wealth, income distribution, political systems, social structure, and economic organization. In the past, some scholars have suggested differentiating states in the developing world by creating additional categories, such as the **Fourth World**, the Fifth World, or the least developed of the less-developed countries (LLDCs). Nevertheless, terms such as "north–south" and "developing world" remain widely employed in diplomatic language, especially in the context of United Nations–sponsored forums.

while growth has been dramatic in some 15 countries in the world, which has brought rising incomes to 1.5 billion people, 100 countries experienced declining or stagnant growth rates. Of these states, 70 have average incomes that are less than they were in 1980. Forty-three countries, many of them African, have lower average incomes today than they did in 1970. Other statistics are just as striking:

- The poorest 20 percent of the world's population saw their share of global income fall from 2.3 to 1.4 percent in the past 30 years, while the share of the richest 20 percent rose from 70 to 80 percent in the same period. This effectively more than doubled the ratio of the share of global income between the richest 20 percent and the poorest 20 percent from 30:1 in 1960 to 74:1 in 1997.

- In the past 30 years the proportion of people enjoying per capita income growth of at least 5 percent a year doubled, from 12 to 27 percent, while in the same period the proportion of those experiencing negative growth tripled, from 5 to 18 percent.

- The gap in per capita income between the industrialized and developing worlds almost tripled between 1960 and 1993, from U.S.$5700 to U.S.$15 400.

- The combined net worth of the richest 358 billionaires in the world exceeds the combined annual incomes of countries with 45 percent of the world's population. Between 1994 and 1998, the 200 richest people in the world doubled their net worth to U.S.$1 trillion.[39]

The relationship between these grim economic figures and quality of life is direct and real. While measures based on monetary shares cannot tell the whole story (some societies with very low per capita GNP rates nevertheless are successful in providing for

basic human needs), the human dimension of these economic statistics is appalling. At the aggregate level, and at the individual level, global inequality has taken a devastating toll on the human condition in much of the world. In all, 1.3 billion people live in abject poverty, without access to basic nutritional requirements, health care, waste disposal, or adequate housing. Put simply, the basic human needs of vast numbers of the world's population are not being met. For example, consider the following statistics:

- *Food, water, and nutrition.* Nearly 800 million people in the world do not receive enough food, and about 500 million are chronically malnourished (unable to maintain body weight). Another 1.3 billion people lack access to safe drinking water, and more than half of the world's people do not have adequate water supplies.

- *Health and health care.* Seventeen million people die every year from treatable infectious and parasitic diseases. The most common are respiratory infections (seven million deaths a year), diarrhea (four million), tuberculosis (three million), and malaria and hepatitis (one to two million). Of the world's 18 million people infected with HIV, 90 percent live in the southern hemisphere. Only 30 percent of the world's doctors practise there, despite the fact that 75 percent of the world's population live there.

- *Children.* More than a third of children in the south are malnourished, and the under-five mortality rate is six times higher than in the north. Every three seconds, a child dies from malnutrition-related problems (more than 1000 an hour, 30 000 a day, 10 million a year).

- *Education.* About 130 million children in the south do not attend primary school, and 275 million (approximately half) do not attend secondary school. One billion people in the world are illiterate.

- *Women.* Seventy percent of the people in abject poverty in the world are women. Two-thirds of illiterate people are women. In the south, maternal mortality rates are 12 times higher than in the OECD countries. Eighty percent of malnourished children are female. For women, the problems of poverty are compounded by inferior social status: female children are less valued; women face barriers in education and career prospects; and women are underrepresented politically, holding only 10 percent of parliamentary seats.

In light of these statistics, it might be useful to reflect on how Canada compares to the rest of the world. The United Nations employs a measure called the Human Development Index, which is based on achievements in basic human capabilities across states. The HDI is measured by life expectancy, educational attainment, and income (GNP per capita). In the 1999 report, Canada ranked number one in the world (as it has since 1992). Of course, this ranking does not mean that Canada does not face problems associated with poverty, homelessness, or the economic and political marginalization of certain groups in society. Nevertheless, it should give Canadians pause to consider what ethical obligations they might have to work to alleviate global inequalities.

THE EMERGENCE OF THE "DEVELOPING WORLD"

In Chapter 2 we examined how the European empires expanded around the world and how non-European empires also expanded and conquered territories abroad, imposing alien systems of economic and political organization. Many of the problems that beset

The struggle of life in Haiti. A woman carries supplies on her head alongside an open sewage drain in the Port-au-Prince slum of Cite Soleil. United Nations soldiers in Haiti ended three years of military intervention in 1997. Although the intervention restored democracy in the Caribbean nation, Haiti remains plagued by crime, poverty, and political instability. (AP Photo/Scott Sady)

the southern states have their origins in the nature of this colonial rule. As we have seen, these empires began to collapse after World War II, and many states gained their political independence. However, the end of colonial rule left most of these former colonies woefully unprepared to govern their political, economic, or social affairs. Although some colonies were better prepared for independence than others, in general the colonies lacked individuals trained or involved in the administration of independent government. Furthermore, the arbitrary nature of colonial borders left many new independent states with complex mixtures of ethnicities, languages, religions, and clans, many of which had historical animosities. The effort to build nationalism around loyalty to the state, as opposed to loyalty to ethnicity or clan, was never very successful, as we saw in our discussion of ethnic conflict in Chapter 6. Finally, a post-colonial dependence lingered: southern states needed northern capital, while northern states continued to exploit southern natural resources and labour. The legacy of imperialism had left the former colonies with the illusion of political freedom but the reality of economic subjugation, which in turn left them vulnerable to political interference and domination. Concern over the north–south split increased during the 1960s and 1970s, and became a major issue at the United Nations (where it is still an issue today). Southern states were now stuck in a cycle of underdevelopment, one that they felt was perpetuated by the investment activities of large corporations, the accumulation of external debt to the north, and the unequal trading arrangement of the world economy.

Efforts to change this situation began at the Bandung Conference in 1955, a meeting of 25 Asian and African states that condemned colonialism. In 1964 a group of developing states in the UN formed the **Group of 77 (G-77)**, which called for the development of favourable terms of trade for developing countries in the GATT. The G-77 did succeed in creating the pressure behind a **Generalized System of Preferences (GSP),** but this concession was not the decisive or major step the developing world was looking for. In 1974, the G-77 called for the establishment of a **New International Economic Order (NIEO)** that would give southern states a better position in the world trading system. Many developing states had evolved into what economists have referred to as "one-commodity countries." Some examples include Bolivia (natural gas), Colombia (coffee), Venezuela (petroleum), Botswana (diamonds), Niger (uranium), Zaire (copper), and Fiji (sugar). The price of such items is susceptible to sudden and dramatic shifts in demand. The NIEO called for commodity agreements that would free states highly dependent on a few products from suffering the effects of wild price fluctuations. It also called for an increase in economic aid from northern states, debt relief by forgiving or postponing repayment, the provision of preferential treatment for Third World exports, transfers of appropriate technology to the south, and for greater southern influence on the boards of the main financial institutions, such as the IMF and World Bank.

These demands, and others associated with the NIEO movement, called for heavy state intervention in the global economy, thus contradicting the principles of free trade on which the GATT trade system was slowly evolving. Despite a modest effort to bolster Third World trade through the European Economic Community in 1975 in the **Lome Convention** (which currently covers trade with some 58 **African, Caribbean, and Pacific [ACP] states**), the overall thrust of the NIEO plan was so anti-market and demanding from the north's perspective that it never had a serious chance of being implemented. Today, the G-77 countries (which now number more than 120) continue to press for changes to the international trading system, but their profile is no longer what it once was.

As efforts to decisively change the global trading system foundered and foreign direct investment proved insufficient, the developing world increasingly relied on financial aid for development. This aid came from three primary sources: loans from the World Bank Group, private capital markets, and Official Development Assistance. The World Bank Group includes the World Bank (IBRD), which has extended loans of more than U.S.$20 billion annually for the past several years. The money in the bank comes from governments (which pay according to a quota) and from borrowing on private financial markets. Loans are extended by a vote, with countries that contribute most to the funds of the Bank having increased voting weight. As a result, the United States is the most important government in the Bank, and the rich countries dominate the voting. The World Bank only approves hard loans, that is, loans that have a good prospect for obtaining returns (repayment with interest). The World Bank Group also includes the **International Finance Corporation (IFC)** (which acts as a bridge between the developing world and private investors and financial institutions), the **International Development Association** (which assists the world's poorest countries in obtaining soft loans, with easier terms of repayment and lower rates of interest), and the International Monetary Fund (which has become a crisis lender to governments in immediate need of funds to balance their payments or compensate for a drop in commodity prices).

The institutions of the World Bank Group have received considerable criticism. Critics charge that the world's richest countries control these institutions (through **weighted voting**), and as a result the institutions lend based not on the need of the developing world but in the interests of capital lenders. The terms of the loans of the World Bank are little better than those from private institutions, and the amount of money dispensed by the Group has never been sufficient to make a decisive difference in the position of the developing world. Finally, the World Bank Group (and especially the IMF) imposes harsh conditions for loans. The **structural adjustment programs (SAPs)** recommended by the IMF and World Bank demand reductions in public spending (which hurt the poor the most) and a focus on trade liberalization and the exportation of natural resources, which harm the environment and curtail more diverse economic development. These measures can increase hardship in developing states and often create political instability.[40]

Through the IFC or through private negotiations, governments in the developing world also obtain finance from private lending institutions, primarily the major international banks. In the late 1960s and through the 1970s, private banks extended massive loans to the developing world. Many of the projects built with these loans failed to yield the expected economic returns, and by the late 1970s and early 1980s, many southern states were facing massive debt crises. Defaults on interest charges began to occur, and many loans were extended or simply written off. As a result, today, private lending institutions are very careful about lending money to the developing world, compounding the capital shortage in poor countries, and paying off the debt has dominated domestic policy decisions.

The third primary source of finance is Official Development Assistance (ODA), which consists of government grants or loans specifically intended for economic development. ODA is extended on a bilateral basis or a multilateral basis (through an international organization). Although the north agreed to maintain ODA targets of 0.7 percent of GNP, they have fallen far short of that goal. Japan is the world's leader in ODA transfers in dollars, with a total of U.S.$9.43 billion in 1997, followed by the United States (U.S.$9.37 billion). As a percentage of GDP, the leading ODA donors in the world are Denmark (1.04 percent), Sweden (0.84 percent), and Norway (0.85 percent). In 1997, Canada's ODA totalled U.S. $1.8 billion, 0.32 percent of GDP.[41] The problem with ODA is that because the lenders are governments, the cause of development is often lost in political considerations. For example, most U.S. ODA goes to a very few allies: Israel, Egypt, Turkey, and Jordan.

The future of foreign aid itself is another topic worthy of discussion here. During the Cold War, development assistance was often an unashamedly political device. Both the United States and the Soviet Union were interested in acquiring what we may term *client states*. Those siding with the West would embrace capitalism and foreign investment; those siding with the East would reject the former and pursue close ties with the USSR. However, with the utter devastation of the latter, development assistance has lost its strategic rationale. What remains, many critics argue, is insufficient for the purpose of meeting basic human needs around the world at a time when the fiscal crisis experienced by many northern states has significantly curtailed their propensity to engage in north–south financial transfers; the need to divert aid to the struggling states of the former Soviet bloc became an important factor in the 1990s.[42]

In the northern states, the provision of foreign aid has become an industry itself, involving government agencies, NGOs, and individual researchers and on-site workers contracted by those institutions, including the large United Nations network. Most aid is tied aid: recipients must use the funds to buy the donor's services. Other conditions, for example, on governance and liberalization measures, may apply as well. It remains to be seen whether development aid can, in the long run, provide the solutions to the more pressing problems facing many southern states. One can argue, with a great deal of certainty, that aid often has a beneficial impact, particularly when it goes to health-related programs such as disease prevention and sanitation improvement. However, many analysts regard aid as a mistake, since it can increase dependency on northern states. And in times of increased fiscal constraint in the north, it would seem to be very dangerous to rely on northern beneficence.

Further, leaders from developing countries complain of the reverse transfer of technology, or *brain drain*, that has often occurred. Developed countries and MNCs have been reluctant to establish research and development and other facilities that employ and train local skilled labour, but they are often willing to take the brightest and hardest working and train them in the north. One study suggested that, between 1960 and 1976, more than 300 000 people migrated from developing countries to work as engineers, scientists, physicians, surgeons, and other technical workers in the United States, Canada, and the United Kingdom alone.[43] The loss of these highly skilled workers makes it even more difficult to develop indigenous technological capabilities. This increases the dependence of southern states on the north, and there is no indication that the trend is reversing.

Alternatives exist to the formal economies states attempt to control. Indeed, the real growth area in Latin America may well be in the informal sector, characterized by low-paying jobs that offer no form of formal social protection but that are often supported by networks of family and friends. We have already mentioned the tremendous amount of domestic work, usually performed by women, that offers monetary compensation but is often rewarded in terms of love of family. Similarly, small communities work to support each other without the help of formal state and international institutions, and we should not overlook this. Up to 60 percent of the African urban workforce is employed in the informal sector, and up to 53 percent in Latin America was in the 1980s (understandably, it is difficult to obtain accurate statistics on this!).[44] We must also recognize the fact that transnational organized criminal activity will generate employment also, whether or not governments act to prevent this (see Chapter 6 for a discussion of international organized crime), ranging from illicit drug growth to prostitution to weapons smuggling. Although northern states want to deal with these human security issues in the public arena, they are part of a system that encourages marginalization on a global level.

CONCLUSIONS

This discussion continues our central theme of paradox in this volume. On the one hand, the global economy displays a trend toward *convergence* in the form of increased trade between countries and peoples, increased levels of global and regional economic cooperation and management, and growing financial interdependence and levels of transactions across state borders. On the other hand, one can also identify trends of *divergence,* in the form of the regionalization of the global economy, the persistence of economic nationalism, and the widening gap between the rich and poor peoples of the world.

All the key variables discussed above, as well as many others, will affect the development of the world economy after 2000. We should keep in mind also that the other topics discussed in this text, such as resource scarcity, overpopulation, international organization and law, and even the military-industrial complex, will affect economic outcomes (according to the Stockholm International Peace Research Institute, American military spending alone was U.S.$260 billion in 1998[45]). The different strands of world politics are so closely woven that it is often impossible to tear them apart. If the world economy stays on its present course, we can predict more expansion, but with occasional turmoil similar to the Asian financial crisis, increased consumption and waste, and increased disparities between rich and poor. This expansion will result in more prosperity for some areas, areas that will be forced to take ever more stringent security measures to protect their accumulated wealth; it will result in a continuation of the cycle of poverty for billions and in the degradation of the environment, both locally and globally.

It is difficult to imagine how all these ongoing concerns will affect the subdiscipline of international political economy itself. During the 1980s it seemed as though the postmodernist account was gaining considerable currency within the discipline, but this is less clear now as analysts return to their roots—be they liberal or mercantilist—and as many of them have become captivated by the globalization debate. Of course, all this is interrelated (much of the literature critical of globalization has postmodernist leanings, for example), and the introduction in this chapter of a distinct environmental perspective further suggests that the field is evolving and expanding as we face the problems of the twenty-first century. What does seem common is that, though increased trade is widely forecasted, and this should bring unprecedented global economic activity, specialists in IPE are increasingly wary about the easy claims of a simplistic faith in globalization. They are concerned with the disparities in wealth that are forming with the new economic order—the distinction between those with access to safe drinking water and information technology (to name but two examples) and those without.

Not all observers hold this view, however; some remain steadfastly optimistic, such as Gwynne Dyer:

> What is actually happening in the world now is akin to what happened in Europe at the end of the feudal era. A new class is emerging, a global middle class, and it will ultimately come to dominate global society both numerically and economically.... The [1996] UNDP report was an extended whine on familiar old themes. It depicted poor countries as the norm, and blamed their poverty on the rich ones.... The report's authors were probably being manipulative rather than just plain ignorant, for it is their job to drum up sympathy and help for the world's poor.[46]

Dyer argues that the overall statistics on economic growth and human welfare are skewed by the inclusion of the "African disaster" (ibid.), but should we really ignore the African disaster (for moral as well as analytical reasons)? Dyer's account is based on a global acceptance of the standards and values of this new middle class, this globalizing cosmopolitan semi-elite. As our discussion on the cultural impact of globalization indicated, this is by no means assured, because people still have a tendency to actually like their cultural identities and even to assert them periodically. Nonetheless, Dyer is certainly right in the assertion that the world economy is changing, perhaps on the level of the great changes that transformed Europe with the advent of capitalism. If this is so, we need to think about the implications of such a shift in world civilization.

In conclusion, although we may marvel at the dramatic surge in trade and financial flows around the world, this affluence is utterly alien to most of the people on this planet. The global economy is exceedingly complex and involves many different actors, and the level of wealth and quality of life vary tremendously across states and within them, so simplification is a perilous exercise. Nevertheless, the socioeconomic character of the world is one of profound division between rich and poor. This division leads to questions about social justice and equality, questions that have been on the IPE and IR agenda for some time but that have often been overlooked because of a primary focus on interstate warfare and trade. We turn to these challenging questions in the next chapter, which examines the complex interplay between human rights and global politics.

Endnotes

1. Quoted in *The Globe and Mail* (17 July 1996), A10.
2. R. Reich, *The Work of Nations* (New York: Alfred Knopf, 1991), 8.
3. The World Commission on Environment and Development, *Our Common Future* (Oxford: Oxford University Press, 1987).
4. J. MacNeil, P. Winsemius, and Taizo Yakushiji, *Beyond Interdependence: The Meshing of the World's Economy and the Earth's Ecology* (Oxford: Oxford University Press, 1992), 32.

5. Vandana Shiva, *Staying Alive: Women, Ecology, and Development in India* (New Delhi: Kali for Women, 1988); and for a critical analysis, see Janet Biehl, *Finding Our Way: Rethinking Ecofeminist Politics* (Montreal: Black Rose Books, 1991).

6. Eric Helleiner, "International Political Economy and the Greens," *New Political Economy* 1 (1996), 59–77, 65.

7. E.F. Schumacher, *Small Is Beautiful: Economics as if People Mattered* (New York: Harper and Row, 1973); M. Bookchin, *Towards an Ecological Society* (Montreal: Black Rose Books, 1991); see also B. Devall and G. Sessions, *Deep Ecology: Living as if Nature Mattered* (Layton: Gobbs Smith, 1985).

8. For a compilation of various authors from this perspective, see W. Sachs, ed., *Global Ecology: A New Arena of Political Conflict?* (London: Zed, 1993).

9. Quoted in Isabel Vincent, "Canadian Mining Firms Lead Charge to Argentina," *The Globe and Mail* (10 January 1994), B1.

10. For an expanded treatment of this section, see P. Stoett, *Human and Global Security: An Exploration of Terms* (Toronto: University of Toronto Press, 1999), 97–118.

11. W. Greider, *One World, Ready or Not: The Manic Logic of Global Capitalism* (New York: Simon and Schuster, 1997). See the book review by M. Miler, "A Rising Tide Sinks All Boats," in *The New York Times Book Review* (19 January 1997), 12.

12. M. Waters, *Globalization* (London: Routledge, 1995), 3.

13. Ibid., 4.

14. R. Cox, "The Global Political Economy and Social Choice," in D. Drache and M. Gertler, eds., *The New Era of Global Competition: State Policy and Market Power* (Montreal/Kingston: McGill–Queen's University Press, 1991), 335–49, 336.

15. V. Kavolis, "Contemporary Moral Cultures and 'the Return of the Sacred,'" *Sociological Analysis* 49 (3) (1988), 203–16, 210–12.

16. R. White, *Global Spin: Probing the Civilization Debate* (Toronto: Dundurn, 1995), 127.

17. Richard Jolly, quoted in J. Stackhouse, "Canada Is the Best, UN Reports," *The Globe and Mail* (17 July 1996), A10.

18. United Nations, *The World's Women 2000: Trends and Statistics* (New York: UN Publications, 2000), 158. See also K. Kempadoo, *Global Sex Workers: Rights, Resistance and Redefinition* (London: Routledge, 1998).

19. See J. Bystydzienski, ed., *Women Transforming Politics: Worldwide Strategies for Empowerment* (Bloomington: Indiana University Press, 1992).

20. See "Per Capita Energy Consumption by Country, 1997," from the World Resources Institute, Washington, DC <www.igc.org/wri/wr-00-01/pdf/ercZn_2000.pdf>.

21. "The Control of Oil," *International Journal* 36 (2) (1981), 273–93.

22. *The Globe and Mail* (15 March 1994).

23. Survey, *The Economist* (18 June 1994), 1–6.

24. P. Sampat, *World Watch* (November/December 1995), 21–3.

25. For an analysis linking southern debt to the north, see Susan George, *Debt Boomerang: How Third-World Debt Harms Us* (Boulder, CO: Westview Press, 1992).

26. This is rather confusing, since international relations scholars use the terms liberal, neoliberal, or even *neoliberal institutionalism,* differently. To add to the confusion, in many states, such as Canada and Great Britain, it has been the Conservative parties that initially implemented the neoliberal economic agenda (no one ever said political science would be a straightforward endeavour).

27. Figures cited in the article by J. Stackhouse, "Rich North, Poor South Divided over Labour Practices," *The Globe and Mail* (9 December 1996), A12.

28. "Floating the Tobin Tax," *The Economist* (13 July 1996), 84.

29. "Eggleton Travels to Poland and Russia to Promote Trade and Investment," Department of Foreign Affairs and International Trade, *News release*, 9 October 1996. In early 1997 "Team Canada" visited South Korea, despite a serious labour dispute in that country.

30. There is a Canadian connection here, since the Council of Canadians, an anti-globalization coalition, were the ones who initially circulated a copy of the proposed MAI over the Internet in April 1997. See T. Clark and M. Barlow, *MAI: The Multilateral Agreement on Investment and the Threat to Canadian Sovereignty* (Toronto: Stoddart, 1997), 21–2.

31. One of the reasons some EU members are fond of the more flexible Euro concept is that the Bundesbank has had such a strong anti-inflationary agenda that it has resulted in a "single-minded fixation on price stability [that] has left Europe facing long-term crisis of joblessness." James Laxer, "Germans Are Creating a Monetary Quagmire," *Toronto Star* (21 July 1996), F3.

32. "EU Tries to Pull Itself Together," *The Globe and Mail* (30 March 1996), A13.

33. See David Long, "Europe after Maastricht," in M. Appel Molot and H. von Riekhoff, eds., *A Part of the Peace: Canada among Nations 1994* (Ottawa: Carleton University Press, 1994), 131–53.

34. B. Coleman, "EU Court Backs Damage Claims," *Wall Street Journal* (6 March 1996), 1.

35. R. Vernon, *Sovereignty at Bay: The Multinational Spread of U.S. Enterprises* (New York: Basic, 1971); R. Barnet and R. Muller, *Global Reach: The Power of Multinational Corporations* (New York: Simon and Schuster, 1974).

36. See, for example, K. Levitt, *Silent Surrender: The Multinational Corporation in Canada* (Toronto: Macmillan, 1970).

37. See John M. Stopford, John H. Dunning, and Klaus O. Haberich, *The World Directory of Multinational Enterprises* (New York: Facts on File, 1980), xxv; *The World Factbook 1994*, US Central Intelligence Agency, 1994 (Washington, DC: US Government Printing Office, 1995); and *Fortune* (7 August 1995), F1–F10.

38. *Human Development Report, 1996* (New York: Oxford University Press, 1996), 2.

39. *Human Development Report, 1996* (New York: Oxford University Press, 1996), 2, and *Human Development Report, 1999* (New York: Oxford University Press, 1999).

40. See Thomas D. Lairson and David Skidmore, *International Political Economy* (Fort Worth, TX: Harcourt Brace, 1993), 65–6.

41. Data from *Development Cooperation, 1997 Report.* OECD Development Assistance Committee (Paris, 1998).

42. However, this is controversial. See Jeanne Kirk Laux, "From South to East? Financing the Transition in Central and Eastern Europe," in Appel Molot and von Riekhoff, *A Part of the Peace*, 172–94.

43. UNCTAD Secretariat, Report of the Secretariat, *Technology: Development Aspects of the Reverse Transfer of Technology* (New York: United Nations, 1979), para. 6.

44. ILO, *World Labour Report 1995* (Geneva, 1993).

45. See *SIPRI Yearbook, 1999* (Stockholm: Stockholm International Peace Research Institute, 1999).

46. "Fiddling the Figures on World Poverty," *Toronto Star* (1 September 1996), F3.

Suggested Readings

Adriaansen, W., and J. Waardensburg, eds. *A Dual World Economy.* Groningen: Wolters-Noordhoff, 1989.

Afshar, H. *Women, Development and Survival in the Third World.* New York: Feminist Press, 1991.

Barber, B. "Jihad vs. McWorld." *Atlantic* 269 (March 1992), 53–63.

Cameron, D., and F. Houle, eds. *Canada and the New International Division of Labour.* Ottawa: University of Ottawa Press, 1985.

Chase-Dunn, C. *Global Formation: The Structures of the World Economy.* Cambridge: Basil Blackwell, 1991.

Cohen, M.G. *Free Trade and the Future of Women's Work: Manufacturing and Service Industries.* Toronto: Garamond, 1987.

Conklin D., and T. Courchene, eds. *Canadian Trade at a Crossroads: Options for New International Agreements.* Toronto: Ontario Economic Council, 1985.

Czempiel, E.-O., and J. Rosenau, eds. *Global Changes and Theoretical Challenges: Approaches to World Politics for the 1990s.* Lexington: Lexington Books, 1989.

Drache, D., and M. Gertler, eds. *The New Era of Global Competition: State Policy and Market Power.* Montreal/Kingston: McGill-Queen's University Press, 1991.

Garten, J. "Lessons for the Next Financial Crisis." *Foreign Affairs* 78:2 (1999), 76–92.

Gill, S., ed. *Gramsci, Historical Materialism and International Relations.* Cambridge: Cambridge University Press, 1993.

Haggard, S., and R. Kaufman, eds. *The Politics of Economic Adjustment: International Constraints, Distributive Conflicts, and the State.* Princeton: Princeton University Press, 1992.

Hettne, B., A. Inotai, and O. Sunkel, eds. *Globalization and the New Regionalism.* Toronto: Macmillan, 1999.

Holm, H.-H., and G. Sorensen, eds. *Whose World Order? Uneven Globalization and the End of the Cold War.* Boulder, CO: Westview Press, 1995.

Jackson, K., ed. *The Asian Contagion: The Causes and Consequences of a Financial Crisis.* Boulder, CO: Westview Press, 1999.

Jomo, K.S., ed. *Tigers in Trouble: Financial Governance, Liberalisation and the Crisis in East Asia.* London: Zed Books, 1998.

Kardam, N. *Bringing Women In: Women's Issues in International Development Programs.* Boulder, CO: Lynne Rienner, 1990.

Katzenstein, P., ed. *Between Power and Plenty: Foreign Economic Policies of Advanced Industrial States.* Madison: University of Wisconsin Press, 1978.

Laferriere, E. "Emancipating International Relations Theory: An Ecological Perspective." *Millennium: Journal of International Studies* 25 (1) (1996), 53–75.

Lele, J., and W. Tettey, eds. *Asia: Who Pays for Growth? Women, Environment and Popular Movements.* Aldershot: Dartmouth, 1996.

Lieber, R. "Oil and Power after the Gulf War." *International Security* 17 (1) (1992), 155–76.

Lopez, G., et. al. "The Global Tide." *The Bulletin of the Atomic Scientists* (July/August 1995), 33–39.

Massiah, J., ed. *Women in Developing Economies: Making Visible the Invisible.* New York: Berg, 1992.

Mittelman, J., ed. *Globalization: Critical Reflections.* Boulder, CO: Lynne Reiner, 1997.

Naisbitt, J. *Global Paradox: The Bigger the World Economy, the More Powerful Its Smallest Players.* New York: Avon, 1994.

Nef, J. *Human Security and Mutual Vulnerability: An Exploration into the Global Political Economy of Development and Underdevelopment.* Ottawa: International Development Research Centre, 1995.

Redclift, M. *Sustainable Development: Exploring the Contradictions.* London: Methuen, 1987.

Ritzer, G. *The McDonaldization of Society.* Thousand Oaks: Pine Forge, 1993.

Rosenau, J. *Turbulence in World Politics.* Princeton: Princeton University Press, 1990.

Sassen, S. *Losing Control? Sovereignty in an Age of Globalization.* New York: Columbia University Press, 1996.

Wade, R. "National Power, Coercive Liberalism, and 'Global' Finance." In R. Art and R. Jervis, eds., *International Politics: Enduring Concepts and Contemporary Issues.* New York: Longman, 2000, 482–89.

Suggested Websites

World Trade Organization
<www.wto.org>

NAFTANET

Virtual Library on International Development
<w3.acdi-cida.gc.ca/virtual.nsf/pages/index_e.htm>

Europa and Internet
    <www.uv.es/cde/euinternet/>

Link to Women's Studies/Women's Issues WWW Sites
    <www.umbc.edu/wmst/links.html>

CHAPTER 9

Human Rights
GLOBAL UNITY AND DIVISION

No one shall be subjected to torture or to cruel, inhuman or degrading treatment or punishment.

—*Universal Declaration of Human Rights,* 1948, Article 5

There is little evidence to suggest that mankind has advanced much beyond [the] level of jungle morality.

—Robert Gilpin[1]

INTRODUCTION: CAN WE INSTITUTIONALIZE ETHICS ON A WORLD SCALE?

The theme of human security, adopted as a guiding principle for Canadian foreign policy, reflects a growing awareness of human rights in the post–Cold War world. The question remains, however, whether this theme can exceed rhetoric and become a truly influential standard for policymaking. This chapter reflects on the challenges and opportunities such a task entails.

In March 1995 the world lamented the passing of a Canadian author who, though virtually unknown outside diplomatic circles, helped pen what may be the most important single document recognized by the global community, the *Universal Declaration of Human Rights.* Professor John Peter Humphrey was the founder and first director of the United Nations human rights division, a post he held for 20 years; he also founded the Canadian Human Rights Foundation and the Canadian branch of Amnesty International, a nongovernmental organization dedicated to protecting citizens from state human rights abuses. However, Humphrey will be most widely remembered for the Declaration itself,[2] but not because the Declaration has become the standard by which all governments run their countries. On the contrary, most observers consider it a largely symbolic work, albeit one of great significance; as a Declaration, it does not carry the status of international law attributed to a convention or treaty. This is but one example of the general frustration with international law encountered by those who would aspire to produce a more standardized world order or human rights regime. Some wonder whether law can even be said to exist if there is no formal, coercive mechanism to enforce it. Indeed, if one needs reliably effective enforcement machinery to establish law, we do not have international law. Though states will often engage in punitive measures to attempt to enforce trade agreements, or to sanction gross violations of human rights such as the institutionalization of apartheid by the former South African government, it is another thing entirely to speak of a systematic law that is applied even-handedly across the globe.

Others, however, argue that the absence of an enforcer does not imply that law, in a less strict sense, does not exist. One might argue that, outside the confines of a domestic

PROFILE 9.1 International Days and Weeks Declared by the United Nations

Note that most of the days and weeks declared by the UN celebrate some sort of human rights–related issue. But does all this celebration really advance these causes?

March 8	International Women's Day	October 1	International Day of the Elderly
March 21	International Day for the Elimination of Racial Discrimination	First Monday of October	World Habitat Day
March 21–28	Week of Solidarity with the Peoples Struggling against Racism and Racial Discrimination	October 9	World Post Day
		October 16	World Food Day
		October 17	International Day for the Eradication of Poverty
March 22	World Water Day	October 24	United Nations Day
March 23	World Meteorological Day	October 24–30	Disarmament Week
April 7	World Health Day	Week of November 11	International Week of Science and Peace
May 3	World Press Freedom Day		
May 15	International Day of Families		
May 17	World Telecommunications Day	November 20	Universal Children's Day
May 31	World No-Tobacco Day	November 20	Africa Industrialization Day
June 4	International Day of Innocent Children Victims of Violence	November 29	International Day of Solidarity with the Palestinian People
June 5	World Environment Day		
June 26	International Day against Drug Abuse and Illicit Trafficking	December 1	World AIDS Day
		December 3	International Day of Disabled Persons
July 11	World Population Day	December 5	International Volunteer Day for Economic and Social Development
September 8	International Literacy Day		
Third Tuesday of September	International Day of Peace	December 10	Human Rights Day

legal system, a law that relies on force alone for its legitimacy is bound to be short-lived and is often more tyrannical than helpful. International law is a system in which consent-granting state leaders choose to participate not because they have to—though no one would deny the fact that some pressure does exist—but because they believe that it will ultimately benefit them. This is perhaps the ultimate example of enlightened self-interest in action.

The Roman and British empires spread law throughout many lands, but it was the law of an empire, not of consensual states. When Hugo Grotius published his *De jure belli ac pacis* (*Law of War and Peace*) in 1625, he was writing in an age when the dominant European colonial powers were defining international law for the rest of the world (see Chapter 5). The periods of decolonization that followed, ending most recently in the 1970s, have changed that perception. Formal state **sovereignty**, and its protection in documents such as the UN Charter, ensures that international law is not something imposed by Romans or Europeans but is something that has gained the acceptance of self-determining members of the international community.

It may be argued, then, that the participation of states in international legal arrangements reflects an even stronger incentive to comply than if that system of law were coercive or imposed. One of the problems with this perspective, however, is that in many areas of international law, including questions about human rights, it is not the people who control the government in power, or those who have consented to participate in international rights regimes, who are threatened by abuses. It is citizens of those states, and the principle of territorial sovereignty does not distinguish between democratically elected leaders and tyrants. Another problem is that conceptions of human rights vary, on both philosophical and political grounds. This variation raises the tricky question of whether the international community has either an obligation or, for that matter, the ability, to institutionalize conceptions of justice, law, and human rights on an international level. We expand on this question below when we discuss human rights law more specifically. For now we will examine the essential divisions of opinion on human rights.

HUMAN RIGHTS DEBATES AND THE STUDY OF GLOBAL POLITICS

As we noted above, serious philosophical differences of opinion exist on the issue of human rights. The first debate concerns the subject matter and definition of human rights; when we speak of human rights, do we focus on the political rights of the individual or the socioeconomic rights of the collective? The tension between the two has been the source of considerable political controversy in global politics. A second debate revolves around the question of whether human rights is a relative or a universal concept. Some charge that human rights is a Western idea, and that civilizations, societies, peoples, and groups have different conceptions of the term. Others argue that basic human rights are universal for all peoples. A third debate concerns the usefulness and effectiveness of international laws on human rights. Each theoretical perspective on global politics that we have introduced in this book regards the issue of human rights very differently.

INDIVIDUAL VERSUS COLLECTIVE CONCEPTIONS OF HUMAN RIGHTS

During the Cold War it became standard for the two opposing camps to each present their vision of human rights as morally defensible and worthy of emulation. The West insisted that the individual is the most important component of any political system, and an individual's rights must be protected from encroachment by the state. The Soviet Union naturally rejected this definition of human rights, arguing that collective rights, or those of entire populations, had to come first. The Communist parties of the East rejected the right to private property, long taken as a fundamental right in the West. They also rejected the right to practise religion freely, and it still is in some societies today where a single religion is instituted as that of the nation-state, such as in Iran.

Naturally, we are engaging in what some might consider *excessive dichotomization* here. Clearly, every society needs some sort of balance between the individual and collective conceptions of rights, such as the right to freedom and the right to be free from poverty. Individual rights can be superseded in the most liberal states by the need to protect collective rights; for example, in the United States, where individual liberties are fairly well protected, the state can still kill people if they are found guilty of treason or other crimes. Sometimes, the logic of group rights can lead to divisive debate. For example, the *Universal Declaration of Human Rights* states that: "the family is the natural and fundamental group unit of society and is entitled to protection by society and the State" (Article 16-3). This statement remains open to interpretation but can be used to challenge the legitimacy of same-sex family status. In Canada, there are various competing conceptions of which should take precedence, the individual or groups such as Francophones in Quebec or First Nations peoples. This philosophical dispute is also at the root of international disputes over human rights and systems of governance. States like Malaysia have argued that Western notions of individual liberty are fine, but they should not be imposed on non-Western states that emphasize collective rights. Human rights groups such as Amnesty International argue that there are some things all individuals should be protected from, including repression and **torture** at the hands of the state.

RELATIVISM VERSUS UNIVERSALISM IN HUMAN RIGHTS

In the African country of Ghana, a few isolated communities still practise an ancient Ewe custom. The custom holds that, for serious crimes against the community such as murder, rape, or theft, "the spirits can be appeased only by the enslavement of young [female] virgins from the offender's family in the shrines of traditional priests." This enslavement of girls as young as 12 demands that the girls participate in sexual acts with the priests. Many Ghanaians are campaigning against the practice, which is said to have enslaved "as many as 10 000 girls." But in the Ghanaian coastal village of Tefle, the village men insist they have the right to practise what they consider to be a vital custom.[3] This is an extreme case; others, such as child labour, invoke similar feelings of horror among Westerners accustomed to a different set of principles. However, many Africans consider the Western tradition of putting older citizens into retirement facilities instead of keeping them at home with extended families to be equally barbaric, and the lack of care for the homeless in major urban centres is viewed with similar disdain. So we realize that there are cultural differences between different societies, as there have always been; the question is whether some practices, such as slavery or genocide, should be universally condemned.

As suggested above, we have to ask also whether it is even appropriate to condemn some states for human rights violations: what gives anyone the right to make such pronouncements? Some reject the premise of a universal moral order, arguing that norms and principles are subject to a specific time and place. In other words, what is morally acceptable today may not be tomorrow; this is certainly the case with some widespread institutions, such as that of slavery in the Americas. It has been suggested that as we progress toward a more civilized world order, we are redefining certain types of behaviour as illegitimate. As described in Chapter 5, the institutionalization of this process of redefinition has been specifically referred to as the social construction of *global prohibition regimes*: they are guided by norms that "strictly circumscribe the conditions under which states can participate in and authorize these activities and proscribe all involvement by nonstate actors."[4] Once we have made some sort of collective decision regarding the immorality of an act or even a sociopolitical system, such as apartheid in South Africa, or state repression in Burma, then we should make an attempt to universalize this decision and spread it around the world, through education or outright coercion.

To many, this sounds rather confusing, for while it may have the most progressive of foundations (such as outlawing slavery, for example), it also implies that the majority (or perhaps merely the strong) has the moral right (or even duty) to impose their will on others. Is this much different from what the imperial powers did during the dark years of colonial administration? Does this simply replace the old political and economic dominance of the West with a new form of **cultural imperialism**?[5] Cultural imperialism usually refers to the imposition of one society's values on another, through either the force of law (as in direct colonialism) or the less overt manipulation of minds through the media (television, radio, newspapers, even the Internet). However, when it comes to standards of international law and human rights in particular, the promotion of Western values with aid policies designed to award liberal democratization are equally suspect, as are rhetoric-laden UN resolutions.

The idea behind cultural relativism is that ethical values (ostensibly the root cause of governments' human rights policies) vary from place to place and over time. As R.J. Vincent writes, this means "that moral claims derive from, and are enmeshed in, a cultural context which is itself the source of their validity."[6] In other words, it may be unfair to criticize the ethical positions of others, since they arise out of the specific conditions faced by them at the time. Japan has always had a strong dependency on seafood, for example; perhaps we should not be surprised or outraged that some Japanese still sell whale meat in restaurants in Tokyo and elsewhere. Amsterdam's "red light" district would appear distinctly unethical in many other areas of the world. While the United States is a powerful proponent of the ethics of democracy, many outsiders point to the increasing use of the death penalty and the disproportionately high incarceration of minorities in that country as an indication of regressive public ethics. Since no states are without human rights problems and controversies, it may not be just cultural imperialism to force one's own values onto the international stage; it may be nakedly hypocritical as well.

Even the more obvious cases can become complicated with a close look. For example, the right to food is often used as an example of a universal human right.[7] However, we must ask whether people have a simple right to adequate amounts of food, or even equitable amounts of food within their own societies (none would pass that test). We might argue that the right to environmental security should be universally applicable, that is, that all people should be able to live in a local environment free from profound ecological threats. However, any attempt to ensure this right would not only challenge sovereignty as an institution but in many cases require the redistribution of resources within societies. At the same time, cultural relativism can become a cloak behind which abusers of basic rights can hide, and we should not let it stop us from analyzing touchy issues. Or, in the words of the distinguished scholar Fred Halliday:

> While an awareness of relativity and difference is essential to an explanation of how and why systems of domination originate and are maintained, such a recognition need not necessarily lead, out of a misplaced anthropological generosity, to denying that forms of oppression do exist and recur in a wide range of societies and historical contexts.[8]

INTERNATIONAL RELATIONS THEORY AND HUMAN RIGHTS

An examination of the theoretical approaches in international relations theory reveals divergent attitudes about the place and role of human rights in global politics. Realists largely reject international law as an essentially inconsequential phenomenon. Since they believe global politics is ultimately about state interests, it is obvious to realists that states simply use international law as yet another tool with which to pursue their own ends. Structural realists would argue that international law on human rights is simply yet another diplomatic apparatus contingent on the power structure of the state system. States may sign treaties related to promoting some conception of equity, but they are motivated by the belief that a rhetorical commitment of this kind would enhance their prestige abroad. Marxists and most critical theorists tend to treat international law as they do domestic law: it is a manifestation of a deeper base of exploitative social relations, part of the superstructure of the capitalist world system. International law simply protects an unjust status quo in which the strong can violate the law with impunity, while the weak are forced to submit to a formal recognition of the justifiability of the system. Human rights law invokes special condemnation because it is regarded as uniquely hypocritical. According to a socialist perspective, the real pursuit of justice and equity would necessarily involve some sort of redistribution of a country's wealth. Measures that fall short of this ideal are not only inadequate but can present the illusion of progress. Liberals and institutionalists, however, place much more importance, if still limited faith, in the rise of international legal agreements. They argue that the complex web of obligations resulting from state participation in various regimes has helped develop a world order with its own set of rules and institutions that can stand on its own, without the nation-state. Slowly, an embryonic world community is forming, in which some standards become universally accepted.

A yet broader issue concerns whether questions of ethics and morality should even be part of the study of international relations.[9] If state sovereignty is sacrosanct, states really have no right to comment on what goes on in other states in the first place. If this were the case, the ethical responsibilities of government leaders would not extend beyond the borders of their own countries.[10] Since the most fundamental principle of international law is state sovereignty, it reinforces, rather than challenges, this perspective. However, leaving questions of permanence aside, this is the age of interdependence. States are highly involved in each other's domestic economies, they often share transnational cultural understandings, and much migration has occurred in the past two centuries. All of this leads us to suggest that, whether they like it or not, government leaders do bear some measure of ethical responsibility for what occurs outside their borders and for what their citizens do outside them as well. While this responsibility has always pertained to the actions of soldiers, it includes the actions of civilians. For example, the Canadian government is joining several other states to make it possible to prosecute Canadians who purchase sex with children when abroad.

Though most would agree that international law not only exists but also can, in fact, reduce the uncertainty inherent in world politics, a more perplexing question is whether or not states have a right or an obligation to institutionalize ethics at the international level, mainly through some forum of the UN. To demonstrate the problematic nature of such efforts, this chapter will focus most exclusively on human rights issues since they demand conceptions of both universal and relative, and individual and collective, rights. But we should keep in mind the fact that many other aspects to international law, public and private, challenge the international community to establish norms and regulations in a relatively disordered and competitive climate. It would not seem radical to suggest that the primary order on which a state must be based is a conception of justice. If we are moving toward an international society capable of such a foundation, what does it look like, and what can be done with it?

HUMAN RIGHTS IN GLOBAL POLITICS

As Sidney Bailey and Sam Daws write, "from a moral point of view, human rights are about the behaviour of individuals. From a legal point of view, human rights are about the responsibilities of governments."[11] Until roughly the mid- to late nineteenth century, human rights concerns were regarded as within the domestic jurisdiction of rulers. Campaigns to abolish the slave trade and to provide humanitarian care for wounded soldiers helped break this confinement, although the principle of nonintervention maintains its prominent place in the UN Charter today. The human rights field has expanded considerably in scope since the end of World War II, the cataclysmic event that so horrified the international community that it began to gradually accept the notion that international law could play a role in avoiding future holocausts (see the section on war crimes below). Where the human rights issue-area departs most noticeably from conventional international legal matters, however, is that it forces us to look beyond the usual tradition that defines international law as law for, and by, states. Even in the World Court, states are still recognized as the sole actors in international law. This distinction becomes increasingly difficult to maintain as global human rights conventions, agreements, and movements flourish, since human rights are ultimately about people and not about the relatively abstract conceptions we call states.

In recent decades, human rights issues have become increasingly prominent concerns for governments, international organizations, and publics. Why has this happened? In the first place, *awareness* has increased. Global communications, travel, and print and television media have made us more aware of what goes on in other countries. States are no longer as capable of controlling information flows across their borders as they once were. Economic interdependence and global communications have provided governments, groups, and individuals with the means to act to promote human rights, through mechanisms such as trade restrictions, boycotts, and public information campaigns and protests. For example, consumer boycotts of multinational corporations (MNCs) have had some success, as many consumers resist buying products produced by victims of repression. Consumer awareness campaigns directed at Heineken, Carlsberg, British Home Stores, and Liz Claiborne compelled those MNCs to leave Burma. Recent campaigns have also been mounted against Royal Dutch/Shell for its operations in Nigeria, Total and Unocal in Burma, Nike in Indonesia, Disney in Haiti, and Zenith and General Motors for gender discrimination in Mexico.[12]

The growth of human rights groups has also given interested individuals the opportunity to devote more time and effort to the cause of human rights. Such nongovernmental organizations (NGOs) include Amnesty International, Human Rights Watch, the International League for Human Rights, and the International Commission of Jurists. As we discussed in Chapter 5, these NGOs work to create awareness and persuade governments to act on human rights issues. As a result, governments are no longer regarded as the primary means of advancing human rights. In fact, governments are increasingly regarded as serious obstacles to progress. Yet they remain an essential piece of the puzzle.

HUMAN RIGHTS AND GOVERNMENTS

Governments are a factor in human rights issues on three levels. First, human rights are a factor in foreign policy decision making. Many governments have participated in efforts to build international law and international regimes to promote them, and they have responded to human rights abuses with diplomatic protests and economic sanctions (such as those directed against apartheid South Africa and against China after the June 1989 Tiananmen Square massacre in which the Chinese military crushed a prodemocracy protest). Other governments have also taken steps to improve human rights in their own societies by prosecuting abusive officials and exposing the stark legacies of

Standing up for liberty. In this now famous photograph, an anti-government protester stands in front of advancing tanks in Beijing's Tiananmen Square on 5 June 1989, at the height of the pro-democracy protests. Deng Xiaoping is believed to have given the final orders for the military suppression of the 1989 Tiananmen Square pro-democracy protests, which claimed hundreds, perhaps thousands, of lives. (AP Photo/Jeff Widener)

their past. For example, the Truth and Reconciliation Commission in South Africa undertook an investigation that has implicated top-level officials in the former South African government (we discuss this later in this chapter). The Guatemalan government acknowledged past abuses and purged the military and the police of the worst human rights offenders. The government of South Korea has convicted two former presidents for their role in a 1980 massacre of civilians by the South Korean military.

Second, governments have displayed inconsistency and a lack of commitment on human rights issues. In particular, governments around the world (including the government of Canada; see Profile 9.2) appear increasingly willing to subordinate human rights concerns to their desire for trade and investment opportunities. Governments have defended this approach by arguing that trade, investment, and interdependence will generate social change in countries with human rights problems and that interdependence will create leverage that can later be used to promote human rights. This "constructive engagement" approach has angered critics, who charge that it amounts to a façade of a human rights policy rather than any genuine commitment.[13] Governments also tend to exert human rights pressure on poor states while not doing the same with economically attractive states, and great powers have often continued to provide Official Development Assistance (ODA) and even military aid to some abusive regimes. Governments have also obstructed efforts to reveal the involvement of their own officials in human rights abuses. The U.S. government, for example, has been reluctant to release documents related to the activities of the Central Intelligence Agency (CIA) in Haiti, Honduras, and Guatemala, obstructing the human rights investigations in progress in those countries.

Third, governments often fail to act on human rights abuses, and many continue to perpetrate abuses at home. Governments were slow to react to the human rights abuses in the former Yugoslavia and to the genocide in Rwanda. Governments in Angola and Cambodia have extended amnesty to human rights abusers. The Japanese government remains unwilling to formally compensate for the treatment of the 200 000 "comfort women" used as sex slaves for the Japanese military in World War II. Many other countries are struggling with political opposition to the investigation of human rights abuses, and some governments attempt to intimidate human rights advocates, harassing many, imprisoning some, and killing others.[14] The role of governments in human rights issues is, therefore, rather poor; although governments can be important agents of progress, all too often they are obstacles to progress or the very source of the problem. This fact complicates related diplomatic initiatives.

Talisman and Sudan

The concept of human security was put to an interesting test in the recent dispute over a Canadian oil firm's investment and operations in the North African state of Sudan. Civil war has raged in that country for almost 50 years. The northern Arab-dominated National Islamic Front government has been fighting the Christian and animist southern region in a brutal confrontation that has killed some 1.5 million southerners and has seen the use of food as a weapon, concentration camps, and reports of southern villagers being taken into slavery by northern militias. (Western Christian groups have engaged in so-called redemption programs, literally buying back slaves from their oppressors, but this has been criticized as well since it drives up the price of slaves.)

In October 1998 Talisman Energy acquired Arakis Energy for C$200 million. This gave Talisman a 25 percent share in the Greater Nile Oil Project, a consortium with China and Malaysia. In southern Sudan, huge oil fields are being drilled and a major pipeline to Port Sudan is planned. The project employs 2000 Sudanese, and more than 100 Canadians are there to train them. However, the southern rebels, in particular the Sudan People's Liberation Army, consider this collaboration with the northern government an affront to their territorial sovereignty and have declared such installations legitimate military targets. As a result the Sudanese government, which takes a share of the revenue generated by the oil extraction, employs military forces to protect the Canadian workers and installations.

Critics charge that this means a Canadian firm is helping to fund a genocidal war. In response, the Canadian government sent African expert John Harker to investigate the situation; his report was largely condemnatory. In early 2000 the government decided that no sanctions would be imposed against Talisman but that they should be encouraged to carefully monitor the situation and perhaps create a trust fund to help southerners after the conflict is over. Human rights activists, who argue that the conflict will not end as long as the Sudanese government is funded by oil revenues, expressed dismay at this decision. The decision also angered the United States, which has imposed tough sanctions (with some notable exceptions) on the Sudan because of suspected terrorist connections. Should the Canadian government have taken steps to force Talisman out of Sudan, or is business just business?

SOURCES: A. NIKIFORUK, "OIL PATCH PARIAH," *CANADIAN BUSINESS*, 10 DECEMBER 2000, 69; "HUMAN SECURITY IN SUDAN: REPORT OF A CANADIAN ASSESSMENT MISSION PREPARED FOR THE MINISTER OF FOREIGN AFFAIRS," OTTAWA, JANUARY 2000; S. THORNE, "CANADA CONSIDERS MORE MEASURES TO ENCOURAGE PEACE IN SUDAN," *CANADIAN PRESS,* 15 FEBRUARY 2000.

HUMAN RIGHTS AND THE UN SYSTEM

In June 1993, the UN-sponsored World Conference on Human Rights in Vienna declared that "the promotion and protection of all human rights is a legitimate concern of the international community."[15] Similar sentiments had been expressed at previous UN conferences and forums. Yet such declarations conflict with the principle of sovereignty enshrined in the UN Charter. As Stephen Marks has observed, "Human rights in the United Nations has been, to a large extent, the story of tension between the principle that the United Nations cannot intervene in the domestic affairs of states and the principle that states must act with the United Nations to realize fully all rights."[16]

While the UN Charter does call explicitly for international cooperation on economic, social, cultural, and humanitarian matters, and the promotion of human rights and fundamental freedoms (Articles 4 and 55, respectively), it is the *Universal Declaration of Human Rights*, adopted by the General Assembly in 1948, that made the most impact on

UN Human Rights Conventions

Note: After each convention appears the year it was opened for ratification and the year it entered into force.

GENERAL HUMAN RIGHTS

International Covenant on Civil and Political Rights, 1966, 1976

Optional Protocol to the International Covenant on Civil and Political Rights, 1966, 1976

International Covenant on Economic, Social, and Cultural Rights, 1966, 1976

UN World Conference on Human Rights: Vienna Declaration, 1993

RACIAL DISCRIMINATION

International Convention on the Elimination of all Forms of Racial Discrimination, 1965, 1969

International Convention on the Suppression and Punishment of the Crime of Apartheid, 1973, 1976

International Convention against Apartheid in Sports, 1985

RIGHTS OF WOMEN

Convention on the Political Rights of Women, 1952, 1954

Convention on the Nationality of Married Women, 1957, 1958

Convention on Consent to Marriage, Minimum Age for Marriage, and Registration of Marriages, 1962, 1964

Convention on the Elimination of All Forms of Discrimination against Women, 1979, 1981

SLAVERY AND RELATED MATTERS

Slavery Convention of 1926, as amended in 1953, 1953, 1955

Protocol Amending the 1926 Slavery Convention, 1953, 1955

Supplementary Convention on the Abolition of Slavery, the Slave Trade, and Institutions and Practices Similar to Slavery, 1956, 1957

Convention for the Suppression of the Traffic in Persons and the Exploitation of the Prostitution of Others, 1949, 1951

REFUGEES AND STATELESS PERSONS

Convention Relating to the Status of Refugees, 1951, 1954

Protocol Relating to the Status of Refugees, 1966, 1967

Convention Relating to the Status of Stateless Persons, 1954, 1960

Convention on the Reduction of Statelessness, 1949, 1951

OTHER

Convention on the Prevention and Punishment of the Crime of Genocide, 1948, 1951

Convention on the International Right of Correction, 1952, 1962

Convention on the Non-Applicability of Statutory Limitations to War Crimes and Crimes against Humanity, 1968, 1970

Convention against Torture and Other Cruel, Inhuman, or Degrading Treatment or Punishment, 1984

Convention on the Rights of the Child, 1989

Convention on the Protection of the Rights of all Migrant Workers and Members of Their Families, 1990

Draft Declaration on the Rights of Indigenous Peoples, 1992

---

legal thinking regarding the obligations of states toward their citizens. More than 60 other instruments were adopted by the General Assembly, including the two international covenants—on Civil and Political Rights and on Economic, Social, and Cultural Rights—collectively known as the International Bill of Rights. Despite considerable dissension, the UN-sponsored World Conference on Human Rights in Vienna (the first in a quarter-century) concluded with a commitment to the idea of universal human rights, and established the post of a UN High Commissioner for Human Rights. The commissioner will help coordinate the work of the 53-member Commission on Human Rights (a subsidiary body of ECOSOC).

In addition, many other bodies in the UN address human rights issues. These include the Committee of Experts of the Racial Discrimination Convention, the Commissioner on Women, the Commission on Discrimination against Women, the High Commissioner for Refugees, the High Commissioner for National Minorities, the International Labour Organization, and the Crime Prevention and Criminal Justice Division in Vienna.

HUMAN RIGHTS AND REGIONAL ORGANIZATIONS

In addition to efforts to promote human rights through the UN, regional IGOs have also made similar efforts, though with varying degrees of commitment and concrete results. In Europe, the foundation for the large body of human rights legislation and institutions is the 1953 European Convention for the Protection of Human Rights and Fundamental Freedoms, drafted to prevent a recurrence of the Nazi crimes against humanity. Two institutions in Europe have built on the principles of the European Convention. The **Council of Europe** maintains the European Court, which, among other cases, has heard charges against the British government alleging that the laws enacted to suppress the Irish Republican Army (IRA) violated the human rights provisions of the European Convention. The Organization for Security and Cooperation in Europe (OSCE—established in 1994 to continue the work of the CSCE) was built on the principles of the Helsinki Final Act of 1975, which provided for the protection of human rights by all signatory governments across Europe (including the USSR) and North America (including Canada and the United States). In 1990, the Charter of Paris committed members to observe the human rights provisions of the CSCE Final Act (and any subsequent amendment) and proclaimed human rights as a "legitimate concern" of all signatory governments. The OSCE mounts periodic fact-finding missions to investigate human rights concerns. In addition, much of the European Convention on Human Rights is reflected in the local laws of several EU member-states, the most recent being that of Britain.

The Organization of American States (OAS) Charter of 1948 has a Declaration of the Rights and Duties of Man, and in 1978 the American Convention on Human Rights (with an inter-American Court of Human Rights) came into force. In Africa, the 1981 African Charter on Human and People's Rights (the Banjul Charter) was adopted by the OAU. In Asia, the Association of Southeast Asian Nations (ASEAN) possesses a human rights commission, and the Asia-Pacific Economic Co-operation (APEC) forum possesses a Human Resources Development Working Group. However, while most of these regional human rights efforts are staffed by dedicated and hard-working personnel, and while many of them perform important roles and tasks on a variety of human rights issues, all of them suffer from the problems of limited financial and human resources and the intransigence (and sometimes the resistance) of member governments.

CONTEMPORARY HUMAN RIGHTS ISSUES

Before looking at specific examples of human rights issues, we should mention the difficulty involved in choosing such examples. As space constrains us from embarking on anything approaching a comprehensive survey, we have chosen several issues that have had a high public profile in the press in recent years. Although this selection is of course arbitrary, we hope we have covered issues of concern to most contemporary students and encourage you to look elsewhere for information on other pertinent topics, such as freedom of speech, the right to food and education, and gay and lesbian rights. In addition, we have not included a discussion of the refugee crisis (which many consider the most pressing and perhaps challenging human rights issue of our time) in this chapter because we deal with it at length in Chapter 11 on population and population movements. We deal with reproductive rights in that chapter as well.

ETHICS AND CONSTRAINTS ON WAR

We include a discussion of the ethical reasoning behind war efforts because war is, at heart, a human rights issue. If war is justified, then killing individual human beings to win one may be justified, and this justification is subject to all the dilemmas inherent in the universal/particular split mentioned above. Have we established a universal code of ethics that tells us when national leaders should declare war on other states, thus risking the lives of their own citizens as well as endangering those of others? The relationship between war and ethics has been a complex one.[17] Most of the world's ethical systems (heavily influenced by religion) deplore the act of killing as a general principle. And yet virtually all ethical systems establish sets of conditions under which such killing is justified or permissible. Ethicists, theologians, and philosophers have established the foundations for the ethical rejection of international violence and war, while at the same time their arguments have been used to support or justify international violence and wars.

There is also the sentiment that war is a distinct human activity in which ethics have no place. *Inter arma silent leges*: in times of war the law is silent. Despite this ethical debate, moral condemnation of the ethics of war tends to be *utilitarian* in nature; that is, the benefits and costs of any act must be judged in moral and ethical terms. As a result, war can be justified in certain cases, such as resisting and punishing aggression, although such wars must still be fought in accordance with certain ethical principles. The problem with utilitarian approaches is that states and groups will manipulate ethical principles to sanction the use of violence, at which point utilitarian ethics may erode into apologies or justifications for the very worst acts of war. *Absolutist* ethics, however, maintain that nothing can justify a certain act, which forms the foundation of the beliefs of pacifists, who maintain that international violence and war are never justified, no matter what the circumstances. The problem with absolutist ethics is that a refusal to use violence or go to war may permit the most horrible acts to take place; inaction itself can be morally bankrupt.

Those who advocate a "just war" doctrine attempt to constrain warfare by establishing the conditions under which it is just to enter into a war and by establishing what level of violence is considered acceptable in the prosecution of that war. This hinges on the distinction between **jus ad bellum** (the justice of a war) and **jus in bello** (the justness of the manner in which a war is fought). In his writing on *jus ad bellum*, Michael Walzer argues that only aggression can justify war, and that wars fought in self-defence are just.[18] The aggressor, once defeated, is to be punished, for punishment will deter future aggression. In society, we punish criminals to deter criminal violence; internationally, aggression is punished to prevent future aggression. From this basic principle are drawn the criteria by which just wars are measured:

- A just war is a war of last resort; all other means of resolution must be explored.
- A just war must be authorized by a legitimate authority, either the state or an international organization.

- A just war must be waged for a just cause, not for aggression or a desire for vengeance.

- A just war must have a good chance of successfully achieving a desirable outcome, and wars fought for good causes that are ultimately hopeless are not justifiable.

- A just war must end in a peace that is preferable to the situation before the outbreak of war.

Jus in bello maintains that a war may also be just or unjust in the manner in which it is fought. A war may have just origins, but it cannot be fought unjustly. Two measures determine the just conduct of a war:

1. A just war must be fought in ways consistent with the principle of proportionality. The potential positives deriving from military activity (such as a bombing campaign) must outweigh the negatives of destruction and death. Military methods must also be limited to the level of violence required to achieve the mission at hand, and any risk to civilians must be proportionate to the military value of the target.

2. A just war must be discriminate—combatants and noncombatants must be treated differently. Civilians cannot be the intentional targets of military operations, and civilian casualties must be minimized when this is possible.

Just war doctrine thus argues that wars should be limited and that the conduct of war is (and should be) governed by rules of behaviour and conduct. It is important to remember that in practice few wars meet all of these criteria, and so debates about the justness of a war generally revolve around examples of when certain principles might have been violated or to what extent a war can be considered just.

Nuclear weapons, and in particular nuclear deterrence, pose a challenge to ethical constraints on war. During the Cold War, most secular and religious ethicists agreed that nuclear weapons are by their very nature indiscriminate and disproportionate, and so nuclear war was generally regarded as inherently unjust. However, nuclear deterrence, the deployment of nuclear weapons in an effort to deter their use, was more controversial. Is it legitimate or just to threaten an action that would be immoral or unjust if it were carried out? The legitimacy of nuclear deterrence was justified on the grounds that it is necessary to avoid a greater evil (aggression by an enemy or subjugation of the free world at the hands of totalitarianism). However, many argued that the arms race invalidated the moral basis of deterrence as a temporary measure; nuclear deterrence was endangering peace, not contributing to it. So, for example, the United Methodist Council of Bishops argued that "the moral case for nuclear deterrence, even as an interim ethic, has been undermined by unrelenting arms escalation. Deterrence no longer serves, if it ever did, as a strategy that facilitates disarmament. Deterrence must no longer receive the churches' blessing."[19] Although the prominence of this issue has receded somewhat, the ethical status of nuclear weapons remains a subject of intense debate, particularly in the context of proliferation and post–Cold War efforts to ban nuclear weapons.

Critics of just war doctrine charge that since the judges of whether a war is just tend to be the very states, governments, or peoples engaged in the violence, a natural tendency exists to frame whatever one side does in good or just terms and to frame everything the opposition does in bad or unjust terms. Nevertheless, to reject just war doctrine outright would be to invite the separation of morality and war. Furthermore, opposition to war is generally founded on judgments of what is considered just. Opposition to the Vietnam War in the United States was largely built on the view of many that the war was unjust, both in terms of its conduct and its origins. Before the Gulf War, extensive efforts were made by governments to convince public opinion that the cause was just. To the extent that support for a war is a function of the extent to which it is just, the criterion of just war doctrine would seem to have some value.

GENOCIDE AND WAR CRIMES

Few words are as connotative as genocide. That the term refers to mass murder is common knowledge; less well known but equally important, it refers to mass murder perpetrated by a state against a specific group of people.[20] This definition is important not only because it recognizes a form of collective rights (freedom from discriminatory murder), but implies that the state—traditionally the guarantor of citizens' rights—can at times become the worst enemy of the people. The Convention on the Prevention and Punishment of the Crime of Genocide (1948) grew out of the recognition of three types of crimes during warfare: crimes against humanity, crimes against peace, and war crimes.

After World War II, trials were held in which the losers—Germany and Japan—were judged by the victors. At the most famous of these trials, the **war crimes trials** in Nuremberg in 1945–46 (the Tokyo war crimes trials are less well known), **crimes against humanity** were considered to be murder, extermination, enslavement, deportation, imprisonment, torture, rape, or persecutions on political, racial, or religious grounds committed against any civilian population (including one's own). The term was first introduced in the London Agreement of 8 August 1945 (issued by the United States, USSR, Great Britain, and France). **Crimes against peace** included planning, preparing, initiating, or waging a war of aggression and participating in a common plan or conspiracy for the accomplishment of war crimes. Nazi aggression was considered a crime against peace, though its chief architect, Adolf Hitler, had killed himself before the bitter end of the struggle in Berlin, thus escaping trial. **War crimes** were considered murder, ill treatment or deportation to slave labour, killing of hostages, and plunder and wanton destruction with no military necessity.

Obviously some measure of overlap exists in these crimes, but they are considered important legal precedents. Polish jurist Raphael Lemkin coined the word genocide during the implementation of Hitler's "final solution." Lemkin had a wide awareness of the atrocities being waged across Europe largely on racial grounds and affecting one ethnic group in particular, the European Jewish community. Thus, he introduced a new term "to denote an old practice in its modern development," derived from the Greek word for race or people, *genos*, and the Latin *caedere* (cide), which means to kill.[21] The Holocaust is still widely considered the ultimate example of genocide. Estimates vary, but at least six million Jews were killed, and many others, including Gypsies, prisoners of war, and German "undesirables," such as people with disabilities and homosexuals.[22] Due to the massive numbers involved, and the administrative efficiency of such systematic murder, the Holocaust remains a singular event in history, but many examples of genocide exist, such as the murder of millions of Armenians by the Ottoman Turks during World War I.

Two events in the 1990s have brought the term genocide and the mechanism of the war crimes trial back into public view. The first was the outbreak of war in the former

Yugoslavia (see discussion in Chapter 6) and the "ethnic cleansing" (see Profile 9.4), concentration camps, mass murders, and rape that characterized the conflict. The second was the outbreak of the carnage in Rwanda in the spring and summer of 1994. This

PROFILE 9.4

Ethnic Cleansing: A Question of Definition?

A term that gained much popularity during the war in the former Yugoslavia is "ethnic cleansing." The term is often used freely without consideration of its meaning. Professor John McGarry has been looking into this troubling question in considerable detail. In a recent paper presented to the Canadian Political Science Association, he writes, "The methods used in ethnic cleansing campaigns are both direct and indirect. Direct methods involve coercive physical expulsions where victim groups are forced onto various types of conveyance and transported or shipped into exile.... Direct expulsions may follow from a unilateral decision by the expelling authorities, as was the case in regions of Croatia and Bosnia in the early to mid-1990s, or they may result from bilateral 'exchange' agreements, where neighbouring states agree to swap their ethnic minorities for compatriots living in other countries. Such agreements were reached between Greece and Bulgaria and between Greece and Turkey just after the first world war, and between Hungary and Czechoslovakia just after the second world war.

"Indirect methods of ethnic cleansing are designed to induce emigration or flight.... Before they proceeded to direct physical expulsions after the Anschluss with Austria in 1938, Nazi authorities openly sought to induce emigration through an array of repressive legislation, particularly the Nuremberg laws of 1935. These laws were supplemented by pogroms such as that which occurred during Kristallnacht [9–10 November 1938: "The night of broken glass"] and they resulted in the migration of 150 000 of Germany's Jewish population.... Zionist settlers in early twentieth-century Palestine sought to induce the emigration of Palestinians by purchasing land from landlords and excluding Palestinian labour from it.... In the former Yugoslavia, a

panoply of different tactics have been employed to induce flight, including the murder or expulsion of elites, mass-killings, psychological warfare, rape, artillery onslaughts on urban areas, use of snipers, commando raids, and destruction of the physical infrastructure on which urban life depends (electricity, heating plants, kiosks selling newspapers, TV and radio transmitters, communal bakeries).

"What this means is that ethnic cleansing can take place even if there are no formal authorised steps to expel minorities. Public officials ... have obvious reasons for refraining from direct methods when indirect ones will do.... Whether expulsions are direct or indirect, perpetrators often claim that the expelled left 'voluntarily' or that they fled fighting rather than being expelled.... On the other hand, minorities which oppose policies unacceptable to them may claim that these policies are designed to force them out, even if such a claim seems implausible. The extent to which these rival assertions are true is often difficult to discover.... Assiduous research, however, can go some way towards destroying myths and establishing what actually happened. There are also two major questions which can be asked to help ascertain if expulsion has taken place: Was there an 'expulsion discourse' in the dominant community before the minority's flight/expulsion? And are the refugees allowed to return home after the fighting has stopped?

SOURCE: JOHN MCGARRY, "ETHNIC CLEANSING: FORCED EXPULSION AS A METHOD OF ETHNIC CONFLICT REGULATION," PAPER PRESENTED TO THE ANNUAL MEETING OF THE CANADIAN POLITICAL SCIENCE ASSOCIATION, BROCK UNIVERSITY, ST. CATHARINES, ON, 2 JUNE 1996, 2–3, 42. REPRINTED BY PERMISSION OF THE AUTHOR. SEE ALSO A. BELL-FIALKOFF, "A BRIEF HISTORY OF ETHNIC CLEANSING," FOREIGN AFFAIRS 72 (1993), 110–21; AND A.M. DE ZAYAS, A TERRIBLE REVENGE: THE ETHNIC CLEANSING OF THE EAST EUROPEAN GERMANS, 1944–1950 (NEW YORK: ST. MARTIN'S PRESS, 1994).

orchestrated campaign of genocide shocked the Western world with images of dismemberment, displacement, starvation, and bloated corpses floating down the Kagera River entering Uganda and Lake Victoria. As a result of just two months of intense violence, United Nations officials estimated the death toll of unarmed civilians in Rwanda at over 500 000.[23] State-employed Hutu militia men are thought responsible for much of the killing, which began after Hutu President Juvenal Habyarimana was killed in a rocket attack on his plane. Rwanda has been plagued with violence, before and after its achievement of independence from Belgian rule in 1962; indeed, it was a massacre of Tutsis in 1959 that originally created an exiled Tutsi community in Uganda, remnants of which returned to Rwanda in 1994 with the currently governing Rwanda Patriotic Front. But nothing in known African history has equalled the recent bloodbath in terms of its scope and, as chilling, the speed with which events took shape.[24] The repercussions of these events spread through the African Great Lakes region in 1996 and 1997, in the form of massive refugee flows and the fall of the long-time president of Zaire, Mobutu Sese Seko.

In 1993, the UN Security Council created the International Tribunal for Violations of International Humanitarian Law in the former Yugoslavia (ICTY) and in 1994 created the International Criminal Tribunal for Rwanda (ICTR). The objective of both of these bodies is to bring the perpetrators of war crimes to justice. The progress of the tribunals has been slowed by financial problems, the active opposition of those who fear exposure and retribution, and an inability to physically apprehend those charged. Nevertheless, the tribunals have been active and have secured convictions (see Profile 9.5).

In what many regard as a sad repetition of history, the ethnic cleansing campaigns as well as the campaigns of systematic rape that have added to the misery of the splintered state of Bosnia have been widely condemned. An international war crimes tribunal has been established to try some of those involved (from all sides) in committing war crimes, and the Dayton Peace Accords signed in 1995 called for the respective sides to the conflict to cooperate with the tribunal (this has been less than forthcoming, however). The tribunal is also supposed to help coordinate the genocide trials now occurring in Rwanda as well, where over 80 000 Hutus have been crammed into jails built for 13 000.

One might argue that the term genocide can be used to describe the manifestations of structural violence as well.[25] Murder, including state murder, takes many forms: the deliberate starvation of entire communities and the use of food as a weapon in general; the lack of clean water supplies in the slums of major cities; the destruction of East Timor by the Indonesian military, or of Tibet by the Chinese, or of parts of Indochina by the Americans, or of political opponents of various Soviet regimes; or the drainage of marshes in southern Iraq. All these cases involve mass death, inflicted with obvious intent. By such an expanded definition, war is genocide. Cultural destruction that has a physical component, commonly called *ethnocide*, is a type of genocide, as are the construction of large-scale dams that displace millions of people, the Himalayan deforestation that has caused floods, and other forms of *ecocide*.

The advent of the nuclear age takes us further toward an alternative and expanded perspective on genocide. It can be argued that nuclear deterrence, based on the threat of mass annihilation, was based on the threat of implementing the ultimate genocidal policy. Of course, one might argue that the threat of nuclear war introduced a new concept to the lexicon, that of **omnicide**. However, since nuclear strategy was predicated on the destruction of a specific enemy, omnicide was not contemplated (though it did not take a considerably bright individual to predict it would result). It is this element of

The Chief Prosecutor

Seeking evidence of atrocity. Former Chief UN War Crimes Prosecutor Louise Arbour, centre, links hands as she listens to Emin Shabnai, right, explain how he lost five members of his family, who were among 13 people killed in a nearby house, as they stand on the grave site in the southeastern Kosovo village of Vlastica. Arbour was on a two-day trip to Kosovo to inspect sites of suspected war crimes. (AP Photo/Visar Kryesiu)

In 1992 the Security Council of the UN created a Commission of Experts to investigate and report on "the evidence of grave breaches of the Geneva Conventions and other violations of humanitarian law in the territory of the former Yugoslavia" (Res. 780, 1992). After the taking of an interim report, which clearly indicated that mass murder had taken place, the Security Council established an international tribunal for the prosecution of individuals responsible (UN Doc. S/Res/808, 1993). In early March 1996 Canadian Justice Louise Arbour was appointed chief prosecutor for the International Criminal Tribunals for the former Yugoslavia and Rwanda. She was previously a member of the Court of Appeals for Ontario. The term of chief prosecutor runs four years and is renewable after that; Arbour left for the Supreme Court of Canada in September 1999 and was replaced by Carla Del Ponte of Switzerland. One would be hard-pressed to think of a more challenging position for anyone in the legal profession. Not only does the tribunal have an impact on the lives of those involved, it is expected to set a precedent, one that the United Nations may or may not be able to meet in the future. One of the most frustrating aspects of the entire procedure is that war criminals are not being brought forth to be tried. Arbour herself has expressed exasperation at the unwillingness of NATO forces to capture or seize war criminals. However, NATO states clearly feel that doing so would endanger not only the peace process but NATO troops as well. Though her position on the Supreme Court is a highly important one, Louise Arbour will be remembered internationally for her vital contribution to the development of international criminal law.

intention, or even incitement, that can lead to the labelling of the nuclear arms race as genocidal. If, as UN officials have recently insisted, we can consider the Rwandan slaughter an instance of genocide because, for example, a Hutu official had given a speech in 1992 in which he "explicitly called on Hutus to kill Tutsis and dump their bodies in the rivers,"[26] then what can we make of a system of national defence that called on thousands of soldiers to take part, if necessary, in the complete annihilation of hundreds of millions of civilians? Or does international, as opposed to civil, war justify such technique? While the Hague Convention[27] merely states that the "right of belligerents to adopt means of injuring the enemy is not unlimited," it is certainly difficult to argue that the use of hydrogen bombs would be limited in any real manner.[28]

FEMALE GENITAL MUTILATION

One of the more complex human rights issues involves the practice commonly called female genital mutilation, which is also often called female castration, circumcision, or genital cutting. It refers to the practice in many Islamic countries of removing or altering parts of the female genitalia at a certain age as a rite of passage. As you can tell, even the question of which name we assign to this practice is highly controversial, for each carries a strong connotation regarding the legitimacy of the act. Two forms of genital mutilation remain prevalent among certain segments of African women: *infibulation*, the severing of the clitoris and labia while the two sides of the vulva are sutured (tied together); and *clitoridectomy*, the partial or complete removal of the clitoris or the removal of both the clitoris and the labia minora. Either procedure comes under severe criticism from many quarters, while it is defended as a cultural priority in others. Several Western states, such as Canada and the United States, have made it illegal for doctors to perform the procedure. This law is not insignificant, since large numbers of recently arrived African women live in both states. No strong opposition to the practice exists at the international level, though UN agencies such as the World Health Organization generally oppose it.

The medical case against female genital mutilation is a very strong one: it can result in excessive bleeding, infection, and even death when improperly performed; and the after-effects include the risk of childbirth complications and of developing obstetric fistulae—holes between the vagina and the bladder, the rectum, or both. Beyond this, however, it represents to many women an act of oppression because it involves removing part or the entire clitoris and thus denies women a basic form of sexual pleasure.[29] Thus, the issue has become a rallying cry for the feminist movement in general. Other Islamic customs, such as *purdah*, have come under intense criticism by Western feminists in particular, but genital mutilation remains the most widely condemned. The international implications of this condemnation can be seen in Canadian refugee policy, which recently adopted the inclusion of women fleeing persecution based on discrimination against their sex as a valid reason to seek asylum. However, most women who undergo the procedure are quite young and are unable to leave their native countries on their own.

Howard French, in an article written for *The New York Times* that explores the issue within the context of the question of cultural relativity, writes about a small group of women in Sierra Leone who are working to ban the practice. One of the group's leaders argues that stopping the practice must be done in as culturally sensitive a manner as possible. For example, genital cutting was traditionally the culmination of a months-long retreat, known as *Bondo*, to mark the passage into womanhood, when older women would share their wisdom with the young. As the years passed, the retreat withered into an increasingly shorter ceremony and was finally represented almost solely by the cutting. Trying to restore the full value of *Bondo* might lead to a greater acceptance of the idea that the circumcision is part of a larger process and may eventually be discarded for hygienic reasons. For many, of course, this approach is far too timid. However, stronger appeals can lead to almost immediate condemnation by religious groups; for example, when a Freetown newspaper published a series of articles critical of the custom, "it became the target of a hostile protest movement by a group of women sworn to defend the rite."[30]

As an issue that forces us to examine the universal/relativist, as well as the gender-related discussions above, female genital mutilation, circumcision, or cutting will continue to outrage many communities. However, those who are campaigning to stop it are in a difficult bind: the harder they work, especially when they manage to publicly question or challenge the legitimacy of the practice, the more the pro-traditional forces will be inspired to resist change. Governments will have to seriously consider this matter when directing development assistance toward health programs abroad, and when determining their own operational definition of refugee status.

TORTURE

The word torture is derived from the Latin word *torquere*, which means "to twist." As a means to ensure the compliance of the people to a ruler's wishes, torture is as old as governance itself. When we mention torture, we are referring essentially to acts committed by governments, though it is clear that nongovernmental forces in wars and even terrorist and resistance groups resort to it as well. Torture is an old and tested technique that can be employed to get people to confess to just about anything, whether or not they have committed the act in question. Historians write of the unspeakable brutality inflicted by Ivan the Terrible and the Spanish Inquisition burnings, both during the 1500s. Torture was an accepted form of public punishment during the early development of the European penal systems, and it was employed as a device to facilitate slavery and colonialism.

The 1789 French Declaration of the Rights of Man forbade torture "forever"; the U.S. Bill of Rights forbade "cruel and unusual punishment." As incarceration in prisons began to replace torture as the chief means of punishing criminals (though many would equate imprisonment with torture as well), it became a less acceptable means of enforcing law and order. During World War II, however, torture came back into vogue— particularly as a device frequently employed by the Nazi Gestapo—and has remained so ever since. The Soviet state under Stalin was renowned for its ability to punish dissidents with psychological torture; but it would be difficult, if not impossible, to find a society where some form of state-sanctioned torture has not occurred at some time.

Torture continues to be employed as a means of extracting knowledge from political participants around the world. It involves the deliberate infliction of pain for this end, and it is often administered by people who have been specially trained as torturers. This distinction is important. The act takes place as a means to something else, be it the suppression of popular dissent or the acquisition of information deemed important by government bureaucrats. Though some individuals involved in its application are no doubt sadistic themselves, they are merely employees in a larger project. This definition helps us distinguish torture in the political sense from that in the criminal sense. Obviously, however, the very definition of torture leaves a great deal open to interpretation. Though the international community has signed many agreements[31] that make the use of torture by governments against the convention of international law, the principle of non-intervention requires that states avoid interfering in the domestic affairs of other states.[32] During the Cold War, many dictatorial or military regimes practised torture, and this was largely ignored for the sake of maintaining alliances (both Western and Eastern). Several Latin American regimes, for example, that in Chile in the 1970s, were infamous for their human rights abuses and torture techniques, and we should note the complicity of the superpowers themselves in many of these cases. In the post–Cold War era, when the old bloc system can no longer be used to justify the toleration of such excesses, some Western governments are moving toward making the receipt of donor assistance contingent on the pursuit of democratic institutions, which would (one might hope) by definition preclude torture.

Nongovernmental organizations such as Amnesty International and Helsinki Watch monitor human rights abuses, including the practice of torture. Several medical institutions have also been established around the world to deal exclusively with helping victims recover from the physical and psychological damage sustained by torture experiences. The very issue of torture is embarrassing to governments that have been involved in its application. Surely we can achieve a universal condemnation here! If we live in a world where torture is accepted, then we are truly in a dark age. What is needed is the vigilant casting of light on such practices where they exist, a subject we will return to below when we discuss the special role played by NGOs in the human rights issue-area.

CHILD LABOUR

Thanks for embarrassing me. Prime Minister John Chrétien shakes hands with child labour activist Craig Kielburger after their meeting in Islamabad, Pakistan. Chrétien's government is often criticized for its emphasis on trade rather than on human rights issues. (CP Picture Archive/Tom Hanson)

As mentioned earlier in this chapter, the international community has condemned slavery for some time, beginning with the major European powers at the Congress of Vienna in 1815. By 1880 more than 50 bilateral treaties on the subject were concluded. At the Brussels Conference in 1890, an anti-slavery act was signed and later ratified by 18 states. This act instituted a number of mutually agreed measures to suppress the slave trade both in Africa and on the high seas, including the right of high seas visits and searches, the confiscation of ships engaged in the trade, and the punishment of their masters and crew. Though slavery is still reported in some parts of the world, such as in the Sudan in Africa, it is generally considered to be outdated.

However, some would argue that the international community has done much less, and should do much more, to suppress another form of economic activity that many feel is the modern-day equivalent to slavery: the use of child labour. It is impossible to provide accurate estimates of the number of children working in the world because of disputes over what constitutes exploitative labour and because many countries refuse to participate in surveys. The United Nations Children's Fund (UNICEF) estimates that the number of children working in exploitative conditions in the world is in the hundreds of millions.[33]

In itself, child labour is nothing new; one might argue that it is only Western notions of adolescence that make the phenomenon recognizable. In other words, before we had anything resembling high school, teenagers simply worked in the fields and factories. It is, therefore, a Western notion of industrial progress that helps us see child labour as abhorrent. However, in some cases we might argue further that there is an absolute abhorrence involved, since it is not unusual to find children as young as 6 toiling away at repetitive and physically demanding jobs in Africa, Asia, and South America. The conditions of children at work around the world are appalling. In Malaysia, children work up to 17-hour days on rubber plantations enduring insect and snakebites. In Tanzania, they pick coffee, inhaling pesticides. In Portugal, children as young as 12 work on construction sites. In Morocco, they sew carpets for export. In the United States, children

Lost childhood. Malova, left, and her sister Bharti sit together on the road near Saundatti in southern India on their way to be initiated as *devadasis,* young girls dedicated to a Hindu goddess. In modern times the religious trappings have all but disappeared, and the devadasi system has become a network for recruiting child prostitutes in India. (AP Photo/Sherwin Crasto)

are exploited in sweatshops. Many children end up working to pay off their parents' debts, and their opportunities for education and an escape from the cycle of poverty are virtually nonexistent. Some young female workers (and many young male workers as well) must also often endure the additional burden of sexual abuse, including the sexually transmitted diseases associated with prostitution.

The products of child labour, many of which are in the textile industry and include clothing and rugs, often end up for sale in North America and Europe. In Bangladesh, textile and clothing exports to the United States have doubled since 1990. As a result of American pressure, some 30 000 children were removed from the country's textile industry between 1993 and 1995. However, one problem that Western governments will have an even harder time dealing with is that many of these children do not end up in school (indeed, many of them are from regions where school is a luxury for the privileged few) but end up on the street, engaging in begging and prostitution to make a living. As an *Economist* editorial suggested, corporate codes of conduct regarding child labour may not end it at all, but "merely shift it to shadier areas of the economy that are far harder to police."[34]

PROFILE 9.6   Canada and Child Labour

Prompted by child rights activists, Western governments are starting to speak loudly about the continued problem of child labour. Canada has joined this international chorus. In 1996, the Canadian government made a contribution of $700 000 to the ILO's International Program for the Elimination of Child Labour. In August 1996 in Stockholm, Minister of Foreign Affairs Lloyd Axworthy, Senator Pearson, and the Honourable Hedy Fry attended the World Congress against the Commercial Sexual Exploitation of Children, along with 700 representatives from 119 countries, more than 100 participants from other international organizations, 500 NGOs and youth delegates, and 500 media representatives. On 18 April 1996, Bill C-27 was tabled proposing amendments to the Criminal Code to allow for the prosecution of Canadian citizens and permanent residents who engage in commercial sexual activities with minors while abroad—a practice commonly known as "sex tourism."

SOURCE: LLOYD AXWORTHY, CANADIAN MINISTER OF FOREIGN AFFAIRS, ADDRESS BEFORE THE PARLIAMENTARY SUB-COMMITTEE ON SUSTAINABLE HUMAN DEVELOPMENT OF THE STANDING COMMITTEE ON FOREIGN AFFAIRS AND INTERNATIONAL TRADE, OTTAWA, 2 OCTOBER 1996.

Foreign investors are often criticized for exploiting local labour, and child labour is part of this as well. Levi Strauss, the jean company, provides schooling for child workers in its suppliers' plants in Bangladesh. This raises yet another ethical dilemma, since one can argue the company is merely reinforcing dependence on it and reaping profits in the process. However, without this schooling, what type of future would the children have?

The question of child labour poses one of the harshest challenges to the concept of universal human rights and the Canadian government's use of the term "human security." Although it may be possible for people in the West to look on child labour as an awful thing, that is because we can afford to. Generally, people in developing states do not force children to work because they derive pleasure from it (sadly, there are exceptions to this, both in the north and south); rather, they do so because they have to ensure the survival of a family. The economic conditions of the underprivileged seem to be worsening, not improving, as time moves on and markets become increasingly global (see Chapter 11). It is difficult to conceive of an end to child labour in light of this fact. Consider the remarks of a mother (a sweeper and latrine cleaner) from India:

> Nearly all our girls work as sweepers. Why should I waste my time and money on sending my daughter to school where she will learn nothing of use?... So why not put my girl to work so that she will learn something about our profession? My elder girl who is fifteen years old will be married soon. Her mother-in-law will put her to cleaning latrines somewhere. Too much schooling will only give girls big ideas, and then they will be beaten up by their husbands or abused by their in-laws.[35]

The split is pronounced between the north and south on the general issue of labour standards. The United States and some other Western countries have expressed a desire to use the World Trade Organization to fight child labour, unfair (i.e., too low) wages, "union-busting," and other practices that they argue may give other countries an unfair advantage in a world moving toward free trade. Southern politicians and economic representatives argue that this effort is really just the old protectionism in new clothing. The International Labour Organization, a UN Special Agency, has for years tried to implement a universal code of conduct regarding conditions of employment, but it is up against opposition in the south and north. Consumers everywhere can investigate the origin of their products and refuse to purchase those made with child labour, but without simultaneous advances in poverty eradication it is of limited use.

SELF-DETERMINATION

To give a more rounded assessment of the concept of collective rights, we turn now to a discussion of the principle of self-determination. Self-determination can be defined variously as the right of all peoples to choose their own government or the right of all peoples to independence and sovereign statehood. As we will see, this issue-area presents all sorts of headaches for national leaders, and cuts to the root of the problems inherent in maintaining a status-quo international system while attempting to institutionalize ethics on a global scale.

In 1996, the Nobel Peace Prize was awarded to Bishop Carlos Belo and Jose Ramos Horta, of East Timor. They had both worked to restore the right of self-determination to the people of East Timor, which has been occupied by Indonesia for more than two decades. This dedication shows how strong the ethic of self-determination remains today, even if it is still unrecognized in many parts of the world. Woodrow Wilson emphasized the right to self-determination in his famous "**Fourteen Points**" following World War I. It was, and still is in many parts of the world, seen as the principle that would guide the way out of colonial domination. States like the United States were born of revolution and war; states such as Canada found their way gradually, eventually achieving the self-determination necessary to become recognized (in the Canadian case, in the League of Nations) as a sovereign state. More recently, the dissolution of the Soviet empire can be seen also as the achievement of self-determination by the peoples of the former USSR and the former Warsaw Pact countries. Some of them, like the Czechs and Slovaks, decided to split even further. Others, such as the Chechens, have become military targets of Moscow instead. Recently, the East Timorese elected to establish full independence, finally ending years of brutal rule by Indonesia; after protracted and intense conflict, a UN-sponsored Australian peacekeeping team entered the country to try to maintain order despite the opposition of some elements of the Indonesian military (see Chapter 7). The situation remains volatile, as many East Timorese who fled to West Timor have not been allowed safe passageway home.

The concept of self-determination remains so difficult, however, because of the collective nature of the right. It begs the further question of just who has the right to self-determination (see Profile 9.7). In the Canadian case, two groups, First Nations peoples and Quebec separatists, argue that they should have the right to self-determination; some of them demand a sovereign state of their own. Even the seemingly monolithic United States has separatist movements emerging in idyllic Hawaii (see Profile 9.8), Puerto Rico, and Texas. The problem is much more acute in areas such as the former Yugoslavia, where pronouncements of sovereignty (and their recognition by the international community) have given rise to ethnic conflict and cleansing. One can argue that the right to self-determination, while acting as a vehicle toward freedom for colonized peoples in the past, invariably creates conflict within states.

PROFILE 9.7 **A Voice for the Unheeded?**

Arvol Lookinghorse, a leader of the North Dakota Sioux community called Lakota Nation, is searching for a way to gain international recognition for his culture and religion. He is not alone. In Hawaii, Mililani Trask is seeking a forum where the voice of an Indigenous nation calling itself *Ka Lahui Hawai'i* can be heard. In Taiwan, Tibet, Kosovo, the Chittagong Hills of Bangladesh, the Crimean Tatars, the Albanians in Greece, and the Ogoni of Nigeria, knocking fruitlessly on the doors of the United Nations and its agencies perennially frustrates people, asking for a hearing. "Even when the debate was specifically about their situations, there was no provision in the UN for these people to address the gathering," said Michael van Walt, who helped these groups come together in 1991 to create a forum for the unheard. He drew on his experience as a legal adviser to the Dalai Lama and to nationalist groups in the Baltic States before the collapse of the Soviet Union gave them back their independence. Ten years later, the Unrepresented Nations and Peoples Organization, or UNPO, has more than 50 members, from Abkhazia to Zanzibar; 4 supporting members that recently moved up to UN membership—Armenia, Estonia, Latvia, and Georgia; and 17 applicants. The organization supports only nonviolent campaigns and works to defuse tensions, not heighten them.

SOURCE: B. CROSSETTE, "A VOICE FOR THE UNHEEDED AT THE UN'S DOORS," *THE NEW YORK TIMES* (18 DECEMBER 1994).

Hawaiian Sovereignty?

We do not usually think of Hawaii as anything more than a popular and expensive tourist destination, but an independence movement there has gained strength over the years. Dozens of pro-sovereignty organizations have appeared, and in 1993 the state legislature passed several laws and resolutions acknowledging sovereignty as a long-term goal. An article in the *Boston Globe* explained the roots of the movement:

In 1920, 20 years after the islands were annexed as a territory and 39 years before statehood, the U.S. Congress passed legislation to which many historians trace the situation today. The Hawaiian Home Act carved out 203 500 of the island's 4.1 million acres—including some of the least productive and poorly situated land—for use by natives. Most of the remaining land was held by private interests or placed under state control, while the U.S. military signed 99-year leases, at $1 each, for several large, strategically located parcels of land. The Indigenous people, known in their language as *kanaka maoli* and defined as those with at least 50 percent Hawaiian blood, have since experienced many of the same difficulties many native peoples face: lower income, higher-than-average alcoholism rates and health problems, and resentment over their "colonization."

SOURCE: A. PERTMAN, "HAWAIIAN SOVEREIGNTY PUSH STEADILY GAINING SPEED," REPRINTED IN *THE GLOBE AND MAIL* (21 MARCH 1996), F5.

HUMAN RIGHTS AND THE SPECIAL ROLE OF NGOs

By now you are no doubt aware that one of the trickiest aspects of human rights work is that the perpetrators of crimes are so often the same people who or institutions that are supposed to uphold and enforce them—in other words, the state itself. For this reason, many people argue that it is short-sighted to trust governments, and that non-governmental organizations, without formal ties to governments, can do a better job of providing information about and evidence of human rights violations. For example, many NGOs have participated in the work of the War Crimes Commission of Experts in the former Yugoslavia, including Amnesty International, the International Committee of the Red Cross, Physicians for Human Rights, Médecins sans Frontières, Helsinki Watch, the International League for Human Rights, the Union for Peace and Humanitarian Aid to Bosnia and Herzegovina, the International Criminal Police Association, the National Alliance of Women's Organizations, and the International Centre for Criminal Law Reform in Vancouver.[36]

The most prominent NGO involved in the human rights issue-area is Amnesty International, which was started in London in 1961 as a campaign by several lawyers and writers. Peter Berenson drew attention to the campaign with an article in London's *Observer Weekend Review*, in which he suggested that the revulsion we often feel regarding human rights violations could be put to good use: "If these feelings of disgust all over the world could be united into common action, something effective could be done."[37] Amnesty now has more than one million members, subscribers, and donors in more than 150 countries, and it seeks to publicize the plight of people who are held as political prisoners around the world. Other groups, such as Americas Watch, Asia Watch, and Africa Watch, monitor human rights adherence by governments, including their foreign policy activities. Church groups are often involved as well, especially in Latin America. The International Committee of the Red Cross is also a prominent player in the human rights issue-area.

NGOs use a wide variety of strategies[38] to call attention to their efforts. They campaign in local settings, exhort members to participate in letter-writing campaigns to pressure public officials to reverse certain decisions, and occasionally participate in protests that result in media coverage as well. Information technology, discussed at greater length in Chapter 12, offers newfound opportunities also. In Thailand, people have referred to the "cellular phone revolution" in which students protesting against the government were joined by relatively affluent Thais with modern phones and fax machines. Protestors used mobile phones to keep in touch after an army crackdown in 1992.[39] During and after the infamous Tiananmen Square massacre of 1989, the Chinese government made a concerted effort to control the flow of information in and out of China. Police monitored incoming faxes, but students were able to use electronic mail on the Internet for some time before authorities detected this and began shutting down computers as well. Indeed, a quick Internet search under the phrase "human rights" will produce a bewildering variety of NGO-sponsored Websites and media reports.

PROFILE 9.9 A Human Rights Advocate: Aung San Suu Kyi

Nobel Laureate Aung San Suu Kyi addresses a crowd in Burma. (AP Photo/Richard Vogel)

Myanmar is small southeast Asian state, formerly known as Burma before a military coup in 1988. Today the State Law and Order Restoration Council, or SLORC, is known as one of the most oppressive governments on earth, severely curtailing freedom of expression and movement and accused of using the forced labour of its citizens. It has actively suppressed opposition with military means. In this context, Aung San Suu Kyi, daughter of Aung San, the founder of the Anti-Fascist People's League, has arisen as the key representative of a democratic voice. She has also been consigned to house arrest and had her movements curtailed. However, she was the winner of the Nobel Peace Prize in 1991, and her status as an international figure has restrained the SLORC from more violent methods of limiting her influence. Aung San Suu Kyi's father was killed in 1947, after leading the struggle for Burmese independence, and she lived in India with her mother and attended Oxford University in England in the late 1960s and 1970s before returning to Burma for the last open multiparty elections there in 1990. Her party won the elections but the SLORC refused to recognize the results. She has never left Burma since and refuses to cease her condemnation of the regime. Sadly, her husband, Michael Aris, died of prostrate cancer in London in March 1999, and she was unable to see him. He was denied entry to Burma, and she feared that if she were to go to him, she would not be allowed back in the country to resume her struggle. Thus are the hardships those committed to such demanding causes must endure.

SOURCE: THE DIGITAL FREEDOM NETWORK: IN THEIR OWN VOICE WEBSITE,
<WWW.DFN.ORG/VOICES?ASIA/BURMA/ASSSK.HTM>.

The increased participation of women in international affairs is obvious, especially if one looks at the proliferation of women's groups active in the transnational context.[40] Though many feminists argue that women have yet to influence the real citadels of power in a meaningful way, the UN has always paid some sort of attention to the gender question. In 1946, the 45-member Commission on the Status of Women was established to collect data on women's rights and make recommendations. It had an immediate impact as the Declaration of Human Rights was being drafted; the original text, borrowing ideas from the American Declaration of Independence, had begun, "All men are brothers … "; the Commission on the Status of Women objected to this sexist language and the draft was amended to read "All human beings are created free and equal in dignity and rights."[41] It was Eleanor Roosevelt, widow of American President Franklin Roosevelt, who played a key role in the writing and passing of the Declaration itself.

In the 1970s ECOSOC (the UN's Economic and Social Council) created the International Research and Training Institute for the Advancement of Women (INSTRAW). As well, the UN Fund for Women (UNIFEM), part of the UN Development Programme, was established in 1976 to provide direct support to women's projects. In 1979 the General Assembly passed the Convention on the Elimination of All Forms of Discrimination against Women (CEDAW), and 23 experts were appointed to oversee that convention's implementation. In 1985, the UN Division for the Advancement of Women was set up following the important outcome of a conference in Nairobi, Kenya, a document called *The Forward Looking Strategies for the Advancement of Women to the Year 2000*. The Fourth UN Conference on Women was held in Beijing in September 1995. The UN has an active Commission on the Status of Women, a 45-member intergovernmental body that meets annually in New York. It prepares reports for ECOSOC. On 8 March 1993, International Women's Day, the Commission on Human Rights adopted by consensus a resolution aimed at integrating the rights of women into UN human rights mechanisms; in December of that year, the UN adopted a Declaration on Violence against Women.

It is obvious that NGOs, including women's groups, will continue to develop their role in the human rights issue-area. They form part of an expanding and increasingly influential network. However, it is not realistic to assume that such organizations can battle the very real power of states that continue to grossly violate their citizens' rights; that takes concerted international efforts as well as change from within. The fall of apartheid in South Africa is a brilliant example of how that combination can succeed, but the continuation of poverty and violence there is indicative of the long road ahead.

THE QUESTION OF JUSTICE

Many of the issue-areas discussed above lend themselves to a discussion of preventive measures. Although it may be impossible to avoid child labour without eradicating poverty or to stop genital female mutilation without a radical change in cultural perspective, it can be argued that crimes against humanity, such as genocide and torture, can be avoided by pursuing what domestic legal experts and judges call the power of deterrence. In other words, if state and military leaders have reason to fear retribution, be it through domestic or international means, they may refrain from excessive atrocities. This was the initial idea behind the Nuremberg War Crimes Trials, discussed above, and it is one of the main justifications for the two international criminal courts described on page 287.

Both of the extant courts have received mixed reviews. The ICTY has more than 1000 staff members from more than 75 countries, and an annual budget of almost U.S.$96 million for the year 2000. It has indicted 94 individuals for various war crimes, including grave breaches of the 1949 Geneva Conventions, violations of the laws or customs of war, genocide, crimes against humanity, and sexual offences. Several individuals have been found guilty, but of course they have the right to appeal and have done so. Similarly, the ICTR has become a fairly major operation; more than 40 Rwandans have been arrested to stand trial, including the former prime minister as well as all senior military leaders and high-ranking government officials, several of whom have been convicted for genocide and crimes against humanity. While fairly widespread support for both courts exists, they face many problems regarding acquisition of both the indicted and evidence; they are often viewed as partial courts, where guilty verdicts are inevitable (and thus they are equated with Nuremberg, largely viewed as a "victor's court"). Maintaining adequate funding is an ongoing concern as well; these are but temporary institutions (though proceedings will no doubt drag on well into the latter half of this decade).

States and NGOs met in Rome in the summer of 1998 to hammer out a treaty to establish an International Criminal Court (ICC), based partly on the ICTY and ICTR experience but also as an effort to deter future acts of state genocide and torture. The resulting Rome Statute has yet to be ratified, as 60 **ratifications** are required for the treaty to enter into force (139 countries have signed the treaty, and 27 had ratified it by the end of 2000). Canada ratified the Rome Statute in July 2000, but several key states, including China and Russia, have refused to sign. The United States initially refused to sign, but did so in December 2000 (although the Senate is unlikely to ratify this decision). Should it be established, the court will focus on genocide, crimes against humanity, war crimes, and aggression (when an agreeable definition of the term is found).[42] Many disputes led to the adoption of the statute: the permanent members of the Security Council insisted the Council had ultimate control over the Court, while others wanted a strongly independent chief prosecutor's office. The Americans also insisted that sections on child soldiers be toned down, and wanted any reference to landmines, chemical, or nuclear weapons removed from the text. Even the clause about "following orders" as an insufficient defence was watered down. Though the American delegation basically got what it wanted, the initial reluctance to sign reflected U.S. wariness of possible consequences for U.S. soldiers serving abroad and concerns in Congress about ceding too much authority to the UN.

Proponents argue that such a court (though it will not have retrospective jurisdiction and can take action only if a national court has declined to do so) is long overdue. The claim that the ICTY and ICTR are inherently unfair suggests that greater level of impartiality is needed for a truly international criminal court, one that can try cases regardless of location. The ICC takes us beyond the capabilities of the ICJ, which can deal only with states and not individuals. In a significant step, the statute does recognize sexual offences as crimes against humanity, including forced pregnancy and sexual slavery. But until the other three permanent members of the Security Council sign on, the court will have limited impact on the ground; and, one might argue, it does little to overcome the concern that there are two sets of international law, one for the powerful and another for the rest. (Although France and the United Kingdom have signed on, they retain what is in effect a veto over the ICC's powers of prosecution action via their Security Council positions.)

Another means to achieve justice is unilateral action, and in this case the recent adventure starring General Augusto Pinochet of Chile provides a promising, but cau-

Justice at last? Relatives of dissidents who disappeared after being arrested under the former dictatorship of General Augusto Pinochet hold portraits of their loved ones as they celebrate outside the Supreme Court building in Santiago, Chile, 8 August 2000. The Supreme Court stripped Pinochet's immunity, clearing the way for the former dictator to be tried on human rights charges. (AP Photo/Eduardo Di Baia)

tionary, tale. Pinochet assumed control of Chile in a brutal coup in 1973 (the former leader, socialist Salvador Allende, was killed; thousands of opponents were jailed and tortured, many of them disappearing altogether during Pinochet's lengthy rule). Chileans rejected his bid to be installed as president-for-life in 1988, but for the plebiscite on this to take place, an agreement was reached that he would be retained as head of the army and that criminal charges would not be laid against members of his regime. While in London for back surgery in October 1998 he was arrested by British authorities, who planned to extradite him to Spain. The Spanish wanted to charge him with various crimes (in the end these were reduced to

the charge of torture) against Spanish nationals during his reign. The international community was quite divided over this issue since it is highly irregular to detain a former head of state who can claim diplomatic immunity. Eventually, British authorities (the Home Secretary), concerned with his failing health, decided he had the right to return to Chile, where he may face charges brought on by his own country. However his health seems to fail whenever such a prospect looms.

At any rate, this was an interesting development because it involved a former head of state. Other developments suggest such people will not be immune from prosecution in the future, with or without an ICC. A judicial investigation has been initiated in Senegal, at the request of a coalition of human rights groups, against the former President of Chad, Hissein Habré, for alleged crimes under international law, including torture, committed during his 1982 to 1990 rule. And Slobodan Milosevic, former president of the Federal Republic of Yugoslavia, is under an international indictment for crimes committed in the former Yugoslavia. However, it could be a chaotic situation if every head of state is brought to justice for crimes committed during his or her rule; few would be exempt, depending on one's definition of crimes. The difficult task of moving on—in Chile's case, difficult indeed, as thousands of relatives and friends of present-day Chileans suffered under Pinochet's iron-fisted rule, or in the case of Cambodia, where over a million citizens were murdered by the infamous **Khmer Rouge** in the late 1970s—remains.

Another path suggests that South Africa's Truth and Reconciliation Commission (TRC)[43] is a superior way to mend the pain of the past while bringing the negative into the open. This is a hard sell in many places, however, and it is dependent on the willingness of both past oppressors and victims (who may prefer to try to forget and move on) to expose themselves to the community at large. The Commission includes three committees. The Human Rights Violations Committee investigated human rights

Seeking truth and opening wounds. Of the Truth and Reconciliation process, chair of the TRC Anglican Archbishop Desmond Tutu wrote in the final report that people "risked opening wounds that were perhaps in the process of healing." (AP Photo/Sasa Kralj)

abuses that took place between 1960 and 1994, established the identity of and located the victims, and referred them to the Reparation and Rehabilitation Committee. A President's Fund, funded by Parliament and private contributions, was established to pay urgent interim reparation to victims in terms of the regulations prescribed by President Nelson Mandela. Finally, and most controversially, the Amnesty Committee considered applications for amnesty from those accused of human rights violations. Applicants could apply for amnesty for any act, omission, or offence associated with a political objective committed between 1 March 1960 and 6 December 1993 (the cutoff date was later extended to 11 May 1994). Archbishop Desmond Tutu chaired the Commission, lending his considerable moral weight to the proceedings. Between early 1996 and mid-1998, the commission heard more than 20 000 people give evidence.

This process was, no doubt, constructive for many. Although one might have a hard time equating appeals for amnesty with repentance, and most of the major administrators of apartheid never appeared before the commission (they do not believe they did anything wrong), it was a progressive step to air old animosities and, importantly, cases in which blacks had engaged in abuse were given equal footing. Even Mandela's own party, the ANC (African National Congress), tried to block the final Report's publication in 1998, concerned about allegations of ANC atrocities committed outside South Africa. At the same time, such a public step could unleash a swell of demands for compensation the state cannot possibly provide; and it might enflame an already volatile country. It was certainly a risk, though in South Africa's case it appears to have been worth it. Whether this could be a means used elsewhere, however, is uncertain. For example, it will be difficult for Indonesia to come to terms with the legacy of the Suharto dictatorship, even if he is forced to pay back some of the hundreds of millions he effectively stole from the country, since the old political machinery is still largely in place in Indonesia. Cambodia's promise to hold a similar truth committee has been criticized as too little, too late by many.

The call for justice and reconciliation will continue to ring out as long as gross human rights violations take place. Students of international relations will remain interested in how the international system responds to human rights violations, and how, in turn, these responses will shape the international human rights context.

CONCLUSIONS

The end of the Cold War has shaken the East–West foundation of the human rights discourse. Although the split between two competing conceptions of human rights (those that protect the individual and those that seek to protect the collective) remains a strong one, governments no longer have the Cold War to blame for ignoring gross rights violations. One might argue that the current debate centres on the legitimacy of a universal approach that seeks common ethical themes we can apply across the globe against a relativist conception of rights that argues each state has its own right to make its own domestic laws and apply them as they deem necessary. As we have seen, human rights as an issue-area covers a diverse range of topics, but they all point toward the difficulty of applying any sort of universal barometer of human well-being at the global level.

We also examined the important role played by NGOs and women in the evolution of an international human rights regime. While NGOs are still relatively powerless compared with the states they seek to monitor, they can publicize cases that may otherwise remain hidden from the international community. Likewise, while the feminist movement has not altered the fundamental discrepancy in power between men and women, women have made considerable progress in popularizing their causes in international forums such as the United Nations. What remains to be seen, however, is whether this progress can be sustained as the economic forces of globalization take precedence in government thinking. We discussed the two opposing policy responses to countries that clearly violate human rights. Though little concrete evidence exists that such states can be forced to change their ways in the short run, the experience of South Africa suggests a sustained drive by the international community—in this case, a sustained rejection of the legitimacy of the policy of apartheid—can make a difference.

We looked also at various efforts to affect post-atrocity justice, including international criminal tribunals and courts, unilateral prosecution, and truth and reconciliation commissions. We should note also, however, that many analysts and activists argue that real justice must involve economic factors as well: that the world is still divided between the very affluent, the middle classes, and the very poor, and that the international system encourages rather than presents an obstacle to this trend. Further, human rights are of little benefit without a survivable environment in which to enjoy them. We turn to the theme of environmental security in global politics in the next chapter, the beginning of the third, and final, section of this text.

Endnotes

1. *War and Change in World Politics* (Cambridge: Cambridge University Press, 1981), 224.
2. For J.P. Humphrey's obituary, see *The Globe and Mail* (16 March 1995), A20. Interestingly, Humphrey was not originally credited with writing the Declaration: "French human-rights activist Rene Cassin, who claimed authorship of the declaration, was honoured with a Nobel Peace Prize in 1968. Yet when researchers pored over Prof. Humphrey's papers at the McGill library [in Montreal], they discovered the original copy in his handwriting."
3. H. French, "Africa's Culture War: Old Customs, New Values," *The New York Times* (2 February 1997), E1.
4. E. Nadelmann, "Global Prohibition Regimes: the Evolution of Norms in International Society," *International Organization* 44 (4) (1990), 481–526, 481.
5. Note, however, that it can be argued that racist conceptions of universal morality delayed the spread of a universalized conception of human rights. Asbjorn Eide reminds us that "there was a long debate in Spanish theological and philosophical discourse on whether the Indians had a soul. This was also the period in which the theories of racism were gaining ground in Europe. From the simplest efforts at classification of human groups by Kant, Linneaus, and Buffon, to full-fledged racist ideologies like that of Gobineau (mid-1850s), these were obstacles to the evolution of universal human rights, as distinct from the Western 'natural rights' which for a long time was limited to the male Caucasian." See "Linking Human Rights and Development: Aspects of the Norwegian Debate," in I. Brecher, ed., *Human Rights, Development and Foreign Policy: Canadian Perspectives* (Halifax: Institute for Research on Public Policy, 1988), 5–30, 27n6.
6. R.J. Vincent, *Human Rights and International Relations* (Cambridge: Cambridge University Press, 1986).

7. See K. Tomasevski, ed., *The Right to Food: Guide through Applicable International Law* (Dordrecht: Martinus Nijhoff, 1987).

8. *Rethinking International Relations* (Vancouver: UBC Press, 1994), 167.

9. See R. Niebuhr's *Moral Man and Immoral Society* (New York: Scribner's, 1947); and T. Nardin, *Law, Morality, and the Relations of States* (Princeton: Princeton University Press, 1983).

10. Thus the title of Stanley Hoffmann's important book, *Duties Beyond Borders* (Syracuse: Syracuse University Press, 1981).

11. *The United Nations: A Concise Political Guide*, 3rd ed. (London: Macmillan, 1995), 87.

12. *Human Rights Watch World Report 1997* (New York: Human Rights Watch, 1996), xxi.

13. Ibid., xiii.

14. Ibid., xxvi.

15. World Conference on Human Rights, *Vienna Declaration and Programme of Action*, Part I, Par. 4.

16. Stephen P. Marks, "Social and Humanitarian Issues," in *A Global Agenda: Issues before the 51st General Assembly of the United Nations* (Lanham: Rowman and Littlefield, 1996), 173.

17. For an important early treatment of this subject, see Q. Wright, "The Outlawry of War and the Law of War," *American Journal of International Law* 47 (1953), 365–76.

18. Michael Walzer, *Just and Unjust Wars*, 2nd ed. (n.p.: Basic Books, 1992).

19. See United Methodist Council of Bishops, *In Defense of Creation: The Nuclear Crisis and a Just Peace* (Nashville, TN: Graded Press, 1986).

20. Article II of the Genocide Convention defines genocide as "any of the following acts committed with intent to destroy, in whole or in part, a national, ethnical, racial, or religious group, such as (a) Killing members of the group; (b) Causing serious bodily or mental harm to members of the group; (c) Deliberately inflicting on the group conditions of life calculated to bring about its physical destruction in whole or in part; (d) Imposing measures intended to prevent births within the group; (e) Forcibly transferring children of the group to another group." The last two are clearly related to the policies employed by the Nazi regime regarding forced sterilization and a program to transfer Aryan-looking children into Aryan families.

21. See his landmark *Axis Rule in Occupied Europe* (Washington, DC: Carnegie Endowment, 1944), 79.

22. R. Hilberg, *The Destruction of the European Jews* (New York: Holmes and Meier 1983); see also H. Fein, *Accounting for Genocide: National Response and Jewish Victimization during the Holocaust* (New York: Free Press, 1979).

23. A United Nations report by three African jurists concluded the killings were part of a larger plan aimed at exterminating the Tutsis; they also noted that "some reliable estimates put the number of victims at close to one million, but the world is unlikely ever to know the exact figure." *The Globe and Mail* (3 December 1994), A13.

24. Detailed accounts are still emerging. See, for example, A. Destexhe, "The Third Genocide," *Foreign Policy* 97 (Winter, 1994–95), 3–17; M. Leitenberg, "Rwanda, 1994: International Incompetence Produces Genocide," *Peacekeeping and International Relations* 23 (1994), 6–10; and H. Burkhalter, "The Question of Genocide: the Clinton Administration and Rwanda," *World Policy Journal* 11 (4) (1994/95), 44–54. The neighbouring state of Burundi has an equally distressing political past and may be on the verge of similar chaos.

25. See P.J. Stoett, "This Age of Genocide: Conceptual and Institutional Implications," *International Journal* 50 (3) (1995), 594–618.

26. *The Globe and Mail* (3 December 1994), A13.

27. Article 22 of the regulations annexed to The Hague Convention of 1907.

28. To quote two international legal experts: "In light of the multifarious effects of hydrogen-bombs, and particularly the area of devastation from 'fall-out' with its unpredictable genetic effects, it could not be said that a belligerent in resorting to thermo-nuclear weapons was adopting a means of injuring the enemy which was 'limited' in any sense of the word." N. Singh and E. McWhinney, *Nuclear Weapons and Contemporary International Law*, 2nd ed. (Dordrecht: Martinus Nijhoff, 1989), 115–6.

29. See A. Walker and P. Parmar, *Warrior Marks: Female Genital Mutilation and the Sexual Blinding of Women* (New York: Harcourt Brace, 1993).

30. French, "Africa's Culture War."

31. The most important of which are the *Universal Declaration of Human Rights* and the (unratified) Convention against Torture and Other Cruel, Inhuman or Degrading Treatment or Punishment.

32. Note also that if torture takes place during war, it is considered a crime against humanity.

33. *The State of the World's Children 1997*, United Nations Children's Fund (Oxford: Oxford University Press, 1997), 26.

34. "Child Labour: Consciences and Consequences," reprinted in *The Globe and Mail* (5 June 1995), A17.

35. Neera Burra, *Born to Work: Child Labour in India* (Delhi: Oxford University Press, 1995), 211.

36. As well, four Canadians participated in a team of 11 women lawyers, sponsored by the Dutch government, who went to the former Yugoslavia to interview victims of sexual assault and collect evidence of the related military tribunals.

37. P. Berenson, "The Forgotten Prisoners," *Observer Weekend Review* (28 May 1961), 21.

38. See, for example, V.P. Nanda, et al., eds., *Global Human Rights: Public Policies, Comparative Measures, and NGO Strategies* (Boulder, CO: Westview, 1981).

39. See P. Shenon, "Mobile Phones Primed, Affluent Thais Join Fray," *The New York Times* (20 May 1992), A10.

40. See S. Shreir, ed., *Women's Movements of the World: An International Directory and Reference Guide* (Essex: Longman, 1988).

41. Bailey and Daws, 90.

42. For text of the treaty, see the UN Website at <www.un.org/law/icc>. As of 17 July 2000, the following states had ratified: Belgium, Belize, Canada, Fiji, France, Ghana, Iceland, Italy, Norway, San Marino, Senegal, Tajikistan, Trinidad and Tobago, and Venezuela.

43. The commission has its own Website:

Suggested Readings

Andrews, J. *International Protection of Human Rights*. New York: Facts on File, 1987.

Arendt, H. *Eichmann in Jerusalem: A Report of the Banality of Evil*. New York: Viking, 1963.

Bauer, J., and D. Bell, eds. *The East Asian Challenge for Human Rights.* Cambridge: Cambridge University Press, 1999.

Brecher, I., ed. *Human Rights, Development and Foreign Policy: Canadian Perspectives*. Halifax: Institute for Research on Public Policy, 1989.

Charlesworth, H., C. Chinkin, and S. Wright. "Feminist Approaches to International Law." *American Journal of International Law* 85 (October–November, 1991), 613–45.

Donnelly, J., and R. Howard, eds. *International Handbook of Human Rights*. New York: Greenwood, 1987.

Falk, R., S. Kim, and S. Mendlovitz, eds. *The United Nations and a Just World Order*. Boulder, CO: Westview, 1991.

Forsythe, D. *The Internationalization of Human Rights*. Lexington: D.C. Heath, 1991.

Hannum, H. *Autonomy, Sovereignty, and Self-Determination: The Accommodation of Conflicting Rights*. Philadelphia: University of Pennsylvania Press, 1990.

Horowitz, I. *Genocide: State Power and Mass Murder*. New Brunswick, NJ: Transaction Books, 1976.

Howard, R., and J. Donnelly. "Human Dignity, Human Rights, and Political Regimes." *American Political Science Review* 80 (3) (1986), 801–18.

James, A. *Sovereign Statehood: The Basis of International Society*. London: Allen and Unwin, 1986.

Johnson, J.T. *Can Modern War Be Just?* New Haven: Yale University Press, 1984.

Kratochwil, F. *Rules, Norms, and Decisions: On the Conditions of Practical and Legal Reasoning in International Relations and Domestic Affairs*. New York: Cambridge University Press, 1989.

Kuper, L. *Genocide*. New Haven: Yale University Press, 1981.

Lemkin, R. *Axis Rule in Occupied Europe*. Washington: Carnegie Endowment, 1944.

Matas, D. "Prosecution in Canada for Crimes against Humanity." *New York Law School Journal of International and Comparative Law* 11 (1991), 347–55.

Matthews, R.O., and C. Pratt. *Human Rights in Canadian Foreign Policy*. Montreal/Kingston: McGill–Queen's University Press, 1988.

McCormick, J., and N. Mitchell. "Human Rights and Foreign Assistance: An Update." *Social Science Quarterly* 70 (1989), 969–79.

Meron, T. "The Case for War Crimes Trials in Yugoslavia." *Foreign Affairs* 72 (3) (1993), 122–35.

Orend, B. *War and International Justice: A Kantian Perspective*. Waterloo: Wilfred Laurier University Press, 2000.

Robertson, A. *Human Rights in the World: An Introduction to the International Protection of Human Rights*. New York: St. Martin's Press, 1982.

Rosas, A. "State Sovereignty and Human Rights: Toward a Global Constitutional Project." *Political Studies* 43 (1995), 61–78.

Rothberg, R., and D. Thompson, *Truth versus Justice: The Morality of Truth Commissions* (Princeton: Princeton University Press, 2000).

Schmitz, G., and V. Berry. *Human Rights: Canadian Policy Toward Developing Countries*. Ottawa: North–South Institute, 1988.

Scott, C. "Indigenous Self-Determination and Decolonization of the International Imagination: A Plea." *Human Rights Quarterly* 18 (4) (1996).

Sheperd, O.W., and V.P. Nanda, eds. *Human Rights and Third World Development*. Westport: Greenwood, 1985.

Shue, H. *Basic Rights: Subsistence, Affluence, and U.S. Foreign Policy*. Princeton: Princeton University Press, 1980.

Steiner, H., and P. Alston. *International Human Rights in Context: Law, Politics, Morals*. Oxford: Oxford University Press, 1996.

Sullivan, M. *Measuring Global Values*. New York: Greenwood, 1991.

Tomasevski, K. *Development Aid and Human Rights*. London: Printer, 1988.

United States, Department of State. *Country Reports on Human Rights Practices*. Washington: various years.

Van den Berghe, P., ed. *State Violence and Ethnicity*. Niwot: The University Press of Colorado, 1990.

Weiss, T., and L. Minear. "Do International Ethics Matter?: Humanitarian Politics and the Sudan." *Ethics and International Affairs* 5 (1991), 197–214.

Suggested Websites

Research Guide to Human Rights
<www.spfo.unibo.it/spolfo/HRLAW.htm>

Human Rights Watch

International Centre for Human Rights and Democratic Development
<www.ichrdd.ca>

Montreal Institute for Genocide and Human Rights Studies (MIGS)
<www.migs.org>

Women, Law, and Development International
    <www.wld.org>

International Law Treaties
    <mprofaca.cro.net/lawsource.html>

Notre Dame Law School

Human Rights Internet
    <www.hri.ca/welcome.cfm>

The Carter Center
    <www.emory.edu/CARTER_CENTER>

Human Rights Web
    <www.hrweb.org>

PART THREE

Directions

In this final section, we will look forward. All the themes discussed here are familiar ones, including environmental degradation and conflict, population growth, migration, dislocation, human rights issues, the impact of technology on global politics, and the possible causes of violent conflict. However, in this section we explore what the future may hold for these themes and elaborate on the scholarly and policy challenges they pose in the twenty-first century. Although the prognostications can at times be bleak, the fact that the human race has survived so far offers some comfort; and, as we discussed in preceding chapters, the chances of cooperation and positive movement are always as high as conflict and despair. However, as usual, sharply contrasting perspectives exist on just what progress in global politics entails and what directions we will (or should) take in the future. We end with a brief chapter that revisits the central questions raised in Chapter 1.

CHAPTER 10

Global Ecopolitics

The whole point of being a doomsayer is to agitate the world into proving you wrong or into doing something about it if you are right.

—Les Kaufman[1]

INTRODUCTION: CAN WE SUSTAIN OURSELVES?

The earth has endured centuries of human population growth, resource extraction, landscape-ravaging wars, and industrial pollution. Can it continue to do so without irreversibly harmful ecological consequences? Can we manage, despite all the divisions and conflicts that have plagued global politics and the international political economy, to combine efforts to prevent the great biospheric collapse feared by many environmentalists? Or have we moved into this millennium under such a dark ecological shadow that there is no way toward sunlight? In other words, is our habitat now beyond preservation? The most common cause of species extinction is not hunting, poaching, or the direct consumption of toxic chemicals. Species extinction is caused primarily by the destruction of habitat. Viewed from a distance, one might conclude that human society has been committing collective suicide over the past century with an unrelenting assault on its own habitat, the **biosphere**. Though some believe in the almost unlimited nature of the earth's resources and the innate ability of humankind to adapt, most see the current situation as reflective of human folly. The symptoms range from the global, such as the depletion of the ozone layer, to the local, such as the erosion of soil that has been overworked in small African communities and the collapse of the cod fishery off Newfoundland.

Though Western environmentalists have long been lamenting the effects of industrial excess in North America, Europe, and Japan, it has become quite clear that environmental problems in Eastern Europe and the former Soviet Union are approaching catastrophic levels. This fact is reflected by the serious health threats faced by citizens of the industrialized former Soviet bloc, a legacy of centralized economic industrialization.[2] In a dubious tradeoff, industrialization in Eastern Europe and the former Soviet Union took place at the expense of that region's environmental security. The implications of this pollution are international: the resultant carbon emissions contribute to both global warming and regional deforestation in Western Europe (of course, the latter region contributes generously to both problems as well). Another immediate danger is the decrepit state of outdated nuclear reactors in these Eastern countries. It is obvious that great technical assistance is needed if further damage is to be mitigated, assistance that will come mainly from a frightened Western Europe.

We use the problems faced in Eastern Europe and the former Soviet Union as only one example of similar dilemmas encountered throughout the global system. Asia, with its unprecedented economic growth, is putting new and disturbing strains on the environment. Disputes over resources remain explosive (see Chapter 13). African farmers suffer from drought and desertification. North American activists are willing to go to jail to protect old growth forests, which are often cut down for short-term profit. The Amazon continues to burn, and rain forest and valuable **biodiversity** are lost to the causes of population pressure and foreign debt. The world has well over six billion people today, and the world's population is expected to reach eight billion by 2025.

What impact will these environmental issues have on the conduct of global politics? A realist, state-centred perspective would argue that states will continue to find the environment a great source of conflict and that the environmental problems discussed below may alter power relations but will not alter the nature of world politics. For example, China and India have sudden, and impressive, bargaining power in a world scared of the global environmental impact of mass industrialization in either of those highly populated states. The old game of power maximization will continue. Liberals will tend to believe that where a problem exists so too can cooperation and that a complex web of international institutions or regimes is slowly evolving that will give us the capacity to deal with environmental problems while the world economy continues to grow. Marxists tend to see deforestation and soil degradation as part of the process of capitalist exploitation in the periphery. The environmental crisis is seen as the most telling evidence that we have taken the wrong collective path; an ecofeminist perspective would certainly concur.

Beyond these differing perspectives, another debate rages over whether it is proper to view environmental problems from the vantage point of international security problems. Of course, national security must include concern for the environment, but there is considerable reluctance by both military strategists and environmental activists to include each other in their circles. Daniel Deudney (himself a critic of linking security and environment) writes that if "the Pentagon had been put in charge of negotiating an ozone-layer protocol, we might still be stockpiling chlorofluorocarbons as a bargaining chip."[3] However, since war has a tremendous impact on the environment and conflict over resources can itself be a cause of war, environmental security will be a part of the study of global politics for some time to come.[4] In this chapter, we introduce some prominent environmental problems and the ecopolitics that surround them. (We address the more specific issue of overpopulation and the movement of peoples in Chapter 11.) As we will see, environmental problems are a source of both convergence and divergence in global politics. On the one hand, states, NGOs, and individuals have cooperated in response to environmental concerns. On the other hand, environmental degradation affects some regions more than others, and states are increasingly clashing over access to resources. We begin our discussion on a scale that is so small that it is often forgotten: the world of microbes and viruses.

THE MICROENVIRONMENT: THE SPREAD OF INFECTIOUS DISEASE

We begin with reference not to trees, oceans, whales, or mountains but to very small bugs known as microorganisms. Human security has always faced its most prevalent and enduring threat from microorganisms. The bubonic plague, or Black Death, first struck Europe in 1348 and wiped out entire towns and villages. The plague bacillus was carried by the rats that infested the overcrowded, unsanitary towns. Between the fatalities caused by the plague and those caused by the Hundred Years' War between England and France (1337–1453), the European population did not recover until the 1500s. After the expansion of European civilization into colonized areas such as the Americas, Indigenous peoples around the world suffered from the sudden introduction of foreign microbes. The historical record aside, some experts argue that the problem is getting worse, not better, despite the advancement of science. The rapid spread of the AIDS virus (see Profile 10.1) and highly publicized events such as the outbreak of the Ebola

AIDS

Though it is impossible to give an accurate figure, an estimated 32 to 34 million people are living with HIV/AIDS today. **AIDS** stands for **acquired immune deficiency syndrome** and it is caused by HIV, the *human immunodeficiency virus*. HIV and AIDS have no known cure or vaccine.

Our immune systems fight off infections, and AIDS destroys this capacity. Thus, people with AIDS are highly susceptible to other sicknesses as well, such as the common cold. HIV-positive people will have antibodies to HIV, which can be discovered with a simple blood test, though the antibodies can take six weeks to a year to show up. A positive HIV test result does not mean someone has AIDS or will necessarily develop it in the future, however.

The most common prescription for avoiding HIV is to refrain from engaging in unprotected sex and from sharing intravenous needles. Intrauterine devices (IUDs), oral contraceptives, male and female sterilization, and natural family planning methods such as rhythm and withdrawal provide no protection against sexually transmitted diseases (STDs).

AIDS is reaching epidemic proportions in areas of Africa (where two-thirds of all AIDS/HIV victims live) and Asia (where the sex industry has proliferated in the past few decades). In Africa, more than 13 million people have already died of AIDS, 2 million in 1999 alone. In the countries most affected, such as Zimbabwe, Botswana, Namibia, Zambia, and Swaziland, 18 to 26 percent of the population has contacted AIDS/HIV. In addition to the suffering AIDS has brought to Africa, the economies of some countries are already being affected. By 2015, the economies of countries such as Zambia and Zimbabwe are expected to fall by 25 percent.

The politics of AIDS are controversial. Conspiracy theories on the origins of AIDS abound. If a vaccine for AIDS is discovered by a northern multinational pharmaceutical firm, will this knowledge be shared with the south and at what price? At a recent international symposium on the epidemic, South African President Thabo Mbeki caused a stir when he suggested that in Africa, poverty was most to blame for the present situation. He read extensively from a World Health Organization report that mentioned "malaria, hepatitis B, HIV-AIDS and other diseases … micronutrient malnutrition, iodine and vitamin-A deficiency … syphilis, gonorrhea, genital herpes and other sexually transmitted diseases as well as teenage pregnancies … cholera, respiratory infections, anemia, bilharzia, river blindness, guinea worms and other illnesses with complicated Latin names." His point—that Africa is confronted with an immense health crisis of which AIDS is but part of the puzzle—should not be ignored. Critics charge Mbeki is trying to shift the focus away from his government's reluctance to seriously fund anti-AIDS education and treatment. An international effort is underway to fight AIDS in Africa and in other parts of the world. The World Bank has pledged U.S.$500 million in aid, but experts argue that more than $3 billion will be required to address the issue. In 2000, Canada raised its anti-AIDS funding to Africa to C$60 million.

SOURCES: A. PICARD, "POVERTY WORSE THAN AIDS, MBEKI SAYS," *THE GLOBE AND MAIL*, 10 JULY 2000, A4; TOM FENNELL AND LAUREN MCNABB, " 'THE SLIM DISEASE' " *MACLEAN'S* (10 JULY 2000), 32–4.

virus in Zaire in 1995 have alerted various authors to the importance of infectious disease.[5] The spread of hoof-and-mouth disease in Europe in 2001 is a frightening agricultual example.

Dennis Pirages argues four major transformations are underway that "seem to be strengthening the microbes' hands."[6] Rapid population growth and urbanization lead to situations conducive to the rapid spread of disease, especially in the teeming megacities of the south, where adequate health care is seemingly beyond reach for the majority of citizens, and in areas where overpopulation has led to mass movements. Many of the refugees fleeing violence in Rwanda in 1994 died from cholera in the resulting overcrowded refugee camps. Population pressure is forcing people to inhabit previously wild areas, and this has had two consequences: new inhabitants are bringing new diseases into these areas, harming the Indigenous people and wildlife; and the newcomers themselves are exposed to new diseases, which are then spread into the general population.

Second, Pirages writes of changes in human behaviour, such as the so-called sexual revolution of the late 1960s and 1970s in the United States and the global spread in the use of drugs, which facilitated the spread of disease. Cramped prison conditions, which help spread tuberculosis, result from policy shifts and increases in crime often linked to poverty. Third, the environment itself is changing in a way that makes it more difficult to control the spread of disease. Sudden or gradual climate change may give a temporary advantage to resident microbes. For example, Pirages suggests that a fatal outbreak of hanta virus in the desert southwest of the United States may have been triggered by sudden rainstorms that increased population growth among the virus-carrying rodents. In the summer of 2000, the West Nile virus surfaced again in mosquitoes in New York, prompting a massive pesticide spray in the city.

Finally, Pirages refers to technological innovations that have increased, rather than decreased, the ability of microbes to travel, such as the invention of the airplane: "Aircraft cabins ... are an excellent place for a rendezvous with cosmopolitan worldtravelling viruses and bacteria."[7] A virus that causes hemorrhagic fever is said to have found its way to Baltimore from Seoul by way of wharf rats that made the journey in cargo ships.[8] These viruses seem to understand what many global politics analysts do as well: a truly interdependent and interconnected world economy presents as much opportunity as it does danger.

THE MACROENVIRONMENT: PROBLEMS OF THE COMMONS

We now move from the very small to the very big. Global environmental problems are often characterized as problems of the commons. According to Wilfred Beckerman, this "refers to situations in which nobody can be excluded from the use of an asset—such as common grazing land, or fishing grounds, or the atmosphere [but] one person's use of the asset reduces the amount available to other potential users ... unrestricted use of the asset can easily lead to over-use, so that only if some voluntary or enforcement mechanism is introduced can the supply be matched to the demand."[9] One example of an area of the commons is the moon. Clearly, the moon does not belong to a single state, single individual, or group of people. The Americans may have landed there first, and they may even have hit a golf ball there, but no state can lay claim to territorial ownership. A treaty does exist that covers the moon, the Treaty on Principles Governing the Activities of States in the Exploration and Use of Outer Space, Including the Moon and Other Celestial Bodies signed in 1967, and signatories have promised not to indulge in military activities there.

Most resources are rather more accessible than the moon. The essential economic problem, then, is that everyone has an incentive to conserve the commons together but an incentive individually to exploit them. This becomes a political problem when cooperation is necessary to balance these counterincentives. Or, as Stephen Krasner puts it, what he terms liberal cooperation theory holds that "the basic challenge for states is to overcome market failure, the situation in which individual rational self-interested policies produce outcomes that leave each state worse off than it might otherwise have been."[10] The added dimension of environmental concern demands we move beyond asking simply how states can share resources to asking how they can simultaneously conserve or preserve them.

Solutions to typical problems of the commons are rather elusive. Many have argued that the privatization of land or other resources will increase the sense of environmental responsibility of those entitled to it. This proposition is, of course, debatable within national confines but is even less clear when it comes to the international arena, where privatization is akin to territorialization. The 1982 Law of the Sea Convention (LOSC) designated new 200-nautical-mile (approximately 370 kilometres) **exclusive economic zones** in which coastal states would have not only resource rights but also inherent environmental responsibilities. The hope was that, inside the 200-mile (370-kilometre) limit, increased coastal authority by individual states would lead to better management. Instead, "coastal countries such as Canada and the United States displaced overseas fleets from Europe and Japan with new programs and subsidies to build up their domestic fleets [then] scooped up cod and salmon on both coasts with alarming speed, and disastrous results."[11]

Further, areas of the commons, such as the open seas and atmosphere, are not amenable to the expansion of national territories. The United Nations Convention on the Law of the Sea took nine years to negotiate (1973 to 1982).[12] One hundred fifty-nine states and other entities signed the Convention. In November 1993, Guyana became the sixtieth state to deposit its instrument of ratification with the United Nations, and the Law of the Sea officially became effective in November 1994. However, the United States was unwilling to sign the treaty owing to what the Reagan administration perceived as its anti–free enterprise character. The Law of the Sea established an International Seabed Authority that would facilitate the sharing of deep-sea resources, particularly any derived from deep-sea mining, among all states. This distribution contradicted the market-based ideology prevalent in the United States. As a result, many other Western states, Canada included, have signed the Law of the Sea but have not ratified it.

One of the central ecopolitical questions that concerns scholars is how dealing with the commons affects national sovereignty, the cardinal principle of the Charter of the UN. Does the rise of transboundary pollution problems justify infringements on the sovereignty of states, as it does in cases of extreme international security concerns and genocide? Does the need to regulate the commons, or at least to avoid the tragedy of the commons, demand a pooling of sovereignty in certain issue-areas? Has the creation of institutions designed to mitigate environmental damage threatened the long-term future of the nation-state as predicted by the older functionalist school (see Chapter 5)? It is quite clear, in the legal sense, that the principle of sovereignty remains sacrosanct. In 1962, the UN General Assembly adopted a resolution that referred to the "inalienable right" of all states to freely "dispose of their natural wealth and resources."[13] Malaysia made particular reference to this precept during the forestry negotiations leading up to the UN Conference on Environment and Development (UNCED) in 1992, and this is a common north–south sticking point as southern elites claim that any global environmental agenda infringes on their sovereignty. Principle Two of the Rio Declaration (from UNCED) asserts that "states have … the sovereign right to exploit their own resources pursuant to their own environmental and developmental policies."

There is also the question of cost distribution or of who should pay for international efforts to save the commons. With issues such as ozone-layer depletion and global warming, an obvious and potentially decisive north–south split exists. The agreements that are reached today, such as the Montreal Protocol to the ozone-layer agreement and the Convention on Global Warming, may have set important precedents regarding cost sharing and the question of sovereignty. R.E. Benedick concludes: "As a consequence of the ozone issue, the richer nations for the first time acknowledged a responsibility to help developing countries to implement needed environmental policies without sacrificing aspirations for improved standards of living."[14] Similar debate clouded the negotiations for a Biodiversity Treaty: "even before the negotiation began, there was a history of disagreement about the allocation of the economic benefits and technological advances derived from Southern biodiversity."[15] Principle Seven of the Rio Declaration makes note of the "different contributions to global degradation" and resulting "common but differentiated responsibilities." The basic argument is that since the south has suffered from the northern states' indulgence in industrialism and, in an even more direct manner, colonialism, future resource-sharing agreements must reflect this precondition.

One of the more fascinating cases of the management of the commons is that of Antarctica.

ANTARCTICA

Antarctica is an important place. To naturalists, this fact is obvious. Antarctica is not, contrary to popular perception, barren of life; its waters contain a diversified ecosystem and what is known as the "fastest ocean food chain." It is in essence the world's largest wildlife sanctuary, home to 100 million birds and six species of seals. Fifteen species of whales, toothed and baleen, summer there. The global scientific value of this place, where the lowest thermometer reading ever was recorded (–89.6°C, at the USSR's Vostok Research Station in East Antarctica), is increasing. Antarctica offers a "window on the sky," especially regarding the growing ozone hole first discovered there in 1985, and a "window on the past." As Lee Kimball writes, "exhuming trapped air in ice cores at depths of more than 2000 metres, halfway down to bedrock, scientists have found a priceless record of some 150 000 years of atmospheric and climate change."[16] Perhaps most important, Antarctica's environment provides us with a planetary early warning system regarding global warming.

The Antarctic Treaty was signed in 1959, and this was in many ways a landmark event. Though several nations have laid (and maintain) claim to specific parts of Antarctica, they all agreed to adhere to a common management scheme. Both the Cold War superpowers signed, and Antarctica became the world's first nuclear-free zone; it has maintained its nonmilitary status since. The treaty provides on-site verification measures on research conducted in the region, and it opened the door for nonclaimant nations to establish research facilities on the continent. Canada participates in the **Antarctic Treaty System (ATS)** as a nonconsultative party (i.e., it has no voting rights in ATS meetings but can attend as an observer). The ATS involves other management regimes, such as the **Convention on the Conservation of Antarctic Marine Living**

Resources (CCAMLR), well known for its ecosystem approach to resource management. The Antarctic marine ecosystem is protected as a whole, not according to strictly delineated territorial lines. Living resources can be harvested only if ecological relationships are unchanged, if ecological changes are potentially reversible within two to three decades, and if harvesting does not interfere with the recovery of depleted populations. As Kimball laments, however, the burden of proof that excessive damage *is* being done lies with CCAMLR's Scientific Committee. (Kimball and others feel that the harvesters should have to prove that excessive damage will *not* be done.)

Other than the treaty and CCAMLR, the third pillar of the ATS was to be the Convention on the Regulation of Antarctic Mineral Resource Activities (CRAMRA). This agreement was highly controversial since it articulated the possibility of managed mining for exploration and, eventually, exploitation in Antarctica. Many parties objected to the very idea, claiming even limited mining would destroy the fragile Antarctic ecosystem. However, CRAMRA was never established since Australia and France (both consultative parties) refused to sign. On 4 October 1991, in Madrid, Spain, the Protocol on Environmental Protection to the Antarctic Treaty was signed. Antarctica was designated a natural reserve, all mineral resources activities were prohibited for at least 50 years, and regulations were extended to cover tourist activity. A group of annexes provide for a comprehensive protection regime, including an environmental impact assessment guideline, the conservation of fauna and flora, waste disposal and management, and the prevention of marine pollution.[17]

Antarctica came onto the UN agenda in 1983, ostensibly because the world community decided to deal with the Law of the Sea Negotiations (UNCLOS) before this second commons problem was tackled. The consultative parties were not fond of what they perceived to be their adequate management system receiving such scrutiny and, with the exception of the issue of South African participation in the ATS (denounced by the UN General Assembly), refused to participate. For example, they did not vote on the General Assembly resolution (44/124B-1989) that called for the establishment of an Antarctic world park. This resolution was very important, since it dispelled fears that nonsignatories were demanding access to decision making on Antarctica simply because they wanted to get in the exploitation game as well. The resolution also challenged the 24 consultative parties' right to exclusive decision-making status on what many felt was indeed part of the **global commons**, not the domain of a select group of states who were capable of conducting scientific research there.

So the protocol mentioned above could be seen in this light: it is an attempt to contain calls for a world park without world management, or common ownership, and it is an attempt to preserve the exclusivity of the ATS and deny the UN system an acquisition that many policy planners think is too much like world government for their comfort. Reactions are mixed. By adopting the moratorium, consultative parties have made it clear that, at least for now, they have temporarily—and 50 years is an extremely long time in world politics—discarded the promise of exploitation of the continent. This decision is a practical and symbolic victory for some, but others are still convinced that Antarctica should be legally recognized, within the UN framework, as part of the global commons.

A great deal of sensible cynicism exists concerning the ATS and not just because it has not evolved into the universal-membership body some hoped it would. Though it is a symbol of peace and cooperation, Antarctica never offered an especially alluring military advantage to anyone. It is difficult to argue that the ATS represents an unusual instance of economic restraint when it is not, as far as we know, worth exploiting in economic terms. No huge mineral deposits have been found. Oil is suspected but not confirmed, and we gave up on the idea of towing icebergs north for fresh water some time ago. In other words, skeptics argue, Antarctica remains so pristine because it is, in conventional terms, worthless. No doubt a grain of truth lies in this realistic appraisal, but it should not belittle the significance of Antarctic cooperation or dampen enthusiasm for the future of Antarctica, which remains, despite the recent protocol, vulnerable to the advances of the industrial world. For a worthless chunk of ice, many people have spent a lot of time in intense negotiations over its future.

It may not be as easy, however, to deal with other problems of the commons, such as climate change.

CLIMATE CHANGE

Beyond nuclear Armageddon, the biggest long-term threat to humanity may well emanate from the prospect of major disturbances to the earth's climate. Our heavy reliance on the burning of fossil fuels (coal, oil, and natural gas) releases billions of tonnes of carbon dioxide into the atmosphere. Deforestation from slash-and-burn agriculture adds billions more. The ozone layer has been affected by industrial chemicals that stay in the atmosphere for more than a century. If the earth is warming and continues to do so, the results could be catastrophic: the ice caps could melt and sea levels would rise and flood highly populated coastal zones; agriculture could dwindle in what are now productive areas; and the tropics could become uninhabitable, forcing millions to flee as *environmental refugees*.

We have seen a major increase in the level of attention politicians have afforded the broad issue of climate change, and most of this attention has been spent on global warming and ozone-layer depletion. Though the talk of politicians is often viewed as cheap, we know global warming is being taken seriously because those most prudent of institutions, insurance companies, are worried about its effects. At international talks in Geneva in July 1996, 57 European insurance firms urged national delegates to hold a climate change conference to reduce carbon emissions.[18] At an intergovernmental meeting in Kyoto, Japan, in December 1997, states committed themselves to self-imposed limitations by the year 2000. The exact formula was different for each state; Canada pledged to reduce emissions to 94 percent of the 1990 level by 2010 (and has made little, if any, progress toward this goal, complicated by the objections of several provincial governments). Overall, Kyoto calls for cuts averaging just over 5 percent from 1990 levels. To make them less painful, countries will be allowed to trade emissions entitlements if they choose—or hand them over to private companies to trade. Countries that plant forests and other "sinks" that soak up carbon dioxide can offset this against their emissions. Another option is to spend money on cleaning up pollution in other countries through joint implementation programs. Clearly, these measures will allow large industrial states to buy time before they actually reduce measures. However, a Conference of the Parties to the UN Framework Convention on Climate Change in fall 2000 at The Hague failed to achieve a unified approach to the issue.

Beyond this, there are many problems behind implementing the Kyoto protocol. The United States, under the new Bush administration, has refused to ratify it, arguing the southern states must make solid commitments first. In the Canadian case, the federal government representatives who went to Kyoto made a promise they couldn't possibly keep. In Canada's federal system, the provinces are responsible for natural resources, and some of them, such as heavily industrialized Ontario or coal- and oil-producing Alberta, do not intend to make changes. A structural explanation would suggest that the competitive nature of the world economy will limit states' willingness to sacrifice economic growth for the sake of future generations unless they are sure that all states will comply, and we are far from such an ideal.

Some debate remains about the validity of the claim that the earth is warming because of excessive industrial pollution and activity. No one doubts the logic of the greenhouse effect, which suggests that the earth's atmosphere traps certain gases that in turn hold the sun's heat. (Carbon dioxide accounts for about half of the greenhouse effect; methane, natural gas, nitrous oxide, ozone, and chlorofluorocarbons make up the rest.) As global temperatures are generally increasing and more of these gases are being released into the atmosphere by modern society, it stands to reason that a correlation exists. Nonetheless, some argue that nature is still the chief cause of fluctuations in global climate patterns. For example, in 1991, Mount Pinatubo in the Philippines erupted, spilling some 22 million tonnes of sulphur dioxide into the stratosphere, affecting weather patterns around the world. Others feel it is premature to conclude that the warming trend will continue or argue that its implications are unclear and that acting to solve the problem would cause undue economic harm. One of the chief causes of global warming is deforestation, since burning trees releases carbon and dead trees cannot absorb carbon. However, stopping the destruction of the rain forest proves rather difficult when those burning it down are doing so to survive. Meanwhile, the average American car is believed to release its own weight in carbon into the atmosphere every year.[19]

This problem is expected to get much worse: carbon dioxide emissions are expected to increase between 1997 and 2020 from 6175 million metric tonnes to 10 009 million metric tonnes per year.[20] Even if scientific consensus is reached on this issue, we still face a daunting ethical proposition because of the scope of the problem in spatial and temporal terms. As two Worldwatch analysts indicate, the question of global climate change is unprecedented in its "geographical breadth and multigenerational time frame … challenging societies to work cooperatively to protect distant populations as well as those yet unborn."[21] The result is a very complex multilateral bargaining situation, one that opens many doors to confusion. The UN Environment Programme is working with the World Meteorological Organization (WMO) to measure changes in climate (as are thousands of other nationally based scientific institutions around the world); and the UN-sponsored Intergovernmental Panel on Climate Change will continue to produce reports (see the section on the role of science in global ecopolitics in this chapter).

The other major problem related to climate change is that of *ozone-layer depletion*. Volatile chemicals known as **chlorofluorocarbons (CFCs)** used in refrigeration, industrial production, and aerosol cans have damaged the stratospheric ozone layer, which protects us from ultraviolet radiation from the sun. CFCs, along with carbon and other so-called *greenhouse gases*, prevent infrared radiation from escaping the earth's atmosphere. The result is not only increased global warming potential but increased rates of skin cancer and eye problems and adverse agricultural effects. Ultimately, entire ecosystems and immune systems could be disrupted. (For example, marine biologists fear the immune systems of whales are being affected by increased ultraviolet ray exposure.) Ozone produced by burning fossil fuels does not replace stratospheric ozone but pollutes the lower atmosphere.

Unlike the global warming issue, which has generated much debate but relatively little firm commitment on the part of industrial states, the problem of ozone-layer depletion has been met with sound action. Once a certain measure of scientific consensus was reached regarding its origin, ozone-layer depletion generated a quick international response through a series of conferences that ended with the signing of the famous Montreal Protocol in 1987. (Montreal has become an important centre for international organizations dealing with environmental problems; see Profile 10.2.) The United States banned the use of CFCs in aerosol cans in the early 1980s. By 1990, 93 states had agreed to halt CFC production altogether by the year 2000 and had set up a $240 million fund to provide technical assistance to southern states to help them develop acceptable substitutes. China and India had refused to sign the Vienna Convention for the Protection of the Ozone Layer unless this help was included. By 1992, most industrial states had agreed to unilaterally phase out CFC use by 1995.

The increase in governmental regulation to prohibit the sale of Freon, a major ozone-depleting substance used predominantly in the air conditioning units of older cars, has been so marked that a black market in the product is flourishing. In the United States, small-scale smugglers have been caught bringing thousands of kilograms of Freon from Mexico (the latter has delayed the prohibition of Freon). As reported in *The New York Times*, the street price for a 30-pound (14-kilogram) cylinder of Freon more than doubled between 1995 and 1996 to more than $500. Thomas A. Watts-Fitzgerald is the American attorney who has coordinated an investigation into the matter named Operation Cool Breeze. He calculates that buying cocaine, converting it to crack, and selling it brings a 4:1 profit ratio, while buying a canister of Freon in another country for $42 and selling it in the U.S. for $550 produces a 13:1 profit ratio.[22] Despite the rise of such regulatory problems, the costs of reducing CFC use are much lower than those of reducing greenhouse gas emissions in general. One might argue that the Montreal Protocol, a fairly demanding document reached in a relatively short time, was successful because remarkable scientific consensus existed regarding the causes of ozone depletion, as did genuine international fear of the consequences. This type of cohesion of knowl-

PROFILE 10.2   The Montreal Connection

Montreal is world renowned for its old-world charm, cosmopolitanism, and summer jazz festival. However, given its location next to the heavily polluted St. Lawrence River, few would expect Montreal to become a magnet for international organizations dealing with environmental problems. Yet, with the support of the federal government (no doubt influenced by continued fears over separatism), Montreal has attracted a great deal of expertise and officialdom to the area. In fact, one can take a cursory glance at the extent of multilateral action on environmental issues with a survey of the bodies that have located there. The following organizations are already located in Montreal:

- the Secretariat of the Multilateral Fund of the Montreal Ozone Protocol
- the North American Commission for Environmental Cooperation (a North American Free Trade Agreement institution)
- the Secretariat of the United Nations Convention on Biological Diversity
- the Montreal office of the World Conservation Union
- the Network of Expertise for the Global Environment
- the International Water Secretariat

Montreal lost a bid for the Desertification Secretariat, which was located in Bonn, Germany.

edge and expectation has yet to be reached in many other areas related to the environment, however.

Global warming and ozone-layer depletion both raise the question of who should pay for the damage that industrial society has unleashed on the world. Northern states have contributed the most to the problem, but they cannot solve it alone, and the newly industrialized countries such as Brazil, India, and China will make similar contributions in the near future. Ultimately, this is a problem of the commons, and we must reach multilateral agreements, which are in turn enforced by governments, to deal with them. It is far from certain we can do so in a competitive world economy.

DEFORESTATION AND LAND DEGRADATION

Another serious global problem is the impact of human activity on the world's land surface, in particular the removal of the world's forests and the decreasing availability of arable land. Deforestation has become an increasingly popular and public issue in the past decade. While tropical rain forest depletion has gathered the most attention, it is important to remember that temperate rain forest depletion is as serious a problem; in fact, many of the world's temperate rain forests in Europe have already vanished, and depletion rates in Canada, the United States, and Russia are very high.

This fact is a source of friction in international efforts to curb deforestation. Developing countries see these efforts as inimical to their own economic development; the industrialized countries, having exploited much of their own forests, are now trying to prevent the developing countries from exploiting their own. However, tropical rain forest depletion is especially severe; every year, an area the size of Belgium is cleared of rain forest, often by slash-and-burn methods. In Brazil's Amazon Basin, more than 11 percent of the jungle has been destroyed since 1975 (an area the size of Morocco), and deforestation continues at even higher rates.[23] Tropical rain forest is also being depleted in Indonesia, Colombia, Thailand, and the Philippines. In Haiti, more than 90 percent of the country's rain forest has disappeared. In the 1980s alone, the world lost about 8 percent of its tropical forests.[24] Rain forest depletion occurs for many reasons, including a local desire for pastureland, cropland, fuel, and a foreign market for hardwood.

Another tragedy of rain forest depletion is the impossibility of full regeneration. Old-growth timber areas (in both tropical and temperate zones) possess ecosystems and biodiversity developed over thousands of

Up in smoke. Indians of the Xingu Reservation in the central Brazilian state of Mato-Grosso walk among charred trees. According to news reports, fires in that state alone burned more than 150 000 hectares and killed at least 400 head of cattle in August 1998. Fires earlier in the year in the Amazon jungle burned an area the size of Belgium. (AP Photo/Humberto Pradera)

years. Replanted or second growth regions never achieve this level of biodiversity. In addition, because in many cases forests are cleared for pastureland or cropland (which is often exhausted after a few years), the forest cannot regenerate because the land cannot support it. Deforestation has several global environmental implications. It reduces the capacity of the earth to produce oxygen and absorb carbon dioxide, which in turn contributes to environmental change. Rainfall patterns are affected, and soil erosion increases because of a lack of root structures.

In addition to loss of forest cover, land and soil degradation is a serious environmental problem. Soil degradation is estimated to affect some 1.2 billion hectares of land worldwide (10 percent of the current agricultural land area).[25] This degradation is once again caused by human activity: deforestation, overgrazing, and agricultural mismanagement. In severe cases, soil degradation can result in desertification and complete loss of land productivity, a condition that affects five to six million hectares of land every year.[26] Because it takes thousands of years to form a few centimetres of topsoil, this problem has severe implications for the world's food supply (see Chapter 13). Taken together, deforestation and land degradation represent a serious assault on the earth's land mass. In the meantime, as our next section indicates, we are fundamentally changing the evolutionary path of the world's species.

SPECIES IMPOVERISHMENT

The physical division of the earth into nation-states is contrary to the flow of nature, and this becomes most apparent when we consider the fate of migratory mammals that do not recognize borders and have their paths disrupted by such constructions. This issue begs a broader question: are the many species of animals and plants that are currently endangered part of the commons, regardless of where they live? From an ecological viewpoint, the crisis presented by dwindling whale and tiger populations and current attempts to save them is really one of biodiversity, or, put more emphatically, what M. Brock Fenton and others term *species impoverishment*.[27] Though there is nothing unnatural and certainly nothing new about extinction, the twentieth century in particular saw more extinctions in the wild world than ever before. The fear of many specialists during the height of whaling was that the great whales were going the same place as the dodo, and they were going there not because of any natural catastrophe but because of human misunderstanding or, worse, greed. The same fear underlies attempts to save what is left of the tropical rain forests today.

Scientists are still debating the causes of the late Cretaceous extinction in which the large dinosaurs were rendered extinct, about 65 million years ago. This is a question partly of effect: as David Jablonski notes in a fascinating essay on the topic, the late Cretaceous extinction is a very complex phenomenon. "Tropical marine groups were more severely affected than temperate or polar ones; open-ocean plankton and larger swimmers, such as the mosasaurs, were affected more than bottom dwellers; and large land dwellers more affected than small ones, even though some larger forms survived as well."[28] Whatever caused this extinction, it did not kill off all the species on earth at the time, nor did it, in fact, even come close to doing so. This is the key difference: it was, by any account, not preventable with human effort (humans weren't around). Humans are believed at least partially responsible for the large extinction of land animals in the Pleistocene period. The development of agriculture so fundamentally changed the human–nature relationship that we have been able to affect the ecosystem, even the biosphere, with our economic activities.

The human tendency to overhunt constitutes a principal threat to biodiversity today. Columbus discovered the Caribbean monk seal, the single tropical pinniped, in what was called the New World. It has not been seen since 1922. The Steller's sea cow was spotted by a Russian hunting expedition in 1741 in the Aleutians; it was regarded as extinct by the late eighteenth century. More recently, we have witnessed massive fish extinctions—more than 200 species—from Lake Victoria in Africa. These extinctions had many causes, including overfishing, pollution, and the introduction of alien species, such as the Nile perch. Les Kaufman has referred to Lake Victoria as the "Hiroshima of the biological apocalypse."[29] Canadian and European commercial fishers know all too well the economic effects of the rapid reduction of fish species such as cod, turbot, and Pacific salmon and the significant role played by overfishing.

The reduction of species populations will, of course, have a severe impact on their reproductive health. While this may increase the chances of survival for some, since there is less competition for limited resources, it may lessen the chances of survival for the group as a whole. An important element here is the gene pool, which itself must be sufficiently diverse for healthy populations: "Gene pools are being converted into gene puddles vulnerable to evaporation in an ecological and evolutionary sense."[30] The loss of genetic diversity may well be the most serious long-term threat to our environment. As James Scarff notes, the

> elimination of a species reduces the genetic capacity of the ecosystem to respond to perturbations or long-term changes in the environment. Such a loss may also initiate irreversible ecological adjustments which destabilize the ecosystem leading to further extinctions. Economically, the extinction of a species represents the permanent loss of a renewable resource of unknown value [as well as] potential uses for medicine, scientific research, human food, education, and recreation.[31]

The international community has taken steps to limit the degradation of wildlife species. We have numerous fisheries agreements and institutions in place, such as the Northwest Atlantic Fisheries Organization (discussed below) and the International Whaling Commission. Early organizations included the International Council for Bird Preservation (1909) and the International Congress for the Protection of Nature (1913). As early as 1886 a Treaty Concerning the Regulation of Salmon Fishing in the Rhine River Basin was signed by Germany, Luxembourg, the Netherlands, and Switzerland. The first international agreement to conserve a marine mammal was in all likelihood the Fur Seal Convention of 1911, signed by Japan, Russia, Great Britain (for pre-independence Canada), and the United States.

Another groundbreaking agreement was the U.S.–Great Britain Migratory Birds Convention, signed in 1916. In the contemporary setting, what Robert Boardman has called the "linchpin of the system"[32] of international conservationist organizations is the **International Union for the Conservation of Nature and Natural Resources (IUCNNR)**, formed in 1948 in conjunction with the **United Nations Educational, Scientific, and Cultural Organization (UNESCO)**. The IUCNNR is a unique umbrella organization that covers intergovernmental and transnational conservation activity, often working laterally with a plethora of other organizations—both state multilateral and nongovernmental in composition—that have achieved global significance. The **Convention on International Trade in Endangered Species of Wild Fauna and Flora (CITES)** is often heralded as a diplomatic success; it has resulted in the controversial international ivory trade ban of 1989 (partially lifted in 1997 to allow a one-time sale of stockpiled ivory from three southern African states to Japan). But CITES is torn between northern states demanding complete protection of species and southern states wanting to trade in animal parts as part of a broader conservation strategy. The role of opposing NGOs lobbying CITES delegations is interesting as well.

The Biodiversity Treaty, signed at Rio de Janeiro in 1992, further committed states to preserving biodiversity and committed the north to paying the south for use of genetic material found in the latter. The treaty, signed by more than 160 countries in 1992 (belatedly including the United States, after Bill Clinton's election later that year), went into effect in 1993. Delegates from all the signatories form a conference of parties, which meets every year to review progress made toward the three central thrusts of the treaty: the conservation of biodiversity, the sustainable use of biological resources, and the equitable sharing of the benefits arising from such use. A Biosafety Protocol for the Convention on Biological Diversity (CBD) was negotiated in 2000.

However, one can argue that all these treaties are meaningless if the broader problem, the preservation of habitat, is not addressed, and that problem requires much more than the regulation of fishing fleets or the ban of alligator-skin purses or the confiscation of exotic plants at borders. It requires creating the conditions in which humankind no longer has the need to destroy natural habitat. Despite encouraging conservation programs around the world, we are a long way from environmental sustainability.

PROTECTING THE GLOBAL ENVIRONMENT: FROM STOCKHOLM TO RIO

When it comes to the environmental impact of the role played by the major development players in the UN system, many analysts are highly critical. In particular, the **International Bank for Reconstruction and Development (IBRD or World Bank)** and the **International Monetary Fund (IMF)** come under fire for promoting large-scale industrialization and **structural adjustment programs** that encourage the depletion of natural resources for export.[33] We should note, however, that the World Bank and others are slowly beginning to take environmental questions seriously, and initiatives such as the Global Environmental Facility, administered by the World Bank, United Nations Environmental Programme (UNEP), and UN Development Program (UNDP) are contributing to the development of environmental technology (see Profile 10.3 for Canada's enivronmental commitments).

In 1972 the United Nations sponsored the Conference on the Human Environment (UNCHE) in Stockholm, where the UN Environmental Programme was created. The UNEP is not an institution or a specialized agency of the UN, such as the World Health Organization. Rather, it is made up of all the activities undertaken within the UN system that deal with the environment. It has a governing council with 58 nations, elected by the General Assembly for a three-year term. It meets every two years and in special sessions whenever necessary. It has a secretariat, based in Nairobi, Kenya; a voluntary Environment Fund; and the Environment Coordination Board (ECB), which attempts to coordinate all the UN bodies involved in environmental areas. The ECB is chaired by the UNEP's executive director, who in the latter half of the 1990s was a Canadian, Elizabeth Dowdeswell (see Profile 10.4). One of UNEP's most important tasks was to aid in the setup of UNCED, held in Rio de Janeiro, Brazil, in June 1992. UNCED was the largest diplomatic summit ever, and it generated a great deal of press coverage around the world. Several outcomes of UNCED deserve mention here. One was the establishment of a UN Commission on Sustainable Development (CSD), which would meet reg-

Canada's Major International Environmental Commitments

1909	Treaty between the United States and Great Britain Relating to Boundary Waters
1916	Convention between United States and United Kingdom for the Protection of Migratory Birds in Canada and the United States
1946	International Convention for the Regulation of Whaling (Canada withdrew in 1982)
1963	Treaty Banning Nuclear Weapons Tests in the Atmosphere, in Outer Space, and under Water
1971	Convention on Wetlands of International Importance
1972	Canada–U.S.A. Great Lakes Water Quality Agreement
	Stockholm Declaration on the Environment
	London Convention on the Prevention of Marine Pollution by Dumping of Wastes and Other Matter
	Convention Concerning the Protection of the World Cultural and Natural Heritage
1973	Convention on International Trade in Endangered Species of Wild Fauna and Flora
1978	Protocol on the International Convention for the Prevention of Pollution from Ships
1979	Convention on Long-Range Transboundary Air Pollution (LRTAP)
1982	UN Convention on the Law of the Sea (signed but not ratified)
1985	Vienna Convention on the Protection of the Ozone Layer
	reduction of sulphur emissions or their transboundary fluxes by at least 30 percent

	Canada–U.S. Agreement Concerning Pacific Salmon
1986	Canada–U.S. Agreement on the Transboundary Movement of Hazardous Waste
1987	Montreal Protocol on Substances That Deplete the Ozone Layer
1989	Basel Convention on the Control of Transboundary Movements of Hazardous Wastes and Their Disposal
1991	Canada/U.S. Air Quality Agreement
	NOx Protocol to the 1979 LRTAP Convention
	Declaration on the Protection of the Arctic Environment
1992	UN Framework Convention on Climate Change
	Convention on Biological Diversity
	Agenda 21
	"Rio Declaration"
	Statement of Guiding Principles on Forests
1993	North American Agreement on Environmental Co-operation
1994	International Tropical Timber Agreement
	Protocol to LRTAP on Sulphur Emission Reductions
1995	UN Agreement on Straddling Fish Stocks and Highly Migratory Fish Stocks (signed but not ratified)
1996	Comprehensive Nuclear Test Ban Treaty
1997	Kyoto Protocol on Climate Change (signed but not ratified)
	Canada–Chile Agreement on Environmental Co-operation
2000	Biosafety Protocol for Biodiversity Convention (signed but not ratified)

ularly and follow up on the conclusions of UNCED, including a major five-year review in 1997. Second, an agreed text for forestry conservation emerged "very slowly and painfully as those developing countries particularly emphatic on the inviolability of their sovereignty in this area (notably Malaysia and India) scrutinized every word."[34]

UNCED produced the Rio Declaration, which was to have been a more all-embracing "Earth Charter," and which we discussed in our section on the commons. UNCED also

Elizabeth Dowdeswell

Canadian Elizabeth Dowdeswell was the executive director of the United Nations Environmental Programme, the most important UN program that deals directly with environmental problems, from 1994 to 1998. Her approach to the many environmental problems collectively faced by nations was a wide one: "We must look beyond regulatory measures," she writes. "Unless local communities benefit from resources, people simply have no incentive to preserve them." With respect to the important question of biodiversity loss, for example, she says, "UNEP will continue to play the role of consensus builder. We will integrate biodiversity studies into a number of related sub-programmes to enhance the understanding of linkages between the major issues, including desertification, climate change and environmental economics." Somewhat ironically, Dowdeswell wanted the Secretariat of the Convention on Biological Diversity to be located at UNEP headquarters in Nairobi but it ended up in Montreal, instead.

SOURCE: *OUR PLANET: THE UNEP MAGAZINE FOR SUSTAINABLE DEVELOPMENT* 6 (4) (1994), 2.

produced the Convention on Climate Change, mentioned above, and Agenda 21, a thick action plan on various aspects of future environmental protection. Since it suggests practical policy initiatives, Agenda 21 is really the core UNCED achievement. It did not, however, obtain stringent financial commitments from the northern states to pay for it.

TRANSBORDER ENVIRONMENTAL ISSUES

States must worry about much more than the problems typically associated with the global commons and multilateral coordination. They must also be concerned with local or regional environmental concerns, especially transborder pollution, which flows from one country into another, often through streams, lakes, and air. Since power differentials usually exist between neighbouring states—one is often more industrialized, or it has a geographic advantage, such as being upstream—realists argue that transborder pollution will be the cause of future violent conflict. However, many states—Canada and the United States, with the **International Joint Commission (IJC),** are often used as an example—co-manage their mutual frontiers on an ongoing basis. Even so, the potential for conflict exists: Canada and the United States argued for years over the effects of acid rain that came to Canada from industrial regions in the United States.

In the past several decades, growing public awareness of the detrimental effect of pollution has come to underscore a variety of measures at the national and international levels to stem the tide of pollution as societies continue to industrialize.[35] Atmospheric nuclear tests in the 1950s created radioactive fallout that travelled thousands of kilometres, raising public concern over the discovery of cesium-137, strontium 90, carbon 14, and various isotopes of plutonium in the environment.[36] This concern helped push the United States toward signing the Partial Test Ban Treaty (see Chapter 6), which limited future nuclear testing to underground facilities.

Perhaps the most famous case of transborder pollution resulted from an accident at the Chernobyl nuclear reactor in Ukraine in April 1986 (at the time, Ukraine was still part of the Soviet Union; it is now an independent state). A meltdown in a reactor unit caused an explosion and fire that spread airborne radioactivity as far away as Italy and

Aftermath of ecological calamity. Workers who constructed the cement sarcophagus covering Chernobyl's reactor in 1986 pose with a banner reading: "We will fulfill the government's order!" next to the uncompleted construction. Thousands of workers who took part in the cleanup of Chernobyl have died from the after-effects suffered during the work, according to information from the "Union-Chernobyl-Ukraine." (AP Photo/Volodymyr Repik)

Sweden. Soviet leaders made matters worse by initially shrouding the event in secrecy. In Scandinavia, nomadic Laplanders were severely affected as their reindeer herds ate toxic grass. A recent low-level leak of radioactive inert gases and iodine from a reactor near St. Petersburg has accentuated the fear that more Chernobyls are waiting to happen. Throughout the Cold War, Eastern Europe had served as a captive market for the Soviet nuclear industry, and Soviet-designed reactors (located in Czechoslovakia, Hungary, Bulgaria, and Eastern Germany) did not always include sufficient emergency core cooling systems or containment vessels.

Since the unprecedented nuclear disaster at Chernobyl, concern has increased over the safety of Soviet nuclear technology and operations. A "nuclear safety account" has been set up at the European Bank for Reconstruction and Develop-ment (EBRD), to which Canada has contributed. The Canadian Nuclear Safety Initiative was established in 1992 to enhance the short-term safety of Soviet-designed plants, in particular the RBMK reactors (which, though they use graphite instead of heavy water, are similar enough to the Canadian produced CANDU reactors to warrant Canadian technical expertise). It is clear that the cash-strapped nations in Eastern Europe and particularly the Commonwealth of Independent States are in no position to discontinue atomic energy use, for they depend on it for such rudimentary necessities as heat and lighting. The long-term outlook, however, is less clear. Meanwhile, nuclear suppliers such as Canada are interested in the possibility of a CANDU reactor marketplace in Eastern Europe once the current reactor styles are finally discontinued or replaced. Canada has also recently engaged in a controversial sale of CANDU technology to China.

Other transborder pollution problems have resulted from industrialization. Several regional agreements aim at reducing acid precipitation (acid rain), which damages trees; for example, in 1988, 24 European states signed a treaty to limit nitrogen oxide emissions to 1988 levels by 1995, and Canada and the United States have a bilateral agreement that is the result of many years of protracted bargaining.[37] However, without funding for effective scrubbers for smokestacks for industries burning lignite (a highly sulphurous coal), acid rain will continue to be a major problem, particularly in Eastern Europe.

Yet another transborder environmental issue is the circulation of pesticides, an issue that illustrates the complexity of both modern science and the world economy. For example, in 1990 U.S. manufacturers exported more than 24 million kilograms of pesticides such as DDT, dieldrin, toxaphene, endrin, ethyl parathion, and other compounds that were banned, restricted, or unregistered for use in the United States. Most of these were shipped to southern states, such as Argentina, Colombia, Ecuador, and the Philippines, though a significant amount went to Belgium, Japan, and the Netherlands. In his excellent recent study of pesticide regulation, John Wargo draws attention to the difficulty of regulating such international commerce in products that are highly hazardous to both human and ecosystem health:

> An active ingredient produced in the United States may be shipped to Switzerland where it is combined with other ingredients and shipped to Egypt. In Egypt, it might be applied as an insecticide to cotton. Cottonseeds may then be harvested and sold to a commodity broker in Israel, who then sells them to a manufacturer of cottonseed oil in Italy. The Italian firm may then sell the oil, perhaps mixed with other oil from seeds grown in Guatemala with the help of another pesticide, to an American food processing company.[38]

Another local and regional environmental issue is access to fresh water. Though recent events, such as flooding in India, Bangladesh, and Mozambique, suggest that the problem of water is one of overabundance, the longer-term issue will no doubt be scarcity. Only about 3 percent of the world's water is fresh, and much of that is frozen in the Arctic icecaps. In effect, less than 1 percent of the world's water is easily accessible fresh water. Global water use doubles every 21 years, and water use now exceeds sustainable consumption limits. More than one billion people in the world lack a safe water supply. Aquifers in many of the world's regions are running dry or becoming contaminated with seawater. Many major rivers are mere streams when they reach the coast due to diversion of water for irrigation. The demand for fresh water comes from agriculture (66 percent of the total consumption), industry (25 percent), and human consumption (9 percent). In some regions, the increased rate of water use has had dramatic consequences. A stark example can be found in the Aral Sea region of Central Asia. During Soviet rule, massive quantities of water were diverted from the river systems feeding the Aral Sea to irrigate a huge agricultural project. The flow of water to the Aral Sea slowed to a trickle, and as a result the lake has now shrunk by one-third. Not only has this devastated the local fishing industry but the dry sea salt is swept up by winds into dust storms, which deposit salt over a wide area, poisoning land and people.[39]

Concern continues about whether shortages of fresh water will provoke conflict between states or peoples in the near future. After all, water is the most essential of resources, perhaps after breathable air; many states share water resources or argue that they have a right to do so. In fact, a new term has been coined to refer to conflicts over water resources: *hydropolitics*.[40] Water conflict has been an acute problem in areas with arid climates, such as Northern Africa and the Middle East. As water consumption increases alongside population and economic growth, the quest for sources of fresh water becomes more dramatic and has already been the cause of conflict between several states. In the Middle East, water has been an issue in the dispute between Israel and the Palestinian people (see Chapter 13).

Not all analysts are as quick to point to water as the source of protracted and perhaps violent future conflict, however. Some argue that shared resources can bring out the best in states, promoting their ability to cooperate when they must to achieve mutual benefits. Thomas Homer-Dixon argues that, though there are historical examples of wars caused by the quest for nonrenewable resources (such as oil and minerals), "the story is different for renewables like cropland, forests, fish and fresh water. It is hard to find clear historical or contemporary examples of major wars motivated mainly by scarcities of renewables."[41] This analytic caution is certainly warranted, but it does not really contradict the claim that conflicts over resources are potential causes of international and civil warfare, as well as factors in long-range geostrategic thinking. In any event, in many of the world's regions, water shortages are already a reality. As the demand for water increases due to population growth, the expansion of agriculture, and industrialization, the pressure on already dwindling supplies will intensify. We return to this theme in Chapter 13 but turn now to a recent resource dispute.

TRANSBOUNDARY RESOURCE CONFLICTS: THE CASE OF THE FISHERY DISPUTE

One can argue that in the modern age it is oil that states fight over most frequently. The Gulf War, examined in detail earlier in this text, suggests this much. However, states have also come into conflict over other resources. Managing fisheries has often proven to be one of the more complex of the many problems of the commons. The so-called cod wars between Iceland and Britain in the 1960s and 1970s provide a historical example of potential conflict over dwindling resources. This conflict became evident to Canadians in 1995, when a dispute over straddling stocks off the coast of Newfoundland assumed international proportions. The case involved the Spanish fishing fleet and an uncharacteristically assertive Canadian government. The Spanish Basques were fishing off the coast of Newfoundland as early as 1530, though they called it *Terranova* then. By the 1580s, French Basque ships were returning from the area loaded with cod and, eventually, whale oil. In March 1995 Canada seized the Spanish trawler *Estai* outside Canadian territorial waters. In 1994, the multilateral **Northwest Atlantic Fisheries Organization (NAFO)** had set limits on the total allowable catch of Greenland halibut (or turbot), allocating national quotas for this resource. The European Union, pressured by Spain and Portugal, rejected the quotas as unfair.

Canada imposed a unilateral moratorium, concerned with the depleting turbot stocks, and eventually seized the *Estai*, claiming that the trawler was not only violating the quota rules but was using illegal fish nets in the process. Since the vessel was on the high seas, Canada was, in effect, breaking international law. Canada's seizure of the Spanish trawler led to international tension, because Canada's international legal jurisdiction stops after the 200-nautical-mile (370-kilometre) limit imposed by the exclusive economic zone provision of the Law of the Sea. Before 1977, Canada had a 12-mile (19-kilometre) limit; it was expanded that year and non-Canadian trawlers, at one point the largest consumers of cod, withdrew.

Seized ship. Onlookers watch the Spanish trawler *Estai* arrive at St. John's on 12 March 1995. A Canadian fisheries patrol vessel fired the first salvo in what became the Great Turbot War between Canada and the European Union. (CP Picture Archive/Fred Chartrand)

Canada and Sustainable Development: Business as Usual?

The most recent White Paper on foreign policy, *Canada in the World*, makes repeated reference to sustainable development, including a pledge to "ensure that Canadian foreign policy promotes sustainable development globally through the careful and responsible balancing of trade, development and environmental considerations" (pages 36–7). The environment, along with basic human needs, women in development, infrastructure services, human rights, democracy and good governance, and private sector development, remains a priority for development assistance. However, the vast majority of Canadian development projects abroad are in the form of tied aid, which obliges the recipient to spend aid money on Canadian products or expertise. There is also the matter of selective assistance: beyond emergency aid situations, Ottawa is primarily interested in developing the newly emerging markets in Southeast Asia and Eastern Europe and in selling CANDU nuclear reactors abroad.

Another controversial facet of the whole human security ideal involves Canadian private sector investment activities abroad. At least three recent events have brought this area under scrutiny: reports suggesting that Talisman, Inc., has been supplying the Sudanese government with funds, which the latter has used to carry out genocide and engage in oil drilling in south Sudan (see Chapter 9), and two industrial accidents with ecological consequences. The most infamous of the accidents occurred in southern Spain on 24 April 1998, when four billion litres of toxic waste spilled from a tailings dam at a Canadian-owned zinc mine. Hundreds of acres of farmland were stained by the sudden flood, and the company involved, Toronto's Boliden Limited, has refused to accept full responsibility. The other accident occurred when a truck carrying sodium cyanide up the Tienshin mountain range crashed in Kyrgyzstan. Again, it was a Canadian-owned firm, Cameco, a gold-mining firm that was running the mine and, again, the company refused to pay compensation to those affected. (Some dispute exists as to the extent of damages in question in both cases.) The cyanide fell into the Barskan River, which supplies a local town with drinking water and eventually runs into Lake Issyk-kal.

These cases tarnish Canada's reputation abroad and challenge the idea that Ottawa is serious about making Canadian-owned firms behave themselves.

However, foreign vessels, often associated with European nations but flying the flags of Central American countries, continued to take cod and other fish immediately beyond the limit on the Grand Banks. Thus, the fishery dilemma quickly became a foreign policy problem.

Understandably, the frustration has been mounting in an already economically depressed area: the East Coast and Newfoundland in particular. Though the links between seal population and cod depletion are tenuous at best, calls have rung out for a massive increase in the hunting of harp seals. This upsets the animal rights movement, which has considerable influence over consumer habits in the European marketplace, and which placed great emphasis on stopping the whiteskin seal harvest in the 1970s. But it is the foreign fishing that raises the greatest concern. One major player, fishers' union leader Richard Cashin, suggested that fishers take direct action to protect "their" area. The anger is reflected in a letter to the editor published in *The Globe and Mail*:

> The world's greatest fishery is on the verge of extinction … what remains of the stock is being exterminated by foreign ships … diplomacy has clearly failed…. Canada's pathetic appeasement of the exterminators just makes us a

laughingstock.... It's about time we used our armed forces where we need them, in the Grand Banks rather than Somalia.[42]

The federal government has repeatedly declared a willingness to block non-NAFO members from sending trawlers into the Grand Banks off Newfoundland. But it was less the issue of cod and more the case of turbot that brought things to a head. Eventually, Canada passed legislation that would make it legal (in the domestic context, if not in the international) to physically stop ships from fishing near the 200-nautical-mile (370-kilometre) exclusive economic zone.[43] To complicate matters, the Spanish have been accused of overfishing near Norwegian waters. (Some analysts feel this was one reason why the Norwegians rejected EU membership in a recent referendum.) This, then, is at least partially an internal policy problem for the EU, since it is clear that the EU Commission has the power to "enforce compliance of environmental obligations among [EU] member-states, including ensuring proper implementation of their Community obligations."[44]

In 1997, Canada became embroiled in another fisheries dispute, this time off the West Coast of Canada. The dispute broke out between Canada and the United States over Pacific salmon quotas and the failure of efforts to negotiate a new Pacific salmon treaty. Tensions escalated between the governments of British Columbia and Alaska, Washington state, and Oregon. At one point, Canadian fishers surrounded an Alaskan ferry in anger. The fishing season ended with no resolution of the dispute. Dwindling stocks of fish on both coasts may lead to increasingly intense disputes in the future.

NONGOVERNMENTAL ACTORS AND THE ENVIRONMENT IN GLOBAL POLITICS

Little doubt remains that the environment has become an important foreign policy issue for most governments. For example, Canada has an official ambassador for the environment, John Fraser, who attends multilateral conferences such as the September 1995 meeting in Geneva that amended the Basel Convention to prohibit the sale of toxic wastes from OECD countries to southern ones for final disposal or recycling.[45] However, despite all this government activity, it would be impossible to approach a thorough treatment of global ecopolitics without reference to the nongovernmental actors that have converged to participate in this field. In fact, many would claim that NGOs have been the principal instigators all along, the ones that forced states to take environmental concerns seriously in the first place.

NGOs are active in many areas with clear international implications. For example, an NGO that has seen recent success in stemming the tide of large-scale infrastructure development is the International Rivers Network, based in Berkeley, California. It led a successful coalition that lobbied strongly against the World Bank's financing of a Nepalese hydropower project and an earlier effort to stop the Bank's funding of India's notorious $3.5 billion Narmada Dam. The World Bank's financing of large dams has dropped from an average of 18 a year between 1980 and 1985 to only 6 a year between 1986 and 1993.[46] Perhaps most symbolically, the Bank is staying away from the Three Gorges Dam on China's Yangtze River, which will involve the resettling of more than one million people. Meanwhile, a Paris-based professional IGO, the International Commission on Large Dams, has a more positive attitude toward dam construction. As some 843 large dams are under construction around the world, this body not only supports the general idea that hydroelectric power is the cleanest and most efficient of energy sources but is willing to help in its development.

The confrontation between environmental groups and large multinational corporations is usually covered in the media. A little-known but important exception is the

The Seikatsu Club

The Seikatsu Club is a consumer group involving some 170 000 households throughout Japan. It was founded by women in the early 1970s in reaction to minimata disease, the fish-borne mercury poisoning that causes neurological disease, paralysis, and death. Recognizing the negative impacts of pesticides and other agricultural chemicals on health and the environment, the club uses its purchasing power to promote the development of organic and ecological farming. After the Chernobyl nuclear accident, the club created the Radiation Disaster Network, which monitored radioactive substances in food imported in Europe.

The Seikatsu Club is one of 13 000 consumer groups in Japan that are advancing Japan's self-sufficiency in food and leading a nationwide movement to reform consumer habits and lifestyles. The objectives of the Seikatsu Club are to learn how to govern society through self-management, to rebuild local societies, and to create locally based economies with cooperative systems of welfare, health, education, and culture.

SOURCE: D. GOLDIN ROSENBERG, "INITIATIVES IN FEMINISM, ENVIRONMENTALISM AND ACTION," *ALTERNATIVES: PERSPECTIVES ON SOCIETY, TECHNOLOGY AND ENVIRONMENT* 21 (1995), 20–1.

longest-running civil suit in British legal history, involving McDonald's, the American hamburger giant, and two unemployed environmentalists. The two belonged to London Greenpeace when it distributed a leaflet in the mid-1980s called "What's Wrong with McDonald's: Everything They Don't Want You to Know." McDonald's sued for libel but may have been sorry it did, since the two alleged libel-mongers have forced the company to defend itself in court. For example, the court has heard evidence that McDonald's paid people to infiltrate London Greenpeace. A nutrition expert employed by McDonald's itself testified that "it is 'very reasonable' to tell the public that 'a diet high in fat, sugar, animal products and salt and low in fibre, vitamins and minerals is linked with cancer of the breast and bowel and heart disease.' That was one of the very allegations in the pamphlet against which McDonald's is complaining."[47]

NGOs have often assumed a watchdog role, reporting on the activities of MNCs and states for the general public; they also influence government policy at the national level. For example, Greenpeace members are included in the official American delegation to the International Whaling Commission, where the United States has consistently opposed lifting the global moratorium on commercial whaling now in place. NGOs also influence the operations of multilateral forums, contributing to CITES and World Conservation Union meetings and their outcomes. At times, they are criticized for insisting on a Western environmentalist ethic, even in local situations where people are more attuned to living on the land than most NGO members have ever been, and for focusing on a few key issues, ones that can aid in fundraising appeals, simplifying complex situations.

THE ROLE OF SCIENCE IN GLOBAL ECOPOLITICS

The current debate over the safety of genetically modified organisms (GMOs) (see Profile 10.7) has drawn attention to role of scientific certainty, or perhaps more precisely, the lack of scientific certainty facing decision makers. The global warming debate is another prime example. Although acceptance of the fact that the earth is currently warming and that the greenhouse effect facilitates this is widespread, less certainty exists

PROFILE 10.7 — Genetically Modified Organisms (GMOs)

Genetic engineering refers to a variety of techniques aimed at deliberately changing the genetic makeup of a cell or organism. Scientists have been able to modify the genes of many crops, including tobacco, tomatoes, corn, squash, potatoes, and cotton. Some genetically engineered crops, such as the FlavrSavr tomato (which is designed to stay fresher longer), are on the market in the United States. The tomato is FDA (Food and Drug Administration—U.S.A.) approved, but critics have argued that the long-term effects on health are unknown. Further, they argue that the cross-pollination effect from farms using genetically modified seeds is unknown. Some plants have been modified to be resistant to weed killers, insects, viruses, or fungi. Corn plants have been genetically modified to help farmers rid their fields of weeds without destroying the crop.

Researchers can also genetically engineer many food animals, including fish, cows, goats, sheep, and pigs. For some animals, scientists can combine genetic engineering with cloning to produce many identical, genetically modified animals. Such animals can be used for research into human health issues and even for organ transplants. Again, critics are concerned about the ethical implications of modifying nature and about possible accidents. The powerful biotechnology industry, most of it located in the United States and Japan, wants the Europeans and others to open their markets to GMOs, while the EU, reflecting public opinion there, is reluctant to do so. The industry argues that such technology improves farming techniques and will, in the long term, provide more food for more people, but concerns remain about the tendency of the industry to force farmers to use its products and the lack of labelling specifying GMO products in supermarkets. Organizations such as Greenpeace have made an anti-GMO stance part of their platform. The Biosafety Protocol of the CBD dealt with the issue to some degree, but it remains a contested trade, public health, and ethical issue.

over whether this will have the effects some have predicted (see above) and over who exactly is to blame.

On 10 September 1995, *The New York Times*, on the front page of its widely read Sunday edition, announced: "Experts Confirm Human Role in Global Warming." This was a highly publicized acknowledgment that the global warming issue—once characterized by a great deal of scientific uncertainty and, therefore, difficult to deal with politically—is becoming less of an uncertain phenomenon. Indeed, from a political perspective, the series of conclusions published by the Intergovernmental Panel on Climate Change could be a vital step toward achieving the type of collective action such global problems demand, confirming what many political analysts have suggested: science is playing an increasingly large role in galvanizing political action, even at the international level. This point is well made in *An Agenda of Science for Environment and Development into the 21st Century*, which is the published summary of a conference held in Vienna in November 1991. The conference, ASCEND 21, which featured presentations by specialists in many interrelated fields such as population, energy, marine and coastal systems, biodiversity, and public awareness, aimed to provide a contribution to the Agenda 21 UNCED process but also made the case for the importance of integrating the social and natural sciences as we strive for necessarily complex solutions to frustratingly complex problems.[48]

What emerges from much of the scientific community is an emphasis on adopting the so-called precautionary principle in environmental management. The principle, which is endorsed in the consensually based Rio Declaration (Principle 15) of 1992, Agenda 21 (Chapter 17, paragraph 17.2), the United Nations Framework on Climate Change (1992), the Convention on Biological Diversity (1992), and the Montreal Protocol on Substances That Deplete the Ozone Layer (1990), insists that governments have an obligation to prevent environmental degradation, and that, in the absence of scientific certainty regarding the future impact of human activity, we should err on the side of caution and resist undertaking threatening actions.[49]

Richard Elliot Benedick, who was a member of the American delegation to negotiations over the ozone protection regime, writes in his book *Ozone Diplomacy*:

> Politicians must ... resist a tendency to lend too much credence to self-serving economic interests that demand scientific certainty, maintain that dangers are remote and unlikely, and insist that the costs of changing their ways are astronomical. The signatories at Montreal knowingly imposed substantial short-run economic dislocations even though the evidence was incomplete; the prudence of their decision was demonstrated when the scientific models turned out to have underestimated the effects of CFCs on ozone.[50]

CONCLUSIONS

Though it would be wonderful to conclude that environmental diplomacy reflects a global consciousness that is transforming old notions of parochial interests, it would also be wrong. As time passes and it becomes increasingly apparent that the larger common threats such as global warming, ocean pollution, and biodiversity reduction are real, then we might see substantive shifts in foreign policy perspectives.

In this chapter, we've discussed several environmental threats to human security: microbes and viruses; the problems of the commons, including global warming and ozone-layer depletion; transborder pollution; and resource conflicts. All these problems are interrelated and require concerted international action to meet the challenges they pose. We've also discussed the important roles of science and NGOs. We return to the theme of human security in the next chapter, where we discuss overpopulation, urbanization, and refugee movements. The conclusion of this chapter is that ecopolitics is here to stay; it is a valid and challenging subfield of the study of international relations.

Endnotes

1. "Why the Ark Is Sinking," in L. Kaufman and K. Mallory, eds., *The Last Extinction*, 2nd ed. (Cambridge, MA: MIT Press, 1993), 1–46, 12.
2. See M. Feshbach and A. Friendly, *Ecocide in the USSR: Health and Nature under Siege* (New York: Basic Books, 1992).
3. D. Deudney, "The Mirage of Eco-War: The Weak Relationship among Global Environmental Change, National Security and Interstate Violence," in I. Rowlands and M. Greene, eds., *Global Environmental Change and International Relations* (London: Macmillan, 1992), 169–91, 178.
4. See P. Stoett, "The Environmental Enlightenment: Security Analysis Meets Ecology," *Coexistence* 31 (1994), 127–46.
5. Two popular books are R. Preston, *The Hot Zone* (New York: Random House, 1994), and L. Garrett, *The Coming Plague: Newly Emerging Diseases in a World Out of Balance* (New York: Farrar, Straus, and Giroux, 1994). See also F. Cartwright, *Disease and History* (New York: Thomas Crowell, 1972).

6. Dennis Pirages, "Microsecurity: Disease Organism and Human Well-Being," *Environmental Change and Security Project Report* (The Woodrow Wilson Center), 2 (1996), 9–14, 10.

7. Ibid., 10.

8. Although not an example of infectious disease, students from the Great Lakes area of Canada and the United States might recall the invasion of zebra mussels, which hitchhiked from Europe in ballast water in cargo ships. The mussels harmed both boats and local water systems.

9. "Global Warming and International Action: An Economic Perspective," in A. Hurrell and B. Kingsbury, eds., *The International Politics of the Environment* (Oxford: Clarendon Press, 1992), 253–89.

10. "Sovereignty, Regimes, and Human Rights," in V. Rittberger, ed., *Regime Theory and International Relations* (Oxford: Clarendon Press, 1993), 139–67. See also P.M. Wijkman, "Managing the Global Commons," *International Organization* 36 (3) (1982), 511–36.

11. M. M'Gonigle and D. Babicki, "The Turbot's Last Stand?" *The Globe and Mail* (21 July 1995), A19.

12. See C. Sanger, *Ordering the Oceans: The Making of the Law of the Sea* (Toronto: University of Toronto Press, 1987).

13. General Assembly Resolution 1803 (XVII), 14 December 1962.

14. *Ozone Diplomacy: New Directions in Safeguarding the Planet* (Cambridge: Harvard University Press, 1991), 207. See also R.R. White, "Environmental Management and National Sovereignty: Some Issues from Senegal," *International Journal* 45 (Winter 1990), 106–37.

15. T. Brenton, *The Greening of Machiavelli: The Evolution of International Environmental Politics* (London: Earthscan, 1994), 202.

16. L. Kimball, *Southern Exposure: Deciding Antarctica's Future* (Washington: World Resources Institute, 1991).

17. For the complete text, see *Antarctic Journal of the United States* [Natural Science Foundation], 26 (4) (December 1991).

18. The Swiss Reinsurance Co. even has a full-time climate-change adviser. P. Knox, "Weather Talk Becoming Urgent," *The Globe and Mail* (27 July 1996), A1.

19. B. McKibben, "Reflections: The End of Nature," *The New Yorker* (11 September 1989), 47–8.

20. Michael T. Klare, "Resource Competition and World Politics in the Twenty-First Century," *Current History* 99 (December 2000), 407.

21. C. Flavin and O. Tinali, *Climate of Hope: New Strategies for Stabilizing the World's Atmosphere*, Worldwatch Paper 130 (Washington: Worldwatch Institute, 1996).

22. C. Goldberg, "A Chilling Change in the Contraband Being Confiscated at Border Crossings," *The New York Times* (10 November 1996), 15.

23. Diana Jean Schemo, "Amazon Is Burning Again, as Furiously as Ever," *The New York Times* (12 October 1995), A3.

24. See UN Food and Agricultural Organization, *Forest Resources Assessment 1990: Tropical Countries*, Forestry Paper 112 (Rome: UN FAO, 1993).

25. *Global Environmental Outlook*, United Nations Environment Programme (New York: Oxford University Press, 1997), 235.

26. Ibid., 236.

27. M.B. Fenton, "Species Impoverishment," in J. Leith, R. Price, and J. Spencer, eds., *Planet Earth: Problems and Prospects* (Montreal/Kingston: McGill–Queen's University Press, 1995), 83–110. See also P. Ehrlich and A. Ehrlich, *Extinction* (New York: Wiley, 1986); N. Eldredge, *The Miner's Canary: Unravelling the Mysteries of Extinction* (New York: Prentice Hall, 1991); and P. Colinvaux, *Why Big Fierce Animals Are Rare: An Ecologist's Perspective* (Princeton: Princeton University Press, 1978).

28. D. Jablonski, "Mass Extinctions: New Answers, New Questions," in L. Kaufman and K. Mallory, eds., *The Last Extinction*, 2nd ed. (Cambridge, MA: MIT Press, 1993), 47–68, 52.

29. "Why the Ark Is Sinking," in L. Kaufman and K. Mallory, eds., *The Last Extinction*, 2nd ed. (Cambridge, MA: MIT Press, 1993), 1–46, 43. See also Kaufman's "Catastrophic Change in Species-Rich Freshwater Ecosystems: The Lessons of Lake Victoria," *Bioscience* 42 (11) (1992), 846–58; and Y. Baskin, "Africa's Troubled Waters: Fish Introductions and a Changing Physical Profile Muddy Lake Victoria's Future," *Bioscience* 42 (7) (1992), 476–81.

30. T. Foose, "Riders of the Last Ark: The Role of Captive Breeding in Conservation Strategies," in L. Kaufman and K. Mallory, eds., *The Last Extinction*, 149–78.

31. "Ethical Issues in Whale and Small Cetacean Management," *Environmental Ethics* 2 (3) (1980), 241–80, 244 n., 14.

32. R. Boardman, *International Organization and the Conservation of Nature* (Bloomington: Indiana University Press, 1981).

33. See, for example, B. Rich, *Mortgaging the Earth: The World Bank, Environmental Impoverishment and the Crisis of Development* (London: Earthscan, 1994).

34. T. Brenton, *The Greening of Machiavelli: The Evolution of International Environmental Politics* (London: Earthscan, 1994), 229.

35. An important contribution to this awareness was the famous text by Rachel Carson, *Silent Spring* (Boston: Houghton Mifflin, 1962).

36. See Catherine Caufield, *Multiple Exposures: Chronicles of the Radiation Age* (London: Secker and Warburg, 1989).

37. See Don Munton and Geoffrey Castle, "Reducing Acid Rain, 1980s," in Don Munton and J. Kirton, eds., *Canadian Foreign Policy: Selected Cases* (Scarborough: Prentice Hall, 1992), 367–80.

38. J. Wargo, *Our Children's Toxic Legacy: How Science and Law Fail to Protect Us From Pesticides* (New Haven: Yale University Press, 1996), 281.

39. See William S. Ellis, "A Soviet Sea Lies Dying," *National Geographic* (February 1990), 73–93.

40. See L. Ohlsson, ed., *Hydropolitics: Conflicts Over Water as a Development Constraint* (London: Zed, 1995). See also J.K. Cooley, "War Over Water," *Foreign Policy* 54 (1984), 3–26, and M. Lowi, *Water and Power: The Politics of a Scarce Resource in the Jordan River Basin* (Cambridge: Cambridge University Press, 1993).

41. T. Homer-Dixon, "The Myth of Global Water Wars," *The Globe and Mail* (9 November 1995), A23. He adds that the alarmist concern with inevitable water wars "distracts the public's attention from the real results of water scarcity. Shortages reduce food production, aggravate poverty and disease, spur large migrations and undermine a state's moral authority and capacity to govern. Over time, these stresses can tear apart a poor society's social fabric, causing chronic popular unrest and violence."

42. Letter is from R. Johnstone, of Newfoundland, and was published in *The Globe and Mail* (27 January 1994), A24. Somewhat ironically, Somalia faces a similar problem. Fishing boats from the EC and Pacific Asia have been harvesting the lobster and tuna grounds off the Somalian coast, and that destitute nation, without a coast guard, has been unable to deter them. "Somali Clans Threaten Foreign Fishing Boats," *The Globe and Mail* (3 February 1994), A9.

43. P. Koring, "Canada to Block Fish 'Pirates,'" *The Globe and Mail* (12 January 1994), A1, A2. Canadian Fisheries Minister Brian Tobin, who made this announcement during a meeting with EC Fisheries Commissioner Vannis Paleokrassas, told reporters: "It's an act of conservation; nobody could call it an act of war. We're out to declare enough is enough when it comes to the desecration of cod stocks by nations that operate outside of any civilized norms."

44. P. Sands, "Enforcing Environmental Security: The Challenges of Compliance with International Obligations," *Journal of International Affairs* 46 (2) (1993), 367–90. For a recent analysis of the Canada–Spain "fish war," see Andrew Cooper, *Canadian Foreign Policy: Old Habits, New Directions* (Scarborough: Prentice Hall Allyn and Bacon, 1997), 142–72.

45. Canada has yet to ratify this convention; it wants to wait to see which wastes the relevant technical committee declares hazardous first. Due to lax environmental standards, disposal costs in southern states are almost always considerably cheaper than in the north. This encourages northern companies to dump their waste in the latter. Canada generates up to five million tonnes of hazardous wastes annually and exports less than 10 percent. R. Matas, "Ban on Shipping Toxic Waste Endorsed by Rich Countries," *The Globe and Mail* (21 September 1995). Canada originally insisted that non-OECD states should be allowed to receive hazardous waste if they had the technological capacity to recycle it, but the overwhelming majority of the 88 states and the European Union supported a complete ban, since it is easy to classify anything as recyclable.

46. Eduardo Lachica, "U.S. Turns Back on Big Dams," *The Globe and Mail* (14 March 1996), A16.

47. Tom Utley, "McDonald's vs. Greenpeace," *Kitchener Record* (29 June 1996), A13.

48. J. Dooge et al., eds., *An Agenda of Science for Environment and Development into the 21st Century* (Cambridge: Cambridge University Press, 1992).

49. D. Freestone, "The Precautionary Principle," in R. Churchill and D. Freestone, eds., *International Law and Global Climate Change* (London: Graham and Trotham, 1991), 21–39; A. Moiseev, "The GEF: Aspects of Purpose, Formation, and Change," M.A. thesis, University of Guelph, 1996, 49–53.

50. *Ozone Diplomacy: New Directions in Safeguarding the Planet* (Cambridge, MA: Harvard University Press, 1991), 204–5.

Suggested Readings

Boyden, S. *BioHistory: The Interplay between Human Society and the Biosphere, Past and Present.* Paris: UNESCO, 1992.

Brown, N. "Climate, Ecology and International Security." *Survival* 31 (1989), 519–32.

Caldwell, L.K. *International Environmental Policy: Emergence and Dimensions.* Durham, NC: Duke University Press, 1990.

Choucri, N., ed. *Global Accord: Environmental Challenges and International Responses.* Cambridge, MA: MIT Press, 1993.

Dalby, S. "Ecopolitical Discourse: 'Environmental Security' and Political Geography." *Progress in Human Geography* 16 (4) (1992), 503–22.

Dauvergne, P. *Shadows in the Forest: Japan and the Politics of Timber in Southeast Asia.* Cambridge, MA: MIT Press, 1997.

Diamond, I., and G. Orenstein, eds. *Reweaving the World: The Emergence of Ecofeminism.* San Francisco: Sierra Club, 1990.

Haas, P., R. Keohane, and M. Levy, eds. *Institutions for the Earth.* Boston: MIT Press, 1993.

Huang, M. "The Anti-Nuclear Power Movement in Taiwan: Claiming the Right to a Clean Environment." In J. Bauer and D. Bell, eds., *The East Asian Challenge for Human Rights.* Cambridge: Cambridge University Press, 1999, 313–35.

Hurrell, A., and B. Kingsbury, eds. *The International Politics of the Environment.* Oxford: Clarendon Press, 1992.

Keohane, R., and M. Levy, eds. *Institutions for Environmental Aid: Pitfalls and Promise.* Cambridge, MA: MIT Press, 1996.

Litfin, K. *Ozone Discourses: Science and Politics in Global Environmental Cooperation.* New York: Columbia University Press, 1994.

MacDonald, D., and H. Smith. "Promises Made, Promises Broken: Questioning Canada's Commitments to Climate Change." *International Journal* LV (1) (1999), 107–24.

Mann, J., D. Tarantola, and T. Netter, eds. *AIDS in the World 1992.* Cambridge, MA: Harvard University Press, 1992.

Meadows, D.H., et al. *The Limits to Growth.* New York: Universe Books, 1972.

———. *Beyond the Limits: Global Collapse or a Sustainable Future.* London: Earthscan, 1992.

Mies, M., and V. Shiva. *Ecofeminism.* Halifax: Fernwood Publications, 1993.

Minger, T., ed. *Greenhouse Glasnost: The Crisis of Global Warming.* New York: Ecco Press/Institute for Resource Management, 1990.

Munton, D. "Dependence and Interdependence in Transboundary Environmental Relations." *International Journal* 36 (1981), 139–84.

Myers, N. "Environment and Security." *Foreign Policy* 74 (1989), 23–41.

Nanda, V.D. *International Environmental Law and Policy.* New York: Transnational, 1995.

Porter, G., and J. Welsh Brown. *Global Environmental Politics.* Boulder, CO: Westview, 1991.

Shiva, V., et. al. *Biodiversity: Social and Ecological Perspectives.* London: Zed, 1991.

Smith, R. "New Problems for Old: The Institution of Capitalist Economic and Environmental Irrationality in China." *Democracy and Nature* 5 (2) (1999), 249–74.

Tickell, C. "The World after the Summit Meeting at Rio." *Washington Quarterly* 16 (1993), 75–82.

Wapner, P. *Environmental Activism and World Civic Politics.* Albany: SUNY Press, 1996.

Young, O., ed. *The Effectiveness of International Environmental Regimes: Causal Connections and Behavioral Mechanisms.* Cambridge, MA: MIT Press, 1999.

Suggested Websites

Envirolink

UNEP
<www.unep.ch>

The Panos Institute
<www.oneworld.org/panos/index.html>

Global Environmental Facility, World Bank

Energy and Environment Links
<zebu.uoregon.edu/energy.html>

Climate Network Europe
<www.climnet.org>

TRAFFIC North America
<www.traffic.org/about/in_field_tna.html>

Environmental Law
<www.nd.edu/%7Elawlib/research/hrtopical4.html#T18>

Green Net

CHAPTER 11

Population Growth and Movement

To couple the concept of freedom to breed with the belief that everyone born has an equal right to the commons is to lock the world into a tragic course of action.

—Garrett Hardin, 1968[1]

The existence of refugees is a symptom of the disappearance of economic and political liberalism.... The basic real solution of the refugee problem, real or potential, is necessarily therefore related to the solution of the great problems of economic and political adjustment in the contemporary world.

—Sir John Hope Simpson, 1938[2]

INTRODUCTION: THE OVERPOPULATION DEBATE

Two of the most obvious trends in the immediate future will be continued population growth and population movements. This chapter will examine the debate over whether overpopulation is as important an issue as is often claimed and will examine urbanization and women's rights in this context. In addition, we discuss trends in migration and government responses, and then look at the problem of refugees.

Two central debates exist concerning the question of human population levels today: is overpopulation even a problem, and if so, who is responsible? It is hard not to consider overpopulation a problem given the social and environmental consequences of high population density around the globe. Therefore, the second debate will be more relevant in the future. Sometime in 1996, the population of Canada finally exceeded 30 million. At the end of the last ice age, when people began migrating to the area we now know as the Americas, the entire earth probably supported fewer than 10 million people. By 1930, there were two billion of us; by 1995, six billion, and, barring some large-scale calamity like nuclear war, there will be well over eight billion by the year 2025. After accounting for deaths, we are adding almost 100 million people a year to the planet (that's more than the population of Germany or Mexico). It is not uncommon to hear estimates of a global population of well over 12 billion in the near future. Demographers liken population growth rates to large cargo ships: one can stop the engines, but it will be some time before one stops the boat. Because so many women are of childbearing age, even if they all had but one child, the population would still increase dramatically since the newborns would be alive at the same time as their parents.

This population growth comes at a time when a major food crisis is looming on the horizon. During the 1960s and 1970s, the so-called green revolution increased crop yields through the use of irrigation, pesticides, and fertilizer, a less viable option today, when almost all prime arable land has been put to use and the excessive use of pesticides has often caused more problems than it has solved. The promise of GMOs (see the previous chapter) remains politically and scientifically contentious. Though enough food is available to feed everyone now and malnutrition and undernourishment are largely a consequence of inadequate distribution, this may not be the case when we have 12 billion people to feed. Current trends indicate that the distribution of food continues to be uneven, creating some areas of overindulgence and others of severe malnutrition.

The so-called **demographic transition** that characterized European development involved the decline of both death and birth rates as industrialization created advanced medical technology and people became more secure and thus less intent on raising large families. High infant mortality rates encourage parents to have more children since their survival is less certain. Demographers expected this pattern to repeat itself elsewhere, but this clearly has not been the case for many southern states, where population continues to rise. Though death rates have dropped in many places, birth rates stay high and populations continue to grow at 2.5, 3.0, and 3.5 percent or higher per year.[3] Several states now have, or will soon have, more than 100 million inhabitants (see Profile 11.1).

With more than a billion people, it is doubtful any sort of transition can stem massive population increases in places like China and India, and many argue that China's one-child policy, while a threat to individual liberty (and to the lives of consequently unwanted babies), was a necessary step that should be followed elsewhere. The idea of a population bomb was popularized in the 1970s by writers such as Paul and Anne Ehrlich, who argued that massive increases in population threatened not just the standard of living of people around the globe, but human life itself.[4] In what has become a classic piece of **neo-Malthusian** literature, "The Tragedy of the Commons," professor of

---

PROFILE 11.1

The Twenty Most Populous States, 1998

(All figures are estimates, rounded off to the nearest million.)

1.	China	1 236 000 000	12. Germany	82 000 000
2.	India	980 000 000	13. Vietnam	77 000 000
3.	United States	270 000 000	14. Philippines	75 000 000
4.	Indonesia	204 000 000	15. Turkey	64 000 000
5.	Brazil	166 000 000	16. Iran	62 000 000
6.	Russian Federation	149 000 000	17. Egypt	62 000 000
7.	Pakistan	132 000 000	18. Ethiopia	61 000 000
8.	Japan	126 000 000	19. Thailand	61 000 000
9.	Bangladesh	126 000 000	20. United Kingdom	60 000 000
10.	Nigeria	121 000 000	(Canada: 30.3 million)	
11.	Mexico	96 000 000		

Note that the science of population estimation is inexact.

SOURCE: *THE WORLD BANK, WORLD DEVELOPMENT INDICATORS 2000* (WASHINGTON: IBRD, 2000), TABLE 2.1.
© WORLD BANK. REPRINTED WITH PERMISSION.

human ecology Garret Hardin argued that we simply cannot afford to allow population increases and that to ensure our future collective survival, even the freedom to reproduce must be limited.[5]

Of course, many dismiss this as an extreme position; some argue population growth will level off with continued economic growth or with famine and disease. Indeed population rates have been slowing dramatically in some states, such as Germany and Russia. Others suggest that high populations themselves are not to blame for the environmental problems we face but rather that the consumption patterns of citizens in the relatively affluent states are unsustainable. According to a classic formula developed in the 1960s, the environmental impacts of population size, affluence (i.e., consumption), and technology are interrelated.[6] This formula suggests that, while absolute increases in population do put added strains on ecosystems, what that population consumes (and how it does so) is just as important. While the northern states have clearly contributed more to global warming and other industry-related problems than the southern ones, the most rapid population growth, by far, has been in the south. So while the question of whether population growth itself is the culprit of all our problems may be misleading, one cannot ignore the substantial impact that millions more people have each year.

It should be clear, then, that both the north and the south have an important role to play in decreasing the negative effects of population growth, but there is the additional ethical question of whether governments are right to impose birth control on their populations. The Chinese government has attempted to impose a one-child only policy on couples; inducements include charging fees for services for second children that were free for the first and rewarding single-child couples with promotions at work and free university education for the child. Abortions are strongly encouraged in the advent of a second pregnancy. In some cases, this policy has even resulted in **infanticide**: since baby boys are more highly valued than girls, couples intent on having a son may resort to murder should a girl be produced. Similarly, families in India, China, and elsewhere have used prenatal amniocentesis and ultrasound scanning to discover the sex of fetuses, and then aborted the females.[7] During the 1970s, China's fertility rate fell from 6 children per woman to about 2.5. Despite this drop, most people would agree that China still has a tremendous overpopulation problem. However, the ethical questions remain and will only become more pronounced as governments and international aid agencies struggle with continued population growth.

While a UN Conference on Population and Development in Cairo in 1994 did produce a plan to prevent world population from exceeding 7.2 billion people over the next two decades, it remains to be seen whether states will actually commit the resources this entails. Ultimately, it is up to individual governments to stem poverty and provide family planning possibilities; the record so far is not encouraging. Two of the more visible outcomes of the population explosion are urbanization and the demand for birth control policies in crowded states.

URBANIZATION

One of the most pronounced effects of population growth and movement is **urbanization**.[8] The city has often been viewed as a primary indicator of "modernity"; urbanization followed industrialization, which meant that **GNP (gross national product)** was increasing and society was advancing toward the Western ideal. Cities came to symbolize a certain notion of progress, but do Bangkok's steel and glass high-rises offer positive

Living with urbanization. Ten-year-old Lina Sumayg, one of hundreds of the Philippines' poorest people, holds onto a prized possession found in the trash in the Payatas slum district of Quezon City, Philippines. (AP Photo/Pat Roque)

proof of Thailand's economic miracle? Or do they merely put a glittering face on the detrimental effects of rapid development? For proletarian migrants, is the quality of life in burgeoning Mexico City an improvement over life in rural Mexico?

The pure logic behind the quest for the city is clear. Big cities with high population densities reduce the *unit costs of infrastructure*: it becomes cheaper to supply essential services (such as water, electricity, and education) to people if they live closer together. Employment opportunities, and the image of a better life, attract migratory labour. Companies are more likely to invest in cities, where both labour pools and urban middle-class markets are easily accessible. And since all this activity is highly concentrated, it can be regulated by government and, to the extent possible under a market economy, urban planning can facilitate a more humane, less alienating centre of human life.

Throwing the environmental question into this equation presents a profound challenge to such logic. If cities produce more pollution than can be safely managed, if traffic congestion not only creates smog but actually impedes transportation, if neighbouring land is degraded because of waste disposal needs and excessive demands on natural resources, and if most rural–urban migrants end up in unsanitary, marginalized shanty towns, is urbanization really a step in the right developmental direction? Increasingly, northern and southern analysts of sustainable development cast rapid urbanization in a negative light. This view is tied, of course, to population growth. Most dramatically, the spectre of rising megacities, great centres of sprawl, chaos, and pollution, looms over projected images of the southern hemisphere's future. In 1975, 1.5 million people lived in cities; by 1995, 2.6 billion people lived in cities. In 2000, half of the world's population lived in cities, and this urbanization is expected to continue, with 5.1 billion people living in cities by 2025 (see Profiles 11.2 and 11.3).

It is hardly questionable that the combination of urbanization, poverty, poor services, and lax regulations can have disastrous environmental effects. Katmandu, Nepal, a city designed for some 40 000 occupants, now has more than 700 000, and the famous Katmandu Valley is covered by a blue haze of pollution from cars, wood fires, kilns, and construction, which forces pedestrians and cyclists to wear cloth masks (a scene common in Mexico City as well). The rapid urbanization of Bhopal, India, was what made the industrial accident there in 1984 so disastrous in terms of human casualties, as leaked gas descended on the sleeping occupants of a nearby shantytown. Only 2 percent of Bangkok is connected to city sewers. The sorry list goes on and on: infrastructure

Megacities

Megacities are those with more than eight million inhabitants. In 1950, there were only two in the world: London and New York. By 2015, it is estimated that there will be more than 30. Below we list the top 10 largest cities in 1996, then the estimated top 10 in 2015. It is very difficult to compare estimates of city size, since different surveys include different areas as part of city centres, and the homeless often go uncounted.

TOP TEN MEGACITIES, 1996

1. Tokyo, 26.8 million
2. São Paulo, 16.4 million
3. New York, 16.3 million
4. Mexico City, 15.6 million
5. Bombay, 15.1 million
6. Shanghai, 15.1 million
7. Los Angeles, 12.4 million
8. Beijing, 12.4 million
9. Calcutta, 11.7 million
10. Seoul, 11.6 million

TOP TEN MEGACITIES, 2015 (ESTIMATED)

1. Tokyo, 28.7 million
2. Bombay, 27.4 million
3. Lagos, 24.5 million
4. Shanghai, 23.4 million
5. Jakarta, 21.2 million
6. São Paulo, 20.8 million
7. Karachi, 20.6 million
8. Beijing, 19.4 million
9. Dhaka, Bangladesh, 19 million
10. Mexico City, 18.8 million

SOURCE: UN HABITAT II, REPRINTED WITH PERMISSION OF THE UNITED NATIONS; J. VIDAL, "THE GLOBAL FORMULA FOR SOCIAL DYNAMITE," *THE GLOBE AND MAIL* (15 JUNE 1996), D4; ALSO SEE N. HAJARA, "BURSTING AT THE SEAMS," *TIME*, SPECIAL ISSUE, NOVEMBER 1997, 30–3.

An Emerging Global Megacity System?

Here is an interesting scenario: as globalization reduces the importance of the nation-state, the megacity replaces it as the primary means of expressing political power and conducting global interaction. The trend toward the megacity is evident in Ontario, where the provincial government amalgamated the different districts of Toronto into one big administration. Business today is conducted between cities, not countries. Likewise, travel is from metropolis to metropolis. As cities increase in size and wealth, devouring more of the countryside around them, the megacity may become the most important political unit. This is not without some historical precedent: in the period 800 to 322 B.C.E., a Greek city-state system flourished. The population of the cities varied: larger states such as Syracuse, Acragas, and Athens had around 50 000 citizens, while smaller cities, such as Siris and Thourioi in Sicily, had but several thousand.* Eventually, Athens formed a far-reaching empire that kept other cities under domination; this move was opposed by Sparta and other cities in the Peloponnesian League. War between the two alliances broke out in 431 B.C.E., and the entire system fell to Philip of Macedonia later that century. Might we see a world where dominant cities such as New York, London, and Tokyo battle it out for commercial and cultural supremacy?

*See K. Holsti, *International Politics: A Framework for Analysis*, 7th ed. (Englewood Cliffs, NJ: Prentice Hall, 1995), 36; he also cites K. Freeman, *Greek City States* (London: Methuen, 1948).

unable to meet city demands, unequal access to the infrastructure that is available, and lack of precautions against the environmental risks, both natural and industrial, that face certain segments of city populations.[9]

WOMEN'S RIGHTS AND BIRTH CONTROL

If we do accept the proposition that overpopulation is a real and urgent problem, we must ask next what we can do about it and what the ethical implications of such actions are. Birth control has been the technological cause of reduced fertility in the industrialized north, combining with higher education levels and higher standards of living to reduce reproductive rates. In the south, irreversible female sterilization is often the most common form of birth control. Concerns are mounting about the health impact of new birth control technologies, such as a drug called *quinacrine*, which is in fact an anti-malarial drug that causes scar tissue if placed directly in the womb. The scarring causes the fallopian tubes to become permanently blocked. Quinacrine also damages DNA in bacteria, so experts worry it might, in fact, cause cancer in women.

Beyond immediate health concerns, many raise questions regarding the ethical appropriateness of encouraging women—largely rural, uneducated women in underdeveloped states—to submit themselves to birth control measures. A common complaint is that the population issue, when it gets into the hands of government leaders and international bureaucrats at the UN and elsewhere, becomes a quantified issue or a numbers game. Groups like the International Planned Parenthood Federation promote birth control as a means toward greater societal stability but thus deflect attention from women's sexuality and reproductive freedom.[10] The abortion issue is even more divisive, since many religious representatives refuse to deal with policies that they think legitimize abortion on demand. During the Reagan and Bush administrations, the United States refused to fund planned parenthood programs because of their acceptance of abortion.

Others argue that instead of focusing on reducing sheer numbers, policies designed to limit population increases should concentrate on infant mortality and women's health. The lack of access to health care is a primary factor here. A recent study released by the **World Health Organization (WHO)** and **UNICEF** estimates that 585 000 women die from pregnancy-related causes each year, with almost all these deaths (99 percent) occurring in low-income states.[11] In the less-developed states, complications associated with pregnancy are often the leading causes of death among women of childbearing age; a high death rate is also associated with sterilization. By the mid-1990s, an African woman faced a 1 in 21 chance of dying as a result of pregnancy; the risk for a North American woman is 1 in 6366.[12]

We should also consider the words of Mahbub ul Haq, a special advisor to the administrator of the **UN Development Program (UNDP)**. While he was the minister of planning and finance in Pakistan (1982–88) he worked hard, aided by a **USAID** grant, to "saturate the villages with condoms." Nonetheless, "it was my greatest policy disaster. Despite the campaign, the population growth rate actually went up, from 3 to 3.1 percent. What went wrong? The answer is that female literacy in the villages was only 6 percent. Without investing in educating women, it was naive to expect investment in condoms to yield any effective results. If I had to do it all over again, I would put almost all that money into boosting female literacy."[13] These are hard-learned lessons, and there simply isn't enough development funding to afford many more of them. Of course, birth control is the responsibility of men as well. Millions of men have undergone vasectomies in the past two decades, and medical advances may make it possible for men to take a birth control pill themselves. Failing this, it is always safer, both to avoid unwanted pregnancy and to protect partners from sexually transmitted diseases, to rely on the good old-fashioned condom.

We now turn to one of the more pronounced effects of a heavily populated world: the rise in mobility of people in the form of both migrants and refugees. One of the primary stimulants to migration has always been employment opportunity, so we begin with a brief look at the contemporary context.

EMPLOYMENT AND MIGRATION

Keeping people busy is no small task. One of the most important functions of government during the Keynesian era has been to provide employment for citizens of states hit by temporary depression or recession. Several shifts in employment patterns can be noted in the industrialized states. Technological development, particularly the rise of microelectronics, has certainly reduced the need for manual labour; this leads to what we call structural unemployment, as opposed to unemployment caused simply by the standard growth–recession cycle. Also, many countries are moving toward smaller and more flexible production units, subcontracting work, and temporary or part-time hiring. These systems allow for rapid adjustment to market conditions and reduce the need to pay employees long-term benefits. Perhaps most important, corporations are increasingly able to use cheaper labour in the southern hemisphere to produce their goods.

Capital mobility, the increase in communications and transportation capability, and the ability to parcel out components of the work process have produced downward pressure on wages, suggesting that the standard of living, measured in real terms, is decreasing in many states, such as Canada and Britain. Unemployment is as high as 12 percent in France and Italy and 22 percent in Spain. Even the powerful German economy, after the reintegration of East and West, stood at 11 percent unemployment in 1995. Only Japan has managed to keep unemployment under 5 percent in the past decade, and this has been problematic given the long-term recession in that economy.[14]

However, unemployment levels will always fluctuate, and one might argue that a new workforce will gradually adapt to the new technology. This adaptation itself will generate employment as information technology educators train people. But this scenario may be a bit rosy and may neglect other factors. For example, former Communist states must deal with massive unemployment alongside privatization. Not only were many companies in these nations too quickly privatized but also now they must compete in world markets with much more efficient and experienced Western firms. It is estimated that, from 1990 to 1992, unemployment in former Eastern bloc countries and the former USSR rose from 100 000 to more than four million (14 percent in Poland, 11 percent in Hungary), and real wages have been declining as well.[15] Strikes are common as workers, fed up with terrible conditions and pay, seek to improve their condition. Even the military personnel so coveted during the height of the Cold War are reportedly undernourished and often go without pay, risking their lives in what are often inadequate safety conditions (epitomized by the sunken submarine *Kursk* in the summer of 2000). Yet, if they leave the army, they are sure to swell the ranks of the unemployed. In short, the crisis of unemployment will surely be one of the toughest and most troubling issues on the agenda of the international community in 2000 and beyond.

It is difficult to imagine the large impact transformations in prevalent technology will continue to have on the global economy. Changes in technology result in changes in the way goods are produced and the manner in which people are—or are not—employed to produce them. Often, people are being replaced by machines through **automation** in the form of **robotics**. Of course, this phenomenon is not new, but the new automation is much more omnipresent, and entire factories run by only a few humans and the robots they service will be commonplace in the future.[16] Japan leads in the field of industrial automation, with some two-thirds of the world's robots currently "employed" there.

The problem with automation, as India's great political and spiritual leader Mohandas Gandhi and others lamented many years ago, is that it displaces traditional workers. While some might view this as a sign of progress since it relieves humans from tedious work, it is a severe unemployment crisis to others (especially to those displaced) and will cause further problems in the future. A globalized economy will mean that capital, more mobile than ever, will seek out rewarding returns wherever they can be found. If cheap labour is available, then it will suffice; but cheap labour may be difficult to find in the future if highly specialized production lines continue to dominate production. Automation may look like an even better path to follow if this is the case.

Economists have long considered migration (the crossing of borders for temporary or permanent stay) the result of push–pull factors. Unemployment, low wages, environmental deterioration, warfare, and other negatives push migrants (or, in more extreme cases, refugees), while the promise of employment, higher wages, education for children, and other positive expectations pull them into big cities and across borders. Employment has always been the central concern for economists dealing with migration, and until recently, it may be argued that migration was largely considered an employment-related phenomenon.

One area where we might see increases in labour demand will involve the north–south trade route. Canada's recent signing of a free trade agreement with Chile is based on the assumption that trade between these two countries will rapidly increase in the near future. Canada stands to gain jobs in several sectors, including machinery and equipment, particularly for use in mining and forestry; telecommunications equipment and expertise; fertilizers; metallurgical and thermal coal; pharmaceuticals; certain chemical and glass products; a range of wood and paper products; aircraft; rail and urban rail equipment; autos and auto parts; and health and medical equipment. At the same time, the south–north labour movement, which would benefit the south by releasing some of the population and unemployment pressure currently growing there, is generally not welcomed by the northern states. As unemployment continues to be a huge problem in shifting economies, migration will increase. The world's labour force is projected to grow by almost one billion during the next two decades, mostly in developing countries hard-pressed to generate anywhere near an adequate number of jobs. Already, the human traffic within countries like China is startling; states will have to grapple with the question of what to do about this movement when borders are involved. Despite the rhetoric of proponents of globalization, borders are a real and determinative factor today. We discuss this below.

WHAT WOULD A TRULY BORDERLESS WORLD LOOK LIKE?

If the world had no sovereign nation-states and no borders that protected them from others, then there would be little political constraint on people's movements. Doubtless, other constraints would limit human movement. Access to transportation would be a key factor, as it has been throughout the ages. However, it is possible to travel long distances, by plane, ship, or train, with modest financial means. Another constraint would be cultural and the link between peoples and the land on which they were born and

From boat to bus to prison. Illegal migrants are escorted to waiting buses in Port Hardy, British Columbia. (CP Picture Archive/Chuck Stoody)

raised. The largest constraint on movement is a rather difficult thing to measure: contentment. If people are relatively satisfied with the standard of living they enjoy, they will not see a need to pick up and move on. The Europeans who flooded the United States and Canada in the late nineteenth century were leaving in search of a better life, just as many migrants from developing states are doing today when they move northward. In a world divided between rich and poor, there is more pressure than ever for northward migration, and were it not for the immigration controls afforded by borders, the flow would be much greater. In 1989, the UN estimated that some 50 million people, or 1 percent of the world's population, lived in countries other than their country of origin, and the World Bank estimated the number of international migrants of all kinds at 100 million.[17]

According to a simple economic model, labour follows capital. In other words, a truly borderless world would mean that people would flock to sources of employment, wherever they might be. As the world economy becomes increasingly integrated, however, the centres of financial power and industrial production would become heavily overcrowded, and it would be increasingly difficult to sustain them. We see this domestically with the process of urbanization, discussed above, but this could occur at a global level as well, as entire areas, megacities, even states attract labour. We do not, however, live in a borderless world (despite what some of the more assertive advocates of globalization have been telling us). In fact, the migration and refugee issue-area reinforces the concept of the state system based on territory and sovereignty, for much of the world lives behind relatively closed borders, and states are increasingly protecting their own citizens before admitting others (see Profile 11.4).

Many argue that increased population pressure and migration will exacerbate divergence in the world system because states still jealously protect their borders from foreign intrusion. This fact is most evident in the **immigration** control issue-area. Trade liberalization encourages capital mobility, but there has not been a commensurate opening of borders to labour migration. If anything, the opposite has occurred as northern governments increase entry requirements and attempt to lure only those migrants who can clearly afford to pay their own way or, better, invest in the economy. Nowhere is this as acute as in Western Europe, where the fall of the Soviet Union and Eastern bloc states has led to **emigration**, from both the former Soviet Union and elsewhere (see Profile 11.5). The war in Yugoslavia, meanwhile, demonstrated the potential for forced migration to take place in the post–Cold War era. We need not stop at Europe, however, for a look at the contemporary **refugee** crisis. Recent mass movements of refugees have occurred in South America, Africa, and Asia.

Migrants and Refugees: What Is the Difference?

Generally speaking, the difference between migrants and refugees is that the former leave their country voluntarily, while the latter are forced to do so. However, the distinction between voluntary and involuntary migration, while important, is also necessarily fuzzy. Not all involuntary migrants would be considered refugees by the international convention on that topic. Anthony Richmond* prefers the terms "proactive" and "reactive" migration.

We should note also the existence of another category of migrants who are usually labelled *nondocumented* (also known as illegal aliens). According to the Program of Action of the International Conference on Population and Development (ICPD), documented migrants are "those who satisfy all the legal requirements to enter, stay and, if applicable, hold employment in the country of destination." See also Profile 11.8 on Civil War Refugees and Canada.

* See his *Global Apartheid: Refugees, Racism, and the New World Order* (Oxford: Oxford University Press, 1994).

Mass Migration and the Former Soviet Union

Few areas have experienced the type of turmoil brought on by the dissolution of the Soviet Union in the late 1980s. One of the more pronounced effects of this political transformation has been a huge exodus of ethnic groups across the region. Since 1989, more than nine million people have left their homes because of ethnic tension or environmental disasters. This figure means that 1 of every 30 residents of the former Soviet Union has migrated! In this case it is clear that we are dealing with forced migration: 3.6 million refugees have fled from the Armenia–Azerbaijan war and the fighting in Chechnya. Many of the migrants were trying to return to ancestral homelands after their previous forced evacuation during the Stalin era. More than 34 million Russians, Ukrainians, and Belorussians were living outside their homelands when the Soviet Union expired. Slavs have been moving from the five new states of Central Asia—Turkmenistan, Uzbekistan, Kazakhstan, Tajikistan, and Kyrgyzstan. The severe environmental decay of the Aral Sea in Central Asia, radiation in the Semipalatinsk nuclear testing range, and the infamous Chernobyl meltdown (see Chapter 10) have also forced citizens to move themselves and their belongings to other areas. All this movement of peoples produces a great deal of confusion, not only within the affected areas but also throughout the Commonwealth of Independent States and the international diplomatic system as a whole.

Concerns continue about a resumption of the old Russian nationalism of the past, perhaps abetted by the introduction of post–Soviet Communists into power in Moscow. Further, Western Europe in particular is concerned with the possibility that many of the forced migrants will eventually find their way into Western Europe, where living conditions continue to be a good deal better. So we see that political, economic, and social factors are all involved in this international dilemma.

SOURCE: SEE R. EVANS, "MASS INTERNAL MIGRATIONS UNSETTLE FORMER SOVIET STATES," *THE GLOBE AND MAIL* (23 MAY 1996).

The sudden influx of refugees into an area disturbs both the political and environmental conditions of the receiving area. Although humanitarian relief is a widely touted principle in the international system, and some states such as Canada have always emphasized this in their foreign policy platforms, the fact is that it is very draining to house and support refugees, especially in states with limited access to resources. Thus, rather than suggest newfound political convergence as free individuals cross borders when they want to, the current migration and refugee situation reflects violence, destitution, and increasing resistance to what we might term the humanitarian impulse. With some notable exceptions, such as the rights of labourers in the European Union, we are far from entering the age of mobility. In short, a truly borderless world would look remarkably different from the one we see today.

THE MOVEMENT OF PEOPLES IN HISTORY

People have always been on the move, for the purpose of escape, enrichment, or just plain adventure. As Sidney Klein has demonstrated, mass migrations "go back millions of years," long before the advent of the modern nation-state.[18] To name just a few examples, early movements in Mesopotamia of Assyrians and Hittites, and of Indo-Europeans into India, date back to 2000 B.C.E. The people who developed Greek civilization filtered down through the Balkan peninsula to the shores of the Aegean Sea about 1900 B.C.E., undermining the older Cretan civilization; and around 1150 B.C.E. other Greek-speaking tribes invaded from the north. The Greeks would go on to form the city-states, such as Athens, Corinth, and Sparta, which many historians view as the beginning of the international system (see Chapter 2).

Many generations later, the industrializing states of Europe used the emigration of tens of millions of Europeans to head off a looming overpopulation problem in the nineteenth and early twentieth centuries; they encouraged immigration in the post–World War II period to provide the labourers needed for reconstruction. In fact, Europe's burgeoning cities would have suffered from unprecedented overpopulation between 1840 and 1940 were it not for the migration of almost 60 million people from Europe to countries such as the United States, Russia, Argentina, Canada, Brazil, and Australia.

The great European exodus was caused by a combination of push and pull factors. Politically, the age of individual liberalism meant that people were for the first time literally free to move. Europeans were pushed out of Europe by rises in population and scarcity of work; in an extreme case, millions fled the famine in Ireland in 1846. As usual, technological advances played a decisive role as well. The steamship made it easier, and cheaper, to cross the sea (an experience enjoyed previously only by the very rich or by sailors). Railroads were instrumental in distributing people to and from ports. Some people were fleeing from political persecution, such as the many Russian and Polish Jews who entered the United States before World War I. On the pull side, many of the receiving states actively campaigned to attract Europeans as valuable labourers and farmers (exceptions to this pattern were Australia and New Zealand, which discouraged the importation of cheap labour). Migrant labourers would be a valuable source of remittances back home, and this transfer of funds continues today (see Profile 11.6). In the early 1920s the United States began to impose quota restrictions on the number of immigrants it would accept, and since then northern states have gradually adopted policies aimed at constricting, not encouraging, emigration.

It is also important to understand that ethnicity and population movements are often closely connected. Two terms that are often used to reflect this are *irredenta* and *diaspora*. Irredenta are "territorially based minorities contiguous to a state controlled by their co-ethnics," people who often call for the right to self-determination.[19] Hitler used Germans living abroad to encourage acceptance of his expansionist foreign policy. A Malay–Muslim majority inhabits Thailand's four southern provinces, though Malaysia

PROFILE 11.6 — Remittances by International Migrant Workers, Selected Countries, Early 1990s

	IN MILLIONS OF DOLLARS	REMITTANCES AS A SHARE OF FOREIGN EXCHANGE EARNINGS
Albania	278	57
El Salvador	789	37
Egypt	4 960	31
Jordan	1 040	26
Bangladesh	942	25
Morocco	1 945	23
Mali	87	23
Greece	2 360	16
Portugal	3 844	15
Pakistan	1 562	15
Philippines	279	13
Turkey	2 919	10
India	3 050	9

SOURCES: WORLD BANK, *WORLD DEVELOPMENT REPORT 1995* (NEW YORK: OXFORD UNIVERSITY PRESS, 1995); AND M. RENNER, *FIGHTING FOR SURVIVAL* (NEW YORK: W.W. NORTON, 1996), 100.

and Thailand have maintained fairly good relations over the last few decades. Irredenta are created by shifts in political geography—the movement of borders induced by occupation or annexation, for example.

Diaspora, however, are created by migration; they are groups of people who live outside their area of ethnic origin. Many diasporas have been very influential because of their cosmopolitan orientation, diverse language skills, and commercial contacts. Examples include Jews and Greeks in the Ottoman Empire, the Germans in Tsarist Russia, and the Chinese in many Asian states, including Thailand and Malaysia. Other diaspora are linked more directly to population movements induced by the opportunity of working abroad, such as the Algerians and Senegalese in France, Jamaicans and Pakistanis in Great Britain, and Mexicans and Filipinos in the United States. These groups often become permanent citizens, and, as in the case of the American Cuban community, they can be quite vocal in political terms.

Migration today takes place all over the world, with heavy south–north and east–west patterns. Migrant workers bring skills that are often employed in host countries because others refuse to do the work, and this generates large remittances that are sent home (see Profile 11.6 for an idea of how important this practice has become in many states today). Some states are highly dependent on receiving these remittances, as they are a chief source of foreign exchange. As migrant workers establish themselves in new countries, they may become citizens or permanent residents and bring the rest of their families over with them. Thus, migration acts to provide labour pools in receiving countries, while it relieves unemployment in sending countries. This is the theory, at any rate: in some cases, migration increases social and economic problems in host countries, while it drains sending countries of valuable human resources (see Profile 11.7).

Another issue related to migration is the spread of disease. Again, this is an old story, since migrants have brought their diseases, and immune systems, with them since the

PROFILE 11.7 — Largest Refugee-Generating Countries and Countries Hosting the Largest Refugee Populations, January 1995

REFUGEE-GENERATING COUNTRIES			REFUGEE-HOSTING COUNTRIES		
COUNTRY	THOUSANDS OF REFUGEES	% of POPULATION	COUNTRY	THOUSANDS OF REFUGEES	% of POPULATION
Afghanistan	2 744	15.0	Iran	2 236	4.0
Rwanda	2 257	29.0	Zaire	1 724	4.0
Liberia	794	26.0	Pakistan	1 055	1.0
Iraq	702	3.0	Germany	1 005	1.0
Somalia	536	6.0	Tanzania	883	3.0
Eritrea	422	12.0	Sudan	727	3.0
Sudan	399	1.0	United States	592	0.2
Burundi	389	6.0	Guinea	553	9.0
Bosnia	321	9.0	Côte d'Ivoire	360	3.0
Vietnam	307	0.4	Ethiopia	348	1.0

SOURCES: UN HIGH COMMISSIONER FOR REFUGEES, *THE STATE OF THE WORLD'S REFUGEES 1995* (NEW YORK: OXFORD UNIVERSITY PRESS, 1995); AND M. RENNER, *FIGHTING FOR SURVIVAL* (NEW YORK: W.W. NORTON, 1996), 102.

days of early trading in the Middle East. When the Europeans began to migrate to the Americas, the result was the death of millions of Indigenous inhabitants who were exposed to European germs. The problem remains serious today, as several case studies demonstrate, especially in the age of AIDS.[20]

PROTECTING MIGRANT WORKERS[21]

Migrant workers often end up in vulnerable positions and are perceived as needing additional, international protection. However, this is a very touchy area, since it falls within the jurisdiction of individual states to govern their own domestic labour laws. Previous work by the International Labour Organization (ILO) helped form the basis for what is arguably the most important UN General Assembly resolution dealing with migrant labour, the International Convention on the Protection of the Rights of All Migrant Workers and Members of Their Families. This is a comprehensive document that, at present, has escaped ratification by the majority of UN states, including Canada. It requests governments to pursue nondiscriminatory practices regarding migrant employees, including nondocumented migrants, and their families. It is, in essence, an attempt to guarantee migrant workers the same rights that are already enshrined in the *Universal Declaration of Human Rights* (1948) and the subsequent International Covenants on Human Rights. For example, Article 10 states that "No migrant worker or member of his or her family shall be held in slavery or servitude"; Article 12 calls for their right to "freedom of thought, conscience and religion," including the right to "ensure the religious and moral education of their children in conformity with their own convictions"; and Article 18 gives migrants "the right to equality with nationals of the State concerned before the courts and tribunals."

At a much more visible level, the UN Conference on Population and Development at Cairo (1994) was precedent setting in that it included migration on its agenda. The most significant outcome was the establishment of the Program of Action of the International

Conference on Population and Development (ICPD). Canada pushed strongly to include migration on the ICPD agenda. Chapters IX and X of the ICPD Program of Action discuss contemporary migration pressures, assuming a broad scope on the topic, including the role of development, documented and undocumented migrants, refugees, asylum seekers, and displaced persons. It suggests that the north–south gap in wealth be reduced; that migrants' remittances be facilitated and channelled into productive investment in developing states; that discriminatory practices that harm migrants, including current outbreaks of racism and **xenophobia** (a fear or hatred of others not in one's social or ethnic group), be stopped; that family reunification of migrants be promoted; that the exploitation of undocumented migrants be prevented; and, related to the latter, that international trafficking in migrants (especially for the purpose of prostitution) be prevented. As with all such sweeping statements, most of this is a lot easier said than done.

MULTILATERAL ORGANIZATIONS AND MIGRATION

Another multilateral effort to aid migrants has been the work of the **International Organization for Migration (IOM).** The IOM has assisted in many efforts to help refugees but also helps migrants settle in new areas and acquire needed job skills. By 1976 the IOM had permanent offices in Indonesia, Malaysia, Singapore, and Thailand. In the 1980s the IOM became increasingly involved in migration and refugee assistance in Latin America and in 1991 was entrusted by the UN Disaster Relief Co-ordinator to organize the **repatriation** of foreigners stranded in the Gulf region after Iraq's invasion of Kuwait; this amounted to some 200 000 repatriations.[22] The IOM has also been involved extensively with the U.S.–Haitian refugee situation, helping with the interview process of boat people in Port-au-Prince (the in-country refugee processing system), Miami (facilitating domestic transportation for approved refugees), and also in Kingston, Guantánamo, and the Turks and Caicos Islands. The IOM prepares case files, coordinates interviews with American immigration officers, arranges for departure assistance, and aids resettlement in the United States for approved refugees.[23] More controversially, the IOM has become involved in the repatriation process as well. The IOM is often criticized for promising more than it can deliver on the policy side of the issue; and since it is dependent on receiving states for funding, it is often accused of being an organization that merely fulfills the wishes of the United States and others.

Many regional multilateral organizations have put migration somewhere on the agenda, if not front and centre. For example, the G-7 states (Canada, Japan, Italy, France, the United Kingdom, the United States, and Germany), which hold annual summits and lesser-publicized ministerial-level meetings to discuss economic coordination, often deal with migration issues; however, it has yet to become a big-ticket item, despite the fact that it is obviously intrinsic to the often-discussed question of unemployment. The OECD surveys migration trends as well, and the European Union has a variety of mechanisms designed to both facilitate labour movement within the Union and limit migration into it.

Canada has been participating in the Intergovernmental Consultations on Asylum, Refugee, and Migration Policies in Europe, North America, and Australia (commonly referred to as either the IGC or the Informal Consultations) based, with its own small secretariat, in Geneva. At present, 15 governments take part in the consultations, which began in 1985, and generate documentation on issues such as temporary protection, asylum procedures, trafficking in illegal aliens, and unaccompanied minors.[24] The **UN**

High Commissioner for Refugees (UNHCR) and IOM both participate in the process, though it has a rather closed-door image. Since the consultations are among countries of destination only, they have been criticized for what one analyst believes is a self-protective focus on "removals, prevention of asylum-seeking, and individuals seeking asylum in order to avoid asylum shopping."[25] However, we should not exaggerate the IGC's ability to realize its goal, since most states—including Canada—remain reluctant to lose their ability to be flexible on asylum, refugee, or migration policies.

REFUGEES

"Everyone has the right to seek and enjoy in other countries asylum from persecution" (*Universal Declaration of Human Rights*, 1948, Article 14).

Refugees are created when people facing persecution flee their circumstances individually or in groups and when people are forcibly expelled from their home state. Though we usually envision the former when we think of refugees, we should also keep in mind that mass expulsions have been common forms of policy throughout history: some 15 million Africans were forced overseas into slavery before 1850 and massive forced movements were notable before, during, and after World War II.[26] During the Cold War, refugee movements were often considered political priorities by the West; however, they now receive a less urgent response and though many states such as Canada have maintained fairly liberal refugee acceptance policies, international refugee assistance is clearly underfunded.

It is, of course, extremely difficult to measure the number of refugees worldwide, especially if one seeks to include people who have been displaced within their home state.

Dislocation in wartime. An unidentified woman carries a wounded boy, injured when local ethnic Albanians threw stones at a camp where Gypsies had taken refuge in the village of Obilicevo, near Pristina, in the Yugoslav province of Kosovo. About 900 Gypsies, fearing attacks from ethnic Albanians who accused them of collaborating with Serbs, left the town of Kosovo Polje and came to the camp in Obilicevo. (AP Photo/Amel Emric)

When G.J. van Heuren Goedhart was appointed the first UN High Commissioner for Refugees in 1951, there were 1.25 million refugees. In 1976, with Sadruddin Aga Khan as High Commissioner, there were 2.8 million recognized refugees. In 1994, by contrast, there were more than 19 million, and this figure was taken before the frenzy of violence in and resultant exodus from Rwanda in April–May 1994.[27] By 1999, the UNHCR was responsible for a total of 21 459 550 persons.[28]

Along with this unprecedented increase in numbers, a much more complex understanding of refugee and migration issues has evolved. While political refugees were once regarded as "the tragic product of an incompatible juxtaposition, whether of faction, class, religion, ideology, or nationality,"[29] other factors such as development, over-population, and the environment play major roles today, necessitating even more complex models. Just as important, we need to look at multilateral efforts to deal with refugee flows, efforts that are aimed not only at mitigating the human suffering of refugees but also at protecting the states into which they flow.

MULTILATERAL RESPONSES TO THE REFUGEE PROBLEM

At the international level, the UNHCR remains the principal organization whose mandate is to aid and assist refugees. The UNHCR is constantly employed today in all corners of the globe. While its primary mandate relates to caring for those Convention refugees who cross borders, it is increasingly dealing with internally displaced persons as well. The UNHCR budget, which is derived from voluntary contributions (largely from states but also from nongovernmental organizations and individuals), is divided into funding for general programs (basic projects for refugee aid and durable solutions, the most important of which is repatriation) and special programs, which include responses to sudden emergencies such as the outflow of more than one million Rwandans from that troubled state in 1994–95.

Several other UN bodies are involved in refugee protection and assistance. Most notably, the United Nations Relief Works Administration (UNRWA), another voluntary, contribution-based international organization, was established in 1949 to deal with the refugee problem generated by the first Arab–Israeli War, and its operations have expanded to include health care and education provision. It had more than 2.5 million people registered in 1991, located in Jordan, Syria, Lebanon, the West Bank, and the Gaza Strip.[30] The UNRWA, with more than 18 000 Palestinian employees, is the single largest operating program within the UN system. Despite the political uncertainty in the region, it "carries on a thankless task, criticized for not doing more while financial contributors grow restive in support of a relief operation that has no end in sight."[31] A Canadian-led international committee, termed the Refugee Working Group, has toured Jordanian refugee camps for Palestinians, with an aim toward incorporating the refugee question into the broader Middle East peace process.

The United Nations Relief and Rehabilitation Administration (UNRRA) was established by the Allies in 1943 to follow them into liberated areas at the close of World War II to provide immediate relief to victims of the war, including concentration camp survivors. UNICEF was established in 1946, and in 1953 moved into longer-term programs beyond Europe and Asia. UNICEF delivers aid to drought- and war-stricken regions and works with the WHO to help meet the nutritional requirements of refugee children. The WHO is also involved with assessing the nutritional requirements of refugee populations; in 1988 an international conference, "Nutrition in Times of Disaster," met at WHO's headquarters in Geneva. More broadly, the UNHCR works in conjunction with the World Food Program in many cases of unexpected refugee flows (see Profile 11.8).

The UNHCR also consults with some 300 NGOs that play roles in relief operations. In 1993, more than a quarter of the UNHCR budget went to NGOs. However, what is arguably the most significant partner is in fact an intergovernmental organization, the **International Committee of the Red Cross (ICRC)** (in Islamic countries, the International Committee of the Red Crescent). Its history dates to 1859, and it was charged in 1864 with overseeing the implementation of the first Geneva Convention. At present the ICRC has 48 delegations operating in 80 countries, and a considerable portion of its operations involve refugee assistance. Examples of heavy ICRC involvement include El Salvador and Nicaragua, Sudan, Angola, Mozambique, Uganda and Somalia, Afghanistan, Pakistan, the Thai/Cambodian border, and the territories occupied by

In 1996, Canada issued new guidelines that reduce the confusion over who can be admitted as a refugee during a civil war. The chair of the Immigration and Refugee Board, Nurjehan Mawani, said these guidelines reflect what many board members were already doing, as well as the precedents set by the Federal Court of Appeal. People fleeing civil war are judged by the risk of persecution they face. Individuals do not have to be personally singled out. If they are members of a large, persecuted group, they are considered refugees under the United Nations refugee convention, which includes persecution based on race, religion, nationality, or membership in a social group. Civilians caught in indiscriminate shelling or looting are not considered refugees unless they are members of an ethnic or religious group that is a target. However, they must show that they cannot flee to another part of their home country or that another group cannot protect them.

SOURCE: LILA SARICK, "GUIDE ON CIVIL-WAR REFUGEES ISSUED," *THE GLOBE AND MAIL* (8 MARCH 1996), A7.

Israel. ICRC represents displaced civilians to governments and armed movements, actively protects them through its ability to achieve legal access (occasionally denied) to refugee and internment camps, provides medical, food, and material assistance, and runs the Tracing Agency, which seeks to reunite displaced and separated families.[32]

ICRC and UNHCR have some overlap in their mandates, but a general division of labour has evolved: the ICRC assumes primary responsibility for persons displaced within a country during wartime, while the UNHCR has exclusive responsibility for refugees in countries of temporary or first asylum. This distinction, however, is not permanent, as was evidenced with the ill-fated Safe Haven plan in Bosnia-Herzegovina, when the UNHCR was used to protect and feed internal displacees. In one case, a UN pullout left the ICRC to service genuine cross-border refugees as well.[33] Though it might appear as if these two agencies overlap considerably, it is essential that each exist independent of the other. The Red Cross is involved with warfare-related situations exclusively, while the UNHCR is not. The Red Cross operates independently from the UN system (although it has observer status in the General Assembly), while the UNHCR does not. The Red Cross is willing to go where the UNHCR is not, and the UNHCR does things the Red Cross cannot. Both are desperately needed today; unfortunately, both are entirely dependent on the voluntary contributions of states and individuals for funding, which is habitually meagre.

Other NGOs play important roles in emergency humanitarian assistance as well. Notably, the Save the Children Fund has played a key role in many refugee relief situations (more than half the world's refugees are children) in places as diverse as Russia, Hungary, Korea, Algeria, Jordan, Gaza and the West Bank, Cambodia, Laos, Central America, Iraq, Rwanda, Zaire, Nepal, and Bangladesh. The Save the Children Fund was founded in 1919 by a British schoolteacher named Eglantyne Jebb, who would draft the Declaration of the Rights of the Child in 1923, adopted by the **League of Nations** in 1923 and, much later, redrafted as the 1989 UN Convention on the Rights of the Child. In 1979 various national units came together under the umbrella of the Geneva-based International Save the Children Alliance (ISCA), which now has 25 members.[34]

On a global level, the refugee situation is particularly acute. If the world community, and especially the primary donor states, wants the UNHCR to deal with emergency refugee flows, then it will have to increase funding for this highly strained organization.

For example, Canada presently funds overseas emergency refugee assistance through the International Humanitarian Assistance (IHA) budget of the **Canadian International Development Agency (CIDA)**; this amounts to less than 3 percent of the IHA budget, and CIDA's overall funding level will be decreasing in the next few years.[35] As for the idea that giving aid to refugees will foster dependence and corrupt the initiative of refugees themselves, this has been widely disputed by scholars such as David Keen.[36]

THE INTERNALLY DISPLACED

Social and environmental problems, including poverty, resource scarcity, and warfare, can induce large-scale refugee movements. However, most displaced people do not cross national borders. There are millions of involuntary migrants who are victims of political violence and environmental degradation yet who are not officially considered refugees because they are not crossing borders. This matter is still considered purely one of domestic policy. Rural–urban migration, population displacement caused by large-scale development projects, deforestation, soil degradation, and even forced expulsions between regions within states are still considered the domestic affairs of sovereign states, and although outside funding agencies can certainly wield influence in directing governments away from these processes, stopping them altogether is not a distinct possibility under the present circumstances.[37]

The government of Indonesia has orchestrated one of the largest internal movements of people. In an effort to reduce overcrowding on the main Indonesian island of Java, some six million people have been moved to outlying islands such as Sumatra, Kalimantan, Sulawesi, and Irian Jaya. Most of those resettled work in agriculture and many now actually own their own land. Lately, the migrants have found work in other areas, such as rubber and coffee plantations, fishponds, and seaweed processing plants. However, despite reforestation projects in eastern Kalimantan, environmentalists complain about the widespread deforestation caused by this mass migration to formerly remote areas, and many of the migrants are living in dire poverty in their new locations. Nonetheless, the program continues, as Jakarta, the main city on Java, continues to grow. It is estimated that the metropolis will have well over 20 million citizens by the year 2015.[38]

Two essential types of internal displacees exist: those who have fled warfare or extreme environmental degradation, and those who have been moved by their governments for the purposes of economic development. In either case, it is still a matter of considerable debate whether the UNHCR or any other body should be permitted to interfere in the internal affairs of a state to help internally displaced people.[39] When Russian forces caused people to flee the war zone in Chechnya, Russia asked the UNHCR to assist in the care of the internally displaced. However, this request was an exception to the rule. More generally, millions of internally displaced people in the next few decades will have a difficult time integrating with the rest of the societies in which they live. This difficulty will in turn increase outward, cross-border migratory pressure as well.

GENDER, THE SEX TRADE, AND TRAFFICKING IN MIGRANTS

Within the subfield of migration studies, several other issue-areas are receiving increasing attention. The question of gender is foremost among them. Women migrants and refugees face a unique set of obstacles as they resettle in new countries.[40] They are often the victims of outright repression in their home states, and, in fact, several states—Canada among them—have gone so far as to accept such women as legitimate Convention refugees.[41] In their new settings, they often find it difficult to obtain employment that can adequately support them and their children. Single women and unaccompanied minors are certainly vulnerable to harm and, especially, sexual abuse, in refugee camps.

As the result of destitution or outright coercion, many women and children migrants become involved in the international sex-trade industry (see Profile 11.9). This represents not only a shameful aspect of the failure to provide basic human rights to those affected but also increases the health risks associated with such work. Most notably, of course, the spread of HIV/AIDS, which is virtually uncontrollable in many regions of the world today, is undeniably accelerated by prostitution, which often assumes the form of a global operation, complete with resorts attracting men from North America, Europe, and Asia. The international community has often dealt with this issue; even the long-defunct League of Nations had a Committee of the Abolition of White Slavery (terminology largely discarded today) and preceding that there was an international Agreement for the Suppression of the White Slave Traffic and related conventions in 1904 and 1910, respectively. It is not possible, therefore, to argue that this issue is too new to deal with. Yet we need more global attention to stop or at least limit this flagrant form of exploitation, as well as domestic legislation discouraging the practice.[42] However, until this issue becomes more prominent and is addressed with more energy, little will be done, as some governments are accomplices in the growth of the sex industry.

The illegal trafficking in migrants is of growing concern worldwide, despite measures such as the Convention on the Rights of the Child, which asserts, "State parties shall take measures to combat the illicit transfer and non-return of children abroad."[43] A recent seminar sponsored by the IOM on the trafficking of migrants concluded that it was part of a much broader pattern of transnational criminal activity and could only be dealt with as an element of an internally coordinated strategy to eliminate that sector.[44] However, this is much easier said than done for a wide variety of reasons that space limitations do not permit us to explore here. In addition, there is the question of the rights of illegal migrants, which is a particularly visible issue in the United States. The Migrant Worker's Convention outlined above would apply to these people as well, and this explains some of the overwhelming reluctance among industrialized states to even sign the agreement.

Discrimination against migrants, especially female migrants, takes many forms around the globe.[45] It might be argued that one of the greatest difficulties involves

---

PROFILE 11.9

Transnational Prostitution: A Resolution

A large traffic in women and children for the purpose of prostitution remains, according to a recent resolution adopted by the United Nations General Assembly. In it, the UN condemned the illicit and clandestine movement of persons across national and international borders, largely from developing countries and some countries with economies in transition, with the end goal of forcing women and children into sexually or economically oppressive and exploitative situations, for the profit of recruiters, traffickers, and crime syndicates, as well as into other illegal activities related to trafficking, such as forced domestic labour, false marriages, clandestine employment, and false adoption.

SOURCE: UN RESOLUTION A/RES/49/166, 24 FEBRUARY 1995.

encouraging governments to accept the idea that all migrants, be they permanent (settlers), temporary contract workers, temporary professional transients, clandestine or illegal workers, asylum seekers, or genuine refugees as defined by the 1951 Convention, are entitled to the same rights. This is simply not an acceptable formula; it would imply, for example, that temporary workers and even illegal migrants would have the right to vote and receive the same social services as regular tax-paying citizens.

CONCLUSIONS: WHITHER THE AGE OF MOBILITY?

Migration policies among the industrialized northern states have, by and large, emphasized the closure of borders.[46] Overall, one might argue that we have seen a shift in how the world community views the migration issue-area: an evolution from what was once viewed primarily as a labour-related question to what is today seen primarily as a population—or, more specifically, overpopulation—question.

Even if the neoclassical framework for development and trade liberalization is effective in stimulating markets, this will not necessarily stop migratory pressure. Georges Tapinos notes this with regard to NAFTA: its initial success might absorb some of the surplus of Mexican labour resulting from industrialization and a decrease in agricultural subsidies, "but the majority will seek employment in the United States.... It is a straightforward illustration of the fact that [trade and investment] liberalization between countries with significant differences in size, endowments and production patterns cannot in the short run simultaneously achieve two objectives: an increase in the standard of living, and a decrease in the propensity to emigrate."[47]

It may be true that members of affluent societies are capable of travelling the globe as they never were before, but this is the post–Cold War era. The East–West dynamic has largely been removed and replaced with concerns not about political refugees who can make a splash in the newspapers when they defect from the Soviet Union but about displaced Russians seeking employment in Western Europe, or people fleeing civil war in the former Yugoslavia or in Burundi to seek haven in neighbouring states, or Haitians trying desperately to cross ocean space in decrepit boats to Florida only to be intercepted at sea and, eventually, returned. While there is little doubt that the age of capital mobility is upon us, we are far from a world in which people travel as freely across borders.

In this chapter we have examined issues related to the large population increases experienced in the twentieth century, including the question of responsibility for promoting sustainable development, urbanization, birth control, and voluntary and involuntary population movements. There can be little doubt that the increase in population puts additional strain on the natural ecosystems on which we all ultimately depend and that overconsumption in both the north and south exacerbate the environmental problems discussed in Chapter 9.

If high populations are a reflection of poverty, so are large population movements. In this chapter, we discussed the push–pull factors involved in migration and then looked at the contemporary refugee crisis, with an emphasis on multilateral responses. Ultimately, however, individual governments will have to cope with both migratory and refugee pressures and the larger problem of internal displacement. Finally, we concluded that rising population levels are encouraging closed borders in the north, thus exposing a rather large hole in the convergence thesis outlined in Chapter 1.

From a global perspective, the problem may well be too large for any one or combination of international organizations to handle, and bilateral initiatives will be needed along with open immigration policies and long-term aid. However, this seems less likely as northern governments continue to experience the crunch of financial realism, which has finally started to seriously shape fiscal policies and external aid budgets. Xenophobia remains a factor in immigration policy and fears of "Third World" population increases provoke it. The south's current condition is at least partly the result of the north's historic exploitation of it, yet the north is in a decreasingly viable position to contribute to long-term solutions.

The global population will continue to rise, especially in the southern hemisphere, in the future. This increase will occur despite tragic epidemics, such as the spread of the AIDS virus in Asia and Africa. The realistic question is not whether things will be moving in this direction but how we will cope with unprecedented numbers of people, millions of whom will be on the move. In the midst of all this humanity, can compassion survive?

Endnotes

1. G. Hardin, "The Tragedy of the Commons," *Science* 162 (December 1968), 1243–48.
2. J.H. Simpson, *Refugees: Preliminary Report of a Survey* (London: Chatham House, 1938), 193.
3. For a standard essay on the demographic transition theory, see H. Frederiksen, "Feedbacks in Economic and Demographic Transition," *Science* 166 (1969), 837–47.
4. See their *The Population Explosion* (New York: Simon and Schuster, 1990).
5. Hardin, "The Tragedy of the Commons."
6. This formula is usually expressed as follows: I = PAT: impact is equal to population size, multiplied by per capita consumption (affluence), in turn multiplied by a measure of the damage done by the technologies chosen to supply each unit of consumption.
7. Amniocentesis uses a sample of amniotic fluid from a pregnant woman's uterus to diagnose possible genetic defects, and reveals the gender of the fetus in the process. See N. Kristof, "Peasants of China Discover New Way to Weed Out Girls," *New York Times* (21 July 1993), A1.
8. Parts of this section are taken from P.J. Stoett, "Cities: To Love or to Loathe?" a review article based on J. Kasarda and A. Parnell, ed., *Third World Cities: Problems, Policies, and Prospects* (London: Sage, 1993); and J. Hardoy, D. Mitlin, and D. Satterthwaite, *Environmental Problems in Third World Cities* (London: Earthscan, 1992), which appeared in *Environmental Politics* 3 (2) (1994), 339–42.
9. See Kasarda and Parnell, *Third World Cities;* Hardoy, Mitlin, and Satterthwaite, *Environmental Problems;* and P. Gizewski and T. Homer-Dixon, "Urban Growth and Violence: Will the Future Resemble the Past?" *Project on Environment, Population and Security* (AAAS and University College, University of Toronto, 1995).
10. See B. Hartmann, *Reproductive Rights and Wrongs: The Global Politics of Population Control and Contraceptive Choice* (New York: Harper and Row, 1987). For an excellent essay dealing with the transnational alliances and networks that have evolved related to population control issues, see B. Crane, "International Population Institutions: Adaptation to a Changing World Order," in P. Haas, R. Keohane, and M. Levy, eds., *Institutions for the Earth: Sources of Effective International Environmental Protection* (Cambridge, MA: MIT Press, 1994), 351–96.
11. "Maternity: Greater Peril?" *Populi: The UNFPA Magazine* 23 (1) (1996), 4–5.
12. *Our Planet* 6 (3) (1994), 11.
13. "Hard Lessons in Population Planning," *Our Planet* 6 (3) (1994), 32.
14. International Labour Organization, *World Labour Report* 1995 (Geneva, 1995).
15. Ibid.
16. Note that the linguistic root of the word "robot" is in fact the Czech word for serf, *robotnik*. See P.B. Scott, *The Robotics Revolution* (New York: Oxford University Press, 1982), 10.
17. L. Hossie, "Migration Increases as Search for Good Life Grows," *The Globe and Mail* (22 June 1993), A10.
18. *The Economics of Mass Migration in the Twentieth Century* (New York: Paragon House, 1987). See also Stephen Castles and Mark Miller, *The Age of Migration: International Population Movements in the Modern World* (New York: Guilford, 1993).

19. M. Esman, "Ethnic Pluralism and International Relations," *Canadian Review of Studies in Nationalism* 17 (1–2) (1990), 83–93.

20. See S. Armstrong, "AIDS and Migrant Labour," *Populi: The UNFPA Magazine* 21 (11) (1994/95), 13.

21. Parts of this section are taken from P.J. Stoett, "International Mechanisms for Addressing Migration," *Canadian Foreign Policy* 4 (1) (1996), 111–38.

22. For a concise history of the IOM and discussion, see R. Appleyard, *International Migration: Challenge for the Nineties* (IOM: Geneva, 1991).

23. *IOM News* 7 (1994), 2.

24. States involved include Australia, Belgium, Canada, Denmark, Finland, France, Germany, Italy, the Netherlands, Norway, Spain, Sweden, Switzerland, the United Kingdom, and the United States.

25. Nazare Albuguerque-Abell, "The Safe Third Country Concept: Deflection in Europe and Its Implications for Canada," *Refuge* 14 (9) (1995), 1–7, 5. The postwar expulsion of millions of Germans from various regions following the **Potsdam Treaty** is particularly notable, if often ignored in popular histories of the war. See Alfred-Maurice de Zayas, "International Law and Mass Population Transfers," *Harvard International Law Journal* 16 (2) (1975), 207–58; Paul Lewis, "U.N. Hopes Number of Refugees Falls," *New York Times* (20 March 1994), 11.

26. The postwar expulsion of millions of Germans from various regions following the Potsdam Treaty is particularly notable, though it is often ignored in popular histories of the war. See Alfred-Maurice de Zayas, "International Law and Mass Population Transfers," *Harvard International Law Journal* 16 (2) (1975), 207–58.

27. Paul Lewis, "U.S. Hopes Number of Refugees Falls," *New York Times* (20 March 1994), 11.

28. This figure includes refugees, asylum seekers, the internally displaced, returned refugees, and returned internally displaced for whom the UNHCR has assumed primary responsibility. They cannot reflect the large number of internally displaced people for whom the UNHCR can do nothing. Source: *Refugees and Others of Concern to UNHCR, 1999 Statistical Overview*, Internet, <www.unhcr.ch>.

29. E. Buehrig, *The United Nations and the Palestinian Refugees: A Study in Nonterritorial Administration* (Bloomington: Indiana University Press, 1971), 3.

30. Palestinian refugees in Israel were initially under the care of the UNRWA, but Israel assumed that responsibility in 1952. See Alexander Bligh, "From UNRWA to Israel: The 1952 Transfer of Responsibilities for Refugees in Israel," *Refuge* 14 (6) (1994), 7–10, 24.

31. Robert Riggs and Jack Plano, *The United Nations: International Organization and World Politics* (Belmont, CA: Wadsworth, 1994), 230.

32. F. Maurice and J. de Courten, "ICRC Activities for Refugees and Displaced Civilians," *International Review of the Red Cross* 280 (1991), 9–21.

33. This occurred in northwest Somalia, where the ICRC extended its operations in aid of Ethiopian refugees after the World Food Programme and UNHCR suspended their activities for security reasons. Ibid.

34. For an excellent essay on the Save the Children Fund in Britain and its constant interaction with the UNHCR, World Food Programme, and other UN bodies, see A. Penrose and J. Seaman, "The Save the Children Fund and Nutrition for Refugees," in P. Willetts, ed., *"The Conscience of the World": The Influence of Non-Governmental Organizations in the UN System* (Washington: Brookings, 1996), 241–69.

35. See M. Hart, "Canadian Overseas Assistance for Refugees," in H. Adelman, ed., *Refugee Policy: Canada and the United States* (Toronto: York Lanes, 1991).

36. *Refugees: Rationing the Right to Life* (London: Zed Books, 1992), 55.

37. See R. Cohen, *Human Rights Protection for Internally Displaced Persons* (Washington: RPG, 1991); and F. Deng, *Protecting the Dispossessed: A Challenge for the International Community* (New York: Brookings, 1993).

38. S. Mydans, "Indonesia Resettles People to Relieve Crowding on Java," *New York Times* (25 August 1996), 4. For a report on a similar situation in Thailand, see D. Hubbel and N. Rajesh, "Not Seeing the People for the Forest: Thailand's Program of Reforestation by Forced Eviction," *Refuge* 12 (1) (1992), 20–1.

39. See R. Plender, "The Legal Basis of International Jurisdiction to Act with Regard to the Internally Displaced," *International Journal of Refugee Law* 6 (3) (1994), 345–61.

40. See S. Martin, *Refugee Women* (London: Zed Books, 1992).

41. See N. Spencer-Nimmons, "Canada's Response to the Issue of Refugee Women: The Women at Risk Program," *Refuge* 14 (7) (1994), 13–8. We should note also the role played by the Canadian Working Group for Refugee Women, a subgroup of the NGO-based Canadian Council for Refugees.

42. Canada has finally joined Sweden, Norway, Denmark, France, Belgium, Germany, Australia, the United States, Finland, Iceland, and New Zealand in moving toward passing legislation making it possible to charge citizens abroad who purchase sex from minors. J. Sallot, "Canada Targets Overseas Child Sex," *The Globe and Mail* (4 April 1996), A4.

43. UN Resolution A/RES/44/25, 20 November 1989, Article 11.

44. "International Response to Trafficking in Migrants and the Safeguarding of Migrant Rights," *International Migration* 32 (4) (1994), 593–603.

45. The question of discrimination against migrants seeking employment came home to Canadians recently as it was suggested that non-White Canadians were having a difficult time finding overseas jobs teaching English. "Asian Schools Avoid Non-White Canadians," *The Globe and Mail* (28 March 1996), A1.

46. For a survey, see D. Kubat, *The Politics of Migration Policies: Settlement and Integration, the First World into the 1990s* (New York: Center for Migration Studies, 1993).

47. "International Migration and Development," *Population Bulletin of the UN* 36 (1994), 1–18, 12.

Suggested Readings

Appleyard, Reginald. *International Migration: Challenge for the Nineties.* Geneva: IOM, 1991.

Castles, S., and M. Miller. *The Age of Migration: International Population Movements in the Modern World.* New York: Guilford, 1993.

Cook, R. "International Human Rights and Women's Reproductive Rights." *Studies in Family Planning* 24 (1993), 73–86.

Cornelius, W., et al. *Controlling Immigration: A Global Perspective.* Stanford: Stanford University Press, 1994.

Cunliffe, A. "The Refugee Crisis: A Study of the United Nations High Commission for Refugees." *Political Studies* 43 (1995), 278–90.

Davies, J. *Displaced Peoples and Refugee Studies: A Resource Guide.* Refugee Studies Programme, Oxford University. London: Hans Zell, 1990.

Dirks, G. "International Migration in the 1990s: Causes and Consequences." *International Journal* 48 (2) (1993), 191–214.

Ferris, E. *Beyond Borders: Refugees, Migrants and Human Rights in the Post–Cold War Era.* Geneva: WCC Publications, 1993.

Fontenau, G. "The Rights of Migrants, Refugees or Asylum Seekers under International Law." *International Migration Quarterly* 30 (1992), 57–68.

Forbes Martin, S. *Refugee Women.* London: Zed Books, 1991.

Ghimire, K. "Refugees and Deforestation." *International Migration* 32 (4) (1994), 561–70.

Gurtov, M. "Open Borders: A Global Humanist Approach to the Refugee Crisis." *World Development* 19 (5) (1991), 485–96.

Hakovirta, H. "The Global Refugee Problem: A Model and Its Application." *International Political Science Review* 14 (1) (1993), 35–57.

Hartmann, B. *Reproductive Rights and Wrongs: Global Politics of Population Control and Contraceptive Choices.* New York: Harper and Row, 1987.

King, R., ed. *Mass Migration in Europe: The Legacy and the Future.* London: Belhaven Press, 1993.

Klein, S. *The Economics of Mass Migration in the Twentieth Century.* New York: Paragon House, 1987.

Kritz, M., et al. *International Migration Systems: A Global Approach.* Oxford: Clarendon Press, 1992.

Lemay, M., ed. *The Gatekeepers: Comparative Immigration Policy.* New York: Praeger, 1989.

Loescher, G. *Beyond Charity: International Cooperation and the Global Refugee Crisis.* New York: Oxford University Press, 1993.

Magotte, J. *Disposable People? The Plight of Refugees.* New York: Orbis, 1992.

Maurice, F., and J. de Courten. "ICRC Activities for Refugees and Displaced Civilians." *International Review of the Red Cross* 280 (1991), 9–21.

Nash, A., ed. *Human Rights and the Protection of Refugees under International Law.* Halifax: Institute for Research on Public Policy, 1988.

Ogata, Sadako. "The UN Response to the Growing Refugee Crisis." *Japan Review of International Affairs* 7 (3) (1993), 202–15.

Rogers, R. "The Future of Refugee Flows and Policies." *International Migration Review* 36 (4) (1992), 1112–43.

Rystad, G., ed. *The Uprooted: Forced Migration as an International Problem in the Post-War Era.* Lund: Lund University Press, 1990.

Sassen, S. *Globalization and Its Discontents: Essays on the New Mobility of People and Money.* New York: The New Press, 1998.

Straubhaar, T. "Migration Pressure." *International Migration* 31 (1) (1993), 5–32.

Suhrke, A. "A Crisis Diminished: Refugees in the Developing World." *International Journal* 48 (2) (1993), 215–39.

Troper, H. "Canada's Immigration Policy Since 1945." *International Journal* 48 (2) (1993), 255–81.

Weiner, M. *International Migration and Security.* Boulder, CO: Westview, 1993.

Zayas, A. "International Law and Mass Population Transfers." *Harvard International Law Journal* 16 (2) (1975), 207–58.

Zolberg, J. "Un reflet du monde: les migrations internationales en perspective historique." *Revu Études Internationales* 24 (1) (1993), 17–29.

Suggested Websites

The Population Council

World Food Programme

The Hunger Web
   <www.brown.edu/Departments/World_Hunger_Program/>

United Nations High Commissioner for Refugees, REFWORLD
   <www.unhcr.ch/refworld/welcome.htm>

Guides: Refugees and Migration
   <www.oneworld.org/guides/migration/index.html>

CHAPTER 12

Global Politics and the Information Age

Technology is now, for better or for worse, the principal driving force behind the ongoing rapid economic, social, and political change. Like any irrepressible force, the new technology can bestow on us undreamed of benefits but also inflict irreparable damage.

—Wassily Leontief, *Economist*[1]

INTRODUCTION: GLOBAL POLITICS AND SOCIAL REVOLUTIONS

The development of human society is often conceptualized in terms of stages or revolutions. Each stage represents a significant leap forward in human development, which lays down the foundation for successive revolutions. In each of these forward leaps, a close relationship exists between technological developments and the evolution of political, economic, and social organizations. For example, the **agricultural revolution** greatly increased food production in eighteenth-century Europe through a combination of mechanical introductions, cropping techniques, and changes in landholding practices. The **Industrial Revolution** represented a shift from agrarian-based economic activity to manufacturing, which profoundly altered the character of society. The very concept of work was changed, and the social relations that sustained manufacturing became the subject of historians such as Karl Marx and authors such as Charles Dickens. The **green revolution**, stimulated by the mechanization of agriculture and the development of new fertilizers, pesticides, and seeds, has had a global impact in the form of increased food production and, arguably, growing population levels.

Others have explored the phenomenon of human development in terms of waves stimulated by technical advances. In the 1920s, the Russian economist Nikolai Kondratieff identified long waves in the world economy approximately 50 to 60 years long. Each cycle was characterized by a surge in economic growth and productivity. In 1939, the economist Joseph Schumpeter explained these waves in terms of clusters of technical inventions, innovations (the development of new techniques and products from these inventions), and diffusion (the spread of these techniques and products around the world). Each wave of inventions, innovations, and diffusion stimulates a surge in economic activity, after which economic growth slows as all the potential from new inventions is realized. Schumpeter characterized these waves as "creative gales of destruction" because they would sweep old industries aside and replace them with new ones. Following Schumpeter's reasoning, four such waves have been identified:

1. The 1780s to 1840s, driven by the steam engine and innovations in textiles and iron

2. The 1840s to 1890s and the era of the railway

3. The 1890s to 1930s, driven by electric power, chemical technologies, and improved steels

4. The 1930s to 1980s, driven by the automobile and petroleum energy[2]

Today, we don't have to stretch our imaginations to argue that the computer and the information revolution constitutes yet another wave, one that is sweeping across the globe, albeit at different speeds. This revolution is built on the advances in microelectronics that have vastly increased the processing power of computers while reducing cost and bulk. Improvements in storage capacity and retrieval have led to an explosion in the gathering, storing, processing, and analysis of information, which has become increasingly vital to political and economic activity. The development of improved communications technologies and the creation of many different international communications channels or links have allowed computers and their users to transmit or disseminate information around the world. Information and data management is now the fastest-growing area of economic activity, prompting suggestions that the industrialized world is heading into a postindustrial society and that the military applications of information technology (IT) could change the face of world politics (we return to the latter theme in the next chapter).

The idea of a postindustrial society sounds encompassing, but to a certain degree it has already arrived in advanced capitalist states such as Canada and Japan, where the service sector is as important as the manufacturing sector, and where the production of information is as important as the manufacture of products. Further, some **futurologists** argue that, just as the industrial society needed an infrastructure of railroads, bridges, and highways, the postindustrial society will be built on the computer and computer networks. Daniel F. Burton predicts the emergence of a "networked economy, an economy in which computing and communications converge to create an electronic marketplace that is utterly dependent on powerful information networks." According to Burton, a new international regime will replace the bipolar Cold War order:

> [This regime] will not be the cold peace of mercantilism that was pioneered by Japan and other Asian nations during the 1980s. Nor will it consist of the different brands of regionalism that have proliferated in Europe, the Pacific, and the Americas in recent years. Instead, the new international order will be built around the brave new worldwide web of computers and communications.[3]

This sounds like a rather brave prediction, and as we will see, there are good reasons not to exaggerate the potential impact of the information age on global politics. However, as realists would remind us, continuities in world politics have spanned one or more of the social revolutions in human history. We should, therefore, see continuity as well as change in the years ahead.

TECHNOLOGY AND THE WORLD ECONOMY

Beyond economic and market forces, and even beyond the active work of governments to promote free trade and link states electronically, one might argue that the real force behind globalization is something that is not even human: the technology we have created to manipulate our environment. There is nothing new about this; the spread of technology has been a consistent companion of the spread of civilizations, a process that continues today in the information age. However, while many southern nations will develop the infrastructure enabling them to use the computer-designed industrial robotics emerging on the stage of world production, producing such innovations is another matter entirely. Southern states may increasingly find themselves on the disadvantaged end of a world divided between the technological innovators and the technologically dependent.

Sociologists interested in technology have introduced a convergence theory that is not unlike the idea of convergence as we have used it in this book. According to this theory, "the opportunities and demands presented by modern technology promote the convergence of all societies toward a single set of social patterns and individual behaviours."[4] In other words, the adoption of Western technology and science will lead to the establishment of political institutions and cultural environments similar to those in the advanced European and American worlds. Thus, globalization will inevitably be realized through technological standardization.

As a theory, however, this leaves some room for healthy speculation. One might point to the spread of capitalism as the source of this convergence instead of to the technology employed. Obvious cases exist where distaste for Western society has led to an assertion of anti-Western political change, such as the Iranian revolution that ushered into power the late Ayatollah Khomeini. In the more general sense, one can argue that culture does not necessarily converge simply because of technological similarities. There are distinct patterns of social interaction within different societies despite a high rate of technological convergence. Japan and the United States and Germany all have adopted industrial technology yet remain quite different in terms of cultural attributes. Though many would argue with this, we can even point to significant cultural differences between countries as similar in technological circumstances as the United States and Canada.

In short, technology will continue to change and affect those working with it and those reliant on it. As James Rosenau argues, technology has "profoundly altered the scale on which human affairs take place, allowing people to do more things in less time and with wider repercussions than could have been imagined in earlier eras."[5] At the same time, technological advances will be jealously guarded in a world still full of competitive states. As two international political economists conclude, technology's "critical nature has led to restrictions, sanctions, thievery, and espionage, all of which prohibit the free flow and testing of ideas.... In the area of technology, the prevalent notion among advanced states seems to be more mercantilist than a liberal economic philosophy."[6]

There is no escape, since information is now a "basic resource needed for technico-economic activity, on a par with matter and energy."[7] As such, some sectors of society will prosper, while those marginalized from evolving levels of access to this resource will only become poorer. The next generation of complex technology to run the economy will no doubt increase wealth and opportunity for those with access to education. We must keep in mind, however, that we live in a world where, despite years of literacy programs, more than a billion adults still cannot read or write and more than 100 million children of primary school age are not able to attend school every year.[8] Rather than view new technology as a potential panacea, we should see it not only as a potential source of liberation from manual work and as a means of expanding intellectual horizons but also as a potential cause of great economic displacement and cultural conflict.

THE IMPACT OF COMPUTERS

If any form of technological change has had a profound impact on the lives of millions of people in recent times, it is the advent of the personal computer (PC). The evolution of the modern computer began in 1946 with the development of the **ENIAC** (Electronic Numerical Integrator and Calculator), widely regarded as the first electronic computer. Initially designed to calculate the trajectories of artillery shells, ENIAC was a remarkable accomplishment for its time. It could execute 5000 arithmetic calculations per second. It was also 3 meters high, 30 meters long, and weighed more than 30 000 kilograms. ENIAC used 18 000 vacuum tubes and consumed 150 000 watts of power. With the invention of the transistor in 1947, computer design was liberated from the limitation of the vacuum tube. Through the 1950s and 1960s, large centralized mainframe computers dominated the computer industry, and International Business Machines (IBM) became a dominant MNC in the 1970s. The combining of many miniature transistors on a single silicon chip (the integrated circuit) in 1959 and the development of the microprocessor (in essence a computer on a chip) in 1971 profoundly altered the computer industry. Microchips rapidly became increasingly powerful. The 486 microprocessor, used in the early 1990s, could execute 54 000 000 instructions per second, weighed only a few grams, and used less than two watts of electricity. Intel's Pentium microprocessors can execute more than 200 000 000 instructions per second. The fact that this type of speed exists is amazing enough, but what is revolutionary, in political terms, is that so many people have access to it.

These advances in miniaturization, processing power, and cost effectiveness made the PC practically and economically viable, placing unprecedented processing power in the hands of individuals. Today's generation of laptop computers are many times more powerful than the mainframe computers of the mid-1970s. With the development of the PC, the number of computers in the world began to grow rapidly. In 1971, there were approximately 50 000 computers in the world. In 1981, there were approximately 4 million. In 1998, there were at least 270 million PCs in use in the world, and the pace of this growth is accelerating. The computer industry has also become increasingly important to the global economy. By 1985, the output of the global electronics industry equalled the world automobile industry's and exceeded the world steel industry's.[9] Similarly, it is difficult to imagine an industry that does not use computer technology today, and this includes governments and military establishments as well. In fact, some authors believe that military developments mirror the technological changes driven by changing economies. For example, the Tofflers write that "as we transition from brute-force to brain-force economies, we also necessarily invent what can only be called 'brain-force-war' "[10] with high-tech laser weapons and computer guidance systems. We will explore these developments in Chapter 13.

We are now entering a new stage in the evolution of the computer: the development of networks. Coupled with advances in communications technologies, users are increasingly linking their computers together to connect with others to facilitate business, communication, financial transactions, and access to information. While the most famous of these networks is the Internet, a wide variety of other computer networks exists, such as local area networks (LANs) and wide area networks (WANs), which facilitate links between the computers of a specified group of people (such as corporate employees, bank branches, or network games players). Future developments in the electronics and computer industry will bring further advances in processing power, miniaturization, and cost reduction. The possibilities for the future application of computers in business, communications, medicine, scientific research, design, and the arts are virtually endless.

For those of us living in the industrialized world, the computer and information revolutions have had an enormous impact on our daily lives. Most of the alarm clocks that awaken us in the morning are operated by a microprocessor. Our kitchen appliances (which may have already begun to make our breakfast or morning beverage before we wake up) are also operated by microprocessors. The television and stereo are increasingly complex electronic devices, as is the telephone. Further, microprocessors are important contributors to the design and manufacturing of these household items. The thermostats in our homes, the electricity grids from which we draw our power, the transportation networks we use, all employ microprocessors to some extent. Many of us also use home computers for household finances, taxes, and record keeping, as well as correspondence, recreation, and education. Increasing numbers of people *telecommute* by working at home and sending their work to the office or to their clients by computer network. Increasingly, we can shop, bank, and earn a living using our home computers. We have increasing access to a wide range of products and investment opportunities. As individuals, we are all highly reliant on technology and increasingly connected to the world economy and global communications systems.

At work, the impact of the computer and information revolution has been dramatic. Computers and communications technologies have increased individual productivity, and have proliferated in the workplace. In 1991, companies spent more money on computer and communications equipment than on industrial, mining, farming, and construction equipment combined.[11] Businesses use computers for communications, data storage and retrieval, business administration, payroll, record keeping, and budgeting. Banking and financial industries are almost entirely dependent on computers and communications links. Manufacturing industries use computers to design new products, operate their production facilities, manage inventories, track shipments, and distribute raw materials, supplies, and parts. Medical sciences use computers and microprocessors in medical instruments and tools, diagnostic aids, and record keeping. The architecture, fashion, and graphic design fields make wide use of computers. Increasingly, education at all levels employs computers in some capacity.

The computer and information revolution has done more than increase individual productivity or alter individual work habits and tools; it has affected the very nature of work in modern industrialized societies as a whole. A massive shift in employment patterns away from agriculture and manufacturing has taken place in the twentieth century. In the United States in the early 1800s, more than 70 percent of workers were engaged in agriculture. Today, agriculture accounts for only some 3 percent of the workforce. In the early 1900s, some 35 percent of U.S. workers were engaged in manufacturing industries. Today, manufacturing industries account for less than 25 percent of the workforce. A similar pattern can be found in Canada, despite continued reliance on the natural resource sector. In the 1950s the majority of workers in the industrialized world were involved in manufacturing or transporting material goods. It has been estimated that by the year 2010, no industrialized country will have more than one-tenth of its workforce in these traditional manufacturing sectors.[12] In 1996 the OECD concluded that there was a clear trend in affluent countries toward an economy in which more than half of the labour force was engaged in the production, distribution, and use of information.[13] High-technology manufacturing now accounts for 25 percent of all manufacturing output in these countries, and knowledge-based services are growing even faster, accounting for 8 out of 10 new jobs.[14] All this leads some analysts and futurologists to suggest that we are heading toward a postindustrial economy.

However, many argue that this postindustrial society will not be one of promise but of increased dislocation, unemployment, and economic hardship for many, if not most, people. Unemployment and stagnant or falling wages and household incomes are growing concerns in most industrialized economies. Commentators speak of the "jobless recovery" from the recession of the early 1990s in which unemployment levels remain unacceptably high despite economic growth and expanding global trade. The cause, many allege, is the computer and information revolution, coupled with the growing globalization of the world economy.

Even as this is happening, advances in telecommunications, trade, and financial flows have increased international competition, prompting firms to downsize (the technical term for firing employees) and facilitating their efforts to shift production to low-wage countries. As a result, unemployment (and the social problems associated with it) is on the rise. In addition, those jobs that are created will be insufficient in number to replace the jobs lost, and many of them will be low-paying service sector jobs with poor benefits and low job security (sometimes called "McJobs"). Globalization and technological change have driven employers and workers farther apart in many sectors of the economy: as profits rise and wages fall, the bulk of income and revenues will go to a few individuals, widening the gap between rich and poor. These conditions have led Ethan B. Kapstein to argue the following:

> The global economy is leaving millions of disaffected workers in its train. Inequality, unemployment, and endemic poverty have become its handmaidens. Rapid technological change and heightening international competition are fraying the job markets of the major industrialized countries. At the same time, systemic pressures are curtailing every government's ability to respond with new spending. Just when working people most need the nation-state as a buffer from the world economy, it is abandoning them.[15]

Alternatively, many argue that these fears are alarmist and that protesters are the equivalent of modern-day Luddites, a reference to the British workers of the early nineteenth century who smashed the machines that threatened their jobs. Advocates of the computer and information revolution argue that predictions that machines will cause unemployment and social dislocation have been common. In the 1930s, automation of manufacturing was blamed for increases in unemployment, and in the 1940s, others predicted that computers would throw massive numbers of individuals into enforced idleness. Today, robotics, computers and their networks, and information-based sectors are being blamed for job losses. Defenders of the new technologies argue that society benefits from technological innovation. Despite the increasing pace of technological change, and indeed because of it, employment, incomes, and living standards have risen steadily. Because computers and information systems enhance productivity, advocates maintain, they will increase real incomes, from either higher wages or lower prices. This increases the purchasing power of the average consumer, which stimulates other sectors of the economy.

One thing is certain: the new information technologies are pervasive. They affect virtually every economic sector, and will revolutionize the way traditional industries produce and distribute their products. In addition, the computer and information revolution will create completely new industries where none existed before. New products create new jobs. Thirty years ago, products such as videocassette recorders, video cameras, Sony Walkmans, cellular phones, global positioning systems, and CD and DVD players did not exist. The pace of development in the computer industry illustrates this point: in 1996 fully 70 percent of the computer industry's revenues came from products that did not exist two years before.[16]

How does this development affect our environmental perspective introduced in Chapter 8? One might argue that the **infrastructure** of the information revolution makes fewer demands on resources and pollutes less. Ships, trucks, railways, and cars require a large amount of raw materials and energy to produce and keep in operation. Furthermore, these products are the source of serious pollution problems. Work in the information age has the potential to reduce the consumption of resources and traffic congestion (through telecommuting and banking or shopping online). However, countries such as Japan are already confronting serious waste disposal problems related to storing obsolete computer products. And all of this technology has greatly increased the demand for electricity, which in itself has serious environmental consequences, especially in an age where renewable energy sources are largely ignored. Increased use of computers has not led to a paperless office; in fact, paper consumption increased from 170 million tonnes a year in 1980 to 298 million tonnes in 1997.[17]

With respect to unemployment, innovation does not mean painful labour market adjustments will not occur, especially in the short term when we will see a pronounced shifting of the job market. The key is that these positions are in new industries rather than in traditional employment sectors. This debate is likely to continue, for it is an inescapable fact that many workers of many different kinds are feeling less secure in their jobs, that unemployment remains high, and that there is general dissatisfaction with economic performance in the industrialized countries. Whether the computer and information revolution is blamed (justly or unjustly), responding to these conditions presents a major challenge to the economic and fiscal policies of the developed world.

TRANSNATIONAL COMMUNICATION

The computer and information revolution is only one dimension of the broader phenomenon of transnational communication. The vast majority of people in the north (and many in the south) have access to unprecedented communications links, including telephone, fax, e-mail, the Internet, television, and international radio services. People are able to communicate and exchange more information more frequently and at less cost than ever before. Much of this communication and information transfer is personal or general in nature. However, much of it is specialized, intended for experts in some scientific or commercial field. The growth of transnational communication, and the challenges and opportunities it poses for individuals, organizations, and governments, is a major issue in global politics.

In the past, the speed of communication was essentially equivalent to the speed of transportation. With the exception of very basic signalling using flags or smoke, messages could only travel as fast as the messenger carrying them. In practice, this meant the use of human, animal, or mechanical transport. While some of these communications methods were relatively swift and effective (such as the pony express system of Imperial China and the use of carrier pigeons), it could take days, weeks, months, or even years to transmit messages or news. In the eighteenth century, a trip around the world took several years by sailing ship. Today, jet aircraft can fly around the world in less than a day carrying large parcels and other mail items. Bulk cargo ships are far faster than the merchant sailing ships of just two hundred years ago. Trucks can haul large amounts of freight over expansive road networks.

However, the remarkable advances have been in the area of electronic communication. As recently as a hundred years ago, the idea of virtually instantaneous global communication would have been dismissed as an unrealistic dream. Today, it is a commonplace reality for an increasing number of people around the world. The dramatic increase in transnational communication is a direct result of technological change. From the development of the telegraph in 1840 to modern satellite communications in the 1990s, technology has improved to enable millions of people to communicate on a near-simultaneous basis with each other using telephones or computer messages.[18] Millions more can access media channels such as television and radio, and receive information, sounds, and images from places around the world. Moreover, the cost of this communication has decreased dramatically. A three-minute telephone call between New York and London fell from U.S.$244.65 in 1930, to $31.58 in 1970, to $3.32 in 1990, to 35 cents in 1998 (in 1990 dollars).[19] Sending an e-mail message from Calgary to Paris costs no more than sending an identical message from Calgary to Edmonton.

Because of these developments, it is possible to speak of a communications revolution and the consequent "death of distance" made possible by the computer, the explosion in information availability, and the proliferation of hard links (physical communications links such as cables) around the world. Fibre optic and laser technologies have dramatically increased the carrying capacity of telephone cables. Computers enable such lasers to transmit several messages simultaneously over a single optical fibre. This is an illustration of the synergistic effect of technological innovation on global communications. Innovations have been melded together to create a whole greater than the sum of its parts. Because of this, it is difficult to predict the future of communications developments. If people living 50 years ago had never even heard of computers, satellites, or digital telephones, what will the next 50 years hold? One trend is identifiable: the increasing use of wireless communications links. With some exceptions, most communications in the twentieth century required a *hard link* of some kind, usually in the form of a copper-based or fibre optic cable. Increasingly, communications are *wireless*, using radio waves to transmit messages and data through the air (or space). Such technologies include cellular phones and satellite receivers and dishes, which enable people to communicate from remote areas or receive television broadcasts even when no physical link is available. Advances in wireless communications technology may be the next wave of the computer revolution.

The scope of the communications revolution can be highlighted by looking at some recent trends and developments.

One of them likes the wireless revolution. A Chinese worker pedals to work along a street in Beijing carrying boxes of products as a rider sits comfortably in the back, using his cell phone. (AP Photo/Bullit Marquez)

Consider a now common household item, the telephone. International phone traffic has increased dramatically. The use of international telephone calls (measured in terms of minutes) jumped from 3.5 billion in 1985 to 6 billion in 1989, with a large amount of this traffic devoted to the transfer of large amounts of data using computer modems. In 1960, a transatlantic telephone cable could carry 138 conversations. Today's fibre optic cables are capable of carrying 1.5 million conversations. The use of telephone satellite communications has facilitated this entire process. In particular, the Intelsat network, which had its first satellite in orbit in 1964 and now has 24 satellites in operation, has increased the carrying capacity of global telephone links. With Intelsat in operation, international phone traffic has been freed from undersea or underground cables linking continents and cities.

Another global communications network that has exploded into public awareness in the past few years is the Internet. The Internet is an international network connecting thousands of independent computer networks through a common set of standards and protocols. The Internet can be conceptualized as a web of linked computers with no centralized focal point or *node*. No central computer *runs* the Internet; rather, it is a system of linked computers, which exist in a nonhierarchical arrangement. Individual computer users can access these linked computers, thus providing people with access to the entire network. The Internet's power and potential is derived from its ability to link different types of computers, software operating systems, and independent networks through a common protocol called TCP/IP. Technical differences between computers and networks do not matter as long as they can communicate using this protocol.

The Internet originally developed out of a military communications project in the 1960s. The United States Department of Defense Advanced Research Projects Agency Network (ARPAnet) was established to ensure that communications between political and military leaders could be maintained even in the event of a nuclear attack. Because the structure of ARPAnet was decentralized, if some sections of the network were destroyed or disabled, the network would still function. ARPAnet was transferred to the National Science Foundation, which renamed the network NSFnet. NSFnet was expanded to universities and government agencies in the 1980s and then turned over to private companies. The beginning of the explosion in Internet use occurred in the late 1980s, as more powerful computers emerged and the World Wide Web (WWW) was created. The WWW software, created by Tim Berners-Lee at the European Particle Physics Laboratory (CERN) in Switzerland, established the common user protocols for addresses, languages, file transfers, and browsers. The Web facilitated the use of the Internet through easier-to-use interface software, thus enabling anyone with a computer, a modem, a browser, and the requisite interest to use the Internet.

The growth of the Internet has been spectacular. The Global Internet Project estimates that 40 to 60 million people worldwide use the Internet every year. More than 100 countries have some form of access to the Internet (although in practice this access may be quite limited). The number of Internet hosts (those computers with a direct connection to the Internet) increased from 100 000 in 1988 to more than 36 million in 1998. It was estimated that by 2000 there would be 250 million Internet users.[20] It is increasingly apparent that the day will soon be upon us when television cable services and Internet reception are linked in most households. (The services are already linked in many households.) Some feel this expanded communicative ability may bring humanity closer together, in a *global village* or *cyberworld* where national borders become irrelevant and a global awareness of a shared human identity and destiny will take shape. In other words, the Internet could be one of the most important instruments of *convergence* in human history.

However, enthusiasm over the Internet must be tempered with some sobering realities. While the Internet promises enormous potential for business, personal communication, and access to information, the use of the Internet is dominated by the industrialized world (in particular, the United States). The vast majority of people on earth have little or no access to the Internet, even if they have heard of it; in fact, half of the world's population has never made a telephone call. Furthermore, like television programming, the quality of the Websites on the Internet varies widely. Some sites are reputable and of high quality; others are virtually useless and contain false or misleading information. The Internet offers a forum to any individual or group that can construct a Website (including hate groups and the pornography industry), which demands a careful critical perspective when viewing information on the World Wide Web. While Web advocates cite the Internet's capacity to promote democracy, diversity, and the free flow of information, all information can be manipulated and controlled. Many governments manage their citizens' access to the Internet (see Profile 12.1). The perspectives and values of the developed world dominate the content on the Internet. English is the language of almost 80 percent of Internet Websites. The content of the Internet is heavily corporate and money matters in terms of vying for viewers (a familiar phenomenon to advertising executives and political campaign managers). The Internet also raises issues related to privacy (including the security of financial and medical information) and copyright (witness the debate over Napster MP3 software). Computer piracy and hacking raise concerns about the security of computer systems and the challenges of responding to this problem in a world of governments with different legal systems.

THE DISSEMINATION OF TECHNOLOGY, INFORMATION, AND IDEAS

The computer revolution and the creation of expanding communications channels have led to an explosion in the availability of information. The volume of information available to us is extraordinary. Technology facilitates the creation, processing, accumulation, storage, and management of information on an unprecedented scale. Desktop computers can now process vast amounts of information and data and create spreadsheets, charts, and multimedia presentations. Single CD-ROMs can store volumes of books and images. Modern libraries are increasingly electronic, storing a growing amount of their information holdings in digital form and offering computerized access to their databases and to the databases of other libraries. Technology has also facilitated the spread, or dissemination, of information; during the past two decades, global communications channels have increased their information-carrying capacity a million times over.[21] Traditional media sources such as newspapers, television, and radio, along with computer networks, allow us to access a wide variety of news items, technical information, images, new product developments, and music. Governments can receive information on domestic political events and international political events within minutes.

Over the longer term, we can expect the availability and dissemination of ideas to have a dramatic effect on the nature of scientific discovery and on innovation. Science can be a lonely enterprise; the image of the lone scientist toiling in a lab into the late hours of the night is an accurate one. However, scientific discovery is also a collaborative enterprise. Scientists often seek out other scientists for assistance or advice. The process of scientific verification and review demands that experiments and discoveries be replicated and evaluated by scientific peer groups. The collaborative aspects of scientific discovery can thus be facilitated and accelerated by communications technology and the dissemination of information within the **epistemic communities**.

In the past, innovations disseminated slowly, spreading only as fast as messages and people could travel. As a result, news of discoveries or innovations took a long time to come to the attention of those that could make use of them. In the television series *Connections*, host James Burke suggested that technological change was largely the result of inventors taking older discoveries, adding an innovation of their own, and applying it to the problem they were concerned with. The result was a new way of doing things, inspired by the borrowing and adaptation of other ideas. Today, the availability and dissemination of information allows would-be innovators to access a vast reservoir of information and ideas from around the world. New ideas and innovations appear almost daily, and those who are interested in certain scientific or technical pursuits can easily access the information they are interested in or need. The potential for scientific and technical progress is therefore extraordinary.

However, the dissemination of scientific discovery and innovation is not always regarded as a good thing. In fact, many scientific discoveries and innovations are kept secret. The belief that national security may be put at risk is one rationale for preventing the dissemination of information. Another may be the commercial potential of the discovery and the desire to profit from it. Of course, there is an increasing trend toward using information networks for **industrial espionage** to steal information and data. This theft raises a number of questions about the security of personal information in an information age. Information about our financial situation, medical history, family records, and backgrounds increasingly resides in computers in electronic form. Access to them is possible. This is a growing problem for the privacy of the individual.

Further, we should not overlook the fact that many technological innovations are derived from military applications. Medical science profited immensely from the battlefield experience of the two great wars, for example, but we have also seen the application of nuclear technology to warfare and an arms race that precluded many other socially progressive possibilities.

FROM EVENT TO LIVING ROOM: THE GLOBAL MEDIA AND HOW THEY WORK

The media (especially radio and television) are rightfully accorded a special significance in the study of global politics. In part, this is because radios and televisions have spread throughout the world, and there are more people listening and watching than ever before. While this is important, it is only part of the story; radio and television networks and their affiliates (or subsidiary stations) have access to an increasingly wide variety of news items. As a result, we increasingly refer to *global media* that deliver information, sounds, and images from political events, wars, natural disasters, and cultural and sporting events. Because of this, global media have had a notable impact on the knowledge and attitudes of individuals, as well as on the policies of governments and policing capabilities (see Profiles 12.1 and 12.2).

The global media can disseminate information and ideas in a variety of different forms, including newspapers and magazines (print media), films, radio, and television. The information and ideas carried by the media can in turn influence the ideas, attitudes, beliefs, and decisions of those who have access to it. The power of the media is enormous, for they are the source of much of the information that people receive about the world in which they live, and what we know of the world is for the most part what we hear or see

PROFILE 12.1 · China and the Internet

China is a good example of a country that is attempting to embrace communications technology while exercising political control over information content. As part of a government plan in place since the early 1990s, China has been developing its communications infrastructure, installing telephone lines at a rate of two million per month in 2000. Internet use has increased from 50 000 users in 1995 to 9 million in 1999, with 20 million expected by the end of 2000. However, the Chinese government continues to impose tight controls on the free flow of information, fearing the consequences for the country's political system. As the late Chinese leader Deng Xiaoping once said, "when you open the window, the flies come in." The Ministry of Information Industry controls Internet traffic entering the country, blocking Websites such as the BBC, CNN, and the *Washington Post*, as well as the Websites of human rights organizations and Chinese dissident groups. Prison sentences have been handed out to Chinese citizens who violate domestic laws on the dissemination of information and protest material over the Internet. As China becomes more connected to the world economy, and as the economic importance of information flows increases, the interaction will become a fascinating case study of the clash between the power of the state and the forces of an electronic borderless world.

PROFILE 12.2 · The Web and Different Perspectives on World Events

One has to be careful with the World Wide Web, because anyone can publish almost anything on it. However, it does provide an alternative to mainstream media. For example, when Peruvian soldiers stormed the Japanese embassy in Lima in April 1997, killing all the members of the *Movimiento Revolucionario Tupac Amaru* (MTRA) who were holding dignitaries hostage, media coverage focused on the military action and not the reasons for the occupation in the first place: namely, that Peru is one of the worst violators of human rights, and the rebels were at least partly protesting this, as well as the entrenched and extreme disparities of wealth in Peruvian society. The MRTA, however, maintain a Website to publicize their side of the conflict. The perspectives and information were obviously tilted toward their interpretation, but it was as believable an account as that offered by the government. Amnesty International also maintained a Website on the conflict, in which they condemned both Peru for human rights abuses and the MRTA for terrorist activities.

SOURCE: JACK KAPICA'S "CYBERIA" COLUMN IN *THE GLOBE AND MAIL* (2 MAY 1997). THIS IS A FASCINATING COLUMN FOR INTERNET USERS.

or read. If we are not exposed to certain information or events, we generally remain unaware of them. As a result, what is reported and what is not is important.

In the past, newspapers, magazines, radio, and movie theatre newsreels (short news presentations shown before a feature film) were the dominant forms of media. Today, the media with the greatest political impact are radio and television. Radio remains a powerful media source largely because it is easily accessible. There are more than two billion radios in the world, and in countries where illiteracy rates are high, the radio is the primary source of information and news about national or international events. International short-wave radio broadcasts, such as Voice of America (VOA), the British Broadcasting Corporation (BBC) World Service, and Radio Canada International, reach into the remotest regions of the world to bring news items, political perspectives, and entertainment to those with short-wave receivers.

However, television is even more politically powerful, largely because of the impact that pictures, or images, can have on human emotions and reactions. Television brings a sense of immediacy, or presence, that other forms of media do not possess. There are over 800 million television sets in the world, and an increasing range of channels is available to most consumers. Cable channels and satellite television channels continue to proliferate, and in North America, some viewers have more than 100 channels to choose from. Like radio, television also has networks devoted to international broadcasting. The U.S.-based Cable News Network (CNN) and the British-based International Television Network (ITN) are the most prominent examples. In 1994, CNN broadcast to over 140 countries. As James Rosenau has argued, "Access to television has become sufficiently global in scope that it must be regarded as a change of [fundamental] proportions."[22] Even the steadfastly anti-Castro American government has permitted CNN to set up shop in Cuba.

All global media networks and many national networks employ foreign correspondents around the world, but if one is not immediately available, a local reporter or his or her video footage will be used instead. The proliferation of privately owned video cameras has allowed many networks and reporters to gain unprecedented access to visual records of events. These videos, taken by citizens, have often provided much of the visual content of certain television reports, such as the police beating of Rodney King that sparked riots in Los Angeles in the early 1990s. Coverage of events is hastily transmitted to the network headquarters by satellite and becomes part of the daily volume of news items that are available for dissemination to national networks or to regional and local network affiliates. Often, national networks or other television networks will use reports, video, and interviews from other networks.

As a result, it is not uncommon for Canadian viewers watching the Canadian Broadcasting Corporation (CBC) to see reports filed by reporters working for CNN, ITN, BBC, or American networks such as CBS, ABC, or NBC. Live reports can be carried over satellite and broadcast in *real time* around the world. Frequently, scheduled broadcasts will be interrupted to give viewers information on a news item that may have occurred only a few minutes earlier on the other side of the world. Often, when a major story breaks, virtually every network in the world will be covering it, and coverage of this event will become part of every local municipal news broadcast. In a sense, this story might become the global news "issue of the day," broadcast by networks in countries around the world (often using the same video images). As we shall see, this process has raised concerns about the gathering and dissemination of media reports, and the **homogenization** of the global media. Another concern is the concentration of international media in a shrinking number of large corporations. In the 1980s, the global media was concentrated in perhaps 50 corporations. Today, some 20 companies dominate the global gathering, processing, and dissemination of programming.

These patterns are of particular concern to developing countries. The rich industrialized world's domination of the global media and information content on the airwaves and the Internet raises concerns about the ability of the developing world to have its voice heard, its concerns expressed, and its cultures and values protected. Developing countries see the rich world's domination of the information age as another factor perpetuating dependence. Of course, some of these concerns are shared by certain industrialized countries (especially France and Canada) worried about the intrusion of American cultural products into their own societies. In the 1980s, the developing world called for the adoption of a New World Information and Communication Order (NWICO) that would establish limits on the domination of the media and information networks and create space for the voices of the southern hemisphere. This effort never overcame opposition from rich countries, but the struggle continues in the form of disputes over cultural protection and control of local independent media establishments around the world.

THE MEDIA AND POLITICAL DECISION MAKING

The media can play a critical role in the formulation of the foreign policies of governments. International events and government priorities will largely determine the foreign policy agenda. International events can compel governments to react, while governments may have particular foreign policy goals they want to achieve while in office. However, as we discussed in Chapter 3, governments are not entirely free to do whatever they want in the foreign policy realm. The agenda facing governments may be influenced by a wide variety of domestic factors. As we discussed in Chapter 3, one of these factors is public opinion, which can be profoundly affected by the media, especially television. As global media continues to become increasingly pervasive, we can expect this question to grow in relevance in the study of global politics. The media can affect foreign policy decision making in a number of different ways.

Agenda Setting

The items on any government's foreign policy agenda are those that are considered important enough to demand government attention. The global media (and the domestic national media) play a role in this process by bringing issues to the attention of the public. This is not done in any purposeful manner; news is seldom intentionally manipulated by radio or television networks themselves. However, in the process of reporting on certain issues (and not reporting on others) the media influence the agenda confronting decision makers. The media may also structure this agenda by influencing perceptions of which issues should have a higher priority than others, because few issues that are raised in the media, and, therefore, brought to the attention of the public, can be ignored by governments. If an issue is a public issue, then it becomes an issue for elected officials, who, after all, must be sensitive to the concerns of their constituents. In Canada and in other parliamentary democratic systems, an issue can be raised in the legislature, at a press conference, or at a public meeting. Elected officials are required to respond in an informed manner, with some explanation of how the government might respond to the issue. As a result, issues brought to the foreign policy agenda by the media become relevant to unelected officials as well. Bureaucracies and bureaucrats pay close attention to media reports, for they know that members of the legislature and ministers must respond to these issues, and will turn to the bureaucracy for advice and assistance in preparing responses. The media bring issues to public awareness; in the absence of this awareness, governments might not have to respond.

Shaping Perceptions

Just as the media can bring issues to public attention, the media can also influence public perceptions of these issues. Media (especially television) can transmit sounds, images, or narrative that engender a strong emotional reaction in the public. Pictures of famine victims, human rights abuses, brutality, and human suffering can create strong pressures on governments to *do something* to alleviate or stop these injustices. In many cases, the media story may blame certain individuals or groups for these injustices and highlight a possible course of action or a possible target for government policy. As a result, not only is the public made aware of the issue but also the media story may influence public perceptions of what ought to be done. This can create policymaking problems, for if governments and those advising them feel that this public perception of what ought to be done is unfeasible or even dangerous, they will be reluctant to act. Alternatively, governments may find another course of action more appropriate and face the task of selling this policy to a public that may have different perceptions of the issue. In addition, the media can also provide the public with a sense of how their own individual feelings about an issue are shared (or not shared) by society. Media coverage of mass protests, rallies, and marches can provide a perception of what the rest of society feels is important. And because many people, from news commentators to protestors to foreign policy experts, have their opinions on what ought to be done solicited and broadcast to the public, the government must respond to the various proposals for action put forward from a wide variety of individuals (see Profile 12.3).

Influencing Decision Makers

The media can often have a direct impact on decision makers themselves. Elected and unelected government officials (including prime ministers and presidents) watch television, listen to the radio, and read newspapers. As a result, they can be directly affected by media stories and media portrayals of the issues. For world leaders, as for publics, news items from global television networks such as CNN or ITN are often the first indication that an event has occurred, and the first source of information on breaking events. Government officials will also monitor media coverage of their own actions and responses to see how their own policies are played out in the media and what reactions government policies are receiving from the public.

PROFILE 12.3 | **Domestic Politics, Canadian Foreign Policy, and Haiti**

In February 1996 the Chrétien government adopted a vigorous (and very public) foreign policy toward Haiti. In part, this foreign policy activism was due to a by-election in the Montreal riding of Papineau-St-Michel. The riding had a high concentration of Haitian voters, and the Liberal candidate, Pierre Pettigrew, could expect to receive strong support from this constituency if Canada was pursuing a strong foreign policy toward Haiti.

Before the by-election, Canada was involved in the UN peacekeeping mission in Haiti; in addition, Pettigrew (not yet a member of the House of Commons) flew to Port-au-Prince to attend the inauguration of President René Préval. There, Pettigrew announced a Canadian government donation of C$700 000 to UNICEF for use in Haiti. Pettigrew won the by-election over Bloc Québécois candidate Daniel Turp.

Embarrassing Government

The ability of the media to discover and reveal events around the world often forces governments to face the consequences of their actions in the international realm. It is increasingly difficult for governments to hide or ignore unfavourable news or politically problematic issues. If governments make mistakes, or make what in retrospect are poor decisions, they will quite likely have to respond to critical reports and investigations in the media. On other occasions, current government policies may be subject to criticism. As a result, governments and politicians often find themselves faced with embarrassing (and potentially politically damaging) inquiries into why the government is pursuing the course of action it is. For example, the efforts of the Liberal government under Jean Chrétien to expand Canadian trade in Asia through the "Team Canada" mission has met with criticism from human rights organizations that the government is not doing enough to promote human rights in Asia. This criticism is accompanied by stories and images of poorly paid workers toiling for long hours under terrible working conditions.

Some might conclude that the power of the media is decisive as a determinant in foreign policy decision making, but this is not accurate. After all, even if the agenda is at least in part set by media reports, in practice governments have a lot of flexibility over how they might actually respond to an issue. When public pressure encourages governments to do something, it seldom specifies what that something should be. Agenda setting is not policy setting. Although media stories may influence the public's perceptions of what their government ought to do, only rarely is public opinion unified on an issue. The fact that public opinion is often split or undecided allows governments considerable room to manoeuvre when making decisions. As for the media affecting government leaders and key officials directly, while this can happen, they are also surrounded by advisers and experts armed with secret intelligence or information, wider historical perspectives, and policy experience. This group enables decision makers to draw on more sources of information and ideas than those presented on television. And while it is harder for governments to escape the consequences of poor decisions, the unintended consequences of their decisions, or even criminal or unethical decisions, the media also provide governments with an unprecedented capacity to explain and defend their actions or even to apologize and acknowledge mistakes.

THE INFORMATION AGE AND GLOBAL POLITICS: THE EROSION OF THE STATE?

The information age may be the final blow to the supremacy of the state in international relations, finishing off the steady erosion in the power of the state brought on by developments in weapons technology and the globalization of the world economy. States have increasingly lost their capacity to secure their territory and populations from attack and have increasingly lost their once dominant grip on their own national economies. Now, the information age promises the flow of ideas, transactions, and communications across the world, virtually unaffected by states and governments. The state is now losing its capacity to control or influence the flow of information within and across its borders, and over what its citizens see, hear, and think. Individuals, groups, and organizations are in increasing contact, creating new communications networks, channels for ideas and debate, business and financial links, and "virtual communities."

Many governments, including the government of Canada, now make little or no effort to directly control this flow of information (though they will make efforts to manipulate it). This is particularly true of those governments in politically open societies. The struggle over the interpretation and portrayal of ideas and events continues.

Domestic critics of government use their unprecedented access to information to criticize the government and its policies in the media. The most open of governments still keep much of their foreign and defence policy affairs (and many other areas as well) behind a veil of secrecy, which the media and citizens' groups often try to penetrate. Governments must continually grapple with issues related to the material content of information flows, as citizens' groups call for the ban or regulation of material they consider immoral or misleading. Governments must also contend with the power of images. During the Vietnam War, largely unfettered television coverage contributed to growing anti-war sentiment. In Russia, television coverage of the conflict in Chechnya contributed to growing public sentiment against the war. In contrast, during the Gulf War and the air campaign against Serbia the press (and especially television) was tightly managed by the coalition and NATO governments.

Many governments also actively attempt to conceal or suppress information or ideas from abroad. For many governments, the free flow of information represents a threat to the power, and even the survival, of the regime. Ideas and information, particularly if they expose lies, abuses, or the controversial nature of ideological claims, can be politically powerful. During the Cold War, the Soviet Union and Eastern Europe jammed foreign radio broadcasts (especially Radio Free Europe, the Voice of America, the BBC World Service, and Radio Liberty) and foreign television broadcasts. Telephone links to the outside world were tightly controlled and monitored; as late as 1987, the Soviet Union possessed only 16 international long-distance telephone circuits.[23] Newspapers were heavily controlled and censored. Photocopy machines were not available to the public. Underground literature (called *Samizdat*) was replicated by hand, on typewriter, and passed from person to person. Today, countries such as North Korea, Sudan, Iraq, Iran, and Myanmar impose draconian restrictions on information flows within and across their borders.[24] And as we have seen, some countries such as China are attempting to restrict access to the Internet.

Despite such efforts, information and communications technologies can be powerful instruments of dissent, even in countries with highly authoritarian political systems. Audio and videotapes have played instrumental roles in the toppling of governments. In the years before the Iranian revolution, audiotapes recorded by the Ayatollah Khomeini in France and smuggled into Iran played a decisive role in the undermining of the Shah's regime and the enormous popularity of Khomeini on his return from exile. In the Philippines, the dictatorship of Ferdinand Marcos fell in part due to the circulation of videotapes showing the assassination of the Philippine opposition leader, Benigno Aquino. Telephone, fax, and computer networks have also played a role in political dissent. During and after the Tiananmen Square protests of 1989, protestors and sympathizers abroad made extensive use of fax machines and e-mail to gather and disseminate information on events at Tiananmen. The Chinese government was forced to respond by placing controls on access to fax machines and supervising incoming messages. In Thailand, protestors against the military government used telephone and fax lines to communicate and coordinate their efforts. When the government employed force to suppress the protests, cutting phone lines and shooting at the demonstrators, the opposition remained in communication using cellular telephones. In Serbia, street demonstrations broke out in protest of the government's cancellation of local election results in 1997. The protesters employed a radio station to combat government domination of the media. When this was shut down, the protestors communicated with each other and the outside world using the Internet. "It used to be that guerrilla fighters lugged AK-47s and sent battlefield news in rolled-up scraps of paper, faithfully carried by couriers through treacherous jungles and mountain passes. Today's revolutionary carries a laptop, and plugs into the Net."[25]

THE INFORMATION AGE AND THE POWER OF THE STATE: A WORLD DIVIDED?

However, governments can also harness the power offered by the computer revolution and the information age. Does this new era of technology-induced freedom from state controls exist primarily in the minds of those who foresee a technological, transboundary world? Is the computer, information, and communications revolution overrated as an agent of change in global politics? After all, information has always been an important element of state power, and computers and communications technologies permit states to access, store, and use information as never before.

States employ this information to their advantage in a number of ways. In their interactions with one another and with nonstate actors, information (or "intelligence") has always been a vital dimension of diplomacy and war. Negotiation, bargaining, and conflict management efforts are facilitated by virtually instantaneous communication and the increasing capability of states to gather information independently. The telephone has become a central tool of contemporary diplomacy; leaders and officials of states often communicate with each other simply by picking up the phone. States also employ information as an instrument of state power, by disseminating information into the international system in the form of radio broadcasts, information services, and statements in the media. Governments may also spread **disinformation**, in a deliberate attempt to mislead other governments (or their own populations). The ability of computers to store and retrieve information offers governments an unprecedented capability to watch over the lives of citizens and keep files on suspected subversive elements. These technologies may, therefore, increase, rather than decrease, the power of the state with respect to the individual.

This raises the issue of information power. It is quite possible that the states that are world leaders in computer development, information production, and communications technology will be the most powerful states in the international system. Just as past technical innovations increased the power of certain societies or states, the information age will increase the power of those states best able to develop and harness the potential of these new technologies. Many observers argue that the country best placed to increase its power and exert leadership in the information age remains the United States:

> Knowledge, more than ever before, is power. The one country that can best lead the information revolution will be more powerful than any other. For the foreseeable future, that country is the United States. America has apparent strength in military power and economic production. Yet its most subtle comparative advantage is its ability to collect, process, act upon, and disseminate information, an edge that will almost certainly grow over the next decade.[26]

Power in the information age will not be dependent on natural endowments of population or resources or geographic position, although these will still have relevance. Instead, power will depend on technological leadership, on political, economic, and social flexibility, and on education. Furthermore, leadership in the information age will also enhance the more traditional measures of power. Technological advances have already led to speculations about a new military-technical revolution and the birth of information warfare. As we will see in Chapter 13, countries that can incorporate information technologies into their military forces will have an enormous advantage on the battlefield and in crisis situations, because they will have a superior capability to gather information about their opponents, a superior ability to communicate, and far superior weapons capabilities. The advantage of a military force equipped with such capabilities over a force that is not was dramatically illustrated during the Gulf War.

The potential for a widening global disparity between states and peoples who can experience and benefit from the information age and those who will not has raised the question of whether we are heading into a world divided between the information and technology haves and have-nots, the info-rich and the info-poor. The proponents of the convergence theme point to the expanded capacity of humankind to communicate as a primary factor in the shrinking of the world. There can be no doubt that the advances made in communications technology, from the invention of the sail to the telephone to the Internet, have resulted in both qualitative and quantitative shifts in the way we communicate with others. However, critics argue that the advent of computer technology has not provided equitable access to the information age. In fact, the computer revolution has exacerbated differentials in the standard of living, and the future prospects, of the world's people. In short, the new technology imposes a two-tier infrastructure on the world economy, in which those with education and access to it have large advantages over those who do not. Optimists argue that these differences will be overcome as the technology spreads; that in the end we will all be better off for it. Pessimists argue that the spread of the technology will be limited to those who can afford it and have the economies to sustain it, and that the mass of the people in the world will be unable to take advantage of the information age.

A GLOBAL CULTURE?

Transnational communications technologies and the global media are shrinking the planet. Individuals around the world can watch the same news reports, listen to the same music, watch the same sporting events, see the same movies, eat the same food, and be exposed to advertising for the same consumer products. As a result, a global culture may be taking form. To be sure, this global culture exists only in a very embryonic form today, if it exists at all. If it does develop, the larger part of the population of the planet will not share in this experience. However, we may be witnessing the beginning of a form of cultural integration or homogenization, borne on the pathways opened by transnational communications technologies and the information revolution.

Television programming, movies, and music have become increasingly globalized. Audiences around the world can watch television programming—particularly in the form of drama series—from other countries. These programs can reveal the nature of life in other countries and other societies, and as a result television can be a powerful educational tool. However, television can also distort the perception of life in other countries; exported Western soap operas have created the impression among many people in other societies that all North Americans and Europeans are rich. Children and family programming is also increasingly globalized, as suggested by the international success of the *Mighty Morphin Power Rangers* (dubbed into English from the original Japanese) and the Canadian television series *Degrassi Junior High*. Movies are also distributed internationally, as are music recordings. Quality cinema is shown at international film festivals (such as the famous Cannes film festival). Classical musicians and conductors move routinely across national borders. In the genres of rock, jazz, and

Sampling Western culture. An Indian holy man sips a soft drink at the opening of the first McDonald's family restaurant in New Delhi. (AP Photo/Ajit Kumar)

blues, tours are often international in scope. Some varieties of music are explicitly international in inspiration, and are sometimes referred to as "world music."

Sporting events have also become internationalized. The Olympic Games and the World Cup (to name only two) are now major international events, watched by hundreds of millions of people. Virtually all athletic and sporting pursuits have some version of a world championship, whether it is in figure skating, ice hockey, or car racing. Frequently, sporting figures will become international celebrities, famous throughout the world. Sports can create a sense of human community, and some suggest that sporting events can be a force for peace, unifying peoples in a shared activity. Of course, sports can bring out intense state or even ethnic nationalism, as people cheer for *their* national team or competitor. Sporting events can also take on a political dimension—witness the intense rivalry of the Canada–Soviet Union hockey confrontations. However, sports bring people (both participants and spectators) together, and the increasing trend toward international competitions, visiting tours of sport teams, and exchanges and trips in youth sports is another example of the blurring of national boundaries.

The wide availability of food and consumer items from other countries (made possible by global trade) also has contributed to the globalization of culture. Many food and consumer products are indistinguishable from the culture that produced them: when one thinks of sushi, one thinks of Japan; when one thinks of Mercedes, one thinks of Germany. In addition, advertising has a powerful cultural dimension, as advertising increasingly links products and the multinational corporations that produce them with music, images, and international celebrities. Icons of certain cultures have spread dramatically, and some are approaching the status of global icons, such as the Golden Arches and Ronald McDonald of the American fast-food chain. However, advertising also carries certain cultural values and messages, and can encourage Western-style consumerism and materialism.

Finally, the language barrier—one of the last barriers to the spread of culture and international communication—is on the verge of being overcome (see Profile 12.4). Computer software that can translate text from one language to another is now available, as are programs that will translate Website pages and allow Internet users to expand their searches to foreign-language Websites. The communications revolution and the information age may be accelerating another remarkable global trend: the increasing dominance of English. Already, 80 percent of all information stored on computers is in English. English is the language of the Internet, and is growing rapidly as the international language of communication. By 2007, according to one estimate, there will be

Toward Unicode?

How can people who speak different languages communicate on the Internet? A North American consortium has developed a universal digital code, named Unicode, that may overcome this obstacle. Computers operate on binary bits: combinations of zeros and ones. For example, ASCII (the American Standard Code for Information Interchange) represents each character by a sequence of seven zeros or ones; but only 128 possible sequences exist, so it is a limited translator. Non-English speaking countries have their own codes, with their own limitations. The developers of Unicode circumvent this by using a sequence of 16 zeros and ones, producing 65 536 different combinations. Thus, any language can have its own sequence for each character in that language. Translating software is also becoming more popular and advanced, and should be widespread in the future. E-mail will present some problems because, as A. Pollack reports, "the informal word usage and unusual punctuations that are common … could further confuse an electronic translator." However, the gist of a message could come through, and efforts are being made to facilitate "translation of messages in transit so that e-mail sent in English, for example, could arrive at the other end in French."

SOURCE: A. POLLACK, "CYBERSPACE'S WAR OF WORDS," *THE GLOBE AND MAIL* (10 AUGUST 1995), A10.

more people who speak English as a second language than there are people who speak it as a first language.[27] English dominates the scientific and intellectual communities, and English-language training is in extremely high demand around the world. As Daniel F. Burton argues, "These technologies will further loosen culture from its geographic moorings, thereby contributing to the creation of a free-floating cosmopolitan class that is not restricted by national identity."[28]

However, considerable concern remains around the world that this global culture may in fact be less of a fusion, or integration, of cultures from around the world than the spread—or, worse, imposition—of Western culture and especially American culture. Instead of a global culture emerging, some would argue, we are witnessing cultural imperialism. The global culture is dominated by the English language, the U.S. film and television industries, American and Western media networks, and advertising for Western-style consumption. Hollywood, for example, dominates global cinema and the television programming industry; it supplies 80 percent of the world's demand for films and 70 percent of the world's demand for television shows. Hollywood already makes more than half its money abroad.[29] The vast majority of Internet users and servers are in the United States; of the estimated 159 million users worldwide in 1998, 88.3 million were in the United States, and 68 percent of all Internet servers are in the United States.[30] This dominance, in turn, may give the United States an important lead in soft power. So even the realist perspective would argue that the information revolution is significant, if only because it can reinforce the importance of state power.

CONCLUSIONS

Where will the computer revolution, the communications revolution, and the information age take us? Innovation is difficult to predict; new discoveries may open up completely new areas of human endeavour, much as the development of the computer has. The question for observers of international relations is how these innovations will affect the interaction of states, groups, and individuals. As we have seen, the impact up to now has been profound.

The consensus is that the information age will accelerate the erosion of the state and enhance global interdependence. A new era of global communication promises improved international understanding and the establishment of new patterns of human interaction across state boundaries. However, the information age may also enhance the power of some states in the international system and serve to make us all more vulnerable to both observation and crime. The pervasiveness of certain cultures and perspectives on computer networks and in the global media may lead to a cultural backlash against transnational communication. We must not forget that the majority of people on this planet are untouched by the information age. What does the information age promise these people? The information age may thus be a force of convergence for many in the international system, but it is also a force of divergence, as so many past revolutions in human history have been.

Endnotes

1. Quoted in Charles W. Kegley, Jr., and Eugene R. Wittkopf, *World Politics: Trend and Transformation,* 5th ed. (New York: St. Martin's Press, 1995), 554.
2. See J. Goldstein, *Long Cycles: Prosperity and War in the Modern Age* (New Haven: Yale University Press, 1988); and C. Freeman, "Diffusion, the Spread of New Technology to Firms, Sectors, and Nations," in A. Heertje, ed., *Innovation, Technology, and Finance* (New York: Basil Blackwell, 1988), 38–70.
3. Daniel Burton, Jr., "The Brave New Wired World," *Foreign Policy* 106 (Spring 1997), 23–24.
4. R. Volti, *Society and Technological Change*, 2nd ed. (New York: St. Martin's Press, 1992), 235.
5. J. Rosenau, *Turbulence in World Politics* (Princeton: Princeton University Press, 1990), 17.
6. R. Walters and D. Blake, *The Politics of Global Economic Relations*, 4th ed. (Englewood Cliffs, NJ: Prentice Hall, 1992), 188.
7. J.-J. Salomon and A. Lebeau, *Mirages of Development: Science and Technology for the Third Worlds* (Boulder and London: Lynne Rienner, 1993), 86. See also Paul Kennedy's *Preparing for the Twentieth Century* (New York: Random House, 1993).
8. This according to the UNDP *Human Development Report 1992* (New York: Oxford University Press, 1992), 2.
9. M. Castels and L. D'Andrea Tyson, "High Technology Choices Ahead: Restructuring Interdependence," in J. Sewell and S. Tucker, eds., *Growth, Exports, and Jobs in a Changing World* (New Brunswick, NJ: Transaction Press, 1988), 57.
10. A. Toffler and H. Toffler, *War and Anti-War: Survival at the Dawn of the 21st Century* (Boston: Little, Brown and Company, 1993), 10–11. See also R. Preston and S. Wise, *Men in Arms: A History of Warfare and Its Interrelationships with Western Society*, 4th ed. (New York: Holt, Rinehart, and Winston, 1979).
11. See Price Pritchett, *The Employee Handbook of New Work Habits for a Radically Changing World* (Dallas: Pritchett and Associates, 1996), 4.
12. P. Drucker, *Post-Capitalist Society* (New York: HarperBusiness, 1993), 40.
13. Dominique Foray and Bengt-Ålce Lundvall, "The Knowledge-Based Economy: From the Economics of Knowledge to the Learning Economy," *Employment and Growth in the Knowledge-Based Economy.* OECD Documents (Paris: Organisation for Economic Cooperation and Development, 1996), 16.
14. P. Woodall, "The World Economy," *The Economist* (26 September 1996), 43.
15. Ethan B. Kapstein, "Workers and the World Economy," *Foreign Affairs* 75 (May/June 1996), 16.
16. Woodall, "The World Economy," 19.
17. Michael T. Klare, "Resource Competition and World Politics in the Twenty-First Century," *Current History* 99 (December 2000), 403–7.
18. See I. de Sola Pool, in Eli M. Noam, ed., *Technologies without Boundaries: On Telecommunications in a Global Age* (Cambridge, MA: Harvard University Press, 1990).

19. See *Global Economic Prospects and the Developing Countries* (Washington, DC: World Bank, 1992), and *Human Development Report 1999* (New York: United Nations, 2000).
20. See Burton, "The Brave New Wired World," 25.
21. Woodall, "The World Economy," 4.
22. *Turbulence in World Politics: A Theory of Change and Continuity* (Princeton, NJ: Princeton University Press, 1990), 339–43.
23. A. Ramirez, "Dial Direct to Moscow and Beyond," *New York Times* (20 May 1992), D1.
24. Some argue that the media in advanced capitalist states are just as manipulative and that there is a connection between the owners of the media and pro–status quo forces in government. The most famous proponent of this view is Noam Chomsky; see for example Noam Chomsky, *Media Control: The Spectacular Achievements of Propaganda* (New York: Seven Stories Press, 1997).
25. Isabel Vincent, "Rebel Dispatches Find Home on Net," *The Globe and Mail* (11 June 1996), A1.
26. J. Nye, Jr., and W. Owens, "America's Information Edge," *Foreign Affairs* 75 (March/April 1996), 20.
27. "Language and Electronics: The Coming Global Tongue," *The Economist* (21 December 1997), 76.
28. Burton, "The Brave New Wired World," 36.
29. "Star Wars," *The Economist* (22 March 1997), 15.
30. See Andrew L. Shapiro, "The Internet," *Foreign Policy* 115 (Summer 1999), 14–27, and Burton, "The Brave New Wired World," 32.

Suggested Readings

Alleyne, M. *International Power and International Communication.* Toronto: Macmillan, 1995.

Baldwin, T., D. McVoy, and C. Steinfeld. *Convergence: Integrating Media, Information, and Communication.* Thousand Oaks, CA: Sage Publications, 1996.

Castells, M. *The Rise of Network Society.* Cambridge, MA: Blackwell Publishers, 1996.

Connor, E. *The Global Political Economy of Communication: Hegemony, Telecommunications and the Information Economy.* New York: St. Martin's Press, 1994.

Dosi, G., et al., eds. *Technical Change and Economic Theory.* London: Frances Pinter, 1988.

Downing, J., Ali Mohammadi, and A. Sreberny-Mohammadi. *Questioning the Media: A Critical Introduction.* Thousand Oaks, CA: Sage Publications, 1996.

Drucker, P. *Post-Capitalist Society.* New York: HarperBusiness, 1993.

Duncan, B., et al. *Mass Media and Popular Culture.* Toronto: Harcourt Brace, 1996.

Dutton, W., ed. *Information and Communications Technologies: Visions and Realities.* New York: Oxford University Press, 1996.

Frederick, H. *Global Communication and International Relations.* Belmont, CA: Wadsworth, 1993.

Hamelink, C. *The Politics of World Communication.* Thousand Oaks, CA: Sage Publications, 1994.

Haywood, T. *Info-Rich and Info-Poor: Access and Exchange in the Global Information Society.* New Jersey: Bowker-Saur, 1995.

Krasner, S. "Global Communications and National Power: Life on the Pareto Frontier." *World Politics* 43 (1991), 336–66.

Martin, W. *The Global Information Society.* Brookfield, VT: Gower, 1995.

Medina, A. "Canada's Information Edge." *Canadian Foreign Policy* 4 (2) (1996), 71–87.

Menzies, H. *The Information Highway and the New Economy.* Toronto: Between the Lines, 1996.

Muszynski, L., and D. Wolfe. "New Technology and Training: Lessons from Abroad." *Canadian Public Policy* 15 (1989), 245–64.

Pirages, D. *Global Technopolitics: The International Politics of Technology and Resources.* Pacific Grove, CA: Brooks Cole, 1989.

Pool, Ithiel de Sola. *Technologies without Boundaries: Telecommunications in a Global Age.* Cambridge, MA: Harvard University Press, 1990.

Robinson, P. *Deceit, Delusion, and Detection.* Thousand Oak, CA: Sage Publications, 1996.

Said, E. *Covering Islam: How the Media and Experts Determine How We See the Rest of the World.* Rev. ed. New York: Vintage, 1997.

Schenk, D. *Data Smog: Surviving the Information Glut.* New York: Harper Collins, 1997.

Smith, A. *The Geopolitics of Information: How Western Culture Dominates the World.* New York: Oxford University Press, 1980.

Suggested Websites

If we began to list even a fraction of the Websites dealing with the topic presented in this chapter, it would be an overwhelming exercise. Our recommendation is that you take some time to do some surfing, to get a feel for the wide variety of material available, noting the cultural, commercial, and political attributes discussed above.

CHAPTER 13

Violent Conflicts of the Future?

Geoeconomics is spreading and becoming the dominant phenomenon in the central arena of world affairs.

—Edward Luttwak[1]

The fundamental source of conflict in this new world will not be primarily ideological or primarily economic. The great divisions of humankind and the dominating source of conflict will be cultural.

—Samuel P. Huntington[2]

It is time to understand "the environment" for what it is: the national security issue of the twenty-first century.

—Morton Kaplan[3]

INTRODUCTION: FUTURE CONFLICTS

In this penultimate chapter, we return to the problem of war in global politics. Our first objective is to explore some of the potential causes of future wars, based on some identifiable trends and examples from the current international system. This discussion is not intended to be exhaustive. After all, wars break out for a variety of reasons and not all of them can be anticipated. In addition, wars between states and groups may continue to break out for the reasons discussed in earlier chapters of this book, such as ideological competition, expansionism, separatism, ethnic strife, and arms races. In fact, two of the possible causes of future wars are disputes over economics and resources, which have been causes of war for centuries. Nevertheless, the changing nature of global politics suggests that some issues may become more relevant as issues of dispute and contention in the future and that these issues will have a qualitatively different aspect than past conflicts. In particular, the changing nature of the global economy, the decline of the state, environmental degradation, and the widening gulf between rich and poor countries and peoples may produce tensions, disputes, and conflicts that could lead to increased international violence and war in the twenty-first century. If we accept that a major component of our ability to prevent future wars will be anticipating their underlying causes and taking steps to ameliorate them, then we must make this effort, despite the hazards inherent in speculating about the future.

Our second objective is to examine the character of these potential future wars. How will these wars be fought? What weapons and techniques will be used? Here we can predict two trends. We can expect future high-intensity conflicts involving one or more countries of the rich industrialized world to be dominated by modern weapons technology and information systems, as mentioned in the previous chapter on the information age. As this technology proliferates through the international system, we can expect more countries to acquire ever more sophisticated weapons systems. However, we can also expect the trend of low-intensity conflict to continue, especially at the substate level. These wars will be characterized by the use of light weapons and the tactics and techniques of communal warfare. Either way, we must not lose sight of the fact that war results in suffering and precludes genuine human development.

FUTURE WARS FOR ECONOMIC POWER?

An intimate link between economics and conflict has always existed. Throughout history, economic concerns or incentives have sparked the outbreak of wars or have influenced the conduct of military campaigns. Through war, states and empires could acquire territory, natural resources, population, and industrial capacity. During war, economic targets have often been a priority. In the ancient period, wells were poisoned and land rendered unsuitable for agriculture (usually by salting the soil). In the modern period, economic blockades and embargoes have been imposed on some states, such as Germany during World War I. In *total wars* states have engaged in the strategic bombing of manufacturing and energy infrastructure to cripple the war effort and weaken the civilian morale of the target nation. Historically, the most powerful countries have possessed the largest and most powerful economies, in part because this wealth has underwritten the development of powerful military capabilities. However, as we discussed in Chapter 4, the importance of economic power has also been the source of economic competition between states. Even when they are not at war in a military sense, states are engaged in a struggle for economic power. In the contemporary international system, concern exists that this historical pattern is reappearing and that we are heading into a future characterized by an intense economic competition between states (in effect, a global economic war) and the possibility that economic competition and economic disputes could escalate into political and military rivalries and possibly even military wars.

After the military confrontation of the Cold War, the perception is that military power has declined in utility and importance. Instead, economic power is the key index of power in the world, and actors in the international system (especially states) are increasingly regarding the health of their economies as a security issue. As a result, economics is becoming the primary arena of competition and conflict between states. As Robert A. Isaac argues, "Although the Cold War has ended, the primacy of insecurity—of the infinite striving for security—has not. Where military security prevails, such as in most of the industrialized democracies, there has merely been a shift in the form of insecurity to the economic or psychological realms, as nations seek to increase economic competitiveness and to reduce unemployment."[4] In this view, the ability of a country to provide a high quality of life to its citizens is a motivating factor in the aim for economic security.

However, Edward Luttwak has suggested that we are entering a world in which states will compete with each other in the economic realm solely to achieve economic power (see Profile 13.1). As Luttwak argues:

> In traditional world politics, the goals are to secure and extend the physical control of territory, and to gain diplomatic influence over foreign governments. The corresponding geoeconomic goal is not the highest possible standard of living for a country's population but rather the conquest or protection of desirable roles in the world economy. Who will develop the next generation of jet airliners, computers, bio-technology products, advanced materials, financial services, and all other high value output in industries

Survival of the Smartest: Geoeconomic Warfare

Many realists predict a return to economic nationalism in the future world economy. In particular, Edward Luttwak makes the following arguments:

- Geoeconomics is spreading and becoming the dominant phenomenon in the central arena of world affairs, but not all states are equally inclined or equally capable of participating in the new struggle.

- Small but well-educated countries can be much more successful in geoeconomics than they could ever be in world politics, where size always counts and may alone be decisive.

- States will tend to act geoeconomically simply because of what they are: territo-

rially defined entities designed precisely to outdo each other on the world scene.

- When there is no strategic confrontation at the centre of world affairs that can absorb the adversarial feeling of the nations, those ill feelings may be diverted into the nation's economic relations.

- The emerging geoeconomic struggle for high-technology industrial supremacy among Americans, Europeans, and Japanese is eroding their old alliance solidarity. Increased geoeconomic activity will characterize their economic relationship, as opposed to free-trade economics.

SOURCE: EDWARD LUTTWAK, "THE COMING GLOBAL WAR FOR ECONOMIC POWER," *THE INTERNATIONAL ECONOMY* 7 (SEPTEMBER/OCTOBER 1993), 20.

large and small? Will the designers, technologists, managers, and financiers be Americans, Europeans, or East Asians?[5]

In other words, states will continue to battle one another not for territory or resources, or for religious, political, or ideological reasons but for economic supremacy. At stake is nothing less than the future power position of all states in the system. Long-term (perhaps permanent) winners and losers will emerge from this economic war. For the winning states, the spoils of victory will include industrial supremacy, technology and information leadership, and the economic capacity to sustain a modern military. The losing states will face the problems created by reduced fiscal resources; reduced economic growth and a smaller economic pie; permanent relegation to the ranks of the resource extraction, branch plant, or cash crop economies; second-rate technology and information systems; and a lack of the economic means to escape a cycle of poverty.

The economic war between states is, therefore, cast in *zero-sum terms*; that is, gains for one side are seen as a loss for the other. This view is different from liberal perspectives on global economic cooperation in which both sides should benefit (and usually do). In fact, predictions of future economic wars are informed by realist views of international relations. Realists would argue that states are concerned with relative economic gains because their economies are the foundation of their power. As Michael Mastanduno argues, "Even if nation-states do not fear for their physical survival, they worry that a decrease in their power capabilities relative to those in other nation-states will compromise their political autonomy, expose them to the influence attempts of others, or lessen their ability to prevail in political disputes with allies and adversaries."[6] As a result, states will compete for economic advantage, not only seeking absolute gains but relative gains in their favour, to prevent other countries from surpassing their own economic power (and therefore their position in world affairs).[7]

Luttwak argues that just as in war, offensive weapons will dominate in the new global struggle for economic power. Luttwak envisions a new mercantile world, with states using unilateral actions to alter the balance of trade in key economic sectors (those sectors identified as desirable). The weapons in this economic competition will be the instruments used by governments and their self-interested bureaucracies to encourage economic development in certain sectors. These instruments include a combination of incentives and trade barriers. Incentives include the following:

- *Research and development programs to encourage the development of certain economic sectors.* For example, the governments of Japan and the United States (as well as the European Union) have established programs to develop new computer and computer-related technologies. In 1990, the United States launched a project to develop a more efficient battery for electric cars. The project was funded by the government and all three major U.S. automobile manufacturers and is aimed, Luttwak argues, at the Japanese auto industry.

- *Subsidies to certain industries.* Governments may also promote certain industries through financial assistance. Luttwak cites Airbus Industrie (a European consortium that produces passenger aircraft in direct competition with U.S. manufacturers such as Boeing) as an example of how governments can offer direct financial support to certain economic sectors. States can also offer subsidies in the form of preferred national treatment, such as government purchase of products on favourable terms. The Japanese government, for example, purchased Japanese computers to assist the development of Japan's computer industry, then in direct competition with the U.S. industry, which is led by IBM.

- *Export assistance to domestic firms to encourage foreign sales.* Governments have also used loans (at low rates of interest) to encourage the purchase of their domestic products. Most exporting countries have export banks that offer loans and credit to finance exports. Purchasers from abroad can secure credit to purchase products at rates lower than they would find in their own countries or in other countries. Of course, if a sale is considered particularly lucrative, governments may compete for that sale by competitively lowering the interest rates offered by their export banks. Luttwak calls this "predatory finance."[8]

States will employ these instruments in an attempt to encourage exports to other countries, acquiring market share abroad, and thus ensuring the health of certain favoured sectors (such as high technology). At the same time, states will erect trade barriers to certain products coming from abroad, to limit the market share foreign firms can acquire in their own domestic economies. Such barriers may take the form of tariffs, customs duties, or regulations on product standards.

Because of the severity of the stakes involved in the struggle for economic power in the future, states will find themselves in an increasingly cutthroat competition for economic development, a competition that could compromise the political relationship between them. This compromise raises the question of whether economic disputes will spill over into political and even military disputes in the future. The Cold War tended to reduce the intensity of economic disputes between countries in the interests of maintaining unity in the face of the mutual threat. Japan, the United States, and Germany may have been economic competitors, but they were security partners. The Cold War is now over, and the concern is that trade disputes could escalate as states retaliate against one another by imposing tariffs, duties, or other barriers to trade. Not only would this have a damaging effect on the global economy (and on the economies of the states themselves) but also it would lead to rising political tensions. If this tension should occur between the major trading states in the future, it would represent the breakdown of the political partnership of the Cold War era. Economic rivals might be increasingly perceived as political and even military rivals, ushering in a new era of political and military competition.

Obviously, Luttwak is no liberal. He assumes economic conflict will predominate over economic cooperation. He assumes that states will not be willing to sacrifice some material economic interests for the sake of greater overall gains from trade and collaboration. Luttwak also assumes that international economic conflict management instruments (in the form of institutions) will be unable to stop self-interested defections from beginning a slide to a new mercantile world. Of course, Luttwak is correct when he points to the existence of economic disputes and competition in the global economy. However, these disputes have yet to compromise the basic cooperative character of most international economic activity. Liberals would argue that the trend toward interdependence, globalization of trade and finance, and the development of institutions of economic management all suggest that cooperation, rather than conflict, is the future for the global economy. In contrast, Marxists would argue that the current economic system is exploitative and predatory. The axis of conflict in the global economy will not be between states; it will be between rich and poor, and cooperation will not be based on the enlightened self-interest of states, but on the interests of the transnational elite.

FUTURE WARS BETWEEN CIVILIZATIONS?

In a controversial article published in the influential journal *Foreign Affairs,* Harvard professor Samuel P. Huntington argued that the primary source of conflict in the world will not be ideology, economics, or nationalism. Rather, future wars will occur between the world's civilizations. As Huntington argues, "Nation states will remain the most powerful actors in world affairs, but the principal conflicts of global politics will occur between nations and groups of different civilizations. The clash of civilizations will dominate world politics. The fault lines between civilizations will be the battle lines of the future."[9] As we discussed in Chapter 1, conflict between civilizations was a fixture of human history before the development of the modern Westphalian state system. Huntington picks up on this historical theme and argues that the principle lines of conflict in world history have evolved through several stages. In feudal periods in Europe and Asia, conflict revolved around monarchs and their power. In the age of the modern nation-state, wars were between states and their respective state nationalisms. Wars then became wars between ideologies (fascism, communism, and democracy). Today, Huntington argues, with the state and state nationalism eroding and the great ideological battles over, we are returning to an era characterized by conflict between cultures, between the civilizations of the world.

Huntington argues that civilizational identity will be increasingly important as a factor in future global politics. He defines a civilization in the following manner: "A civilization is a cultural entity. Villages, regions, ethnic groups, nationalities, religious groups, all have distinct cultures at different levels of cultural heterogeneity.... Arabs, Chinese, and Westerners, however, are not part of any broader cultural entity. They constitute civilizations. A civilization is thus the highest cultural grouping of people and the broadest level of cultural identity people have short of that which distinguishes humans from other species."[10] Huntington argues that there are eight major civilizations in the world: Western, Confucian, Japanese, Islamic, Hindu, Slavic-Orthodox, Latin American, and possibly African. Increasingly, the conflicts of the future will take place along the fault lines where these civilizations meet. These fault lines have a history of tension and conflict, which reflects the clashes between cultures. Many recent and current conflicts in the contemporary international system are taking place along these fault lines, in places like the former Yugoslavia, Azerbaijan, Armenia and Georgia, the Horn of Africa, Russia and Chechnya, India and Pakistan, and India and China. Huntington offers several explanations as to why civilizational disputes are growing and will become the basis for most future conflicts.

- Civilizations are more basic than the state; for everything we are, we owe less to the state than to the civilization we belong to. Civilizations are differentiated by history, religion, language, culture, and tradition. Differences among civilizations are, therefore, fundamental and very enduring. As a result, differences among civilizations have generated the longest and most violent conflicts and will do so increasingly in the future.

- Increasing global interdependence, interaction, and contact between peoples of different civilizations, rather than contributing to understanding and accommodation, is making more people aware of differences between them. Interdependence and globalization are contributing to civilizational consciousness among the peoples of the world.

- Economic and social change around the world is altering the relationship between individuals and traditional social institutions. In particular, the state is in decline and religion is replacing it. The revival of religion around the world means a world increasingly united around the religious heritages of civilizations rather than the nationalist heritage of nation-states.

- The spread and power of Western civilization is provoking a counterreaction in other civilizations. Civilizational consciousness is in part a reaction to the encroachment of Western culture and values on traditional, civilizational belief systems. An anti-Western return to civilizational roots is underway around the world, from Asianization in Japan, to the Hinduization of India, to the re-Islamization of the Middle East and the Russianization of Russia.

- Civilizational differences are less subject to change or flexible adaptation. Negotiations, compromises, and resolution of disputes that have a civilizational aspect are more difficult to achieve.

- Economic patterns are assuming civilizational forms and shapes. The development of trade blocks will add another element to the growing cohesion of civilizations and the divisions among them. Civilizational links will become more important factors in the creation of economic zones of activity, with peoples of shared civilizational heritage more disposed toward doing business with each other than they are with peoples of other civilizations.

Ultimately, Huntington argues, civilizational identity is becoming increasingly important as an influence on the perceptions of peoples around the world. This influence will create an "us versus them" mentality, which will drive intercivilizational differences on a whole range of international issues from human rights to immigration to trade, and from commerce to the environment.

Huntington argues that the global spread of Western culture and power is already provoking a backlash against the West. The future may be one of "the West against the rest." This argument (as Huntington himself points out) is not an original one. Kishore Mahbubani has argued that the central axis of conflict in the world in the future will be between Western civilization and the non-Western civilizations of the world.[11] This conflict will have two dimensions. On the one hand will be a struggle for military, economic, and institutional power. The non-Western world regards the shape and form of the global economy as inherently discriminatory toward developing countries, and while the rich (mostly Western) world grows richer, the developing (non-Western) world benefits little. For example, the West largely controls international institutions such as the United Nations and the International Monetary Fund. Military activities such as the Gulf War showed the willingness of the West to attack non-Western countries, while at the same time failing to respond quickly in Rwanda or in Bosnia or in East Timor. The effort to prevent the flow of arms to states like Libya, Iran, Iraq, and North Korea is an example of the West trying to preserve its military superiority over the rest of the world. On the other hand will be a struggle over culture. As we discussed in Chapter 9, the rest of the world often sees the effort of Western countries to encourage democracy and human rights as a form of cultural imperialism.

The response of the non-Western world in this struggle has been (and will continue to be) varied. Some non-Western states will adopt a policy of isolation, in effect sealing off their societies and economies from the West, thus protecting themselves from the corruptive influences of Western ideas and the economic dependency created by the global economic system. However, this path has proved largely unsuccessful, with the countries that have pursued it (North Korea and Burma) experiencing increased poverty and economic collapse. A second response is to join the West and adopt Western values and institutions, including democracy, law, and human rights. The difficulty with this course of action is that it involves the import of value systems that are very different from those shared by the majority (or a significant portion) of the population. This may create social and political unrest between those who want to "Westernize" and those who want to protect the history and culture of the society. A final option is to acquire military and economic power to resist the West and to make common cause with other non-Western peoples in this effort. Huntington argues that for those civilizations for which Westernization is neither feasible nor desirable, the preferred course of action is resistance and the development of the military capacity to confront the West.

The reaction of the West will also be crucial. In the long term, Huntington argues that the West must recognize that the dominance of Western civilization around the world is ending and that other civilizations will begin to re-exert their place and influence on global politics. The West, along with all of the world's civilizations, will have to develop an increased understanding of the philosophical and religious differences between them. There will be no universal civilization but a world of civilizations.

Huntington's thesis has stirred considerable debate and a strong response from those skeptical of his view. Huntington's critics argue that the boundary between civilizations is far from distinct and that conflict within a civilization—that is, intracivilizational conflict—may be more frequent than clashes between civilizations. Many take issue with Huntington's definition of the major civilizations of the world. Others stress that states are a far more decisive force than Huntington suggests. Instead of civilizations motivating the actions of states, it is truer that states control civilizations and cultures. Huntington has also been criticized for overestimating the role played by culture in the world. Most peoples and governments are motivated not by cultural concerns but by concerns over economic growth. The world is characterized not by the triumph of religious and culturally oriented governments, but by the failure of such governments. The West, far from being increasingly despised, is still a source of admiration and attraction for non-Western peoples, in particular the young. Huntington's thesis, therefore, is not without its flaws. However, it remains a serious point of discussion in the debate about the origins of the wars of the future.

ENVIRONMENTAL DEGRADATION AND ENVIRONMENTAL CONFLICT

As we discussed in Chapter 10, environmental issues have received increasing attention from individual members of the public, private groups and associations, the governments of states, and international organizations. Much of this attention is focused on the local, regional, or global environmental problems created by human activity on the planet. Much of the urgency surrounding environmental problems comes from a belief that they are going to get worse, not better. Environmental degradation is regarded as a global problem (some would say the problem) in and of itself. While this is true, environmental degradation has also been identified as a source of international conflict and war. Furthermore, as environmental degradation worsens, it may be an increasingly important cause of war in the future. As a result, environmental degradation has been regarded increasingly as a security issue in the study of international relations.[12] However, the conceptualization of the environment as a security problem is not without its detractors. Skeptics argue that it is inappropriate to characterize environmental issues as security issues because the environment is not an enemy and environmental issues cannot be addressed through traditional military means. Others argue that little hard evidence exists to support the link between environmental degradation and conflict and war.[13]

The hypothesis that environmental degradation is a cause of conflict in the international system is built on the logic of scarcity. Both renewable and nonrenewable resources are finite in quantity. As the population of the planet increases, and as industrialization and consumption continue to grow and spread, the scarcity of resources will become increasingly acute, for three main reasons:

- Human activity will increasingly consume more resources, degrading the quality and availability of resources.

- Population growth will increase the number of people making demands on a shrinking resource pie.

- Resources will not be distributed equally, and the concentration of resources in a small segment of the population will decrease the availability of that resource to the rest of the population.

As available resources deteriorate or are depleted, competition for access to these resources will increase. Conflict and war over resources will be the inevitable result. Indeed, some would argue that this process has already begun. A major Canadian-led international research project on environmental scarcity and violent conflict reached the following conclusion:

> Scarcities of renewable resources will increase sharply. The total area of high quality agricultural land will drop, as will the extent of forests and the number of species they sustain. Coming generations will also see the widespread depletion and degradation of aquifers, rivers, and other water

resources; the decline of many fisheries; and perhaps significant climate change … environmental scarcities are already contributing to violent conflicts in many areas of the world. These conflicts are probably the early signs of an upsurge of violence in the coming decades that will be induced or aggravated by scarcity.[14]

A number of different environmental issues have been cited as causes of existing or future conflicts:

- The degradation and loss of arable land, with consequent implications for crop and livestock production
- The destruction of forests and consequent loss of forestry-related employment, revenue, topsoil, and species diversity
- The depletion and degradation of fresh water supplies
- The depletion of strategic minerals, including oil
- The overexploitation and consequent depletion of fisheries resources

Two links exist between environmental degradation, resource scarcity, and conflict and war. First, environmental degradation and resource scarcity may cause resource wars between states. Second, environmental degradation and resource scarcity may cause intrastate conflicts between peoples.

RESOURCE WARS BETWEEN STATES

An intimate link has always existed between resource scarcity and interstate conflict and war, and this link was evident in the twentieth century. One study of 12 twentieth-century conflicts found that access to oil or strategic minerals was an issue in 10 of those conflicts.[15] Perhaps this fact should come as no surprise, as oil and strategic minerals are the lifeblood of industrialized economies and modern military capabilities are regarded as a defining factor in the power of a state.[16] In contrast, the study found that only 5 of the 12 conflicts studied involved renewable resources, such as cropland or fish. During the Cold War, there was a view (mostly held in Washington) that the Soviet Union was seeking to expand its influence over critical resources and strategic minerals in the Persian Gulf and South Africa.[17] A recent example of a war involving oil or strategic minerals was the Gulf War, which was fought at least in part to prevent one country from gaining control over a significant percentage of Middle Eastern oil reserves. In the contemporary international system, the dispute over the Spratly and Paracel Islands in the South China Sea carries the potential for interstate conflict over the right to exploit oil and mineral deposits on the seabed (see Profile 13.2).

However, in the future one renewable resource is likely to become an increasing cause of interstate war: fresh water. Fresh water is fundamental to all living things and is essential for all forms of economic activity. However, supplies of readily accessible fresh water are unevenly distributed, leaving many of the world's regions seriously short of this vital resource. As Peter H. Gleick argues,

> As we approach the twenty-first century, water and water supply systems are increasingly likely to be both objectives of military action and instruments of war as human populations grow, as improving standards of living increase the demand for fresh water, and as global climatic changes make water supply and demand more problematic and uncertain.[18]

The Spratly Islands Dispute

Claiming the Spratlys. A Chinese flag flies from one of the two newly finished concrete structures on the Mischief Reef, off the disputed Spratly group of islands in the South China Sea. The U.S. State Department has said that Chinese construction on the disputed islands is potentially provocative and urged China to continue direct discussions with all parties involved. China claims that the structures are only for their fishers seeking shelter. (AP Photo/Aaron Favila)

The Spratly Islands are a group of 500 small islands situated in the South China Sea. Six states lay claim to some or all of the Spratly Islands or their territorial waters: Brunei, China, Malaysia, the Philippines, Taiwan, and Vietnam. Although most of the islands are mere outcroppings of rock or coral, they possess strategic value for three reasons: they are located in the middle of an important international sea lane, their territorial waters are rich in fish stocks, and their seabeds contain oil and mineral deposits. The Spratly Islands dispute has had a violent dimension, particularly between Vietnam and China. These two countries have clashed over some of the islands in 1974, 1982, 1988, and 1992. Most countries that lay claim to some or all of the islands maintain military garrisons on selected islands, and all maintain an air force and naval presence in and around the islands. Despite calls for a regional conference on the future of the islands, and the opening of talks between China and Vietnam, the Spratly Islands remain a subject of intense interstate dispute. There are concerns that this dispute could result in armed conflict at any time.

Water and water-related facilities have often been targeted in times of war. In the ancient period, wells were poisoned to deny water to the enemy, a practice that continued for centuries. In the twentieth century, hydroelectric dams were targets during World War II and the Korean War. Irrigation systems in North Vietnam were bombed by the United States during the Vietnam War, and Syria and Israel had violent clashes over water in the mid-1960s. In the Gulf War, Kuwaiti desalination plants were destroyed by Iraq, while coalition bombing largely destroyed Iraq's water supply system.

It is feared that in the future, the increasing scarcity of water will lead states into regarding access to water as a national security matter, provoking conflict and wars between them. The threat of war over water will be most acute in arid regions, where water resources (in the form of lakes, rivers, or aquifers) are controlled by a number of states with a history of antagonistic relations. The most prominent example of an area in which water has had security implications is the Middle East.[19] Two sources of Middle Eastern water are a particular focus of concern: the Nile and the Jordan River Basin (see Profile 13.3).[20]

Disputes over water are not confined to the Middle East. In central Asia, the flow of water in the tributary rivers of the shrinking Aral Sea has been a cause of concern for the newly independent states of the former Soviet Union. Similarly, tensions have risen in south Asia over access to the waters of the Ganges and Indus rivers. In the Americas, conflict may grow over the waters of the Colorado, the Rio Grande, and the Great Lakes (see Profile 13.4). Water is not the only resource that might spark future conflicts, but

Water and Interstate Conflict in the Middle East?

THE NILE

The Nile River is one of the most famous and historic rivers of the world. It is also a river of tremendous regional economic importance. The Nile is the primary source of water for both human consumption and agriculture in northeast Africa, in particular Egypt and the Sudan. In fact, almost all of Egypt's water is drawn from the Nile. However, almost all of the source water of the Nile originates outside of Egypt, in the seven countries that straddle the Nile River Basin: Sudan, Ethiopia, Kenya, Rwanda, Burundi, Tanzania, and Zaire. The exploitation of water resources in these countries would reduce the flow of water to the Nile and to Egypt. To the Egyptian government, this is a major security concern, prompting former Egyptian president Anwar Sadat and former foreign minister Boutros Boutros-Ghali to warn that conflict over water might result in Egypt going to war.

THE JORDAN RIVER BASIN

The Jordan River Basin is a valley in the central Middle East that collects most of the rainwater that falls on the region. Syria, Lebanon, Israel, Jordan, and the West Bank are heavily dependent on the Jordan Basin for their water supplies, and since the creation of Israel in 1948 access to this water supply has been a factor in the Arab–Israeli conflict. In fact, approximately 40 percent of Israel's ground water originates in the territories occupied by Israel in 1967. Water demands in Israel are rising as the population increases, and this has resulted in an increased dependence on water drawn from the Jordan Basin. Israel has also drawn water from pumping ground water aquifers, which are becoming saline from overuse. Israel runs a *water deficit*, drawing out more water than nature replaces. Water has become a crucial point of discussion and dispute between Israel and the Palestinian people (who have had their access to water restricted by the Israeli government), as well as between Israel and neighbouring Arab states. Conflict over water could easily spark a wider conflagration in a region already beset with conflicts and high levels of tension, and resource sharing must be part of any future peace negotiations.

SOURCE: SEE MIRIAM R. LOWI, *WATER AND POWER: THE POLITICS OF A SCARCE RESOURCE IN THE JORDAN RIVER BASIN* (CAMBRIDGE: CAMBRIDGE UNIVERSITY PRESS, 1993).

given the increasing consumption and decreasing availability of this vital resource, water may become as much a factor in war between states as oil and strategic minerals have been in the past.

RESOURCE WARS BETWEEN PEOPLES

In addition to provoking conflict and war between states, environmental degradation and resource scarcity can provoke political upheaval, social instability, and wars within states. Just as states may clash violently over the control of vital resources, in some cases communal groups within states (or across state boundaries) may clash violently over the control of resources. Environmentally induced intrastate conflict will occur largely in the developing world, where states are weak and individuals or groups in society already face high levels of economic deprivation. In such cases, environmental degradation and resource scarcity contribute to increased economic deprivation, and are part of an interrelated web of social pressures, along with population growth, migration, and poverty. In the face of such pressures, the capacity of the state to provide services or maintain its authority or legitimacy erodes. As Thomas Homer-Dixon argues, "Resource degradation and depletion often affect economic activity in poor countries and thereby contribute to deprivation."[21]

PROFILE 13.4   Canada's Freshwater Supply

Canada has a large supply of fresh water and this is expected to be a growing issue in its relations with the United States. In both Canada and the United States, water demand continues to increase, making successful management all the more important in the future.

- Between 1972 and 1991, Canada's water usage increased from 24 billion cubic metres per year to over 45 billion cubic metres per year—a rise of more than 80 percent; in the same period, population increased only 3 percent.

- Freshwater lakes, rivers, and underground aquifers hold only 3.5 percent of the world's water. By comparison, saltwater oceans and seas contain 95.1 percent of the world's water supply.

- Canada has about 9 percent of the world's fresh renewable water supply, compared with 18 percent for Brazil, 9 percent for China, and 8 percent for the United States.

- The Great Lakes constitute one of the largest systems of freshwater reservoirs on earth, with 18 percent of the world's fresh surface water.

- About 7.6 percent of Canada is covered by fresh water in lakes and rivers—755 165 square kilometres. To this can be added 195 059 square kilometres of perennial snow and ice.

SOURCE: ENVIRONMENT CANADA, <WWW.EC.GC.CA/WATER/>.

Environmental degradation and resource scarcity increase demands on government finances and services. For example, shortages of water require expensive dams or new irrigation systems. The loss of rural incomes from environmental degradation provokes migration to cities, increasing demands for transport, energy, water, sanitation, food, and health care. As economic activity is affected by environmental degradation, government revenues decline, reducing the ability of governments to maintain services and order. As Homer-Dixon argues, "A widening gap between state capacity and demands on the state, along with the misguided economic interventions such a gap often provokes, aggravates popular and elite grievances, increases rivalry between elite factions, and erodes a state's legitimacy."[22] As a result, conflict between communal groups within a state, or conflict between governments and disaffected communal groups, will intensify as competition to control resources and wealth grows. In many cases, political elites will hoard whatever surplus wealth is produced, and use it to maintain their power and their privileged lifestyles. The rest of the population will struggle for what share of the resource pie is left, or they will seek to overthrow the political elites. The overall result is the erosion and collapse of social order, and the disintegration of the state as different factions and groups do battle over a shrinking economic base, often destroying what little in the way of resources, facilities, or livelihoods that remained to them. This condition of near anarchy exacerbates environmental degradation and economic deprivation. Where there is no government or system of order, there are no regulations or laws governing the use of natural resources. Conservation and preservation become impossible. In the worst cases, these factors can converge into a horrific blend of violent conflict, crime, poverty, disease, and starvation and malnutrition. All of this occurs in those areas of the world least equipped to respond to such crises or to manage them effectively.[23]

In the face of such conditions, a natural reaction of people is to flee to escape the violence of war or the hardships of economic deprivation. Environmentally induced conflicts can thus create large refugee movements, migrations of peoples that move to new locations within a country or from one country to another.[24] These migrations have been identified as another source of potential conflict, for refugee movements create tensions and disputes in the regions or countries that receive them. As Nazli Choucri has argued, "The masses of forcefully uprooted persons … might become a key element in the lethal feedback dynamic between environmental degradation and violent conflict."[25]

Refugee movements can create or spread conflict because the influx of a large number of refugees can alter land availability and distribution patterns, disturb economic relations, alter the political and social climate, and upset the local ecological balance. This can provoke communal conflicts between migrant peoples and the peoples in the receiving region. This is true of international refugees (those who cross state borders) and internally displaced refugees (those who flee from one area of a country to another). In the Canadian study on environmental degradation and violent conflict, Homer-Dixon argued that: "There is substantial evidence to support the hypothesis that environmental scarcity causes large population movement, which in turn causes group identity conflicts."[26] Similarly, Nazli Choucri claimed that: "environmental degradation forces people to move, sometimes across borders, and most assuredly to impinge on and ultimately challenge [host] populations."[27]

However, because migrations and the effects they produce are influenced by a wide variety of factors, the link between environmental refugees and the spread of conflict is not an automatic one. In fact, according to Astri Suhrke, conflict will occur "only under conditions of zero-sum interaction—whether actual or perceived. The alternative is a value-added model, where migrants are incorporated into the host society without collective strife, typically by providing needed labour and skills. Nor does ethnic differentiation between host population(s) and newcomers necessarily make the incorporation process conflictual."[28] There are also constraints on the capacity of refugees to create conflict. Refugee populations may be isolated in refugee encampments in relatively remote regions. They may be too weak or disorganized to be regarded as a threat. In many cases, refugee movements that are regarded as a threat have the support of a neighbouring state, and therefore the refugees are seen as an instrument of foreign interference. As a result, many refugee movements do not produce conflict and violence, but misery and death.[29]

Environmentally induced intrastate conflicts are already in evidence, and some observers have postulated that they will spread to include larger and larger regions, eventually to include the northern hemisphere as well.[30] Some of the most dramatic examples of the link between environmental degradation, resource scarcity, and economic deprivation can be found in West Africa, although the stresses caused by environmental degradation can also be found elsewhere, such as the Philippines and Haiti. In his article "The Coming Anarchy," Robert Kaplan vividly describes his experiences in western Africa in general and Sierra Leone in particular:

> West Africa is becoming the symbol of worldwide demographic, environmental, and societal stress, in which criminal anarchy emerges from the real "strategic" danger. Disease, overpopulation, unprovoked crime, scarcity of resources, refugee migrations, the increasing erosion of nation-states and international borders, and the empowerment of private armies, security firms, and international drug cartels are now most tellingly demonstrated through a West African prism.[31]

Tragically, the picture is similar in many areas of central Africa. According to Dr. Bukar Shaib of the World Commission on the Environment, Africa's crises are essentially environmental in origin: "Africa is dying because her environment has been plundered, over-exploited and neglected."[32]

In the Philippines, economic deprivation has been a root cause of internal conflict for decades. The primary problems are shortages of cropland and deforestation. Population growth and unequal distribution of land have forced poor peasants to migrate to the cities or the highlands. In the cities, the migrant poor swell the shantytowns and place even more pressure on already stretched government resources. In the highlands, the migrants clear the forests to create land for crops. This contributes to soil erosion, the silting of rivers, and the destruction of yet more forests when the productivity of cleared land is exhausted. In either case, the migrants become chronically poor and understandably frustrated with the lack of attention given to their plight by governmental authorities.

The link between environmental degradation, resource scarcity, and political upheaval and violence can also be found in the plight of Haiti. A combination of population growth, land shortages, and corrupt leadership bent on expropriating available wealth has left Haiti the poorest country in the Western hemisphere. Haiti's forests have virtually disappeared, cut down to create more land for cultivation. Poor Haitians move up the mountainsides, clearing more forests and exhausting the land. The loss of the forest contributes to soil erosion, which has rendered almost half of the countryside unsuitable for farming. This, coupled with population growth, has led to a fall in per capita incomes. People have migrated to the cities, especially Port-au-Prince, a teeming city dominated by enormous slums. Many others have fled Haiti as refugees. Political instability and civil strife have characterized recent Haitian politics as the rich political classes use increasing levels of force and repression to maintain their control over the country. In 1986 the "Baby Doc" Duvalier regime collapsed, and international intervention restored civilian rule. However, the severity of environmental degradation in Haiti raises doubts about the country's long-term economic and political future.

In Brazil, fears persist that the unequal distribution of land and wealth could create domestic instability and increasingly violent conflict in the future. Although Brazil ranked ninth in the world in gross domestic product in 1996, the distribution of wealth in Brazil is highly unequal. In fact, the poorest 40 percent of the Brazilian population receives only 7 percent of total income. Land distribution is even

The human impact of resource wars. Women carry their belongings past a destroyed house during fighting in 1996 between Angolan troops and rebel soldiers in the Cabinda enclave, a corner of central Africa wedged between Congo and Zaire, administered by Angola but separated from the country by a finger of Zairian territory. The rebels complain that people in Cabinda live in miserable poverty while the Angolan government strips the region of its riches: diamonds, manganese, timber, and oil. (AP Photo/Nestor Ebongo)

more unequal, with less than 1 percent of all landowners controlling almost half of Brazil's privately held land. As a result, Brazil has some 12 million landless peasants while more than 180 million hectares of farmable land lie unused.[33] Many of these peasants have migrated to the cities, feeding Brazil's expanding urban slums. Lack of housing, jobs, and access to government services, as well as extreme poverty have led to a soaring crime rate. Recently, there has been a move to return to the land, in the form of squatting and occupying unused tracts of land. This has brought the landless peasants and the Landless Workers Movement, the organization that represents them, into conflict with local landowners and the police. This confrontation has not always been peaceful: more than 1700 people have been killed in the past decade. More radical organizations committed to armed struggle have grown rapidly. Unless meaningful land reform is enacted over the opposition of the politically powerful landowning class, a violent conflict over land distribution may be in Brazil's near future.

Despite the caution over the link between refugee movements and conflict, there are examples of environmentally induced refugee movements provoking political and social upheaval and violence. Refugee flows from Bangladesh into northeast India (arising largely from population growth and land scarcity) have provoked communal conflict between migrant and indigenous peoples. In Assam, the Lalung peoples have reacted angrily and sometimes violently against the Muslim Bengali migrants, whom they accuse of appropriating scarce farmland. In Tripura, an eight-year insurgency was conducted by Tripuris over access to land, which was in short supply due to a massive influx of refugees from Bangladesh. Efforts by the Indian government to return dispossessed land and stop the flow of migration have met with mixed success in the face of continued environmental stresses on land resources in the region.[34]

If projections of future stresses on the environment and consequent resource scarcities are correct, then we can expect conflicts that are provoked (in whole or in part) by environmentally induced grievances to become an increasing fixture of conflict and war in global politics.

However, we must be cautious when making predictions about the environmentally induced implosion of entire regions of the world. Conflict-torn areas and countries such as West Africa and Haiti are in desperate condition, but little sign exists of the grim predictions of the coming anarchy on a larger scale. Most peoples in most parts of the world go about their daily lives trying to make a living; they are not under an imminent threat of environmentally induced social collapse. Making such predictions may lead to a fearful siege mentality in the rich industrialized world, prompting a retreat into a global gated community designed to shut out the chaos of the rest of the world in what ever form it might take, from televised images to refugees. Instead we must recognize the need for an effective international response to such crises, and the need for long-term changes to economic development policy to prevent such human disasters from defining the twenty-first century.

A REVOLUTION IN MILITARY AFFAIRS?

What will future wars look like? As we discussed in Chapter 12, the rapid pace of technological change has affected (and perhaps even transformed) the global political economy, information flows and financial markets, and global cultural politics. Technology has altered patterns of work, communication, and recreation in the industrialized world. Technology has also dramatically increased the capacities of modern weapons and military communications and information systems. Indeed, many security studies experts argue that we are witnessing a profound shift in the traditional method of fighting wars. A widely held assumption among security studies scholars is that the historical development of military capabilities has not progressed in a steady fashion. Rather, increases in military capabilities have been characterized by sudden surges in the effectiveness of weapons and military technique. These surges originate from technological, organizational, and larger social and economic innovations. It can hardly be surprising that against the backdrop of the computer and information revolution, declarations have been made that we are experiencing a parallel revolution in military affairs (RMA).

An RMA is the relatively swift onset of a qualitative transformation in the effectiveness of military technologies that fundamentally alters the conduct of military operations and the nature of the strategic environment. One key concept that distinguishes changes in military technologies, doctrines, and organizations (which are not rare) from revolutionary developments (which are rare) is *discontinuity*. That is, revolutions are characterized by transformations in the nature of the conduct of military operations such that previous technologies and techniques are rendered obsolete. Early revolutions are associated with gunpowder, the rise of the national armies of the Napoleonic period, and the Blitzkrieg warfare of World War II (see Chapter 2). It's worth emphasizing that technological developments are not sufficient indicators of military revolutions, although weapons developments are almost always central to any revolution that has ever been identified. Military revolutions are also based on organizational innovation and are grounded in larger economic, social, and political changes which impact on military capabilities.

What are the components of the current RMA? Advocates of this concept point to the following:

- A decrease in the relationship between distance and accuracy, made possible by modern electronics. Precision-guided munitions are now capable of hitting targets over long distances with a high probability of success (though not as high as is often advertised by weapons manufacturers and governments).

- The increased capacity of some weapons systems to act autonomously from human operators. These military versions of robots promise a transition from current semi-autonomous warfare (a human fires the weapon which guides itself to the target) to fully autonomous warfare (the weapons system decides when and where to fire based on its programming).

- The development of stealth technology, which renders some weapons systems extremely hard to detect by conventional radars.

- An increase in the capability to conduct surveillance and reconnaissance over the battlefield through the employment of remotely piloted vehicles, satellites, and signal-intelligence equipment.

- An increase in the capacity to store, analyze, and disseminate information in real time (no time delay) through communications and battle management systems, thus reducing the "fog of war."

- An increased capacity to fight at night and in all weather conditions with minimal degradation of effectiveness.

- An increased ability to engage in offensive information warfare to disrupt the opponent's military and civilian communications and thus influence the political and psychological dimensions of the conflict.

- The increased use of space.

- The development of doctrine and training and leadership skills assisted by realistic simulations.

- The potential to reduce civilian casualties and *collateral damage* associated with the use of military force.

As noted above, developing technologies also promise new methods of conducting information warfare, and managing the public relations and imagery of wars and interventions. In this sense, future wars will not only take place between combatants and their weapons systems, but also in the arena of public perception and opinion, the media, and in information and misinformation efforts mounted by governments, groups, and individuals.[35]

Not surprisingly, the leading proponent of the RMA concept is the United States, which is developing its armed forces for an RMA future. The objective is to ensure that the U.S. armed forces remain preeminent on the battlefield in the twenty-first century—a key element, realists would say, of maintaining U.S. hegemony. Some U.S. allies (including Canada) are expected to remain interoperable with the U.S. military to ensure that their forces can cooperate effectively on the battlefield (a major issue in allied or coalition operations). However, few if any countries have the resources to implement RMA techniques and weapons with the enthusiasm displayed by the Americans. However, as we discussed in Chapter 6, as weapons technologies continue to diffuse through the international system, more countries are acquiring modern weapons. These may not always be the most modern weapons, but they are far more capable and destructive than previous generations of hardware and software. As a result, we can expect future interstate wars to be fought with progressively more sophisticated technologies.

Considerable controversy is associated with the RMA. Some security studies experts doubt that RMAs even exist, disputing the notion of historical discontinuities in the development of warfare. Others point out that it is essentially an American enterprise, and is, therefore, motivated more by the U.S. military and its corporate suppliers than by any sense of security requirements. Still other argue that the RMA is relevant to U.S. military requirements, but the danger is that the United States will move so far ahead of the rest of the world (including its key allies) in military capabilities that it will be less disposed toward multilateralism and more disposed toward unilateralism. (This is a particular concern in Canada, where the Canadian government has always tried to encourage the United States to pursue multilateral solutions to problems.) This concern has accelerated as the United States considers the development and deployment of a national missile defence system, designed to intercept and destroy a limited number of ballistic missiles attacking North America. There is also the question of the effectiveness of the new technologies. For every measure there is a counter measure, and even the most sophisticated weapons can be defeated using relatively simple techniques. Doubts exist as to whether RMA capabilities will be effective in forest or jungle terrain. During the bombing of Serbia, the Serbian military made wide use of decoys, which proved effective against many high-technology weapons. As for ballistic missile defences, they can be circumvented by using delivery systems as low tech as a boat or a truck. In other cases, controversies may erupt concerning the use of certain weapons; witness the debate over the alleged health effects of depleted uranium munitions in the Gulf War and in the former Yugoslavia. Finally, some question the relevance of the RMA in an era where major war may be obsolete.[36] RMA capabilities will not enhance the ability of military forces to conduct peacekeeping missions or low-intensity conflicts, which are precisely the kinds of missions they will be required to conduct in the future.

This last point raises the question of whether the RMA is an effort to prepare for the wrong kind of war, and therefore we should not pay an undue amount of attention to it. The vast majority of recent and current wars are fought not with the weapons and techniques of the twenty-first century but with the weapons and techniques of the twentieth. As we discussed in Chapter 6, almost all these wars have been fought between communal groups at the substate level. The character of war in the future is therefore likely to be bifurcated between two styles. First, wars or interventions involving advanced industrialized states will feature modern weapons systems, highly trained professional personnel, and the organizational techniques characteristic of information age societies. Second, other wars (likely more numerous) will feature communal groups or weak states using light weapons and the techniques of nineteenth-century warfare or insurgency conflicts. States with active peacekeeping commitments, such as Canada, will have to adapt to both types of military technology in the future.

CONCLUSIONS

This chapter has examined three different perspectives concerning the causes of war in the future, and two different perspectives concerning the future character of war. Having done so, we must remind ourselves that our capacity to predict the outbreak of specific wars (whether they be interstate wars or intrastate wars) is very limited. The Gulf War, for example, came as a complete surprise to many, as did the collapse of Yugoslavia and the NATO air campaign against Serbia. However, economic, cultural, and environmental trends may be increasingly important as the causes of future wars. The changing nature of global politics suggests that the nature of the global economy, the decline of the state, environmental degradation, and the widening gulf between rich and poor countries and peoples may produce tensions between states and peoples that could lead to increased interstate and intrastate violence and war in the twenty-first century.

At the same time, we proceed armed with substantial knowledge about the impact of environmental change, population displacement, ethnic conflict, new weapons systems, and many of the other topics raised in this chapter. Increasing our understanding of these dynamic and interrelated factors, and thus our ability to prevent episodic violent conflict, remains the principal task of students of international relations today.

Endnotes

1. Edward Luttwak, "The Coming Global War for Economic Power," *The International Economy* 7 (September/October 1993), 20.
2. Samuel P. Huntington, "The Clash of Civilizations?" *Foreign Affairs* 72, 3 (Summer 1993), 22.
3. Morton Kaplan, "The Coming Anarchy," *Atlantic Monthly* (February 1994), 58.
4. Robert A. Isaac, *Managing World Economic Change: International Political Economy*, 2nd ed. (Englewood Cliffs, NJ: Prentice Hall, 1995), 30.
5. Edward Luttwak, "The Coming Global War for Economic Power," *International Economy* 7 (September/October 1993), 20.

6. Michael Mastanduno, "Do Relative Gains Matter? America's Response to Japanese Industrial Policy," *International Security* 16 (Summer 1991), 78.

7. Joseph M. Grieco, "Anarchy and the Limits of Cooperation: A Realist Critique of the Newest Liberal Institutionalism," in Charles W. Kegley Jr., ed., *Controversies in International Relations Theory: Realism and the Neoliberal Challenge* (New York: St. Martin's Press, 1995), 151–71.

8. Edward Luttwak, "The Coming Global War for Economic Power," 20.

9. Huntington, "The Clash of Civilizations?" 22.

10. Ibid., 23–4.

11. Kishore Mahbubani, "The West and the Rest," *The National Interest* (Summer 1992), 3–13.

12. See, for example, Olivia Bennet, ed., *Greenwar: Environment and Conflict* (London: Panos Institute, 1991); Norman Myers, "Environment and Security," *Foreign Policy* 74 (1989), 23–41; Neville Brown, "Climate, Ecology, and International Security," *Survival* 31 (November/December 1989), 519–32; and Peter H. Gleick, "Environment and Security: Clear Connections," *The Bulletin of the Atomic Scientists* 47 (April 1994), 17–21.

13. See, for example, Marc S. Levy, "Is the Environment a National Security Issue?" *International Security* 20 (Fall 1995), 35–62, and Astri Suhrke, "Environmental Change, Migration, and Conflict: A Lethal Feedback Dynamic?" in Chester A. Crocker, Fen Osler Hampson, and Pamela Aall, eds., *Managing Global Chaos: Sources of and Responses to International Conflict* (Washington, DC: United States Institute of Peace Press, 1996), 113–27.

14. Thomas F. Homer-Dixon, "Environmental Scarcities and Violent Conflict: Evidence from Cases," *International Security* 19 (Summer 1994), 5–6.

15. Arthur Westing, ed., *Global Resources and International Conflict: Environmental Factors in Strategic Policy and Action* (Oxford: Oxford University Press, 1986), 204–10.

16. See Ronnie D. Lipschultz, *When Nations Clash: Raw Materials, Ideology, and Foreign Policy* (New York: Ballinger Publishing, 1989).

17. Jock A. Finlayson and David G. Haglund, "Whatever Happened to the Resource War?" *Survival* 29 (September/October 1987), 403–15.

18. Peter H. Gleick, "Water and Conflict: Fresh Water Resources and International Security," *International Security* 18 (Summer 1993), 79.

19. See Thomas Naff and Ruth Matson, *Water in the Middle East: Conflict or Cooperation?* (Boulder, CO: Westview Press, 1984).

20. See Gleick, "Water and Conflict," esp. 85–86, and Miriam R. Lowi, "Bridging the Divide: Transboundary Resource Disputes and the Case of West Bank Water," *International Security* 18 (Summer 1993), 113–38.

21. Homer-Dixon, "Environmental Scarcities and Violent Conflict," 24.

22. Ibid., 25.

23. See Paul Kennedy, *Preparing for the Twenty-First Century* (New York: Random House, 1993).

24. We addressed the issue of migration and refugees in more detail in Chapter 11. Here, we explore the link between environmental refugees and the spread of violent conflict and war.

25. Nazli Choucri, "Environment, Development, and International Assistance: Crucial Linkages," in Sheryl J. Brown and Kimber M. Schraub, eds., *Resolving Third World Conflict: Challenges for a New Era* (Washington, DC: United States Institute of Peace Press, 1992), 101.

26. Homer-Dixon, "Environmental Scarcities and Violent Conflict," 20.

27. Choucri, "Environment, Development, and International Assistance," 101.

28. Astri Suhrke, "Environmental Change, Migration, and Conflict: A Lethal Feedback Dynamic?" in Chester A. Crocker, Fen Osler Hampson, and Pamela Aall, eds., *Managing Global Chaos: Sources of and Responses to International Conflict* (Washington, DC: United States Institute of Peace Press, 1996), 116.

29. Homer-Dixon, "Environmental Scarcities and Violent Conflict," 21.

30. See Robert Kaplan, "The Coming Anarchy," *Atlantic Monthly* (February 1994), 44–76.

31. Ibid., 48–66.

32. Quoted in F. Akpan, "Environment and Development," *APRI Newsletter* 5 (September–October 1990), 18.

33. Fabio L.S. Petrarolha, "Brazil: The Meek Want the Earth Now," *Bulletin of Atomic Scientists* (November/December 1996), 21–2.

34. See Shaukat Hassan, "Environmental Issues and Security in South Asia," *Adelphi Paper* No. 262 (London, International Institute for Strategic Studies, 1991).

35. Michael Ignatieff, *Virtual War* (Toronto: Penguin Books of Canada, 2000).

36. Michael Mandelbaum, "Is Major War Obsolete?" *Survival* (Winter 1998/99), 20–38.

Suggested Readings

Arnett, Eric, ed. *Science and International Security: Responding to a Changing World.* Washington, DC: American Association for the Advancement of Science, 1990.

Bennet, Olivia, ed., *Greenwar: Environment and Conflict.* London: Panos Institute, 1991.

Buzan, Barry. *People, States, and Fear.* 2nd ed. Boulder, CO: Lynne Rienner, 1991.

Encarnation, Dennis J. *Rivals beyond Trade: America versus Japan in Global Competition.* Ithaca, NY: Cornell University Press, 1992.

Kennedy, Paul. *Preparing for the 21st Century.* New York: Random House, 1993.

Lairson, Thomas D., and David Skidmore. *International Political Economy: The Struggle for Power and Wealth.* Orlando, FL: Harcourt Brace Jovanovich, 1993.

Lipshutz, Ronnie D. *When Nations Clash: Raw Materials, Ideology, and Foreign Policy.* New York: Ballinger Publishing, 1989.

Renner, Michael. *Fighting for Survival: Environmental Decline, Social Conflict, and the New Age of Insecurity.* New York: Norton, 1996.

Thurow, Lester C. *Head to Head: Coming Economic Battles among Japan, Europe, and America.* New York: Morrow, 1992.

Volden, Ketil, and Dan Smith, eds. *Causes of Conflict in the Third World.* Oslo: North/South Coalition and International Peace Research Institute, 1997.

Weiner, Myron, ed. *International Migration and Security.* Boulder, CO: Westview Press, 1993.

Westing, Arthur H., ed. *Global Resources and International Conflict: Environmental Factors in Strategic Policy and Action.* Oxford: Oxford University Press, 1986.

Suggested Websites

Institute for the Study of Advanced Information Warfare
<www.psycom.net/iwar.1.html>

DefenseLink

Project Ploughshares

CHAPTER 14

Global Politics in the Twenty-First Century

Pessimism over the future of the world comes from a confusion between civilization and security. In the immediate future there will be less security than in the immediate past, less stability.... But, on the whole, the great ages have been unstable ages.

—A. North Whitehead[1]

REVISITING SOME CENTRAL AND STILL PERPLEXING QUESTIONS

In this final chapter, we revisit the themes of this book in terms of the origins, currents, and future directions of global politics. We are living in a world of transition, but as you no doubt gathered from the historical material in this text, the world has always been in transition. The difference today is the pace of that transition. Political developments, technological innovation, and international transactions all happen so rapidly that the study of global politics can be both bewildering and overwhelming. It is our hope that this textbook has provided you with a foundation for understanding the world in which we live, and that your interest in global politics will not end here. This is only the beginning of a lifelong attentiveness to the challenges we will all face in the future.

The range of topics covered in this text has been very broad, but we assure you it is in no way exhaustive. Whether the concern is with commerce or weapons systems, the rights of children or the impact of democratization, space exploration or cultural relativism, global politics is a subject area that challenges us to think as broadly as possible. In the future, new issues will arise, ones that have not been anticipated by scholars, politicians, or futurologists. Therefore, it is important to keep an open mind, develop the analytical tools we use for thinking and reflecting on global politics, and maintain an appreciation of the shape and form of global politics today.

In Chapter 1 of this book, we introduced some of the most fundamental questions facing observers of global politics today. In light of the material we have covered in this book, is it possible to answer some of those questions?

Which theoretical perspective best describes and characterizes the global political system?

As this text has illustrated, debates about theory are important. Theory provides us with a framework for looking at the world, with a structure for organizing and prioritizing the bewildering array of issues and events that make up global politics. Despite the fact that liberalism is in ascendancy among international relations scholars, there is no universally accepted theoretical wisdom on the nature and dynamics of global politics. This is why so much disagreement exists on the issues covered in this book. We have introduced several contending perspectives, such as idealism, realism, liberalism,

Can we learn from experience? A huge mushroom cloud rises above Bikini atoll in the Marshall Islands, 25 July 1946, following an atomic test blast, part of the U.S. military's Operation Crossroads. The dark spots in the foreground are ships that were placed near the blast site to test what an atom bomb would do to a fleet of warships. (AP Photo)

neomarxism, and feminism, among others. We can derive perspectives on global issues from each of these perspectives. Realists see a cyclical struggle for power in an anarchic world. Liberals see increasing interdependence. Neo-Marxists and dependency theorists see harmful hierarchies and patterns of dominance. Feminists stress a gendered perspective of global political processes and structures. For environmentalists, the world is viewed in terms of ecological sustainability. If it is impossible to point to one of these theories and say that it is the right one, the theories remain valuable as tools for examining world events. When something happens in global politics, it can be useful to ask the question, how would a realist explain this event? How would a liberal, or a Marxist? In this way, you can discover possible alternative explanations that may shed light on your understanding of the issues.

What are the lessons of the past?

This text has pointed out how important an awareness of past events can be in any effort to understand the present. To an extent, we are all products of past events, and the world in which we live is the product of the evolution of historical forces and human decisions. Does history repeat itself? Are we living in a world (as realists suggest) that would be recognized by Thucydides and Sun Tzu? Certainly, we can find past examples of issues that occupy us today (such as the problem of controlling armaments, and neomercantilist trading policies), and we can point to the existence of dynamics that took place during the Peloponnesian Wars in today's politics (such as the position of weaker actors and balance of power activity). However, while it is important to be aware of past events, it is a mistake to rely on them to the exclusion of other factors. Many times, scholars and politicians draw on the past to justify their arguments about the present. In most cases, however, the comparisons may be inappropriate, because there are significant differences between the two situations. In addition, as this text has illustrated, many things have changed; new issues have arisen, new technologies developed, new global processes created. We do live in a different world, although it is not so different that we can afford to ignore our past.

Is the international system fragmenting or integrating?

This text has suggested that we live in a world characterized by two forces: convergence and divergence. The question is, which is the stronger? The two phenomena seem to exist side by side in the international system. We see convergence in the increasing interdependence between states, the growth of IGOs and NGOs, awareness and action devoted to transnational issues such as the environment, and growing contact, travel, and transactions between the peoples of the world. However, we see divergence in the continued conflict between states, the disintegration of some states, ethnic conflict, the increasing gap between the rich and poor, and the split between the technological haves and have-nots. At this point, identifying a dominant trend is impossible, although it is clear that for some convergence is the reality in their lives, while for others divergence is the more powerful influence. In Canada, we are very privileged in many ways but we are not immune from these forces. Even as globalization links us to the world of trade, travel, and telecommunications, it stimulates national debates about our economic future and our culture. The enduring national unity debate is a reminder that we are not immune from the forces of divergence.

Are states becoming obsolete?

The rise of transnational issues and challenges to the cohesiveness of the state have called into question the status of states as the dominant actors in global politics. State borders have become increasingly porous in the face of weapons technology, trade, financial flows, international travel, and the Internet. States such as the Soviet Union and Yugoslavia have collapsed. Substate actors are becoming more prominent, as are transnational issues that cut across state borders, such as pollution, refugee flows, and environmental degradation. And we have seen the rise of other international actors, such as IGOs, NGOs, and multinational corporations. Yet, the state survives. Diplomatic activity is still conducted by states and more specifically by the politicians and officials who govern them. States still exert a tremendous influence on all our lives, whether as objects of our loyalty or as providers of services we value. The sovereignty of the state has not yet eroded to the point where we can speak of the imminent demise of the state in world politics.

Is military power less relevant?

Is economics the new currency of power in the world? Has the usefulness of military power declined to the point that we may speak of a geoeconomic, rather than a geopolitical, world? Or perhaps the future will be a liberal world of peaceful trading states? In either scenario, economics prevails. Certainly, the profile of economic issues has been raised. As this text has pointed out, governments are increasingly preoccupied with concerns about trade and wealth. We have seen efforts by states—on both a global and a regional basis—to establish free trade principles and practices, and to expand these practices to more and more areas of economic activity and to more and more countries around the world. At present, economic cooperation seems to be prevailing against economic competition; but lest we forget, there have been other times in history when this pattern reversed itself. Or is the military instrument still the most important and most relevant instrument of power in global politics? Certainly, we have seen numerous examples of the use of force, from Bosnia to Kosovo. Military preparedness is still seen as vital in many (if not most) countries of the world. Perhaps we should not dismiss the importance of military power too quickly.

What are the causes of war, and how can conflicts be managed or prevented?

This is a question of enduring importance in international relations, and as this text has demonstrated, we are still struggling to find answers and solutions. The problem of war is still one of the priorities (and some would say the priority) of international relations.

What we have seen, however, is a shift in the agenda from traditional interstate wars (although these still occur and will again in the future) to intrastate conflicts between communal groups. We have also seen that the record of arms control and conflict management is on the whole rather bad. War is one of the enduring characteristics of global politics, and yet the mechanisms we have at our disposal to prevent, control, or stop it are still limited. The Canadian and Norwegian emphasis on human security, which stresses the need to provide care for individuals affected by war, is welcome; but questions concerning the legitimacy of humanitarian intervention complicate the issue further.

How can the proliferation of conventional weapons and weapons of mass destruction be stopped?

The flow of weapons of mass destruction, sophisticated conventional weapons, and small arms to areas of tension and conflict is a pressing international concern. The spread of these weapons creates regional tensions, destabilizes local military balances, and, according to some scholars, increases the likelihood of war. The possibility that weapons of mass destruction will increasingly fall into the hands of terrorist groups adds an additional urgency to this issue. How this flow of arms might be stopped is a prominent feature of the contemporary arms control debate. Canada's recent initiatives (in tandem with a coalition of NGOs) to create an international ban on the use of landmines are some of the more prominent examples of progress in conventional arms control.

What is the future of the international economy?

This text has offered three main visions of the future of the global economy. One suggests that states will turn to mercantilist practices based on economic nationalism. Another suggests that we are heading into a world of increasingly liberal free trade, with barriers to goods and services falling steadily. Another suggests that the world economy is becoming increasingly divided into trading blocs, which may come to compete against each other. At this time, it seems as if the liberal model of free trade is in ascendance, manifested in the creation of the World Trade Organization and the expansion of free trade areas. However, there are also reactions against such policies, in the form of domestic protests and government concerns about sovereignty and independence. In most countries, there is powerful political opposition to increasing free trade, and concerns about the effects of free trade treaties on jobs, the environment, health and safety standards, and culture. We have also discussed the expanding role women are playing in the global economy today, the uncertainty surrounding energy sources and prices, the persistence of high government debt loads, and a continued increase in the capability and employment of advanced technology. All of this takes place in the context of what some term *globalization* and others term *neoimperialism*.[2]

Are international organizations getting stronger or weaker?

This text has examined the extent to which international organizations of various kinds are involved in international politics, whether they are sustaining military alliances or the regulation of international standards on travel, monitoring human rights, or providing aid to victims of war or natural disaster. International organizations are a key manifestation of cooperation in international affairs. Some would argue that they serve to enhance and reinforce cooperation. Yet, all too often these organizations are ignored, poorly supported, or regarded with suspicion or outright hostility. Many international organizations are showing signs of decay, while others are struggling to adapt to a new international environment or reduced levels of finance. The one certainty is that international organizations, whether they are composed of states or individuals, depend on the commitment of their members for their survival. Canada has a strong, if at times inconsistent, tradition of supporting multilateral institutions, but will this continue in an era of reduced spending? Meanwhile, the study of multilateral institutions has a bright future in the discipline.[3]

How will environmental issues affect global politics?

As we have noted, the environment has exploded into public consciousness in the last few decades, and especially in the last decade. Environmental degradation has emerged as a serious global issue, a serious regional issue, and a serious public policy issue within states. The question is whether environmental pressures such as climatic change and resource scarcity contribute to increased cooperation or increased conflict among states and peoples. As we have seen, there is potential for both. There are increasing international efforts to manage environmental problems through the establishment of treaties and multilateral institutions, such as the Convention on Biological Diversity. Environmental NGOs, such as Greenpeace and Friends of the Earth, have widened the scope of their activities. New political perspectives have emerged with the environment as the core concern. On the other hand, we have witnessed the failure of some prominent management efforts, such as The Hague conference of 2000. We have seen political friction on issues such as access to fresh water and dwindling fish stocks. The environment has emerged as a major issue between the south and the north as the debate on overpopulation and overconsumption continues. We have seen clashes between environmental protection and economic concerns such as competitiveness, growth, and jobs, though these may be compatible goals in the end. As northern states, such as Canada, struggle to develop a coherent global warming strategy, fundamental questions about our lifestyle surface. One thing is certain: the environment is here to stay as an issue in global politics.

What will be the impact of the information revolution on global politics?

Some of us are living in the middle of the information revolution; most people are not. Nevertheless, there is no doubt that technological developments have led to a massive increase in the flow of information and ideas across borders, and the increased role of information as an engine of economic activity. Will the information revolution promise a world of improved communication, understanding, and sharing of knowledge leading to a global community, or a world of the information rich and the information poor? Unfortunately, both eventualities are likely to occur. We can see the evidence for this today, as information technologies transform how people do work—in a very few privileged countries. In other countries, people have no access at all to these innovations, and those who do are the political and economic elites. We must also be aware of the extent to which these new technologies may come to serve as instruments of disinformation, propaganda, crime, and war, for they are already in use for these purposes today. On the other hand, if it is true that knowledge is power, information technology could serve as a liberating tool for the oppressed.

How will increasing migration of people affect global politics?

As we have seen in this book, people are on the move around the world, in the form of emigrants, refugees, and migrant workers. People are fleeing areas devastated by conflict, environmental degradation, economic hardship, and political and religious repression. They are attracted by hopes of a better life, jobs, security, freedom, or by the basic human needs: food, shelter, and clothing. Increasing hardship and population pressures in the southern hemisphere suggest that even larger population movements will occur in the future, posing hard questions for immigration and refugee policy in traditional receiver states, such as Canada. We see many examples of generosity and compassion in the form of immigration and aid NGOs. We also see many examples of a siege mentality, such as purposefully restrictive immigration policies and the exploitation of migrant peoples. Perhaps this will lead to efforts to change the root conditions that lead to migrations in the first place. Perhaps it will lead to more and more people travelling the world's regions, unwanted, with no place to go.

What will be the future impact of the power differential between the developing and developed world?

This text has pointed out the massive and appalling discrepancy between the rich and the poor people of the world. An ever-widening gap in economic and political power exists between the rich countries of the industrialized world, including Japan and some other rising Asian states, and the poorer regions of Latin America, Asia, and Africa. Unfortunately, it is difficult to avoid the conclusion that these disparities will continue to widen, as environmental degradation and pollution disproportionately affect poorer regions, as population and migration place pressure on limited resources, as economic development in the south continues to lag behind that in the north, and as new technologies and techniques are introduced into the rich information-age economies. As a result, the north–south debate is likely to intensify. Canada has scaled back its development assistance programs in recent years, and can no longer claim to be a leader on this issue.

What are the best strategies for development and aid?

This text has addressed the problem of global disparities in wealth. The question of what to do about this disparity has been the subject of intense debate. As we have seen, liberal approaches to development suggest one path, while dependency theory suggests another. Neither approach has been uncontroversial or a panacea for the plight of the poor. Perhaps sustainable development strategies will have successes in the future, and efforts to promote the role of women in development will increase the socioeconomic stability of poor areas in the world. We hope that we have moved beyond the simplistic **paradigm** that equates human and societal development with the replication of the Western mode of industrialization. New approaches favour small-scale improvements, gender analysis, and culturally and environmentally appropriate technology. It is too early to tell if these approaches will bear fruit. As this text has pointed out, the stakes—both economic and human—are enormous.

CONCLUSION: HUMANITY AND WORLD POLITICS

This text has covered a wide variety of topics, but we justify this with reference to the subject matter at hand: global politics must be approached from many perspectives and relates to so many interconnected issues that some frustration and confusion is inevitable, even among the most seasoned of observers. At least two themes run throughout the text. First, the links between the three sections—origins, currents, and directions—should be clear at this stage. Without an understanding of the past, and the present, we cannot hope to make even fragmentary estimations concerning the future. Similarly, the academic discipline of IR is hardly a static one, and though there are several perennial themes and some entrenched polemical positions, theoreticians are always struggling with the task of making sense of past, present, and future events and conditions. Second, as discussed in our introductory chapter, the paradoxically twinned themes of convergence and divergence continue to dominate the discussion on global politics. It would be an error, we believe, to emphasize one at the expense of the other, for they are part of the same historical path.

It is tempting to look back at the collective experience of international relations and sigh, resigned to the depressing state of human relations and the immense problems involved in achieving international cooperation on the vital issues we face today and in the future. Yet our perspective must change in spite of (and indeed because of) what appears to be the increasing parochialism of humanity. In our interdependent world we remain, in the words of none other than Henry Kissinger (hardly a naive idealist), "stranded between old conceptions of political conduct and a wholly new conception, between the inadequacy of the nation-state and the emerging imperative of global community."[4] Given the continuing threats nations collectively face—from poverty to planetary environmental degradation—it is clear that decision makers must think as globally as possible. Barring the construction of large isolation tanks, states and peoples cannot deal with the increasingly transnational global agenda in a unilateral fashion. In terms of future survival, cooperation is essential. Without it, all else is impossible. States with extensive multilateral ties, such as Canada, have a vital role to play; more to the point, we all do. The first step toward solving such problems is learning about them, and we hope this text has provided a start.

Endnotes

1. A. North Whitehead, *Science and the Modern World* (New York: New American Library, 1953), 208.
2. On globalization, see Claire Turenne Sjolander, "The Rhetoric of Globalization: What's in a Wor(l)d?" *International Journal* 50 (1996), 603–16.
3. See especially J. Ruggie and H. Milner, eds., *Multilateralism Matters: New Directions in World Politics* (New York: Columbia University Press, 1993). See also T. Keating, *Canada and World Order: The Multilateralist Tradition in Canadian Foreign Policy* (Toronto: McClelland and Stewart, 1993).
4. Henry Kissinger, 1975, quoted in C. Kegley and E. Wittkopf, *World Politics: Trend and Transformation,* 4th ed. (New York: St. Martin's, 1993), 10.

Suggested Readings

Behnke, A. "Ten Years After: The State of the Art of Regime Theory." *Cooperation and Conflict* 30 (2) (1995), 179–97.

Cox, Robert, and T. Sinclair. *Approaches to World Order.* Cambridge: Cambridge University Press, 1996.

Dewitt, David, David Haglund, and John Kirton, eds. *Building a New Global Order: Emerging Trends in International Security.* Toronto: Oxford University Press, 1993.

Doyle, M. *Ways of War and Peace: Realism, Liberalism, Socialism.* New York: Norton, 1997.

Falk, R., S. Kim, and S. Mendlovitz, eds. *The United Nations and a Just World Order.* Boulder, CO: Westview, 1991.

Gordon, N., and B. Wood. "Canada and the Reshaping of the United Nations." *International Journal* 47 (1992), 479–503.

Hastedt, G., ed. *One World, Many Voices: Global Perspectives on Political Issues.* Englewood Cliffs, NJ: Prentice Hall, 1991.

Head, Ivan. *On the Hinge of History: The Mutual Vulnerability of South and North*. Toronto: University of Toronto Press, 1991.

Keating, T. "The Promise and Pitfalls of Human Security." Paper presented to the Canadian Political Science Association Annual Meeting, Quebec, July 2000.

Nossal, Kim Richard. *The Politics of Canadian Foreign Policy*. 3rd ed. Scarborough, ON: Prentice Hall, 1997.

Roberts, A. "A New Age in International Relations?" *International Affairs* 67 (July 1991), 506–25.

Rochester, J.M. *Waiting for the Millennium: The United Nations and the Future of the World Order*. Columbia, SC: University of South Carolina Press, 1993.

Toffler, A. *Power Shift: Knowledge, Wealth, and Violence at the Edge of the 21st Century*. Toronto: Bantam, 1990.

White, R. *North, South, and the Environmental Crisis*. Toronto: University of Toronto Press, 1993.

Glossary

This glossary contains very brief descriptions of important terms used in the textbook. The glossary has been compiled using a number of sources, including the "Historical Glossary" found in H. Morgenthau, *Politics Among Nations: The Struggle for Power and Peace, Brief Edition,* revised by K. Thompson (New York: McGraw-Hill, 1993), Cathal Nolan's *The Longman Guide to World Affairs* (White Plains, NY: Longman, 1995), and our own general knowledge. We gratefully acknowledge the suggestions of an anonymous reviewer of an earlier draft of this manuscript as well. We have put these terms in **bold** where they appear for the first time in the text.

ABM Antiballistic missile, designed to intercept and destroy incoming ballistic missiles. The development and deployment of ABMs has been restricted by the 1972 ABM Treaty.

Absolute poverty The condition of being unable to meet basic subsistence needs of food, clothing, and shelter.

Acid rain Sulphur dioxide and nitrogen oxide combined with precipitation; caused by industry, automobiles, and power plants. Harms forests and acidifies lakes.

Acquired immune deficiency syndrome (AIDS) A fatal disease that destroys the body's immune system; spread mainly through sexual contact or injection with infected blood.

Adjudication Deciding a legal issue through the courts or some other third party that can make a binding decision.

Advisory opinion An ICJ (International Court of Justice) nonbinding legal opinion for the UN or a specialized agency.

African, Caribbean, and Pacific States (ACP) Fifty-eight states associated with the European Union.

African National Congress (ANC) South African political party, founded in 1912, that for years opposed apartheid but is now governing that state. Its leader, Nelson Mandela, was released from prison in 1990 and served as South Africa's first president.

Agricultural revolution Large-scale shifts in prevailing food production methods that have an impact on the whole of society.

Alexander the Great King of Macedon, 336–323 B.C.E. Conquered Thrace, Illyria, and Egypt; invaded Persia and northern India; virtual leader of Mediterranean centre of civilization.

Alliance cohesion The degree to which alliance members hold common goals and coordinate policy.

Alliances Groups of actors who pool their resources for a common cause, usually in relation to national defence.

American Civil War 1861–65. War between the United States of America (Union) and the secessionist southern Confederate States of America (Confederacy). The war ended the dreams of an independent south and ended slavery.

Anarchy In its most basic form, the absence of central government. A prominent part of the realist perspective's ontology. More generally, it refers to lawlessness.

Angell, Norman 1874–1967. Famous British pacifist who wrote *The Great Illusion 1910.* Somewhere between an idealist and a liberal.

Antarctic Treaty System (ATS) Signed in 1959 by 12 so-called consultative parties with claims on Antarctica and able to demonstrate a substantial scientific interest in Antarctica. Established the area as a demilitarized zone; various subsequent agreements have been added.

Anti-Semitism Prejudice, discrimination, or persecution against Jewish people.

Apartheid Racial separation policy in South Africa until the early 1990s.

Appeasement An attempt to satisfy a potential aggressor by making territorial or other concessions to that potential aggressor. This technique failed to satisfy Adolf Hitler.

Arab League Founded in March 1945, a voluntary association of 22 Arab states.

Armistice A general term for a negotiated peace, but most often used to describe the end of World War I.

Arms control Any diplomatic effort designed to regulate levels or types of arms (bilaterally or multilaterally, with conventional or nuclear arms).

ASEAN (Association of South East Asian Nations) Formed by the Bangkok Declaration 1967; includes Indonesia, Malaysia, the Philippines, Singapore, Thailand, Brunei, Burma, and Laos.

Asian Development Bank A multilateral bank similar to the World Bank with a regional focus; headquarters established in 1966 in Manila, Philippines.

Atlantic Charter Statement of general principles, signed by Roosevelt and Churchill in August 1941, related to postwar order, including principles of national self-determination, opposition to aggression, disarmament, and equal access to trade and raw materials.

Atomic bomb A weapon based on the rapid splitting of fissionable materials, thereby inducing an explosion with deadly blast, heat, and radiation impact; a nuclear weapon.

Authoritarianism Political system in which individual freedom is subordinate to the power of the state, concentrated in one leader or group that is not accountable to the people.

Automation The replacement of human workers with machines. See **robotics**.

Balance of payments The net flow of money into, and out of, a state. Encompasses trade, tourist expenditures, sales of services, foreign aid, debt payments, profits, etc.

Balance of power A term used to describe a contemporary or historical system (regional or global) in which no one state has the power to dominate all the others.

Balance of trade The relationship between exports and imports.

Balfour Declaration A British policy announced in 1917 by foreign secretary Arthur Balfour legitimizing the return of Jews to Palestine.

Ballistic missile A missile using a ballistic guidance system influenced by gravity and friction and employing no thrust after its initial boost phase. Some missiles travel 300 metres; others can travel halfway around the world.

Basic human needs Adequate food intake (calories, vitamins, protein, minerals, etc.), disease-free and toxin-free drinking water, minimum clothing and shelter, literacy, sanitation, health care, employment, and dignity.

Bay of Pigs Part of the Cuban coastline where in 1961 a group of Cuban refugees staged a failed invasion under American auspices.

Beggar-thy-neighbour policies Attempts to alter a trade balance by devaluing currency and raising barriers to imports.

Berlin Wall Constructed in 1961 by East Germany, the Berlin Wall encircled West Berlin, a part of the city controlled by the Western allies during the Cold War. Constructed to prevent people from fleeing East Germany into the West, the wall was a symbol of East–West division until it was dismantled in 1989 as the Cold War ended.

Bilateral Any political or economic activity between the governments of two states. See **multilateral**.

Biodiversity Greatly varied flora and fauna in a habitat; is under threat in many areas of the world.

Biosphere Life and living processes at or near the earth's surface, extending from the ocean's floors and the lithosphere to about 75 kilometres into the atmosphere.

Bipolarity Global political system with two competing poles of great power, such as during the U.S.–USSR Cold War era.

Bipolycentrism A distribution of power in which there are two main poles of power as well as a number of other less powerful, but still significant, power centres.

Bolsheviks Members of the radical minority in the Russian Social Democratic Party (1903–17), led by Vladimir Lenin. Carried out the communist revolution of 1917.

Boycott The refusal of a country to import goods and services from another country; done for punitive reasons.

Bretton Woods system The post–World War II international monetary order, named after the 1944 conference held at Bretton Woods, New Hampshire. Main institutions in the system were the IMF, IBRD, and GATT.

Bureaucratic politics model An approach to the study of foreign policy that focuses on bargaining and compromises among governmental organizations and agencies pursuing their own interests.

Camp David A mountain retreat for the U.S. president in Maryland and site of the famous Camp David Accords, signed in 1978 by President Anwar el-Sadat of Egypt and Prime Minister Menachem Begin of Israel.

Capital-intensive production Industry (such as computers) that depends on infusions of capital investment to acquire the technology necessary to be competitive.

Capitalism An economic system based on the private ownership of property and commercial enterprise, competition for profits, and limited government interference in the marketplace.

Capital mobility Ability of international investors to invest in foreign countries with minimal constraints.

Cartel An international agreement among producers of a commodity that attempts to control the production and pricing of that commodity. See **Organization of Petroleum Exporting Countries.**

Catherine the Great (Catherine II), Tzarina of Russia (1762–96). Expanded and strengthened the Russian Empire, chiefly at the expense of Turkey.

Chlorofluorocarbons (CFCs) Gases used as aerosols, refrigeration chemicals, and in the manufacture of plastics; thought to be largely responsible for ozone layer depletion.

Churchill, Winston 1874–1965. British prime minister (1940–45, 1951–55), naval officer, and author.

CIDA Canadian International Development Agency.

Clausewitz, Karl von 1780–1831. Prussian general and author of military strategy; wrote *On War*.

Client states States highly dependent on great powers for military or economic aid.

Cold War Hostility between the United States and the Soviet Union in the bipolar era (roughly, 1947–90).

Collective security Mutual multilateral consent to an agreement that declares that aggression by one state on any other is an attack on the whole; the primary security mechanism created by the United Nations Charter.

COMECON Council for Mutual Economic Assistance, established in 1949 to increase trade within the Soviet bloc; dissolved in 1991.

Commonwealth Voluntary association of former dominions, colonies, and other overseas territories of Britain. Forty-nine states belong; annual meeting of heads of state generates some attention.

Commonwealth of Independent States (CIS) Arrangement among many of the former republics of the USSR, formed in December 1991. Includes Armenia, Azerbaijan, Byelorussia (Belarus), Kazakhstan, Kirghizia (Kyrgyzstan), Moldavia (Moldova), Russia, Tadzhikistan (Tajikistan), Turkmenistan, Ukraine, and Uzbekistan.

Concert of Europe A system of consultation established among the European powers after the defeat of Napoleon (1815). The aim of the Concert was to maintain the peace and manage the balance of power in Europe, which it did with considerable success until the outbreak of the Crimean War (1854–56).

Congress of Vienna 1814–15. Peace conference following the Napoleonic Wars at which the great powers—Austria, Russia, Prussia, Great Britain, and France—agreed on territorial and political terms of settlement.

Conscription A policy requiring all men of a certain age to serve in the military, during peace or war. Also referred to as the "draft"; conscription is very controversial in Canada and the United States but more accepted in most other countries of the world.

Constructive engagement Trying to influence a state's domestic policies by maintaining trade and diplomatic ties, as opposed to the use of sanctions.

Containment The United States' grand strategy during the Cold War, designed to contain the perceived military, political, and ideological threat of the Soviet Union.

Convention on International Trade in Endangered Species of Wild Fauna and Flora (CITES) 1973 multilateral accord that regulates export, transit, and importation of endangered animal and plant species.

Convention on the Conservation of Antarctic Marine Living Resources (CCAMLR) Promulgated in 1980 by consultative parties to the Antarctic Treaty to protect environment and resources of Antarctic seas region.

Council of Europe International body created in 1949 by representatives of Great Britain, France, Belgium, the Netherlands, Luxembourg, Norway, Sweden, Denmark, Ireland, and Italy; joined by Greece and Turkey in 1950; aimed toward a European federation.

Crimean War 1854–56. France, Great Britain, and Turkey allied against Russia and fought a bitter war on the Crimean peninsula.

Crimes against humanity Genocide, enslavement, rape, deportation, imprisonment, murder, torture, or persecutions on political, racial, or religious grounds committed against any civilian population.

Crimes against peace Generally, planning, preparing, initiating, or waging a war of aggression and participating in a common plan or conspiracy for the accomplishment of war crimes.

Cruise missile A missile, guided remotely (from satellites in some cases), that can fly low enough to escape radar detection and can deliver conventional or nuclear warheads.

Cultural imperialism Imposition of values on one society by another by direct administrative means (such as education) or more subtle means (such as television commercials).

Currency speculation Purchasing of foreign currency with an aim to sell it when, and if, its value increases. Can distort government efforts to manage the economy.

Customs union A common external tariff is applicable to all imports from outside the area; internal barriers to trade are removed. Different from a free trade area, in which internal barriers are removed but external barriers remain up to individual states.

Deficit The amount by which a government's spending exceeds its revenues in any fiscal year.

Demographic transition theory Argues that the decline in the industrialized state's birth rate is a direct consequence of social and economic development, and that with time other states will follow.

Dependency theory Contends that the north has created a neocolonial relationship with the south, which is dependent on northern capital.

Desertification Process in which potentially productive land is transformed into arid, desert-like territory. A severe form of land erosion.

Détente A relaxation of tensions or a decrease in the level of hostility between the superpowers during the Cold War.

Deterrence Persuading an opponent not to attack by making sure it is aware that a counterattack would follow. Pertains especially to the nuclear strategy of the superpowers during the Cold War.

Disinformation Spreading of false propaganda or forged documents to confuse counterintelligence or create political confusion, unrest, and scandal. Some would argue that governments do this with their own citizens as well.

Doves Informal term used to describe elected or unelected political figures who advocate less hard-line or confrontational approaches to their countries' enemies.

Duty Special tax applied to imported goods, based on tariff rates and schedules.

Ecocide Deliberate destruction of the environment for military purposes.

Economic Community of West African States (ECOWAS) Founded in 1975 to promote cooperation in west Africa, with 16 member states.

Embargo The refusal of one country to export goods to another, for punitive reasons. Most famous example is the American embargo on Cuba.

Emigration Leaving one's home country to live in another.

ENIAC The first computer. It was so large that it filled an entire room.

Epistemic community A global network of knowledge-based professionals in scientific and technological areas that often have an impact on policy decisions.

Ethnic cleansing The forced removal of an ethnic group from their area of residence using tactics that include executions, the destruction of homes, and rape to instill fear in the target population. In its ultimate form, genocide.

Euro The common currency of European Union states, introduced gradually in the late 1990s, and now in use in 11 EU states; began strong but eventually faltered against the American dollar.

European Economic Community See **European Union**.

European Monetary System Established in 1979 as the first major step toward the establishment of a common currency in the European Union. System collapsed in 1993, but was revived.

European Union (EU) Previously the European Economic Community, established by the Treaty of Rome, signed on 25 March 1957, and further cemented by the Maastricht Treaty (though it was rejected by some members) of 1991. Includes Austria, Belgium, Denmark, Finland, France, Germany, Greece, Ireland, Italy, Luxembourg, Netherlands, Portugal, Spain, Sweden, and the United Kingdom. States have coordinated policies in a number of areas, such as migration and currency, but have fallen short of a common security and foreign policy.

Exchange rate The values of two currencies relative to each other. For example, one Canadian dollar may be worth 70 cents of an American dollar.

Exclusive economic zone The 200-nautical-mile or 370-kilometre (area in which coastal states have jurisdiction over the resources of the sea and the seabed (i.e., beyond their 12-mile or 19-kilometre territory) but not territorial rights. Accepted as customary law.

Exports Products shipped or otherwise transferred to foreign states.

Export subsidies Special incentives, including direct payments to exporters, to encourage foreign sales.

Extraterrltoriality In diplomatic practice, the tradition that visiting diplomats are exempt from local legal jurisdiction.

Fascism An authoritarian ideology that subsumes individuals before the state; popular in Italy, Spain, and Germany in the period leading up to World War II.

Food and Agriculture Organization (FAO) Formed in 1945 as a UN specialized agency to deal with food production; based in Rome.

Foreign direct investment (FDI) Buying stock, real estate, or other assets in a foreign country with the aim of gaining a controlling interest (usually over 50 percent) of foreign enterprises. Differs from portfolio investment, which involves investment solely to gain capital appreciation through market fluctuations.

Fourteen Points U.S. President Woodrow Wilson's formulation of Allied war aims and of a general peace program, delivered to Congress 8 January 1918.

Fourth World An expression that is usually meant to include the very least developed, or poorest, states.

Free trade International movement of goods unrestricted by tariffs or nontariff barriers.

Functionalism International cooperation in largely technical areas (communications, travel, trade, environmental protection) and related theories about possibly resultant political integration.

Futurologists People who attempt to predict the future based on present trends. (Some claim they are scientists, others do not.)

Game theory A mathematical approach to modelling political behaviour. It is used by international relations scholars to evaluate decision-making patterns among two or more actors under certain proscribed conditions.

General Agreement on Tariffs and Trade (GATT) Concluded in 1948, followed by successive rounds of negotiations culminating in the establishment of the World Trade Organization in 1995. General aim is to facilitate expanded international trade with the reduction of trade barriers.

General Assembly The democratic core of the United Nations, where all states are equally represented; more than 185 states are currently represented.

Generalized System of Preferences (GSP) A system approved by GATT in 1971 that authorizes developed countries to give preferential tariff treatment to less-developed countries.

Genetic engineering Biotechnological process by which the insertion of foreign genes results in the genetic modification of existing plants and animals, producing genetically modified organisms. A contentious ethical and trade issue today.

Geopolitics A form of foreign policy analysis that emphasizes the link between geographic variables (such as location, resources, and topography) and political behaviour. Political action is seen as largely determined by geography.

Glasnost The Soviet policy of increased openness, developed and implemented under the leadership of Mikhail Gorbachev in the late 1980s.

Global commons Elements of the earth and atmosphere (oceans, seabed, atmosphere, outer space) that are the property of no one nation or individual but are deemed to be the property of all.

Golan Heights Contested territory adjacent to Israel, which has occupied it since the 1967 war.

Good offices Services, roles, and functions provided by a third party in an effort to resolve a dispute. Often refers to the secretary-general of the UN.

Great Depression Severe unemployment and financial collapse of the early 1930s; international in scope.

Green revolution The increase in agricultural production in many developing countries in the 1950s and 1960s, made possible by genetically engineered grains, fertilizers, and more efficient use of land.

Gross domestic product (GDP) A measure of national income that excludes foreign earnings.

Gross national product (GNP) The sum of all the goods and services produced by a state's nationals, whether in that state or abroad.

Grotius, Hugo 1583–1645. Dutch jurist and humanist, often called the father of international law.

Group of Eight (G-8) The eight largest economies (the United States, Japan, Germany, France, Russia, Italy, the United Kingdom, and Canada); government representatives meet often to coordinate monetary policies.

Group of Seven (G-7) The seven economically largest free-market states: Canada, France, Great Britain, Italy, Japan, the United States, and Germany. Russia is now a participant in what are now referred to as G-8 conferences.

Group of 77 The 77 Third World states that co-sponsored the Joint Declaration of Developing Countries in 1963 calling for greater equity in north–south trade. Presently includes more than 120 members.

Groupthink The tendency of decision makers to develop, in groups, a common perception of an issue or problem and exclude those with different opinions or ideas.

Hague Conventions Resulting from the Hague Peace Conferences of 1899 and 1907; provided for Permanent Court of Arbitration, defined the laws and usages of land warfare, rights and obligations of neutrals, etc.

Hapsburg Ruling house of Austria 1282–1918; provided the emperors of the Holy Roman Empire from 1438 to 1806.

Hard power A reference to traditional measures of power, such as economic capability, population, and especially military strength.

Hawks An informal term for those elected or unelected officials who advocate more uncompromising or confrontational policies toward their country's enemies.

Head of state An individual who represents the sovereignty of a state. In many cases, this individual is different from the head of government (e.g., the British monarch and the British prime minister; the Queen of Canada, represented by the lieutenant-governor, and the prime minister of Canada; in the United States, the president assumes both roles.

Hegel, Georg Wilhelm Friedrich 1770–1831. German philosopher, inspiration for Karl Marx and others.

Hegemon A dominant state that uses its military and economic power to establish global rules and institutions in accord with its interests.

Hegemonic powers States with extraordinary influence—viewed as stabilizers by some and imperialists by others.

Hegemonic stability Theory that a leading state can provide the public good of stability in the global political system, on the condition that it can maintain its contested hegemonic status.

Hegemony Political dominance; either undisputed leadership in politics or dominance in the realm of ideas.

High politics Traditionally considered the politics of war between states; military security and diplomacy.

Hobbes, Thomas 1588–1679. English political philosopher. Author of *Leviathan*.

Hobson, John 1858–1940. English economist who wrote on imperialism.

Holy Roman Empire 962–1806. Western European political entity claiming to be successor to the Roman Empire (suspended in 476); a European commonwealth; lost importance after Thirty Years' War (1618–48).

Homogenization Any process in which different entities become increasingly similar; the diminishment of diversity.

ICBM (intercontinental ballistic missile) A ballistic missile capable of flying from one continent to another, but especially one capable of flight between North America and Eurasia. Central to modern nuclear deterrence.

Immigration The arrival of foreigners in a country for the purpose of taking up residence. A vital source of economic production.

Imperialism A policy of establishing political and economic control over foreign territories and all the intellectual accompaniments. At times used to refer to the spread of Western capitalism and the current processes of globalization.

Imports Products brought into a state from abroad. See **exports**.

Industrial espionage The use of human or electronic means to covertly acquire industrial secrets.

Industrial Revolution The mechanization of industry and associated changes in social and economic patterns in Europe (and especially Great Britain) in the late eighteenth and early nineteenth centuries.

Infanticide The deliberate killing of children.

Infrastructure The industrial and transportation assets of a state. Infrastructure includes factories, roads, bridges, power plants, and storage facilities.

Interfirm alliances The cooperation of MNCs to maintain operations in different countries, for various reasons.

International Bank for Reconstruction and Development (IBRD) Development-based lending agency affiliated with the United Nations, commonly referred to as the World Bank.

International Civil Aviation Organization A specialized agency of the UN, organized in 1947; formed to expand international air trade and promote safety. Headquarters are in Montreal.

International Committee of the Red Cross (ICRC) Referred to as the International Committee of the Red Crescent in Muslim societies. A neutral humanitarian relief organization, founded in 1859, based in Switzerland. It cares for wounded during battle and observes rights of prisoners of war.

International Court of Justice (ICJ) The World Court, which sits in The Hague, Netherlands, with 15 judges.

International Development Association An affiliate of the World Bank (IBRD) that provides interest-free, long-term loans to developing states.

International Finance Corporation (IFC) Created in 1956 to finance overseas investments by private companies without necessarily requiring government guarantees; borrows from the World Bank.

International Joint Commission (IJC) Canada–U.S. body established by the Boundary Waters Treaty of 1909 to deal mainly with transborder water resource questions. Consists of three Canadian and three American commissioners. Provides analysis and rulings related to transborder environmental issues, such as Great Lakes pollution.

International Monetary Fund (IMF) Autonomous but affiliated with the UN since 1947; designed to facilitate international trade, reduce inequities in exchange, and stabilize currencies.

International Office of Weights and Measures Intergovernmental organization established in 1875 to standardize weights and measures, affiliated with the UN since 1949.

International Organization for Migration (IOM) Assists migrants as they settle in new countries; also helps with refugee assistance. Headquarters are in Geneva.

International Telecommunication Union Established 1934 as an amalgamation of the International Telegraph Union (established 1865) and the International Radiotelegraph Union (established 1906).

International Union for the Conservation of Nature and Natural Resources (IUCNNR) Promotes sustainable development and preservation of nature; involves both governments and NGOs; based in Geneva. Also known as the World Conservation Union.

Internet An information network of computers that enables users to communicate and access information from all linked computers. Originated in a U.S. military communications project.

Intifada **(resurgence)** A series of minor clashes between Palestinian youths and Israeli security forces in the occupied territories that escalated into a full-scale revolt in December 1987.

Iron Age The historical epoch characterized by the widespread use of iron in tools and weapons.

Isolationism A foreign-policy approach emphasizing self-reliance and limited economic or political interaction with the international system.

Jus ad bellum Principles used to decide whether a war is just.

Jus in bello Principles used to decide what types of violence are permissible in war.

Kant, Immanuel 1724–1804. German philosopher; wrote of a transnational political possibility.

Kellogg–Briand Pact Pact of Paris signed in 1928 by 44 states, renouncing war and promoting peaceful dispute settlement; named after U.S. Secretary of State Frank Kellogg and French Foreign Minister Aristide Briand.

Kennan, George 1904– . American diplomat and historian, ambassador to the Soviet Union, 1952.

Khmer Rouge (Red Cambodians) Communist rulers of Kampuchea, 1975–79, under Pol Pot and Leng Saray; still a political force in the region.

Korean War North Korea attacks South Korea June 1950; UN forces under American command join late June; Chinese communists join North Korea November 1950; armistice concluded July 1953. Korea remains what many would consider to be the last Cold War front.

La Francophonie Group of French-speaking states that meets to coordinate development policies.

League of Nations The international organization that existed, without American membership, between the end of World War I and the end of World War II.

Lenin, Vladimir I. 1870–1924. Russian revolutionist and statesman; founder of Bolshevism, the Third International, and the Soviet Union.

Less-developed countries (LDCs) Those states in the lowest economic rankings, usually with a per capita GNP of less than U.S.$400 (1985).

Locke, John 1632–1704. English philosopher, promoted individual liberty and the right to private property.

Lome Convention Agreement concluded between the EU and 58 African, Caribbean, and Pacific countries (ACP), allowing the latter preferential trade relations and greater economic and technical assistance.

Long cycles The theory that hegemons rise and decline in regular patterns, which in turn influence the international economy and the outbreak of hegemonic wars.

Low politics Label given to those aspects of international relations that were (or still are) believed to be less important or decisive than military power, alliances, and diplomacy. Included trade, international organizations and nongovernmental organizations, culture, and travel.

Luxemburg, Rosa 1870–1919. German Marxist; founded Spartacus Party during World War I; wrote on imperialism.

Maastricht Treaty Signed by European Community in December 1991, outlining steps toward further integration. See **European Union**.

Machiavelli, Niccolo 1469–1527. Italian political philosopher, strategist, and statesman.

Mackinder, Halford 1861–1947. British geographer; formulated the idea of the Heartland (Europe) as the key to world rule.

Mahan, Alfred Thayer 1840–1914. American historian, naval officer; formulated doctrine of sea power.

Malnutrition Results from inadequate or unbalanced diet, usually deficient in protein, vitamins, or minerals.

Marketization Movement away from state-controlled economy toward private property rights, open competition, trade liberalization, open investment, and floating currency.

Marshall Plan U.S. Secretary of State George Marshall's 1947 plan to aid the reconstruction of European industry after World War II.

Marx, Karl 1818–83. German economist and historian. Founder of the ideology of Communism; proponent of historical materialism.

Mercantilism The perspective holding that international trade should be regulated by the state to maximize national income. Also known as economic nationalism and neomercantilism.

MERCOSUR A trade agreement linking Argentina, Brazil, Paraguay, and Uruguay.

Middle powers Countries that do not possess the power attributes of the great powers but that can have a significant impact on international politics in certain specific regions or in certain specific issue-areas. Canada is often described as a middle power, though some call it a satellite of the United States.

Mill, John Stuart 1806–73. English philosopher and economist.

Montreal Protocol 1987 agreement calling on states to limit production and use of ozone-depleting CFCs.

Multilateral Involving three or more states; usually connotes cooperative action.

Multilateral Agreement on Investment (MAI) Originally an OECD-coordinated effort to protect foreign investors from governmental intrusion; disbanded but still on the larger WTO agenda.

Multinational corporation (MNC) A profit-seeking enterprise with operations in at least two states. Powerful actors in global politics today.

Multipolarity A distribution of power in which there are a number of poles, or great powers, in the system. This was characteristic of the pre–World War I era, and some analysts believe it can lead to instability.

Mutual assured destruction (MAD) The underlying nature of the nuclear stalemate between the superpowers during the Cold War. Both the United States and the Soviet Union possessed such large and capable arsenals that each side knew that if it attempted to attack the other with nuclear weapons, it would receive a devastating nuclear blow in return. As a result, both sides were deterred from using nuclear weapons against each other.

Napoleon Bonaparte I 1769–1821. Emperor of France, 1804–15. Strategist, military and political.

Napoleonic Wars 1796–1815. Waged by France under Napoleon against England, Austria, Prussia, Russia, and most of the other countries of Europe. Ended with France's defeat at Waterloo.

Nation People tied together by common ethnic, linguistic, or historical bonds; not necessarily members of the same state.

Nationalization A government's assumption of the ownership of property, often previously owned by citizens from another state. Famous cases include the nationalization of the Suez Canal, and Cuban and Iranian appropriation of American commercial property.

Neo-Malthusian Argument that resources will be outstripped by population growth in the modern era; has led to calls for strict population control.

New International Economic Order (NIEO) Statement of priorities adopted at the Sixth Special Session of the UN General Assembly in 1974, calling for equal participation of LDCs in the north–south dialogue.

Nonaligned Movement (NAM) An effort begun in 1955 by developing countries to cooperate on issues of joint interest, especially decolonization, neutrality in the Cold War, and a more favourable international economic environment for their products. The NAM is largely moribund today.

Nongovernmental organizations (NGOs) Groups that do not represent the views of governments; usually operating for the purpose of charity or value propagation. INGOs are those NGOs with operations or members in at least two states.

Nontariff barriers Erected by a government to discourage imports. Formal and voluntary quotas, prohibitions of certain imports, discriminatory restrictions, licensing requirements. Now the main way governments restrict international trade.

North American Free Trade Agreement (NAFTA) Trilateral economic agreement reducing barriers on trade between Canada, the United States, and Mexico; contains side agreements on labour rights and environmental protection.

North Atlantic Treaty Organization (NATO) Collective defence alliance created in 1949 to prevent the Soviet Union from attaining political influence or territorial conquests in Europe. Composed of 16 states by 1982, the alliance has restructured itself after the Cold War and admitted three new members in 1997. Headquarters are in Brussels.

Northwest Atlantic Fisheries Organization (NAFO) Multilateral body established to regulate fishing in the northwest Atlantic; includes Canada, the EU, and several Asian states, but not the United States.

Nuremberg War Crimes Trials 1945–47. Trials of Nazis for war crimes by an international military tribunal; several were subsequently executed. See **war crimes trials**.

Omnicide Literally, the killing of all life, as might result from a nuclear war.

Organisation for Economic Co-operation and Development (OECD) An organization of industrialized states.

Organization for Security and Co-operation in Europe (OSCE) A multilateral forum for discussing a wide range of political questions in Europe; includes Canada, the United States, Russia, and all of the

European states. Established in 1995 to give permanent staff and headquarters to the Council on Security and Co-operation in Europe (CSCE).

Organization of American States (OAS) Intergovernmental organization of 35 states of North and South America formed in 1948 as a forum for political dialogue. Canada joined in 1994.

Organization of Petroleum Exporting Countries (OPEC) Producers' cartel setting price floors and production ceilings of crude petroleum; the Arab oil producers (Saudi Arabia, Kuwait, the United Arab Emirates, Qatar, Iraq, Algeria, and Libya), Ecuador, Gabon, Nigeria, Venezuela, and Indonesia.

Paradigm An intellectual framework that structures analysis and is widely accepted as legitimate.

Per capita Putting aggregate statistical information, such as GNP, into per-person form.

Perestroika Economic reform policies instituted by Mikhail Gorbachev in the Soviet Union in the late 1980s.

Permanent Court of International Justice Established 1921 pursuant to the Covenant of the League of Nations; terminated in 1945 when its functions were transferred to the International Court of Justice provided by the Charter of the UN.

Peter the Great (Peter I) 1682–1725. Founder of the modern Russian state.

Petrodollars U.S. dollar holdings of capital surplus by OPEC countries; helped create Third World debt crisis because southern countries borrowed heavily in the 1970s.

Polarity The number of poles, or concentrations of power, in a region or in the international system. Systems with one dominant concentration of power are unipolar, those with two are bipolar, while those with many are called multipolar.

Politburo The supreme decision-making body of the Soviet Union during the Cold War.

Portfolio investment Buying shares in foreign firms but not directly controlling them. Also, taking out government loans and buying bonds.

Potsdam Treaty Result of a conference among the United States, USSR, and Great Britain at Potsdam, Germany, in the summer of 1945; chief authority in Germany given to American, British, Soviet, and French occupation authorities; laid down terms for denazification, demilitarization, democratization, and expulsion of ethnic Germans in Eastern Europe.

Propaganda Deliberate attempt to influence the attitudes and opinions of a target population through systematic dissemination of information.

Protectionism Using tariffs and nontariff barriers to control or restrict the flow of imports into a state; usually associated with neomercantilism.

Proxy wars Wars, usually in the south, where the great powers are indirectly involved.

Public good Publicly funded and regulated services or infrastructure, open to use by all members of a society; in the international sense, the provision of political, military, and economic stability by a hegemon.

Quota A quantitative limitation imposed by government, usually applied to inflows of goods or migrants.

Ratification Official governmental acceptance of a treaty.

Recession Rise in unemployment, decline of investment and growth; usually a period of less than a year. Recessions in important markets cause international concern.

Refugee A person who has fled his or her country of origin because of fear of persecution, discrimination, or political oppression.

Regime Rules, principles, and decision-making procedures governing international behaviour in certain issue-areas.

Repatriation The resettlement by a refugee in his or her home state.

Reprisal A hostile, illegal act that is rendered legal when carried out in response to a previous illegal act.

Resolution Formal decision of UN body, usually either registering a widely held opinion or recommending some sort of action to a UN body or agency.

Robotics Use of highly complex machines to perform complicated manufacturing tasks. See **automation**.

Rousseau, Jean Jacques 1712–78. French philosopher, author of *The Social Contract*. Influenced the concept of popular sovereignty.

SALT Strategic Arms Limitation Treaties between United States and USSR; treaties signed 1972 and 1979.

Sanctions Punitive measures, such as boycotts or embargoes, imposed on states by the international community in either a bilateral or multilateral context.

Satisficing Propensity of decision makers to select an alternative that meets minimally acceptable standards.

Schlieffen Plan The German military strategy for the conquest of France, put into action in World War I. The plan called for German armies to sweep through neutral Belgium and envelop Paris.

Secretariat The administrative organ of the United Nations, headed by the secretary-general; more generally, the administrative branch of any international organization.

Secretary-General Chief administrative officer of the United Nations who also plays an important, if controversial, diplomatic role.

Security Council Fifteen states (five permanent members) sit on this chief collective security organ of the UN.

Security dilemma A product of international anarchy in which states seek to rely on their own means to ensure their security by developing their military forces. In doing so, they inspire fear and distrust in their neighbours, who also arm. This reaction starts an arms race in which none of the participants is any more secure (and may in fact be less secure) than it was initially.

Self-determination The claim that people have the right to self-rule.

Shiite Islam The smaller of the two major branches of Islam, often equated with Islamic fundamentalism, consisting of those who regard Ali, son-in-law of Muhammad, as the prophet's legitimate successor. The Koran is the only source of political authority.

SLBM (submarine-launched ballistic missiles) A ballistic missile launched from a nuclear-capable submarine.

Soft power Elements of state power, such as ideological attractiveness, culture, information capacity, and education, that have traditionally been disregarded (especially by realists) in favour of military or economic strength.

Solidarity Self-governing trade union movement in Poland that began in 1980 and eventually played a major role in changes there; led by Lech Walesa, elected president of Poland in December 1990.

Sovereignty A government's ability to manage internal affairs and independently represent itself externally. A principle securing noninterference from other states, the keystone of the Charter of the United Nations.

START Two treaties, START I and START II, reached between the United States and the USSR/Russia that will make deep cuts in the nuclear arsenals of both countries.

State A political entity possessing determined territory, permanent population, active government, and sovereign recognition by other states. Can also refer to the governing element of society with a monopoly on legitimate coercive violence; also, the instrument of the ruling economic classes.

State terrorism The use of state power to terrorize civilians into compliance.

Structural adjustment programs (SAPs) Attempts by indebted governments to limit their spending, eliminate subsidies, and promote trade liberalization. Usually part of an IMF-sponsored or World Bank–sponsored loan package.

Sunni Islam The dominant branch of Islam consisting of those who regard the first four caliphs as legitimate successors of Muhammad.

Superpowers The former USSR and the United States during the Cold War era.

Synthesis An idea formed by a combination of other ideas.

Tariff A tax levied on imports. Free traders aim to eliminate them.

Thirty Years' War 1618–48. General European war fought mainly in Germany; petty German princes and foreign powers (France, Sweden, Denmark, England) against the Holy Roman Empire (Hapsburgs in Austria, Germany, Italy, the Netherlands, and Spain); also a religious war of Protestants against Catholics. Ends with the Treaty of Westphalia.

Thucydides c. 460–400 B.C.E. Athenian historian. Wrote of security dilemma dynamics.

Torture Deliberate inflicting of pain, physical or psychological. Often state induced.

Trade Exchanges of products, services, or money between states.

Trilateral An agreement or arrangement between three states or groups of states, such as NAFTA or the **Trilateral Commission** (United States, Western Europe, and Japan).

Truman Doctrine Outlined to Congress by U.S. President Truman in March 1947 in support of the Greek–Turkish aid bill; calls for the containment of Communism by giving aid to like-minded governments.

UN Conference on Trade and Development (UNCTAD) A coalition of southern states that began meeting in 1964.

UNDP UN Development Program, coordinates and assists development projects related to UN.

UNESCO UN Educational, Scientific, and Cultural Organization, Paris.

UNHCR UN High Commissioner for Refugees.

UNICEF UN Children's Fund; assists millions of destitute children around the globe; originally established to help war refugees in 1946.

Unilateral One-sided initiatives; the actions of a single state.

Unipolarity A region or international system in which there is one dominant actor. Some argue that the current international system is a unipolar one, with the United States as the one remaining superpower.

Universal Postal Union Established in 1875 with headquarters in Bern, Switzerland; became a specialized agency of the UN in 1947.

Urbanization The process of growth, often rapid, of cities.

USAID American foreign-aid department.

Verification Process of determining that all sides of an international agreement are in compliance.

Versailles Treaty The principal treaty terminating World War I.

Veto The right to prohibit certain actions. The permanent members of the Security Council have a veto over the Council's substantive actions.

Vienna, Congress of 1814–15. Peace conference following the Napoleonic Wars at which the great powers—Austria, Russia, Prussia, Great Britain, and France—agreed on territorial and political terms of settlement.

War crimes Includes perpetrating mass murder, ill-treatment, deportation, or forced labour of prisoners, killing hostages, plunder, and wanton destruction with no military necessity.

War crimes trials Prosecution of war criminals by an international tribunal, following World War II at Nuremberg and Tokyo, and presently at The Hague. May also take place within domestic jurisdiction of states.

Warsaw Pact A treaty signed by the Soviet bloc states in 1955 pledging mutual military allegiance to the Soviet Union; dissolved in 1991.

Weighted voting A system of voting, such as that used in the IBRD, where the value of a member's vote is determined by the contribution (usually financial) the member makes.

Weimar Republic 1919–33. German state established under a democratic federal constitution passed by a constitutional assembly in the city of Weimar.

Wilson, Woodrow 1856–1924. Twenty-seventh president of the United States, 1913–21; known for his internationalism.

World Health Organization (WHO) Specialized agency of the UN, founded in 1948; assists in health programs, including children's immunization, around the globe. Headquartered in Geneva.

World Trade Organization (WTO) Organization that was formed in 1993 to supervise the GATT and arbitrate related trade disputes. Began operations in 1995; headquartered in Geneva.

Xenophobia A strong dislike, fear, or suspicion of other nationalities.

Yalta Conference A February 1945 summit meeting with Franklin Roosevelt, Josef Stalin, and Winston Churchill at which major postwar issues were discussed, such as the status of Poland and voting arrangements in the UN.

Zero-sum game A relationship in which a gain for one actor is equal to a loss for another actor. Realists saw the Cold War as a zero-sum game.

Index

sustainable development and, 328
World War I and, 41
World War II and, 52
WTO rulings, 251
Canada–Chile Free Trade Agreement,
254, 344
Canada–U.S Free Trade Agreement, 255
Canada in the World, 5
Canadian International Development
Agency (CIDA), 354
Canadian Nuclear Safety Initiative, 325
CANDU reactors, 325
Capital-intensive production, 151
Capitalism, 97, 113
Capital mobility, 343
CARE International, 142–43, 145
Carr, Edward Hallett, 161
Cartel, 118
Carter, Jimmy, 78, 205
Carter Doctrine, 78
Cashin, Richard, 328
Castro, Fidel, 76
Catherine the Great, 32
Cellular phone revolution, 296
Central Intelligence Agency (CIA), 279
CFE Treaty, 211
Chanakya, 27
Chechnya, 91, 175–76
Chemical weapons, 180–82
Chemical Weapons Convention
(CWC), 210
Chemical Weapons Destruction
Agreement, 206
Chernobyl nuclear disaster, 324–25
Chiang Kai-Shek, 46, 73
Chicken, 86
Child labour, 291–93
Child prostitution, 292, 355
Chile, 254, 299, 344
China. *See* People's Republic of China
Chlorofluorocarbons (CFCs), 317–18
Choucri, Nazli, 397
Chrétien, Jean, 102, 122
Churchill, Winston, 50, 73
Civilizational disputes, 389–92
Civilizational systems, 242
Clash of civilizations, 4
Classical model, 80
Classical realism, 11
Claude, Inis, 134
Clausewitz, Karl von, 35
Client states, 64, 265
Climate change, 316–19
Clinton, Bill, 233, 256, 322
Clitoridectomy, 289
Coalitions, 57
Cobden, Richard, 228
Codification, 146
Cod wars, 327
Cohesive alliances, 58
Cold War, 3, 64–94
  end of, 20, 86–94
  and foreign policy decision making,
  78–86
  geopolitical dimension, 67–68
  ideological dimension, 66–67
  international dimension, 71–78
  international security and, 161–63
  origins, 66–78
  persistent themes, 65
  strategic dimension, 68–71

Collective security, 44, 139, 147
Colonies, 36
Combs, Cindy, 187
"Coming Anarchy, The" (Kaplan), 397
Commission for Environmental
Cooperation (CEC), 255
Commission on the Status of Women,
297
Committed thinking, 83
Commons, problems of, 312–14
Commonwealth, 141
Commonwealth of Independent States
(CIS), 89
Communal conflicts, 170–77
Communal groups
  nature of, 170–71
  types of, 171
Communication, transnational, 367–70
Communications revolution, 368
Complex interdependence, 12
Complex interdependence theory, 12
Complex international interdependence,
105
Comprehensive Test Ban Treaty (CTBT),
150, 208–10
Computers. *See* Information revolution
Concert of Europe, 34
Conference on the Human
Environment (UNCHE), 322
Conflict management
  democratic peace, 231–34
  diplomacy, 197–203
  disarmament/arms control, 203–13
  economic interdependence, 228–29
  humanitarian intervention, 226–28
  international law, 213–14
  international organizations, 214–17
  sanctions, 229–31, 232–33
  UN peacekeeping, 217–26
Congo Crisis, 220, 221
Congress of Vienna, 34
Connections, 371
Conscription, 40
Constructive engagement, 232, 279
Constructivism, 14, 109
Consumer awareness campaigns, 278
Containment, 72–73, 92
Content analysis, 83
Convention on Biological Diversity, 332
Convention on the Conservation of
Antarctic Marine Living Resources
(CCAMLR), 314–15
Convention on the Elimination of All
Forms of Discrimination Against
Women (CEDAW), 297
Convention on International Trade in
Endangered Species of Wild Fauna
and Flora (CITES), 321–22
Convention on the Prohibition of
Military or Any Other Hostile Use
of Environmental Modification
Techniques, 206
Convention on the Regulation of
Antarctic Mineral Resource
Activities (CRAMRA), 315
Conventional Forces in Europe (CFE)
Treaty, 141, 211
Conventional weapons, 182–85
Convergence, 4, 266, 406–7
Convergence theory, 363
Cooperation, 56

Core–periphery, 151
Corn Laws, 112
Correlates of War Project (COW), 164
Couloumbis, Theodore, 149
Council for Mutual Economic
Assistance (COMECON), 120
Council of Europe, 282
Counterdominant actors, 9
Cox, Robert, 241
Crimean War, 35, 98
Crimes against humanity, 285
Crimes against peace, 285
Critical perspectives, 13–14
Cruise missiles, 190
Cuban Missile Crisis, 76, 90, 94
Cultural imperialism, 259, 275–76
Cultural relativism, 275–76
Currency speculation, 119, 248
Currie, Arthur, 41
Customary law, 147

Dallaire, Romeo, 224
Davis, Sam, 139
Dawes, Charles G., 114, 144
Dawes Plan, 114
Daws, Sam, 277
Dayton Peace Accords, 224, 287
Decision-making theory, 78–86
Declaration of Principles (Atlantic
Charter), 133
Deconstructionists, 13
Deficit, 100
Deforestation, 319–20
De Jura Belli et Pacis (Grotius), 146
de Klerk, F.W., 232
Del Ponte, Carla, 288
Democratic peace, 231–34
Democratization, 87
Demographic transition, 338
Department of Humanitarian Affairs
(DHA) (UN), 225
Department of Peacekeeping
Operations (DPKO) (UN), 225, 226
Dependency theory, 13, 107–8
Détente, 67, 78
Deterrence, 71
Deudney, Daniel, 310
Deutsch, Karl, 215
Developed world, 259, 410
Developing world, 259, 262–66, 410
Diaspora, 347–48
Diefenbaker, John, 198
Diplomacy, 197–203
Diplomatic immunity, 148, 198
Disarmament, 203–13
Discourses, The (Machiavelli), 24
Disease, 310–12, 348–49
Disinformation, 378
Distribution of power, 57–60
Divergence, 4, 266, 407
Dollar crisis, 117
Dollar shortage, 116–17
Domino theory, 77
Dougherty, James, 79
Doves, 67
Dowdeswell, Elizabeth, 322, 324
Doyle, Michael, 233
Drugs, and organized crime, 193
Dumbarton Oaks Conference, 133
Dyer, Gwynne, 267

Roosevelt, Eleanor, 297
Rosecrance, Richard, 229
Rosenau, James, 142, 363, 373
Rousseau, Jean Jacques, 56
Ruggiero, Renato, 121
Rush–Bagot Treaty, 204
Russett, Bruce, 233
Russia, 91. *See also* Soviet Union
Russian *mafiya*, 192
Russian Revolution, 42, 113
Rwanda, 224, 286–87

Salami tactics, 77
Sanctions, 98, 147, 229–31
Satisficing, 80
Save the Children Fund, 353
Scarff, James, 321
Schlesinger, Arthur, Jr., 11
Schlieffen Plan, 40
Schumacher, E.F., 240
Schumpeter, Joseph, 361
Science
  dissemination of information and,
    370–71
  role in global ecopolitics, 330–32
Seattle, "battle" in, 250, 252
Secretariat (UN), 132, 139
Secretary-general (UN), 129, 139
Security. *See* International security
Security communities, 215
Security Council (UN), 66, 138–39, 147
Security dilemma, 55–57
Seikatsu Club, 330
Self-determination, 162, 293–95
Semi-periphery, 108
Serbia, 226–27
Sex trade, 355
Shaib, Bukar, 398
Shelley, Louise, 192
Shiite Islam, 25
Signalling, 199
Simon, Mary, 144
Simpson, Sir John Hope, 337
Singer, J. David, 164
Singh, Nagendra, 148
Sino–Soviet split, 74
Six Great Triads, 192
Sixth Committee of the General
  Assembly, 149
Slavery, 153, 291
Small states, 60
Smith, Adam, 103–4
Smoot–Hawley tariff, 114
Socioecological insolvency, 152
Soft power, 10, 55
Soil degradation, 320
Solidarity, 170
Somalia, 82, 175, 224
South Africa, 232, 279, 297, 299–300
South Asia, nuclear weapons in, 179–80
South Korea, 279
Sovereign states, 34
Sovereignty, 56
Soviet Union
  birth of, 46
  Cold War (*see* Cold War)
  collapse of, 88–89, 91–93, 99
  invasion of Afghanistan, 78
  mass migration, 346
  reform program, 87, 91, 93
  Sino–Soviet split, 74

suppression of information, 377
Special drawing rights (SDRs), 118
Species impoverishment, 320–22
Speth, James Gustave, 238
Sporting events, 380
Spratly Islands dispute, 394
Stag hunt allegory, 56
Stalin, Joseph, 46
Standard operating procedures (SOPs),
  82–83
Standby Arrangements program, 225
Star Wars, 78
State, 4, 34
  classifying, 60–61
  survival of, 407
State level of analysis, 9
State terrorism, 187
Stock market crisis (1929), 113–14
Strategic Arms Limitation Treaty
  (SALT), 77, 205–7
Strategic Arms Reduction Treaty
  (START), 205–7
Strategic Defence Initiative (Star Wars),
  78
Strategic studies, 161
Strategic triangle, 59
Structural adjustment programs
  (SAPs), 247, 264
Structural realism, 12
Structural unemployment, 343
Submarine-launched ballistic missiles
  (SLBMs), 205
Sudan, 176, 280
Suez Crisis, 75, 219
Suhrke, Astri, 397
Summit diplomacy, 199
Summit of the Americas, 199, 252
Sunni Islam, 25
Sun Tzu, 28, 54
Superpowers, 52
Supranational institution, 130
Systemic level of analysis, 9

Talisman Energy, 280
Tapinos, Georges, 356
Tariffs, 100
Team Canada, 102, 249, 376
Technology. *See* Information revolution
Telecommuting, 365
Telephone, 369
Television, 373
Territorial principle, 147
Terrorism, 186–91
  changing character of, 188–89
  combating, 189–91
  international agreements, 191
  origins/causes, 187–88
Thatcher, Margaret, 81, 147
Third-party mediation, 200
Third World, 259, 261
Thirty Years' War, 23, 28–30
Threat analysis, 161
Threshold Test Ban, 206
Thucydides, 22, 230
Tiananmen Square, 278, 296, 377
Tito, Joseph, 174
Tobin tax, 248
Toffler, Alvin and Heidi, 115, 364
Tokyo subway attack, 181, 189
Torture, 290–91
Touval, Saadia, 224

Toyotism, 243
Track two diplomacy, 198
Trade, 100
Trade deficit, 100
Trade surplus, 100
Trafficking of migrants, 355–56
"Tragedy of the Commons, The"
  (Hardin), 338
Transborder environmental issues,
  324–29
Translating software, 381
Transnational communication, 367–70
Transnationalist, 12
Trask, Mililani, 294
Treaties, 146–47
Treaty Limited Equipment (TLE), 211
Treaty of Brest–Litovsk, 46
Treaty of Versailles, 41, 42
Trilateral Commission, 122
Tripolar systems, 58–59
Trudeau, Pierre Elliott, 10, 101
Truman, Harry S., 72
Truman Doctrine, 72
Trusteeship Council, 139
Truth and reconciliation commissions,
  299–300
Tucker, Robert, 68
Turkey, 46
Tutu, Desmond, 200

ul Haq, Mahbub, 342
UN arms register, 211
Uncommitted thinking, 83
UN Conference on Environment and
  Development (UNCED), 123,
  313–14, 322–24
UN Conference on Population and
  Development, 339, 349
UN Conference on Trade and
  Development (UNCTAD), 130
UN conferences on Conventional
  Weapons, 214
UN Convention on the Rights of the
  Child, 353, 355
Unemployment, 343–44, 365–67
UN Environmental Programme
  (UNEP), 130, 317, 322, 324
UN Fund for Women (UNIFEM), 297
UN High Commissioner for Refugees
  (UNHCR), 351–54
UNICEF, 244, 352
Unicode, 381
Unified Task Force (UNITAF), 224
Union of Soviet Socialist Republics
  (USSR). *See* Soviet Union
Unipolar system, 59
United Nations, 127–30, 133–40
  Charter, 146–47
  collective security and, 44, 139, 147
  environmental issues and, 322–24
  human rights and, 280–82
  IJC, 149–50
  international days/weeks, 273
  location, 135
  member-states of, 137–38
  origins, 66, 133–35
  overview (chart), 136
  peacekeeping, 217–26
  problems, 139–140